Resurgent China

Resurgent China

Issues for the Future

Edited by

Nazrul Islam

First published 2009 by
PALGRAVE MACMILLAN

Palgrave Macmillan in the UK is an imprint of Macmillan Publishers Limited,
registered in England, company number 785998, of Houndmills, Basingstoke,
Hampshire RG21 6XS.

Palgrave Macmillan in the US is a division of St Martin's Press LLC,
175 Fifth Avenue, New York, NY 10010.

Palgrave Macmillan is the global academic imprint of the above companies
and has companies and representatives throughout the world.

Palgrave® and Macmillan® are registered trademarks in the United States,
the United Kingdom, Europe and other countries.

ISBN-13: 978–0–230–53807–8 hardback
ISBN-10: 0–230–53807–X hardback

This book is printed on paper suitable for recycling and made from fully
managed and sustained forest sources. Logging, pulping and manufacturing
processes are expected to conform to the environmental regulations of the
country of origin.

A catalogue record for this book is available from the British Library.

Library of Congress Cataloging-in-Publication Data

Resurgent China : issues for the future / edited by Nazrul Islam.
    p. cm.
Includes index.
ISBN 978–0–230–53807–8
    1. China – Economic policy – 2000– 2. China – Economic
conditions – 2000– 3. Economic development – China. I. Islam, Nazrul.

HC427.95.R47 2008
330.951—dc22   2008036947

10 9 8 7 6 5 4 3 2 1
18 17 16 15 14 13 12 11 10 09

Printed and bound in Great Britain by
CPI Antony Rowe, Chippenham and Eastbourne

To the people of China

Contents

Tables

Figures

Foreword

New books on China are appearing almost every week, if not every day. Adding another book to this crowded field therefore needs some justification. To justify the publication of this volume, we may cite its following five distinctive features. First, while most books on China are single-issue focused, the current volume addresses a whole range of important issues facing China. Single-issue focused books have the scope of investigating a particular issue more intensively. The downside is that they cannot do enough to reveal the connections among different issues. Yet, understanding of these connections is very important for correctly dealing with the issues. By discussing the issues together, this volume can better reveal their interconnections. Second, many books are focused on explaining what happened in the past. By contrast, this book focuses on the future. It analyzes the past and current trends in order to make useful suggestions and conjectures for the future. Third, many volumes on China are put together as a collection of disparate papers, written often for a conference. This book instead is the outcome of a two-year long research project organized at the International Centre for the Study of East Asian Development (ICSEAD). It is therefore the result of a thoughtful design, implemented through careful selection of topics and authors, who then collaborated among themselves, participating in two workshops (held in January and July of 2006 at ICSEAD), where preliminary and final drafts of the chapters were presented and discussed by the authors. Thus, instead of being a collection of individual papers written in isolation, this volume represents the outcome of a collaborative effort. Fourth, while most books on China represent scholars from one or two countries, this volume represents scholars from almost all major countries of China scholarship, including China itself, Japan, the United Kingdom, and the United States of America. Such a wide-scale international collaboration in producing a volume on China is rather rare. Fifth, although this volume is written by experts, mostly economists, it is, for its most parts, accessible by non-economists too. This volume will therefore prove useful to policy makers and all those who take an interest in China.

Hoping that the above distinctive features justify the production of this book, it is now necessary to acknowledge all those who made it possible. First of all, thanks are due to ICSEAD and its Director, Shoichi Yamashita, who encouraged me to undertake this "China Growth Project," gave an almost free rein to design it, and then provided all kinds of assistance to actually implement it. I also appreciate the cooperation from ICSEAD's Research Director, Susumi Hondai, and other researchers, who were not direct participants of this project. ICSEAD administrative staff members brought in their Japanese meticulousness and efficiency to the logistics of the workshops, making it easier for me to focus on the academic side of the project.

Most of all, I would like to thank the contributors themselves, who generally took my comments and suggestions in stride, tried to maintain the schedule, and finally reposed their trust in me, waiting patiently as the manuscript went through the motions of the publication process, which, as is not unusual, took more time than was originally anticipated. Taking this opportunity, I would like to thank, for their valuable comments, the referees engaged by Palgrave to review the manuscript. Thanks are also due to Katsuji Nakagane and Kazuyuki Motahashi, who offered valuable comments and advice and participated in the workshops. It is also my pleasure to thank, for his support and encouragement, Dale Jorgenson, my advisor at Harvard, who was always ahead of me by several decades and notches, no matter which particular area I chose to work on, including China's development problems. I would also like to thank Mosharraf Hossain, my teacher from Dhaka University, for his support and encouragement at different stages of my life.

The process of publication of the volume led to nice interaction with the representatives of Palgrave, in particular, Alec Dubber and Taiba Batool, and later on with Vidhya Jayaprakash, of New Gen Imaging, who handled the production of the book.

Finally, I would like to thank my immediate family, – my wife, Tanvira, my son, Rahul, and my little daughter, Nusaybah, – who have to endure my long hours, stretching into the weekends. I would also like to thank members of my extended family, back home in Bangladesh, my mother, sisters, and brothers. My late father, from whom I inherited the knack of writing, always comes to my mind prominently whenever I see my writings in print. The support and encouragement from my friends was also always very reassuring.

Unlike many other books on China, this one has a very practical goal, namely to help the Chinese people, to whom this book is dedicated, to understand and confront better the issues that their country currently faces. The effort of the authors, and all those who contributed to the production this book, will prove successful if it can, even by a small measure, achieve that goal.

Nazrul Islam
August, 2008

Contributors

Robert Ash Professor of Economics and Director, SOAS Taiwan Studies Programme, School of Oriental and African Studies, London University, UK.

Erbiao Dai Research Associate Professor, International Centre for the Study of East Asian Development (ICSEAD), Japan.

Shiro Hioki Associate Professor, Graduate School of Economics and Management, Tohoku University, Japan.

Ken Imai Senior Research Fellow, Institute of Developing Economies (IDE), Japan.

Nazrul Islam Senior Economic Affairs Officer, Development Policy Analysis Division (DPAD), Department of Economic and Social Affairs (DESA), United Nations, USA.

Reiitsu Kojima Professor of Emeritus, Daito Bunka University, Japan.

Ding Lu Professor of Economics, University of the Fraser Valley, Canada.

Nobuhiro Okamoto Associate Professor, Faculty of International Relations, Daito Bunka University, Japan.

Kexi Pan Associate Professor, School of Social Development and Public Policy, Fudan University, China.

Xizhe Peng Professor and Dean of the School of Social Development and Public Policy and Director of the Institute for Population Research, Fudan University, China.

Li Qi Assistant Professor, Department of Economics, Agnes Scott College, USA.

Eric D. Ramstetter Research Professor, International Centre for the Study of East Asian Development (ICSEAD), Japan, and Visiting Professor, Graduate School of Economics, Kyushu University, Japan.

Thomas G. Rawski Professor of Economics and History, University of Pittsburgh, USA.

Hiroshi Sakamoto Research Assistant Professor, International Centre for the Study of East Asian Development (ICSEAD), Japan.

Kazuhiko Yokota Research Associate Professor, International Centre for the Study of East Asian Development (ICSEAD), Japan.

Juan Yu Fudan University, China.

1
Resurgent China: Issues for the Future

Nazrul Islam

1.1 Introduction

China has been experiencing very fast economic growth for three decades now. As a result, China's per capita income has increased almost ten-fold from $224 in 1978 to $2,055 in 2007.[1] Surpassing other G-8 countries, China has become the second largest economy in the world in Purchasing Power Parity (PPP) terms, and she is already the world's top exporter country. This fast economic growth has been associated with fundamental changes in China's institutions. From a centrally planned economy and very egalitarian society, China has become by and large a market-based economy and an unequal society. China has also become more integrated with the rest of the world.

The rise of China is having repercussions all across the world. On the one hand, China has become the workshop of the world, supplying low-cost manufacturing goods to almost every part of the globe. On the other hand, China's demand for energy and other industrial raw materials is affecting their world prices. As a result of her success in export, China now has the largest foreign currency reserve, much of which is invested in the US securities market, so that the economies of the United States and China have become interdependent in more ways than are readily visible. The world strategic balance is shifting as a result of China's growth.[2]

In the Middle Ages, China thought of herself as the center of the world, naming herself as the Middle Kingdom, and the rest of the world was drawn to her because of her wealth, technology, and culture. However, China stagnated later and, after losing out in the Opium Wars in the mid-nineteenth century, found herself subject to a quasi-colonial rule by European powers.[3] After a long period of wars and revolutions, China is now staging a spectacular comeback, and the question that is engaging the minds of scholars and policy makers alike is what lies ahead of this resurgent China, and how her resurgence will influence the world. Will China be able to sustain her growth? Will she be able to deal with the new issues that are arising internally as a consequence of her growth process? Will China be able to accomplish her "peaceful rise" in the international arena, as proclaimed by her recent government declaration? These are some of the sweeping questions that are drawing increasing attention.

Answers to these broad questions however depend on the resolution of a wide range of issues that have accompanied or arisen in the course of China's growth. This volume is an attempt to identify these issues and offer an understanding of how they are likely to play out in the future. For this purpose, the volume brings together discussions by experts on most of the important issues that China now faces. This introductory chapter provides an overview and synthesis of these issues, drawing upon the remaining chapters. It begins in Section 1.1 with a discussion of the demographic issues, followed by a discussion in Section 1.2 of interrelated issues of employment, migration, urbanization, and industrialization strategies. Section 1.3 examines China's industrialization from the viewpoint of the Lewis growth model. Section 1.4 discusses issues concerning inequality and disparity. Section 1.5 discusses issues regarding China's internal economic integration. Section 1.6 examines issues concerning productive asset ownership and reform of State Owned Enterprises (SOE). Banking and financial sector reform issues are discussed in Section 1.7. Section 1.8 discusses issues concerning sources of China's growth and its sustainability in the light of the accumulation vs. assimilation debate. Section 1.9 discusses issues concerning resource constraints and environmental problems faced by China. Section 1.10 concludes.

1.2   Demographic issues

Economic growth begins and ends with people. This volume therefore begins with demographic issues discussed by Peng in Chapter 2. The biggest issue that China faces with regard to demographics concerns what to do next with her "One Child" policy.

1.2.1   Demographic transition

China has witnessed a dramatic demographic transition in the last few decades. The population growth rate per annum has decreased from 1.06 percent in 1995 to 0.76 percent in 2000 and 0.53 percent in 2006. A sharper decline in the birth rate has made this possible, because the process was accompanied by a decline in the mortality rate too. General socio-economic development of course had an important role in the decline of the birth rate. However it is well known that China's One Child policy, adopted in the late 1970s, played an important role in this regard.

Many outsiders do not know that China allowed considerable variation in the implementation of her One Child policy. For example, the policy was enforced relatively strictly in urban areas, while in rural areas two children were generally allowed on the ground that rural families needed labor for work on the farm and also for support during old age. Similarly, the One Child policy was enforced for the majority *Han* people, while the national minorities were largely exempted. Finally, there were large variations in the rigor of implementation of the policy, giving rise to considerable variations in the actual outcomes even of the same policy.

The One Child policy and the variations in its implementation have resulted in many desirable and not-so-desirable outcomes, and as a result China now faces quite a few dilemmas. The most desirable outcome of course has been the above mentioned dramatic decline in the birth rate and the consequent dramatic decline in the population growth rate. As a result, China can now see an end to her population growth. According to some projections, China's population will peak at 1.4 billion in 2050 and then decline.[4] Such a turnaround will no doubt come as a great relief to those who were haunted by the specter of a population explosion in China.

1.2.2 Demographic bonus

Another positive, albeit transient, consequence of the demographic transition has been the "demographic bonus" or "demographic window of opportunity" that China is currently enjoying and passing through. This refers to the fact that China now has more people in the working age group relative to the number of elderly and young, allowing her to enjoy a low overall dependency ratio. We will come back to the issue of China's demographic bonus shortly.

1.2.3 Gender and regional imbalances

The One Child policy has had some negative consequences too. One of these is the imbalance in the male-female ratio resulting from abortion of female fetuses.[5] With wider availability of ultra sonogram technology, the problem may become severe in the near future despite official efforts to prevent the practice. A second problematic outcome has been an imbalance, so to speak, in population growth across urban and rural areas and across regions. For the reasons mentioned above, the rural population has grown faster than the urban population (excluding migrants). Similarly, the population of provinces having more non-*Han* people and/or with lax implementation of the One Child policy has grown faster. Such an uneven pace of population growth has resulted in some important employment issues, as we will discuss later.

1.2.4 Aging

Another consequence that may be related to the One Child policy is aging of the Chinese population. The general decline in the birth rate, together with an increase in the longevity (resulting from improvements in healthcare and general socio-economic conditions), has caused the Chinese population to age faster. In 2005, average longevity in China reached 72 years and the proportion of the population aged 65 and above reached more than 7.69 percent. While it took Sweden and the United Kingdom 85 and 45 years, respectively, for the proportion of their populations aged 65 and higher to increase from 7 to 14 percent, China is projected to witness a similar increase in only 27 years. In addition, aging in China is occurring at a much lower per capita income level. For example, while Japan reached the median age of 32.6 years in 1980 with a per capita income of $15,600, China is projected to reach the same median age with a per capita income of only $1,200.

Aging of the population is pushing the issue of old age security to the foreground. The issue is also related, via pensions, to the issue of employment. China is far from having any comprehensive formal social security arrangement. In rural areas, such arrangements are largely absent. In urban areas, the arrangement, in the form of pensions provided by employers, is generally limited to only the formal sector. Meanwhile, aging implies that there will be fewer working age people relative to the number of old and retired people. What China does with the One Child policy therefore also affects the tasks that she faces with regard to aging and old age security.

1.2.5   Dual impact of economic prosperity on fertility behavior

As in many other countries, China's rising economic prosperity is affecting fertility behavior in two opposite directions. On the one hand, by increasing the opportunity cost of time and decreasing the necessity of children for old-age support, prosperity is reducing the desire of many families to have children. This impact is helpful for non-coercive implementation of the One Child policy. On the other hand, by making children more "affordable," prosperity is increasing the desire of some families to have more children. This desire conflicts with the One Child policy, invoking more resistance to its implementation. The problem is exacerbated by the fact that many local governments see fines and confiscated property of violators of the One Child policy as a source of their revenues, leading to some arbitrariness in the policy and its implementation and often causing social unrest.[6]

1.2.6   Issues for the future

Despite some of the undesirable consequences, the impact of the One Child policy on the whole has been profoundly positive, allowing China to gain control over her population growth. Thus a total abandonment of the One Child policy is neither suggested by most experts nor is envisaged by the policy makers. However, China can hardly avoid the necessity of introducing changes in the way the One Child policy is implemented in the future. As a general goal, it would be desirable for China to gradually switch to various material and moral incentives rather than coercion as a way of implementing her demographic policies. An important issue facing her therefore concerns how to use skillfully the dual impact of rising prosperity on fertility choice in order to achieve the above switch. China also faces the task of revisiting the variations that are currently allowed in the implementation of the One Child policy and of making necessary adjustments. She also faces the challenge of matching her evolving demographic reality and policies with the big gaps she faces with regard to social security and in particular old age security. Resolving the demographic issues will also require eradication of arbitrariness and corruption that now often characterize implementation of the One Child policy by local administrations. In this sense, demographic issues also intersect issues concerning reform of China's public administration and finance.

1.3 Employment, migration, urbanization, and industrialization strategy issues

An interrelated set of issues that China faces concerns employment, migration, urbanization, and spatial nature of industrialization. These issues are discussed by Ash and Kojima in Chapters 3 and 4, respectively. Peng too provides an introduction to some of these issues in Chapter 2. One question that provides a converging point for many of these issues concerns what to do in future with the Chinese household registration system, *Hukou*.

1.3.1 Twin employment challenges facing China

The starting point of employment and migration issues is provided by the "demographic bonus" discussed in Section 1.2. What is "bonus" from the viewpoint of demographics can be a "challenge" from the viewpoint of employment. As Ash points out, China faces twin challenges with regard to employment. One is of urban origin, arising from restructuring of SOEs. Outside observers are often not aware of the vast and heart-wrenching labor retrenchment and turnover that China's SOE restructuring has involved.[7] This process is not yet fully complete. However, it seems that China has been successful, by and large, in managing the SOE surplus labor problem.[8]

The second and more daunting employment challenge is of rural origin and is intimately connected with China's past demographic and social policies. The bulge in the working age population, referred to as the "demographic bonus," is concentrated mainly in rural China. One of the historical reasons for such concentration lies in China's *Hukou* system. Peng offers a useful discussion of the origin and evolution of the *Hukou* system, under which the Chinese were and still are not free to leave their rural adobes. In pre-1978 years, the *Hukou* system was complemented by the collectivist framework of Communes, which allowed mobilization of the "surplus" rural labor for various infrastructure and other collective projects. This collectivist framework also provided a certain type of social security, in the form of "Eating from the same iron bowl." Dismantling of Communes made the "surplus" labor visible in several ways. First, the practice of surplus labor mobilization for collective rural infrastructure projects was either discontinued or lost the previous vigor. As a result, labor no longer required for direct agricultural and other production operations became "surplus." Second, the switch to household farming led to some efficiency improvement, rendering more labor as "surplus." These processes together led to a "huge rural unemployment overhang," creating an enormous pressure on the economy.

The explosive growth of Township and Village Enterprises (TVEs) provided the first valve relieving this pressure. Since mid-1980s, TVEs have absorbed about 125 million rural laborers, allowing them to "Leave agriculture, but not the village!"[9] Why and how TVEs appeared in China is an instructive story that has been told by researchers elsewhere.[10] What is important to note is that TVEs represented, in a sense, a continuation of the practice of surplus labor mobilization for collectivist purposes by China's local authorities as represented by the Communes in pre-1978 years. To the extent that after 1978 many administrative functions of the Communes were taken over by local Township-Village governments, it was not entirely unexpected that they would take the initiative to set up TVEs, especially when other conducing factors converged. From a pre-existing small base, TVEs grew fast to account for almost one-third of China's industrial output and to surpass the formal industrial sector in terms of total employment. An important issue for China's future therefore concerns how much more of China's rural "surplus" labor TVEs can absorb and what role in China's future industrialization TVEs can play.

The second valve relieving China's rural "surplus" labor pressure was provided by migration. As with TVE-employment, getting the exact number of migrants is difficult, with estimates ranging from 125 to 150 million. The nature of migration is also complex, as Ash describes in detail in Chapter 3. Much of the migration is within-province (particularly in the eastern and coastal provinces) and not necessarily to provincial capitals. However, long distance migration across provincial borders has become more important over time, with the ten coastal provinces being the principal destination and the central and western provinces being the main origins.

Both demand and supply side factors have encouraged migration. The main supply side factor was of course the very availability of "surplus" labor in the countryside. Second, the relaxation of the *Hukou* system (which, in part, also reflected demand conditions) helped rural laborers move out and take up residence in urban areas. Third, agricultural reforms since 1978 and industrial reforms since 1984 made food and other commodities available in open markets, allowing migrants to subsist in urban areas without having to rely on the government supply system (restricted to registered urban residents).

On the demand side was the labor requirement of the new industries. The most dramatic in this regard was of course the explosion in coastal provinces of labor intensive manufacturing that took advantage of Special Economic Zones initially set up in these areas. Even outside of these zones and in the internal provinces, the relaxed economic conditions and the introduction of the Dual Track system in the industry in 1984 allowing out-of-plan economic activities by SOEs themselves, generated new labor demand. Finally, economic reforms led to the development of thriving private and informal sectors, demanding labor that rural migrants were eager to supply.

However, as Ash emphasizes, despite the TVE growth and migration, a huge amount of "surplus" labor still remains in rural areas, and this amount will increase with mechanization of the Chinese agriculture. Fan (2005), for example, estimates that a total of 300–400 million people will have to be relocated to non-farming sectors in the next 40–50 years in China.[11]

1.3.2   Which industrialization-urbanization strategy to choose?

In confronting the enormous employment challenge, China seems to have a difficult choice. One option is to abolish the *Hukou* completely and let the surplus labor migrate freely to urban areas, and thereby let the current coastal urban centers to become mega-sized. For short, this may be called the "mega-industrialization/urbanization" (or simply "mega-industrialization") strategy, something similar to that of Japan, where a major part of the nation's economic activity is concentrated in a series of almost contiguous cities along the coast stretching from Tokyo to Fukuoka. Another, opposite in nature, option is to take industry where the labor is, following the TVE spirit. This may be called the "rural industrialization" strategy, which would not require an abolition of the *Hukou* system.

Judging the merits and demerits of these two strategies requires a more detailed understanding of the consequences of internal migration. On the one hand, migration has supplied labor to fuel the growth of industry, construction, and service sectors in both formal and informal sectors in urban areas and even in rural areas of coastal provinces. On the other hand, alongside taking off the pressure of rural unemployment, migration has generated remittance income, increasing thereby consumption and investment in rural areas. These reverse beneficial effects amplify when migrants themselves return with their accumulated savings, experience, and ideas.

However, migration also had some negative consequences, for both rural and urban areas. Kojima draws attention to some of the negative effects on rural areas, such as localized depopulation and deterioration of the rural education system. The urban problems of migration are more visible. Though open markets of food and other products allow migrants to feed and clothe themselves, they are generally excluded from public housing, education, and health facilities, which are restricted to registered urban residents. Migrants also remain outside the pension and social insurance systems that are generally limited to the formal sector employing mostly registered urban residents. On the one hand, these various exclusions generally make migrants' lives in urban areas precarious, since private sector supplies of health, education, and housing services are not yet adequate. On the other hand, partly as a result of the above deprivation, migrants often cause law and order and civic problems. China therefore finds herself in an awkward situation with her migrants. On the one hand, she cannot do without them; on the other hand, she cannot quite embrace them fully. China needs to find a solution to this conundrum soon, because the phase of enjoying migrants' labor without giving them adequate rights cannot go on for ever.

The "mega-industrialization" strategy may provide to this problem one type of solution, by replacing the *Hukou* system with an open urban social system that embraces migrants on an equal basis. However there are many potential problems with this strategy too. First, this strategy will require creation of necessary physical infrastructure in the mega-cities to accommodate the migrants. This is no mean task, given the prospects of another 300 to 400 million prospective additional migrants. Second, even if mega-industrialization proves to be physically and financially feasible, questions remain regarding its desirability from the viewpoint of social and regional balance, because the strategy implies hollowing out of much of inland China and concentration of population and economy along the coast. While suitable for a relatively small and island country like Japan, it is not clear whether such a coastal concentration is suitable for a big country such as China with vast inland territories and population. In terms of physical dimensions, China is better compared with the United States than Japan. However, the US coastline extends along three sides of her border, allowing for a much more dispersed industrialization and urbanization even if economic activities gravitated to the coast.[12] By contrast, China's coastline is limited to one side only, implying that gravitation of economic activities to the coast would mean a much greater degree of geographical concentration in China.

If "mega-industrialization" is not suitable, can "rural-industrialization," driven by further expansion of TVEs, be the way out? The spectacular success of TVEs can be a reason to feel encouraged about this idea. Such a strategy also promises to be much less disruptive in terms of settlement pattern and social makeover. However, there are serious concerns regarding the viability of this strategy. Ash, for example, sees several factors likely to constrain the spread of TVEs in interior provinces. Some of these relate to the availability of capital and markets in these provinces, characterized as they are by lower per capita income. The western provinces may thereby be caught in a vicious circle whereby the absence of TVEs and similar productive employment opportunities make their per capita income low, which in turn limit the possibility for TVEs to grow in these provinces for want of markets! Another issue with "rural industrialization" strategy is the ecological fragility of China's western provinces. Many have argued that due to this fragility the density of economic activity that wide replication of TVEs implies will not be environmentally suitable for western provinces. Finally, there is the important issue of economies of scale and benefits of agglomeration involving dynamic externalities necessary for successful growth of many industries. Thus rural-industrialization, appealing as it may be from certain considerations, may not be viable as a general industrialization strategy for long term success in the contemporary competitive global economy involving rapid technological change.

In view of the limitations of the mega-industrialization and rural-industrialization strategies, the Chinese leadership seems to be trying to steer a middle course. The idea is to encourage industrialization and urbanization not only along the coast, but in the inland provinces too. This may be called the "dispersed industrialization/urbanization" or simply "dispersed-industrialization" strategy. There is no clear government declaration about such a strategy choice, and hence the evidence is only indicative and circumstantial. However, the Chinese leadership's current goal of "harmonious" development seems to accord with such a middle-way, and an array of projects, programs, and pronouncements also seem to agree with it.

The Great Western Development Project (GWDP) can be taken as an example.[13] Launched in 2000, this project was apparently intended to break the vicious circle in which western provinces are seemingly caught. It envisages (a) development of infrastructure, (b) enticement of foreign investment, (c) increased attention to ecological protection, (d) promotion of education, and (e) retention of talent.[14] As of 2006, one trillion Yuan ($133 billion) has been reportedly spent on building infrastructure in western China. The Three Gorges Dam project is also put forward as a component of this strategy. The idea here is to use the increased navigability of the Yangtze River to implement a *T*-shaped development process, with the Yangtze delta (Shanghai area) as the head and interior cities along the bank of the Yangtze as the stem. Another example of the government's effort towards "dispersed-industrialization" can be seen in the recent attention given to the development of small and medium sized towns and cities.[15]

However, it is difficult to say how clear the government is about a "dispersed industrialization" strategy and how committed it is regarding different projects seen as having an important role in the implementation of this strategy. For example, commenting on the GWDP, Goodman (2004) notes that this project was introduced almost casually in the political process and without any fanfare that is usually associated with introduction of large projects. Also significant is that the project does not entail any large commitment of state resources.[16] There is also evidence that, in the wake of major problems that have arisen vis-à-vis GWDP, regional emphasis seems to have shifted toward central provinces, as well as to rejuvenation of the Northeast. Such lack of clarity of purpose and methods may be a concern in view of the fact that China, left to the spontaneity of market forces, is likely to gravitate to the "mega-industrialization" route. Tugging China away from this gravity pull, and leading her toward "dispersed-industrialization" will require considerable effort.

1.3.3   Issues for the future

How China will absorb another 300 to 400 million laborers from her agriculture sector into industry and service sectors remains one of the most important issues facing China in the future. China has declared the goal of reaching a 50 percent urbanization rate by 2020. However, China is yet to develop a coherent strategy for achieving this goal. Despite the move away from central planning toward market, the Chinese authorities still hold considerable leverage over the economy in order to be able to influence the course and spatial nature of industrialization and urbanization. The issue is whether the government will be able to use these levers properly in order to solve the problem of the "rural unemployment over-hang" in a smooth manner, do away finally with the *Hukou* system that puts up an artificial barrier among the people of the same country, and achieve a more dispersed-industrialization and urbanization. In short, formulation of a viable industrialization-urbanization strategy and development of an integrated action plan for implementation of that strategy are among the crucial issues facing China in the future.

1.4   China's industrialization in the light of the Lewis growth model

Are there theoretical models that can shed light on the interrelated issues of employment, migration, urbanization, and industrialization discussed in the section above? The neoclassical growth model, with its assumption of full employment, perfect mobility of factors, equality of marginal products with factor returns, even if suitable for describing the functioning of an already industrialized economy, does not seem appropriate for analyzing the industrialization process that usually involves transfer of underemployed labor from the traditional sector to the modern sector. Islam and Yokota show in Chapter 5 that the growth model presented by Arthur Lewis is more suited for the latter purpose. The authors then present an empirical analysis testing the Turning Point hypothesis of the Lewis model for China.[17] The main questions that arise in this regard are whether China is heading toward the Turning Point, and, if so, how close it is to this point and what the implications are.

1.4.1   Relevance of the Lewis model for China

In view of Ash's discussion in Chapter 3 and that of Peng in Chapter 2 there is hardly any dispute that widespread un- and underemployment, particularly in the agricultural sector and/or rural areas remain a fundamental feature of the Chinese economy. The discussion also establishes the fact that migration of rural labor to urban areas has been one of the main aspects of China's industrialization process. Low rural wage and income level are indicative of low marginal product of labor in China's agriculture and other rural sectors. The family organization of the Chinese agriculture allows laborers to enjoy an average income that is higher than labor's marginal product, which is pushed to a very low level in order to maximize output (rather than profit) using family labor. The large difference between rural and urban labor incomes indicates that perfect labor mobility and equalization of factor returns across sectors may not hold true for China. These empirical facts point to a match between China's reality and the assumptions of the Lewis model, which took transfer of labor from low productivity traditional sector to high productivity modern sector as the defining aspect of development.

1.4.2   The Lewis Turning Point hypothesis

Lewis growth model finds its concentrated expression in the Turning Point hypothesis, which follows from the assumption that the presence of "surplus" labor (in the traditional sector) allows entrepreneurs of the modern sector to enjoy an "unlimited" (perfectly elastic) supply of labor at the going wage rate. With no rise in wages, entrepreneurs can have more economic surplus, which they can reinvest, and the resulting capital accumulation then allows further labor absorption in the modern sector. A mutually reinforcing process unfolds, propelling industrialization forward. However, with time, as surplus labor gets exhausted, the marginal product of labor starts to increase in the traditional sector, catching up with the wage level, and ultimately pushing up wages. The wage curve, after remaining quite flat for a long time, reaches a Turning Point and starts to rise in tandem with the rise in marginal product. The economy then becomes fully employed and attains certain characteristics described by the neoclassical model.

1.4.3   Turning point for China

The question therefore is whether empirical facts of China conform to the dynamics implied by the Lewis Turning Point hypothesis. In their empirical exercise, Islam and Yokota test this hypothesis by estimating a production function for the

Chinese agriculture sector, which they take as the empirical counterpart of the "traditional" sector of the Lewis model. The estimated production function allows computation of the marginal product of labor. Comparing this marginal product with "wages," the authors find that while the former is still below the latter in the agriculture sector, the gap between the two is narrowing, suggesting that China is approaching the Turning Point, even though she has not crossed that point yet. The finding matches with the empirical facts regarding the "overhang of rural underemployment" that makes it unlikely for China as a whole to have already reached the Turning Point. At the same time, with the huge migration that has already taken place and the explosion in the TVE employment, it is also true that a considerable dent has been made in the vast reservoir of un- and underemployed labor that existed in China at the time when reforms began. Further, China is a big country with considerable restrictions on migration still holding in the form of *Hukou* and other formal and informal rules and norms, so that even though China as a whole may still be away from the Turning Point, it is not unlikely that some labor shortage and wage push are already experienced in certain coastal cities, as indicated by some recent formal and anecdotal evidence.

1.4.4   Issues for the future

Looked from the viewpoint of the Lewis model, the main issue for the future is whether China will be able to proceed smoothly to the Turning Point and thus complete successfully the basic industrialization process. Despite China's remarkable progress so far, China's reaching the Turning Point is fraught with many potential problems, some of which are external, while others are internal. On the external side, the important issue is of sustainability of export growth, which has so far acted as the engine of China's growth. China's success at export has already caused imbalances leading to pressures on China by her international trading partners. Meanwhile, the very working of the Lewis dynamics (in the form of a flat wage curve), together with a very high saving rate, the state's withdrawal from provision of many essential services, and other sources of distributional inequality, have restricted the growth of China's home market. In face of limited domestic consumption demand, high investment rates have been the mainstay of China's recent growth. However, a combination of high investment rate and declining productivity (to be discussed soon) is not sustainable in the long run. There is also the issue of material resource constraint, also to be discussed soon. These various hurdles indicate that China's smooth progression toward the Lewis Turning Point is not guaranteed. Whether China will be able to overcome the above hurdles, reach the Turning Point, and thereby complete the transition from a "surplus labor" economy to a fully employed, industrialized economy is an important issue facing China in the future.

1.5   Issues of inequality and disparity

The issues of employment, immigration, industrialization, and urbanization discussed above are closely related with issues of inequality and disparity. As already noted, China has morphed from one of the most egalitarian societies to one of the more unequal societies, and the rising inequality has now become a threat to social stability and continued economic growth. Ramstetter, Dai, and Sakamoto discuss the inequality issues in Chapter 6. These issues also appear in the discussions by Ash in Chapter 3 and by Peng and Kojima in Chapters 2 and 4, respectively. How to mitigate inequality and disparity without jeopardizing China's industrialization is one of the most important issues facing China in the future.

1.5.1   Rising social and regional inequality

The Gini-Coefficient of income distribution for China already exceeds 0.4, making her more unequal than many developed capitalist countries of the world. As is the case with migration, the inequality picture of China is complex, with the following three generally recognized its dimensions: (a) regional inequality; (b) urban-rural inequality; and (c) social inequality, meaning inequality across different social strata as identified by income levels.

Data problems make quantification of the relative importance of these different dimensions of inequality in China difficult. Until recently, Chinese national accounts data were province-based, and often the provincial data did not tally with corresponding national figures. Also, while national accounts data can help to quantify regional inequality, they generally do not shed light on either urban-rural inequality or social inequality. For the latter purposes, surveys are necessary. Chinese survey data may be broadly classified into two groups, namely official and unofficial. However, surveys generally differ in terms of methodology and scope and hence often yield different results.

Ramstetter, Dai, and Sakamoto present a detailed analysis of data from these different sources and reach the following main conclusions: (a) Regional inequality, according to national income data, has increased in terms of income and also, though less so, in terms of consumption. Survey data however show a smaller increase in income inequality. (b) Official survey data show a marked increase in rural-urban inequality during the early 1990s and since 1998, both nationally and in most regions. (c) Official survey data also show social inequality to have risen at an accelerated pace since the late 1990s, both nationwide and in most regions. (d) Findings from unofficial survey data broadly confirm the above findings obtained from the official survey data. (e) The distribution of income and consumption is generally more equal within regions than nationwide. (f) Intra-regional distribution tends to be more unequal in the East than in the Center and the West. (g) Urban inequality measures would be higher if migrants (ignored by most surveys) were included in the surveys.[18] (h) Cross-province studies show some convergence in per capita income during the early years of reform followed by divergence since the beginning of 1990s.[19]

Overall, the authors conclude that the distribution of income and consumption has become markedly more unequal in many respects during the late 1980s and early 1990s and then again in the late 1990s and the early twenty-first century. To understand what China can do to mitigate inequality, it is necessary to understand the reasons behind China's inequality.

1.5.2 Reasons behind inequality

Several factors have converged to make China so unequal. The reasons behind the rise of regional inequality are not difficult to understand. First, the eastern provinces benefited from the agricultural reforms with which the Chinese reforms started in 1978. Later when China launched her export-oriented, labor-intensive industrialization through the establishment of Special Economic Zones in the coastal provinces, the economic advantage of these provinces was sealed. In this sense, the rise in regional inequality has a lot to do with China's geography itself.

With respect to rural-urban inequality, it may be noted that during the initial (1978–1984) years, when reforms concentrated on agriculture, the rural income increased at a faster rate than the urban income, narrowing the rural-urban income gap to a certain extent. However, with the shift of reforms to industry, the urban income started to rise faster, particularly in the eastern/coastal provinces. The rural-urban inequality was exacerbated by the gradual shrinkage of the government role in the provision of education, health, and other services to the rural population. The expansion of TVEs helped to support rural income to some extent. However, the export-led industrialization unleashed in coastal urban areas surpassed the TVE growth in terms of the impact on income differentiation. Migration, by helping to fuel coastal urban economies, exacerbated rural-urban inequality, even though it supported rural income through remittances and by relieving unemployment pressure on the rural economy.

The reason why social inequality increased lies primarily in the development strategy that China pursued since 1978. From "Eating from the same iron bowl," China embraced the Deng dictum that "It is glorious to be rich!" and then "It is all right for some to get rich first!" The latter was an official sanctioning of inequality, albeit assumed as a temporary expedient. The direct and indirect effects of switching from collective to household farming already allowed income differentiation to emerge in rural areas. With the industrial reforms of 1984, income differentiation could rise in urban areas too. Both these processes were compounded by private and cooperative entrepreneurship, now allowed in both urban and rural areas. Finally, establishment of Special Economic Zones and almost free-wheeling capitalism involving both foreign and domestic capital inside them made income differentiation inexorable. Thus, unleashing of market forces, together with private entrepreneurship, and absence of adequate redistribution mechanisms played the main role in creating and exacerbating social inequality in China in the recent period.

1.5.3 Effects of inequality

From certain perspectives, some rise in inequality is inevitable in the process of industrialization. The Lewis model, as we saw, suggests some rise in inequality during the industrialization process, at least until the economy has reached the Turning Point. As pointed out in the previous section, wages for unskilled labor, according to this model, will not increase much during the initial stage of industrialization, so that economic surplus will be concentrated in a greater proportion in the hands of entrepreneurs who can then save more and invest. The rise in inequality, in the Lewis model, is thus necessary for boosting capital formation. Kuznets (1955) also propounded an empirical relationship, often known as the Kuznets Curve, suggesting exacerbation of inequality during the initial stage of development.

However, there are important weaknesses both in the theory and empirical regularity proposed above. First of all, the propensity to save may be high even among low income families, a proposition that seems to be particularly true for many Chinese. Second, an efficient financial system can readily mobilize small savings of many and make them available for investment in large projects. In fact, China has been very successful at such financial intermediation.[20] Third, the rich may not actually save and invest more at home, preferring rather to squander money on conspicuous consumption and/or siphoning it off to "safe havens" abroad. In view of the above, it is not surprising that empirical findings regarding the relationship between inequality and growth often point to the opposite direction, showing countries more unequal in distribution experiencing lower rates of economic growth.[21]

It is therefore an open question whether a very high degree of inequality was necessary for China's recent growth. Even if it was necessary, there is certainly no such necessity now, at least from the viewpoint of generation of savings, because China currently seems to suffer from rather "excess" savings. The Chinese saving rate currently hovers around 40 percent, and in some years gets close to 50 percent. By contrast, and partly as a result, the share of consumption in GDP is low. According to many observers, the high degree of social inequality is contributing to these imbalances and is making growth unsustainable by restricting the domestic market for consumption goods, conducing to very high investment rates, and leading to inefficiency of capital.[22] To make her growth sustainable, China therefore needs to address the issue of inequality by moving toward a more balanced distribution of her GDP between export and domestic use and a more balanced distribution of the latter between consumption and investment. China needs to address the issue of inequality also to influence the migration pattern towards "dispersed-industrialization" and away from "mega-industrialization." We thus see a connection between the inequality issue and the issues of industrialization and urbanization strategy, and this connection goes in both directions.

The sustainability issue is not only economic; it has a socio-political dimension too. Even if China succeeds for a while in expanding her export opportunities and thus not find the domestic-market constraint arising from inequality to be binding, her growth process may face a social constraint in the form of social unacceptability or even resistance caused by inequality. According to some media reports, the number of reported incidents of social unrest in China appears to be rising.[23] In many cases, these incidents are caused by rural inhabitants' general grievances, aggravated often by unjust confiscation of their land by local authorities and developers. In other cases, they involve rural migrants in urban areas who represent the other inequality fault-line in the contemporary Chinese society. A conflagration of such social unrests may put the very growth process at risk, as it did in 1989.

1.5.4   What to do about inequality?

Of the three dimensions of inequality, the more tractable one seems to be regional inequality. The link between the task of overcoming regional disparity and the goal of achieving "dispersed-industrialization" is obvious. The GWDP and, to a certain extent, the Three Gorges Dam Project, may be thought of as projects also meant to mitigate regional inequality. China seems to be making other efforts along this line. For example, she is trying to create a growth process involving her far western provinces and the erstwhile Soviet Central Asian republics. Similarly, China is trying to create a growth triangle involving her southern and southwestern provinces and Myanmar, Bangladesh, and north-eastern provinces (states) of India. There is also the idea of making central China the new growth center so that it can serve as a conduit for achievements and resources of eastern China to percolate to the west.[24] Nevertheless, overcoming regional inequality is an uphill task, and it remains to be seen how successful China will be in this respect in the future.

So far as rural-urban inequality is concerned, the Chinese government has recently abolished the Agriculture Tax to reflect its awareness of the issue. However, this abolition is likely to have only marginal effect on the rural-urban inequality problem, whose source is manifold and more serious, and whose mitigation therefore requires a more comprehensive effort. Among other measures, it will certainly require a reversal of the government withdrawal from provision of education, health, and other social services, including old-age security, to the rural people. China also needs to revisit the price issue in order to eliminate any discrimination or adverse terms of trade faced by the agriculture and rural sector and to stimulate the sector. This task has become all the more important in the light of the recent food crisis. Another important task in this regard is to use more creatively and energetically the returnee migrants' potential.[25] Finally, as is the case with regional inequality, the resolution of the rural-urban inequality has to be sought in the context of the general goal of "dispersed-industrialization."

The problem of social inequality is more difficult to address. There are broadly two routes in this regard, namely (a) the direct route, working via employment and wages, and (b) the indirect route, working via redistributive mechanisms. So far as the direct/wage route is concerned, China faces a dilemma. On the one hand, she is intent on continuing market oriented reforms, increasing the role of the market and private sector, and thereby having less government control over wages. Yet, left to the market only, the wage-route may not be that effective. As noted in the previous section, viewed from the Lewis growth model, unskilled wages in China may not increase at a rapid pace until the Turning Point is reached. Left entirely to market forces, it is therefore difficult to expect economy-wide wage increases robust enough to reverse the inequality trend any time soon. On the other hand, it is widely feared that inept interventions in the labor market may disrupt China's export-led industrialization and abort China's progression toward the Lewis Turning Point.

The above dilemma does not mean that China should feel paralyzed and do nothing along the direct/wage route to mitigate social inequality. First of all, China certainly needs to prosecute aggressively and stop cases of coerced labor and other such malpractices. Second, she may prod her trade unions to be more active in collective bargaining and to participate in the wage-setting process more vigorously. Third, China may pay more attention to upgrading the quality of her labor force (though more education and training), thus climb up the ladder of skill intensity of commodities produced, so that wages can increase while not throttling the export-led growth. Finally, China may accelerate the growth of her home market, so that the constraints on wage growth arising from her current dependence on exports become less severe.

Nevertheless, in view of the dilemma above, indirect, redistributive measures (using instruments of public finance) may have more appeal as a mechanism for mitigating social inequality in China, at least for now. For example, China can reform her taxation system to make it more progressive and fair. Second, there is no reason why China's commitment to market reforms should mean withdrawal of the state from provision of public goods and services to the population, both urban and rural. With rising economic prosperity, China should be financially more capable of providing these services and thus redress inequality and promote vertical mobility in the society.

It may be noted that China's experience with regard to inequality differs from what was observed in this respect in other East Asian economies such as Japan, South Korea, and Taiwan, which could achieve export-led industrialization without letting inequality become too high and are therefore often put forward as evidence of "growth with equality." It is difficult to see why China should not be able to emulate this East Asian experience when she is basically following a similar model of catch-up industrialization. China may therefore examine more carefully and benefit from the experience of her neighboring economies about how to use both the direct/wage route and the indirect/redistributive route to keep inequality low while industrializing.

1.5.5   Issues for the future

Rising inequality has become one of the most important issues facing China. Inequality is giving rise to both economic and social constraints on China's growth. After the initial euphoria from allowing some "to get rich first," the Chinese leadership seems to be waking up to the potentially destabilizing effects of excessive inequality. There is some reflection of this awareness in its current goal of "harmonious" development. However, no comprehensive plan to address the issue of inequality is yet in sight. There is apparently not much awareness about the links between inequality and disparity issues with issues of industrialization strategy and macroeconomic imbalances. The inequality issue is all the more important for China in view of her goal of establishing a socialist, which in general means a more egalitarian, society. Given the goal of socialism, it should be embarrassing for China to have a higher degree of inequality than in many advanced capitalist countries. Excessive inequality may raise questions about the sincerity of the socialist goal and unravel the implicit social compact that currently holds the Chinese society together. It is therefore necessary for China to address the inequality and disparity issues with some urgency.

1.6 Domestic economic integration issues

An important issue that China faces concerns integration of her domestic economy. It has been argued that in the process of growth and greater integration with the outside world, the Chinese economy has become domestically fragmented into self-sufficient, autarkic local units. Such fragmentation, it is argued, goes against regional specialization based on comparative advantage, reflects inefficient resource allocation, and hence is harmful for the economy and its future growth. Hioki and Okamoto in Chapter 7 and Qi in Chapter 8 discuss this important issue. How to increase economic integration among its regions while at the same time increasing interaction with the outside world and ensuring growth is a serious issue facing China in the future.

1.6.1 Earlier findings by Young and Poncet

Earlier Young (2000) drew attention to the fragmentation issue by presenting several types of evidence, the most important of which is convergence of GDP structure of the provinces. He showed further that the convergence was not the result of China's opening up to international trade. Young was worried by the finding, because the observed autarky meant that China has allowed distortion and "irrational factor allocation," resulting in economic inefficiency.

Poncet (2003, 2005) echoes Young's views and reports a decline in the relative importance of inter-provincial trade since the end of 1980s. According to her data, while in 1987 a Chinese province on average consumed 53 times more goods imported from the "Rest of China (ROC)" than from the "Rest of the World (ROW)," the ratio has declined to 15 by 1997. At the same time, while in 1987 an average citizen consumed 12 times more local (provincial) goods than goods imported from ROC, this ratio increased to 16 in 1992 and 27 in 1997. Together these data show increased dependence on local and ROW goods and decreased reliance on ROC goods, implying that while China's provincial economies have become more integrated internationally, they have become disintegrated domestically.

To find the proximate reasons behind the decline in the importance of ROC goods, Poncet uses what is known as, the "border effects method" of analysis.[26] With trade flow data up to 1997, Poncet finds that the "tariff equivalent of border effects" between China and her international partners has decreased from 123 percent in 1987 to 112 percent in 1997, while the "tariff equivalent" of impediments to inter-provincial trade within China has increased from 37 percent in 1987 to 41 percent in 1992 and to 51 percent in 1997.[27] Thus while impediments to ROW flows have decreased, impediments to ROC flows have increased.

Poncet also investigates whether fragmentation is more prominent in the coastal provinces (because of their greater integration with the international economy) than in the interior provinces. She finds that impediments to inter-provincial trade are in fact lower in the coastal provinces than in the interior provinces. This finding contradicts the claim that lower inter-provincial trade is a consequence of greater international trade engagement. As Poncet (2003) notes, "internationally engaged provinces are also the most domestically integrated (p. 15)."[28]

1.6.2   Findings by Hioki and Okamoto

Hioki and Okamoto raise the analysis to a more sophisticated level using input-output multipliers and qualitative input-output analysis. They divide China into seven regions, namely (a) Northeast, (b) North, (c) Central, (d) East, (e) South, (f) Northwest, and (g) Southwest. A comparison of input-output multipliers computed on the basis of input-output tables of 1987 and 1997 helps to show the change that has occurred in the strength of the multipliers over the period. The qualitative input-output analysis, on the other hand, helps to reveal the changes in the direction of the linkages of the economies of China's various regions.

The findings of Hioki and Okamoto show that over the sample period, intra-regional linkages have become stronger than interregional linkages, indicating some increase in regional self-sufficiency or decrease in interdependence among China's regions. Their analysis also reveals the specific ways in which the economies of different regions have changed, and these findings may be summarized as follows:

- Northeast China has undergone considerable de-industrialization, with the importance of its heavy industry as a purchaser of industrial output of the surrounding regions decreasing markedly.
- North and Central regions have become pronouncedly autarkic in terms of both forward and backward linkages. However, the provinces of these regions have become more dependent on some industries in East China as outlets for their products. Central China has become more important as a purchaser of intermediate products made in the Northwest.
- East China has emerged as a growth pole with positive spillovers to surrounding areas. However, it has become less important as a supplier of intermediate products to other regions.
- South China, with its concentration on export-oriented industries, caters mostly for the international market, and has become less important as a supplier of intermediate products to other regions. Unlike East China, it has not emerged as a growth pole.
- Northwest China has become isolated and dependent on the demand from Central China for its minerals.
- Southwest China has also become more isolated and self-sufficient.

Hioki and Okamoto examine whether the observed tendency towards self-sufficiency is due to data deficiency, such as the failure of the Chinese data collection systems to keep pace with the growth in inter-provincial/regional trade. The authors conclude that corrections for such data deficiencies would not change the basic results.

1.6.3   Explanation of increased regional self-sufficiency

Despite the agreement regarding the rise in regional self-sufficiency, researchers differ with regard to its causes. Poncet (2003) actually does not deal with this question, limiting herself rather to observing that provincial autarky is the result of "a tendency for self-sufficiency and autarchy notably in interior provinces in addition to a substitution effect between domestic products and international products in favor of the latter (p. 16)." This statement is however somewhat tautological, and Poncet does not ask the question what may explain the "tendency for self-sufficiency."[29]

Young (2000), by contrast, makes the underlying cause of self-sufficiency an important, if not the main, focus of his paper. He offers a politico-economic hypothesis, according to which the observed self-sufficiency is a "pitfall of partial reform." Young characterizes "devolution" as the main feature of the Chinese reform, and maintains that provincial governments used their power obtained under devolution to engage in protectionism. According to him, they have been able to do so, because the reforms were "partial," dismantling planning at the national level, yet allowing local governments to continue planning and not give free rein to market forces. According to Young, local governments made the best use of this opportunity, engaged in rent-seeking behavior, and as a result China moved "from having one central plan to having many, mutually competitive, central plans," resulting in "a fragmented internal market with fiefdoms controlled by local officials (p. 1129)."

Young (2000) particularly worried that the distortions caused by partial reforms might become a long term pernicious feature of the Chinese economy, persisting even after the rent-seeking opportunities that gave rise to them disappeared.[30] He thought that local authorities' control over prices, output, and investment, though better than the control by central authorities, cannot be conducive to long term prosperity. He therefore made an ardent call to the Chinese authorities to wake up to the danger, wrest back the power given to provinces under devolution, and enact the "moral equivalent" of the US constitution's "interstate commerce clause," under which states are barred from putting up obstructions to across-state trade and factor flows. Young thought that such a change, if unaccompanied by attempts to revive old style central planning at the national level, will allow China to benefit from the "virtuous aspects of interregional local government competition" while avoiding its negative aspects.[31]

Hioki and Okamoto however do not believe that "partial reform" or "fiefdom" of local authorities is the key to explaining the observed autarky. They point to studies examining integration of markets of individual commodities, such as rice, wheat, maize, soybean, hog, beer, lumber, etc. showing long term spatial integration. Based on their reading of the literature, Hioki and Okamoto conclude that while protectionism of local governments might have been one reason for the observed autarky, it did not have as much of a role as argued by Young. Hioki and Okamoto instead point as explanatory factors to the following: (a) substitution of domestic trade by international trade, (b) formation of industrial clusters in coastal areas, and (c) aggregation-level of the analysis.

With regard to the first, Hioki and Okamoto calculate the ratio of international (ROW) goods to non-local (i.e., ROC) goods and find the average value of this ratio for the seven regions to have increased from 8.4 percent in 1987 to 26.3 percent in 1997, indicating that domestic autarky has increased alongside an increase in integration with ROW. This finding is qualitatively similar to what Poncet (2003) reported.[32] With regard to the second, Hioki and Okamoto note that clusters and agglomerations have indeed formed in the Pearl River and the Yangtze River Delta Zones and, within such clusters, industries are expected to have denser linkages with each other, thereby increasing the relative importance of intra-regional linkages. Coming to the third, Hioki and Okamoto point out that their "regions" are much larger than provinces, which were the unit of analysis of Young and Poncet, and note that self-sufficiency is more likely to be observed within such larger units, because many linkages that are inter-provincial are intra-regional in their study.[33]

It is important to note that despite the difference in methodologies of the two studies, the data used by Poncet as well as Hioki and Okamoto extend to 1997. A decade has since passed, and it is important to know how things have changed during this time. That is what Qi does in her analysis presented in Chapter 8, where she also subjects to a more detailed analysis Young's contention regarding devolution and its role in the observed self-sufficiency of the Chinese regions.

1.6.4   Devolution as part of Chinese reforms

Qi proceeds by first giving an account of China's fiscal "devolution," noting the following two stages of this process:

(a) Fiscal contracting/responsibility system (*caizheng chengbao zhi*) or, for short, "Fiscal Contracting System (FCS)," was introduced in 1978 and after some initial experimentation was consolidated into a uniform system in 1983. The spirit of the system was similar to that of agricultural reforms (introduced at about the same time), under which farming households were allowed to retain output exceeding their pre-set quota. Before FCS, China had a basically "province collects and center spends" system of public finance, under which provincial governments collected taxes through local tax bureaus and then passed on to the central government its due.[34] Under FCS, the center's due was fixed mostly in terms of absolute amounts (often in nominal terms) and not as a share (percentage). This arrangement gave local governments great incentives to collect revenues, because they could retain what was over and above the contracted amount to be remitted to the center. This also led to an increase in extra-budgetary revenues (relative to budgetary revenues) collected by local governments, because these revenues were not subject to sharing by the central government, and the local governments could use their authority to determine the tax rates and fees that fell under the extra-budgetary revenue category.[35]

One important consequence of FCS was "fiscal decline" that refers to the relative decline in central government's share in revenue collection. The decline took place particularly after 1984 when FCS was consolidated and the industrial reforms began to precipitate the explosion of TVEs, which were under the jurisdiction of local governments. These reforms weakened the tax base of the central government by exposing SOEs to competition from TVEs and the private sector and by allowing SOEs to retain part of the profit, while expanding the tax base of local governments. As a result of the fiscal decline, the revenue share of the center declined from 30 percent in 1985 to 22 percent in 1993.[36]

(b) Tax Sharing System (TSS) (*fenshuizhi*) was introduced in 1994 in order primarily to halt the fiscal decline. An important organizational change that accompanied TSS was the establishment by the central government of its own collection agencies in the form of National Tax Services (NTS) in all provinces to collect central taxes and shared taxes. Local tax bureaus were now to collect only local taxes. The central government's dependence on provincial governments for tax collection thus ended. Along with this radical organizational change came a change in the definition of the center's due. Under TSS, taxes were assigned either to the central or local governments. Central taxes included such big ticket items as custom duties, income taxes from centrally owned enterprises (usually large SOEs), consumption tax, turnover tax, etc. Local taxes, on the other hand, included income taxes and profit remittances of locally owned enterprises, personal income taxes (of minor importance in China) and other such items. A few other taxes were shared by central and local governments. TSS also clarified the division of spending responsibilities.

Provinces naturally resisted the switch from FCS to TSS, but the center placated them by offering to return part of the shared revenues to ensure that provincial revenues would not drop below the 1993 level. TSS successfully reversed the fiscal decline. The revenue share of the center rose from 22 percent in 1993 to 55.7 percent in 1994. Despite this early reversal, the central share has since fallen once again, though still remains higher than its level at the time of FCS. The reason for this recent decline lies in the relatively faster expansion of the base of many local taxes and slower growth of the sources of central taxes.

The above account shows that it is incorrect to characterize TSS simply as recentralization. It is true that TSS reflected the center's attempt to regain control over the economy's financial resources, and the establishment of the NTSs ended provinces' bargaining power as tax collectors. However, TSS also allowed considerable freedom for local governments and provided them with strong incentives to enlarge local tax base by encouraging local business development. As Zhang (1999, p. 6) notes, these reforms led to "self-financing regimes for both the center and the provinces." The financial autonomy granted to the provinces through FCS was retained in a modified form in TSS as well.

1.6.5 Evolution of the consequences of fiscal devolution

Young was correct to highlight "devolution" as a characteristic of Chinese reforms. However, his analysis suffers from two deficiencies. First, fiscal devolution is just one aspect of the Chinese reform process, which is of much broader scope, encompassing reforms in agriculture, industry, foreign economic relations, financial sector, administration, legal set up, etc. Reducing this whole range of complicated reforms to just "devolution" is not accurate. Even within the limits of fiscal reform, the change from FCS to TSS, as noted above, was not a unidirectional and linear move toward devolution. Instead it was a complicated change involving both advance and retreat at the same time.

Second, Young's prediction about provincial protectionism becoming a permanent feature of the Chinese domestic economy did not prove correct. It should be mentioned in this connection that the "rent-seeking behavior," "protectionism," or "fiefdom" on the part of the provincial governments that Young emphasized are not always the same as rent-seeking for private gains type of behavior observed in many developing countries. As Young himself notes, in their protectionist behavior, the Chinese provincial governments were motivated mostly by the desire to "protect employment, avoid social instability arising from radical restructuring, help grow new industries, etc." More importantly, the financial autonomy itself over time prompted the provinces away from protectionism and towards a virtuous competition focused on liberalization and removal of distortions. It is true that Young does mention the possibility of "virtuous aspects of interregional competition." However, in his scheme of things, this was only possible if the center "wrested back enough power from the regions." What the subsequent Chinese experience has shown is that the "virtuous aspects" of interregional competition may materialize even with provinces retaining much of their financial autonomy. Some researchers have used the expression, "market preserving federalism" in order to capture this particular Chinese phenomenon.[37] Qi notes in Chapter 8 that "never before did local governments play such a vital role in managing local economies," and yet, "the induced competition among jurisdictions provides the incentives for local political officials to develop and maintain hospitable environments for markets and economic factors."

1.6.6   What do the recent data show?

Is there any empirical evidence showing that Chinese provinces are using their financial autonomy to switch from protectionism to liberalization and removal of distortions? Qi thinks that there is such evidence and offers an empirical exercise to support her claim. She poses the question, "Are…policies such as erecting trade barriers to impede market forces sustainable in the long run?" Echoing Montinola, Qian, Weingast (1996), Qi answers that while there may be strong local protectionism in the early stages of reform, protectionism yields to liberalization in later stages of reform. In other words, protectionism did not prove to be the long-run equilibrium for Chinese provinces. As local governments with poor economic performance learnt from other regions' success, they realized that protectionism did not necessarily bring prosperity and help to reap the dynamic gains. Competition among regions led to imitation of the best practice, which in this case was liberalization.

Qi's empirical analysis focuses on the industrial Concentration Ratio (CR). She draws attention to the fact that more segmentation would lower the CR. Qi's results show that while the CR fell during the initial years, indicating segmentation, it has been rising in more recent years, indicating weakening of segmentation. Qi bolsters the finding by investigating the variation of CR with respect to profitability of industry and share of SOE in the industry. Generally it is suggested that protectionism would be greater in industries that are more profitable, for obvious reasons, and in industries that are dominated by SOEs, as their presence makes it easier for governments to intervene. This would imply an inverse relationship (negative correlation) between CR and "Tax Plus Profit Margin (TPM)," the general indicator of profitability, and between CR and the SOE share of the industry. Qi's data show that between 1993 and 2002, the CR has rather increased (from 0.63 to 0.66) in the most profitable industries and dropped (from 0.68 to 0.62) in the least profitable industries. Similarly, Qi shows that SOE share is rather high in industries with high CR ratio and low in industries with low CR ratio. Overall, Qi concludes that protectionism based on TPM or SOE share is not what is driving the current changes in China's industrial structure.[38]

Thus, China's experience with regard to fiscal devolution provides another example of the reform's dialectical nature that finds one of its manifestations in "time-specificity," whereby the same institutional arrangement can produce different outcomes depending on (changing) circumstances. A dynamic view is therefore necessary in order to anticipate and appreciate the mutability of the impact of a reform measure depending on the context and time, as could be noticed with regard to China's fiscal devolution. Unfortunately, many researchers often take a static and mechanistic view of the reform process and lament about the "partial" or "gradual" character of reform, when in fact it is this "gradual" and "partial" nature of reform that ensures its success.[39]

1.6.7   Issues for the future

China is big and diverse. Distance and physical terrain make communication and transportation difficult and expensive. The interior and western provinces are far away and different from the coastal provinces in many respects. Given this physical setting, it is easy for Chinese provinces and regions to become isolated, self-contained units. Much therefore depends on the institutional setting that can counteract the centrifugal forces rooted in geography and ensure integration, reaping of economies of scale, and specialization on the basis of regional comparative advantage. The incentive scheme within which Chinese provincial governments operate is therefore very important. It is a welcome development that after an initial phase of protectionism, the provinces are now using their fiscal autonomy and other powers to move toward liberalization and removal of impediments to inter-provincial trade and factor flows. It remains an important task for China in the future to ensure the continuation of this process so that a truly integrated internal economy emerges.

An advantage that China has in achieving the goal of domestic economic integration is that she can use both economic and political levers. China has a highly integrated political system, within which provincial leaders compete for further rise in their careers. Good stewardship of the provincial economy is generally thought to be an important criterion in judging the performance of provincial leaders. How to combine optimally the economic and political levers to prod Chinese provinces further along the path toward integration is an important issue for China in the future.

1.7 Productive asset ownership and SOE reform issues

An important set of issues facing China concerns ownership of productive assets. China's move away from central planning to market is also associated with a move away from state- to private ownership of productive assets. Where this process should end or what concrete form the state ownership should take are fundamental question for China's economic and social make-up. Imai discusses some of these issues in Chapter 9 in relation to China's ongoing reforms of her industrial State Owned Enterprises (SOE). Whether or not to retain a substantial state ownership over productive assets, and, if so, how to ensure economic efficiency and technological progress while retaining state ownership are some of the crucial issues facing China in the future.

1.7.1 The issue of land ownership in China's agriculture sector

The scope of the ownership issue extends to the agriculture sector, where the question of land ownership remains yet to be fully settled. When China began her agricultural reforms with the introduction of the household responsibility system, allowing households to produce in part for the market, the step also involved transfer of user rights to land from Communes to farming households. China now faces the issue of what to do next with regard to land-use rights and ownership.

There are some who argue that the productivity of the Chinese agriculture, after some improvement following the transfer of land-use rights to farming households, has now stagnated, because necessary investments are not forthcoming in view of the uncertainty created by lack of ownership over land. According to this viewpoint, the solution lies in transfer of full ownership, in short, privatization, of land. It is argued that such a transfer will, in addition to removing uncertainty, allow land to gravitate, through sale and purchase, to those who can use it more effectively. Finally, according to this view, such a step will also help protect farming households from illegal and/or unjust confiscation of their land by local authorities and developers.

There are, however, strong arguments against privatization of land too. First, it is pointed out that long term user rights are all that is required for investment necessary for effective utilization of land. Thus lack of ownership should not be an obstacle to investment in land improvement, agricultural equipments, and other related items. Second, sale and purchase ensuing from transfer of ownership rights will lead to land concentration, a situation similar to what existed in China before the 1949 revolution. Such a concentration will aggravate rural inequality and raise further questions about the sincerity of China's socialist goal. Finally, in a situation of weak law enforcement, privatization will not be able to prevent unjust confiscation of land, and governance-related reforms are instead required for this purpose.

An important task facing the Chinese authorities is to weigh these different arguments in the light of the agricultural productivity situation and other considerations and to decide about which course to pursue with regard to land ownership in the coming years.

1.7.2 Transformation of ownership in non-agriculture sectors

The ownership issue is more prominent in non-agricultural sectors. Since the beginning of reform, the role and extent of public (meaning government or state) ownership has shrunk while that of private ownership has expanded. This has happened in several ways, as described by Imai in detail in Chapter 9. The first is through the new growth of the private sector, both inside and outside Special Economic Zones. The second is through privatization of pre-existing public enterprises. A special, third way is represented by TVEs, which emerged under local government and/or cooperative ownership after the reform, but later were and continues to be converted into private ownership. Given that TVEs account for about one-third of industrial output, their transfer to the private ownership represents a large change in the ownership structure of the Chinese industry.

The process of privatization of pre-existing public enterprises, generally known as SOEs, is linked with the industrial reform that began on a wide scale in 1984. Initially the reform was focused on improving the performance of SOEs while keeping their ownership unchanged. The reform in SOE management through the introduction of the Dual Track system, along with competition from burgeoning private and TVE sectors, indeed led to some improvement in SOE performance. However with time the reform reached a second stage, when in order to further improve efficiency it was decided to privatize Small and Medium Enterprises (SMEs) and corporatize large ones, pluralizing their ownership.

The process began in earnest following Deng's southern tour in 1992 and reaffirmation by the Chinese government of its commitment to pursue market reforms. In particular, the Party Resolution of 1993 authorized local governments to experiment with "various measures" including outright sale of small SOEs. This came at a time when the performance of small and medium SOEs under the jurisdiction of local governments was deteriorating in the face of competition from private enterprises and TVEs. The move also coincided with the fiscal reform involving the switch from Fiscal Contracting System to Tax Sharing System, a move that increased the pressure on local governments to generate their own revenues. As a result, and with a view to reducing the financial burden, many local governments resorted to a whole scale sellout of small and medium SOEs, particularly the ones that were incurring losses.

Meanwhile, corporatization and selling of a part of the shares led to the emergence of a new type of enterprises, which are "state controlled" (because of the state's dominant share) though not fully "state owned." SOEs therefore now have two subtypes, namely "Wholly State-Owned Enterprises" (WSOE) and "State Controlled Enterprises" (SCE). As a result of the privatization process, the number of SOEs decreased by almost half from 253,525 in 1995 to 137,753 in 2004. The decrease was mostly due to the reduction in the number of small SOEs, which were under the jurisdiction of municipal, county, and ward governments.[40] In terms of methods of privatization, Management Buy Out (MBO) and Management and Employee Buy Out (MEBO) have played a major role.[41] As of 2004, there still remained more than 100,000 small and medium SOEs, though Imai thinks that their eventual privatization is just a matter of time. It needs to be noted that in contrast to the reduction in the number of small and medium SOEs, the number of large SOEs has increased, indicating a process of consolidation, and showing that merger also played an important role in the process.

One important finding of Imai is that, despite the sharp decrease in the number of SOEs, the share of SOEs in the total industrial output has remained very stable. This share was 34 percent in 1997, and it remained 34.2 percent in 2005, fluctuating in the intervening years between 33.2 and 35.7 percent, except in 2004 when it rose to 37 percent. Beneath this "paradoxical stability" there has been, however, a considerable shift in importance from WSOEs to SCEs. According to data presented by Imai, while the share of the WSOEs in the industrial value added declined from 23.4 percent in 1999 to 13.5 percent in 2003, the analogous share of SCEs increased over the period from 11.2 to 22.0 percent.[42] Similarly, while the number of WSOEs decreased from 79,731 in 1994 to 23,228 in 2003, the number of SCEs increased from 7,353 to 11,052 over the same period.

The stability of SOE share achieved through increase in the number and share of SCEs reflects, to a certain degree, the success of SECs. Imai shows that there are broadly two types of successful SCEs. One is represented by "traditional" SOEs, which operate in oligopolisitc industries involving high sunk costs and high entry barrier. Imai presents SINOPEC as an example of this type of SCEs. The other is represented by "manager-controlled" SCEs operating in very competitive industries. Imai presents "Doublestar" as an example of this type of SECs.[43]

Despite the success of some SCEs and stabilization of the SOE share, the issue of industrial ownership is not fully settled yet, as is reflected by the fact that the ownership situation of both SINOPEC and Doublestar remains unstable. With regard to Doublestar, the instability arises from the very reason that lies behind its success, namely the personal role of its manager, who as a "virtual private entrepreneur" helped to create Doublestar asset value but does not have a legal claim on it. In the current environment of China, this is creating a tension which is finding its resolution through a very gradual and surreptitious process of privatization of the company. As for companies such as SINOPEC are concerned, to the extent that no particular individual's performance played an important role in their success, the question of their outright privatization does not arise. However, the tension lies between the necessity of market oriented management, on the one hand, and the dominance of state ownership, on the other. In order to resolve the latter tension, China has been encouraging its corporatized SCEs to get listed in the country's stock markets (set up in Shenzhen and Shanghai), and pluralizing their ownership through sale of their shares in these markets. In fact, based on a 2001 survey, 80.5 percent of the 1,050 companies listed in these markets were SCEs with either the central or local government as the dominant share holder. Viewed from another angle, nearly 60 percent of shares issued by listed companies in China are estimated to be owned by the State in 2006.[44]

The listing of companies in the stock market has of course been helpful in raising low-cost capital from the public. However, the state-owned shares were initially made non-tradable. The dominance of state shares, together with their non-tradability, frustrated to a great extent the other important purpose of listing in stock markets, namely letting the market influence the management performance of the companies. Non-tradability also hindered the development of the stock markets themselves.[45] Responding to this conundrum, the Chinese government allowed in 2005 conversion of non-tradable shares into tradable. Since then, as Imai points out, such conversion has proceeded "at an unprecedented rate," and both domestic private and foreign capital are buying into SCE shares.[46] It is therefore clear that the ownership structure of the Chinese industrial sector is still very much in a flux.

1.7.3 Issues for the future

China faces the important issue of reaching an equilibrium in the process of transformation of ownership of productive assets. The apparent stability of the SOE share in the industrial value added does not represent such an equilibrium. China needs to determine where to draw the line between state and private ownership and what concrete form the state ownership should take.

As in other countries undergoing reform, the case for privatization is generally argued on the ground of efficiency. A related argument has been made that state ownership over businesses acts as a source of macroeconomic instability by causing banks to lend money to SEC-related, but economically unsound, investment projects (a behavior pattern that also contributes to inefficiency). However, large state sectors exist in many developed capitalist economies too. These economies seem to have found a way of combining market-governed management with dominant state ownership. Singapore, for example, has many large companies with the state having the dominant share. Some observers indeed think that China is following the Singaporean model.

However, China also has to keep note of the issue of equality. Further expansion of private ownership through conversion of non-tradable SOE shares into tradable shares and expansion of the private sector is likely to exacerbate the already high degree of social inequality observed currently in China. Excessive inequality and unbridled power of private corporations over the society are generally deemed to be features of capitalism that are better to avoid, particularly if the goal is to build a socialist, egalitarian society.

Can China strike a better balance between the goals of efficiency and equality? Responding to these twin demands, will China be able to generate innovative institutions not previously seen elsewhere in the world? TVEs, for example, were a unique Chinese innovation that played an important role in her transition. Given her desire to have a more productive economy while retaining the socialist goal, can China serve as a laboratory for new institutions to emerge, as West Europe did at the advent of the modern period and gave birth to joint stock companies and share markets? Can China offer alternative new contents, different ways of realization, of state or public ownership? Can direct democracy made possible on a wider scale by the Internet help to overcome some of the informational problems and thereby open new ways for members of a society to produce, exchange, distribute, and consume? Is there anything in the currently unfolding Chinese economic reform processes that may point to such possibilities?

These are some of the momentous questions that the Chinese leadership will have to face in the coming years. From this point of view, what happens in China in future is of interest to all who are trying to grapple with the difficult issue of appropriate forms of ownership over productive assets in a post-modern world.

1.8   Banking and financial sector reform issues

The main issues that China faces for future with regard to her banking and financial sector are somewhat similar to and linked with the issues pertaining to her industry and concern whether to retain substantial state ownership and if so, how to ensure efficiency and equity under such ownership. Lu discusses these issues in Chapter 10.

1.8.1   China's success in financial intermediation

Many outside observers do not know about the crucial role that China's banking sector has played in China's reform.[47] As Lu points out, the banking sector's "systematic efforts to attract deposits and mobilize savings" played an important role in ensuring China's high saving and investment rate. As a result, China's banking sector assets grew by about 35 percent per year, reaching 37.5 trillion Yuan ($4.7 trillion) by the end of 2005. Unlike in Russia, where the Big Bang reform led to substantial demonetization, China's reform was characterized by unusual financial depth. In fact, while the M2-to-GDP ratio is near 60 percent in most developed market economies, in China this ratio reached 60 percent in late 1980s and 100 percent in 1990s, and rose to 185 percent by 2004. The capitalization of the domestic equity market rose from virtually zero in 1990 to 4.6 trillion Yuan ($31 billion) at the end of 2000. Given the plunge towards barter economy that the Chinese economy took during the Cultural Revolution of 1966–1976, such financial sophistry from the very beginning of reform has been quite remarkable. How was it possible for China to accomplish this feat?

1.8.2   Banking sector reforms

Lu provides a detailed account of the financial sector reforms that China has carried out so far. He notes that the 1984 industrial reforms, which replaced "repatriation of profit" by "tax" and "budgetary grants" by "bank loans," necessitated financial reforms too. Accordingly, China moved from the previous mono-bank system to a separation of central banking from commercial banking. The People's Bank of China (PBC) was therefore reconstituted in 1984 into a central bank, while the big state-owned "specialized banks," namely Bank of China (BC), Agricultural Bank of China (ABC), the China Construction Bank (CCB), and the Industrial and Commercial Bank of China (ICBC) were reorganized to take over regular, commercial banking. At the same time, PBC started experimenting with more conventional central banking instruments, rather than relying on commands.

These reforms accelerated when CPC's 1992 (October) Congress set establishment of a "socialist market economy" as the goal, and in November, announced the 50-article Decision of the CPC Central Committee (CC) setting out strategies of further reform. The promulgation in 1995 of the Central Bank Law and the Commercial Bank Law marked the formal end of the mono-bank system and firmly grounded the post-reform modern central banking system based on fractional reserves. To take off the load of policy loans, three policy-loan banks, namely the State Development Bank (SDB), Agricultural Development Bank of China (ADBC), and Export and Import Bank of China (EIBC), were created in 1994. The "asset-liability management method" was introduced into the accounting system of the state-owned banks to consolidate their financial independence and business autonomy. A nationwide inter-bank market started operation in 1996.

These developments at the top were accompanied by a growth of second tier financial institutions. Some of the non-bank institutions, such as Rural Credit Cooperatives (RCCs) had existed in the pre-reform era, but these were now restructured to suit the new business environment.[48] Local governments, not unexpectedly, played an important role in the growth of the second tier financial institutions. As a result, by the end of 2005, China had in her banking sector over 30,000 financial institutions, displaying the enormous diversity and complexity characterizing China's financial system.[49] As a result of this diverse growth, there is no longer a monopoly of state ownership of banking capital. In fact in 2005, state owned banks accounted for only 52.5 percent of the banking sector assets.[50]

Alongside the growth of banking institutions, there were moves away from quantitative national credit planning to market-based regulation. From 1998, the PBC discontinued the practice of formulating a national credit plan and allowed state-owned commercial banks to make their own lending decisions. A loan classification system was introduced to promote sound lending decisions. To reduce provincial governments' interference in bank lending, the PBC consolidated its 30 provincial branches into nine regional centers. In 2000, PBC began to liberalize interest rates by lifting the control on foreign currency rates for deposits larger than $3 million with the eventual goal of deregulation of all foreign currency and Chinese Yuan interest rates. In April 2003, China set up the China Banking Regulatory Commission (CBRC) as the central regulator of the banking system, entrusting it with the task of regulating the commercial banks, so that PBC could focus on formulating and implementing monetary policy as well as enacting safeguards to ensure financial stability.

1.8.3 The problem of non-performing loans

An important problem facing China's banking sector is that of Non-Performing Loans (NPL), which became widespread by the late 1990s.[51] The general causes of NPL are similar to those observed in many other transitional and developing countries. The industrial reform switched SOEs from budgetary finance to bank credit at a time when increased competition from private enterprises and TVEs led to a deterioration of SOE performance and increased their credit need, which the state-owned banks were almost obliged to satisfy. Lu characterizes this practice of pressuring banks to issue loans out of policy considerations as *ex-ante* intervention by the government in the operation of the banking sector. The problem has been compounded by *ex-post* intervention by the government in the form of bailing out both troubled SOEs and the banks lending to them, encouraging thereby moral hazard type behavior, including undue risk-taking by the banks.

The Chinese government did make various efforts, including writing off bad debts and a "debt-for-equity" swap, to lessen the NPL problem. To let commercial banks improve their performance, the central bank, PBC, allowed further flexibility in determining interest rates to be charged on deposits and loans. PBC also took measures to strengthen supervision, in particular to meet the capital ratio of 8 percent of risk-weighted assets as decreed by Basel I, the global standard. Banks were required by CBRC to lower their NPL ratio to below 15 percent by 2005. Also, CBRC required all commercial banks to meet the Basel I capital ratio by January 2007 or face severe sanctions, including removal of senior management.[52] Under these pressures, the Chinese banks did make some effort to lower the NPL ratio, and as a result there was some decline since 2002 of both NPL balance and NPL ratios, a phenomenon referred to as "double declines." Progress was also made by the banks in meeting Basel I capital adequacy ratio. Between 2002 and 2005, the Chinese banks also diversified their loan portfolio, moving away from investment loans to consumer loans, and substantially increased their pre-tax profits.

A closer examination however reveals that the observed "double decline" was not as robust as it appeared, because much of it was attained through transfer of bad loans to asset-management companies and through attempts to "grow out" of the problem via increased lending.[53] Several factors helped banks to expand their lending. One is the high savings ratio, reaching almost 50 percent of GDP, as a result of which banks were flooded with deposits that savers could not use in the stock market. A second factor is the undervalued currency. Expectation of Yuan's revaluation invited a huge inflow of hot money, leading to surging speculative investment in domestic assets.

However, this lending boom led to overheating of the economy and deterioration in the quality of investment projects, as reflected in China's increasing Incremental Capital Output Ratio (ICOR), which has increased from 2.8 during 1991–1995 to 5.1 during 2001–2005. By comparison, Japan's ICOR during 1961–1970 was 3.2, Korea's during 1981–1990 was 3.2, Taiwan's during 1981–1990 was 2.7, and India's during 1995–2004 was 4.1. The rising ICOR poses important questions of efficiency of capital use and sustainability of the China's growth process.

The less-than-satisfactory experience in reducing NPLs prompted the Chinese authorities to consider more radical steps, in particular that of pluralizing the ownership of the state-owned banks. The fact that non-state, shareholding banks had lower NPL ratios further encouraged this line of thinking.[54] Such pluralizing however requires corporatization and the use of the stock exchange, as is also the case with state-owned industrial enterprises. This coincidence illustrates the central role that China sees of her stock markets in further continuation of the reform process. In fact, China had earlier set 2005 as the deadline by which to have major state banks listed in the stock market, and many of the above described measures to improve performance, ways of functioning, and balance sheet were taken with this goal in mind. China even took some unorthodox measures to improve the financial worth of the banks by recapitalizing them using the country's foreign exchange reserves.[55] Since January 2005, CBRC has also worked in cooperation with local governments to implement debt-for-equity restructuring of local deposit institutions, write off bad loans, and close down some insolvent credit coops and local banks. The question now is whether China's stock markets are ready to play the important role that is envisaged for it.

1.8.4 Progress and problems of China's stock markets

The two stock market exchanges in Shanghai and Shenzhen were already functioning on an experimental basis since 1990. The process got a boost with the formation in October 1992 of China Securities Regulatory Commission (CSRC) and passing in July 1999 of China's first Securities Law that strengthened CSRC's supervisory power. Building up the institutional structure for efficient functioning of China's stock markets is however made difficult by a power struggle among the PBC, the Ministry of Finance, and other bureaucracies over the control of the securities industry. The regulatory framework therefore remains fragmented, and the CSRC itself is given conflicting missions of providing preferential capital access for SOE and increasing their values, on the one hand, and of being an impartial supervisory and regulatory authority, on the other.

As noted earlier in the context of industrial SOEs, the non-tradability of the state-owned shares limited the ability of the stock markets to discipline the management and also hindered further development of the stock market, which, according to Lu, was perceived "as a vehicle for the government to unload the financial burdens of keeping those mammoth SOEs to the retail investors." Also, poor accounting standards, weak corporate governance, lack of transparency, and scandals of insider trading further damaged public confidence in China's stock markets. Partly as a result of the above, China's stock market went into a slump in the early 2000s (following China's accession to WTO), making savings head to the banking system and leading to the credit expansion noted earlier.[56]

To improve the situation, China in October 2005 made a legislative overhaul of its two laws, namely the Law of Financial Securities and the Law of Corporations.[57] More importantly, as already noted, China decided in April 2005 to make all non-tradable shares held by state agencies convertible into tradable ones, giving an impetus to further development of the stock market. Lu informs that by mid-2006 out of a total 1,300 listed companies as many as 1,092 (about 85 percent and accounting for 81.25 percent of all listed companies' market value) had either completed or were on the way to complete this conversion.

In pluralizing bank ownership using the stock market, China is paying particular attention to forming strategic partnership with foreign banks. This is driven, in part, by conditions to which China agreed while accessing WTO requiring opening up of the banking sector to external investments.[58] However, China also seems to be trying to use the pluralizing process as a short cut to "introducing foreign management, technology, and financial products." To facilitate the process, China is encouraging its banks to seek "strategic," and not just random, investors.[59]

As Lu informs, the strategy has been hugely successful.[60] Foreign banks have been eager to accept China's offer to be strategic investors in her banks. By the end of October 2005, as many as 17 domestic commercial banks have had foreign strategic investors. These include CCB, BOC, BoCom, five of the 13 shareholding commercial banks, and seven city commercial banks. The total investment pledged by these foreign strategic investors amount to $16.5 billion. Among the foreign financial institutions that have formed strategic partnership with Chinese banks are HSBC, Bank of America, Temasek Holdings (Singapore), Royal Bank of Scotland, Goldman and Sachs, American Express, and Allianz (Germany).[61] To facilitate the process further, rules and regulations have been amended in accordance with the WTO National Treatment principle. China is considering revising her corporate bankruptcy law and establishing a credit bureau. She also plans to remove gradually the lending floor rate and the deposit ceiling rate between 2006 and 2009 and between 2008 and 2010, respectively.

In yet another development, PBC, CBRC, and CSRC have taken the step, in early 2005, of allowing a limited number of commercial banks to enter into the fund management business on a trial basis. This is to allow banks, which now depend on interest income for 90 percent of their revenues, to diversify their sources of revenue. The step is also expected to help the capital market grow and facilitate the financial deepening process.

1.8.5   Issues for the future

Despite the significant progress made, China faces many important issues for future with regard to her banking and finance. Some of these are listed below.

Misallocation of banking capital: A disproportionate amount of China's bank lending still goes to SOEs. As of 2003, WSOEs received 35 percent of the bank credit (and accounted for all equity and bond issues) when their contribution to GDP was 23 percent. The other side of this SOE-bias is credit deprivation by SMEs, which account for 75 percent of jobs and 55 percent of GDP and yet in 2003 received only 16 percent of bank loans. Many SMEs are thus forced to resort to high-cost borrowing from informal sources.[62] China has to find ways to end this capital misallocation, which is costing her in terms of efficiency and stability.

Unbalanced financial structure: As of now, investment in China has been mediated mainly through the banking sector, which intermediates about 75 percent of the capital in the economy. By comparison, this ratio is 43, 35, 33, and only 19 percent in India, Japan, Korea, and the United States. As a corollary, China's equity and bond market capitalization rate remains very low. This reliance on bank loans as the cheap (due to the lingering restrictions on interest rate) source of investment, and the resulting misallocation and inefficiency may cause problems for sustainability of China's growth. China therefore faces the issue of rectifying the currently lopsided nature of her capital raising method.

Uncertainty about the efficacy of strategic partnership with foreign banks: Though China is betting on strategic partnership with foreign banks as a solution to her banking problems, questions remain about how successful this strategy will ultimately prove to be. The worry is that with limited stake-holding, foreign banks may be interested more in sharing "the privilege and market-power" of the Chinese banks than in "rocking the boat" by trying to introduce real changes in their management and ways of doing business. In this regard, China faces a similar dilemma as that highlighted in the previous section with regard to ownership of industrial SOEs. Giving up the state's majority share may encourage foreign strategic partners to take more charge of the management of the Chinese banks. However, given her socialist goals, it may be difficult for China to relinquish the state control over the financial levers to private hands, and in this case private foreign hands. China is yet to find a resolution to this dilemma.

Avoiding speculative- and over-financialization: As China strives to use stock market to discipline her companies, both industrial and financial, it is important to avoid the dangers of speculative- and over-financialization. In recent years, financing in developed capitalist countries has witnessed the growth of a new layer, in the form of derivatives, hedge funds, and other exotic financial instruments, which no longer have a direct connection with real production processes and rather actually mask the true risks from not only retail investors but even institutional investors. As a result, rather than facilitating efficient allocation of capital, stock markets under capitalism, in many cases, are serving as an additional mechanism for transfer of income and wealth from small, ordinary investors to "big players." In another dimension of over-financialization, developed capitalist economies, in many cases, have become extremely leveraged, whereby ordinary citizens, companies, and even the governments, are drowning under debt. Such an over-leveraged situation magnifies hugely the role of interest payment and income, which, as a source of income, is the furthest removed from actual production processes. Over-financialization is therefore not only exacerbating inequality, but also contributing to the volatility of capitalist economies. In her enthusiasm to use stock markets to attain a more efficient allocation of capital, China needs to be aware of the dangers of speculative- and over-financialization to make sure that stock markets stay true to their original purpose and help all members of the society to have an equitable share in the returns to capital.

1.9 Sources of growth (productivity vs. accumulation) issues

Discussions above of both SOE and financial sector reform already led to the issue of declining capital productivity in China, as manifested in the rising ICOR. One potential reason for declining capital productivity is Total Factor Productivity (TFP) growth slowdown, which has important repercussions for sustainability of China's growth. Islam and Dai discuss this issue in Chapter 11. How China can prevent a premature deceleration in productivity and thereby sustain its rapid growth for a longer period is one of the important issues facing China in the future.

1.9.1   Previous research on Chinese productivity

The debate concerning China's productivity is, in a sense, an extension of the earlier similar debate focused on East Asian Newly Industrialized Economies (NIE) such as Hong Kong, Singapore, South Korea, and Taiwan. Krugman (1994) drew popular attention to this debate through his *Foreign Affairs* article, in which he claimed that much of East Asian growth was the result of accumulation of inputs and hence would soon face diminishing returns, as it did earlier in the Soviet and other East European economies.

The productivity issue for China can hardly be overemphasized. With another 300 to 400 million people still to be transferred from agriculture, China cannot afford to lose steam at this stage. This issue has therefore received considerable attention from researchers, generating a considerable body of literature.[63] The discussion has generally revolved around the following two questions: (a) What has been the relative importance of input accumulation and productivity growth in China's recent growth performance? (b) Is productivity growth slowing down in China?

There are many different ways to measure productivity. Labor productivity and capital productivity are the easier ones to compute and understand.[64] However, both of them are partial measures of productivity, and the knowledge of one cannot quite tell what is happening to the other. The concept of TFP tries to overcome this weakness by offering a measure of output growth that is over and above what can be attributed to the growth in measured inputs. No wonder that TFP is often called as the "residual" or the "costless part" of growth.[65]

In the varied answers that researchers have provided to the two questions above, two broad tendencies have surfaced. On the one side are those who have reported very high TFP growth rate and thus attributed much of the recent Chinese growth to productivity growth instead of accumulation of inputs. Many of these researchers have also reported a rise in TFP growth rate over time, suggesting productivity acceleration. On the other side are those who have reported very low rates of TFP growth, implying that much of China's recent growth has been due to input accumulation and not productivity growth. These researchers have also generally reported a slowdown in China's TFP growth rate, suggesting productivity deceleration.

An important hurdle to arriving at correct answers to the two questions above lies in the difficulties with respect to data. Most researchers investigating these questions have estimated TFP growth rates using the "Primal Approach," which relies almost exclusively on National Income Accounts (NIA) data. However, the Chinese NIA data suffer from many problems that cannot but affect the results obtained from this approach. By contrast, the "Dual Approach" to growth accounting does not have to rely on the NIA data and can use data on wage and rate of return to capital obtained from independent sources. Results obtained from the Dual Approach can therefore provide an independent check on the TFP results obtained from the Primal Approach and help resolve the controversies. Islam and Dai provide such an exercise for China in Chapter 11.[66]

1.9.2 Evidence regarding Chinese productivity

Independent data on dynamics of wages and rate of return to capital are however not easy to obtain. Of the two, it is easier to get hold of such data for wages. By contrast, information on the rate of return to capital is harder to obtain. This is particularly true for China because of the absence of well-functioning capital markets in the past and limitations of those that exist now. In absence of readily observable rates of return to capital in the market, one is forced to compute these rates proceeding from more basic data. Such computation however requires data not only on profits (the numerator) but also on the value of capital stock (the denominator), none of which are easily available.

Fortunately, some information relevant for the purpose is available for the manufacturing sector in the *China Industry Economy Statistical Yearbook (CIESY)*. This information, together with investment information that can be used to compute capital stock following the perpetual inventory method, allows computation of the rate of return to capital in the "manufacturing" sector, r_M. However, such direct information is not available for computation of r_O, the rate or return to capital in the non-manufacturing, "Other," sector (comprising mostly of agriculture and services). In view of this problem, Islam and Dai present three possible alternative routes.

The first of these is referred to as the "CIESY-route," because it involves substitution of r_M for r_O. Estimates following this route show relatively low rates of TFP growth for China, because r_M, as expected, witnesses a sharper decline. The second route is referred to as the "Hybrid-route," because it involves computation of r_O in a residual manner using data from both CIESY and NIA. Estimates obtained from the Hybrid route show very high TFP growth rates, which is not surprising in view of the fact that r_O obtained in this manner has, by construction, a tendency to rise. This happens because the rate of return to capital for the economy as a whole obtained from NIA data displays a tendency to remain stable. The r_O obtained as a residual therefore has to rise to offset the declining r_M in order to ensure a stable rate of return for the economy as a whole. Another weakness of the Hybrid route lies in the fact that, for computation of r_O, it falls back on NIA data, which the Dual Approach intends to avoid.

In view of the limitations of the "CIESY-route" and the "Hybrid-route," Islam and Dai propose the "Neutral Route," that avoids imposing either a declining or a rising trend on r_O and instead adopts a neutral (or agnostic) position by allowing it to remain unchanged over the period. Estimates obtained from the Neutral route show that China's TFP growth rate for the entire 1978–2002 period was 2.26 percent per annum. However, this rate for the initial 1978–1984 sub-period was higher, 4.59 percent, and it declined to 3.21 percent during 1991–2002.[67] These findings show that China did enjoy high TFP growth rate during the initial years of reform, and this rate remains at a respectable level even now. However, the TFP growth rate in China seems to have undergone substantial slowdown, which in turn affects negatively both labor and capital productivity. The findings of Islam and Dai therefore agree with the decrease in capital productivity noted earlier on the basis of ICOR.

1.9.3   Explanation of TFP dynamics

From one viewpoint, some slowdown in China's TFP growth rate was inevitable. During the initial years of 1978–1984, reforms were focused on agriculture, and the thrust was on an institutional change, namely a switch from collectivist to household farming. This switch did not generally involve expenditure of additional capital. Also, the labor utilized was mostly self-employed, members of farming households themselves, so that their increased exertion might not have found reflection in recorded labor input. Thus it is not unexpected that most of the agricultural output growth during this period would appear to be "costless" and show up as TFP growth.

The situation became more complicated as reforms progressed and expanded to other sectors, in particular, industry. Industrial reforms also involved institutional changes, which continue to this date, as noted in previous sections. However, unlike agriculture, increases in China's industrial output generally required capital expenditure and employment of hired labor, both of which involve costs. As the focus of reforms shifted from agriculture to industry, and the initial impact of the institutional change wore off in the agriculture sector, it was therefore expected that the role of TFP growth would decrease.[68]

However, as a late industrializing country, China still has a considerable scope to enjoy TFP growth owing to technological diffusion. This is the "advantage of backwardness," emphasized earlier by Gerschenkron (1952) and other researchers, referring to the fact that late industrializing countries can benefit from technologies available in already industrialized and technologically frontier countries without paying the full cost that was originally necessary to invent and develop those technologies. Unfortunately, there is no well-developed and agreed theory or model of technological diffusion, despite its huge importance in real world.[69] It is generally agreed that the extent to which a follower industrializing country will benefit from technological diffusion depends on the size of its "technology gap" with the technology frontier, on the one hand, and on its own capability for technology absorption, on the other. The precise nature of this dependence is unclear, but is likely to be complicated and non-linear. Other things remaining the same, as the follower economy gets closer to the technology frontier, the "technology gap" decreases, so that the scope for benefiting from technology diffusion may become more limited, causing TFP growth to slow down. On the other hand, as the follower economy advances, its capability to absorb technology may improve, so that, for a given size of the gap, it can benefit even more from the technology diffusion process. The latter, positive effect from increase in technology absorption capacity may even outweigh the negative effect from narrowing of the technology gap, so that in net terms the follower economy's TFP may even accelerate. These are however theoretical conjectures and what happens in a particular country at a particular point of time remains largely an empirical question.

Looking at China from these perspectives, it may be noted that China's per capita income, despite considerable progress, is still a fraction of that in developed countries. To the extent that per capita income can be a proxy of the general technological level, China is therefore still far from the frontier. Meanwhile, her capability for absorption of frontier technologies has definitely improved. Taking these factors together, there seems no reason for China's TFP to decelerate so soon.

In view of the above, the slowdown in TFP growth rate as reported by Islam and Dai and other researchers before them should be of some concern to China. As of now, unusually high saving and investment rates have allowed China to enjoy high GDP growth rates despite the productivity deceleration. However, as noted above, this process has already created imbalances, and unless appropriate measures are taken, these imbalances are likely to increase with time, potentially jeopardizing the growth process itself.

1.9.4   Issues for the future

China faces a serious issue in the form of productivity slowdown, because sustainability of China's high growth rates depends crucially on TFP growth rates being high. Falling TFP growth rate and rising ICOR seem to suggest that the main problem lies in inefficient allocation and use of capital. Problems of institutional nature may have a more important role in the productivity slowdown than exhaustion of possibilities of technological diffusion.

Productivity slowdown seems to have emerged as a focal point for convergence of several, more underlying issues faced by China. On the one hand, discussions by Imai and Lu suggest that competition among local governments and undue influence of governments and government-owned companies are often leading to excessive investment, some of which is not that productive. According to Lu, the SOE-bias of the banking and finance sector is preventing bank credit from reaching SMEs, which are more productive. The issue of productivity slowdown is therefore related with issues of SOE reform and banking and financial sector reform. On the other hand, discussions in Sections 1.2–1.4 show that productivity slowdown is also related with the issue of GDP composition and source of growth. Addressing the issue of productivity slowdown will therefore require the Chinese authorities to look beneath the surface phenomenon, identify the various factors that are causing it, grasp the interconnections among these factors, and then devise a comprehensive, multi-pronged strategy to overcome the problem and ensure continuation of China's high growth period.

1.10   Material resource and environmental issues

In addition to the issue of economic sustainability, China's growth faces an issue of physical sustainability. China's growing resource requirement is leading to exhaustion and pushing up world prices of many important resources. Many have linked the recent hike in petroleum prices to China's growing demand. At the same time, the negative environmental impact of China's growth has caused some alarm both inside and outside China. Resource exhaustion and environmental degradation are two sides of the issue of physical sustainability of China's growth. Peng, Pan, and Yu discuss in Chapter 12 the issues of resource constraint and environmental impact, while Rawski in Chapter 13 focuses on China's efforts to confront some of the environmental problems. How to ensure the physical sustainability of her growth by lowering the natural resource requirement and reducing the negative environmental impact of economic growth is a crucial issue facing China in the future.

1.10.1 China's ecological footprint

Peng, Pan, and Yu, in Chapter 12, begin by noting that due to her huge population, China's per capita availability of such basic material inputs as land, water, and mineral resources, is limited and much less than corresponding global per capita availability levels. They note that there is already a shortage of domestic supply of one-quarter of the 45 major natural inputs required for industrial development. This rising shortage implies that if the current trend continues China will have to seek more and more resources from external sources, exacerbating concerns that China's growth will lead to resource shortage at the world level.

   To illustrate the point, Peng, Pan, and Yu, use the concepts of "ecological footprint" and "ecological deficit." The former is a measure of how much land and water resources are required for the population to produce what it consumes and to absorb its wastes, based on the prevailing technology. The latter refers to the difference between the "bio-capacity" and the "ecological footprint." Peng, Pan, and Yu offer a computation of China's bio-capacity and ecological footprint from 1961 to 2001 and find that China had an "ecological deficit" for quite some time now. It appears from this computation that the mainland China's use of natural resources exceeds the regenerative capacity of her ecosystem by more than 43 percent. The authors also note important regional variation in this regard. While most provinces suffer from ecological deficit, wealthy urban centers are extending their eco-footprints deep into backward rural areas. The authors also provide a detailed analysis of China's ecological deficit with regard to water and energy resources.

1.10.2 Water

According to the analysis by Peng, Pan, and Yu, China is over-utilizing her water resources, causing an increasing gap in water demand and supply. The average annual runoffs in the Yellow, Huai, and Hai Rivers have dropped by 10 to 40 percent. At the same time, the total area of lakes in China has shrunk by 1.30 million square kilometers, and on average twenty lakes have disappeared each year. Similarly, groundwater overdraft has created 72 depression cones with a total area of 61,000 square kilometers. China also suffers from the important problem of regional imbalance in water supply, with the supply being particularly limited in the northern and western provinces. In order to reduce the imbalance, China is envisaging and undertaking large projects to divert water from the upper, middle, and lower reaches of the Yangtze River towards north and northwest. Peng, Pan, and Yu, however emphasize that to solve her water problems, China will have to restructure the entire economy in order to make it more water-efficient. They note, for example, that in 2000 China's national irrigation water efficiency was 0.43 compared with 0.7 for developed countries. In industry, China's water use per unit of value added in 2003 was about five to ten times higher than that in developed countries. Similarly, China needs to increase the efficiency of water use for household purposes.

In addition to the problem of water availability, China faces serious problems of water pollution and soil erosion that contribute to the degradation of rivers and other water bodies. As Peng, Pan, and Yu report, half of the major rivers and 75 percent of the lakes of China are polluted. According to their study, of a sample of 1,118 cities, 97 percent had polluted ground water and 66 percent had seriously polluted ground water.

1.10.3 Energy

China's per capita energy consumption is still low, standing at 1.7 tons of standard oil, in comparison with 11.7, 5.5, and 6.8 tons of the United States, Japan, and OECD, respectively, and 2.1 ton of the world as a whole. However, due to its huge population, China is already the second largest, after the United States, consumer of energy in terms of volume, with most of it (66 percent in 2002) coming from coal, the most polluting of fossil fuels.

What is disturbing is that China is using energy very inefficiently. Her energy requirement per unit of GDP is 3.9, 6.3, and 9.2 times that of the United States, Germany, and Japan. Similarly, the share of terminal use of coal is very high in China, with only 41 percent used for electricity generation in 2000, as compared with 90, 84, and 90 percent in the USA, Australia, and South Africa, respectively. It is therefore troubling to think of China trying to reach per capita GDP levels of currently developed countries with such inefficient energy use. One of the reasons behind China's energy inefficiency is artificially maintained low prices. For example, China's current consumption tax on oil is only 10 percent of the price, as compared with 75, 60, and 32 percent in the European Union, Japan, and the United States, respectively.

Also important is the fact that China does not have sufficient domestic reserves to meet her projected demands. The import dependence (as a share of total energy consumption) already increased from 7.5 percent in 1993 to 33.8 percent in 2000. As a result, China is scouting for energy all across the world. Such external dependence for energy may however put China in economic and political conflict with other energy demanding nations, jeopardizing her goal of a "peaceful rise" in the international arena.

China also faces serious energy-related environmental problems. On the one hand, roughly 700 million Chinese rural people meet 80 to 90 percent of their energy needs from traditional biomass briquettes, which cause serious indoor pollution and accompanying health threats in rural areas.[70] In addition, roughly 70 million people in China do not yet have electricity. China therefore needs to increase her electricity generation capacity to meet these vast current unmet demands and future needs of the growing economy. On the other hand, her dependence on coal-generated electricity is already causing serious problems of emission and acid rain.[71] Further expansion of coal-generated electricity is very likely to exacerbate the problem.

The issue is important further in view of China's role and responsibility with regard to global warming and climate change. Proceeding from the proposition of "Common but Differentiated Responsibility," China was left out of the Annexure 1 of the Kyoto protocol. However, China has now replaced the United States as the largest emitter of Greenhouse Gases (GHG), and is experiencing the largest absolute increase in GHG emission.[72] It is therefore difficult for China now to reject a role in the international effort to reduce GHG emission, even though her per capita emission is relatively low (about one-sixth of that of the US) and of more recent origin.

1.10.4   China's pro-environmental efforts

It is encouraging that China is displaying increasing awareness about environmental problems, of both local and global nature. In her 11th Five Year Plan (2006–2010), China has set the aim to reduce by 20 percent her consumption of energy per unit of GDP, reduce by 30 percent water consumption per unit of industrial output, increase by five percentage points the utilization ratio of mineral resources, increase by 60 percent the use of industrial solid waste, and reduce by 10 percent emissions of major pollutants. Overall, a goal of resource-saving and environment-friendly production mode and lifestyle has been announced.

As steps toward meeting some of these goals, China has announced a ban on the use of solid clay bricks in urban areas by 2010 and has declared the goal of equipping all coal-fired generators with sulfur-removing systems before 2015. In February 2005, China passed a law, implemented since January 1, 2006, to promote renewable energy and to have provisions for long term development plan, R&D, geographic surveys of resources, technology standards, and financing mechanisms in the field of renewable energy. China is also promoting recycling, and the 11th Five Year Plan put forward specific targets in this regard too.

1.10.5   Historical and comparative perspective

China's attention to some dimensions of local pollution finds support from the analysis presented in Chapter 13 by Rawski, who provides historical and comparative perspectives to show that the pollution problems facing China are not unusual for an industrializing economy, and that China is making progress in dealing with some of them. He therefore offers considerable optimism in the midst of the general alarm with regard to the environmental impact of China's growth.

Rawski's study focuses on urban air pollution. Having shown the seriousness of the Chinese urban air quality problems, he draws attention to the fact that the current levels of China's urban air pollution are not unusual by comparison with what was experienced by currently developed countries, such as the United States and Japan, when they were industrializing. In fact, in many cases, pollution in the latter countries exceeded what is currently experienced in China. To prove the point, Rawski presents historical data on Total Suspended Particulate (TSP) of Pittsburgh, Tokyo, Seoul, and Kitakyushu, and compares them with the average TSP level of 36 major Chinese cities. The comparison shows that while being higher than current TSP levels of these other cities, the Chinese average TSP level is lower than the historical peak level of Pittsburgh (reached in 1923). The comparison also shows that the Chinese average TSP level has dropped significantly from its peak, reached in the 1990s, a peak that was however lower than the historical peak level of Tokyo, reached in 1968, and is now approaching the level of Seoul of the 1980s. Despite this descent of the average, some individual Chinese cities however continue to have ambient pollution levels that are higher than the Tokyo historical peak. This is particularly true for the western Chinese cities, which suffer from the sand problem, and for industrial cities in the coal area which suffer from sulfur in the air.

Expanding further on the issue of variation across cities, Rawski categorizes cities into two groups, namely "administrative" and "industrial." Focusing on the former, he compares Chinese cities of Beijing, Shanghai, and Guangzhou with Tokyo and Seoul. The evidence shows that none of these Chinese administrative cities had ever reached the peak TSP level of Tokyo of 1968, and TSP levels of Shanghai and Guangzhou seem to follow a declining track that is almost parallel to that of Seoul with a ten-year lag. With respect to industrial cities, Rawski shows that TSP levels of such Chinese cities as Taiyuan, Lanzhou, Shenyang, and Chongqing exceeded the Tokyo peak level of 1968, and of these Taiyuan and Lanzhou even exceeded the Pittsburgh 1923 peak, with Lanzhou still hovering around that peak. However, TSP levels of the three remaining cities have since declined to a great extent and have reached the Seoul levels of 1980s.

Rawski shows that the situation is similar with regard to the other important air pollutant, SO_2. The Chinese average for major cities is higher than the current levels of Pittsburgh, Tokyo, Kitakyushu, and Seoul. However, this average has been much lower than historical peaks of Pittsburgh, Tokyo, and Seoul, and it is declining. With respect to NO_x, the average ambient level of China's major cities has been all along much below the level of Tokyo and, in most years, of Seoul. It is close and sometimes below the level of Kitakyushu too. This is largely because of the much less, as of now, prevalence of cars in Chinese cities.

Rawski notes that the reduction of urban air pollution in China was quite rapid. The average Chinese urban TSP level for 2003 is less than half of that for 1986. The pace of decline of the SO_2 level was more dramatic. The average SO_2 level for major Chinese cities in 2004 was less than half of what it was in the early 1980s and is lower than the New York City level of 1972.

Such rapid reduction of urban air pollution in China is however not entirely surprising. Some researchers have put forward the notion of "Environmental Kuznets Curve (EKC)" as a way of conceptualizing the relationship between industrialization and environmental quality.[73] According to EKC, the environmental quality of an industrializing country will first deteriorate and improve later. Earlier, Islam (1997) pointed out that the relationship between income level and pollution in late industrializing (currently developing) countries was likely to be different from that observed in early industrializing (currently developed) countries. He suggested that the EKC was likely to have steeper ascents, lower and earlier peaks, and steeper declines in the former countries relative to that in the latter. Both demand and supply side reasons were offered as explanation for these differences. On the demand side is the increased awareness (often under the influence of the international discourse, events, and funding) about pollution and its harmful effects. On the supply side is the availability of pollution reducing technologies (both "in-process" and "end-of-process" types).[74]

Rawski's analysis of China's pollution dynamics supports many of the propositions above. He puts forward the useful idea of using share of the primary sector labor in total labor as an indicator of the level of industrialization of a country. By plotting against this share the Chinese average urban ambient levels of TSP and SO_2 along with those for Tokyo, Seoul, and Kitakyushu, Rawski shows that the Chinese ambient levels have indeed began to decrease at a much earlier level of industrialization. He finds that the Chinese ambient concentrations of TSP began their downward move when the share of primary labor in the national labor force was approximately 50 percent. By contrast, Japan and Korea had to wait for such descent till this share declined to about 20 to 30 percent. Similarly the Chinese SO_2 level started to decrease when the primary sector labor share reached 35 to 40 percent, whereas in Japan and Korea such decent had to wait till this share reached less than 15 percent. Absence of data does not allow Rawski to extend his analysis beyond the major Chinese cities. However, his preliminary study based on constructed data indicates that similar dynamics apply to smaller Chinese cities too, though with a considerable time lag.[75]

1.10.6 Issues for the future

How to overcome resource constraints and contain the adverse environmental effects of industrialization is a big issue facing China for the future. In order to confront this issue, China has to both improve the efficiency of resource use and contain pollution, and these two tasks are often related.

With regard to water, China needs to launch a vigorous campaign to stop water pollution and loss of water bodies. She faces the important threat of the Three Gorges Dam causing the upstream Yangtze River to be polluted. More generally, China may need to rethink about her grandiose plans to divert water from the Yangtze River to the north and northwest parts of the country. Each river develops in its basin a unique ecology, which suffers damage from large-scale transfer of river flow. Experience shows that such transfers, despite some initial benefits, eventually prove harmful for the destination areas too.[76] Instead of promoting the zero-sum game of transfer, China may focus more on conservation and increasing the efficiency of water use.

Increasing energy efficiency is a big issue for China. To achieve this goal, apart from taking technological initiatives, China has to bring her domestic energy prices closer to their economic costs, including the costs of negative externalities. Correct pricing of energy may help China also to reduce her GHG emission and thus improve her image and position in the international arena with regard to the climate change issue.

China's success in bringing down the ambient levels of TSP and SO_2 in her major cities is encouraging, and this success needs to continue. Meanwhile, China faces the big issue of controlling the NO_X level that continues to rise with the spread of automobiles. China still has the scope to choose whether to become a country of private cars, with the associated environmental and other negative consequences and the related welfare loss, or to become a country with public transportation as the primary mode of transportation. This choice is intertwined with the choice of settlement pattern, because an emphasis on public transportation is likely to promote compact urbanization, which, by reducing infrastructure costs, may also make it easier for China to accommodate another 300 to 400 million people who need to be transferred from rural, agricultural sector. This shows the interconnection among various issues confronting China.

Some researchers, such as Banuri and Opschoor (2007), have put forward the proposition that it may be easier for newly industrializing countries, than the already industrialized ones, to achieve greener economy, because it is more convenient to incorporate green technologies while constructing new structures than while retrofitting pre-existing structures. The choice regarding transportation mode and settlement pattern that China can still make provides an example of such possibility. The recent Chinese initiative to construct entirely new, environment-friendly cities is a welcome sign of the awareness about this possibility. The CPC 17th Congress has pledged "to produce balanced and environment-friendly growth." In particular, the Party has committed itself "to promote a conservation culture by basically forming an energy- and resource-efficient and environment-friendly structure of industries, pattern of growth, and mode of consumption." The issue for China now is to follow up these commitments in a resolute and comprehensive manner and thus establish herself as a global leader in protecting environment and climate rather than be a shadow-box for both justified and unjustified punches in these regards.

1.11 Conclusions

China seems like a giant that is reawakening after several centuries of slumber. In a few decades, China may again become the largest economy of the world, as she was in the Middle Ages. However, in order to reach that stage, China needs to confront a host of issues in the near future. The overview presented in this chapter shows that the list of such issues is long and the issues themselves are complicated and interrelated. The following chapters of the book provide further details concerning each of these issues. Readers going through them will find a wealth of information and insightful analyses and will hopefully emerge with a deeper understanding of the issues.

The issues faced by China may be classified broadly into two types. The first consists of those not concerned directly with the fundamental questions of ownership. Among these are issues related to demographics, spatial aspects of industrialization and urbanization strategy, regional integration and disparity, resource constraint, environment, etc. Resolution of these issues should therefore be less controversial, though by no means easy. The second type of issues concern deep questions regarding ownership of productive assets. These include issues related to SOE reform, banking sector reform, land rights, social inequality, etc. Resolution of these issues will involve more controversy and will influence the fundamental make-up of the Chinese society. Will China evolve into a regular capitalist society, as the proponents of "internal evolution" hope for, or will she strive to be some-thing different, a new type of post-modern society? According to the official ide-ology, China's goal is to build "socialism with Chinese characteristics." However, what this means in concrete terms is yet to be spelt out fully.

It is well known that Deng Xiaoping wanted to postpone these debates for "a hundred years" and focus meanwhile on developing China's productive capacity using whatever means that prove effective.[77] However, development of produc-tive forces does not occur in a vacuum. Instead it requires as a precondition and brings about as a consequence changes in production relations or in the content and form of ownership, and these changes and their ramifications may be too important to ignore. The recent flip-flop over the issue of whether or not to allow private entrepreneurs to become members of the CPC shows how issues often impose themselves on policy makers whether or not they like to confront them. Actual events may therefore force China to resume the debates that Deng wanted to postpone and avoid.

The CPC's recent success in guiding China through the recent phase of industri-alization has been remarkable, particularly in the light of the debacle suffered by the former Communist Party of the Soviet Union (CPSU). Even if China ultimately evolves into a regular capitalist country, the CPC will deserve the credit of guiding the huge Chinese society through this transformation orderly and successfully rather than self-destroying itself and letting the economy and the country into a free fall, as the CPSU has done. However, whether or not the CPC will be able to go beyond and offer the theory and practice of something new in the development of human societies is a question that only the future will answer.

Meanwhile, no matter which of the two types of issues mentioned above is dealt with, China will require a lot of discussion, both within the CPC and in the Chinese society at large, so as to arrive at a shared understanding of the issues and marshal the national energy necessary to resolve them. The effort embodied in this volume will prove successful if it can, even by a small measure, aid that discussion and thus contribute to the great process of China's development.

Acknowledgments

I would like to thank all the authors of this volume, whose chapters provided the basis for this synthesis chapter, and who provided valuable comments on its earlier drafts. In particular, I would like to thank Robert Ash, Erbiao Dai, Eric Ramstetter, and Thomas Rawski for their helpful suggestions. All remaining errors and short-comings are mine. The views expressed in this chapter are author's personal and should not be ascribed to the institutions with which he is associated.

Notes

1 These data, based on official exchange rates, are from the UN Statistics Division: http://unstats.un.org/unsd/ (accessed on July 13, 2007). The numbers vary to some extent depending on the data source. According to Penn World Tables, which use Purchasing

Power Parity (PPP) adjusted values, the Chinese per capita GDP increased from $667.82 in 1978 to $5,333.39 in 2004, signifying an increase by eight-fold.

2   The former World Bank President, James Wolfensohn, has recently talked about a "tectonic shift" of economic power towards developing nations, such as China (*The Daily Star*, September 23, 2007).

3   For historical perspectives on China, see Fairbank and Reischauer (1960, 1965) and Fairbank, Reischauer, and Craig (1989).

4   Projections offered by various sources differ regarding China's population peak size and year. According to the UN projections, the peak population size will be 1.5 billion.

5   This "sex bias in natality" aggravates the problem of "missing women" made (in) famous by Amartya Sen. See Sen (1992, 2003).

6   According to Xinhua report of May 24, 2007, seven towns in the Guanxi region erupted in violence amid tensions over fines and other punishments imposed for having too many children. *The Daily Star*, May 24, 2007. See the story on "Situation Tense after Family Planning Riots in China."

7   See McGuckin and Spiegelman (2004) and Deng and McGuckin (2005) for a detailed account of this process.

8   Many think that unemployment resulting from SOE labor restructuring was one of the main reasons behind China's 1988–1989 political turmoil.

9   The estimates regarding TVE employment, not unexpectedly, vary, depending on the data source.

10 See for example Islam (2008) and Sachs and Woo (2000).

11   The real long term challenge is to create enough jobs for the rural people. Recently, I did some calculations with reference to agriculture and agricultural employment, in Japan, the US, and Australia. Using their experience as guidance, China eventually may only need, approximately 40–60 million farmers to farm the relatively small area of cultivable land in China – which means that in the long run, over the next 40–50 years, a total of 300–400 million people should be relocated from agriculture to the non-farming sector. But the present situation is that in each year, at the current level of technological progress, we shall only create 10–12 million new jobs. This means that over the long term, even with rapid GDP growth, there will still be a huge under-employment situation in rural areas and even more people will flock to the cities looking for jobs. Fan (2005, p. 17).

12 For the United States, the Great Lakes, together with the St. Lawrence River, allow even part of her northern border to have a coastal character. Drawing attention to the coast and importance of the coast as a location of the US economic activities, Rappaport and Sachs (2003) have argued that the United States should be viewed as a coastal nation.

13 This project, initiated through the formation of a Leadership Group by China's State Council under the leadership of the then Prime Minister, Zhu Rongji, is also known by several other names, such as "China Western Development Program" and "Open Up the West Program."

14 There was also an attempt to allow western provinces to specialize in areas in which they were identified to have comparative advantage. I am thankful to Robert Ash for pointing this out.

15 See Kojima (1995) for more discussions on China's urbanization efforts.

16 The following comment regarding this project by Goodman (2004, p. 317) is of note:
       The new campaign to "Open Up the West" that commenced in January 2000 is interesting not only because of its dramatic goal of developing the western and interior regions of the PRC but also because of the ways it has been articulated. Although presented in some ways as a major state project, it was introduced almost casually into the political process, with none of the usual fanfare and perhaps even more remarkably with no great commitment of state resources. Moreover, though it has been in progress for only a relatively short period, it is already clear that uncertainties attend its aims, progress, and potential impact. The contested nature of the campaign to

Open Up the West becomes particularly apparent if, as the case here, the topic is approached from provincial and local levels as well as from the national perspective.

17   See Islam and Yokota (2006) for an earlier discussion of China's industrialization in the light of the Lewis model.

18   It may be noted that, interestingly, inequality among migrants is more pronounced than among residents. This is because while most of the migrants work as laborers, some of them turn out to be entrepreneurs and become very rich.

19   For a recent study of convergence across the Chinese provinces, see Sakamoto and Islam (2008).

20   See McKinnon (1994) and Islam (2008) for details.

21   There is a large literature on the relationship between inequality and growth, and a good part of it focuses on the cross-country relationship between the two. See Alesina and Rodrik (1994, p. 465), who conclude that "inequality in land and income ownership is negatively correlated with subsequent economic growth." Barro (2000, p. 5), in a more recent study based on panel data for a larger sample, concludes that there is "little overall relationship between income inequality and rates of growth and investment," and that "higher inequality tends to retard growth in poor countries."

22   For a recent discussion of these macroeconomic imbalances, see Lardy (2007).

23   According to some press reports the number of social unrest incidents was about 80,000 in 2005.

24   See Ash's discussion in Chapter 3 on this point.

25   See Ash's discussion on migrants' potential in Chapter 3.

26   This method relies on regression using trade flow data with specifications derived from the gravity model of trade and augmented by inclusion of terms representing "border effects." Naughton (1999) used the method earlier to study the issue with data covering 1987–1992 and concluded that "Overly simple characterizations of Chinese provinces as quasi-autarkic protected economies simply don't fit facts."

27   These results are based on an assumed value of nine for the elasticity of substitution between any two varieties of goods traded.

28   Poncet (2005) takes the analysis to the industry level and tries to find the determinants of the barriers to China's internal trade. She also modifies the analysis to ascertain the role of public versus private consumption in the preference for local goods. The findings are similar to those presented in Poncet (2003). "Locally produced goods supply a growing share of provincial consumption to the detriment of goods produced in the rest of the country (Poncet 2005, p. 5)."

29   Poncet (2003, p. 17) however shares Young's alarm about the consequence of regional autarchy, noting that "our results seem to confirm the pertinence of alarming forecasts concerning the danger of China's move towards internal disintegration."

30   "It seems plausible that the endogenous response of actors to the rent-seeking opportunities created by gradualist reform could give rise to new distortions, whose lifespan far exceeds that of the rents which motivated their arrival (Young 2000, p. 1128)."

31   See Young (2000, pp. 1129–1130).

32   Poncet also showed that autarchy was more pronounced for the interior provinces even though these were relatively less integrated with the outside world than were eastern provinces. Hioki and Okamoto (Chapter 7), on the other hand, interpret the finding as "indicating that a part of the relative weakening of interregional linkages can be explained by the substitution of international trade for domestic trade."

33   In fact, based on some analysis of provincial data, Hioki and Okamoto conclude that greater degree of self sufficiency at the level of their regions was actually the result of more trade across provinces within the regions.

34   This does not mean that China had an unchanged fiscal system during the pre-reform years, and Qi provides a good discussion of the upheavals that the system witnessed during that period.

35   Qian and Weingast (1996) report that before the reform, extra-budgetary revenue was 10 percent of GNP in 1978 compared to the budgetary revenue of 31 percent of GNP.

By 1992, the extra-budgetary revenue was up to 16 percent of GNP while the budgetary revenue was down to 14 percent of GNP.

36 Qi also notes that FCS induced local governments to conceal their revenue capacities, as the center tended to revise sharing rules and penalize those provinces with high growing revenues.

37 As Qian and Weingast (1996, p. 8) note, "a particular form of decentralization, called 'market preserving federalism, Chinese style,' provides the critical foundations for market success."

38 Qi confirms that labor is quite mobile across provinces despite *Hukou* and other restrictions. Distinguishing the "commercial sector" from the "official sector," she also shows that "commercial sector" capital is also quite mobile across provinces.

39 For further discussion of these issues, see Islam (2008).

40 Data suggest that roughly a third of this decrease was due to bankruptcies.

41 As in other transition and developing countries, China's privatization process is also awash with complaints of price fixing and other malpractices.

42 WSOE share in industrial value added was 51.5 percent in 1993.

43 Despite the dissimilarities in the markets in which they operate, the two types of SOE share a common structure. Their core business has been reorganized into subsidiary Joint Stock Companies (JSCs), which have been then listed in stock exchanges enabling them to cash in on the growth of China's capital market.

44 "Individual and families" dominated 10.7 percent of the companies. Five percent of the companies did not have any dominant shareholder. Collectives, employee shareholders, and foreigners dominated another 2.4, 0.7, and 0.7 percent of the companies, respectively.

45 This issue will be discussed in more detail in the next section.

46 There are, however, some restrictions regarding the sectors in which foreign capital can enter.

47 See McKinnon (1994) and Islam (2008) for further discussion of this role.

48 In fact it is the RCCs, which, from the very beginning of the reform process, played a vital role in mobilizing savings of the Chinese rural households to the financial system. See McKinnnon (1994) and Islam (2008) for details.

49 These include three policy banks, four major state-owned commercial banks, 13 shareholding commercial banks, 115 urban commercial banks, 57 rural coop banks, 626 Urban Credit Cooperatives (UCCs), 30,438 RCCs, 238 foreign banking institutions, 4 state management companies, 59 ITIC (International Trust and Investment Corporations), 74 business group financial companies, 12 financial leasing companies, 5 automobile finance companies, and a nationwide network of postal saving system.

50 Shareholding banks accounted for another 15.5 percent; urban commercial banks accounted for 5.4 percent, and various other types of institutions accounted for the remaining 26.6 percent.

51 As Lu reports in Chapter 10, according to Citigroup estimates, at the beginning of 2002, the NPL ratio at the four biggest state-owned commercial banks was about 35 percent, and the average capital adequacy ratio (CAR) of these four banks decreased to only 5 percent. In fact these four became "technically insolvent."

52 As Lu reports in Chapter 10, the average capital-adequacy ratio of China's banks (7.8 percent) is much lower than those of other major Asian economies, including India (12.9 percent), Indonesia (19.9 percent), and Thailand (12.7 percent).

53 As Lu reports in Chapter 10 quoting Farrell et al (2006), of the substantial reduction of NPL of the big-four state-owned banks between 2001 and 2005, about 59 percent was due to transfer of bad loans to asset-management companies. The remaining reduction came from NPL resolution and dilution due to growth in new loans. According to the *Economist*, to meet this requirement set by RCBC, the banks "went on a lending binge between 2003 and 2004, partly 'to grow out' of their bad loan problem."

54 As Lu reports in Chapter 10, "the NPL ratio for the shareholding banks has been much lower than that of the state-owned commercial banks (the big four) and the urban commercial banks (mainly owned by local city/municipal governments). Among all commercial banks, the foreign ones have had the lowest NPL ratio." The motivation behind the new stage of banking reforms is well described by Liu Mingkang (December 5, 2005), head of CBRC, through the following statement:
>   A very important issue of reforming the state-owned banks is to fundamentally change these banks' sole ownership by the state through pluralizing the ownership structure. Only when the shareholding and stake-holding are pluralized, it will not be possible for the state budget to "pay the bill" for the losses made by the state-owned commercial banks in violation of the market principle of fair competition. This reform will not only eliminate the institutional cause of moral-hazard behavior in business operation of these banks but also motivate them to be innovative and market-oriented, stand on their own, and improve management and organization.

55 Thus, in January 2004, PBC injected $45 billion from the country's foreign exchange reserves (equivalent to 1/10 of the total reserves), to boost the capital-adequacy ratios of China Construction Bank (CCB) and Bank of China, two of the four big state-owned commercial banks. Similarly, in 2005, the authorities started restructuring of the Industrial and Commercial Bank of China (ICBC) costing over $80 billion, including another $15 billion capital injection from foreign exchange reserves and writing off 170 billion Yuan of the Ministry of Finance's equity in the bank.

56 The capitalization ratio (to GDP) fell from 53 percent in 2000 to 20 percent in 2005. The diminished importance of the stock market as a source of capital was accompanied by expansion of the credit market during 2000–2003 period, which witnessed the fastest credit expansion since the earlier credit boom around 1993.

57 The former now grants CSRC more power to supervise the market. The latter now has lowered the minimum registered capital to start a business for all industries and allows up to 70 percent of the registered capital to be non-cash contributions.

58 Lu notes that in accessing WTO, China had to swallow conditions that are much "more stringent than those imposed on other developing countries by the WTO or its predecessor GATT."

59 To achieve this objective, China has set the following five requirements for foreign banks to purchase shares of the Chinese banks: (a) The stake should be no less than 5 percent and not more than 20 percent (25 percent in case of multiple foreign strategic investors). (b) The holding should not be less than three years. (c) The strategic investor must send personnel to join the bank's board, participate in senior management. (d) The strategic investor must have strong background in banking business. (e) Each foreign strategic investor may not invest in more than two Chinese banks.

60 China has already implemented the corporatization-listing-pluralizing formula for three of the big four, namely CCB, BOC, and CICB. As Lu informs in Chapter 10:
>   By 2005 Fall, Huijin (the agency created to manage and re-capitalize the big state owned banks before they go for IPO) has injected $60 billion of China's foreign exchange reserves into the three banks. One year after it was set up in September 2004, the CCB Co. Ltd. successfully launched its IPO in the Hong Kong stock exchange on October 27, 2005 raising $8 billion from foreign investors for 12 percent of its shares. On May 24, 2006, the BOC raised $9.7 billion (for 10.5 percent of its shares) via its IPO in Hong Kong market.

61 The first big deal to engage foreign strategic investors was the $1.7 billion HSBC paid in August 2004 for a 19.9 percent stake in BoCom, the fifth largest bank in China that was listed early on in overseas stock markets. The CCB received $4 billion even before its IPO by selling 9 percent shares to Bank of America and 5 percent to Temasek Holdings, a Singaporean government investment agency. The Royal Bank of Scotland led an investment consortium to invest $3.1 billion in the BOC, and the consortium of Goldman and Sachs (United States), Allianz (Germany), and American Express (United States) closed a

deal to acquire a 9.9 percent stake in the Industrial and Commercial Bank for a similar sum.

62 Seen from another point of view, private and foreign companies, which serve as the engine of China's growth and account for 52 percent of her GDP, received only 27 percent of bank loans. Estimates indicate that such high cost borrowing by SMEs may equal to about one-fourth of the total bank deposits, indicating the quantitative importance of the issue.

63 See Islam, Dai, and Sakamoto (2006) for a recent review.

64 In fact, per capita GDP can give an approximate and crude, but ready, measure of labor productivity. Similarly, ICOR, reported in Section 1.8, is a measure of capital productivity.

65 For discussions of the concept and measurement of TFP, see Hulten (2001) and Islam (1999).

66 China is not unique to have problems with NIA data. Earlier, suspecting problems with Singaporean NIA data, Hsieh (2002) estimated TFP growth rates for Singapore and several other East Asian economies using the Dual Approach. Islam, Dai, and Sakamoto (2006) provide an earlier analysis of China's TFP growth using the dual approach. The paper also presents a more detailed discussion of the Chinese NIA data problems and the effort to overcome them.

67 The overall average, 2.26 percent, is lower than the average rate for both the initial and recent sub-periods, because during the intervening period of 1984–1991, that includes the years of political turmoil involving the Tiananmen incident, the TFP growth rate fell to negative 0.61 percent per year.

68 However, as already noted, there are researchers who report acceleration of productivity in the more recent period and explain it as the effect of further deepening of reforms, pointing to graduation of reforms from management changes to ownership pluralizing.

69 See Islam (2004) for relevant discussions of the issue of technological diffusion.

70 Several studies ascribe most of the 1.4 million deaths in China from chronic obstructive pulmonary disease to indoor air pollution.

71 China is already the leading producer of raw coal (1.67 billion tons in 2002).

72 Chinese CO_2 emissions in 2020 will be 2.38 billion tons of carbon equivalent compared to 800 million tons in 1995.

73 The parallel between EKC and the concept of Kuznets Curve with regard to the relationship between industrialization and inequality should be obvious.

74 See Islam (1997) for a detailed discussion of these issues.

75 Rawski recognizes that his study is focused on just one dimension of pollution, namely air quality, and that consideration of other dimensions may alter the picture.

76 An example is the Soviet experience of transferring flows of the Amu Darya and Syr Darya Rivers to Kazakhstan. The project ended up harming these rivers and Lake Aral (to which they used to flow) and causing water logging and salinity in Kazakhstan. For a discussion about alternative approaches to rivers, see Islam (2006).

77 This idea is often expressed through the following, attributed to Deng, dictum: "It is not important whether the cat is white or black; what is important is whether it can catch mice!" For a discussion of Deng Xiaoping's economic ideas, see Naughton (1993).

References

Alesina, Alberto and Dani Rodrik. 1994. "Redistributive Politics and Economic Growth," *Quarterly Journal of Economics*, Vol. 109, No. 2 (May), pp. 465–490.

Banuri, Tariq and Hans Opschoor. 2007. Climate Change and Sustainable Development, UN DESA Working Paper No. 56 (October), New York.

Barro, Robert. 2000. "Inequality and Growth in a Panel of Countries," *Journal of Economic Growth*, Vol. 5, No. 1 (March), pp. 5–32.

Deng, Haiyan and Robert McGuckin. 2005. "The Dynamics of China's Labor Market: Job Creation and Destruction in the Industrial Sector," *East Asian Economic Perspectives*, Vol. 16, No. 2 (August), pp. 58–92.

Fairbank, John and Edwin O. Reischauer. 1960. *East Asia: The Great Tradition*, Boston: Houghton Mifflin Company.

Fairbank, John and Edwin O. Reischauer. 1965. *East Asia: The Modern Transformation*, Boston: Houghton Mifflin Company.

Fairbank, John, Edwin O. Reischauer, and Albert Craig. 1989. *East Asia: Tradition and Transformation*, Boston: Houghton Mifflin Company.

Fan, Gang. 2005. "Coming Collapse or Continued Economic Growth?" in David H. Brown and Alasdair MacBean (eds.), *Challenges for China's Development: An Enterprise Perspective*, London: Routledge, p. 17.

Farrell, Diana, Susan Lund, Jaeson Rosenfeld, Fabrice Morin, Niyata Gupta, and Ezra Greenberg. 2006. *Putting China's Capital to Work: The Value of Financial System Reform*, San Francisco: McKinsey Global Institute.

Gerschenkron, Alexander. 1952. "Economic Backwardness in Historical Perspective," in Bert F. Hoselitz (ed.), *Progress in Underdeveloped Areas*, Chicago: Chicago University Press.

Goodman, David, S. G. 2004. "The Campaign to 'Open Up the West': National, Province Level and Local Perspectives," *The China Quarterly*, No. 178, pp. 317–334.

Hsieh, Chang Tai. 2002. "What Explains the Industrial Revolution in East Asia? Evidence from Factor Markets," *American Economic Review*, Vol. 92, No. 3 (June), pp. 133–138.

Hulten, Charles R. 2001. "Total Factor Productivity: A Short Autobiography," in Hulten, Charles, Edwin Dean, and Michael Harper (eds.), *New Developments in Productivity Analysis, Studies in Income and Wealth*, Vol. 63, National Bureau of Economic Research, Chicago: University of Chicago Press.

Islam, Nazrul. 1997. "Income-Environment Relationship: How Different is Asia?" *Asian Development Review*, Vol. 1, No. 1, pp. 18–51.

Islam, Nazrul. 1999. "International Comparison of Total Factor Productivity: A Review," *Review of Income and Wealth*, Series 45, No. 4 (December), pp. 493–518.

Islam, Nazrul. 2004. "New Growth Theories: What Is in There for Developing Countries?" *Journal of Developing Areas*, Vol. 38, No. 1 (Fall), pp. 171–213.

Islam, Nazrul. 2006. "The Commercial Approach vs. the Ecological Approach to Rivers," *Futures*, Vol. 38, pp. 586–605.

Islam, Nazrul. 2008. "Vietnam's Lesson for China: An Examination of the Sachs-Woo Hypothesis," *Comparative Economic Studies*, Vol. 50, pp. 111–157.

Islam, Nazrul and Kazuhiko Yokota. 2006. "An Initial Look at China's Industrialization in the Light of the Lewis Growth Model," *East Asian Economic Perspectives*, Vol. 17, No. 2 (August), pp. 103–132.

Islam, Nazrul, Erbiao Dai, and Hiroshi Sakamoto. 2006. Role of TFP in China's Growth," *Asian Economic Journal*, Vol. 20, No. 2 (June), pp. 127–159.

Kojima, Reiitsu. 1995. "Urbanization in China," *The Developing Economies*, Vol. 33, No. 2 (June), pp. 121–150.

Krugman, Paul. 1994. "The Myth of East Asian Miracle," *Foreign Affairs*, Vol. 73, No. 6 (Fall), pp. 62–78.

Kuznets, Simon. 1955. "Economic Growth and Income Inequality," *American Economic Review*, Vol. 45, No. 1 (March), pp. 1–28.

Lardy, Nicholas. 2007. "China: Rebalancing Economic Growth," Chapter 1 in *The China Balance Sheet in 2007 and Beyond*, published by the Center for Strategic and International Studies and the Peterson Institute for International Economics (May), pp. 1–24.

McGuckin, H. Robert, and Matthew Spiegelman. 2004. "Restructuring China's Industrial Sector: Productivity and Jobs in China," *East Asian Economic Perspectives*, Vol. 15, No. 2 (August), pp. 60–79.

McKinnon, Ronald I. 1994. "Financial Growth and Macroeconomic Stability in China, 1978–1992: Implications for Russia and Other Transitional Economies," *Journal of Comparative Economics*, Vol. 18, No. 3 (June), pp. 438–469.

Montinola, Gabriella, Yingyi Qian, and Barry Weingast. 1996. "Federalism, Chinese Style: The Political Basis for Economic Success in China," *World Politics*, Vol. 48, No. 1, pp. 5–81.

Naughton, Barry. 1993. "Deng Xiaoping: The Economist," *The China Quarterly*, No. 135 (Special Issue: Deng Xiaoping: An Assessment), September, pp. 491–514.

Naughton, Barry. 1999. How Much Can Regional Integration Do to Unify China's Markets? Conference for research on economic development and policy research, Stanford University, Palo Alto, CA.

Poncet, Sandra. 2003. "Measuring Chinese Domestic and International Integration," *China Economic Review*, Vol. 14, pp. 1–21.

Poncet, Sandra. 2005. "A Fragmented China," *Review of International Economics*, Vol. 13, No. 3 (August), pp. 409–430.

Qian, Yingyi and Barry R. Weingast. 1996. "China's Transition to Markets: Market Preserving Federalism, Chinese Style," *Journal of Policy Reform*, Vol. 1, pp. 149–185.

Rappaport, Jordan and Jeffrey D. Sachs. 2003. "The United States as a Coastal Nation," *Journal of Economic Growth*, Vol. 8, No. 1 (March), pp. 5–46.

Sachs, Jeffrey and Wing Thye Woo. 2000. "Understanding China's Reforms," *Journal of Policy Reform*, Vol. 1, No. 1, pp. 1–50.

Sakamoto, Hiroshi and Nazrul Islam. 2008. "Convergence across Chinese Provinces: An Analysis Using Markov Transition Matrix," *China Economic Review*, Vol. 19, pp. 66–79.

Sen, K. Amartya. 1992. "Missing Women," *British Medical Journal (BMJ)*, 304, pp. 586–587.

Sen, K. Amartya. 2003. "Missing Women – Revisited," *British Medical Journal (BMJ)*, No. 327, pp. 1297–1298.

Young, Alwyn. 2000. "The Razor's Edge: Distortions and Incremental Reform in the People's Republic of China," *Quarterly Journal of Economics*, Vol. 115, No. 4 (November), pp. 1091–1135.

Zhang, Le-yin. 1999. "Chinese Central-Provincial Fiscal Relationships, Budgetary Decline, and the Impact of the 1994 Fiscal Reform: An Evaluation," *The China Quarterly*, No. 157, pp. 115–141.

2
Demographic Factors in China's Economic Growth

Xizhe Peng

2.1 Introduction

China is the most populous country in the world, with its population passing the 1.3 billion mark on January 6, 2006. Population is one of the decisive factors shaping the pattern of China's economic growth. On the one hand, the huge population has provided China a massive labor force, making China the "factory of the world." On the other hand, the gigantic population also puts great pressure on China with regard to employment, social welfare, natural resource, and environment.

The major characteristics of China's current population are its uneven regional distribution, rapid aging process, huge internal migration, and rural-urban segregation. In 2005, about 562 million persons, constituting 43 percent of the overall population, were classified as urban population, while the remaining about 745 million persons, constituting 57 percent of the population were rural.[1] China has already entered into the phase of an aging society as more than 7.69 percent of the population, numbering about 101 million, were 65 years and older in 2005. China's population is highly concentrated in the central and eastern parts of the country. However, an unprecedented large-scale rural-urban migration, generally with the eastern coastal region as the destination and numbering about 147 million, has been a major demographic event over the past two decades. The migration has changed the spatial distribution of China's population, affected patterns and path of her urbanization, and exerted great impact on China's socio-economic development.

The goal of this chapter is to provide an overview of China's current demographic situation, identify the main trends, offer some projections, and discuss in broad terms the impact of the demographics on China's future economic growth, employment, urbanization, and pension system.

The discussion of the chapter is organized as follows. The general demographic dynamics of China are discussed in Section 2.1. Section 2.2 reviews China's demographic transition and presents population projection for the future. The role of government population policy in shaping China's population dynamics is discussed in Section 2.3. The rapid process of population aging, which is one of the major features of China's current population dynamics, is examined in Section 2.4. The rest of the sections examine the impact of demographics on China's economic growth, including labor force and unemployment (Section 2.5), urbanization and migration (Section 2.6), and pension system and health care system (Section 2.7). Section 2.8 provides a brief conclusion of the chapter.

2.2 Demographic transition

Over the last half a century, China witnessed a profound demographic transition. Both mortality and fertility have declined, in a more rapid and dramatic way than in any other part of the world (Figure 2.1). Life expectancy in China rose from 43 to around 72 years during the 1950–2000 period, while fertility level dropped from more than six to less than two children per woman over the same time period.

China experienced an impressive decline in death rates, particularly among infants, and a high, even rising birth rate in the 1950s due mainly to great improvement in people's living conditions and social stability in those years after continuous wars during the 1930s and 1940s. As a result, population growth in China speeded up to an alarming level. This was followed by a demographic crisis, accompanied by massive excessive mortality and a sharp decline in the birth rate, occurring during 1959–1961, and caused mainly by the great famine.[2] Even negative population growth was recorded in 1960. China recovered from this crisis in the next few years with a compensating birth peak in the middle 1960s. Overall, during the 15-year period of 1949–1964, China's population increased from 500 million to 700 million, an average annual growth of 13 million.

Fertility decline began first in urban China in the 1960s, and this was followed by the nationwide fertility reduction in the 1970s. Total fertility rate dropped

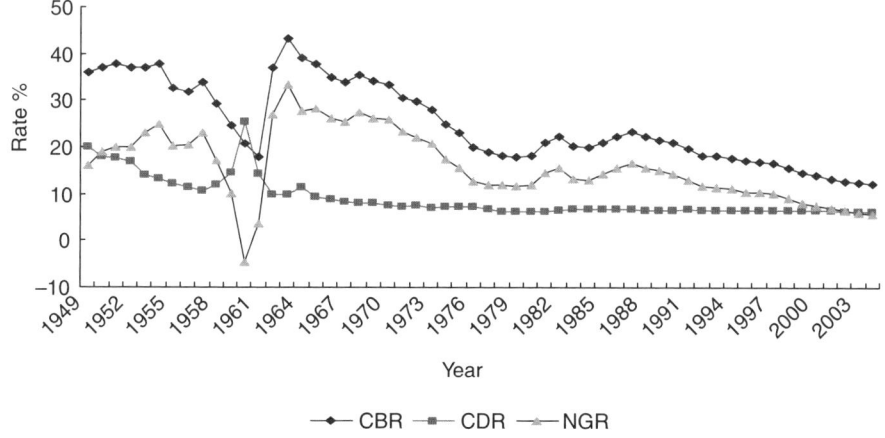

Figure 2.1 China's population dynamics: 1949–2004

Source: China Statistical Yearbook 2004, China Statistical Publishing House, 2005.

from 5.8 in 1970 to 2.8 in 1979 and decreased further to below replacement level in the 1990s. Over the same period, China's mortality level continued its gradual decline. Consequently, the demographic pattern of China transformed from one characterized by high birth, high death and high growth to one characterized by low birth, low death and low growth.

The quality of Chinese population statistics is one of the most debated topics.[3] This is a result partly of shortcomings of China's statistics reporting and collection system, and partly of complexity of relevant issues. Although there are disagreements about the data accuracy, it is commonly accepted that China's current total fertility rate stands at around 1.8. As a result of the fertility decline, it is estimated that in the last three decades, roughly 300 million births were avoided.[4]

Entering into the twenty first century, China's population continued its growth, but the speed has slowed down further. The population natural growth rate declined from 10.55 per thousand in 1995 to 7.58 per thousand in 2000 and further down to 5.87 per thousand in 2004. Nevertheless, due mainly to population momentum, the annual number of births in China remained as high as 16 million, and the annual net increment in population stood at 7.6 million in 2005.

There are marked regional and rural-urban variations in the path and timing of demographic transition. For instance, China's urban fertility transition started as early as the mid-1960s, while similar fertility decline in rural China occurred in the early 1970s. By the late 1990s, the Total Fertility Rate (TFR) ranged from below one in big metropolitan cities like Shanghai and Beijing, to 3.11 in Tibet autonomous region. Such regional diversity can be observed with respect to many other aspects of China's demographics. The serious imbalance in sex ratio at birth is another example.

The abnormal sex ratio at birth was first reported in the 1980s, and has got worse since then. It was reported that in 2005 for every 100 new-born girls, there were 124 boys, compared to 119.92 in 2000 and 111.42 in 1990. There are marked regional differences in this regard. In general, sex ratio at birth in western provinces and autonomous regions is more or less within the normal range, while serious abnormalities of this ratio are reported for the central and southern parts of China.

Variations in demographic transition, on the one hand, have been the consequence of regional variation in socio-economic and cultural conditions (Figure 2.2 and Table 2.1). On the other hand, they influenced local development. In particular, regional variation in economic development is one of the major causes of nationwide population migration.

It is certain that China's population will continue to grow in the near future (Figure 2.3). The peak of the total population and the turning point of the population growth are important factors for future economic growth pattern in China. Various population projections have been made based on different assumptions regarding future trends in fertility and mortality.[5] China's total population, even according to the lowest projection, will increase by at least 100 million to

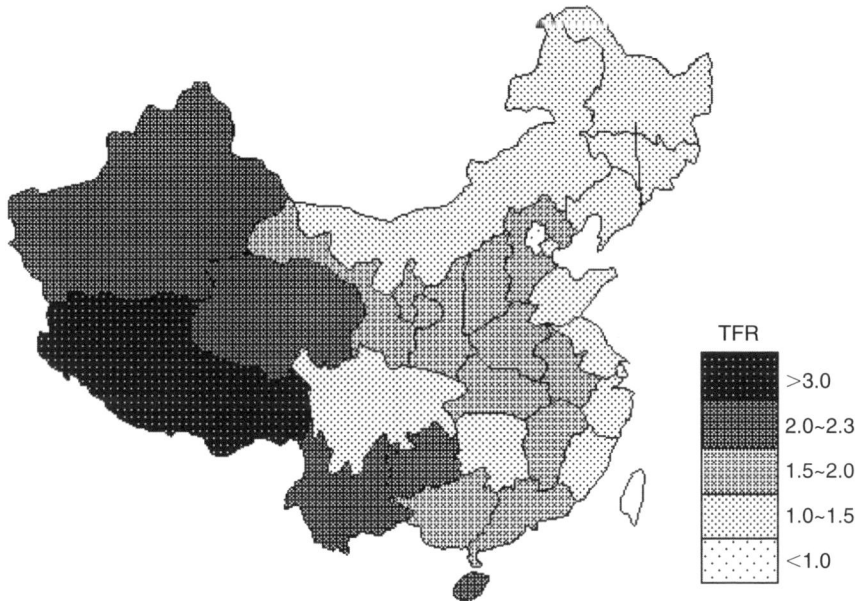

Figure 2.2   Provincial fertility pattern in China, 1997–1999

Source: Based on estimation by China's State Family Planning Commission. Data for Taiwan, Hong Kong, and Macao are not included.

Table 2.1   Provincial pattern of abnormal sex ratio at birth in China, 2000

Sex ratio at birth	Number of provincial units	Provinces, metropolitans and autonomous regions
Below 103	1	Tibet
103–107	1	Xinjiang
107–110	5	Guizhou, Neimenggu, Yunnan, Ningxia, Heilongjiang
110–116	13	Qinghai, Beijing, Shanghai, Jilin, Shandong, Tianjin, Shanxi, Liaoning, Hebei, Zhejiang, Jiangxi, Gansu, Chongqing
116–120	4	Sichuan, Jiangsu, Fujian, Henan
Higher than 120	7	Shannxi, Guangxi, Hunan, Anhui, Hubei, Guangdong, Hainan

Sources: China's 2000 population census.

1.4 billion before the growth finally stops around the middle of the twenty first century. The medium-growth scenario projected by the United Nations based on the assumption of continuation of current demographic patterns anticipates that in the next half century the population of China will reach 1.5 billion, a net increase of 200 million from the present figure. About two thirds of the growth

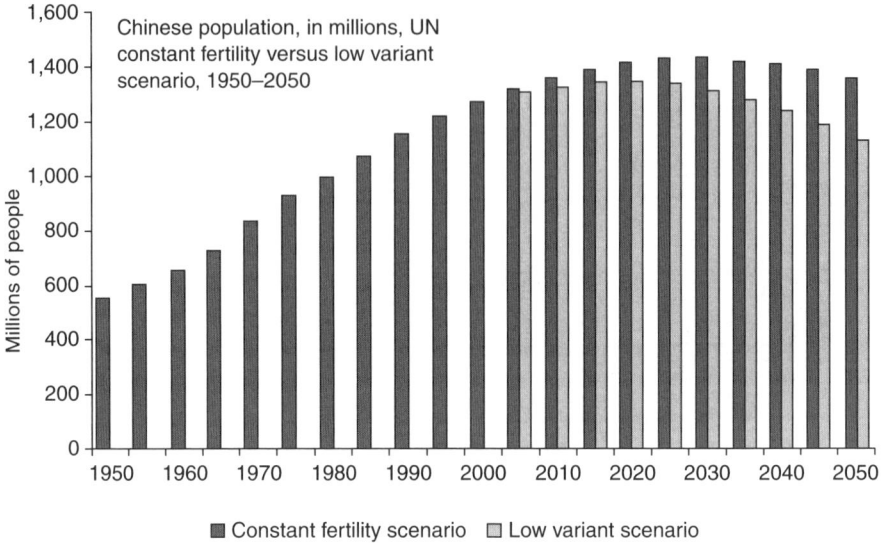

Figure 2.3 Projections for China's population

Source: United Nations Population Division, 2003.

is anticipated to occur between 2000 and 2025, and China's population will eventually stop growing before the middle of the twenty first century. India will finally overtake China as the country with the largest population in the world around 2030.

The future population growth will be largely determined by China's government population policy and future socio-economic development. Although there have been continued debates on whether China should give up its "One Child policy (OCP)" that has been in effect over the last about 30 years, it seems most likely that Chinese government will stick to its current population policy, at least for the near future.

2.3 The role of government population policy

Socioeconomic development is certainly a decisive factor facilitating demographic transition. To a large extent, lower birth and death rates are by-products of socio-economic development. Higher incomes contribute to infant mortality decline by raising nutritional standards and to lower birth rates by raising the market value of women's time and, hence, the opportunity costs of childbearing. Other features of social and economic development, particularly the educational attainment of women, may play an even more important role. With the passage of time, the importance of the socioeconomic factors on fertility trend has been rising. Nevertheless, government polices related to fertility behavior have played a profound role in bringing about the demographic transition in China, and shaping the regional pattern of China's demographic dynamics.

China's demographic transition was initialized by strong and effective government-sponsored public health and family planning programs. China witnessed a very rapid population growth during the 1964–1974 period. Its total population increased from 700 million to 900 million in only ten years, prompting the government to promote the family planning program. The program implementation began in the urban areas in the 1960s, and expanded to the rural areas in the early 1970s. The program focused on the slogan of "Later, Longer, and Fewer", meaning later marriage and later childbearing, longer birth interval, and fewer children. The proposal of "OCP" was first put forward in 1979 and became fully operational in the early 1980s. One of the notable features of China's family planning program is its decentralized policy formation and program implementation. China's current local family planning regulations can be grouped into five major categories (see Table 2.2). In general, regulations are more flexible in rural areas than in urban areas, more rigid for the Han people than for the national minorities. Had all Chinese couples followed the local family planning regulations, the total cohort fertility rate in 1990 would have been 1.62 and 1.50 in 2000, as more people became urban residents and thus changed their birth control categories.[6] Therefore, the notion of "OCP" is actually an oversimplification even though the term is widely accepted.

The differential local birth control regulation is to a large extent a compromise between the central guidance on population control and the local situation, both in terms of socioeconomic development and the political commitment of the local government. For instance, Chinese farmer families can have two children in general, and this is rationalized on the ground that farmer families depend on family labor for agricultural production and for old-age support (primarily support by married son[s]) , as there is almost no well-covered government-sponsored pension system operating for Chinese farmers. Therefore, the relatively rigid family planning regulation is expected to be implemented in regions with better socio-economic conditions, with more concentration of state-owned enterprises, and more people engaging in non-agricultural economic activities in general.

Table 2.2 Comparison of various local family planning regulations, 1990s

Group	Major policy regulations	Coverage
1	One child with very few exceptions in allowing couples to have two children	All urban residents and rural couples in Jiangsu and part of Sichuan province
2	Two children if the first one is a girl	Most rural couples
3	Two children with a four-year spacing	
4	Two or three children	Minorities in the rural areas of minority autonomous regions
5	No numerical regulation	Rural Tibetan population

Sources: Details of provincial family planning regulations are available at www.cpirc.org.cn (accessed on August 15, 2002).

There are always exceptions. It is interesting to note that for a long time the family planning regulation in Guangdong province, one of the rich provinces in China, was a slack one compared to that in many other Chinese provinces, while the regulation in Sichuan province was rigid relative to its socio-economic condition.

Both incentive and disincentive measures have been used to operate and manage the program. Incentive measures rely heavily on the financial capacity and other social welfare resources of local government. When such capacity and resources were lacking, local government often resorted to punitive packages, which in some cases took coercive nature. Such practices were widely used particularly in the 1980s. Levying fines from those parents who gave birth outside the birth control quota was treated as one of the most effective ways of implementing the program. However such fines were also one of the causes of social tension between cadres and the public, especially in the rural areas.[7] The introduction of family planning responsibility system for government agencies at all levels in the 1980s manifested the commitment of the Chinese government to slowing down the population growth. In recent years, more attention has been paid to the provision of social welfare to the rural elderly who followed the government family planning policy regulation in the past.[8] This new measure indicates a significant shift of China's family planning from purely "punishing those who have many children" to "rewarding those who have fewer children". Also, this long-awaited program is one of the major policy measures manifesting the "pro-people" orientation of the present Chinese leadership.

As the imbalance in China's sex ratio at birth has been deteriorating, the Chinese government's attitude toward the problem has recently changed from denying the problem in earlier years to more active condemnation of abortion of female fetuses and prevention of this unfortunate practice. Tough regulations have been introduced to crack down on illegal sex identification and to prevent pre-birth selective abortions of female fetuses. However, as technologies, such as ultrasound examination, become widely available at affordable cost to Chinese farmers, and also due to lack of efficient implementation of these laws and regulations, the problem remains serious. The government's plan to bring the situation back to normal in the near future is fraught with difficulties.

It seems most likely that the current population policy will remain in effect at least for the next five years, but more modifications will be implemented first at provincial level and then extended nationwide.[9] The current population policy will be implemented in a much more comprehensive manner, together with other social policies and along with gradual transformation of governance patterns at the local community level.

2.4 Rapid population aging

One of the major consequences of China's demographic change is rapid population aging. In 2000, the proportion of the elderly (people over 65 years) in the total population for the first time in China's history exceeded 7 percent, indicating that China, as a whole, has become an "ageing society". The total number of eld-erly population increased from 86.87 million in 2000 to 100.45 million in 2005, accounting for 7.69 percent of the overall population, and signifying an increase by 13.58 million over this five-year period. The number of the elderly people is expected to increase by three times over the first half of the twenty first century. If age 60 is used as the criteria, the number of the elderly in China would be much higher. It is reported that in 2005 the number of people aged 60 and over amounted to 144.08 million, an increase by 0.76 percentage point compared to that of 2000.[10]

Along with the size, the proportion of the elderly in the total population is anticipated to rise quickly in the near future. According to the UN estimation, the median age of China will increase by 12.2 years from 32.6 years in 2005 to almost 45 years in 2050.[11] Consequently, the potential support ratio, based on present retirement arrangements, will change from currently 11 elderly persons per 100 working age persons to 39 elderly per 100 working age persons in 2050. The working age population in China will eventually stop growing around 2011, while the growth of the elderly population will continue.

While the major cause of rapid aging in China is fertility decline, improvement in longevity is another salient factor in this regard. In 2004, the life expectancy at birth for all Chinese was 72 years with 70 years for males and 74 years for females.[12] Although the Chinese people nowadays live ten years less than the Japanese, they live on average eight years longer than the Indians. However, marked regional variations exist in China with respect to longevity. The life expectancy at birth for people living in big Chinese cities such as Shanghai has already reached a level similar to that of Japan (83 for female and 79 for men). However the analogous figures are much lower in inland rural areas (Zhao, 2006).

An aging population has long been a major challenge facing many cities and wealthier rural areas in the eastern region, while the vast western provinces are lag-ging behind the national trend with respect to aging (Figure 2.4). Shanghai is one of the "eldest" provincial units in China. It entered the aging stage (people aged 60 and over accounting for more than 10 percent of the total population) in 1979, and 19.58 percent of the city population, 2.66 million in number, was reported to be 60 and older by the end of 2005. On the other hand, Qinghai province is projected to enter the aging society stage not until 2014. Regional variation in population aging is very similar to the regional variation in current fertility, indicating that the aging process is mainly determined by the path of fertility transition. The acceler-ated aging process in some eastern regions and big city centers has already resulted in ballooning of fiscal burden, weak consumption, and poor market innovation. These problems are likely to deteriorate further in the near future.

Attention should be paid to certain features of the regional data on aging, par-ticularly data for the cities, as most of these data were based on people holding the permanent local household registration status (*Huji* population, in Chinese), so that migrants were excluded. For instance, if the calculation was based on long-term residents of Shanghai (people living in Shanghai longer than six months regardless of the *Huji* status), the proportion of the elderly aged 65 and over in

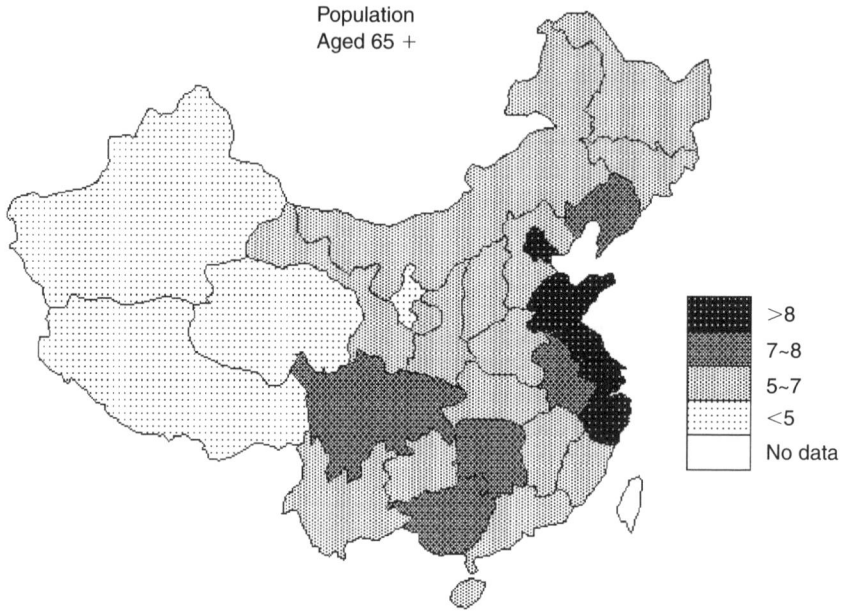

Figure 2.4   Regional variations in population aging, 2000
Source: China's Population Census for 2000.

Shanghai in 2005 would be 11.94 percent rather than 14.97 percent calculated for *Huji* population. Therefore, migration, especially inflow of young migrants, can have a significant effect in slowing down the aging process in China's urban areas.

Unlike many developed countries, aging in China is coming at a much earlier stage in terms of the level of socioeconomic development. For example, Japan reached the median age of 32.6 years in 1980 when her real per capita income was US$15,600. By contrast China has reached the same median age with a real per capita income of US$1,200 only. The transition to an aging society is also occurring over a shorter time span in China. It took Sweden 85 years, United Kingdom 45 years and Japan 28 years to have the proportion in total population of persons aged 65 and over increase from 7 to 14 percent. The comparable demographic shift will be achieved in China in only 27 years.[13] It is also estimated that by the middle of this century, while India will overtake China to become the most populous country in the world, China will become the country with the world's largest elderly population.[14]

2.5   Labor force and employment

China is abundant in labor supply. Among the 1.3 billion people in mainland China in 2003, 760.75 million were economically active, representing the largest labor force in the world. Moreover, the population of working age is growing at the fastest rate during the past decade, increasing by 13.6 million annually on average. This continued growth is mainly caused by the large birth cohorts born two decades ago, and is resulting in low dependency ratios for both the young and the elderly. The proportion of working age population (aged 16–59) to total population has remained at a level around 68 percent over the past decade. The abundant labor supply is one of the major driving forces behind China's rapid economic growth over the years. By mobilizing an almost unlimited and cheap labor supply, China has become the factory of the world. China is harvesting the demographic bonus created by favorable age structure caused by demographic transition.

However, this abundance may change soon as the opportunity window is gradually closing. The annual rate of increase of the working age population in China for 2000–2015 is projected to be only 0.9 percent, much lower than the world average rate of 1.4 percent. It is also projected that while the total Chinese population may peak in 2030, the working age population would peak much earlier, around 2020. The total labor force in China may show a negative growth thereafter as the large cohort of baby boomers who were born in the 1950s will gradually retire in the next decade, while the new comers will not be able to replace them in the same number.[15] Labor shortage has already been widely reported, particularly in the Guangdong province in 2005. The very low wage is one of the causes of the phenomenon. However, the gradual decline in the overall labor supply is another potential cause for the shortage. The future economic growth in China will therefore rely more on the improvement in labor quality rather than on the increase in quantity.[16]

In 2003, 744.32 million Chinese were formally engaged in economic activities. The employees in urban areas accounted for 34.4 percent of the total and those in rural accounting for the remaining 65.6 percent. China's urban labor force used to enjoy full employment but with low salaries. For a long time, jobs were assigned by the State to individuals, and neither workers nor the enterprises had any say in the matter. This "Iron rice bowl" employment system ended in the early 1980s, when contractual employment was introduced nationwide. The 1990s witnessed a further economic restructuring involving both changes in ownership and upgrading of the industrial structure. The transformation of the centrally planned economy towards a market oriented one has made the labor force increasingly mobile, and people have been given much more freedom to choose jobs. As a result of these changes, urban unemployment has emerged, and a relatively large proportion of "excess" workers has been laid off or transferred to other economic activities. It was reported that during the five years of 1998–2003, the total number of laid-off workers from state-owned enterprises had been 28.18 million, of whom over 17 million were reemployed.[17] The rapidly expanding sector of foreign joint ventures and private businesses has been able to absorb millions from the labor force. Employment in China has therefore become quite diversified, and this diversity is increasing continuously. It is projected by the Chinese authorities that in the next five-year period, an additional 50 million labor force will enter China's urban labor market, though the urban economy

Table 2.3 Number of employed and unemployed in China since 1990

Year	Total employees (in millions)	Unemployment (million persons)	Rate of unemployment (%)
1990	639.09	3.832	2.5
1991	647.99	3.522	2.3
1992	655.54	3.369	2.3
1993	663.73	4.201	2.6
1994	671.99	4.764	2.8
1995	679.47	5.196	2.9
1996	688.50	5.528	3.0
1997	696.00	5.768	3.1
1998	699.57	5.710	3.1
1999	705.86	5.750	3.1
2000	711.50	5.950	3.1
2001	730.25	6.810	3.6
2002	737.40	7.400	4.0
2003	744.32	8.000	4.3

Source: "China's Employment Situation and Policies", White Paper issued by The Information Office of the State Council, China, April 26, 2004.

can absorb only 40 million of them. In other words, the urban unemployment is expected to increase by about 10 million by the year 2010.[18] Hence, China will continue to face urban unemployment in the future (Refer Table 2.3 and Figure 2.5).

It is estimated that there are more than 200 million rural surplus laborers who need to be transferred from the agricultural sector. These laborers have been, for a long time, in an underemployment situation and kept to their shrinking land, or partly absorbed by rural industries. As the economic reforms removed many restrictions on geographic mobility, the rural surplus labor force has become visible in the form of large-scale migration driven mainly by economic opportunities available in the places of in-migration. A huge number of migrant workers have restructured the urban labor market.

Migrant laborers now account for 30 percent of China's rural labor force, and they have now become an indispensable part of the urban labor force. It is commonly accepted that the so-called floating population currently numbers about 140 million compared to 70 million in 1993, suggesting that more than 10 percent of the Chinese population are on the move. Another 130 million rural laborers work in the rural industrial sector represented by Town-Village Enterprises (TVEs). Consequently, the number of rural laborers who are engaged in non-agriculture economic activities has already exceeded the traditional urban labor force.

Migrant workers are often blamed to be the competitors of urban jobs and to have made the urban unemployment problem more serious. However, many

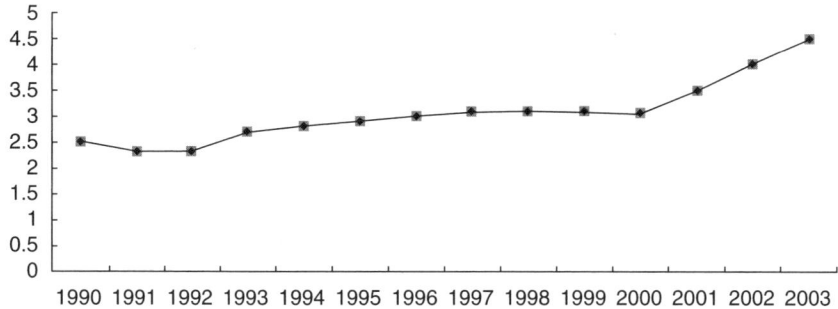

Figure 2.5 Registered urban unemployment rate (%), 1990–2003

Source: "China's Employment Situation and Policies", White paper issued by the Information Office of the State Council, China, April 26, 2004.

studies have shown that migrant workers are more likely to be supplement rather than compete with the local urban labor force. Migrant workers provide an almost unlimited and flexible supply of cheap labor, reducing labor cost in urban sector and easing the shortage of urban low-paid manual workers by usually taking up dirty, demanding, and dangerous jobs that urban workers are no longer willing to take. There is therefore now a segmentation of the urban labor market, with migrant workers concentrating on certain occupations and little labor mobility across the segmented parts. Migration helps reduce labor cost in urban sector as their wages are commonly low and their employers have no obligation to provide for them social security contributions, which in the case of Shanghai, is equivalent to 46 percent of the total wage.

As for the sectoral structure of employment, more people now work in the tertiary industry than ever before, while the number of workers in primary industry declines. In 2003, 218.09 million employees, accounting for 29.3 percent of China's total labor force, worked in the tertiary industry, compared to 18.5 percent in 1990. On the other hand, the proportion of those employed in primary industry dropped from 60.1 percent to 49.1 percent with the number of laborers standing at 365.46 million in 2003.

Viewed from another angle, informal employment has gradually become a major form of employment in China, and it is now treated as one of the very important ways to cope with the urban unemployment problem. The ILO term "informal employment" was first introduced to China in the early 1990s, and was used by researchers before being accepted by the government. Informal employment in China covers various employment forms that differ from the dominant employment form based on the industrialized factory system in such respects as labor hours, the form of reward and income, the working conditions, social security and the fringe benefits, and labor relations.[19] At present, terms such as "informal sector", "informal employment" and "informal worker" are often used with some confusion. There is no clear-cut definition of "informality", and the term "informal employment" was not even mentioned in the recent government

White Paper entitled "China's Employment Situation and Policies" issued by the Information Office of the State Council of China on April 26, 2004. Instead, Chinese officials often use the term "flexible employment." In spite of this confusion, there is no doubt that the importance of informal employment in China's economy has increased significantly. It is estimated that the number of laborers engaged in informal economic activities in China's urban sector ranges from 108 to 125 million. The figure would be much higher if all migrant workers are included in the estimation.[20]

Despite rapid expansion of China's high education system over the past decade, there are only 67.64 million persons having a college level education. In other words, there are only 5,175 college graduates in every one million population. This suggests that China has to put in much more effort in raising the education level of the population. China therefore also needs to prepare more earnestly for the phase when enhancing the quality of labor will be the only way to enhance the labor input.

2.6   Urbanization and migration

China's population is highly concentrated in the eastern part of the country, especially in the coastal zones. Roughly one billion Chinese live in only a little more than 30 percent of the country's land area. In contrast, 50 percent of China's inland areas are very sparsely populated. China is under-urbanized given its level of economic development. According to the *1 percent National Population Sample Survey* conducted in November 2005, 561.57 million mainland Chinese are classified as urban residents living in 662 cities and 20,358 towns. Thus, urban population accounted for about 43 percent of the national population in 2005 as compared to 36.22 percent in 2000. The potential for urban growth in China is therefore substantial. China has launched its ambitious urbanization program aiming at transferring more than ten million rural farmers annually into urban areas over the next 20 years.

With the process of urbanization, a large number of people are increasingly concentrated in small geographic regions, particularly in the Yangtze River delta, the Pearl River delta and the Beijing-Tianjin region. These big metropolitan regions have played an overwhelmingly important role in China's recent economic growth. For instance, in 2003, more than 21 percent of China's total GDP was produced in the Yangtze River delta area covering 110,000 square kilometers (1.14 percent of the national total) and 16 prefecture-level cities including Shanghai, Hangzhou and Nanjing, with a population of 82 million (6.32 percent of the national total). The rapid development of big metropolitan areas or urban concentrations has certainly benefited from the "openness" policy initiated by late Deng Xiaoping in the 1980s, and also indicates a shift of China's urbanization strategy from focusing on small and medium-sized towns and cities to a balanced development of big, medium and small cities and towns. Urbanization is viewed as one of the decisive factors driving future economic growth in China.

As China's economic growth during the reform period (except for the initial years) has been mainly concentrated in urban sectors, the ratio of urban to rural per capita income (urban disposable income to rural net income) increased from 1.86 in 1985 to 3.11 in 2002. If public housing subsidies, private housing imputed rent, pension, free medical care, and educational subsidies were included, as the China Human Development Report 2005 points out, the urban to rural income ratio would be four or higher instead of 3.2 as acknowledged by official document.[21]

This rise in urban-rural income difference is caused partly by China's dual development path. China has been for a long time a dual society with an overt socio-economic line drawn between urban and rural part of the country, based on the household registration system, known as *Hukou* in Chinese. The *Hukou* system has developed over the last half a century. The system was formally established in 1953 with the initial function of public security. In 1956, food rationing was introduced in urban areas based on *Hukou* status, and the urban-rural division began to surface. It was in 1958 that for the first time, as stipulated by the government "Regulation on Household Registration", households were divided into agricultural households and non-agricultural households. The recovery of the economy from the Great Leap Forward movement and the great famine of 1961 led to further control on migration, and kept the system in effect for more than 20 years.

The dual system was a kind of institutional arrangement for China's industrialization. Based on the system, the State purposely lowered the price of agricultural products, and collected a huge amount of financial resources from the agricultural sector to invest in the industrial sector. With the passage of time, more functions were added to the *Hukou* system. As a result, the system led to discriminative treatment of rural population in dispensation of almost all public resources, including education, employment, and social welfare entitlement. Without urban *Hukou*, one would not qualify for job assignment, which was the only method of gaining employment in urban areas before the 1980s, because private employment virtually did not exist. Without urban *Hukou* and formal urban employment, it was impossible to have housing and difficult to gain access to other major necessities for living, because these were rationed to urban residents before the mid-1980s.

The functions of *Hukou* have been gradually diminishing since the launch of economic reform in the early 1980s. However, as *Hukou* has been functioning as a base for social segregation with respect to social welfare and many other entitlements as well as an essential tool of political and social control for a long time in China. It is likely to take a long time to change the system in a systematic and comprehensive manner.

The large-scale rural-urban migration that China has been witnessing in recent years can be a very efficient vehicle for social enlightenment, with profound social and political implications and entailing relatively very small cost, particularly for the government. The demographic impact and economic contribution of the migration are apparent in both rural and urban areas. It is estimated that the rural-urban labor mobility contributed to about 16–20 percent of China's GDP increase in the 1990s. The remittance sent back by those migrants has become a very important source of income for rural families. Therefore, migration is viewed by the Chinese government as one of the best ways to alleviate poverty and to make rural surplus labor force employed.

On the other hand, the migration is also creating a number of problems, including generation of social tensions between regular city dwellers, on the one hand, and temporary migrants, on the other. Arrival of migrants in large numbers has also given rise to a challenge to the existing governance structure of the cities.

Many institutions established in the central planning era have remained as obstacles to rural-urban integration. Migrant workers are generally excluded from the urban social welfare system although some efforts have been made recently to protect the basic rights and to improve the general living and working conditions of migrant workers. Measures have been taken to include migrants into urban "formal" labor market, so that an integrated urban labor market could be established. One of the specific steps necessary is to include migrants into the urban social security system.[22] Such a step, on the one hand, can extend the contribution base of urban social security funds, and thus partially solve the problem of an increasing deficit in the urban pension system, caused mainly by rapid population aging in urban areas. On the other hand, the step will help to reduce the labor cost gap between local urban workers and migrant workers. To the extent that migrants generally originate from and maintain connection with Chinese farming households, improvement in the conditions of the former will have beneficial effects on the latter too.

2.7   Demographic impact on pension system

Rapid aging process has brought to the forefront the issue of a social welfare system. At present, there is no nationwide pension system in place in China. After two decades of reform, the current pension system still suffers from various shortcomings and faces tremendous difficulties, especially in the old industrial regions where the extent of population aging is greater. Even the coverage of the urban pension system is limited. By the middle of 2005, China's urban pension system covered a total population of 168.68 million only, including about 42 million pensioners and 125 million employees who contributed to the pension fund. This means that only 30 percent of all urban residents, and 15 percent of all employees, were covered by the program.

On the whole, the Chinese pension system is still a pay-as-you-go system, though a partly funded multi-pillar system has been introduced in the 1990s. Under this system, individual pension accounts were set up, but their scope and impact have still remained very nominal. Also, the current system is burdened by unfunded liabilities from the old system, called the Legacy Debt.[23] It is reported that the total annual net inflow from China's Government revenue into the pension fund to balance the system amounted to 52.4 billion Yuan in 2004, and the accumulated inflow reached 170 billion between 1998 and 2005. Nevertheless, there is still a total deficit of 2.5 trillion Yuan in China's urban pension system.[24]

The estimated ratio of Implicit Pension Debt (IPD) to national GDP ranges from 80.8 percent to 145.4 percent, based on different assumptions of the discount rate used in the simulations.[25]

Such a huge pension burden will inevitably affect the investment capacity of Chinese economy in future, as any effort to tackle the great deficit will involve funds in stock market, banking operation, and enterprise financing. The future demographic changes (with relatively fewer workers relative to the population) will put significant downward pressure on household saving.[26] The ratio of pensioners to contributors in urban China has reached 33 percent in 2003 compared to 19 percent in 1989, and is expected to rise further in the near future if no significant change occurs in the system (Wang and Mason, 2007).

China's current state-supported pension system and other social welfare provisions are highly urban biased. There is very limited social welfare provision for the rural elderly. A few exceptions are the "five-guarantee system" and poverty relief subsidies. In some rich rural areas, a community-based old-age support system has been set up. However, children remain the almost only source of support for many elderly in the rural areas. The fertility transition is facilitating the decline of the average family size and nuclearization of the family structure. The reductions in economic returns from cultivated land, out-migration of rural youngsters, and the weakening of family support have made the elderly in the countryside more vulnerable. It is an extremely difficult task for China to

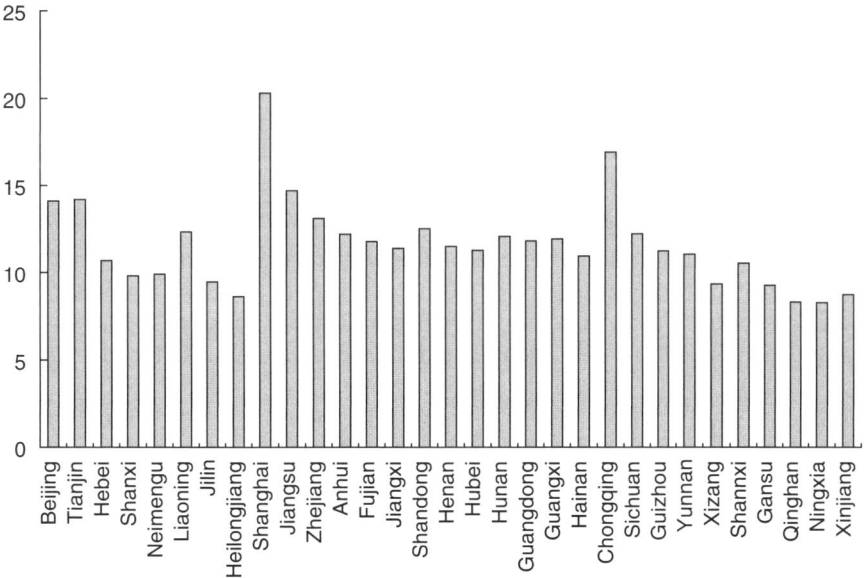

Figure 2.6   Aged dependency ratio in China's provinces

Source: Calculated by author using data from 2005 National Population Survey conducted by State Statistics Bureau of China.

establish a pension system that will cover the entire rural population, given the fact that there is already a 2.5 trillion Yuan deficit in China's urban pension system, as mentioned earlier.

We already noticed that due mainly to different paths to demographic transition, the aged dependency ratio, defined as the number of retirees (60 and over for men and 55 for women) as a percentage of the working age population, varies across regions. This regional variation in the aging process will certainly affect the regions' economic burden for old-age support. As already observed China's present pension system is a highly fragmented and decentralized one. Contribution rate, coverage, and scale of pooling are quite different across regions, so is the management. The administrative infrastructure relative to the demands on it is seriously deficient. The lack of a national pool of pension funds leads to huge disparities and inequalities within the system.

Overall China's pension system is facing a serious challenge. At present, the government is insufficiently prepared, and is still exploring proper ways to cope with the problem. Efforts have been made by both scholars and officials to search for possible solutions. The issues investigated include rural-urban division and possible options for its abolition, decentralized financing and administration and its advantages and disadvantages, inclusion of immigrants in urban pension schemes, and reform of the pension administration structure.[27] Debates continue on whether the rural system should be established independent of the urban pension system, or whether it should be an extension of the urban system. No matter what the final strategic decision turns out to be, it is certain that developing a pension system covering all the elderly in China will require a huge amount of resources, thereby reducing resources for investment. On the other hand, further economic growth may prepare China better to bear the burden of an increasingly aged society.

2.8   Conclusions

China is going through a period of the "demographic bonus" with the richest supply of labor and the lightest burden of population dependency. If enough jobs can be created during this period, China can benefit from an abundant labor force for economic growth before the aging population peaks in 2030.

Regional differentials in the demographic transition resulted in a varied population situation, leading to varied local conditions regarding labor supply and pressure on the social security system. Internal migration can be the bridge to match the conditions necessary for harvesting the demographic bonus in both rural and urban areas. Migration provides economic opportunities to those migrating from poor rural areas while at the same time solving the problem of shortage of young laborers in the urban areas. Even though exporting and losing a young able working force, rural areas are benefiting from migration through reduction of the unemployment rate and from remittances. On the other hand, migrants from rural areas are providing an almost unlimited labor supply for the growing urban economy.

With the rapid aging process, the favorable age structure and the current golden opportunity for economic growth will disappear in about 20 years' time nationally, and the demographic window will close thereafter. An aged China will eventually face the overall shortage of a young labor force, and this will lead to significant shifts in the economic structure.

Acknowledgments

The author is grateful to Nazrul Islam, the editor of the book and organizer of the ICSEAD's China growth project, and other colleagues who participated in the project and its two workshops and provided valuable comments on earlier versions of the paper. They are however not responsible for remaining errors.

Notes

1 Unless specified, major population data in 2005 are from "Communiqué on Major Data of 1 Percent National Population Sample Survey in 2005," announced by National Bureau of Statistics, March 16, 2006.
2 The author provided one of the detailed studies on this demographic crisis. See Xizhe Peng. 1987. "Demographic Consequences of the Great Leap Forward in China's Provinces," *Population and Development Review*, 13: 4, pp. 639–670.
3 In a recent article, Guangyu Zhang and Zhongwei Zhao provided some detailed analyses on China's demographic data, see: "Reexaming China's Fertility Puzzle: Data Collection and Quality over the Last Two Decades," *Population and Development Review*, June 2006, 32: 2, pp. 293–321. It is my own opinion that government statistics remain one of the best data sources at present even though they suffer from misreporting. This is particularly true concerning the national data.
4 This is an officially reported estimate. See Yang Kuifu et al. Zhongguo jihua shengyu xiaoyi yu touru (Input and Benefit of China's Family Planning) (Beijing: China Population Publishing House, 2001).
5 There are different projections about the future population growth in China, primarily based on different fertility assumptions. See for example, Zhai Zhenwu, "Population of China: Prospects and Challenges," in Peng Xizhe and Guo Zhigang. 2000. pp. 246–256; and Cao Guiying, "The Future Population of China: Prospects to 2045 by Place of Residence and Level of Education," Interim Report, IR-00-026, 2000, International Institute for Applied Systems Analysis, Austria.
6 This is viewed as the "policy fertility", a weighted average assuming that the reproductive behavior of all couples of different nationalities in different locations conforms to the local government family planning regulations. Details can be found in Guo Zhigang et al. (2003).
7 The penalty system was often criticized as a coercive measure and a source of local corruption. It was replaced by a social support fee in 2004.
8 Details of the program can be found in the speech at the Press Conference on The System of Social Support for Some Rural Families Practicing Family Planning By Ms. Pan Guiyu, the vice minister of the NPFPC on June 9, 2005.
9 Whether or not China's population policy should be changed is a very topical issue for the present. For relevant discussion, see Peng (2004) and Wang (2005).
10 See China National Statistics Bureau (2006).
11 The UN Population Division, The World Population Prospects: The 2004 Revision.
12 Annex table 1, Basic indicators, The World Health Report 2006, WHO.
13 See Kevin Kinsella (2000).

14 It is estimated by China's Family Planning Commission that the total number of Chinese over 65 will reach 332 million by 2050.
15 Projection made by Cai Fang, *China Youth News*, September 4, 2006.
16 Qiao Hong, in *Goldman Sachs Global Economic Paper*, No. 138, February 14, 2006.
17 White Paper titled "China's Employment Situation and Policies" issued by The Information Office of the State Council, China, April 26, 2004.
18 *Development Outline of Labor and Social Security in China for the Eleventh Five-Year Period*, The Ministry of Labor and Social Security, 2006. Also see *China Daily*, November 10, 2006.
19 Yue Guo (2006) "Informal Employment in China," http://210.218.209.2/emate-gw/seminar.nsf/allview (accessed on July 5, 2007).
20 Wu Yaowu. 2006. Informal Employment: Size and Characteristics, Unpublished Internal Report, Institute of Population and Labor Economics, Chinese Academy of Social Sciences, Beijing.
21 China Human Development Report, 2005. 2006. China Development Research Foundation, Beijing: UNDP.
22 For example, Shanghai's municipal government announced in November 2006 that all qualified migrant workers in Shanghai can get Shanghai's residential registration identification, and should be covered by a package of social welfare provisions that is usually available only to urban residents.
23 See Thanara Trinh (2006).
24 Announced by China's former Financial Minister Xiang Huancheng. See *Guoji Jinrongbao* (International Financial news), October 24, 2005, or http://news3.xinhuanet.com/fortune/2005-11/11/content_3764172.htm (accessed on December 13, 2005).
25 IPD refers to the present value of benefit commitment that a pension scheme makes to current workers and pensioners. See Xin Wang (2004).
26 Louis Kuijs. 2003. Investment and Saving in China, World Bank China Research Paper Series No.1.
27 For example, see Robert Stowe England. 2005. *Aging China: The Demographic Challenge to China's Economic Prospective*, The Washington Papers.

References

China, Development Research Foundation. 2006. *China Human Development Report 2005*, Beijing: UNDP.

China, National Statistics Bureau. 2006. *Communiqué on Major Data of 1% National Population Sample Survey in 2005*, Beijing: China Statistics Publishing House.

Guo, Zhigang, Zhang Erli, Gu Baochang, and Wang Feng . 2003.The Diversity of China's Fertility Regulations Based on Policy Fertility Measures, *Population Studies*, 9 (in Chinese).

The Information Office of the State Council of China, "China's Employment Situation and Policies", White Paper issued on April 26, 2004, Beijing.

Kevin, Kinsella. 2000. "Demographic Dimensions of Global Aging", *Journal of Family Issues*, Vol. 21, No. 5 (July), pp. 541–558.

The Ministry of Labor and Social Security of China. 2006. "Development Outline of Labor and Social Security in China for the Eleventh Five-year Period", Beijing.

Peng, Xizhe. 1987. "Demographic Consequences of the Great Leap Forward in China's Provinces", *Population and Development Review*, Vol. 13, No. 4, pp. 639–670.

Peng, Xizhe. 2004. "Is it Time to Change China's Population Policy?", *China: An International Journal*, Vol. 2, No. 1 (March), pp. 136–149.

Peng, Xizhe and Guo Zhigang (ed.) 2000. *The Changing Population of China*, Oxford: Blackwell Publishers.

Thanara, Trinh. 2006. "China's Pension System: Caught between Mounting Legacies and Unfavorable Demographics". Deutsche Bank Research Paper, February 17.

Wang, Feng. 2005. Can China Afford to Continue its One-Child Policy, *Asia Pacific Issues*. 17 Honolulu East-West Center.

Wang, Feng and Andrew Mason. 2007. "Population Aging in China: Challenges, Opportunities, and Institutions", in Zhongwei Zhao and Fei Guo (ed.) *Transition and Challenge: China's Population at the Beginning of the 21st Century*, Oxford: Oxford University Press, pp. 177–196.

Wang, Xin. 2004. "China's Pension Reform and Capital Market Development", *China and World Economy*, Vol. 12, No. 3, pp. 3–16.

Zhang, Guangyu and Zhongwei Zhao. 2006. "Reexaming China's Fertility Puzzle: Data Collection and Quality over the Last Two Decades", *Population and Development Review*, June, Vol. 32, No. 2, pp. 293–321.

Zhai, Zhenwu. 2000. "Population of China: Prospects and Challenges", in Peng Xizhe and Guo Zhigang (eds.) *The Changing Population of China*, Oxford: Blackwell Publishers, pp. 246–256.

Zhao, Zhongwei. 2006. "Income Inequality, Unequal Health Care Access, and Mortality In China", *Population and Development Review*, 32, pp. 461–483.

3
Employment and Migration: A Chinese Rural Perspective

Robert Ash

3.1   Introduction

The reforms of the last 25 years have made China an increasingly urbanised society, and the process of urbanisation will accelerate in the coming years. For the time being, however, China remains a predominantly *rural* society. Some 745 million people – 57 percent of the total population – are officially registered as rural.[1] Two-thirds of total employment takes place in the countryside,[2] and agriculture alone still accounts for almost 45 percent of all jobs.[3] These are formidable numbers. No assessment of China's future economic and social development can fail to take close account of the challenges posed by this "rural bias" and its implications for government economic and social policies.

Much recent analysis has rightly highlighted the potentially acute threat to China's future development posed by increasingly serious pressure on resources (especially water, land and energy). Such pressures, as well as those associated with widening inter-regional and inter-sectoral economic and welfare gaps, have in recent years pushed the Chinese government toward a major strategic initiative grounded in the imperative of achieving a more sustainable pattern of economic and social development. It is still too early to assess the impact of this new strategy. It is, however, clear that against the background of urban unemployment pressures and even greater problems caused by the massive overhang of rural under-employment, sustainability in the Chinese context cannot succeed unless it effectively addresses these and associated issues. From this perspective, the recent shift toward a more "harmonious" and "people-centered" development trajectory merely underlines the importance of facilitating a steady increase in employment in both urban and rural China.

This chapter investigates the major challenge that faces the Chinese government in its efforts to accommodate employment pressures within the rural sector. It comprises four main sections. The first and second sections seek to provide an overview of rural employment conditions, viewed from both national and regional perspectives. They are followed (Section 3.3) by an examination of patterns of migration within and from the rural sector, with brief consideration also given to the phenomenon of returnee migration to the countryside. The fourth section addresses some of the important employment policy implications of the preceding analysis. Finally, there is a brief summary and conclusion.

3.2   Rural employment conditions in China

In the 1980s economic diversification in the Chinese countryside was so rapid that by 1990 the contribution of non-farming activities to rural value-output had already overtaken that of agriculture. This is a process that has since intensified, both in the agricultural economy "proper", where animal husbandry and aquatic production have expanded disproportionately compared with crop cultivation growth, and in the non-farming rural economy. The extent of economic diversification in the countryside is captured in Table 3.1.

Remarkably, over 80 percent of gross rural income in China now derives from non-agricultural activities, and almost 60 percent comes from rural *industry* alone. A further significant share derives from other non-agricultural activities, such as construction and services. In 2004[4] the value-added of industrial activities in rural Township and Village Enterprises (TVEs) was higher than that of all agricultural activities, and more than two times that of value-added from crop cultivation.[5] As Table 3.1 shows, gross income from all rural non-agricultural activities is

Table 3.1   Rural economic diversification – the situation in 2004

	Gross income from farming and non-farming rural activities (b. yuan)	As % of gross rural income
Gross rural (farming and non-farming) income Of which:		
INCOME FROM AGRICULTURE	15,117.3	100.0
Crop cultivation	2,752.2	18.2
Forestry	1,505.9	10.0
Livestock husbandry	99.3	0.7
Fishing and aquatic production	785.2	5.2
Other	215.4	1.4
INCOME FROM NON-FARMING	146.4	1.0
Rural activities	12,365.1	81.8
Rural industry	8,659.2	57.3
Rural construction	853.8	5.6
Rural transport	628.8	4.2
Rural commerce and catering	1,383.8	9.2
Services	387.9	2.6
Other	451.5	3.0

Source: China Ministry of Agriculture, *Zhongguo nongye fazhan baogao, 2005* (China Agricultural Development Report). 2005. Hereafter *Baogao*, Beijing: Nongye chubanshe, p. 179.

now well over four times that of gross farm income. Indeed, rural economic diversification has assumed an importance that transcends China's domestic economy: in 2004 the value of TVE export deliveries was about US$205 billion.

These developments are mirrored in employment trends. Official statistics suggest that between 1978 and 2005 TVEs on their own generated more than 114 million new jobs in the rural sector.[6] The strong trend toward diversification in rural, non-farm employment between 1978 and 2004 is shown in Table 3.2.

The decline in the share of farm workers in total employment – from 90 percent to less than one-third – is testimony to the remarkable degree of rural employment diversification that has taken place in China since 1978. But it is a salutary reminder of the continuing employment challenge posed by agriculture that although it has been in decline since 1991,[7] the number of workers still tied to farming in 2004 was still 31 million (11 percent) more than in 1978.

Perhaps the most dramatic manifestation of employment change in the Chinese countryside since the early 1980s is reflected in the mushrooming of the TVEs. The impact of the expansion of this sector on rural employment is captured in Table 3.3, which also shows the functional distribution of the TVE labor force.

Over 70 percent of those working in rural TVEs are now engaged in industrial and commercial activities, and a further 10 percent in construction. The success of TVEs is without doubt one of the most remarkable features of China's social and economic development under reform. As will be shown in the following section, their geographical distribution is highly concentrated in a very small number of provinces, although (as is also argued below) it is too simple to suggest that the further geographical extension of TVEs offers a realistic basis for the formulation of future rural employment expansion policies.

The ownership pattern of TVEs has also undergone rapid change, although disentangling the reality of such changes is extremely difficult.[8] According to official sources, in 1980 all TVEs were collectively owned. By 1985, however, one-third of their workforce were categorised as "individual self-employed".[9] Subsequently, there was also a rapid expansion of privately owned enterprises. By 2002 over a quarter of all rural TVE employees were working in private enterprises, and with a further 45 percent working on an individual self-employed basis, only 37 percent of TVE employees were in collectively owned units.

Concealed in these figures are interesting findings relating to changes in the average size of TVE, measured by number of employees. It would appear that the average enterprise size in all ownership categories has increased over time, although private and self-employed units have remained smaller than Collectively Owned Enterprises (COEs).

Data also suggest that average labor productivity in collectively owned TVEs has outstripped that of both other ownership categories.[10] To what extent this reflects a trade-off between the fulfilment of efficiency and employment goals is an interesting question that deserves further investigation. The answer may partly lie in the adoption of more modern, capital-intensive technology by larger collective TVEs – a process perhaps also matched in recent years by the private TVE sector.

Table 3.2 Rural employment diversification, 1978–2004

	Total employed labor force (rural + urban)	Total rural employed labor force	Number (million) and proportion (%) of rural workforce engaged in following rural activities:					
			Crop farming, forestry, husbandry and fisheries	Manufacturing	Construction	Transport, storage, posts and tele-communications	Wholesale and retail trade, and catering	Other
1978	401.52	306.38	274.88 (89.7)	17.34 (5.7)	2.30 (0.8)	0.80 (0.3)	0.52 (0.2)	5.21 (5.6)
1980	423.61	318.36	283.34 (89.0)	19.42 (6.1)	2.83 (0.9)	0.90 (0.3)	0.67 (0.2)	5.88 (1.8)
1985	498.73	377.08	303.52 (80.5)	27.41 (7.3)	11.30 (3.0)	4.34 (1.2)	4.63 (1.2)	25.88 (6.9)
1990	647.49	428.04	333.36 (77.9)	32.29 (7.5)	15.23 (3.6)	6.35 (1.5)	6.93 (1.6)	33.88 (7.9)
1995	680.65	450.42	323.35 (71.8)	39.71 (8.8)	22.04 (4.9)	9.83 (2.2)	11.70 (2.6)	43.80 (9.7)
2000	720.85	479.62	327.98 (68.4)	41.09 (8.6)	26.92 (5.6)	11.71 (2.4)	17.52 (3.7)	54.42 (11.3)
2004	752.00	487.24	305.96 (62.8)	54.39 (11.2)	33.81 (6.9)	13.61 (2.8)	27.02* (5.5)	52.45 (10.8)

Note: *Includes accommodation services.

Source: China Ministry of Labour and Social Security, Zhongguo laodong tongji nianjian, 2005 [China Labour Statistical Yearbook, 2005], hereafter LDTJNJ, Beijing: Tongji chubanshe, p. 31.

Table 3.3   Employment trends in TVEs, 1978–2004

	Total employ-ment in TVEs	Number (m.) and proportion (%) of workers in following TVE branches:						
		Farming	Industry	Construction	Transport and storage	Wholesale and retail trade	Hotels and catering	Other
1978	28.27	6.08 (21.5)	17.34 (61.3)	2.36 (8.3)	1.04 (3.7)	1.44 (5.1)	–	–
1985	69.79	2.52 (3.6)	41.37 (59.3)	7.90 (11.3)	1.14 (1.6)	16.85 (24.1)	–	–
1995	128.62	3.14 (2.4)	75.65 (58.8)	19.33 (15.0)	9.52 (7.4)	16.77 (13.0)	2.25 (1.7)	1.97 (1.5)
2000	128.20	2.22 (1.7)	74.77 (58.3)	15.81 (12.3)	8.98 (7.0)	15.57 (12.1)	8.64 (6.7)	2.30 (1.8)
2004	138.66	2.85 (2.1)	81.61 (58.9)	13.76 (9.9)	8.44 (6.1)	16.99 (12.3)	8.18 (5.9)	6.83 (4.9)

Source: LDTJNJ, 2005, p. 495.

Table 3.4   Changing ownership composition of township and village enterprises (TVEs), 1978–2002

	Total workforce of all TVEs	Number (m.) and proportion (%) of workers in TVEs in following ownership categories		
		Collective	Private	Self-employed individual
1978	28.27	28.27 (100.0)	–	–
1980	30.00	30.00 (100.0)	–	–
1985	69.79	41.52 (59.5)	4.75 (6.8)	23.52 (33.7)
1990	92.65	45.92 (49.6)	8.14 (8.8)	38.58 (41.6)
1995	128.62	60.60 (47.1)	8.74 (6.8)	59.27 (46.1)
2000	128.20	38.33 (29.9)	32.53 (25.4)	57.34 (44.7)
2001	130.86	33.72 (25.8)	36.94 (28.2)	60.20 (46.0)
2002	132.88	38.01 (28.6)	35.02 (26.4)	59.84 (45.0)

Source: China National Bureau of Statistics, *Zhongguo tongji nianjian, 2003* [China Statistical Yearbook, 2003], hereafter *TJNJ*, Beijing: Tongji chubanshe. 2003. p. 447. Comparable data for later years are not available in subsequent editions of *TJNJ*.

Table 3.5 Changing average size of TVEs by ownership category

| | **Average number of workers per TVE** | | |
	Collective	Private	Self-employed
1978	18.5	–	–
1990	31.6	8.3	2.4
2002	52.0	15.2	3.3

Source: *TJNJ*, 2003, op. cit., pp. 447–448.

Overall, China's success in rural job creation since 1979 has been remarkable. Yet so strong remains the legacy of the rural bias in so many aspects of development during the Mao Era that even allowing for the serious labor consequences of urban state-owned enterprise restructuring in recent years, it is in the countryside that China faces the greatest employment challenge. The origins of this challenge lie in two structural features.[11] First, the existence before 1978 of large-scale concealed unemployment has, under the impact of later reforms, been transformed into a more *visible* and therefore more challenging problem. It would be wholly wrong to suggest that under-employment is a purely post-1949 phenomenon in China. On the contrary, there is plentiful evidence to indicate that throughout the first half of the twentieth century – no doubt, much earlier too – the seasonal nature of farm work dictated that periods of intense activity alternated with those, often much longer, of inactivity. Data collected by Buck in his famous survey of farm conditions in China during the pre-war period[12] highlight the complexity of agricultural employment conditions in the countryside. On the one hand, only 35 percent of able-bodied men between the ages of 16 and 60 were engaged full-time in farm work – a figure which, however, rose to 93 percent if those engaged on a part-time basis were included.[13] On the other hand, Buck's study also reveals that only 19 percent of farms recorded *no* agricultural labor shortage throughout the year.[14] Such findings are not mutually contradictory. Rather, the unambiguous message conveyed in Buck's investigation is that under-employment, not open unemployment, was the major problem facing labor management in rural China.[15] One of the strengths of farm organization during the Mao years was that collectives maximized employment through effective, if not efficient mobilization of available labor supplies for purposes of rural capital formation, such as irrigation and other kinds of infrastructural construction. However, the dismantling of the collective framework in the early 1980s left a vacuum in this regard that has not been filled. In addition, efficiency-enhancing rural reforms exacerbated under-employment by raising farm workers' productivity. The outcome was a massive overhang of surplus farm labor, manifested most obviously among crop cultivators. Despite the creation of tens of millions of new non-agricultural jobs in the countryside, the problem has persisted. Even today, there probably still exist 130–150 million surplus rural laborers – some sources suggest even more – most of whom are farmers.[16] This would suggest that up to 45 percent of the agricultural labor force, or 30 percent of the entire rural labor force, are in surplus. Survey findings revealed that in 2002 a member of the rural labor force worked, on average, for 9.83 months per annum (6.7 in agriculture and 3.13 in rural non-farm activities).[17] Regional differences apart,[18] such average estimates conceal wide variations in work attendance rates and anecdotal evidence suggests that the marginal productivity of many under-employed farmers who work for no more than a few weeks in the year is close to zero.

The second structural feature to which reference should be made is the occupational profile of farming itself. Chinese agriculture has traditionally been dominated by crop, and especially grain, farming. Alongside rural economic diversification, the rapid expansion of livestock farming and fishing since the 1980s has also generated a much more diversified *agricultural* economy.[19] During the same period, the share of crop farming in the Gross Value-Output (GVO) of agriculture declined from 80 percent to marginally less than 50 percent, while the combined contribution of husbandry and fishing has risen to 44 percent. The changes in profile of farm production have, however, not been matched by changes in the structure of agricultural employment, which is still dominated by crop farming. Comprehensive time-series data showing the changing employment composition of farming appear not to be available, but there is little doubt that the proportion of workers tied to crop cultivation remains extraordinarily high. One authoritative source shows that out of a total farm labor force of 365.71 million in 2000, some 349.4 million workers – almost 96 percent – were engaged in growing crops of one kind or another.[20] A figure in excess of 90 percent no doubt exaggerates reality. That is, it includes both those whose involvement in crop farming is part-time – even marginal, as measured by the value of Labor's Marginal Productivity (MP_L). But the inference that farm under-employment is heavily concentrated in the cropping sector is confirmed by the findings of China's first "National Agricultural Census", which provides the following breakdown of rural employment, as shown by farmers' "main economic activity":

Table 3.6   Composition of farm employment, 1996

	Number (m.) and share (%) of persons engaged in each branch of farming
All farm activities	425.00
Crop farming	403.74 (94.9)
Animal husbandry	14.84 (3.1)
Forestry	1.04 (0.2)
Fisheries	2.93 (0.7)
Agricultural services	2.44 (0.6)

Sources: China, National Agricultural Census Office and Food and Agricultural Statistics Centre, *Abstract of the First National Agricultural Census*, Beijing: China Statistics Press, 1999 (2nd printing), p. 59.

It is noteworthy too that between the early 1980s and the early 1990s,[21] the expansion of the farm workforce, *in absolute terms,* and its maintenance at a high level could not be explained by changes in sown area or in its composition. Such findings appear to underline the severity – probably increasingly so – of the problem of farm under-employment that China has faced under the impact of post-1978 reforms.

An important observation relating to farmers' welfare also deserves to be made. It is that since the sown area under grain still accounts for two-thirds of the total sown area,[22] most crop farmers – almost certainly, a disproportionately high proportion of them – are to a greater or lesser extent dependent for a living on the least remunerative of farming activities (namely, grain cultivation). The government's imperative of grain self-sufficiency has imposed a high cost in terms of efficiency, as measured *inter alia* by the distribution of labor in agriculture. In 2004, for example, the GVO of cereal farming accounted for only 35 percent of agricultural GVO,[23] although (as indicated above) it absorbed a far larger share of the work time of the farm labor force.

3.3   Regional variations in rural employment conditions in China

It is a truism that China's continental size makes generalizations about any aspect of its social and economic change hazardous. Accordingly, analysis of the regional dimension and implications of national developments is an essential part of any exercise. In the context of this chapter, for example, it is noteworthy that off-farm rural job creation has been heavily concentrated in China's coastal provinces. In 2004, for example, 57 percent of all TVE workers throughout the country were employed in just ten eastern coastal provinces,[24] whose higher efficiency than elsewhere was also highlighted in their disproportionate contribution (72.5 percent in *2003*[25]) to TVE value-added.[26] By contrast, in the same year the 12 provinces that are the focus of the national strategic initiative to "open up the West"[27] accounted for barely 20 percent of total TVE employment (2004) and a mere 13 percent of value-added (2003).

The implications of differences in the regional composition of employment are implicit in the estimates shown below in Table 3.7. They point to the existence of a regional employment triptych, associated with the different balance between rural farming and non-farming activities. In 2004, whereas the farm sector accounted for little more than half of rural jobs in eastern coastal areas – not coincidentally, the region containing the provinces that had benefited disproportionately from post-1978 reforms – in non-coastal central provinces the corresponding figure was 64 percent, and in western China, 76 percent. From east to west, industrial manufacturing alone absorbed 19 percent, 9 percent and 5 percent of rural employment in the three regions. Stated differently, the regional analysis highlights the higher proportion of the rural labor force engaged in non-farming – which means higher-income – activities in the east, compared with other parts of China. Concealed in the figures is the additional important finding that of those working solely or primarily in farming, a higher proportion in interior regions is dependent for a living on agricultural activities, especially crop farming, that offer relatively low incomes than is the case among farmers in eastern coastal provinces.

In short, since the mid-1980s increases in rural income accruing to those living in the coastal regions have derived – increasingly so, as time series data would show – from higher-return, non-farming activities. At the same time, the evidence shows that for those coastal residents still tied to farming for a living, rises in *agricultural* income have come increasingly – and to a greater extent than in other regions – from the pursuit of farming activities outside the cropping sector (above all, from fishing and animal husbandry). Such findings have important implications for employment policy in China.

Reference was made earlier to the massive overhang of surplus rural labor – the phenomenon is in fact overwhelmingly agricultural – inherited from the Mao Era. Putting a figure on the scale of the surplus poses seemingly intractable difficulties. Suffice to say that at the time of writing this, Chinese sources continue to refer to the existence of 150 million potential migrants "awaiting to transfer from rural to urban areas."[28] Nor should one automatically assume that continuing rapid economic growth will bring a swift resolution to the employment challenge posed by the huge numbers of under-employed farmers and rural laborers. In a recent (2005) article, it was suggested that by 2020 between 100 and 150 million surplus rural laborers would have joined the flow of migrants out of the countryside.[29]

Recent estimates of the regional distribution of surplus laborers do not appear to be available. A priori reasoning would, however, point to the likelihood of higher agricultural and rural under-employment existing in interior regions than along the coast. The following table (Table 3.8), showing the extent of surplus farm labor in each province of China in 1998, lends support to this supposition.

The regional distribution of surplus rural labor can be characterized in terms of a rough dichotomy between eastern and western, coastal and interior regions. In terms of the regional triptych referred to earlier, the most striking finding for 1998 is the sharp difference in rural labor supply conditions between western China and the rest of the country. It is instructive, for example, that the 12 western provinces, which in 1998 contained 30 percent of China's rural population, accounted for 41 percent of its surplus labor. By contrast, the corresponding figures for the nine central and north-eastern provinces were 34 percent and 32.5 percent; and for the ten coastal provinces, 35.8 percent and 26.8 percent.[30]

However, the degree of disaggregation captured in this table is fairly small, and concealed in the estimates for each broad region are major differences in the scale of rural under-employment between individual provinces. In interpreting the provincial figures, a distinction may usefully be made between levels and rates of surplus labor. For example, in 1998 a surplus labor ratio in excess of 60 percent existed in five western provinces, compared with only one in their central and north-eastern counterparts – and none along the coastal seaboard.[31] But

Table 3.7 Regional patterns of rural employment, 2004

	Total rural labor force	Cropping, forestry, husbandry and fisheries	Manufacturing	Construction	Transport, storage, posts and tele-communications	Wholesale & retail trade, and catering	Other
		Number (million) and proportion (%) of rural workforce engaged in following rural activities:					
China	487.24	305.96 (62.8)	54.39 (11.2)	33.81 (6.9)	13.61 (2.8)	19.28 (4.0)	60.19 (12.4)
10 eastern provinces	173.79	88.79 (51.1)	32.39 (18.6)	14.41 (8.3)	6.10 (3.5)	9.80 (5.6)	22.30 (12.8)
9 north-eastern and central inland provinces	173.38	111.06 (64.1)	14.86 (8.6)	11.15 (6.4)	4.61 (2.7)	5.43 (3.1)	26.27 (15.2)
12 western provinces	140.07	106.11 (75.8)	7.14 (5.1)	8.25 (5.9)	2.90 (2.1)	4.05 (2.9)	11.62 (8.3)

Notes: '10 eastern provinces (municipalities)': Beijing, Tianjin Shanghai, Liaoning, Hebei, Shandong, Jiangsu, Zhejiang, Fujian and Guangdong.
'9 north-eastern and central inland provinces': Jilin, Heilongjiang, Shanxi, Anhui, Jiangxi, Henan, Hubei, Hunan and Hainan.
'12 western provinces': Tibet, Xinjiang, Ningxia, Inner Mongolia and Guangxi Autonomous Regions, and Qinghai, Gansu, Shaanxi, Sichuan, Chongqing, Yunnan and Guizhou provinces.

Source: LDTJNJ, 2005, p. 31.

Table 3.8   Estimates of surplus labor in Chinese provinces (provincial-level units), 1998

	Labor requirements	Labor availability	Surplus labor units	Surplus labor ratio (%)
China	**176.59**	**324.35**	**147.76**	**45.6**
10 eastern provinces	**59.05**	**98.72**	**39.67**	**40.2**
Beijing	1.19	0.65	−0.54	−81.9
Tianjin	1.28	0.79	−0.48	−60.9
Hebei	97.48	162.00	64.54	39.8
Liaoning	50.76	62.43	11.67	18.7
Shanghai	0.86	0.73	−0.13	−18.6
Jiangsu	13.31	15.33	2.02	13.2
Zhejiang	4.84	11.07	6.22	56.2
Fujian	3.59	7.71	4.13	53.5
Shandong	12.52	24.98	12.45	49.9
Guangdong	6.91	15.02	8.11	54.0
9 north-eastern & central inland provinces	**63.96**	**111.99**	**48.03**	**42.9**
Jilin	2.97	5.12	2.25	43.1
Heilongjiang	4.59	5.79	1.20	20.8
Shanxi	5.44	6.33	0.89	14.1
Anhui	12.84	19.65	6.81	34.6
Jiangxi	6.91	10.89	3.99	36.6
Henan	10.18	29.03	18.85	64.9
Hubei	10.05	12.66	2.61	20.6
Hunan	9.72	20.74	11.02	53.1
Hainan	1.29	1.69	0.39	23.6
11 western provinces	**53.29**	**113.64**	**60.35**	**53.1**
Inner Mongolia	2.96	5.12	2.16	42.2
Guangxi	7.90	15.90	8.00	50.3
Sichuan	18.50	38.22	19.73	51.6
Guizhou	5.52	13.83	8.31	60.1
Yunnan	8.67	16.54	7.87	47.6
Tibet	0.34	0.91	0.57	62.4
Shaanxi	3.36	10.46	7.10	67.9
Gansu	2.61	6.80	4.19	61.6
Qinghai	0.44	1.38	0.94	68.0
Ningxia	0.61	1.45	0.84	58.0
Xinjiang	2.38	3.03	0.65	21.3

Note: Unless stated otherwise, all figures in millions. Small inconsistencies reflect rounding-up of original data.

Source: Liu Jiang (Chief Editor). 2000. *Ershiyi jichu Zhongguo nongye fazhan zhanlüe* (China's Agricultural Development Strategy in the twenty first century), Beijing: Nongye chubanshe, p. 600.

while the western region includes the province with both the highest recorded surplus rural labor ratio (Qinghai) and the highest absolute level of surplus labor (Sichuan), it is noteworthy that in 1998 the provinces that ranked second, third, fourth and fifth after Sichuan in terms of absolute under-employment were in central and eastern China.

The inference I draw from the estimates shown in Table 3.8 is that while they are certainly carry important employment policy implications, they are not a sufficient basis on which to make policy *recommendations*. The reality of demographic and employment conditions in China has been and remains extremely complex. The most obvious finding that emerges from the figures is the huge potential for rural out-migration contained in them. From the perspective of 1998, this potential was already being realized and the momentum of such migration has been maintained down to the present day. But the factors shaping population movements are enormously complex and patterns of migration reflect more than the mere existence of large labor surpluses and high rural surplus ratios. So much is apparent from the fact that three coastal provinces which have been major recipients of rural migrants – Zhejiang, Fujian and Guangdong – had the highest surplus labor ratios in the entire seaboard region in 1998. An analysis of the main provincial sources of rural migrants reveals similar apparent anomalies.

What the estimates show unambiguously is that except for Yunnan and Xinjiang, the most remote south-western and north-western provinces of China faced the most serious incidence of agricultural under-employment. Inherent in this finding was the likely existence in these regions of a vicious circle. On the one hand, the burden they faced in finding employment outlets for surplus farm labor was greater than in other parts of the country. On the other hand, the remoteness of these regions and their innate poverty deprived them, to a greater extent than elsewhere, of the means – whether in terms of the availability of funding or of markets – whereby they might successfully embark on a program of indigenous rural employment creation. This is a point to which I return below.

3.4 Migration

Migration undertaken by Chinese peasants is a complex phenomenon. It does not refer only to movements from countryside to city, nor even to movements across provincial boundaries. Significant numbers of migrants move from one rural location to another; many move between locations within a given province. Transferring from a rural to an urban location does not necessarily mean moving to a large city: in 2000, for example, only 30.2 percent of city migrants were employed in provincial capitals.[32] Nor should migration be thought of as an irreversible and permanent one-way process. Many migrants who leave the countryside, whether for cities or another rural location, maintain close links with their home villages. In addition, a process of "cultural institutionalization" had encouraged many migrants – both successful and unsuccessful – to return to their native villages. In other words, return migration is also an important phenomenon in China.[33]

Something of the complexity of movements undertaken by rural migrants is captured in the Table 3.9.[34]

The estimates reveal a clear pattern and trend. During the period shown, there was a steady increase in numbers of people who left their home counties in search of work. Moreover, of those crossing county borders, an increasing number – both

Table 3.9   Employment destinations of rural migrants, 1997–2000

	Total number of rural residents leaving their home villages	Number (million) and proportion (%) of rural migrants relocating to the following destinations		
		Outside home village, but remaining in home county	Outside home county, but remaining in home province	Outside home province
1997	38.90 (100.0)	12.88 (33.1)	11.14 (28.6)	14.88 (38.3)
1998	49.36 (100.0)	17.18 (34.8)	13.46 (27.3)	18.72 (37.9)
1999	52.04 (100.0)	15.82 (30.4)	14.97 (28.8)	21.25 (40.8)
2000	61.37 (100.0)	16.24 (26.5)	16.80 (27.4)	28.33 (46.2)
2001	63.65 (100.0)	14.13 (22.2)	18.87 (29.6)	30.65 (48.2)

Source: Cai Fang, *Zhongguo renkou yu laodong wenti baogao*
(Report on Questions of Population and Labour in China), No. 4, 2003, Shehui kexue wenxian chubanshe, p. 180.

in absolute and relative terms – sought employment in a different province. Indeed, by 2001 almost half of all migrants crossed their provincial boundaries, compared with only 38 percent four years earlier.[35]

An inference of the figures shown in Table 3.9 – one that is supported by overwhelming empirical evidence – is that accompanying structural changes in rural employment, large-scale migration out of the countryside has also become a defining characteristic of rural change in post-1978 China. By such means a highly motivated and, by the standards of poor countries, a quite skilled pool of labor has been made available to sectors and regions of high growth in the economy. The process has also facilitated capital accumulation and technical progress within the rural sector itself, as migrants have sent or brought back to their native villages and towns income and expertise gained from working outside farming and/or in the urban sector.

During the 1980s, deregulation and loosening controls over rural residents resulting from the weakening of the household registration (*Hukou*) system, alongside easier access to food in urban markets, facilitated rural-urban migration on an increasingly large scale. Rural industrialization also created new towns populated by former peasants, while rapid economic growth – especially in areas such as those of the Pearl and Yangtze River Deltas[36] – provided job opportunities for migrants. In some cases – the most striking example was the Pearl River Delta region – migrants found jobs in burgeoning labor-intensive industries. Elsewhere, many became self-employed in a wide range of informal, mainly unskilled and menial, activities.

The demographic impact of migration is captured in statistics showing the residential status of the population. Data for 2004, shown in the "One Percent Sample Survey on Population Change", are set out in Table 3.10.

The sample survey data indicate that in 2004 almost 9 percent of China's population – almost 114 million people – was living somewhere other than in the place where they were officially registered. Comparison with earlier years would show that this proportion had risen over time.[37] Given that the benefits of post-1978 growth have accrued disproportionately to coastal provinces, it is not in the least surprising that well over half of these "migrants" were living in eastern China, where the proportion of total population living away from their official domicile was almost 13 percent, compared with only 6–7 percent in interior regions.

Such figures point to a distinctive regional pattern of migration having emerged in China under the impact of reform, and support the statement made in the Ministry of Labour and Social Security's (MoLSS) 2002 Report that

"[t]he cross-provincial flow of rural labour is mainly from provinces and municipalities in the central region and the western region such as Sichuan, Chongqing, Jiangxi, Anhui, Hunan, Henan, Guizhou and Guangxi to provinces and municipalities in the eastern region such as Guangdong, Zhejiang, Shanghai, Beijing, Fujian and Jiangsu".[38]

Elsewhere, a MoLSS source noted that in 2002 these six provinces had absorbed an astonishing 80.2 percent of the flow of rural cross-provincial migration.[39] By far the most important provincial destination for rural migrants was Guangdong, which accounted for 47.6 percent of the total.[40]

But what of the provincial origins of the flow of rural-urban migration? Apart from the availability of local alternative employment opportunities, the man-land ratio is likely to have been a major determinant of provincial outflows of labor. Available data lend strong support to this supposition. The estimates in Table 3.11 indicate the main provincial sources of rural migration in 2002.

Reference to estimates of rural labor force and arable area in each of these provinces[41] will confirm that all of them are characterized by high man-land ratios. It is true that some other provinces, not shown in Table 3.11, had equally high ratios. But these – for example, Guangdong, Fujian and Zhejiang – were areas in which rapid growth offered considerable non-farming and non-rural employment opportunities to residents without the necessity of crossing provincial borders.[42]

A more detailed, but less current, picture of inter-provincial flows is available from the 1995 "One Percent Sample Survey of Population Change". For reference purposes, these are shown in Table 3.12.

With adjustment for sampling, the figures indicate that the coastal provinces were the net recipients of almost 36 million migrants. Of these, the net labor outflow from just nine central and north-eastern provinces accounted for almost two-thirds, the balance being made up for by 12 western provinces (including Chongqing). In general, the provinces with the largest net inflows and outflows coincide with those listed earlier for 2002.

Reference has already been made to the existence of a strong correlation between man-land ratios and levels of rural migration. Other familiar push and

Table 3.10   Residential status of China's population, 2004

	Total population (thousand)	Population living in town, township or sub-district in which they were registered (thousand)	Population not living in town, township or sub-district in which they were registered (thousand)	Proportion of population living in town, township or sub-district other than that in which they were registered (%)
China	1,253.605	1,143.642	109.963	8.77
East China	466.703	406.678	60.025	12.86
Beijing	14.213	9.902	4.311	30.33
Tianjin	9.868	8.533	1.335	13.53
Hebei	66.078	61.848	4.230	6.40
Liaoning	41.100	37.008	4.092	9.96
Shanghai	16.702	14.000	2.702	16.18
Jiangsu	72.295	64.942	7.353	10.17
Zhejiang	45.682	37.780	7.902	17.30
Fujian	34.048	26.780	7.268	21.35
Shandong	89.072	80.999	8.073	9.06
Guangdong	77.645	64.886	12.579	16.43
Northeast & Central Inland China	425.928	396.903	29.025	6.81
Jilin	26.397	25.162	1.235	4.68
Heilongjiang	37.241	34.760	2.481	6.66
Shanxi	32.352	29.572	2.780	8.59
Anhui	62.575	57.689	4.886	7.81
Jiangxi	41.524	37.870	3.654	8.80
Henan	94.372	88.609	5.763	6.11
Hubei	58.510	55.066	3.444	5.89
Hunan	65.041	60.927	4.114	6.33
Hainan	7.916	7.248	0.668	8.44
West China	329.882	311.04	18.842	5.71
Inner Mongolia	23.233	20.141	3.092	13.31
Guangxi	47.408	44.781	2.627	5.54
Sichuan	84.919	81.079	3.840	4.52
Guizhou	37.780	35.567	2.213	5.86
Yunnan	42.720	40.753	1.967	4.60
Tibet	2.636	2.617	0.019	0.72
Shaanxi	36.022	33.595	2.427	6.74
Gansu	25.409	24.668	0.741	2.92
Qinghai	5.213	4.899	0.314	6.02
Ningxia	5.662	5.218	0.444	7.84
Xinjiang	18.880	17.722	1.158	6.13

Note: The sampling fraction is 0.966 percent.

Source: NBS, Dept. of Population and Employment Statistics, Zhongguo renkou tongji nianjian (China Population Statistical Yearbook). 2005. (Beijing: Tongji chubanshe), pp. 98–99.

Table 3.11 Provincial origins of rural migration (2002)

	Proportion of cross-provincial rural labor outflows from the following provinces (municipalities) (%)
Anhui	12.59
Sichuan	11.77
Jiangxi	11.54
Hunan	10.49
Hubei	10.10
Henan	7.65
Guangxi	7.12
Chongqing	5.72
Guizhou	5.25
TOTAL	82.23

Source: *2003–2004 nian: Zhongguo jiuye baogao*, p. 214.

pull factors have also encouraged rural laborers to leave their domiciles to seek work elsewhere. At the most aggregate level, evidence of a steadily widening gap between rural and urban incomes underlines the material inducement to look for employment in cities. Between 1990 and 2005, average per capita net rural income rose, in nominal terms, from 345.5 to 3,255 yuan, whereas per capita disposable income increased from 1,002.2 to 10,493 yuan. As a result, the urban-rural income ratio rose from 2.2: 1 to 3.2: 1.[43] Concealed in these figures are important regional and functional income variations. For example, in 2004 average net rural income in eastern China (3,987 yuan) was 46 percent higher than in central provinces – and 91 percent above that of western China.[44] Such figures help explain why interior regions generated a disproportionately high share of rural migrants.

A regional analysis of changes in the structure of the rural economy since the 1980s is also revealing in helping explain migration trends. It shows that in eastern coastal provinces, the contribution of rural industry and other non-farming rural activities to the rural GDP has risen more rapidly than in other parts of the country and has reached a much higher level. It follows that while a reduction in the contribution of farming has been a national phenomenon, the extent of the decline has differed between regions. This is of course an important finding, given that the rewards from farming are lower than those from other activities. It is also significant that within agriculture, farmers in the interior tend to be more dependent on crop cultivation – especially grain farming – than on higher-return activities, such as husbandry and aquatic production. To turn this statement on its head, compared with their central and western counterparts, eastern coastal provinces have benefited from increases in farm income, which have increasingly derived from high-return, non-cropping farm activities. Against this background,

Table 3.12 An interpretation of migration from household registration and current residency status data: The situation in 1995, as shown by that year's one percent sample survey

	Total population by registration (persons)	Actual population (persons)	Outflow (+) or inflow (−) (persons)
East China	**122,168**	**157,176**	**− 35,008**
Beijing	7,801	13,855	− 6,054
Tianjin	3,703	5,417	− 1,714
Hebei	10,874	10,138	+ 736
Liaoning	11,398	13,882	− 2,484
Shanghai	6,182	12,280	− 6098
Jiangsu	21,681	24,868	− 3,187
Zhejiang	13,647	10,920	+2,727
Fujian	8,088	9,122	− 1,034
Shandong	14,863	14,772	+91
Guangdong	23,931	41,922	− 17,991
Northeast & Central Inland China	**91,945**	**68,972**	**+ 22,973**
Jilin	7,375	6,031	+ 1,344
Heilongjiang	16,558	14,677	+ 1,881
Shanxi	4,357	5,220	− 863
Anhui	12,916	6,301	+6,615
Jiangxi	8,979	5,508	+3,471
Henan	13,391	8,251	+5,140
Hubei	11,022	10,583	+ 439
Hunan	15,480	10,160	+ 5,320
Hainan	1,867	2,241	− 374
West China	**76,678**	**64,643**	**+ 12,035**
Inner Mongolia	7,555	9,138	− 1,583
Guangxi	10,701	6,206	+ 4,495
Sichuan	28,270	15,333	+ 12,937
Guizhou	6,516	5,449	+ 1,067
Yunnan	8,198	9,248	− 1,050
Tibet	266	539	− 273
Shaanxi	5,149	4,898	+ 251
Gansu	4,649	3,879	+ 770
Qinghai	1,985	2,153	− 168
Ningxia	904	949	− 40
Xinjiang	2,485	6,851	− 4,366

Note: The sampling fraction is 1.028 percent.

Source: *Zhongguo renkou tongji nianjian* (China Population Statistical Yearbook). 1997. Beijing: Tongji chubanshe, pp. 223–234.

it is no surprise that central and western regions should have generated the largest shares of rural migrants since the 1980s.

The departure of a farmer from a village by no means implies an absolute loss of income to the community. On the contrary, migrants have been an extremely important source of income to their home communities in China.[45] According to a recent investigation, the value of migrant remittances in 2004 and 2005 may have been as high as 223 billion yuan and 250 billion yuan, respectively (US$27.6 and $30 billion).[46] Most of those who migrate from the countryside in China are farmers and the significance of remittances may be gauged by comparing them with the value of farm production. From this perspective, it is telling that the estimated potential value of remittances in 2004 was equivalent to 21.1 percent of agricultural value-added in the same year.[47] Bearing in mind that average net rural per capita income in China was only 2,936 yuan in 2004, the significance of Cheng and Zhong's finding that the average value of migrant remittances was 3,500 yuan – typically sent in between three and six installments during the year – requires little comment. The figure may be compared with information given to Rachel Murphy during her fieldwork studies in Jiangxi province, which suggested that remittances contributed up to 30 percent of local rural income.[48] Such remittances not only facilitate rises in living standards, but also enhance the revenue-collecting capacities of local governments. To what extent they help promote growth, it is difficult to say. My own guess is that such is the poverty of many of the home regions of migrants that their remittances serve mainly to boost family consumption, rather than increase investment. What seems undeniable is that in their absence, material living standards of migrants' families would have been significantly lower – and in some cases, may even have fallen below subsistence levels.[49]

In many developing countries, migration is assumed to be an irreversible phenomenon. This assumption is often misleading in the Chinese context. Emotional and cultural factors encourage many migrants to return to their home villages, where their newly acquired skills, knowledge, work experience and savings promise to benefit the local community. Migration establishes linkages between countryside and cities, and facilitates return flows of workers – usually young and better-educated – as well as of skills, capital, commodities and information. As such, it has the potential to make a significant contribution to rural economic and social development, not least in more remote regions.[50] To what extent such potential can be fulfilled depends critically on the efficacy of government policy. It is instructive that just as push and pull factors generate rural out-migration, so a similar combination results in the return of many migrants to the countryside and their original villages. Since the mid-1990s, a significant – probably increasing – proportion of the "floating migrant population" has returned, in some cases permanently, to the rural sector. Some migrants return home having accumulated sufficient savings to invest in new rural ventures – usually outside of farming. Others do so, having failed to find rewarding work elsewhere. For both those who have succeeded and those who have failed, anti-migrant discrimination in cities frequently provides an added inducement to return to the rural sector.[51] It is against this background that, as one observer puts it, "both planners and migrants internalize the belief that the return of rural workers to their villages is inevitable".[52] The policy inference seems clear. It is incumbent on the central government to maximize the positive contribution of such migrants, both in the interests of Chinese aspirations to become a 70 percent urbanized society by the middle of the century, and in those of the more vigorous economic and welfare growth of the rural sector.

In the end, urban and rural employment issues in China cannot be separated. It is no coincidence that alongside the persistence of a massive reservoir of surplus rural – above all, agricultural – labor, large-scale migration from the countryside into the cities has become such a defining feature of recent changes in the disposition of the work force. Such migration acts as a safety-valve, which serves to mitigate economic hardship and alleviate rural unrest. But it sometimes does so at the expense of generating new tensions in cities. Even if migrants do not directly compete with urban workers and more often than not take jobs that registered members of the urban labor force are not prepared to do, they place serious strains on urban infrastructure. When they fail to find employment, social stability can be undermined as a result of rootless migrant youths turning to crime, no doubt exacerbating more general prejudice that is felt by both urban residents and officials toward migrants.

3.5   Policy dimensions of the rural employment challenge

Until recently, rapid economic growth is the touchstone by which Chinese governments have been judged. Deng Xiaoping's maxim that "to get rich is glorious" and his willingness to "let some people get rich first" are at the heart of a trend toward "growth with inequity", which has characterized China's development trajectory since at least the mid-1980s. The result has been an outstanding growth record, but one that has been achieved at the expense of increasing social and economic polarization, as well as huge resource and environmental strains. The emergence of widening differentials – intra and inter-regional, intra- and inter-sectoral – is a critically important parameter of efforts to accommodate rural employment pressures. It is also central to understanding the government's recent shift toward a strategy of sustainable development, captured in the new imperatives of creating a "people-centered" and "harmonious" society.

Shifting to a new strategy frequently generates dilemmas for policy-makers. In the context of this essay, an interesting question is to what extent there may exist a trade-off between attainment of a more sustainable pattern of growth and the maintenance of the momentum of employment creation. What can be regarded as axiomatic is that rapid growth is a necessary condition of increasing job opportunities. This fact is highlighted in official statistics. Revised data issued by the National Bureau of Statistics (NBS) show, for example, that between 1993 and 2001, alongside a quite sharply declining trend in national GDP growth between the early 1990s and 2001,[53] there was also a sharp slowing in the rate of employment creation. The impact of slowing growth on job creation seems clear in the finding that whereas between 1978 and 1993, the rate of job creation increased annually by 3.5 percent p.a., thereafter until 2003, the corresponding figure was a mere 1.1 percent.[54] Since 2001, however, the rate of employment expansion has so far failed to match the acceleration in GDP growth.

However, aggregate GDP indicators offer only a proximate view of the rela tionship between economic growth and employment. The *structure* of economic growth is also critically important, since the employment response to output expansion depends on the values of employment elasticity associated with the different economic activities. At a national level in China, the average value of employment elasticity fell sharply between the 1980s and 1990s (from 0.32 to 0.11).[55] But this decline in part reflected low agricultural growth relative to that in both industry (manufacturing and construction) and services. The implications for employment of this structural shift deserve emphasis, for there is strong international evidence to suggest that the employment elasticity in agriculture is significantly lower than that of industry and, especially, services. In China between 1979 and 2000, for example, sectoral average values of employment elasticity varied from 0.06 (primary sector) to 0.34 (secondary) to 0.57 (tertiary sector).[56] Such findings highlight the need for growth strategies to accommodate, as far as possible, structural features that can simultaneously serve employment goals.

The regional distribution of growth, to which reference has already been made, is another important issue. The increasingly strong shift in the economic centre of gravity toward China's coastal provinces has worked to the detriment of employment opportunities in the interior, especially in western China. Coastal regions have benefited disproportionately in terms of fixed investment receipts:[57] it is noteworthy that in 2004 the ten coastal provinces of eastern China absorbed 67 percent of rural fixed investment, compared with one-third in the remaining 21 interior provinces.[58] This is clearly relevant to understanding why rates of rural trans-provincial migration have been highest in central and western provinces. The strategy to "open up the west",[59] announced in 2000, is one initiative that was designed to redress the skewed regional economic profile in China. In the event, its hoped-for returns do not appear to have materialised. Recent reports point to continuing major difficulties in the region and certainly there is no clear evidence that the initiative has yet had a significant impact on employment there. On-going problems have been acute in the north-west – especially in Shaanxi, Gansu, Qinghai, Ningxia and Xinjiang – where rapid population growth has placed severe pressure on natural resources and inadequate education, low labor productivity and a lack of employment opportunities have created a vicious circle of poverty.

This is the background against which, since spring 2005, increasing priority has been given to the development of c*entral* China (Shanxi, Henan, Anhui, Jiangxi, Hubei and Hunan) – a region that contains a quarter of the Chinese population and contributes almost a quarter of national GDP. The choice of central provinces as a new focus of China's regional strategy reflects inherent structural, geographical and resource advantages, as well as its greater susceptibility than western provinces to the positive trickle-down effects of more rapid growth in neighboring coastal regions. If, as is intended, central China becomes a major transport, commercial and distribution hub, it will facilitate the creation of closer linkages between east and west to the potential benefit of employment in western provinces. The most recent regional strategic shift also promises to have direct pay-offs for employment in individual central provinces. As the experience of the Pearl River Delta shows, the fulfillment of Anhui's destiny as a major new labor-intensive manufacturing base, if it happens, will have a significant pay-off in terms of absorbing surplus farm labor in neighboring and other interior provinces.[60,61]

All these observations are relevant to rural employment policies. They high-light the importance of maintaining an appropriate momentum of urban, as well as rural economic growth. They also underline the need for careful investigations of regional, as well as national employment elasticities in order to maximize job opportunities through the implementation of an appropriate *structural* pattern of growth.

The rural sector is no exception to the general finding that since the 1980s, employment elasticity has been in decline. However, an important qualification to this statement is that the employment elasticity of farming is lower than in rural construction, industry and service activities. Alongside the declining rate of labor absorption associated with the overall pattern of change, falling rates of growth in agriculture and rural industry have also sometimes constrained the potential for job creation in the countryside.

Under the impact of reform, agricultural employment – those engaged in crop farming, forestry, animal husbandry and fishing – has been in decline since 1991.[62] Continuing structural change in the farm sector and rises in productivity are likely to further reduce the demand for labor in the farm sector. The policy challenge implicit in declining farm employment is dramatically captured in one commentator's observation that in the long run the agricultural share of the total employed labor force will fall from the current level (44 percent) to a mere 10 per-cent.[63] The inescapable inferences are that the number of surplus farm laborers – already huge – will rise to even higher levels, and that this huge surplus will remain the central focus of government employment efforts in the rural sector.

One of the most noteworthy features of China's rural employment strategy has been the transfer of enormous numbers of laborers out of farming into non-farm work located in the countryside. In this respect, most impressive of all has been the development of TVEs – nearly all of them small or medium-scale, and many of them reliant on quite labor-intensive technologies. In the face of the further downsizing of the farm labor force, the pressure to establish new TVEs in order to expand rural employment may be expected to intensify. On the surface, the potential labor absorptive capacity associated with the further expansion of TVEs would seem to be considerable, not least given the heavy geographical concen-tration of existing rural enterprises within a few provinces. In reality, however, analysis of current conditions in China counsels caution in advocating employ-ment policies based on a further major expansion in rural industrialization. Not least, it is instructive that employment growth in the TVEs has declined sharply since the mid-1990s.[64] This falling off in the employment contribution of TVEs reflected a variety of factors, including the impact of the Asian financial crisis, the introduction by the Chinese government of tighter credit, policies, declining government support for TVEs in the face of a trend toward their privatization and the adoption of more capital-intensive techniques by a growing number of rural enterprises.

The geographical concentration of TVEs in a small number of coastal provinces lends an obvious attraction to suggestions that they be established much more widely – especially in interior regions of the country. But to be effective, such a policy recommendation requires the fulfillment of certain conditions, such as the availability of labor of appropriate skills, access to capital, the attainment of appropriate levels of per capita income and the existence of adequate markets. Availability of labor is least likely to pose a major constraint. By contrast, however, capital and market constraints are likely to be much more real and serious. In these respects, it is revealing that average per capita net rural income in China's interior provinces is less than 60 percent of the corresponding figure in coastal regions.

In short, inherent in rural conditions there are severe limitations on the extent to which a policy of accelerated rural industrialization, based on the establishment of TVEs over a wider geographical area of China, is likely to succeed. Future labor absorption by rural industrial enterprises will be contingent on changes not only in the relative price of capital and labor, but also in market conditions in the Chinese countryside. Advocacy of wider rural industrialization is necessarily subject to the ability to overcome such constraints.

From this perspective, it is noteworthy that rural industry by no means defines the full scope of the rural, non-agricultural economy in China. In fact, it accounts for only 60–70 percent of rural, non-agricultural output, the remaining 30–40 percent coming from rural construction, transportation, commerce and other services. This has important implications for rural employment, since many of these rural non-manufacturing activities are inherently labor intensive and/or allow for significant substitution of labor for capital. It also helps explain the Chinese government's increasing advocacy of the expansion of rural tertiary occupations.

At the heart of China's rural problems is the issue of farmers' poverty.[65] To look for solutions outside farming is a rational response to this problem. But it is also important not to ignore employment creation possibilities *within* the farm sector. Both in absolute and relative terms, farm employment will continue to contract in the coming years, but it will be many years before its share of total employment falls to the low level to which official sources aspire. In the meantime, efforts are needed not only to generate income growth from primary farm production, but also to promote intra-agricultural diversification, based on a recognition that the prevailing imperative of maintaining a 95 percent degree of grain self-sufficiency may be neither necessary nor desirable. Most important of all, intensified efforts are needed to create a system of agriculture embodying a higher degree of integration between farming, processing and other associated farm-related operations – in other words, the development of agro-industry and agribusiness.

Government policies that address *migration* in a creative, flexible and positive manner will be crucial to accommodating rural employment pressures. Even allowing for the social and economic strains of large-scale movements of population, migration contains the potential to make a major contribution to rural economic development through skill enhancement, capital formation and employment promotion. The behavior of rural migrants and Chinese attitudes to migration lend added significance to this contribution. Unlike their counterparts in some other Asian countries, migrants working in Chinese towns and cities remit significant funds to the families they have left behind in the countryside. In recent years, these have been increasingly important in boosting lagging farm incomes, but they also contain the means to raise agricultural investment. There is evidence too that the marginal propensity to save is quite high among migrants, many of whom aspire to return to the countryside. The role of such returnee migrants is an important one, and China's experience shows how the entrepreneurial and other skills they have acquired in an urban environment can enhance and transform backward rural economies to the benefit of economic development and community welfare.

Migration attracts those who are strong, innovative and relatively better-educated, and their return home promises to benefit both the rural economy and local community through the financial resources, skills and work experience that they bring back with them. Hence, the importance of recent government initiatives to provide, and improve training in, new skills and other techniques (managerial, organizational, etc.) in order to improve the quality of returnee migrants and maximize their modernizing impact on local economies. It is unrealistic to suppose that returnee migrants will seek to use their resources – both financial capital and skills – in farming. More significant is their likely contribution toward the creation of small towns – a key focus of current rural policy – the modernization and expansion of rural industry, and the development of rural tertiary activities. The wider horizon of returnees enables them to access resources, both inside and outside the local community, which may be unavailable to indigenous entrepreneurs. Meanwhile, the fulfillment of such goals demands the formulation and implementation of appropriate preferential policies, such as temporary tax reduction and preferential access to resources (including credit, land, raw materials, water and electricity). Local governments should also provide practical help to facilitate reintegration of returnees into the local community, including the provision of schooling for their children. The potential benefits to the rural economy of returnee migrants' financial and human capital are huge.

3.6   Summary and concluding remarks

In the past, the most important demographic determinant of employment in China was the rate of population increase; today, it is the age structure of China's total population. Recent experience suggests that China is capable of finding productive employment for new entrants into the labor force. By far the greatest employment challenge faced by the government is finding productive employment for unemployed members of the existing labor force. These include two main categories: unemployed urban workers who have been laid off from state-owned enterprises and failed to find new jobs; and – by far the more important compo-nent – the massive overhang of surplus farm laborers in the countryside. Trying to accommodate the job aspirations of the urban and rural unemployed and under-employed is a challenge that will tax the ingenuity of the government for at least two more decades. Not until around 2030 will the combined impact of past low fertility rates and the aging process at last begin to erode China's super-abundance of labor.

The macroeconomic environment will be a major determinant of the Chinese government's ability to fulfill its employment creation goals during the com-ing decades. At the same time – not least, against the background of increasing rural social instability in recent years –the employment impact, both direct and indirect, of the government's macroeconomic policies will necessarily assume a high priority. Meanwhile, the shift, since 2004, toward a strategy of develop-ment sustainability carries potentially very real implications for employment. Fulfillment of the new strategy's goals may, after all, necessitate a sacrifice in terms of economic growth, since a one percent reduction in GDP growth will – to a greater or less extent, depending on the sector(s) most affected and the rel-evant value(s) of employment elasticity(ies) – have a significant knock-on effect on employment.

China's development trajectory since the mid-1980s has embodied a widen-ing economic gap and increasing social polarization between different regions of China. The benefits – including employment gains – of post-1978 economic growth have accrued disproportionately to coastal regions. One of the most dif-ficult employment challenges facing the Chinese government is to find ways of promoting more rapid growth and changes in the structure of the economy that will enhance job creation in interior regions, especially in the far west.

Although recent large-scale lay-offs from state-owned enterprises have exacer-bated unemployment in Chinese cities, to argue that excess labor supply alone is the main cause of urban unemployment is too simple. Important too has been the institutional segmentation of urban labor markets and the maintenance of institutionally determined high urban wage rates. Here is one area in which the existence of western-style trades unions might exacerbate employment condi-tions through demands for restrictions on in-migration of cheap rural labor. One of the important messages of this chapter is that policy-makers need to take account of potential urban-rural synergies, and devise policies that will facilitate competition between urban and rural enterprises, without the imposition of such restrictions.

In the countryside, the rapid expansion of rural non-agricultural activities – most notably, the development of rural industrial enterprises – has made a huge contribution to easing labor pressures associated with the existence of massive under-employment. Small-scale enterprises have proven themselves to be a low-cost, flexible instrument of labor absorption. Another message of this chapter is, however, that although the employment potential of the further development of such enterprises has not been exhausted, their further expansion – especially in poorer interior regions of the country – will be constrained by prevailing low levels of per capita income and the absence of developed market networks. At the same time rural industrialization is not the sole manifestation of non-agricultural economic activities in the countryside. Both construction and the service sector are also important destinations for surplus rural laborers, accounting for about one-third of all rural enterprise employment, and well over 20 percent of rural non-farm jobs. Such activities are, it is true, susceptible to the vagaries of cyclical growth and may therefore offer less secure employment opportunities than manufacturing employment. But their potential role is considerable, and it is no coincidence that tertiary sector employment has been an increasingly important focus of employment policy in recent years.

Migration should also be viewed as a positive instrument of employment policy, even if its consequences are not always uniformly beneficial. To regard the role of rural-urban migration simply as a safety-valve that serves to ease employment pressures and relieve social strains in the countryside is too conservative and passive. There is overwhelming evidence that those who leave their villages in search of work tend to be young, better-educated, better skilled and more resourceful. During their absence, migrants contribute much to their home communities through the regular remittances which many of them make. If they eventually return to the rural sector, the potential economic return for those communities accruing from the fruits of their urban experience – measured not only in terms of the savings they bring back, but also entrepreneurial and other skills that they have learned – is also likely to be significant. In short, returnees are a force for local economic growth – especially for rural, non-farm development – the benefits of which promise to accrue not just to themselves and their families, but also – through employment and income generation – to the wider local community. Facilitating the developmental and welfare-enhancing role of returnee migrants should be regarded as a core objective of job-creation and skill-enhancement policies in rural China.

The forces bearing on China's rural development are complex and, in some respects, mutually antagonistic. Nobody can doubt that the growth and welfare record of post-1978 rural reforms is a remarkable one. But it would be foolish to underestimate, let alone ignore, the problems generated by those reforms. This essay has tried to highlight the profound employment consequences of rural reforms, and to suggest some of the ways in which they can be addressed. If the underlying issues are complex, the ultimate message is simple. It is that the failure to meet the rural employment challenge will pose a serious threat to the sustainability of China's social and economic development.

Acknowledgements

I am grateful for the many valuable suggestions on the original version of this paper provided by colleagues involved in this project. I am especially indebted to Nazrul Islam for his kindness in accommodating complications arising from my inability to attend the conference at which the papers in this volume were first discussed. Of course, any remaining errors are entirely my own responsibility.

Notes

1 Making such a simple statement is fraught with difficulty. The figure cited above is given in National Bureau of Statistics (NBS), *Zhongguo tongji zhaiyao, 2006* (China Statistical Abstract, 2006), hereafter *Zhaiyao*, Beijing: Tongji chubanshe, 2006, p. 39. However, reference to official Chinese sources reveals major differences in estimates of rural population. Take the situation in 2004: on the basis of the 2004 National Sample Survey on Population, China's rural population in that year was 757.05 m. (NBS, *Zhongguo tongji nianjian, 2005* [China Statistical Yearbook, 2005] hereafter *TJNJ*, Beijing: Tongji chubanshe, 2005, p. 93) – a figure that compares with the Survey's finding that 737,066 out of a sample population of 1 m. were rural (*Zhongguo renkou tongji nianjian*, 2005, p. 13) (sample fraction: 0.966 percent). Contrast this, however, with a rural population of 942.54 m. in 2004, cited in NBS, *Zhongguo nongcun tongji nianjian, 2005* [China Rural Statistical Yearbook, 2005], Beijing: Tongji chubanshe, 2005, p. 29. The two sources use the identical term – *xiangcun zong renkou* – to refer to "rural population", but the difference between the two estimates – 185.49 m. – is almost 25 percent. Moreover, whereas the former source shows rural population to have contracted by 84.33 m. (1990–2004), the latter points to an *increase* of 46.63 m. during the same period.

2 The two sources cited in note 1 are much closer in their estimates of rural employment in 2004 (*xiangcun jiuye* or *xiangcun congye*): 487.24 m. (*ZTN*) and 496.95 m. (*ZNTN*). *Zhongguo tongji zhaiyao, 2006* shows rural employment to have been 484.94 m. in 2005.

3 The precise size of the agricultural labor force is also susceptible to debate. For example, see Thomas Rawski and R. Mead (1998, pp. 767–781), who have argued that official Chinese data significantly exaggerate farm employment.

4 Where possible, I have included data for 2005. However, at the time of writing, many statistics are available only up to 2004.

5 The relevant figures can be found in *Baogao*, op. cit., pp. 162 and 179.

6 In 1978 the number of people working in TVEs was just under 28.3 m. (see Ministry of Agriculture, *Zhongguo nongcun jingji tongji daquan, 1949–1986* [Statistical Compendium on China's Rural Economy, 1949–1986], Beijing: Nongye chubanshe, 1989, p. 286. The corresponding figure for 2005 was 142.72 m. (*Zhaiyao*, 2006, p. 43).

   This simple comparison is, however, misleading to the extent that it fails to take count of annual fluctuations in TVE job creation – in particular, the severe contraction in employment that took place in 1997, from which recovery was not achieved until 2003.

7 In 1991 the agricultural labor force (those engaged in crop farming, forestry, animal husbandry and aquatic production) numbered 341.86 m.

8 There is widespread consensus that many enterprises officially recorded as collectively-owned were, and are, de facto private.

9 That is *geti qiye*.

10 Cf. the following (*TJNJ*, 2003, op. cit., pp. 447 and 449):

	Average value-added per worker (*yuan*)		
	Collective	Private	Self-employed
1978	737.0	–	–
1990	3,642.7	2,429.5	1,642.3
2002	31,746.3	25,178.2	19,217.7

11 See also Ash. 2006.

12 See Buck. 1937/1964. Buck's survey was undertaken throughout China between 1929 and 1933.

13   See Buck. 1937/1964, p. 294. In southern rice regions, 38 percent of men engaged full-time in agriculture, compared with 30 percent in northern wheat regions. Some 80 percent of farm "idleness" occurred during November–February – months during which many farmers engaged in important income-enhancing non-farm subsidiary handicraft activities.

14   Labor shortages were most serious during the short time usually available for harvesting, although lack of labor was also a problem during the transplanting period in double-cropping rice and rice-wheat regions.

15   In a comment relevant to post-1949, even post-1978, employment policies in Chinese agriculture, Buck observed,

   [t]he amount of man labour in China is almost unlimited and one of the great problems is the discovery of enough productive work to keep this vast human army profitably employed. Paradoxicall.y, the problem is also one of reducing the amount of human labour required during periods of peak labour requirements for important farm operations, such as planting and harvesting and for tasks which man labour alone cannot accomplish such, for instance, as pumping water to great heights or distances. Buck 1937/1964, p. 289.

16   Measuring the precise extent of under-employment is notoriously difficult. The two main ways in which attempts have been made to quantify it are: first, based on labor norms, to measure the difference between labor availability and requirements; second, based on estimates of Labor's Marginal Productivity (MP_L), to trace trend changes in MP_L in an attempt to confirm the existence of surplus labor (defined in terms of a zero MP_L). It is estimated that in the 1990s, some 160–180 m. labor units were needed to meet crop farming requirements. Set alongside estimates shown below in Table 3.4, this would suggest a surplus of in excess of 140–160 m. laborers – a figure that is in line with the 130–150 m. figure cited in the text.

17   Mo Song (Chief Editor), *2003–2004 Zhongguo jiji jiuye zhengce de shixian* (Actively fulfilling China's employment policies, a.k.a. The Blue Book of Chinese Employment), Beijing: Ministry of Labour and Social Security (MoLSS), 2004, p. 204.

18   In western China the average amount of time engaged in farming was 7.55 months p.a., compared with 6.25 in eastern regions; the corresponding figures for time spent in rural non-farm work were 2.45 and 3.98 mths. (Ibid.). See also next section on regional variations in rural employment conditions.

19   Between 1978 and 2005, the average nominal rate of growth of crop farming GVO was 11.2 percent p.a.; the corresponding figures for animal husbandry and fisheries were 16.6 percent and 21.3 percent. Forestry grew by 13.4 percent p.a. (*Zhaiyao, 2006*, op. cit., p. 123).

20   Cai Fang (Chief Editor), *Zhongguo renkou yu laodong wenti baogao*, 2002 (Report on population and labor issues in China, 2002, a.k.a. Green Book on Population and Labour), (Beijing: Shehui kexue wenxian chubanshe), 2002, p. 51. The figures given in this source are taken from survey material. Note that the total farm labor force (That is those engaged in crop farming, forestry, husbandry and fisheries) given in the 'Green Book' (365.71 m.) is 11.5 percent higher than the corresponding figure for 2000 cited in *TJNJ*, (2003, p. 411).

21   The agricultural labor force peaked in 1991. But its subsequent decline has been slow, and in 2004 the agricultural labor force was 12.5 percent below the 1991 level, implying an average annual rate of contraction of barely 1 percent (from data in *LDTJNJ, 2004*, op. cit., p. 9, and NBS, *Zhongguo nongcun tongji nianjian, 2005* (China Rural Statistical Yearbook, 2005), hereafter *NCTJNJ*, Beijing: Tongji chubanshe. 2005, p. 31).

22   In 2005 China's total sown area was 155.5 m. ha., of which 104.3 m. ha. were planted under food grains (*Zhaiyao, 2005*, op. cit., p. 125).

23   Estimated from data in *NCTJNJ, 2005*, op. cit., p. 109.

24   Beijing, Tianjin, Shanghai, Liaoning, Hebei, Shandong, Jiangsu, Zhejiang, Fujian and Guangdong. Just four provinces – Shandong, Jiangsu, Zhejiang and Guangdong – contained 38 percent of all TVE workers. The relevant data are in *LDTJNJ, 2005*, op. cit., p. 496.

25 At the time of writing, I do not have estimates for 2004. The 2003 figure is from Ministry of Agriculture, *Zhongguo nongye tongji ziliao, 2004* (China Agricultural Statistical Materials, 2004), Beijing: Zhongguo nongye chubanshe, 2005, p. 186. Notice that Shandong, Jiangsu, Zhejiang and Guangdong accounted for almost half of aggregate value-added.

26 The employment bias toward TVEs in these ten provinces is highlighted in the finding that they contained less than 36 percent of China's rural labor force (*TJNJ, 2005*, op. cit., p. 121).

27 The autonomous regions of Tibet, Xinjiang, Ningxia, Inner Mongolia and Guangxi, and the provinces of Qinghai, Gansu, Shaanxi, Sichuan, Chongqing, Yunnan and Guizhou.

28 Xinhua News Agency, May 29, 2006, quoting Chinese government sources.

29 The potential fallacy in merely assuming that rural under-employment must contract is also highlighted in the source from which the figures in Table 3.8 (below) are taken, which projects an increase in rural surplus laborers from 147.8 m. (1998) to 180 m. in 2005 (*Ershiyi jichu Zhongguo nongye fazhan zhanlüe*, p. 600).

30 Rural population estimates for 1998 are available in *NCTJNJ, 1999*, p. 41.

31 If provinces with a surplus labor ratio in excess of 50 percent are included, the figures rise to eight (west), two (central) and three (eastern coastal).

32 Huang Ping and Zhan Shaohua, "Internal Migration in China: Linking it to Development" (paper presented at a Regional Conference on Migration and Development in Asia, held in Lanzhou on March 14–16, 2006 and co-sponsored by the International Organisation for Migration, the UK Department for International Development and the PRC Ministry of Foreign Affairs).

33 The phrase is Rachel Murphy's. See her seminal study of return migration – *How Migrant Labour is Changing Rural China*. Murphy (2002).

34 I have not been able to find comparable data for the years since 2002.

35 The number of rural migrants should not be confused with the number of people who transferred to new jobs. MoLSS statistics indicate that for the period shown in the table, only a little over half of job transfers were made by people seeking work outside their home villages and townships. For example in addition to the 63.65 m. rural residents who left their home villages in search of jobs, a further 60.82 m. found new jobs in those same villages. This is just one indicator of the success of government injunctions to "leave the soil, but not the countryside" (*li tu bu li xiang*). The MoLSS *China Employment Report (2001–2002)* notes that "the proportion of rural transferred getting employment outside township started to be higher than ... [that] getting employment inside township in 1998" (prepared in 2002 for the MoLSS-ILO China Employment Forum, 2003), p. 104.

36 In 2000 37.22 percent of all migrant workers were reported to be working in these two Delta regions (Huang Ping and Zhan Shaohua, "Internal Migration in China," op. cit., p. 4).

37 For example in 1997 the corresponding figure was 5.6 percent (around 67 m. people).

38 *China Employment Report*, op. cit., p. 109. The Report added that these six provinces (municipalities) had absorbed 78.2 percent of all cross-provincial rural migrants.

39 See MoLSS, *2003–2004 nian: Zhongguo jiuye baogao* (China Employment Report, 2003–2004), Beijing: Zhongguo laodong shehui baozhang chubanshe, 2004, p. 214. This Chinese-language source is not the same as the English-language *China Employment Report*, referred to earlier in this section.

40 Zhejiang took 9.9 percent, followed by Shanghai (6.8 percent), Beijing (6.7 percent), Jiangsu (5 percent) and Fujian (4.2 percent). Ibid., p. 214.

41 For example, see *TJNJ, 2005*, op. cit., pp. 446–447.

42 A 1993 investigation revealed that migration across provincial borders accounted for only 21.2 percent of total rural migration in eastern China, compared with 38.7 percent and 39.9 percent in central and western regions. See Ministry of Agriculture. (2001). *Nongmin shouru yu laodongli zhuanyi* (Rural Income and Rural Labor Transfers) Beijing: Zhongguo nongye chubanshe, p. 181.

43 Ministry of Agriculture, *Zhongguo nongye fazhan baogao* (China Agricultural Development Report). (2005) (Beijing: Zhongguo nongye chubanshe), p. 171, and NBS, "Statistical Communiqué of the PRC on the 2005 National Economic and Social Development," (February 28, 2006).

44 *Zhongguo nongye fazhan baogao*, op. cit., p. 171. Rural per capita net income in 2004 is shown for all 31 Chinese provincial-level units in *TJNJ*, 2005, op. cit., p. 360.

45 According to Rachel Murphy, remittances by Chinese migrants are part of a deliberate "strategy for 'rural livelihood diversification'" (see her "Domestic Migrant Remittances in China: Distribution, Channels and Livelihoods," paper prepared for the International Organisation for Migration Research Series, 2006 No. 24 [Geneva: International Organization for Migration], p. 5). Murphy also makes the interesting observation that "[t]he world over, off-farm activities generate more income than agriculture and it is access to this cash rather than the size of land allocations that determines wealth inequalities within rural communities" (Ibid.).

46 Cheng Enjiang and Xu Zhong, "Domestic Money Transfer Services for Migrant Workers in China", Consultative Group to Assist the Poor, 2005, p. 4. Note that the national estimates of remittances are "potential" (Cheng and Zhong) in the sense that they reflect extrapolations from the findings of a sample survey conducted in Zhejiang province. There is no doubt room for a significant margin of error in the estimates.

47 The value-added figure – 1,182.77 billion yuan – is given in *Zhongguo nongcun tongji nianjian*, 2005, op. cit., p. 94.

48 See Murphy (2002, p. 38).

49 It is in this sense that Huang and Zhao's remark to the effect that "[h]ad there been no, or much less migration, the socio-economic gap between rural and urban societies would have been much wider" is, I believe, best understood ("Internal Migration in China", op. cit., p. 6).

50 A path-breaking study of returnee migration is Murphy (2002, chapters 5–7).

51 Temporary workers talk most about the fact that, no matter what, the local public security officials come in the middle of the night and inspect the *hukou*, and if there is no temporary residence card, the migrant is fined whatever sum enters the official's head. Those who run are pursued and beaten. There is no human dignity. This makes the workers feel as though they are lost in an alien land, and that the home village is the best after all. (from a Chinese source, quoted by Murphy, *How Migrant Labour is Changing Rural China*, op. cit., p. 44)

52 Ibid.

53 The statistical revisions were made public in January 2006. For further information, including the full revised GDP series, see http://www.stats.gov.cn/english/newsand-comingevents/t20060110_402300302.htm, accessed on November 14, 2006.

54 Based on figures in *LDTJNJ*, 2005, op. cit., p. 8 and *Zhongguo tongji zhaiyao*, 2006, op. cit., p. 43. Notice that the data in these sources differ from those in *TJNJ*, 2005, op. cit., p. 118.

55 The underlying implication is that incremental job creation associated with a 1percent increase in GDP growth fell by almost a third during this period.

56 The differences reflect differing technological coefficients of production. In particular, in services, there is more scope for substituting labor for capital than in industry, where the capital-labor ratio is both higher and – especially in heavy industry – more fixed.

57 In 2005 ten coastal provinces (excl. Guangxi nor Hainan) absorbed 56 percent of national fixed investment (*Zhongguo tongji zhaiyao*, 2006, op. cit., p. 56), and around 85 percent of utilised FDI.

58 The 12 far western provinces accounted for a mere 13 percent of national rural fixed investment (*TJNJ*, 2005, op. cit., p. 157).

59 *Xibu da kaifa*.

60 Two other central provinces – Henan and Jiangxi – have been designated as nodes of modern *agricultural* development. This concept implies farmers' involvement not

only in production, but also in processing and distribution, and therefore also carries potentially important implications for rural employment creation.

61 Since 2003 another regional priority has been the revitalisation of the economy of the Northeast (Liaoning, Jilin and Heilongjiang) – the former heartland of China's centrally-planned industrial economy and a major casualty of SOE restructuring. The core of these efforts has been industrial diversification based on the extension of private sector activities, as well as the implementation of social security initiatives designed to lessen the social impact of restructuring and maintain basic living standards for lay-offs. Although some progress has been made toward fulfilling such goals, financial constraints remain an obstacle to more rapid improvements, and the transformation of the industrial bases of Liaoning and other parts of the Northeast will be a long term process, with a correspondingly minor short-run impact on rural employment.

62 See above, Table 3.2.

63 Thomas Scharping. 2003. *Birth Control in China 1949–2000: Population Policy and Demographic Development* (London and New York: RoutledgeCurzon), p. 335. Another indication of the huge burden of long-run urbanization is afforded by a report in a Chinese newspaper (*Guangming ribao*) in July 2002 that by 2050, more than 600 million people would have moved from rural to urban areas (many of them living in small or medium-sized rural-based cities.

64 The decline in TVE employment growth was dramatic – from 5.95 percent p.a. (1985–1995) to 0.84 percent p.a. (1995–2004). Rural industrial employment expansion fell from 4.9 percent p.a. to 3.6 percent p.a.

65 The official Chinese rural poverty line is defined as the level of income below which income can no longer provide for the subsistence needs – That is, food, clothing and shelter – of the rural population. Subsistence income in these terms is US$0.66 per head per day in constant 1985 Purchasing Power Parity (PPP) US dollars. But estimates of poverty levels are highly sensitive to the choice of measures used, and China's official poverty line is significantly lower than that used by many international agencies. For example, application of the World Bank's US$1 per day criterion would show the incidence of rural poverty to have fallen from 490 million at the beginning of the 1980s to about 76 million as of mid-2005. Chinese sources recognize such anomalies in their acknowledgement that in addition to the 26 million farmers who live in abject poverty, there are almost 50 million more low-income earners in the countryside who would be reduced to destitution in the face of serious illness or a natural disaster. Official statistics also reveal that the number of rural residents in receipt of minimum living allowances rose from 3.6 to over 14 million between 2000 and 2004.

References

Ash, Robert. 2006. "The Long-Term Outlook for China's Economic Reform," *Asia Europe Journal*, Vol. 4, No. 2.

Buck, John Lossing. 1937, rep. 1964. *Land Utilisation in China,* New York: Paragon Book Reprint Corp.

Cai, Fang (Chief Editor). 2002. *Zhongguo renkou yu laodong wenti baogao* (Report on population and labor issues in China, 2002, a.k.a. Green Book on Population and Labour), Beijing: Shehui kexue wenxian chubanshe.

Cheng, Enjiang and Xu Zhong. 2005. "Domestic Money Transfer Services for Migrant Workers in China," China, Consultative Group to Assist the Poor.

China, Ministry of Agriculture. 1989. *Zhongguo nongcun jingji tongji daquan, 1949–1986* (Statistical Compendium on China's Rural Economy, 1949–1986), Beijing: Zhongguo nongye chubanshe.

China, Ministry of Agriculture. 2005a. *Zhongguo nongye fazhan baogao, 2005* (China Agricultural Development Report, 2005), Beijing: Zhongguo nongye chubanshe.

China, Ministry of Agriculture. 2005b. *Zhongguo nongye tongji ziliao, 2004* (China Agricultural Statistical Materials, 2004), Beijing: Zhongguo nongye chubanshe.

China, Ministry of Labour and Social Security. 2004. *2003–2004 nian: Zhongguo jiuye baogao* (*China Employment Report*, 2003–2004), Beijing: Zhongguo laodong shehui baozhang chubanshe.

China, Ministry of Labour and Social Security. 2005. *Zhongguo laodong tongji nianjian, 2005* (China Labour Statistical Yearbook, 2005), Beijing: Zhongguo tongji chubanshe.

China, National Bureau of Statistics. 2005a. *Zhongguo nongcun tongji nianjian, 2005* (China Rural Statistical Yearbook, 2005), Beijing: Zhongguo tongji chubanshe.

China, National Bureau of Statistics. 2005b. *Zhongguo tongji nianjian, 2005* (China Statistical Yearbook, 2005), Beijing: Zhongguo tongji chubanshe.

China, National B ureau of Statistics. 2006. *Zhongguo tongji zhaiyao, 2006* (China Statistical Abstract, 2006), Beijing: Zhongguo tongji chubanshe.

Huang, Ping and Zhan Shaohua. 2006. "Internal Migration in China: Linking it to Development" (paper presented at a Regional Conference on Migration and Development in Asia, held in Lanzhou on March 14–16, 2006 and co-sponsored by the International Organisation for Migration, the UK Department for International Development and the PRC Ministry of Foreign Affairs).

Liu, Jiang (Chief Editor). 2000. *Ershiyi jichu Zhongguo nongye fazhan zhanlüe* (China's Agricultural Development Strategy in the 21st Century), Beijing: Zhongguo nongye chubanshe.

Mo, Song (Chief Editor). 2004. *2003–2004 Zhongguo jiji jiuye zhengce de shixian* (Actively fulfilling China's employment policies, a.k.a. The Blue Book of Chinese Employment), Beijing: Ministry of Labour and Social Security.

Murphy, Rachel. 2002. *How Migrant Labour is Changing Rural China*, Cambridge: Cambridge University Press.

Murphy, Rachel. 2006. "Domestic Migrant Remittances in China: Distribution, Channels and Livelihoods" (paper prepared for the International Organisation for Migration).

Rawski, Thomas and Robert Mead. 1998. "On the Trail of China's Phantom Farmers", *World Development*, Vol. 26, No. 5, pp. 767–781.

Scharping, Thomas. 2003. *Birth Control in China 1949–2000: Population Policy and Demographic Development*, London and New York: RoutledgeCurzon.

4

China's High Economic Growth and the Emergence of Structural Contradictions

Reiitsu Kojima

4.1 Introduction

China has realized "high economic growth" since the introduction of reform and "opening up" policy in 1979. We define "high economic growth" as real economic (GDP) growth rate of 6 percent or more, sustained for more than three years. This chapter has the following three objectives. The first is to analyze China's economic performance since 1979 by comparing it with earlier economic growth experiences of Japan, Taiwan, and Korea, which also realized high economic growth during the latter half of the twentieth century. In this regard, the focus will be on the main players and factors that caused the high economic growth. In particular, we will consider the question of how long China's high growth will continue, and whether or not the length of China's high growth period can match that of Taiwan and Korea. The second objective of the chapter is to identify the emerging contradictions that China faces. Failure to resolve these contradictions in a timely manner will lead to social and political difficulties, which in turn may put an end to China's high growth period. Third, the chapter will discuss the new economic issues that China is likely to face in the coming decade. Finally, the chapter will combine the analysis of emerging contradictions with discussion of new issues in order to point to steps and policies that are necessary for China to maintain its high economic growth and attain healthy economic development.

The discussion of the chapter is organized as follows. Section 4.2 compares China's economic growth record with that of Japan, Taiwan, and Korea. Section 4.3 identifies the emerging contradictions. Section 4.4 discusses the factors that may slow down the Chinese growth. Section 4.5 offers the concluding remarks.

4.2 China's high economic growth in the light of the experiences of Japan, Taiwan, and Korea

4.2.1 China's growth measured by real GDP

Figure 4.1 compares economic growth rates of China and Japan. Japan entered a period of high economic growth in the middle of 1950s. Before that, her growth

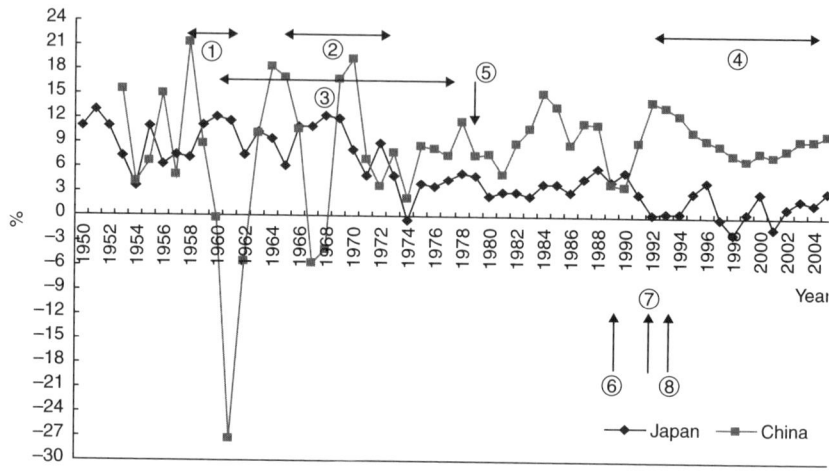

Figure 4.1   Annual real GDP growth rate of Japan and China

Notes:

① *Great Leap Forward* period
② *Cultural Revolution* period
③ International blocked period
④ Introduction of large amount of foreign funds
⑤ Beginning of Reform-Opening policy
⑥ Tiananmen Square event
⑦ Publication of Deng Xaoping's *Southern Trip Speech*
⑧ Resolution of socialistic market economy

Sources:

Japan
1950–1955: Nihon no Hyakunen (Japan's 100 Years). Revised 2nd edition. Kokuseisha Press, 1986, p. 94.
1956–1999: Ibid., revised 4th edition. Kohtaroh Yano Memorial Association Press. 2000. p. 108.
2000–2002: Nihon Kokusei Zue (Japan's Statistical Outlook), Kohtaroh Yano Memorial Association Press. 2004. p. 89.
2003–2005: Nihon Keizai Shinbun (The Japanese Economy Newspaper), September 4. 2006. p. 14.

China
1953–2000: *China's Statistical Yearbook.* 2001 edition. p. 51.
2001–2004: Ibid., 2005 edition. p. 53.
2005: People's Daily, August 31, 2006.

had been fairly rapid, but in many ways this was a recovery from the destruction caused by the American air bombing during the Second World War. During the decade from 1959 to 1969, Japan's annual growth rate was more than 11 percent, with the exception of two years. The high economic growth period for Japan ended in 1974, as a result of the first oil shock which took place in the autumn of 1973. Thus, Japan's high economic growth lasted 18 years with an average annual growth rate of 9.3 percent.

Although there were episodes of high growth (as per our definition above) in pre-1978 years in China, this period was characterized by three major periods of ups-and-downs (Figure 4.1). These were caused mainly by political struggles within the Chinese Communist Party (CCP), as politics controlled the economy. Genuine continuous high economic growth in China therefore started in 1979. Since then, China has maintained a high growth rate of more than 6 percent, with the exception of the three years of 1981, 1989, and 1990. The average annual growth rate during the 27 years between 1979 and 2005 has been 8.6 percent. It seems that China's high growth period will continue through 2006 and beyond.

Figure 4.1 does not show the growth rates of Taiwan and Korea. However, it is known that Taiwan entered a period of high growth at the end of 1950s. It ended in 1998 when the Asian financial crisis broke out. Korea began to grow rapidly at the beginning of 1960s and was also severely hurt by the Asian financial crisis. It adopted a tightening policy suggested by the IMF, and achieved a temporary recovery in 1999. Taiwan's annual growth rate averaged to 8.3 percent for a period of 40 years, and Korea's annual average growth rate was 8.6 percent for nearly the same four decades. Taiwan and Korea may thus far hold the world record for high economic growth, both in terms of the annual growth rate and the length of the period. The interesting question therefore is whether China will be able to surpass Taiwan and Korea with regard to growth performance.

4.2.2   The main factors behind China's high economic growth

There are three main factors behind China's high economic growth. The first is the large expansion of exports. The second is the high rate of fixed capital investment, and the third is the rapid urbanization.

The first factor was made possible by the introduction of a large amount of foreign loans and foreign direct investment and two devaluations of the *Yuan*, by 6.8 percent in 1986 and 50 percent in 1994. China ranked 26th in the world in terms of exports in 1980, and climbed to be 15th in 1990, accounting for 1.8 percent of world total exports. In 2000, China rose to the seventh rank, with a 3.9 percent share of world exports, and in 2005 it surpassed Japan, reaching the third rank and accounting for 6 percent of world exports. It should be noted that foreign invested enterprises account for 60 percent of China's exports (Shinohara, 2003).

The second factor has been a key to China's high economic growth (Kojima, 2002). Capital investment consists of investment in infrastructure, real estate construction (including housing), equipment and machinery of enterprises, and inventory stock. Figure 4.2 shows the GDP share of consumption and investment in China and Japan over the years. We see that when Japan started its rapid economic development, fixed capital formation accounted for 20 percent of her GDP. This share jumped to more than 35 percent within several years, and remained at this level until 1975. After the first oil shock, the share fell to around 30 percent, and continued to be at that level until 1996. Since the end of the Japanese bubble economy in 1992, the Japanese government has spent a large amount of public money on infrastructure construction to promote a recovery from the recession, with little or no positive result.

In China, soon after the Tiananmen Square incident, the ratio of fixed capital investment to GDP jumped to 32.2 percent in 1992 from 28 percent in the previous year and remained at the 35 to 38 percent level for several years. Since 1999, this ratio

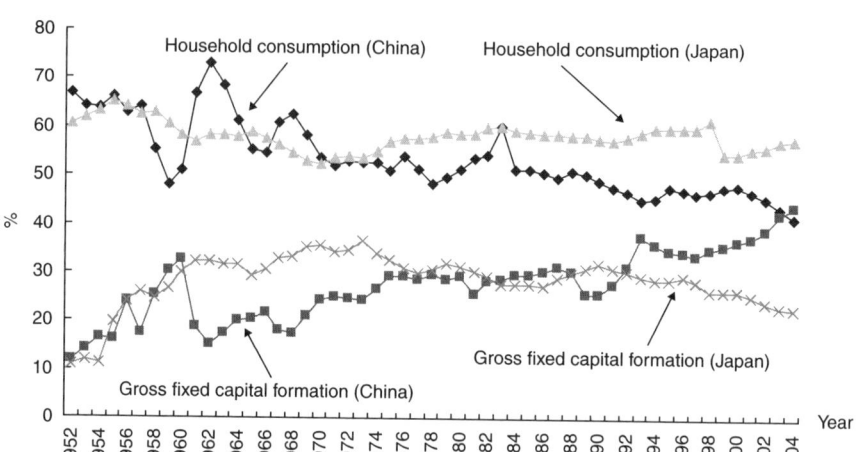

Figure 4.2 Ratio of household consumption and gross fixed capital formation in GDP of Japan and China

Sources:

Japan
1951–1954: Nihon no Hyakunen (Japan's 100 Years). Revised 2nd edition. Kokuseisha Press. 1986. p. 94.
1955–1998: Nihon no Hyakunen (Japan's 100 Years) Revised 4th edition, Kohtaroh Yano Memorial Association Press. 2004. pp. 104–105.
1999: Nihon Kokusei Zue (Japan's Statistical Outlook). Kohtaroh Yano Memorial Association Press. 2003. p. 92.
2000–02: Ibid., 2004/05 edition. p. 92.
2003–2004: Ibid., 2006/07 edition. p. 93.

China
1952–1995: Department of National Economic Accounting, State Statistical Bureau (ed.), Zhongguo guonei shengchan zongzhi hesuan lishi ziliao (the Gross Domestic Product of China: 1952–1995), Dongbei University of Finance and Economics press. 1997. pp. 25, 43, 50.
1996–2003: *China's Statistical Yearbook.* 2004 edition. pp. 65–66.
2004: Ibid., 2005 edition. pp. 63, 64.

has risen further, reaching nearly 39 percent in 2002. In 2004, the ratio surpassed 40 percent, reaching 43.8 percent, which is larger than the ratio of household final consumption to GDP for that year. A ratio of fixed capital investment to GDP above 35 percent is regarded as abnormal in the economic history of advanced countries. A ratio above 40 percent is perceived to be excessive. As a result of the steady rise in the share of investment in GDP, the share of household final consumption in GDP in China fell below 50 percent at the beginning of 1990s. With the onset of the 2000s, this share fell further and by 2004 reached a low of 41.4 percent.

The Japanese household final consumption to GDP ratio is around 60 percent (Figure 4.2), and the ratio is similar in Taiwan and Korea. In Western Europe and the United States, this ratio is around 70 percent. China's consumption to GDP ratio is therefore extraordinarily low. One reason is that this ratio is extremely low in rural areas. This suggests that for a balanced growth, China must find ways to raise household final demand in rural areas.

Table 4.1 shows the contribution of household final consumption and gross fixed capital investment to annual GDP growth rates. As can be seen, already in 1992 and 1993, fixed capital investment contributed to more than half of the Chinese annual GDP growth. From 1998 onwards, the extent of this contribution rose further, reaching in some years almost 70 percent (as in 2003). We may therefore conclude that China's high growth is led by fixed capital investment.

Table 4.1 also provides the breakdown of fixed investment into its various constituent parts and shows their annual rate of growth. In China, fixed capital investment is divided into four types, namely (a) new construction project investment (b) construction for renovation (c) real estate investment, and (d) other. As we can see, during 1992–1993 and in more recent years (since 2000), real estate investment has played the most important role among the four types.

Table 4.1 Contribution to GDP growth and rate of increase of different components of fixed capital investment

	Contribution (%) to GDP growth rate		*Annual rate (%) of increase of different components of fixed capital investment*				
			Total fixed capital investment				
	Household final demand	**Fixed capital investment**	**Total**	**New construction project investment**	**Construction by renovation**	**Real estate investment**	**Others**
1990	31.6	21.2	2.4	9.8	5.2	−7.1	−3.8
1991	40.6	40.8	23.9	24.2	23.3	32.7	22.5
1992	46.8	51.9	44.4	42.4	42.8	117.5	35.7
1993	37.3	54.0	61.8	53.2	50.3	165.0	50.4
1994	42.1	31.8	30.4	39.5	32.9	31.8	18.7
1995	51.9	29.1	17.5	15.0	13.0	23.3	20.2
1996	52.5	30.6	14.8	16.3	9.8	2.1	22.0
1997	41.2	27.7	8.8	15.7	8.5	−1.2	5.5
1998	50.3	60.3	13.9	20.2	15.2	13.7	5.5
1999	65.8	50.3	5.1	4.2	−0.7	13.5	5.4
2000	53.4	47.2	10.3	7.8	13.9	21.5	6.7
2001	32.5	45.3	13.0	10.4	16.0	27.3	7.7
2002	33.4	57.2	16.9	19.2	14.0	22.8	11.5
2003	27.9	68.5	27.7	29.7	27.8	30.3	22.9
2004	30.5	53.5					

Notes:
(1) Based on GDP calculated along the expenditure approach.
(2) The 2004 figures on components of fixed capital investment are not included in the *China Statistical Yearbook*, 2005 edition.

Sources: (1) *China Statistical Yearbook*, 2005 edition, pp. 63–64; (2) Ibid., 2004 edition, pp. 188–193.

Taking 1990 as the benchmark, real estate investment by 2003 has increased by 40-fold, compared to 12.5-fold increase in total fixed capital investment, 13.5-fold increase in new construction project investment, and 10.4-fold increase in renovation investment. This suggests that China's high economic growth since 1990 has been led mainly by fixed capital investment, within which investment in real estate played the main role.

There are three reasons for the expansion of real estate investment. One is the rapid urbanization; the second is housing construction; and the third is infrastructure construction. As is well known, beginning in 1961 the Chinese government adopted an anti-urbanization policy (Kojima, 2005). For many years, population inflows into cities from rural areas were prohibited except for entry into the army and university. After the dismantling of the people's communes at the beginning of the 1980s, peasants began to flow illegally from rural areas into the cities and designated towns, even though strict restrictions and various administrative barriers were in place in the cities. In a sense, the urbanization during the 1980s can be understood as a recovery from the effects of the earlier anti-urbanization policy. In the 1990s, China's rate of urbanization was comparable to those of other countries at similar economic level, even though urban areas still continued to restrict the inflow of peasants. During the decade of 1990s, the annual rate of increase of non-farming population of both cities and designated towns proved to be 4.8 percent, a fairly high rate but lower than in some countries in Africa or Latin America. The elasticity of urbanization to the GDP growth rate is 0.6, meaning that a 1 percent increase in the real GDP growth rate leads to a 0.6 percent increase in urban population.

Table 4.2 shows the decomposition of the Chinese urban population by the size of cities (and designated towns). It also shows the rate of urban population growth in cities (and designated towns) of different size. We see that from 1985 to 1994, the rate of growth of population in cities with populations below 300,000 was quite high. Since 1995, however, the situation has reversed. These small cities suffered population loss, while the megalopolis cities experienced the highest population increase. From this table, we can safely say that China has entered into a period of megalopolis urbanization (Kojima, 2006).

Construction or redevelopment of large cities are however extremely costly. This is one reason for the increase in fixed capital investment in China. Table 4.3 presents information on housing investment. We see that until 1991, housing construction investment in rural areas was larger than that in urban areas. The reverse has been the situation since 1992. In urban areas housing construction investment increased by 22 times between 1990 and 2004, while in rural areas the increase has been only 3.7 times. The shares of urban and rural housing investment in the total were 18 and 82 percent, respectively, in 2004 (People's Bank, 2005).

In addition to the urban housing construction investment, there are the gigantic infrastructure projects. Many big projects were launched in the 1990s. Among them are the Three Gorges Dam Project, the Great Western Development Project including natural gas pipelines stretching 4,200 km, the railway project connecting Tibet, a water canal project from a branch of the Yangzi River to the Beijing

Table 4.2 Structure of cities by population size and annual rate of population growth

	Share (%) of population by city size			Annual rate (%) of increase	
	1984	**1994**	**2002**	**1985–1994**	**1995–2002**
Above 10 million			4.5 }10.4	7.9	6.1
5–10 million	6.1	7.5	5.9		
2–5 million	19.9	12.6	16.7	1.1	5.4
1–2 million	13.4	15.3	18.7	7.1	4.3
500,000–1 million	21.0	14.8	19.2	2.1	5.1
300,000–500,000	13.4	14.6	17.7	6.6	4.2
100,000–300,000	21.3	29.6	14.0	9.3	–7.9
Below 100,000	4.9	5.6	3.2	7.3	–5.5

Source: Calculated based on the following sources:
1984: *Zhongguo Chengshi Tongjinianjian (China City Statistics Yearbook)*, 1985 edition, pp. 35–42.
1994: Ibid., 1995 edition. pp. 19–23.
2002: Ibid., 2003 edition. pp. 31–37.

area, and industrial and commercial mall and park construction. In the middle of the 1990s, many transportation and communication national network plans for express highways, oil and gas pipelines, and optical fiber networks were initiated. These networks have been built at a rapid speed. In 1990, China had just 500 km of express highways. By 2004 this number rose to 34,300 km, making China second in the world (after the United States with 90,000 km) in terms of the length of highways. Japan began its construction of highways at the beginning of 1960s, and completed 8,000 km over four decades. On the other hand at the current pace of highway construction, China is likely catch up with the United States within the next decade.

4.2.3   The main players in fixed capital investment

There are three main players encouraging fixed capital investment. They are local governments, developers, and four state-owned commercial banks. The central government is in charge of major projects at the national level, using budgetary finance. Local governments above the provincial-level cities also take the initiative for provincial-level projects. Under the supervision of provincial governments, county and county-level cities have been very active, especially in the construction of industrial parks and commercial sites.

Once projects are given recognition by government at various levels, they are undertaken by developers, most of which were separated from governmental organs during the 1990s and are supposed to be independent construction enterprises. The projects are financed mainly by the four state-owned banks. After the completion of a development project, the government sells the land to users through bidding. At this stage, a land price emerges, and local governments

Table 4.3   Housing investment

	Housing investment (Billion Yuan)			Increase index (1990 = 100)			Share (%) in housing investment	
	Total	Rural	Urban	Total	Rural	Urban	Rural	Urban
1990	116.45	66.61	49.83	100	100	100	57.2	42.8
1991	141.74	77.66	64.08	121.7	116.6	128.6	54.8	45.2
1992	171.69	70.34	101.35	147.4	105.6	203.4	41.0	59.0
1993	272.58	82.17	190.41	234.1	123.4	382.1	30.1	69.9
1994	380.64	110.21	270.42	326.9	165.5	542.7	29.0	71.0
1995	473.67	145.85	327.82	406.8	219.0	657.9	30.8	69.2
1996	519.85	187.23	332.62	446.4	281.1	667.5	36.0	64.0
1997	537.07	205.10	331.97	461.2	307.9	666.2	38.2	61.8
1998	639.38	208.30	431.08	549.1	312.8	865.1	32.6	67.4
1999	705.88	200.79	505.09	606.2	301.4	1,013.6	28.4	71.6
2000	759.41	215.89	543.53	652.1	324.1	1,090.8	28.4	71.6
2001	833.91	207.76	626.15	716.1	311.9	1,256.6	24.9	75.1
2002	940.71	215.82	724.89	807.8	324.0	1,454.7	22.9	77.1
2003	1,079.23	216.75	962.48	926.8	325.4	1,931.5	20.1	89.2
2004	1,346.51	245.50	1,101.01	1,156.3	368.6	2,209.5	18.2	81.8

Sources: Section on Fixed Capital Investment of the State Statistical Bureau, ed., *Statistics on Investment in Fixed Assets of China (1950–2000)*. China Statistical Press, 2002, p. 32; *China Statistical Yearbook*, 2005 edition, p. 191.

including city governments can get fairly significant amount of revenues through these sales and through land tax. Developers also get a large profit, which is estimated to be 30 to 40 percent of the final sale price. Governments at the county or county-level city get around 20 to 30 percent (of the sale price), while towns and village governments get about 10 to 20 percent. In contrast, peasants, whose land is expropriated, get only several percent of the final sale price (Chang, 2006). The profits of developers are so high that banks are willing to give them loans, even though the central bank and/or the central government often issues orders to restrict financing to them. We thus have a trinity of local governments, developers, and banks. It is the symbiotic relationship embodied in this trinity that is one reason behind the extraordinarily high fixed capital investment ratio observed in current China.

4.3   Newly emerging contradictions – immiserization of peasants

4.3.1   Emergence of depopulated areas

A population decrease in rural areas during the period of high economic growth is a normal and natural phenomenon. As long as the peasants remaining in the rural areas are successful in raising productivity and upgrading the existing rural communities into new developed ones, the population decrease does not have negative consequences. What has been the case in this regard in China?

The fifth national census of 2000 carries two kinds of population data, namely family registration and current residence. If the population measured by an area's family registration is larger than that measured by current residence, it means that that area is losing population. In the opposite case, the area is gaining population. Calculation shows that 12 out of 31, or 38.7 percent of provincial-level administrative regions lost population, as did 192 among 350 (45.1 percent) prefectural-level administrative regions and 869 out of 1,186 (73.3 percent) of county-level regions. For county-level regions, the calculation was limited to just 14 provinces rather than the 31 provincial-level regions. Rural areas are mainly in county-level regions. Overall, the data show that in and around 2000, 70 to 80 percent of rural areas were losing population.

The loss of rural population is caused mainly by young workers flowing out from rural areas. It is estimated that as of 2004, around 140 million peasants have left rural areas (NBSC, 2005). They are abandoning agriculture, especially cultivation of main traditional crops such as grains, soybean, and cotton. Data compiled in Table 4.4 illustrate the process. We see that during a period of about 20 years, sown area under miscellaneous cereals and spring wheat shrank by three-fourths, and that under early ripening indica rice by half. Meanwhile, production of soybean and cotton has increased. However, import of these two commodities increased faster leading to a decrease in the self-sufficiency ratio, as can be seen in Table 4.5. This means that agricultural product processing industries in rural areas are shrinking, with accompanying job losses. Unless job growth in alternative new rural industries offset these losses, the process leads to a net loss of job opportunities in rural areas. This seems to be what is happening in the rural areas of inland provinces.

There are some worrisome developments in the tertiary sector of rural areas too. As a result of the one child policy and population exodus, many primary

Table 4.4 Decline in sown areas of miscellaneous cereals, spring wheat, and early ripening Indica rice (Indexes with 1980 or 1982 value as 100)

Miscellaneous cereals		Spring wheat		Early ripening Indica rice	
1980	100.0	1982	100.0	1980	100.0
1990	69.2	1992	99.2	1989	84.3
1999	33.4	1999	67.0	2000	61.4
2003	25.3	2003	25.8	2003	50.3

Source: *China Agricultural Yearbook*, 1981, 1983, 1990, 1991, 1993, 2000, 2004 editions.

Table 4.5 Imports and self-sufficiency ratio of soybeans and cotton

	Soybean		Cotton	
	Import ('000 ton)	Self-sufficiency ratio (%)	Import ('000 ton)	Self-sufficiency ratio (%)
1985	10	112.2	0	109.1
1990	10	109.2	420	94.7
1995	2,940	100.6	786	86.3
2000	10,410	60.2	84	104.6
2004	20,230	46.7	1,910	76.9
2005	26,160		2,500	69.2

Notes:
(1) Self-sufficiency ratio = production/apparent consumption.
(2) 2005 figures are calculated from January to November figures as published.

Sources: 1985–2000: *China Agricultural Development Report*, 2004 edition; 2004: *China Statistical Yearbook*, 2005 edition; 2005: *China Farmer's Daily*, January 10. 2006. p. 6, January 20, 2006, p. 5.

schools and junior high schools in rural areas have been closed down or amalgamated with those in county capitals or cities. Tables 4.6 and 4.7 show the case of Zhejiang province, while Table 4.8 shows the case of the Chengdu prefecture-level administrative region of Sichuan province. The number of schools providing primary education in rural areas of Zhejiang province decreased by about 95 percent between 1990 and 2000, and the number of teachers decreased by about 80 percent. Similar tendencies can be observed in Zhejiang rural areas with respect to junior high school education. The opposite can be seen in the urban areas, where the numbers of both students and teachers have increased. The same phenomena can be observed in Chengdu of Sichuan province, whose economic level is far lower than of Zhejiang province. As a whole therefore rural areas in China are facing a decline.

4.3.2 Landless peasants

As mentioned earlier, since the beginning of 1990s, the annual growth rate of urban population in China has been 4.8 percent or more. This is fairly high by international standards (Kojima, 2005). Such rapid urbanization automatically leads to expansion of urban city areas. It is estimated that a 1 percent increase in urban population leads to an expansion of urban area by 2.26 percent in cities that are above middle scale. Gigantic infrastructure projects also require land. How is the land for such urban expansion and infrastructure construction obtained? Under the land law, arable land is collectively owned, and cannot be sold or used for another use. Only if the land is reclassified as to be under state ownership, can it be legally expropriated for non-agricultural use (Chang, 2006).

If a town or village devises a plan to develop a certain land area for industrial or commercial use, it must get administrative permission from a higher government level. The level differs depending on the acreage, but it was generally the

Table 4.6 Changes in the education sector of rural areas of Zhejiang province (1990 = 100)

	1990	1995	2000	2003
Primary education				
Number of schools	100	29.2	11.9	5.2
Number of pupils enrolled	100	32.2	22.5	12.9
Number of teachers	100	36.8	32.7	20.9
Junior high school education				
Number of schools	100	38.5	27.8	16.7
Number of pupils enrolled	100	46.5	35.5	18.7
Number of teachers	100	43.4	40.3	23.1

Source: Zhejiang Xiang Cheng Statistical Yearbook, 2000 edition, p. 3.

Table 4.7 Changes in the education sector of designated cities of Zhejiang province (1990 = 100)

	1990	1995	2000	2003
Primary education				
Number of schools	100	370.0	217.0	160.0
Number of pupils enrolled	100	243.6	257.2	267.2
Number of teachers	100	243.6	289.0	309.9
Junior high school education				
Number of schools	100	201.9	194.8	194.3
Number of pupils enrolled	100	201.9	259.0	300.0
Number of teachers	100	184.8	252.5	306.2

Source: Estimated by subtracting figures of rural areas from the whole provincial figures in Table 4.6.

county level or the provincial-level government which used to grant the permission. However, in order to prevent abuses, the central government in 1999 moved the right to give permissions from the county level to the provincial level. When permission is granted, the land is placed under state ownership. Once local governments get the permission for development, the peasants on that land lose all rights and are merely paid a certain sum for compensation prescribed in the land law. The sum paid for compensation is usually six to ten times the annual revenue derived from the land. In coastal areas an additional sum equaling to four to six times of annual revenue is paid for resettlement.[1] In the central and western areas, the compensation is lower. The compensation is far lower for land

Table 4.8 Changes in the education sector of rural areas, county seats, and designated cities in Chengdu PRLR, Sichuan Province

	Rural areas			County seats			Designated cities		
	1999	2002	Change (%)	1999	2002	Change (%)	1999	2002	Change (%)
Primary education									
Number of schools	2,087	171	−91.8	332	264	−20.5	182	154	−15.4
Number of pupils enrolled	69,919	59,037	−15.6	35,104	41,693	+18.8	19,997	20,821	+4.1
Number of teachers	21,778	19,175	−12.0	13,006	15,571	+19.7	8,245	7,844	−4.9
Junior high school education									
Number of schools	147	124	−15.6	188	216	+14.9	48	43	−10.4
Number of pupils enrolled	34,130	24,277	−28.9	75,088	77,482	+3.2	29,787	30,463	+2.3
Number of teachers	4,712	4,300	−8.7	11,931	14,032	+17.6	5,828	6,330	+8.6
Senior high school education									
Number of schools	1	0	−100.0	442	94	−78.7	56	54	−3.6
Number of pupils enrolled	91	0	−100.0	20,326	46,685	+129.7	3,921	18,291	+366.5
Number of teachers	77	0	−100.0	13,227	5,856	−55.7	2,633	3,015	+14.5

Note: Chengdu PRLR consisted of is a prefectural level region consisting of seven districts, eight counties, and four cities in 1999, and nine districts, six counties, and three cities in 2002.

Source: Chengdu Statistical Yearbook, 2000 edition, p. 321. 2003 edition. p. 304.

to be used for public use, such as infrastructure or construction of government buildings. Since arable land cannot be marketed, peasants cannot reap capital gains. The local governments choose the developers, and when the development is completed, they sell the land to users. As already mentioned, most of the revenue from sale goes to developers, local governments, and banks, leaving very little for the peasants. In the case of land for public use, the land price is fixed at negligible levels. This is one reason for the construction of wide roads and monumental governmental and university buildings in China.

By the beginning of 2005, applications for the development of more than 850 industrial parks or commercial sites had been made by various local governments, including those of towns. This is because local governments hoped to gain revenue through land management to pull themselves out of financial crisis. In 1994, the central government introduced a new tax system eliminating taxes that had been lucrative for local governments. As a result, the financial performance of local governments, especially town- and village governments, deteriorated rapidly. The accumulated debt of town and village governments is estimated to be about 1 trillion yuan in 2005, equaling to 7.2 percent of GDP. This may be compared with its 1998 value of 326 billion, equaling to 4.1 percent of GDP in that year.[2] More than 60 percent of these debts are considered to be bad loans. No wonder that local governments try to generate revenues from land sales in order to improve their financial position.

This is the background of the emergence of landless peasants (Cai, 2006). Their emergence is the other side of the coin of the real estate investment wave. The number of landless farmers increases as more fixed capital investment is carried out. Their total number is now estimated to be between 40 and 50 million. They receive no social welfare support from the central government and have difficulty finding new occupations, as most of them are over 40 years old. Some scholars call these people *sanwu nongmin* (peasants with no land, no social welfare, and no occupation).

At the People's Congress in March 2006, the central government decided to abolish the agricultural tax and to give financial support to compulsory education in rural areas. This is an epoch-making step in the Chinese history. However, these two policies will not be sufficient to stop the immiserization of peasants. The abolition of the agricultural tax will lead to a further deterioration of the financial situation of town- and village governments, as this tax was one of their most important sources of revenue (Li and Li, 2004; Lou, 2003). For many years, education in rural areas was financed by rural communities rather than by the central government. Given this background, the new policy represents a step forward. However, it comes too late. This kind of policy should have been introduced in the 1980s. There is still policy discrimination between rural and urban areas. For example, people in rural areas have to construct infrastructure at their own expense and receive no social welfare from the central government. The question now is whether or not the central government will adopt a policy to redistribute the gains from high economic growth to the underprivileged classes. If it fails to do so, the new contradictions will become social or political issues. To prevent this possibility, a basic financial reform is needed aimed at dissolution of the trinity of local bureaucrats, developers, and state-owned banks.

4.4.   Factors that may slow down economic growth

In this section, we consider certain factors that may slow down Chinese economic growth.

4.4.1   Declining efficiency of fixed capital investment

Table 4.9 shows the efficiency of fixed capital investment, measured as additional GDP divided by total fixed capital investment undertaken in that year. We see that fixed capital investment efficiency has declined over time. While the efficiency measure ranged between 0.7 and 0.4 until mid-1990s, it has since declined to values ranging between 0.3 and 0.1 in more recent years.

This decrease may be a result of wasteful and lavish designs in public infrastructure projects. Roads, for example, are planned so that each side has three lanes, then a green belt, and then one or more extra lanes, sometimes for tractors or bicycles. What is more, gorgeous memorials can be found at each crossroad or roundabout. However, there are often very few cars on these roads. Similarly, Chinese local governmental office buildings are often larger and more splendid than those of the Japanese central government! Different local governments seem to be competing with one another in terms of grandeur and lavishness.

How is it possible that the Chinese local governments can construct such big and gorgeous roads and buildings? One possible reason is that they do not have to pay for the land they acquire for the construction purposes. This is a form of institutionalized wastage. This system lowers the efficiency of fixed capital investment.

4.4.2   Two factors slowing down export expansion

There are two factors that may potentially slow down China's export expansion. One of these is the possible appreciation of the value of the Chinese currency

Table 4.9   Efficiency of fixed capital investment

Year	Efficiency	Year	Efficiency
1985	0.62	1997	0.26
1990	0.39	1998	0.15
1991	0.50	1999	0.12
1992	0.55	2000	0.20
1993	0.67	2001	0.25
1994	0.72	2002	0.21
1995	0.58	2003	0.27
1996	0.43	2004	0.33

Source: China Statistical Yearbook, 2005 edition, pp. 63–64.

Yuan, by at least 10 to 20 percent in the near future. We refrain from a detailed discussion of this point in this paper.

The other factor is the rise in wages. During the rapid economic growth periods in Japan, Taiwan and Korea, land prices, wages and retail prices rose simultaneously. In China, though land prices in urban areas have generally increased, retail prices and wages have not kept pace with this increase. However, this is changing. Figure 4.3 shows the annual nominal GDP growth rate and annual increase in the nominal wage in urban areas. We see that since 1998, the annual rate of increase in wages has surpassed the nominal GDP growth rate. It is to be noted that this happened 20 years after rapid economic growth started in China in 1978. Such a long delay in rise in wages was possible because China had a large surplus labor in rural areas.

Until 1998, wages rose only for high-class staff or skilled laborers, or in new industries, such as finance, real estate, and media, but not in manufacturing. The wage levels in export industries, such as textile, miscellaneous industries, and even electronic appliances, have remained unchanged. With the beginning of the twenty-first century, this situation has changed. A general labor shortage is

Figure 4.3   Annual growth rate of nominal GDP and worker's average wage

Sources: *China's Statistical Yearbook,* each edition.
China: *China Statistical Yearbook* (1986 edition, p. 103) for 1982; Ibid (1994 edition, p. 18) for 1993; Ibid (2004 edition, p. 104) for 2003.
Japan: *Jinkou no Doukou(Population Dynamics)*, 1996, 2000, 2001/2002, 2003 editions.
(1) China: Up part of Bar graph refers to ratio of 2003; Middle part: 1993; Bottom part: 1982;
    Japan: Up part of Bar graph refers to ratio of 2003; Middle part: 1990; Bottom part : 1980.
(2) 7.14 percent: Aging society.
(3) Above 14 percent: The Aged Society.
(4) It is expected that in 2030 the ratio in China will reach to the largest.

Table 4.10   Estimation of new labor supply in rural areas ('000)

	New labor supply
1996–2000 yearly average	7,340
2001	7,770
2002	8,960
2003	11,430
2004	9,300
2005	10,130
2006	9,970
2007	4,540
2008	2,470
2009	530
2010	–2,060

Note: The estimation is not always accurate because if the enrollment ratio from junior high school to senior high school rises, the new labor supply will decrease.
Source: Zhongguo Nongcun Jingji (China Rural Economy), August 2000.

surfacing. This represents the effects of China's one child policy and the spread of compulsory education. Table 4.10 presents some projections about incremental labor supply in China up to the year 2010. Of course, such projections cannot be accurate given the state of the data and other uncertainties. However, we see a gradual decline leading to a negative value in 2010. Anecdotal evidence also points to the emergence of a situation of labor shortage in certain parts of China (State Council, 2006). For example, in 2004, the regulated minimum wage was raised by 20percent to 40percent in many cities. Most observers agree that since 2002 Guangdong area has been experiencing a shortage of young labor, and this shortage is gradually spreading to the Shanghai economic zone.

These two factors, namely the appreciation of yuan and the increase in wages will surely raise the cost of export unless China is able to implement technological innovation at a sufficient pace. China is now at a turning point, where it may no longer be possible to increase exports on the basis of low wages alone.

4.4.3   Future prospects seen from the viewpoint of population dynamics

It is necessary to emphasize two points in making judgments about China's long-term future. The first is the rapid ageing of the population. Internationally, a society is said to have become an "ageing society" when the ratio of the population above 65 years of age to the total population reaches 7 percent. When this ratio

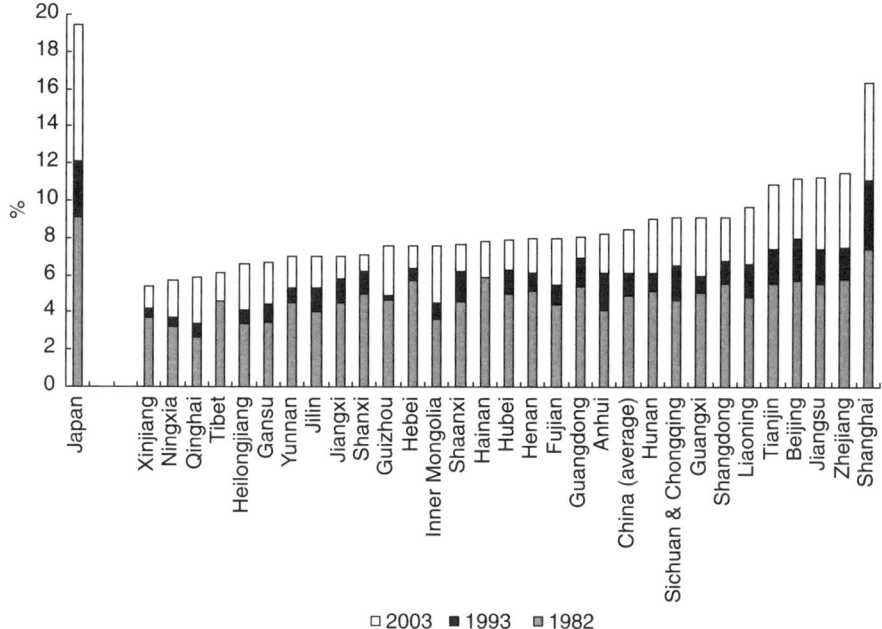

□ 2003   ■ 1993   ■ 1982

Figure 4.4   Ageing in China: ratio of population above 65 to total population

Sources:
China: *China Statistical Yearbook* (1986 edition, p. 103) for 1982; Ibid (1994 edition, p. 18) for 1993; Ibid (2004 edition, p. 104) for 2003.
Japan: *Jinkou no Doukou (Population Dynamics)*, 1996, 2000, 2001/2002, 2003 editions.

Notes:
(1) China: Upper part of Bargraph refers to ratio of 2003; Middle part: 1993; Bottom part: 1982;
    Japan: Upper part of Bargraph refers to ratio of 2003; Middle part: 1990; Bottom part: 1980.
(2) 7.14 percent: Ageing society.
(3) Above 14 percent: The Aged Society.
(4) It is expected that in 2030 the ratio in China will reach to the largest.

crosses 14 percent, the society is called an "aged society." Figure 4.4 illustrates these dynamics at the Chinese provincial level. It also provides comparison with Japan, which is considered to have become an aged society at the fastest pace. However, China may soon surpass Japan's record. Shanghai is already approaching Japan in this regard.

In section 4.1 we noted depopulation of Chinese rural areas caused by exodus of the young. We observed that 73 percent of county and county-level cities have already entered into a depopulation phase. Taking care of the older folks left behind in depopulated rural areas is therefore emerging as a serious new problem. Since urbanization has proceeded so rapidly, China as a whole has not yet prepared itself for tackling this emerging problem.

It also needs to be emphasized that according to our projections, China will reach a static population stage some time between 2020 and 2023. Many Chinese scholars on population issues anticipate that the population will stabilize in or around 2030, at a level of approximately 1.6 billion. However, we think that this projection involves overestimation.

Figure 4.5 shows changes in the total fertility rate of Japan and China. Approximately 30 years or so after the total fertility rate falls below the 2.1 line, the population of a nation begins to decrease. Japan's total fertility rate fell below 2.1 in 1974, and in 2005 its total population began to decrease. China's total fertility rate is now around 1.15, a figure far below Japan's 1.25 in 2005. China's fertility rate seems to have fallen under 2.1 around 1993, although the statistics are not always accurate. Taking these points into consideration, we think that China's population will stabilize sometime between 2021 and 2023, at 1.52 billion. Thus, China will arrive at the stationary stage of population earlier, unless the Chinese government changes its "one child policy."

These two factors, namely rapid aging of the population and cessation of population growth, will work to slow China's economic growth down. One important policy for avoiding a fall in the economic growth rate in the coming 10 to 15 years is to implement in China's financial system a drastic change aimed at redistribution of the dividends of the rapid economic growth to the poor and poor areas. This policy will require a struggle against the current formidable trinity of local bureaucracy, developers, and state-owned banks.

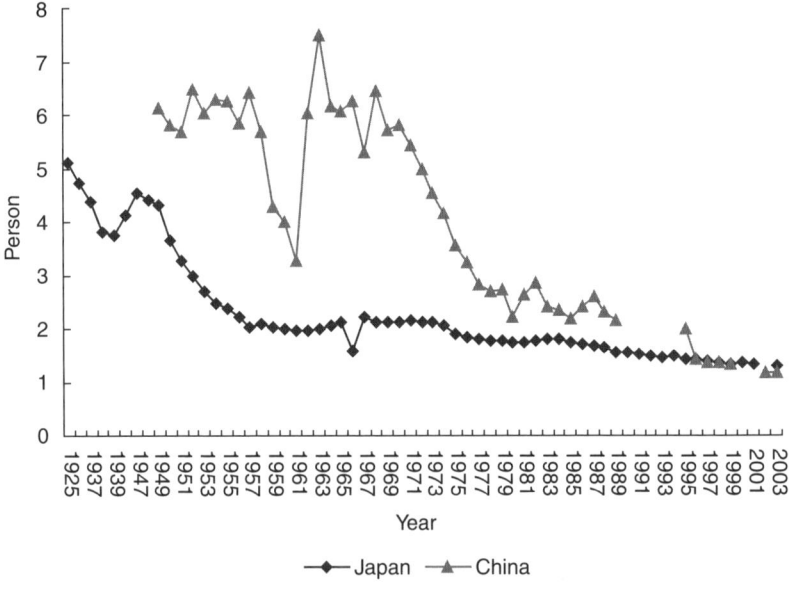

Figure 4.5   Total fertility rate of Japan and China

Sources:
(1) Institute of Population problems (eds.), *Jinkou no Doukou (Population Dynamics)*, each edition, Kousei Tokei Kyokai.
(2) Keiko Wakabayashi, *Dokyumento Chugoku no Jinkou Kanri (Document China's Population management)*, Nihon Hyoronsha, p. 411.
(3) *China's Statistical Yearbook*, each edition.

4.5 Concluding remarks

An international comparative perspective is useful in assessing China's growth performance. So far the record holders of high growth are Taiwan and Korea, which have experienced high economic growth lasting for about 40 years. Japan's high growth period lasted for 18 years. By comparison, China's high growth period has so far lasted 27 years. This puts her ahead of Japan, but still short of Taiwan and Korea.

China's high growth has been achieved through high rates of fixed capital investment and of export growth caused in turn by a large amount of foreign direct investment. In addition to the equipment and machinery investment, the fast pace of infrastructure build-up and investment in real estate and urban housing construction (induced by rapid urbanization) have contributed to China's high investment ratio. The trinity consisting of local governments, developers, and four state-own banks, has been one of the main propelling forces behind this investment spree.

China's high economic growth and rapid urbanization have however given rise to some new contradictions that cannot be ignored. Among these are: (a) decline of the rural economy (especially in inland and mountainous areas, which are traditionally not rich), manifested in large-scale depopulation (b) emergence of a class of landless peasants, and (c) emergence of urban poor, including peasant migrants. These contradictions have already graduated from being economic problems into becoming social problems. Unless the government deals with these problems effectively, these may turn into political problems. In fact, the number of various disturbances has been increasing over the past years. More than half of these are related to land expropriation by governments and developers. It will be difficult for China to sustain high growth without resolving those newly emerging contradictions.

Changing population dynamics will also affect China's economic growth prospects in the near future. There are three anticipated changes. First, new supply of young labor will decrease sharply in the near future owing to the continued enforcement of the "one child policy" and the rapid spread of education at senior high school level and above. The growing tightness of the labor market finds manifestation in the fact that wages have been rising since 2002. This is bound to affect China's exports. Second, the Chinese society is aging at the fastest rate in human history. Taking care of the aged, who will now comprise a higher proportion of the population, will entail a greater financial burden on the government and the society. Third, the total population of China will reach a stationary state around 2020, much earlier that previously projected.

In view of the emerging contradictions and the population dynamics, it is necessary for the Chinese government to bring about changes in its policies. In particular, it has to change the financial redistribution system, which has so far favored the trinity comprised of local governments, developers, and state-owned banks, and make it work more in favor of the poor and the needy. At the same time, China needs to change her industrial policy to make it more congruent with the goal of sustainable development.

Acknowledgements

The author would like to thank Nazrul Islam and other participants of ICSEAD's China Growth Project for their comments on earlier drafts of the paper. Special thanks are due to Erbiao Dai for his help in processing this paper. They are however not responsible for remaining errors.

Notes

1   Chang Hongxiao, *Tudi Jiemi* (Disclosure of land secrecy), *CAIJING* (*Finance and Economy*), February. 20 issue, 2006, No. 153. Caijing Magazine Publishing Company: Beijing.
2   DW News.com (Duowei Xinwen), April 15, 2006.

References

Cai, Jianwen. 2006. *Zhongguo Nongmingong Shengcun Jishi* (*Record of Peasant laborers in China*), Dangdai Zhongguo Publishing Company: Beijing.
Chang, Hongxiao. 2006. "Tudi Jiemi (Disclosure of Land Secrecy)," *Caijing (Finance and Economy),* February 20, 2006, 153. Caijing Magazine Publishing Company: Beijing.
Kojima, Reiitsu. 2002. "On the Reliability of China's Economic Statistics with Special Reference to GDP," *The Journal of Econometric Study of Northeast Asia*, 4, 1. Economic Research Institute for Northeast Asia: Tokyo.
Kojima, Reiitsu. 2005. *Urbanization in China in the Light of International Experiences*, Paper written for the World Bank, Washington D.C., October, 2005. (Not yet published)
Kojima, Reiitsu. 2006. The Rapid Urbanization of China and Its Impact on the Development and Decline of Small Cities and Towns, Paper written for the World Bank, Washington D.C., March 2006. (Not yet published).
Li, Yizhi and Li Yanfang. ed. 2004. *Nongcun Caizheng Jingrong* (*Rural Finance and Banking*), China Financial Publishing House: Beijing.
Lou, Yixing. 2003. *Difang Caizheng Xinlun* (*A New Analysis on Local Finance*), Zhongguo Caijing Publishing Company: Beijing.
National Bureau of Statistics of China (Rural Social and Economic Survey Section of NBSC). 2005. *Zhongguo Nongcun Laodongli Diaoyan Baogao 2005* (*Research on Rural Labor of China in 2005*), China Statistics Press: Beijing.
People's Bank (Real Estate Financial Analysis Team of People's Bank). 2005. *2004 Zhongguo Fangdichan Jinrong Baogao* (*Report of Chinese Real Estate Financial Analysis in 2004*), August 5, 2005. China People's Bank: Beijing.
Shinohara, Miyohei. 2003. *Chugoku Keizai no Kyodaika to Hong Kong* (*The Big Expansion of Chinese Economy and Hong Kong*), Keisoshobo Publishing Company: Tokyo.
State Council (Project Research Team of State Council). 2006. *Zhongguo Nongmingong Diaoyan Baogao* (*Research on Rural labor of China*), Zhongguo *Yanshi* Publishing Company: Beijing.

5
China's Industrialization Viewed from the Lewis Growth Model

Nazrul Islam and Kazuhiko Yokota

5.1 Introduction

This chapter examines China's industrialization in the light of the Lewis growth model. Even casual observation suggests that the Chinese economy has many of the features that the Lewis model tries to capture. Yet, while the Lewis model has been applied to study industrialization of other countries, surprisingly little, if any, effort has been made in this respect with regard to China.[1] This chapter is an attempt to fill this void.

The chapter begins with a brief perusal of Lewis' own writings and those of Fei and Ranis in order to clarify certain aspects of the assumptions and predictions of the Lewis model. The review shows that, despite subsequent extensions, the main prediction of the model remains what is known as the Turning Point prediction. According to this prediction, the wage of unskilled labor in the "modern" sector will remain fairly flat for a considerable period of time before reaching the Turning Point and rising thereafter rapidly. This prediction also applies to the "traditional" sector wage curve, which in fact is expected to reach a similar Turning Point earlier, though the curve as a whole remains below the modern sector wage curve. Eventually the two curves get closer, signifying the equalization of wages in the two sectors (subject to caveats) and the disappearance of the duality of the economy.

In their empirical work inspired by the Lewis model, some researchers focused on testing directly the model's *assumptions*, such as duality, existence of surplus labor, etc. Scholars following this line of query often used micro data and adopted the methodology of comparative-statics.[2] However, as Lewis himself, and Fei and Ranis following him, frequently pointed out, the Lewis model is mainly a story about long run macro dynamics, even though, as Sen (1966, 1967a, 1967b) shows, the story does not contradict rational optimizing behavior at the micro level. Other researchers however have rightly focused on macro dynamic *predictions* of the Lewis model and, in particular, examined the wage data to see whether the Turning Point prediction held, and if yes, how long it took the economies to reach the Turning Point, and what forces were important in propelling the process.

Testing the Turning Point prediction is however not easy, as recognized by Lewis himself and other researchers. The challenges range from problems regarding the correspondence between the dual sectors of the "theory" and the "empirical" sectors for which actual data are available to problems regarding the type of wage to examine. Despite these difficulties, many researchers have used the Lewis model and produced instructive results. For example, Williamson (1982) presents unskilled labor wage data for England during the first industrial revolution and shows that the wage curve remained essentially flat for about 40 years before starting to rise. Fei and Ranis offer compilation and analysis of wage data for Taiwan and Korea showing that the marginal product in agriculture increased much faster than wages in these countries.

Much research using the Lewis model was conducted on Japan, with a prominent role played in it by Minami (1964, 1966, 1967, 1968), who offered five criteria to identify Lewis Turning Point. Denoting marginal product of labor and wage in the traditional sector by MP_L^T and w^T, respectively, Minami's Criterion-I simply notes that, according to the Lewis model, $MP_L^T < w^T$ in the traditional sector until the Turning Point is reached. Based on a meticulous analysis focused on this criterion, Minami shows that Japan reached the Turning Point in the post Second World War period, and not during the 1920s, as was suggested earlier by Ranis (1957).

When it comes to China, the application of the Lewis model faces some additional difficulties arising from her specific institutional features, such as (a) the legacy of central planning, (b) restrictions on rural-urban migration, (c) frequent changes in the administrative jurisdiction of urban and rural counties, and (d) the establishment of modern industrial enterprises in rural areas in the form of Township and Village Enterprises (TVE). Earlier, based on a graphical analysis, Islam and Yokota (2006) showed that the Chinese wage curves appeared to display the Turning Point feature and that, according to the results from the Fei-Ranis style decomposition, capital accumulation played the main role in propelling the economy toward that point.

This chapter takes the analysis to a deeper level by using Minami's Criterion-I to identify the Turning Point for China. According to this criterion, the Turning Point is reached when the marginal product of labor in the traditional sector rises from below to become equal to the wage. In applying this criterion, the paper takes the "agriculture" sector as the empirical counterpart of the "traditional" sector of the Lewis theory, and estimates the production function for the agriculture sector of China for various years using provincial data. The estimated production function is used to obtain estimates of the marginal product of labor, which are then compared with the wage. The sample period extends from 1987 to 2005.

The analysis produces the following main results. First, the agricultural wage has increased over time, implying that the traditional sector wage curve has not remained entirely flat. This is however not surprising, because the Lewis model does not rule out some increase in the wages before reaching the Turning Point. Second, the marginal product of labor in the traditional sector (MP_L^T) has been increasing at a much faster rate than the wages. The trend of increase accelerated since 1998, even though more recent years witnessed some deceleration. Third, even though the MP_L^T curve is rising more steeply than wages, so that the gap between the two is narrowing, the average wage curve as a whole still remains above the MP_L^T-curve. Together these results indicate that China is steadily progressing toward the Lewis Turning Point, though it has not reached that point yet.

From a theoretical perspective, the findings lend support to the duality postulated by the Lewis model and the Turning Point prediction that ensues from it. The neoclassical growth model, with its assumption of full employment, perfect mobility, and equalization of factor returns across the sectors may therefore not provide the right description of the Chinese economy. However, as Lewis himself noted, once the economy reaches the Turning Point and the duality disappears, the postulates of the neoclassical model may become applicable, though the issue of finding a satisfactory explanation of the technological progress, a task that the new growth models are struggling with, will still remain.[3]

The discussion of the chapter is organized as follows. Section 5.2 offers a brief recapitulation of the salient features of the Lewis model in order to clarify its assumptions and predictions. Section 5.3 considers the extensions to the Lewis model suggested in particular by Ranis and Fei. Section 5.4 reviews previous applications of the Lewis model in studying industrialization. Section 5.5 presents the empirical analysis and the results. Section 5.6 concludes.

5.2 Lewis model of growth: A brief recapitulation

More than half a century ago, Arthur Lewis published his article, "Development with Unlimited Supply of Labor," which together with his subsequent writings gave rise to the famous "Lewis Growth Model," the hallmark of which is the assumption of a dual structure of the economy.[4] Various terminologies have been used to express this dualism, such as urban-rural, capitalist-non capitalist, modern-traditional, capitalist-subsistence, industrial-agricultural, commercial-non-commercial, etc. Lewis himself started with the "capitalist-non capitalist" characterization of this duality, but later recognized the possibility of other characterizations. In this paper, we will use the "modern-traditional" terminology to express the Lewis dualism.

As Lewis (1972) explains, the difference between the two sectors is analytical, and not descriptive. The first analytical difference postulates that the same type of labor has higher productivity in the modern sector than in the traditional sector. Denoting the marginal product of labor in traditional and modern sectors by MP_L^T and MP_L^M, respectively, the Lewis proposition therefore suggests that $MP_L^M > MP_L^T$.[5] This inequality signifies a departure from the neoclassical paradigm of perfect mobility and equalization of factor returns, and it implies that the economy may grow by transferring labor from the traditional to the modern sector.[6]

The second analytical difference between the two sectors concerns distribution. According to Lewis, distribution in the modern sector follows the "marginal productivity rule" of distribution, so that $w^M = MP_L^M$, where w^M denotes the wage in the modern sector. However, it is assumed that in the traditional sector,

$w^T > MP_L^T$, where w^T denotes the wage in the traditional sector. This inequality is possible, because distribution in this sector is governed by a different rule that Ranis and Fei refer to as the "kinship/community rule." This difference in the rule of distribution signifies another departure from the neoclassical economy, according to which the same "marginal product rule" of distribution applies to all sectors of the economy.

The institutional setting of the "kinship/community rule" of distribution can be diverse. The most immediate case is provided by family farms which are constrained (for various institutional reasons) to employ their family labor only on their farms. Such farms will engage in "output maximizing" rather than "profit-maximizing" behavior, and will push application of labor to very low marginal productivity levels (assuming that they have abundant labor relative to land and other inputs). The average product per labor of such farms, considered as "wage," will obviously be higher than the marginal product.

It may be argued that the average product per labor in a family farm is not "wage" in its strict sense.[7] However, the "kinship/community rule" of distribution is assumed to extend beyond the family and hold at the community (village) level, and thus pertain to non-family, hired labor too. In some countries and during the pre-industrial era, villages indeed represented close-knit communities, members of which felt affinity among themselves.[8] Due to this affinity, even families hiring farm labor would pay institutional wage that was higher than the marginal product.[9] Chinese communes themselves provide another example of institutions permitting "wages" to be higher than the marginal product, because these Communes may also engage in "output-maximizing" (rather than profit-maximizing) behavior, and thus push marginal product to very low levels (assuming again that labor is abundant relative to land and other inputs available to the Communes). The *Hukou* (household registration) system that restricts rural-urban migration may further conduce to this outcome.

Ranis and Fei often use the expression "non-commercial organization" as the distinctive feature of the Lewis model's "traditional" sector in order to emphasize its non profit-maximizing behavior that contrasts with the modern sector's commercial principle of profit maximization and the associated "marginal product rule" of distribution. It should be noticed here that the underlying factor behind the postulated duality is the abundance of labor relative to land (and other inputs), which (in conjunction with non-commercial organization and barriers to mobility) depresses the marginal product of labor below the wage in the traditional sector, and makes them both to be less than the modern sector wage and marginal product. All together, we therefore have the following relationship: $MP_L^T < w^T < w^M = MP_L^M$.

The dualism of the economy creates the possibility for the modern sector to expand through absorption of traditional sector's labor without having to increase its wage offer. The relocation of labor from the traditional to the modern sector increases MP_L^T. However, as long as $MP_L^T < w^T < w^M$, such increases do not lead to increases in w^T, and therefore w^M does not have to respond. The modern sector can expand with w^M more or less unchanged, thus creating the possibility

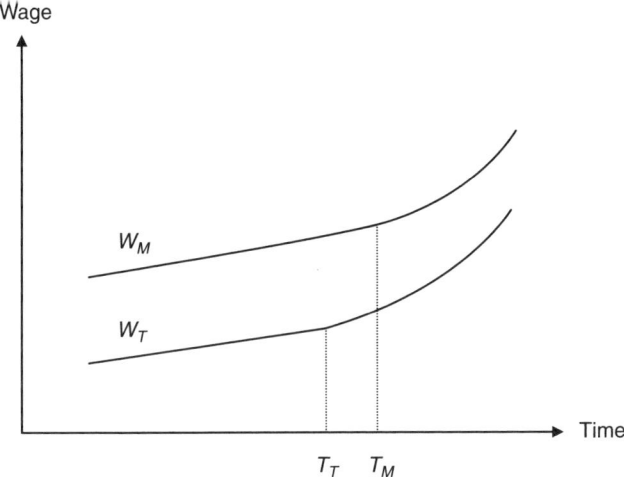

Figure 5.1   Turning Point hypothesis of the Lewis model

Note: Figure 5.1 presents the Turning Point hypothesis of the Lewis model. In it w_T and w_M represent the wage curves of the traditional and modern sector, respectively. The figure shows that (a) both the wage curves are characterized by the presence of a Turning Point, (b) the Turning Point for w_T (denoted by T_T) may precede that for w_M, and (c) eventually the two curves come closer as the duality of the economy disappears.

Source: Authors.

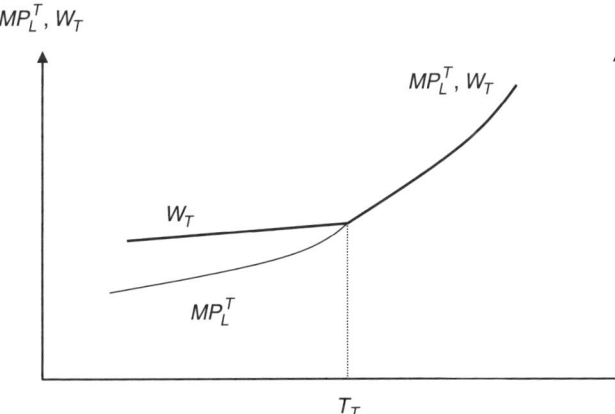

Figure 5.2   Marginal product and wage in the traditional sector

Note: Figure 5.2 illustrates the underlying process that causes the Turning Point. Initially the marginal product of labor in the traditional sector (MP_L^T) is very low, due to output-maximizing behavior. The wage in the sector (w_T) is higher than MP_L^T due to the "kinship/community rule" of distribution. As the economy industrializes and more labor from traditional sector finds employment in the modern sector, and due to other productivity improvements, MP_L^T rises, but does not affect w_T until the Turning Point (T_T) is reached, from which point onwards w_T rises in tandem with. MP_L^T

Source: Authors.

of "unlimited" or "perfectly elastic" supply of labor for the modern sector. Only when the withdrawal of labor pushes up MP_L^T sufficiently high so that it gets closer to w^T, further withdrawal leads to increases in w^T, in turn creating pressure for w^M to rise. This is when the economy reaches the Turning Point, which is first experienced by w^T and then by w^M. With further progress of the process, the equality $MP_L^T = w^T = w^M = MP_L^M$ is reached, the duality of the economy disappears, and the economy starts to correspond to the neoclassical description. Figures 5.1 and 5.2 display the above processes in a graphical form.[10]

Figure 5.1 shows the long run wage curves of the traditional and modern sectors featuring the following properties predicted by the Lewis model: (a) Turning Point of the traditional sector wage curve precedes the same of the modern sector wage curve; (b) the modern sector wage curve stays above the traditional sector wage curve; (c) the gap between the two wage curves narrows over time. Figure 5.2 reveals the reasons for the shape of the wage curves shown in Figure 5.1. It shows that transfer of labor from the traditional sector cannot affect wages as long as the marginal product remains less than the wage, causing the flatness of the wage curves seen in Figure 5.1. However, the Turning Point is reached when the marginal product equals the wage, and after that wages rise steeply.

5.3   Extensions of the Lewis model

In their extension of the Lewis model, Ranis and Fei (1961) emphasize that the Lewis economy is characterized not only by an "organizational dualism" but also by a "product dualism." The latter makes terms of trade between the two sectors an important determinant of the outcome, because wages of the modern sector are mostly spent on output of the traditional sector.[11] They draw attention to the fact that unless productivity in the traditional sector rises, expansion of the modern sector may worsen its terms of trade and choke the modern sector's expansion before reaching the Turning Point. The process of industrialization can thus get aborted.

Other researchers however have pointed out that the terms-of-trade apprehension may be unwarranted, because it applies only to a closed economy.[12] Oshima (1963, p. 449) for example notes that "it seems highly artificial to assume a closed system in a theory which makes the worsening of the terms of trade a cornerstone." Once external trade is assumed, this danger recedes, and Ranis and Fei (1963), in their reply to Oshima, basically concede to the point.[13]

In their extension of the Lewis model, Ranis and Fei suggest several other points in the wage curve. In doing so, they assume that the marginal product curve of the traditional sector is characterized by three phases. In the first phase, the marginal product is zero, so that the transfer of labor from the traditional sector to the modern sector does not lead to any reduction in the traditional sector's total output, and instead releases an amount of wage-goods (output of the traditional sector) that is equal to what is needed to employ the labor in the modern sector. This phase however comes to an end when the marginal product of labor in the traditional sector becomes positive, signifying the beginning of the second phase. Ranis and Fei call this point as the "Shortage Point," noting the fact that the traditional sector output now released will fall short of the amount of wage goods required by the laborer in the modern sector. However, to the extent that the marginal product is less than the wage (in the traditional sector), transfer of labor at this stage does not create pressure on the wage to rise.

This second phase ends with the advent of phase three when marginal product catches up with the wage, and any further transfer of labor now pushes up both the marginal product and the wage in the traditional sector to more or less the same degree. Ranis and Fei refer to this point as the "Commercialization Point," pointing to the fact that the advent of this point signifies the end of non-commercial principle of the traditional sector and the associated "kinship rule of distribution."[14]

A general goal of Fei and Ranis is to bring more rigor to the Lewis discussion,[15] and in doing so, they declare that the Lewis Turning Point coincides with the shortage point, and suggest that Lewis' "unlimited" supply curve of labor is defined by the horizontal portion of the marginal product curve of labor in the traditional sector.[16] A closer observation however shows that the horizontal portion of the marginal product curve is not the same as the horizontal part of the Lewis wage curve, either in the traditional or in the modern sector. The wage curve remains horizontal in both phase one and two, as long as $MP_L^T < w^T < w^M$, while the marginal product curve (for the traditional sector) is horizontal only in phase one. Actually, many researchers doubt marginal product being zero and want to drop phase one altogether.[17] Oshima (1963, p. 451, ff no. 4), for example, notes that once this is done "the flat portion of the total and marginal productivity curve in the model will be replaced by a gently rising slope," and then *"the first phase loses its distinctive character and becomes merged with the second* as far as industrial supply curve of labor is concerned (italics added)." In such a scheme of things the Shortage Point of Fei and Ranis disappears.

According to Ranis and Fei (1963), Lewis refers to the following two things to happen for the Turning Point to occur: (a) the worsening of terms of trade for the industrial sector, and (b) the "exhaustion of surplus labor" in the traditional sector. Given that the first of these do not apply to an open economy, it is only the second that warrants attention. However, "exhaustion of labor surplus" happens only at the end of the second phase of the Fei-Ranis construct and not at the end of phase one. The Lewis Turing Point therefore corresponds to their Commercialization Point, and not the Shortage Point. Fei and Ranis themselves elsewhere seem to correct their position by noting that *"after the turning point the agriculture sector becomes completely commercialized* (Ranis and Fei, 1963, p. 305, italics added)," adding that "after the *turning point* the general level of real wages rises for the first time, as the disguised unemployed in the agricultural sector disappears and no longer plays the role of a 'reserve army.'"

Noting the efforts by Ranis and Fei and other researchers at extending his model and the controversies that arose, Lewis (1972) himself ventures to streamline the ideas.[18] He explains that there are three different versions of the model. In Model-I, the economy is closed, and there is no trade between the two sectors. In this model the Turning Point is reached when "the labor supply ceases to be infinitely elastic and the wage starts rising through pressure from the non-capitalist sector (Lewis, 1972, p. 83)." In other words, under Model-I, outputs of both sectors are fully convertible into each other (or are the same), and hence the issue of shortage (of wage good) and of the Shortage Point does not arise.[19]

Model-II continues with the closed economy scenario, but now assumes that the two sectors produce different goods and hence trade with each other. This is therefore basically the Fei-Ranis model that emphasizes product dualism. We already saw that while the Shortage Point is a possibility in this model, it does not represent the Lewis Turning Point, which instead corresponds to the Commercialization Point. This model allows diverse outcomes with regard to the Turning Point depending on the relative productivity growth in the modern and traditional sectors.[20]

Model-III allows international trade (an open economy situation) so that a rapidly growing industrial sector faced by a too slow agricultural sector can import agricultural products and pay for the imports by exporting its own product. Model-III therefore is equivalent to Model-I, in the sense that products of the two sectors again become convertible, albeit indirectly, via international trade. The terms of trade now enter into the picture, and Lewis notes that in order to export more, the producers may have to lower the prices thus causing a dent in their profit margin.[21] He advises that "a country must plan its development in such a way as to be sure that its exports will keep pace with needed imports," and warns that "if it fails to do this, the rate of growth of output will be constrained by the rate of growth of export earnings (p. 94)."

It needs to be noted that equating Lewis (1954, 1955) original papers with the closed economy Model-I, as is often done, is not accurate, because these original papers actually devoted considerable attention to cross-border *factor flows* (both labor and capital) and their impact (either directly or via terms of trade). For example, Lewis (1954) notes that progress towards the Turning Point may be checked by mass immigration and export of capital.[22] He also notes indirect consequences of export of capital. For example, he observes that export of capital, on the one hand, may cheapen the goods that workers import or raise the wage costs in competing countries, and thus facilitate the progress toward the Turning Point. On the other hand, capital export may raise the cost of imports or reduce costs in competing countries and thus make reaching the Turning Point difficult. Lewis notes the possibility of import of capital too. He notes that capital inflow will not generally raise wages as long as surplus labor exists, but would hasten the progress toward the Turning Point (Lewis, 1954, p. 191).[23] In short, the economy of Lewis (1954) was open to factor flows and the terms of trade consequences of such flows.

In their subsequent work extending the Lewis model, synthesized in Fei and Ranis (1997), the authors propose four points, namely (a) Commercialization Point (b) Reversal Point (c) Export Substitution Point, and (d) Switching Point (p. 290). The first thing to observe is that the list no longer includes the Shortage Point, vindicating the problems with this point mentioned earlier. Second, the

Commercialization Point, as noted above, is basically the Lewis Turning Point, though Fei and Ranis amplify on further properties of this point in the context of an open dualistic model.[24] Third, a close perusal shows that the remaining points on the wage curve identified by Fei and Ranis depend on particularistic assumptions and do not necessarily follow from the general construction of the Lewis model. These points also do not have particular *locus standi* or clear implications for the macro wage curves. For example, the "Reversal Point" is reached when the traditional sector starts to witness absolute decline in its labor force. Next comes, according to Fei and Ranis, the "Export Substitution Point," and finally there is the "Switching Point," when the country becomes a net importer of agricultural goods.[25] The particularistic nature of these points is clear from the fact that not all industrializing economies are to follow the same import-substitution and export-promotion sequence and/or are destined to become net importers of agricultural goods.[26]

The above review shows that subsequent extensions by Ranis, Fei, and others do not change the Lewis model's basic prediction, which remains the prediction of a Turning Point.[27] The extensions however introduce added possibilities and help to understand the likely causes that lead to these possibilities. The knowledge of these extensions should therefore prove useful in interpreting the results presented in this paper.

5.4 Empirical application of the Lewis model

5.4.1 Methodological problems in testing the prediction of the Lewis model

Many methodological problems arise in applying the Lewis model to real experiences of industrialization. One of these concerns the empirical counterpart of the theoretical dualism of the Lewis economy. As noted earlier, there is considerable ambiguity even with regard to the theoretical description of the dualism, with Lewis and other researchers using different versions. No matter which of these different theoretical versions is preferred, there is never a perfect match between them and the empirical counterparts that may be chosen in the light of data availability and other feasibility considerations.

A second methodological problem concerns the type of labor to be studied. It is clear that the Turning Point prediction of the Lewis model concerns the wage of unskilled labor that can be easily transferred from the traditional to the modern sector. Therefore not all labor of the manufacturing sector falls under the purview of the Lewis model. Yet, distinguishing unskilled labor separately within the modern sector is not always easy due to data and definitional problems.

A third problem concerns the type of wage to study, given the type of labor selected for examination. As Lewis himself noted, "Real wage has many meanings." Expanding on the issue, he drew distinctions among "cost of living wage," defined as (w/c), where w is the nominal (money) wage and c is the cost of living; "factoral wage," defined as (w/a), where a is "the income of the non-capitalist worker;" "ratio of wages to prices," defined as (w/p), where p is the index of the "price received by capitalists;" product wage, defined (wL/vQ), where L is the quantity of labor, Q is real output, and v is the value added price of output; and finally (wL/pQ) which is what product wages reduces to when no imported raw materials are used in production (Lewis, 1972, pp. 85–86).

Given the multiple choices possible with regard to each of the three issues above, it is clear what a bewildering variety of possible combinations a researcher has to confront in deciding about the empirical strategy for application of the Lewis model.

Another type of problem arises with regard to the marginal product. Unlike wage, marginal product is unobservable and needs to be estimated using econometric methods, which in turn is fraught with many conceptual and computations problems. Many scholars are averse to the concept of production function necessary for estimation of the marginal product. Even if the concept is accepted, there remain many issues with regard to specification and estimation.

5.4.2   Empirical evidence from other countries on Lewis wage curve

Despite the methodological difficulties, researchers have applied the Lewis model and produced instructive results. A quick review of this research will provide a useful background for considering the results obtained for China.

England: Lindert and Williamson (1983) and Williamson (1982) show that the real wage remained almost constant for nearly 40 years (1780–1820) in England during the Industrial Revolution, with the wage in the modern sector being almost two times higher than in the traditional sector. The near constancy of the agricultural wage in the face of substantial increase in agricultural productivity after the Enclosure Movement presented additional supportive evidence of the Lewis process at work. The evidence led Lindert and Williamson to comment that "(Lewis was) right in viewing the rural sector as an industrial labor reserve such that the urban sector could draw on rural labor supplies during expansion." Commenting on England's experience, Fei and Ranis note that the classical economists were impressed by the stability of the real wage and saw in it the proof of the "iron law of wages," believing it to be ordained. However, they were soon proved wrong, because following on the heels of the classical writings, the Turning Point was reached, and the real wage started to increase sharply. By the time the Turning Point was reached, about 45 percent of the labor force of the countryside was absorbed into England's industrial sector (Fei and Ranis, 1997, p. 109).

Malaysia: The work by Huang (1971) on Malaysia shows that the marginal product of labor in agriculture increased at a significantly faster rate than the real wage in three separate regions of the country. The study also shows that the gap between the marginal product and wage decreased only when the country approached the Turning Point (Fei and Ranis, 1997, p. 156).

Taiwan: A good part of the research by Fei and Ranis themselves was focused on Taiwan,[28] with results showing that while the Taiwanese agricultural real wage remained very stable for a long time (extending from 1958 to 1973), the marginal product increased steadily (since 1963). The research also showed that the Taiwanese industrial wage remained fairly stable for a long time, from 1957 until

1968, when it started to rise, and all the while remained above the agricultural wage. (For details, see Fei and Ranis, 1997, p. 157. Ranis (1995) also presents similar results.)[29]

Korea: Ranis (1995) provides a study of the Korean wage data showing the marginal product rising much faster than the real wage during 1960–1975. The study also shows Korean unskilled industrial wage to be higher than the agricultural wage during the period.[30]

5.4.3 Empirical evidence on Turning Point in Japan

Japan occupies a special place in the literature on application of the Lewis model. The work started with Ranis (1957), showing on the basis of his findings regarding "capital shallowing" that Japan reached the Turning Point during the early twentieth century.[31] Disagreeing with Ranis, Minami offered a thorough application of the Lewis model to Japan's case, distinguishing the following five criteria for identifying the Turning Point:[32]

  I. Comparison between wages and marginal product of labor in the subsistence sector;
 II. Correlation between wages and marginal productivity of labor in the subsistence sector;
III. Movements in real wages in the subsistence sector;
IV. Changes in wage differential (between skilled and unskilled labor); and
 V. Elasticity of labor supply from the subsistence to the capitalist sector.[33]

Minami shows that the Criterion-I offers the most rigorous test of the Turning Point and dominates the other criteria, so that a Turning Point satisfying this criterion will also satisfy the other criteria. Minami's list of criteria also shows that in identifying the Turning Point he focuses on the traditional sector. There are several reasons for this choice. The first is the earlier noted fact that the Turning Point in the traditional sector wage curve has the logical and chronological precedence over the Turning Point in the modern sector wage curve. Second, the comparison of the marginal product and wage in the traditional sector, as noted earlier, helps reveal the underlying process that finds reflection on the surface in the wage curves. The third advantage relates to practicality and data availability. As observed earlier, the Turning Point hypothesis applies to the wage of labor that is easily transferable from the traditional to the modern sector. From this point of view, Minami distinguishes within the modern sector three sub-sectors, namely (a) "traditional," (b) "semi-modern," and (c) "modern," and observes that it is the labor of "traditional" and "semi-modern" sub-sectors that is substitutable by labor of the "agriculture" sector. By contrast, the labor of the "modern" sub-sector, which requires a higher degree of skill, is not substitutable by agricultural labor. That is why Minami thought that "the theory of the turning point is not applicable to the "modern sector" (pp. 69–70)."[34]

Following the classification above, the Turning Point hypothesis should be examined either in the context of the wage of the "traditional" and "semi-modern" sub-sectors of the "modern" sector or in the context of the wage of the "agriculture" sector. Unfortunately, wage data for the former two sub-sectors separately are often difficult to get, and this difficulty makes testing of the Turning Point hypothesis on the basis of the traditional sector's wage data an appealing and feasible alternative.[35]

Having set out the criteria and explaining the reasons for focusing on the traditional sector, Minami (1973) presents a meticulous study of the Japanese agricultural wage data showing that Japan crossed the Turning Point some time during the 1950s and not during the 1920s, as claimed earlier by Ranis.[36]

5.5 Applying Lewis model to China

5.5.1 Particular problems with China

In applying the Lewis model to China, one faces several additional problems caused by her specific institutional features. First, the analytical/theoretical "modern-traditional" dichotomy, as already noted, is not the same as the empirical "urban-rural" or "agriculture-industry" dichotomy. This is more so in the case of China, because, on the one hand, her urban/modern sector has a large presence of informal enterprises using pre-industrial technologies. On the other hand, her rural economy is heterogeneous too, particularly due to the phenomenal growth of TVEs that use industrial technologies right inside what are administratively classified as rural areas. The problem is aggravated by the fact that formal boundaries of urban and rural areas in China undergo frequent changes due to administrative and political considerations, so that these boundaries often do not correspond to their expected economic content.

A second problem concerns movement of labor between traditional and modern sectors. The Lewis model assumes that the flow proceeds in an unrestricted fashion as industrialization progresses. This assumption does not hold true for China, because of its *Hukou* (household registration) system that restricts internal migration. Over time *Hukou* restrictions have been relaxed and/or modified, making internal migration easier. However, the system remains, and the situation is still not one of a free flow of labor from the traditional to the modern sector.

The *Hukou* system is actually a concrete manifestation of a more general institutional characteristic of China, namely the legacy of central planning. As noted earlier, Lewis conceived his model to explain *capitalist* growth of developing countries. That may be a reason why researchers have not been that enthusiastic about applying the Lewis model to China, even though it has been applied extensively to Japan, Taiwan, and other East Asian countries. Since wages (and other prices) under central planning are determined by command or administrative methods, it might have been thought that the Lewis model, which in a sense relies on the market rationale, was not the appropriate model to be used. However, industrialization in a dual economy faces the same economic fundamentals even when it is carried out under alternative, non-capitalist institutions. In fact, Lewis himself mentions that the experience of the (former) Soviet Union (along with that of the United Kingdom) served for him as the empirical reference for his model.[37] Nevertheless, in considering industrialization under non-capitalist institutional frameworks, one has to keep in mind that the planners may not always go by the economic fundamentals, and may instead try to impose choices inspired by political or ideological considerations.[38] China's situation is further complicated by the fact that currently it is neither under central planning nor under entirely market conditions. It is rather in a transition from the former to the latter. This complex institutional context, on the one hand, makes the analysis more challenging, and on the other hand, offers more opportunities to see whether and how institutions influence the underlying economic process of industrialization and expansion of the modern sector through absorption of labor from the traditional sector.

5.5.2 Empirical analysis and results

For the empirical analysis, we use Minami's Criterion-I to test the Lewis Turning Point hypothesis. The exercise requires comparison of the marginal product and wage of labor in the traditional sector, which for China we equate with the "agriculture" sector rather than the "rural" sector as a whole, because of the already mentioned large presence of industrial enterprises in the form of TVEs in the Chinese countryside. As noted earlier, while wage is a directly observable variable, marginal product is not and requires econometric estimation. For this purpose, the paper assumes the following Cobb-Douglas production function for the Chinese agricultural sector:

$$\ln V_i = \alpha + \beta_1 \ln L_i + \beta_2 \ln K_i + \beta_3 \ln R_i + \varepsilon_i, \tag{1}$$

where V, K, L, and R stand for the value added, capital, labor, and land, respectively, and i is the subscript for the province. Value added data are taken from *The China Rural Statistical Yearbook* of respective years. Other variables, including the consumer price index, are obtained mainly from *The China Statistical Yearbook* of respective years. In view of lack of relevant data, capital is proxied by the number of large and medium sized tractors.[39] The sample period runs from 1987 to 2004. Value added is measured in 100 million Yuan; labor in 10,000 persons; and land in 1,000 hectares. The value added figures are in constant 2000 prices. The summary statistics of the data are presented in the Appendix Table 5.A.1.

The equation (1) is estimated for each year of the sample period using provincial data. In order to minimize the influence of seasonal and/or business cycle fluctuations, three-year moving averages are used. For example, to estimate the production function for the year of 1991, the averages for 1990, 1991 and 1992 are used. Given the heterogeneity of the Chinese provinces, particularly with respect to size, heteroskedasticity of the error term is quite likely, and Breusch-Pagan test for the presence of heteroskedasticity confirms this suspicion. To deal with the problem, White's heteroskedasticity-consistent ordinary least squares (OLS) estimator is used.

Table 5.1 presents the main set of results. Before turning to individual coefficients, we may first look at the sum, shown in column (5), of the coefficients for land, labor, and capital, and the values of the F-statistic, shown in column (6), of the test of the hypothesis that this sum equals to one, implying Constant Returns

Table 5.1   Estimated values of the coefficients and results of CRS test

Year	Estimated value of β_1, coefficient of labor (L)	Estimated value of β_2, coefficient of capital (K)	Estimated value of β_3, coefficient of land (R)	Sum of the coefficients: ($\beta_1 + \beta_2 + \beta_3$)	F-value from the test of the null H_0: $\beta_1 + \beta_2 + \beta_3 = 1$
(1)	(2)	(3)	(4)	(5)	(6)
1988	0.2950*	0.1137	0.5725**	0.9813	0.05
1989	0.2514	0.0964	0.6003*	0.9481	0.39
1990	0.2816*	0.1053	0.5629*	0.9497	0.40
1991	0.2467*	0.0960	0.6145***	0.9572	0.30
1992	0.2252	0.0572	0.6579***	0.9403	0.56
1993	0.1315	0.0099	0.7908***	0.9321	0.73
1994	0.1316	0.0159	0.7882***	0.9357	0.63
1995	0.1032	0.0190	0.8204***	0.9427	0.54
1996	0.1774	0.0480	0.7311***	0.9565	0.32
1997	0.2091	0.0636	0.6885**	0.9612	0.63
1998	0.2848*	0.0757	0.5948***	0.9553	0.48
1999	0.3297*	0.0749	0.5397***	0.9443	0.66
2000	0.3598**	0.0577	0.5133**	0.9308	0.95
2001	0.4078**	0.0616	0.4575**	0.9270	1.04
2002	0.3758*	0.0471	0.4872**	0.9101	1.55
2003	0.3475	0.0340	0.5388**	0.9204	1.12

Note: *, **, *** indicate that the estimated coefficient is different from zero at the statistically significant level of 15, 10, and 5 percent, respectively. t-statistics are calculated based on the White heteroskedasticity-consistent estimator. The F-values in the last column are from the test of the null hypothesis H_0: $\beta_1 + \beta_2 + \beta_3 = 1$ that implies constant returns to scale (CRS). The 5 and 1 percent critical values of F (1,26) are 4.23 and 7.72, respectively, showing that the CRS assumption cannot be rejected.

Source: Authors' calculation.

to Scale (CRS). The F-values indicate that the CRS assumption cannot be rejected. Given the divisibility of inputs (a consequence of the lack of mechanization), the evidence for CRS is not surprising.

Turning to the individual variables, we find that the coefficient for land proves to be highly significant for almost all years, and the coefficient for labor proves to be generally significant. The coefficient for capital, however, appears to lack significance. There may be several reasons for the latter result. The first is the general lack of mechanization of the Chinese agriculture, so that the capital requirement (other than land) is not high, a fact that actually justifies taking agriculture sector as the traditional sector. Second, there may also be some problems with the variable (namely the number of large and medium size tractors) used to proxy for capital. In general the lack of significance of capital coefficient agrees well with the general observation that capital equipments as yet play a relatively minor role in the Chinese agriculture.

Given the log-log specification, the coefficients also represent the elasticity of output with respect to corresponding inputs, and given the Cobb-Douglas specification, they also represent the shares of the respective inputs in the value added. Looking from this point of view, we see again that the coefficient for land dominates, accounting for about 60 percent of the value added. Next in importance is labor, accounting for about 30 percent of the value added. To the extent that the Chinese agriculture is now predominantly household "owned" and operated, the value added imputed to land actually accrues to the farm household members, who generally are also the suppliers of labor. This shows that a large part of the income of agricultural households is of non-labor source. Capital turns out to be of the least importance, accounting for about ten percent of the value added.

Looking across years, we see that the importance of land has declined somewhat, decreasing from about 60 percent or more of the value added to about 50 percent in recent years. The share of labor, on the other hand, has increased, rising from about 25 percent to about 35 percent over the sample period. The importance of capital also seems to have declined, decreasing from about ten percent of the value added to about five percent in the recent years. However, given the general insignificance of capital in the regressions, this result may not deserve much attention.

The results presented in Table 5.1 are next used to compute the marginal product of labor. Given the Cobb-Douglas specification, the marginal product of labor (MP_L^T) can be obtained using the relationship: $MP_L^T = \beta_L \, AP_L^T$, where AP_L^T is the average product, given in this case by $\left(V/L \right)$. Table 5.2 presents the values of AP_L^T and estimated values of MP_L^T in columns (2) and (3), respectively. We see that the average value added (AP_L^T) has witnessed a steady increase from 1683 Yuan in 1988 to 3194 Yuan in 2003 (except a slight fall in 1989). The marginal product, in the long haul, has also increased, from 497 Yuan in 1988 to 1110 Yuan in 2003, with however checkered dynamics in between. It decreased initially from 497 Yuan in 1988 to 259 Yuan in 1995. Since then it increased rapidly, almost fourfold to 1141 Yuan by 2001. However, in very recent years, beginning with 2001, the marginal product seems to have undergone some deceleration.

Having obtained the estimated values of the marginal product, we may now turn to the comparison with wage. To facilitate the comparison, Table 5.2 presents the data on real wages in column (4). Figure 5.3 presents the comparison in graphical form. Before commenting on the comparison, a few words regarding the wage data may be in order. Data on real wage in the agriculture sector is actually hard to obtain. We therefore use average net income per labor in the farming sector as a proxy for real agricultural wage, and calculate it using the following formula:

Real Wage = $(F^*P)/(L^*D)$,

where, F is the net per capita income in the agriculture sector, P is the number of persons in a family, L is the number of laborers in a family, and D is the deflator, taken to be equal to the consumer price index. All these variables are national averages and data on them for different years of the sample period are obtained from respective issues of *The China Rural Statistical Yearbook*.

Table 5.2   Average and marginal product and wage of labor

Year	Average value product (V/L)	Marginal value product (MP_{L})	Wage
(1)	(2)	(3)	(4)
1988	1,683.3	496.6	878.3
1989	1,668.3	419.4	789.6
1990	1,687.0	475.0	1,077.3
1991	1,769.8	436.6	1,001.0
1992	1,860.1	418.9	990.3
1993	2,043.4	268.7	1,095.5
1994	2,297.2	302.3	1,174.3
1995	2,510.7	259.1	1,340.0
1996	2,632.0	467.0	1,436.8
1997	2,686.8	561.9	1,432.4
1998	2,690.5	766.2	1,411.3
1999	2,695.1	888.5	1,407.6
2000	2,716.9	977.5	1,269.0
2001	2,798.0	1,141.0	1,302.5
2002	2,922.3	1,098.2	1,291.9
2003	3,194.0	1,110.0	1,271.8
2004			1,430.2

Note: The marginal product of labor is calculated from the product of output elasticity of labor (coefficient of labor) and the average product (V/L). The real wage rate per labor is calculated from the Department of Rural Survey, National Bureau of Statistics of China, *The China Rural Statistical Yearbook*, various issues.

Source: Authors' calculation.

Looking at the wage data, we first notice that the real wage in the agriculture sector has increased over time, from 878 Yuan in 1988 to 1,430 Yuan in 2004, an annual increase of 2.5 percent. Thus, the traditional sector wage curve was not completely horizontal. This should not be surprising, because the Lewis model does not rule out some increase in wage even before the Turning Point is reached.[40] The traditional sector neither remains nor is it expected to remain as placid in practice as is assumed in Lewis theory. Instead it may witness some capital accumulation and technological upgradation leading to a rise in productivity (outward shift of the production function). In fact, as Ranis and Fei emphasized, some improvements in the productivity of the traditional sector is actually necessary for the progress toward the Turning Point. Such improvements in agricultural productivity may lead to increases in agricultural wage.

Thus we see that both the wage and marginal product have increased. What is important is to find out whether the marginal product is increasing at a faster rate than the wage. We just noticed that over the sample period, the wage has increased at an average annual rate of 2.5 percent. Earlier we noticed that, over

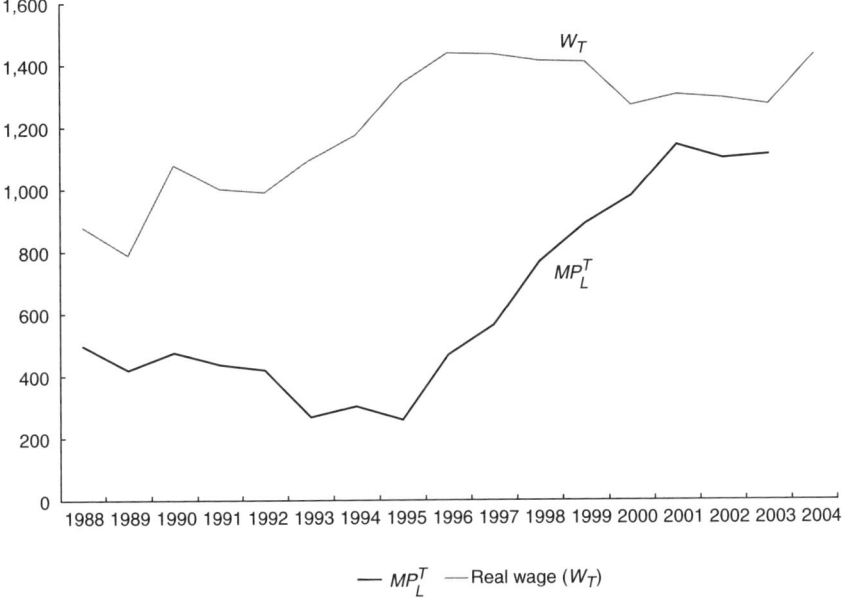

Figure 5.3 Marginal product and wage of labor (Yuan in constant 2000 prices)

Note: Figure 5.3 presents a graphical presentation of the results compiled in Table 5.2. MP_L^T and w_T denote marginal product and wage of labor in the traditional sector. On the long haul both witnesses increase, however, MP_L^T is seen to be rising (from below) faster than w_T closing the gap between the two, as the Lewis model predicts. The Turning Point will be reached when MP_L^T curve will intersect with w_T. The Figure thus shows that the Chinese economy is progressing toward the Turning Point, but has not reached that point yet.

Source: Authors (based on results presented in Table 5.2).

the same period, the marginal product increased from 496.6 Yuan to 1,110.0 Yuan, implying an average annual rate of increase of 5.5 percent, which is almost double the rate of wage increase. In fact, if only the later ascending period (i.e. the period since 1995) is considered, marginal product is seen to increase from 259 Yuan to 1,110 Yuan (in 2003), implying an average annual rate of increase of almost 20 percent. Thus, there is clear evidence that in the Chinese agricultural sector, during the 1988–2003 period, the marginal product of labor has increased at a much faster rate than wage, narrowing the gap between the two, as Figure 5.3 demonstrates graphically.

However, despite the faster rate of increase and narrowing of the gap, the marginal product curve as a whole still remains below the wage curve, showing that while China is progressing toward the Turning Point, it has not reached that point yet. This finding corresponds well with the general perception among scholars and Chinese policy makers that China still faces an enormous challenge of finding more productive employment for a huge pool of underutilized rural labor. Fan (2005, p. 17), the prominent Chinese economist, formulated China's long term employment challenge recently in the following way:

> "The real long term challenge is to create enough jobs for the rural people. Recently, I did some calculations with reference to agriculture and agricultural employment, in Japan, the US, and Australia. Using their experience as guidance, China eventually may only need, approximately 40–60 million farmers to farm the relatively small area of cultivable land in China – which means that in the long run, over the next 40–50 years, a total of 300–400 million people should be relocated from agriculture to the non-farming sector. But the present situation is that in each year, at the current level of technological progress, we shall only create 10–12 million new jobs. This means that over the long term, even with rapid GDP growth, there will still be a huge under-employment situation in rural areas and even more people will flock to the cities looking for jobs."

The question that may be of interest here is why in Chinese agriculture the wage rate proves to be greater than the marginal product. In pondering about this question, we may note that in post reform China, with the dissolution of Communes, agriculture has come to be dominated by family farming. Facing abundant labor, it is quite rational on the part of these farms to engage in "output-maximizing" rather than "profit-maximizing" behavior, and thus to push the marginal product to low levels. Second, despite their dissolution, the tradition of Communes and the recent socialist past can have a lingering effect allowing the "kinship rule of distribution" to have a greater influence in the agriculture of China than in the agriculture of many other "labor surplus" developing countries.

Whatever the reason for wages to be higher than marginal product in the Chinese agriculture, the findings of this paper indicate that the gap between the two has narrowed. With continued faster increase, resulting from further transfer of labor from the rural to the urban sector and other improvements, the marginal product seems to be on its way to catch up with the wage. In other words, China is moving toward the Lewis Turning Point, though it has not reached that point yet.

5.6   Conclusions

Casual observations suggest that China, more than many other developing countries, displays the characteristics that the Lewis model tries to capture. Yet, very few, if any, attempts have been made to study China's industrialization from the viewpoint of the Lewis model. This paper is an attempt to fill that void. Earlier, using a graphical analysis, Islam and Yokota (2006) found that the China's wage curves appeared to conform to the Lewis model's Turning Point prediction. This paper takes the analysis to a deeper level applying Minami's Criterion-I to test for the presence of the Turning Point in China's wage curves. To implement the test, the paper estimates an aggregate production function for the Chinese agricultural sector, which is taken as the "traditional sector" of the Lewis theory, and computes the marginal product of labor for each year of the 1988–2004 sample period. The estimated values of the marginal product

Table 5.A.1 Summary statistics of variables

Province	Value-added		Labor		Capital		Land	
	Mean	Std. Dev.	Mean	Std. Dev.	Mean	Std. Dev.	Mean	Std. Dev.
Total	254.7	197.8	1067.5	888.4	26972.8	30291.6	4964.0	3418.3
Beijing	50.6	5.0	71.3	8.2	11949.6	1261.7	508.9	101.3
Yianjin	42.3	4.8	83.8	4.2	9279.4	1333.1	557.5	25.5
Hebei	422.1	142.4	1696.4	84.0	44298.4	19707.3	8812.6	155.7
Shanxi	113.0	25.5	632.7	24.1	26369.3	4715.9	3928.5	115.7
Inner Mongolia	165.3	52.6	502.0	23.6	37766.7	6572.5	5291.4	586.6
Liaoning	250.3	55.4	621.8	31.8	38593.9	9668.3	3663.8	91.6
Jilin	218.9	57.1	521.4	28.5	37352.4	9310.6	4245.3	329.4
Heilongjiang	283.8	75.2	575.9	138.9	85288.1	14525.4	9003.1	567.4
Shanghai	39.1	4.4	74.3	8.7	9174.6	2343.7	553.8	74.6
Jiangsu	565.7	108.2	1532.2	161.4	32126.1	13889.2	8026.9	243.8
Zhejiang	320.5	67.4	1136.7	163.0	6423.3	1122.4	3826.7	526.9
Anhui	379.8	73.3	1920.3	73.7	14702.1	5662.9	8521.4	345.8
Fujian	221.9	69.6	768.8	28.5	3892.5	2063.9	2749.8	142.3
Jiangxi	217.8	48.6	1066.3	65.9	13531.4	7345.1	5652.3	285.9
Shandong	657.7	153.6	2459.1	116.7	129414.1	33166.7	10952.1	167.2
Henan	584.4	169.3	3006.2	295.7	59826.6	15026.4	12492.4	643.7
Hubei	389.6	64.3	1296.5	130.1	74622.6	9669.1	7394.7	212.4
Human	400.4	101.8	2109.6	89.3	7804.2	3226.6	7841.0	172.5
Guangdong	497.4	87.7	1532.0	79.8	7843.2	3020.6	5308.8	257.2
Guangxi	269.1	83.2	1566.4	32.1	18047.0	14380.9	5726.6	604.3
Hainan	67.9	23.7	170.2	10.0	3108.1	745.0	854.8	64.7
Chongqing	199.9	21.7	891.8	64.0	2743.0	3195.8	3530.9	95.5
Sichuan	583.5	85.6	3441.1	778.9	12037.2	5796.3	11215.6	1549.1
Guizhou	154.1	35.0	1323.7	82.9	11422.7	2614.4	4157.8	503.4
Yunnan	222.8	60.4	1601.3	97.1	16615.6	7462.4	5069.8	604.2
Tibet	13.5	4.9	87.4	2.2	2487.9	944.8	222.2	8.8
Shaanxi	177.5	34.4	1007.5	46.5	22348.2	3869.6	4615.0	274.8
Gansu	115.5	36.2	689.0	35.7	15915.4	3874.2	3676.3	78.1
Qinghai	16.1	3.0	130.0	10.5	3330.5	913.9	536.4	32.8
Ningxia	28.3	6.7	137.1	13.0	5389.5	1996.1	972.2	97.6
Xianjiang	184.8	60.2	293.2	26.1	56304.8	13500.9	3180.5	228.1
1987	195.8	162.5	1064.5	915.0	30377.6	29475.9	4831.9	3472.9
1990	198.3	151.5	1111.2	982.2	27117.1	27551.7	4945.4	3497.3
1995	274.1	205.0	1077.8	939.1	22394.9	24832.0	4996.0	3523.1
2000	280.8	208.3	1058.0	860.5	31437.0	36839.1	5041.9	3446.0
2004	357.0	269.1	987.0	782.2	36085.0	46785.1	4953.3	3498.8

Notes and Sources: Value added is measured in 100 million Yuan (in constant 2000 prices), labor is in 10,000 persons, capital is measured by the number of large and medium size tractors in units, and land is in 1,000 hectares. The data are obtained from various issues of *China Statistical Yearbook*, published by the National Bureau of Statistics (NBS) of China and *China Rural Statistical Yearbook*, published by the Department of Rural Survey of the NBS.

are then compared with the wage of corresponding years. The results show that the marginal product has increased (from below) faster than wage, as envisaged by the Lewis model, so that the gap between the two has narrowed over time. The findings therefore indicate that China is gradually moving toward the Lewis Turning Point though has not reached that point yet. Such a conclusion agrees with the general perception of China observers. At a broader level, the analysis indicates that the Lewis model, with its assumption of dualism, conforms better to the reality of over-populated developing countries, such as China, than do the neoclassical model which assumes perfect mobility and equality of factor returns across sectors.

There remain many weaknesses in this study. First of all, there are generic problems with empirical application of the Lewis model. These include (a) difficulty in finding empirical sectors that correspond well to the duality of the theory, (b) ambiguity with respect to the type of wage to examine, (c) conceptual and econometric problems with estimation of marginal product, and (d) hurdles in finding the right kind of data, etc. In the case of China, the above generic problems are aggravated by specific problems arising from her certain special institutional characteristics, such as (a) household registration (*Hukou*) system restricting mobility of labor, (b) arbitrary and frequently changing definition of urban and rural areas (c) legacy of central planning, (d) weak statistical system, etc. In implementing Minami's Criterion-I, particular problems are faced with regard to data on capital employed and wage prevailing in the agricultural sector. More efforts, in terms of both data collection and analysis, are therefore required before firmer conclusions can be reached. The analysis and findings presented in this paper may therefore be only a beginning of what can be a very rewarding line of research.

Acknowledgements

The authors would like to thank the participants of ICSEAD's China Growth Project and its two workshops for their helpful comments on earlier drafts of the paper. They are however not responsible for remaining errors and shortcomings. The views expressed in this chapter are authors' personal and should not be ascribed to institutions with which they are associated.

Notes

1   Yingfeng Xu (1994) is a paper that refers to the Lewis model. However, it does not really focus on testing the Lewis model's assumptions or predictions in the context of China. Similarly Putterman (1992) refers to dualism but does not engage in an application of the Lewis model to the case of China.
2   For a review of this line of literature, see for example Rosenzweig (1988).
3   See Islam (2003, 2004) for further discussions.
4   See Lewis (1954 and 1955) for the original exposition of the model. For recent discussions of the Lewis model, see the December 2004 special issue of *Manchester School*, the journal in which the original Lewis (1954) paper appeared. The special issue is based on the papers of the symposium organized by the journal to celebrate 50 years of Lewis (1954). See in particular, Fields (2004), Kirkpatrick and Barrientos (2004), Ranis (2004), and Tignor (2004). See also Gersovitz, Diaz-Alejandro, Ranis, and Rosenzweig (ed.) (1982).

5 The institutional underpinnings of this assumption are not always clearly stated, but they seem to include formal or informal restrictions on labor flow (migration), efficiency wages required for the modern sector, labor unions restricting entry, etc.

6 Assuming that more is saved out of the modern sector's increased output, this provides the necessary capital to absorb the relocated labor. This is basically what drives growth in the Lewis model.

7 This is true even without bringing up the issue of contribution of land, implements, and other family owned non-labor inputs that are employed in production.

8 The economy therefore exhibits some properties of the "shared economy" described by Weitzman (1984).

9 Measurement of marginal product in the agriculture sector is particularly problematic at the micro level. To the extent that the agricultural production process extends over a long period with labor requirement varying at different points in time, the marginal product of labor at a particular point of time cannot be determined without considering the labor application profile over the entire production period. Given the seasonality and quasi-fixed requirement of labor per unit of land cultivated, the marginal product may not be as low when the entire crop period is considered as it appears when just the short span during which the labor is actually engaged. Despite these difficulties in conceptualization and estimation, it is generally argued that the distribution principle in such rural communities (traditional sector) does have a "kinship/community" feature enabling wages to be higher than the marginal product. Also, of note is the fact that wages in such situations generally correspond to a subsistence level, so that there may also be some efficiency argument for wages being higher than the marginal product. The average income is already so low that payment below a certain (subsistence) level may just fail to produce the labor that is necessary to carry out the production operations.

10 It needs to be noted that the wage curve in the classical economics is also flat and fixed at the subsistence level. This similarity and the associated departures from other neoclassical assumptions often led to the characterization of the Lewis model as belonging to the classical school. Lewis (1954) himself promoted the idea to some extent. However, it is important to note that the flatness of the wage curve in the Lewis model is not the same as the flatness in the classical economics. The latter, rooted in Malthusian population dynamics, continues in perpetuity (with temporary fluctuations around it) while the former disappears as industrialization progresses. Thus although there is some connection with overpopulation, the nature of the connection is very different in the Lewis model than in the classical model.

11 For elaboration of the point by these authors see Fei and Ranis (1963, 1969), Ranis (1963), Ranis and Fei (1963).

12 For related discussions see Choo (1971), Findlay (1980), Harris and Todaro (1970), Jorgenson (1961, 1967), Leeson (1979), and Nelson (1956).

13 They note that "relaxation of our closed-economy assumption would represent an important next step in the evolution of our model; such relaxation would considerably soften the balanced growth constraint by relaxing a source of rigidity in the system (Ranis and Fei 1963, pp. 452–3)." Elsewhere they note that "the open economy can (indeed) be of considerable help in loosening the strait-jacket of resource constraints and inherited autarky, aiding the domestically driven growth of the dualistic LDC (Fei and Ranis 1997, p. 283)."

14 To facilitate our later analysis, let us refer to the boundary between phases 1 and 2 as the "shortage point" signifying the beginning of shortages of agricultural goods as indicated by the fact that AAS (average agricultural surplus) falls below the minimum wage; let us also refer to the boundary between phases 2 and 3 as the "commercialization point" signifying the beginning of equality between marginal productivity and the real wage in agriculture (Ranis and Fei 1963, p. 540).

15 According to Ranis and Fei (1963, p. 539),
    Lewis himself explains the turning point rather *loosely* as occurring when one of the following events puts an end to the horizontal supply curve of labor: (a) the worsening of the terms of trade for the industrial sector, and (b) the exhaustion of the labor surplus in the agricultural sector.

16 As Ranis and Fei (1963, p. 540) puts it, "The Lewis Turning Point…coincides with the shortage point and the upward movement of the industrial real wage is accentuated at the commercialization point." They think that "Lewis' 'unlimited' supply curve of labor is defined by the horizontal portion of the supply curve, that is St (the portion that pertains to phase 1). When this supply curve turns up, unlimitedness comes to an end (Ranis and Fei, 1963, p. 536)."

17 Oshima (1963, p. 451) observes that
    empirical studies are necessary to substantiate the concept of an institutional wage, i.e. a caloric-minimum wage substantially higher than MPP which the landlord is willing to pay in order to prevent wage levels from falling to caloric levels too low for efficient work. This assumes that the redundant workers have no other place to go and that cultivable land is fixed in the long run. And it contradicts the usual practice of sharp struggles between landlord and tenant in Asian countries. I think a stronger case can be made for assuming wages to be below MPP.

18 See also Lewis (1979, 1980, and 1984).

19 Lewis also mentions of a second Turning Point, which is reached when "the marginal product is the same in the capitalist and non-capitalist sectors, so that we have reached the neo-classical one-sector economy (Lewis 1972, p. 83)." In a footnote, Lewis notes that
    The second turning point is exactly the same as in Fei and Ranis (1964, p. 201–5). The definition of the first turning point is also the same, but the mechanism for reaching it is different, since Fei and Ranis are working with Model-II, in which the capitalist sector depends on the non-capitalist sector for agricultural products. (Lewis, 1972, p. 83)

20 Following Johnson's trade model, Lewis shows that the terms of trade between the two sectors will remain constant if the relative growth rates of industry and agriculture are the same as the relative income elasticities of demand for product of these two sectors. As Lewis (1972, p. 93) explains, "even if the terms of trade are rising, industrial expansion will not necessarily cease. Productivity is rising in the industrial sector, so if real wages (w/c) are constant, the profit margin will not fall unless the terms of trade rise faster than industrial productivity." According to Lewis, this will happen particularly if the productivity growth in the agricultural sector lags much behind that in the industry sector so that the price of agricultural products rises faster than those of the industrial sector. However, even if the terms of trade rise (deteriorates) for the industry, its expansion may not cease if the productivity growth in this sector outpaces the rate of deterioration in the terms of trade. (This is however a little confusing, because the rate of deterioration in the terms of trade itself depends on the rate of productivity growth, and hence two are not independent.) The concrete outcome will then depend on the relative rates of productivity increase in the two sectors and the resulting impact on the terms of trade and movement of the real wage.

21 As Lewis (1972, p. 94) argues,
    In order to export more it may have to lower its prices, thus squeezing its profits. Its real wages, in terms of agricultural products, are fixed by definition. If we take as given the propensity to import and the inflexibility of the agricultural sector, we can see that the possible rate of growth of such an economy is determined by its propensity to export.
    One can see here some influence of the "export pessimism" propounded by Raul Prebisch and others on Lewis thinking.

22 "The country is still surrounded by other countries which have surplus labor. Accordingly, as soon as its wages begin to rise, mass immigration and the export of capital operate to check the rise." Lewis (1954, p. 190).

23 "The importation of foreign capital does not raise real wages in countries which have surplus labor, unless the capital results in increased productivity in the commodities which they produce for their own consumption." (Lewis, 1954, p. 191).

24 Fei and Ranis (1997, p. 290) explain that commercialization "indicates the end of the surplus labor condition. From this point on, the real wage in agriculture equals the marginal product of labor, which signifies that labor is now a scarce factor and the wage increases rapidly." They further explain that the definition of this point remain unchanged for the open economy. As they put it, "this concept (of commercialization point) is also applicable to the open dualistic economy (p. 290)." See Islam and Yokota (2006, p. 108) for further details regarding Fei and Ranis notion of the Commercialization Point in an open economy.

25 See Fei and Ranis (1997, pp. 292–97) and Islam and Yokota (2006, p. 108–9) for further details regarding these additional turning points.

26 Apart from trade flows, an open economy can or does witness other flows, namely of capital, technology, and even labor. As already noted, Lewis (1954) did consider factor flows, albeit in a rudimentary form, and at the very end of the article. Fei and Ranis (pp. 306–319) provide a perceptive discussion of how these other flows can affect the development process of a dualistic economy.

27 Fei and Ranis (1997, p. 283) too recognize this outcome, announcing that "domestic balanced growth remains the centerpiece of success in the open economy, even in relatively small country cases."

28 See for example, Ranis (1973, 1978, 1992, and 1995) and Ranis and Fei (1975).

29 As Fei and Ranis (1997, p. 156) report,
Figures A3.6 and A3.7 present indices of the real wage and the marginal product of labor in the agricultural sectors of Taiwan and Japan during their well-known successful periods of transition. The indices, normalized to begin at the same point, unambiguously illustrate that in both nations the marginal product of labor in agriculture rose significantly faster than the real wage.

30 See also Fields (1994).

31 Fei and Ranis (1997, p. 158) present Figure A3.7. Panel (a) showing "Japanese agricultural real wage index" and "Japanese agricultural marginal product-index." It is seen that the latter always exceeds the former during the 1886–1928 period, with the gap narrowing towards the end of the period. Panel (b) of the Figure compares "Japanese non-agricultural real wage" and "Japanese agricultural real wage," showing the former always to exceed the latter, with the gap rising over the period (1886–1928).

32 See Minami (1964, 1966, and 1968) for his early works on Japan. Minami (1973) compiles his research on Japan's Turning Point. Minami perceives the Turning Point prediction to be so central that he christens the Lewis model and its extensions as the "Theory of the Turning Point." See Minami (1973) for details.

33 It may be noted that Minami uses the "subsistence sector – capitalist sector" terminology to refer to the Lewis dualism.

34 There is a possibility of terminological confusion here. Minami uses the "capitalist-subsistence" terminology to express the Lewis duality, and that is why it is not a problem for him to name a sub-sector of the capitalist sector as "traditional." This naming is however confusing from the point of view of the terminology, namely "modern-traditional" that this paper uses to express the Lewis duality.

35 It is not that skilled labor entirely escapes the purview of the Lewis model. Minami notices that one of the implications or predictions of the Lewis model is that the wage gap between unskilled and skilled labor will increase over time before decreasing. This is in fact his fourth criterion that can be used to find the turning point.

36   See also the related contribution by Reubens (1964).
37   As Lewis (1972, p. 87) puts it, "When the first article was written, the historical wage data uppermost in my mind were those for the cost of living wage in Great Britain in the first half of the nineteenth century, and the USSR in the 1930s." This may suggest that Lewis thought his model to be applicable for the analysis of industrialization in a dual economy under socialism (central planning) too.
38   Bramall (2000) provides a good discussion of the influence of political considerations in deciding about economic matters in China during the Mao years.
39   Lin (1992) too uses the number of tractors as a proxy for capital in the different context.
40   As Lewis (1972, p. 93) explains,
Real wages cannot be constant if agricultural productivity is rising significantly, since this would be moving the factoral terms of trade against industry. So what will happen to profits in any particular case will depend on a race between agricultural productivity, industrial productivity, real wages (which may rise on their own for exogenous reasons), and the commodity terms of trade. If one makes precise assumptions about these magnitudes one can get precise answers, as Fei and Ranis have done.

References

Bramall, Chirs. 2000. *Sources of Chinese Economic Growth 1978–1996*, Oxford: Oxford University Press.

Choo, Hakchung J. 1971. "On the Empirical Relevance of the Ranis-Fei Model of Economic Development: Comment," *American Economic Review*, Vol. 61, No. 4 (September), pp. 695–703.

Department of Rural Survey, National Bureau of Statistics of China. Various years. *The China Rural Statistical Yearbook*. Beijing: China Statistical Press.

Fan, Gang. 2005. "Coming Collapse or Continued Economic Growth?" in David H. Brown and Alasdair MacBean (eds.), *Challenges for China's Development: An Enterprise Perspective*, London: Routledge.

Fei, John C. H. and Ranis Gustav. 1963. "Innovation, Capital Accumulation, and Economic Development," *American Economic Review*, Vol. 53, No. 3 (June), pp. 282–313.

Fei, John C. H. and Ranis Gustav. 1969. "Economic Development in Historical Perspective," *American Economic Review*, Vol. 59 (No. 2, May), pp. 386–400.

Fei, John C. H. and Ranis Gustav. 1997. *Growth and Development from and Evolutionary Perspective*, Oxford: Basil Blackwell.

Fields, Gary S. 1994. "Changing Labor Market Conditions and Economic Development in Hong Kong, the Republic of Korea, Singapore, and Taiwan, China," *World Bank Economic Review*, Vol. 8, pp. 395–414.

Fields, Gary S. 2004. "Dualism in the Labor Market: A Perspective on the Lewis Model after Half a Century," *The Manchester School*, Vol. 72, No. 6 (December), pp. 724–735.

Findlay, Ronald. 1980. "On Arthur Lewis' Contribution to Economics," *Scandinavian Journal of Economics*, Vol. 82, No. 1, pp. 62–76.

Gersovitz, Mark, Carlos F. Diaz-Alejandro, Mark Rosenzweig, and John C. H. Fei (eds.) 1982. *The Theory and Experiences of Economic Development: Essays in Honor of Sir W. Arthur Lewis*, London: Allen and Unwin.

Harris, John and Todaro Michael. 1970. "Migration, Unemployment, and Development: A Two-Sector Analysis," *American Economic Review*, Vol. 40, pp. 126–142.

Huang, Yukon. 1971. "Tenancy Patterns, Productivity, and Rentals in Malaysia," *Economic Development and Cultural Change*, Vol. 23, No. 4 (July), pp. 703–718.

Islam, Nazrul. 2003. "What Have We Learnt from the Convergence Debate? A Review of the Convergence Literature," *Journal of Economic Surveys*, Vol. 17, No. 3 (July), pp. 309–362

Islam, Nazrul. 2004. "New Growth Theories: What is In There for Developing Countries?" *Journal of Developing Areas*, Vol. 38, No. 1 (Fall), pp. 171–212

Islam, Nazrul and Yokota Kazuhiko. (2006). "An initial look at China's industrialization in light of the Lewis growth model," *East Asian Economic Perspectives*, 17, pp. 103–132.

Jorgenson, Dale W. 1961. "The Development of a Dual Economy," *Economic Journal*, Vol. 71 (June), pp. 309–334.

Jorgenson, Dale W. 1967. "Surplus Agricultural Labor and the Development of a Dual Economy," *Oxford Economic Papers*, New Series, Vol. 19, No. 3 (November), pp. 288–312.

Kirkpatrick, Colin and Armando Barrientos. 2004. "The Lewis Model after 50 Years," *The Manchester School*, Vol. 72, No. 6 (December), pp. 679–690.

Leeson, Phil F. 1979. "The Lewis Model and Development Theory," *The Manchester School*, Vol. 57, No. 3, pp. 196–210.

Lewis, Arthur W. 1954. "Economic Development with Unlimited Supplies of Labor," *The Manchester School*, Vol. 22, No. 2, pp. 139–191.

Lewis, Arthur W. 1955. *The Theory of Economic Growth*, Homewood, IL: Richard D. Irwin.

Lewis, Arthur W. 1972. "Reflections on Unlimited Supplies of Labor," in L. E. diMarco (ed.), *International Economics and Development (Essays in Honor of Raul Prebisch)*, New York: Academic Press, pp. 75–96.

Lewis, Arthur W. 1979. "The Dual Economy Revisited," *The Manchester School*, Vol. 47, No. 3, pp. 211–229.

Lewis, Arthur W. 1980. "Autobiographical Note," *Social and Economic Studies*, Vol. 29, No. 4, pp. 1–4.

Lewis, Arthur W. 1984. "Development Economics in the 1950s," in G. Meier and D. Seers (eds.), *Pioneers in Development*, Oxford: Oxford University Press, pp. 121–137.

Lin, Justin Yifu. 1992. "Rural Reforms and Agricultural Growth in China," *American Economic Review*, Vol. 82, No. 1 (March), pp. 34–51.

Lindert, Peter H. and Williamson Jeffrey. 1983. "English Workers' Living Standards during the Industrial Revolution: a New Look," *The Economic History Review*, Second Series, Vol. 36, No. 1 (February), pp. 1–25.

Minami, Ryoshin. 1964. "Economic Growth and Labor Supply," *Oxford Economic Papers*, New Series, Vol. 16, No. 2 (July), pp. 194–200.

Minami, Ryoshin. 1966. "A Model of Economic Development from Classical to Neoclassical Stages," *Weltwirtschaftliches Archiv*, Vol. 97, No. 2, pp. 345–354.

Minami, Ryoshin. 1967. "Population Migration Away from Agriculture in Japan," *Economic Development and Cultural Change*, Vol. 15, No. 2, Part 1 (January), pp. 183–201.

Minami, Ryoshin. 1968. "The Turning Point in the Japanese Economy," *Quarterly Journal of Economics*, Vol. 82, No. 3 (August), pp. 380–402.

Minami, Ryoshin. 1973. *The Turning Point in Economic Development: Japan's Experience*, Economic Research Series No. 14, The Institute of Economic Research, Hitotsubashi University, Tokyo: Kinokuniya Bookstore.

National Bureau of Statistics of China. Various years. *The China Statistical Yearbook*, China Statistical Press, Beijing.

Nelson, Richard R. 1956. "A Theory of the Low-Level Equilibrium Trap in Underdeveloped Economies," *American Economic Review*, Vol. 46, No. 5 (December), pp. 894–908.

Oshima, Hary T. 1963. "The Fei-Ranis Model of Economic Development: Comment," *American Economic Review*, Vol. 53, No. 1, pp. 448–452.

Putterman, Louis. 1992. "Dualism and Reform in China," *Economic Development and Cultural Change*, Vol. 40, No. 3 (April), pp. 467–494.

Ranis, Gustav. 1957. "Factor Proportions in Japanese Economic Development," *American Economic Review*, Vol. 47, No. 5 (September), pp. 594–607.

Ranis, Gustav. 1963. "Allocation Criteria and Population Growth," *American Economic Review*, Vol. 53, No. 2 (May), pp. 619–633.

Ranis, Gustav. 1973. "Industrial Sector Labor Absorption," *Economic Development and Cultural Change*, April. **21**, pp. 387–408.

Ranis, Gustav. 1978. "Equity with Growth in Taiwan: How Special is the Special Case?" *World Development*, Vol. 6, No. 3, pp. 397–409.

Ranis, Gustav. 1992. *Taiwan: From Developing to Mature Economy*, Boulder, CO: Westview Press.

Ranis, Gustav. 1995. Another Look at the East Asian Miracle, *World Bank Economic Review*, Vol. 9, No. 3, pp. 509–534.

Ranis, Gustav. 2004. "Arthur Lewis's Contribution to Development Thinking and Policy," *The Manchester School*, Vol. 72, No. 6 (December), pp. 712–723.

Ranis, Gustav and John C. H. Fei. 1961. "A Theory of Economic Development," *American Economic Review*, Vol. 51, No. 4 (September), pp. 533–565.

Ranis, Gustav and John C. H. Fei. 1963. "The Ranis-Fei Model of Economic Development: A Reply," *American Economic Review*, Vol. 53, No. 3 (June), pp. 452–454.

Ranis, Gustav and John C. H. Fei. 1964. "Capital-Labor Ratios in Theory and in History: Reply," *American Economic Review*, Vol. 54, No. 6 (December), pp. 1063–1069.

Ranis, Gustav and John C. H. Fei. 1975. "A Model of Growth and Employment in the Open Dualistic Economy, the Cases of Korea and Taiwan," *Journal of Development Studies*, 12. pp. 32–63.

Reubens, Edwin P. 1964. "Capital-Labor Ratios in Theory and in History: Comment," *American Economic Review*, Vol. 54, No. 6 (December), pp. 1052–1062.

Rosenzweig, Mark. 1988. "Labor Markets in Low Income Countries," in H. Chenery and T.N. Srinivason (eds.), *Handbook of Development Economics*, Vol. 1, North-Holland: Elsevier Science Publishers B.V. Amsterdam, pp. 713–762.

Sen, Amartya K. 1966. "Peasants and Dualism with and without Surplus Labor," *Journal of Political Economy*, Vol. 74, pp. 425–450.

Sen, Amartya K. 1967a. "Surplus Labor in India: A Critique of Schultz's Statistical Test," *Economic Journal*, Vol. 77, pp. 154–161.

Sen, Amartya K. 1967b. "Review of J. C. H. Fei and G. Ranis, 'Development of the Labor Surplus Economy: Theory and Policy,'" *Economic Journal*, Vol. 77, pp. 346–349.

Tignor, Robert. 2004. "Unlimited Supplies of Labor," *The Manchester School*, Vol. 72, No. 6 (December), pp. 691–711.

Weitzman, Martin. 1984. *The Share Economy, Conquering Stagflation*, Cambridge, MA: Harvard University Press.

Williamson, Jeffrey. 1982. "The Structure of Pay in Britain, 1710–1911," *Research in Economic History*, Vol. 7, pp. 1–54.

Xu, Yingfeng. 1994. "Trade Liberalization in China: A CGE Model with Lewis Rural Surplus Labor," *China Economic Review*, Vol. 5, No. 2, pp. 205–219.

6

Recent Trends in China's Distribution of Income and Consumption: A Review of the Evidence

Eric D. Ramstetter, Erbiao Dai, and Hiroshi Sakamoto

6.1   Introduction

It is well known that China's economy has grown very rapidly in recent years, though there is some controversy over precisely how fast economic growth has been. For example, the new (revised) series on Gross Domestic Product (GDP) suggest that between 1993 and 2004, China's per capita GDP increased 4.1 times in nominal terms and 2.7 times in real terms (Tables 6.1, 6.2).[1] The old national estimates suggest a somewhat slower increase, 3.6-fold and 2.3-fold, respectively, but the old region-based estimates indicate a more rapid increase for the nation, 4.4-fold and 3.0-fold, respectively. The new national series is probably the most accurate because it incorporates new data and estimation techniques.

Rising production and incomes are an important indication of improvements in living standards. In a country like China where many citizens remain relatively poor, increasing incomes of the poor is also a particularly high priority. In this respect, the rapid increase in per capita household consumption, 3.5-fold (old national series) or 3.7-fold (old region-based series) in nominal terms during 1993–2004 (Table 6.3), is another important indicator of the large improvements in living standards during this period. This indicator is particularly relevant to poorer households because they devote a relatively large portion of their income to consumption. In short, trends in per capita GDP and per capita household consumption are both important indicators that China has continued its rapid economic progress in recent years.

Despite this progress, a growing literature has also highlighted concerns with substantial increases in various measures of inequality in recent years. Chinese policy makers also appear to be devoting more attention to inequality issues. The most important reason for concern with equity-related issues in China is probably political, reflecting the desire to avoid marginalizing social groups economically, and thereby reducing the chances of related social unrest. In China, the country's socialist legacy and related social perceptions of equality's importance are also key considerations for policy makers.[2]

Table 6.1 Per capita GDP and per capita disposable income by regional group (national data in current yuan; regional figures are ratios to national estimates)

Indicator	1988	1993	1998	2000	2002	2004
GDP PER CAPITA, PRECISE CALCULATIONS						
National, New Series	–	2,998	6,796	7,858	9,398	12,336
National, Old Series	1,355	2,939	6,308	7,086	8,214	10,561
National, Old Region-based Series	1,337	2,937	6,744	7,823	9,382	13,006
East (11 provinces)	1.40	1.49	1.50	1.53	1.53	1.53
Beijing, Shanghai, Tianjin	3.20	3.08	3.16	3.33	3.37	3.29
Center (8 provinces)	0.83	0.75	0.77	0.76	0.75	0.74
West (12 provinces)	0.68	0.65	0.62	0.59	0.60	0.59
GDP PER CAPITA, ARITHMETIC MEANS OF PROVINCIAL GROUPS						
National, arithmetic means	1,512	3,255	7,337	8,589	10,354	14,098
East (11 provinces)	1.54	1.63	1.66	1.69	1.69	1.69
Beijing, Shanghai, Tianjin	2.73	2.66	2.80	2.91	2.94	2.93
Center (8 provinces)	0.78	0.71	0.73	0.71	0.70	0.70
West (12 provinces)	0.66	0.61	0.58	0.56	0.57	0.57
URBAN DISPOSABLE INCOME, ARITHMETIC MEANS OF PROVINCIAL GROUPS						
National, sample means	1,181	2,577	5,425	6,280	7,703	9,422
National, arithmetic means	1,171	2,572	5,404	6,271	7,527	9,159
East (11 provinces)	1.14	1.22	1.24	1.25	1.24	1.26
Beijing, Shanghai, Tianjin	1.28	1.34	1.50	1.61	1.55	1.59
Center (8 provinces)	0.87	0.84	0.83	0.82	0.85	0.85
West (12 provinces)	0.96	0.91	0.89	0.89	0.88	0.86
RURAL DISPOSABLE INCOME, ARITHMETIC MEANS OF PROVINCIAL GROUPS						
National, sample means	545	922	2,162	2,253	2,476	2,936
National, arithmetic means	591	1,010	2,320	2,429	2,730	3,265
East (11 provinces)	1.36	1.47	1.43	1.46	1.49	1.48
Beijing, Shanghai, Tianjin	1.84	2.04	1.91	2.01	2.13	2.15
Center (8 provinces)	0.85	0.81	0.89	0.85	0.84	0.85
West (12 provinces)	0.85	0.76	0.74	0.73	0.72	0.72

Note: The East is Beijing, Tianjin, Hebei, Liaoning, Shanghai, Jiangsu, Zhejiang, Fujian, Shandong, Guangdong, and Hainan; the Center is Shanxi, Jilin, Heilongjiang, Anhui, Jiangxi, Henan, Hubei, and Hunan; the West is Inner Mongolia, Guangxi, Chongqing, Sichuan, Guizhou, Yunnan, Tibet, Shaanxi, Gansu, Qinghai, Ningxia, and Xinjiang.

Sources: National Bureau of Statistics (2000, 2005a; 2006; various years).

The primary purpose of this chapter is to examine trends and patterns observed in China's distribution of income and consumption expenditures during the rapid growth of the 1990s and the early twenty-first century. Unfortunately, this apparently simple task is also quite daunting for several reasons. First, there are many types of distributions which are potentially important and it is impossible to consider all of them simultaneously. In this paper, we will focus on the

Table 6.2 Real per capita GDP and implicit deflators for GDP by regional group (national data in 1993 yuan; regional figures are ratios to national estimates)

Indicator	1988	1993	1998	2000	2002	2004
REAL GDP PER CAPITA, PRECISE CALCULATIONS (National data in 1993 yuan; regional figures are ratios to national estimates)						
National, New Series	–	2,998	4,625	5,306	6,183	7,397
National, Old Series	2,055	2,939	4,460	5,075	5,826	6,901
National, Old Region-based Series	1,949	2,937	4,924	5,779	6,908	8,805
East (11 provinces)	1.39	1.49	1.55	1.57	1.57	1.57
Beijing, Shanghai, Tianjin	3.25	3.08	3.20	3.30	3.35	3.30
Center (8 provinces)	0.83	0.75	0.74	0.73	0.72	0.71
West (12 provinces)	0.69	0.65	0.59	0.58	0.58	0.57
GDP DEFLATORS (1993 = 100)						
National, New Series	–	100	147	148	152	167
National, Old Series	66	100	141	140	141	153
National, Old Region-based Series	69	100	137	135	136	148
East (11 provinces)	69	100	133	132	133	144
Beijing, Shanghai, Tianjin	67	100	135	137	137	147
Center (8 provinces)	69	100	143	141	140	154
West (12 provinces)	67	100	142	139	140	153

Notes and Sources: See Table 6.1.

distributions of income and consumption, primarily because they are meaningful economic indicators and are relatively easy to measure in the Chinese case. However, it is also important to recognize that distributions of other economic indicators such as productive assets or educational opportunities can be equally important. Second, there are many ways to measure any distribution. Primarily because this paper puts a high priority on incorporating the most recent information available, it focuses on simple measures obtained from published sources. Nonetheless, as will become clear below, these calculations have some important shortcomings and the paper will carefully compare patterns and trends in published data with those observed in compilations using alternative data sources and/or more sophisticated methodologies. Third, as illustrated by the variety of GDP estimates discussed above, there are important measurement issues to address. On the other hand, it should also be recognized that many Chinese data are generally relatively good for a country of its income level.

Because the primary purpose of this chapter is to review recent trends in distribution, it begins with an overview of recent trends that can be observed in the published data (Section 6.2). The chapter then compares the trends observed in official estimates to those identified in previous studies of China's distribution, many of which try to address some of the measurement problems in the official estimates (Section 6.3). Finally, some concluding remarks are offered (Section 6.4).

Table 6.3 Per capita household consumption by regional group (National data in current yuan; regional figures are ratios to national estimates)

Indicator	1988	1993	1998	2000	2002	2004
NATIONAL ACCOUNTS' ESTIMATES, PRECISE CALCULATIONS						
National, Old Series	704	1,344	3,022	3,452	3,884	4,696
National, Old Region-based Series	675	1,266	2,755	3,130	3,650	4,638
East (11 provinces)	1.26	1.28	1.34	1.36	1.37	1.36
Beijing, Shanghai, Tianjin	2.11	2.28	2.46	2.77	2.93	2.91
Center (8 provinces)	0.88	0.86	0.86	0.85	0.85	0.86
West (10–12 provinces)	0.78	0.78	0.73	0.71	0.69	0.68
NATIONAL ACCOUNTS' ESTIMATES, ARITHMETIC MEANS						
National, arithmetic means	741	1,373	2,907	3,364	3,971	4,974
East (11 provinces)	1.31	1.37	1.47	1.51	1.53	1.52
Beijing, Shanghai, Tianjin	1.88	2.00	2.25	2.48	2.58	2.60
Center (8 provinces)	0.85	0.85	0.84	0.81	0.80	0.83
West (10–12 provinces)	0.78	0.74	0.68	0.65	0.65	0.64
SURVEY ESTIMATES, URBAN HOUSEHOLDS						
National, sample means	–	2,111	4,332	4,998	6,030	7,182
National, arithmetic means	–	2,112	4,342	5,034	5,953	7,078
East (11 provinces)	–	1.22	1.22	1.22	1.22	1.22
Beijing, Shanghai, Tianjin	–	1.39	1.48	1.55	1.56	1.58
Center (8 provinces)	–	0.83	0.83	0.83	0.82	0.83
West (10–12 provinces)	–	0.90	0.90	0.92	0.92	0.91
SURVEY ESTIMATES, RURAL HOUSEHOLDS						
National, sample means	–	770	1,590	1,670	1,834	2,185
National, arithmetic means	–	819	1,659	1,750	1,930	2,313
East (11 provinces)	–	1.36	1.36	1.38	1.40	1.40
Beijing, Shanghai, Tianjin	–	1.79	1.82	1.82	1.93	1.96
Center (8 provinces)	–	0.83	0.88	0.86	0.86	0.84
West (10–12 provinces)	–	0.76	0.75	0.75	0.73	0.74

Note: See Table 1 for definition of regions; all estimates exclude Chongqing in 1988 and 1993; urban household estimates exclude Tibet in 1993 and 1998.

Sources: National Bureau of Statistics (2005a; various years); State Statistical Bureau (various years).

6.2   Recent trends in distribution

This section summarizes recent trends observed in the distribution of income and consumption using annual data from the national accounts and the official surveys of urban and rural households coordinated by the National Bureau of Statistics (NBS). These data are chosen because they are easily updated from the *China Statistical Yearbook* (National Bureau of Statistics various years; State Statistical Bureau various years) or the *China Compendium of Statistics 1949–2004* (National Bureau of Statistics, 2005a).[3] Both data sources have important weaknesses, which will be pointed out as relevant below.

6.2.1   Distribution among regions

The disparity of per capita GDP among regions is among the most commonly cited evidence regarding China's uneven and widening income distribution (Table 6.1). Average per capita GDP was higher than the national average in 11 Eastern provinces (Beijing, Tianjin, Hebei, Liaoning, Shanghai, Jiangsu, Zhejiang, Fujian, Shandong, Guangdong, and Hainan) but much smaller in eight Central provinces (Shanxi, Jilin, Heilongjiang, Anhui, Jiangxi, Henan, Hubei, and Hunan) and 12 Western provinces (Inner Mongolia, Guangxi, Chongqing, Sichuan, Guizhou, Yunnan, Tibet, Shaanxi, Gansu, Qinghai, Ningxia, and Xinjiang).[4] The differentials between the East and the other two regions also tended to widen over time. For example, per capita GDP in the East increased from 1.40 times the national average in 1988 to 1.49–1.50 times in 1993 and 1998, and then slightly more in 2000–2004.[5] In the three richest, primarily urban, provinces of Beijing, Shanghai, and Tianjin, per capita GDP increased from 3.08 times the national average in 1993 to 3.29–3.37 times in 2000–2004. At the other extreme, per capita GDP in the West declined from 68 percent of the national average in 1988 to 65 percent in 1993 and 59–60 percent in 2000–2004. Per capita GDP in the Center also declined from 83 percent of the national average in 1988 to 75 percent in 1993, but remained largely unchanged thereafter.

Disparities in per capita disposable income have apparently been much smaller than disparities in per capita GDP, however. For example, according to data from official household surveys, mean disposable income in the East was only 1.14–1.26 times the national average in urban areas and 1.36–1.49 times in rural areas (Table 6.1).[6] Likewise, disposable incomes in the West were also much larger relative to the national average, 86–96 percent in urban areas and 72–85 percent in rural areas, than per capita GDP was. Compared to per capita GDP, there was also less inequality of disposable income in urban areas in the Center, but more in rural areas. Because the household surveys are compilations of information from relatively large samples of households, errors in the survey data are likely to be smaller than in the national accounts, which include considerable extrapolation from raw survey data for households and firms alike.

On the other hand, the household survey data also need to be used with care for the following reasons. First, one-third of the sample households are rotated annually and it is possible that samples for certain years could be peculiar in one respect or another, though related problems should be minimized by large sample size and attempts to choose the sample so that it represents the universe of Chinese households. Second, the household survey data are likely to underestimate disposable income because government transfers to households are often not recorded or underreported in the household surveys. In this respect, it is also important to recognize that many Chinese households, especially richer ones, are hesitant to report high incomes and consumption.[7] Third, official survey data also thought to underestimate urban incomes relative to rural ones because urban households are eligible for large subsidies (e.g., for education and medical care), pensions, unemployment insurance, and minimum living allowances that rural households are not eligible for or receive in much smaller amounts (China, Development Research Foundation, 2005, pp. 26–27).

Although estimates of per capita GDP and per capita disposable income suggest different levels of regional inequality, both the per capita GDP data and the disposable income indicate similar trends in inequality among regions. The most obvious common trend was a fairly large increase in disparity between the East and the national average in 1988–1993 followed by a much slower increase in 1993–2000 and relatively little change thereafter (Table 6.1). Incomes in the West also deteriorated relatively rapidly compared to the national average in 1988–1993, but the deterioration was less rapid in 1993 to 1998/2000, depending on the measure, and slower yet in subsequent years. In the Center, there was also a notable deterioration of per capita GDP through 1993, but the fall in per capita disposable income was relatively small in both urban and rural areas, and all measures of per capita income in the Center remained relatively constant compared to the national average after 1993. For the three richest urban provinces, precise calculations and arithmetic averages reveal different trends, probably because of the small number of provinces in the group and the small size of Tianjin compared to Beijing and Shanghai. Arithmetic averages suggest that per capita GDP in these three provinces fell relative to the national average through 1993. This contrasts to the rise of per capita incomes through 2000 in Eastern urban areas and large fluctuations in rural areas.

The comparisons made above and in Table 6.1 have one potentially important shortcoming, however. Namely, they fail to account for regional differences in inflation. The bottom half of Table 6.2 (precise calculations) suggests that GDP inflation has been relatively low in the East (e.g., 44 percent in 1993–2004) compared to the Center and West (e.g., 53–54 percent in 1993–2004). However, these data suggest that interregional differences in inflation were relatively small. Correspondingly, after the base year 1993, real per capita GDP in the East tended to be only slightly larger compared to the national average than nominal per capita GDP (e.g., 1.57 versus 1.53 in 2004). Similarly, real per capita GDP in the other regions tended to be slightly lower compared to the national average than revealed in current price calculations (e.g., 0.71 vs. 0.74 for the Center and 0.57 versus 0.59 for the West in 2004).

There are at least two additional, well-known problems with China's national accounts that mandate caution when interpreting the trends and patterns observed in per capita GDP, however. First, as highlighted by a recent revision of national estimates discussed in the introduction (the new GDP series in Table 6.1), previous estimates of GDP have underestimated services sector GDP in China and the scope of this underestimation appears to have increased over time. Thus, revised estimates of GDP per capita were 17 percent higher than previous (old series) national estimates in 2004, compared to only 2 percent higher in 1993. Second, region-based estimates, which are based on the old series methodology, imply slightly lower GDP per capita than the old series for the nation in earlier years (1 percent in lower 1988), but much higher levels in recent years (7 percent higher in 1998, 10 percent in 2000, 14 percent in 2002, 18 percent in 2003, and 23 percent in 2004).[8] Unfortunately, estimates for China's regions do not yet reflect the large upward revisions of services sector GDP made at the national level, and the disparity between even the most recent revisions of the old series of regional and national estimates is still quite large. Thus, it is impossible to know how addressing these problems would affect the distribution of per capita GDP across regions, though the disposable income figures suggest that trends in regional distribution are likely to be similar even after the necessary revisions are made.[9]

Household consumption is usually somewhat easier to measure than GDP or disposable income. For example, region-based estimates of household consumption reported in the national accounts are always smaller than corresponding national estimates, and these differentials were relatively small (−4 to −9 percent in 1988–2002 and –1 percent in 2004, Table 6.3).[10] Moreover, changes in household consumption often have more important implications for household welfare than changes in income, especially among poorer households in the short-run, making it an important indicator of household welfare. It is thus significant that the national accounts data suggest that regional differentials in household consumption were markedly smaller than corresponding differentials in GDP per capita (Table 6.1).[11] On the other hand, household survey data suggest regional differentials were rather similar whether measured in terms of disposable income or household consumption. There were two major exceptions where relatively small discrepancies were observed in household consumption, urban households in the West in 2000–2004 and rural households in the East in all years.

The national accounts estimates (arithmetic averages) of household consumption per capita are also similar to corresponding GDP estimates in suggesting relatively rapid increases relative to the national average in the East and relatively slow growth in the West in 1988–2000, but relatively little change thereafter (Table 6.3). However, survey estimates of household consumption contrast by indicating small changes in both urban and rural households in all three major regions. There was a slight deterioration relative to the national average among both urban-rural households in the West, while the reverse was true in the East. Nonetheless these changes were so small they could be considered negligible. There were some increases compared to the national average in the three urban provinces, but in general the survey data suggest that the regional distribution of household consumption remained remarkably constant during this period.

The household survey data also indicate that the regional discrepancies tended to be larger among rural households than among urban households. For example, both disposable income and household consumption were relatively low in the urban East and relatively high in the urban West, compared to corresponding rural areas. On the other hand, ratios of the Center to the national average were similar in both urban and rural areas, for both disposable income and household consumption.

6.2.2   Urban–rural differentials

In addition to examining to the regional differences, it is also common to examine urban-rural differentials using data from the household surveys. There is of course some correlation between regional and urban-rural distributions because the East is more urbanized than other regions and the West less urbanized. However, this correlation is not straightforward, partially because definitions of urban and rural areas change with the degree of urbanization, which in turn varies by region and over time. Most of China's urban areas have been expanding and there are thus a much larger number of urban areas than there were a decade or two ago, for example.

Revised time series on disposable income in urban and rural areas are published annually in both current prices and in constant prices. Except for 1993 (the base year used here), the urban-rural differential was always somewhat larger if calculated in real terms (Figure 6.1). However, reflecting trends in inflation, the urban-rural differential increased more in nominal terms than in real terms during 1985–1993 (1.50-fold versus 1.23-fold), but this was reversed in 1993–2004 (1.15-fold versus 1.28-fold).[12]

Measured in current prices, urban-rural differentials have generally been largest in the West and smallest in the East, whether measured in terms of disposable income or household consumption per capita (Figures 6.2, 6.3). Differences in urban-rural differentials have been particularly large for household consumption in the West since 1999. As indicated above, interregional differences appear slightly smaller in the household consumption data than in the disposable income data (i.e., the lines in Figure 6.3 are generally closer together than in Figure 6.2), but the urban-rural ratios themselves are generally a bit larger if measured in terms of consumption than in terms of income. The fact that urban-rural ratios are generally larger in terms of consumption in turn suggests that urban-rural differentials may have particularly important implications for household consumption and short-term welfare in relatively poor, rural households.

Put another way, these data suggest that urban households in the West tended to spend a larger portion of their income on consumption than urban households elsewhere (Figure 6.4). The gap between urban households in the West and in other regions became conspicuous after the mid- to late-1990s, when the consumption-income ratios stagnated in the 81–83 percent range in the West but fell gradually to 75 percent by 2004 in the East and the Center. In rural households, consumption-income ratios also fell precipitously in all regions

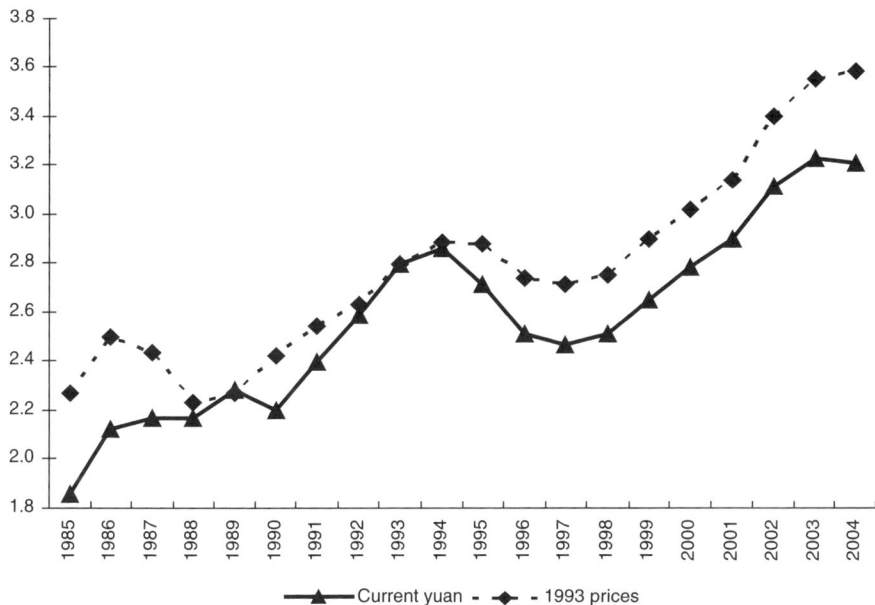

Figure 6.1 National urban-rural ratios for disposable income (Sample means)

Sources: National Bureau of Statistics (2000, 2005a; various years).

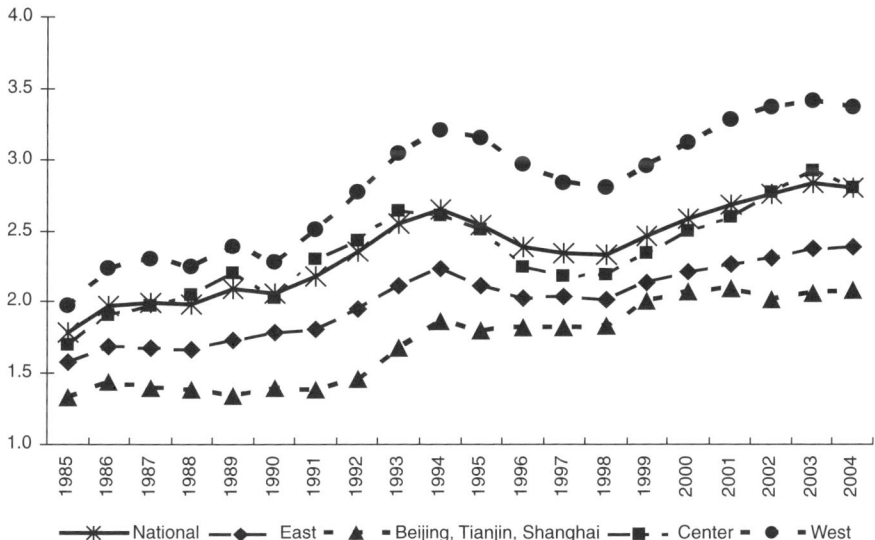

Figure 6.2 Urban-rural ratios for disposable income by region (Calculated from arithmetic means in current yuan)

Sources: National Bureau of Statistics (2000, 2005a; various years).

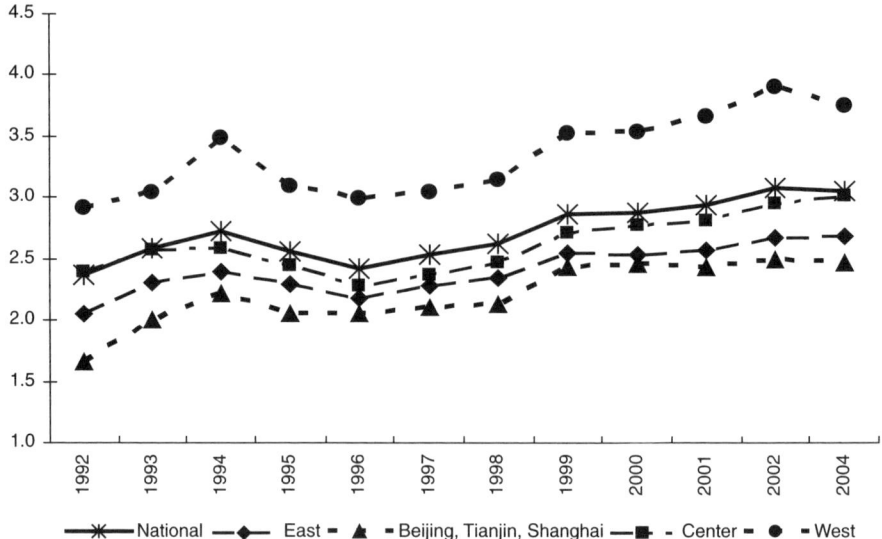

Figure 6.3 Urban-rural ratios for consumption by region (Calculated from arithmetic means in current yuan)

Sources: National Bureau of Statistics (various years); State Statistica Bureau (various years).

between the mid-1990s and 1999 (Figure 6.5). However, after 1999 these ratios also stagnated in rural households in all regions. The consumption-income ratio is a particularly important indicator of the ability of poorer households to make welfare-improving investments in capital goods and education, among other things. Thus, the inability to sustain declines of the consumption-income ratio in rural households and in urban households in the West suggests that growth has not resulted in increases of such investments among these households in recent years.[13]

6.2.3   Distribution among income groups

Although distributions among regions and between urban and rural households are important, a large portion of the income distribution literature focuses on distribution across income groups. This is difficult in the Chinese case because published data have not included compilations by income groups for rural households until very recently. In contrast, data for urban households are available for the entire 1988–2004 period, indicating that both income and consumption tended to grow relatively rapidly among relatively high-income groups, and that growth rates were particularly high in the top (rich) end of the distribution in recent years (Table 6.4). For example, between 1993 and 2004, incomes increased only 2.4 times in the poorest quintile 1, 3.0–3.7 times in the middle quintiles (2, 3, and 4), but a much higher 4.8 times in the richest quintile. Corresponding

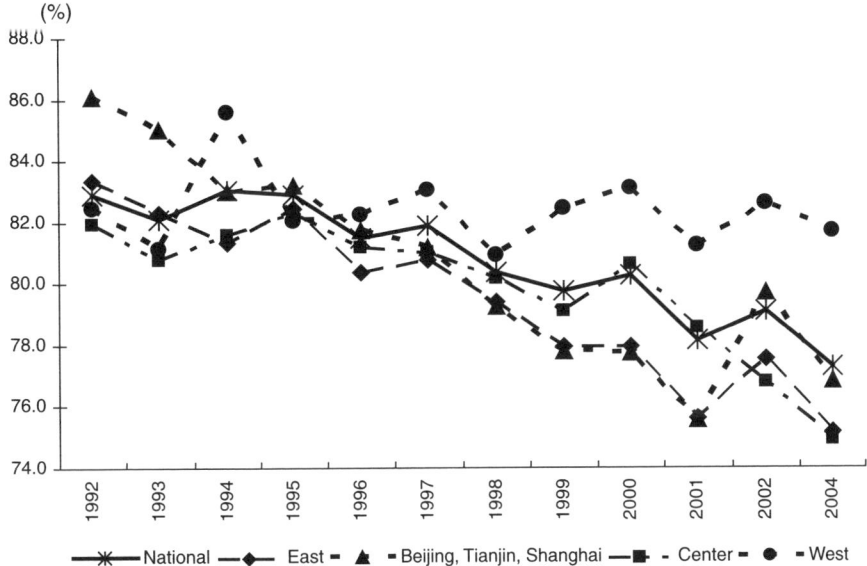

Figure 6.4 Consumption-income ratios for urban households by region (Calculated from arithmetic means in current yuan)

Sources: National Bureau of Statistics (2000, 2005a; various years); State Statistical Bureau (various years).

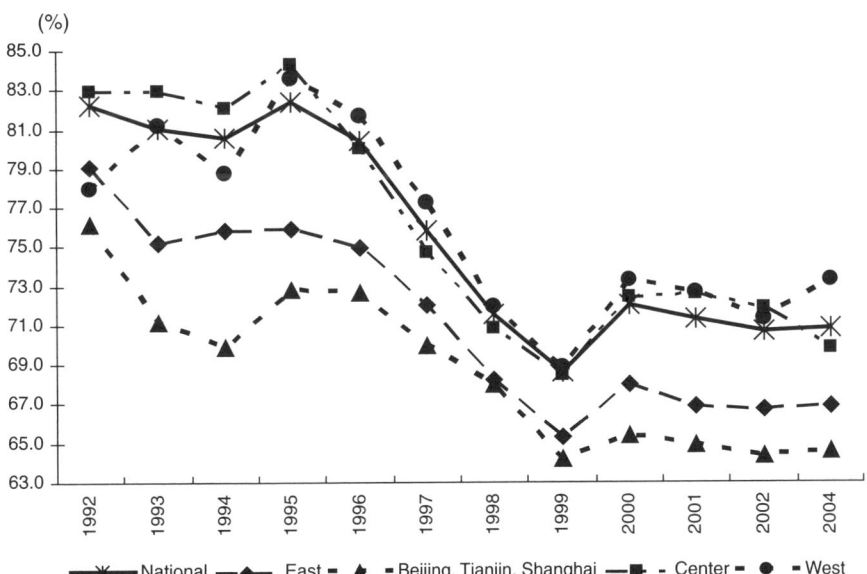

Figure 6.5 Consumption-income ratios for rural households by region (Calculated from arithmetic means in current yuan)

Sources: National Bureau of Statistics (2000, 2005a; various years); State Statistical Bureau (various years).

growth rates of consumption were somewhat slower than growth rates of income but had a similar pattern, 2.4-fold in the poorest quintile, 2.9–3.5-fold in the middle quintiles, and 4.3 fold in the top quintile. In 1988–1993 there was also a similar though less pronounced pattern of relatively rapid income growth among richer urban income groups, but little difference in consumption growth among income groups.[14]

Reflecting relatively rapid growth in rich households, ratios of the richest quintile to the poorest one increased from 2.4 in 1988 to 2.8 in 1993 and 5.5 in 2004 for per capita disposable income (Table 6.4). Ratios of the rich top quintile to middle-income quintiles 2 and 3 also increased rather steadily though less rapidly. Similar trends are also observed in corresponding ratios for household consumption after 1993. On the other hand, ratios of the top quintile to the fourth quintile increased much more slowly through 2000, before increasing more rapidly thereafter. Ratios of the middle-income quintile 3 to the two poorest quintiles 1 and 2 also increased at a relatively slow pace. Thus, gaps between the top and the middle- to low-income groups appear to have increased rapidly in China's urban areas during the last decade.[15]

In 2002 and 2004, ratios of disposable income in the top quintile to income in the other four quintiles were all larger for rural households than corresponding ratios for urban households (Table 6.4). There was a particularly large (6.9-fold) difference between incomes in the top quintile of rural households and the bottom quintile in 2004. However, corresponding ratios calculated in terms of household consumption were generally similar in rural and urban areas. Perhaps the most conspicuous difference in rural areas was the relatively low ratio of the top to the bottom quintile. Thus, although income appears to have been more unevenly distributed in rural areas in recent years, consumption appears to have been distributed a little more equally.

Reflecting low absolute income levels, ratios of household consumption to disposable income were 95 percent or higher for the poorest two quintiles of urban households in 1988 as well as the poorest quintile of rural households in 2002 and 2004 (Table 6.4). This indicates that these households were so poor that they used almost all their income or had to borrow to finance consumption during these periods. After 1988, consumption-income ratios for all urban income groups were much smaller than in earlier years, which might suggest a marked increase in saving and welfare among urban households. However, these declines were not sustained in the bottom two quintiles where consumption-income ratios changed very little after 1993. Consumption-income ratios also increased for the bottom two quintiles of rural households in 2002–2004. In contrast, consumption-income ratios were generally lower and tended to decrease in high-income households, reflecting the fact that richer households are better able to generate funds for saving. By 2004, consumption-income ratios had fallen to 68 and 76 percent, respectively, for the top 2 quintiles in urban areas, and to 60 and 68 percent, respectively, for the same groups in rural areas. Although it is difficult to attach much importance to trends in the short rural series, the urban trend and

Table 6.4 Distribution of disposable income and consumption among urban and rural households by income quintile

| Indicator | Urban Households | | | | | | | Rural | | Urban/Rural | |
	1988	1993	1998	2000	2002	2004	2002	2004	2002	2004
PER CAPITA DISPOSABLE INCOME (yuan)										
Quintile 1	759	1,525	2,890	3,143	3,029	3,646	857	1,007	3.53	3.62
Quintile 2	985	2,029	4,107	4,624	4,932	6,024	1,548	1,842	3.19	3.27
Quintile 3	1,159	2,440	5,119	5,898	6,657	8,167	2,164	2,578	3.08	3.17
Quintile 4	1,367	2,971	6,371	7,487	8,870	11,051	3,030	3,608	2.93	3.06
Quintile 5	1,847	4,245	9,420	11,373	15,384	20,174	5,896	6,931	2.61	2.91
RATIOS										
Quintile 5/quintile 1	2.43	2.78	3.26	3.62	5.08	5.53	6.88	6.88	0.74	0.80
Quintile 5/quintile 2	1.87	2.09	2.29	2.46	3.12	3.35	3.81	3.76	0.82	0.89
Quintile 5/quintile 3	1.59	1.74	1.84	1.93	2.31	2.47	2.72	2.69	0.85	0.92
Quintile 5/quintile 4	1.35	1.43	1.48	1.52	1.73	1.83	1.95	1.92	0.89	0.95
Quintile 3/quintile 1	1.53	1.60	1.77	1.88	2.20	2.24	2.52	2.56	0.87	0.87
Quintile 3/quintile 2	1.18	1.20	1.25	1.28	1.35	1.36	1.40	1.40	0.97	0.97
PER CAPITA CONSUMPTION (yuan)										
Quintile 1	735	1,395	2,688	2,908	2,824	3,399	1,006	1,248	2.81	2.72
Quintile 2	931	1,770	3,503	3,948	4,206	5,096	1,310	1,581	3.21	3.22

Continued

Table 6.4 Continued

Indicator	Urban Households						Rural		Urban/Rural	
	1988	1993	1998	2000	2002	2004	2002	2004	2002	2004
Quintile 3	1,092	2,056	4,180	4,795	5,453	6,498	1,645	1,951	3.31	3.33
Quintile 4	1,270	2,404	4,981	5,895	6,940	8,346	2,087	2,460	3.33	3.39
Quintile 5	1,655	3,172	6,799	8,176	10,980	13,796	3,500	4,129	3.14	3.34
RATIOS										
Quintile 5/quintile 1	2.25	2.27	2.53	2.81	3.89	4.06	3.48	3.31	1.12	1.23
Quintile 5/quintile 2	1.78	1.79	1.94	2.07	2.61	2.71	2.67	2.61	0.98	1.04
Quintile 5/quintile 3	1.51	1.54	1.63	1.71	2.01	2.12	2.13	2.12	0.95	1.00
Quintile 5/quintile 4	1.30	1.32	1.36	1.39	1.58	1.65	1.68	1.68	0.94	0.98
Quintile 3/quintile 1	1.49	1.47	1.55	1.65	1.93	1.91	1.63	1.56	1.18	1.22
Quintile 3/quintile 2	1.17	1.16	1.19	1.21	1.30	1.28	1.26	1.23	1.03	1.03

Note: For urban data, quintiles 1 and 5 are estimated as the averages of deciles 1 and 2, and deciles 9 and 10, respectively; disposable income for 1988 and 1993 is estimated as total income in each year times the average ratio of disposable income to total income because revised, consistent data on disposable income are not available before 1997.

Sources: National Bureau of Statistics (various years); State Statistical Bureau (various years).

the high levels of consumption-income ratios in both urban and rural areas suggest that poorer households have continued to have difficulty generating savings in recent years, despite rapid overall growth.

For 2004, we have also assembled estimates of distribution among income groups by region for urban households in 30 of the 31 provinces and rural households in 11 provinces (Table 6.5). These data illustrate a number of important points. First, distributions among income groups are almost always more equal within the three geographical regions (East, Center, and West) than nationwide. In other words, interregional differences appear to be an important source of overall inequality nationwide. Second, distributions among income groups are markedly less equal in the relatively wealthy East than in the Center or the West, though small sample size makes it difficult to know how meaningful this pattern is for rural households. Third, differences in distributions among urban income groups between the East, Center, and West are relatively small for household consumption but larger for disposable income. Fourth, again for urban households, consumption-income ratios are highest in the East, and particularly high in the three richest, primarily urban provinces. This suggests that the urban poor may be somewhat worse off relative to other income groups in the East than in the other regions. Fifth and finally, consumption-income ratios are quite high (82 percent or more) in the bottom two deciles in both urban and rural areas in all of the three regions. In short, these data suggest that the poorest 40 percent of China's households does not appear to have much income they can devote to saving.

6.3   The economic literature and its implications for inequality trends in China

This section reviews the economic literature analyzing trends in China's distribution and their causes with the aim of facilitating a realistic interpretation of the trends described in the previous section. The review first examines the numerous alternative estimates of inequality in China. Although the most recent studies covered in this review only analyze data through 2002 or 2003 at the latest (because of the time lag between authorship and academic publication), there is sufficient overlap to illustrate important similarities and differences observed in the official data and the results of economic studies, which are often able to address known shortcomings in the official data.[16] Second, the review examines the important and interrelated implications of the Chinese system of classifying households by *Hukou* (residence permits or family registers) and migration for inequality measures in China. Third, the review summarizes results of studies that use decomposition analyses to identify the sources of changes in inequality. Fourth and finally, the review summarizes some major results from the now voluminous literature on convergence among China's regions.

Table 6.5 Distribution of disposable income and consumption among urban and rural households by income quintile and regional group, 2004

	Urban Households				Rural Households			
	East (10 provinces)		Center (8 provinces)	West (12 provinces)	East (6 provinces)		Center (1 province)	West (4 provinces)
Indicator	Group Average	Beijing, Shanghai, Tianjin			Group Average	Beijing, Shanghai		
PER CAPITA DISPOSABLE INCOME (yuan)								
Quintile 1	4,871	6,422	3,527	3,505	2,115	2,868	1,242	1,034
Quintile 2	7,703	9,736	5,583	5,767	3,673	4,832	2,180	1,642
Quintile 3	10,409	12,834	7,356	7,669	5,025	6,573	2,827	2,150
Quintile 4	14,120	17,097	9,550	9,836	6,705	8,571	3,641	2,807
Quintile 5	24,419	29,186	15,423	15,392	11,779	14,519	5,429	4,482
RATIOS								
Quintile 5/quintile 1	5.01	4.54	4.37	4.39	5.57	5.06	4.37	4.33
Quintile 5/quintile 2	3.17	3.00	2.76	2.67	3.21	3.00	2.49	2.73
Quintile 5/quintile 3	2.35	2.27	2.10	2.01	2.34	2.21	1.92	2.08
Quintile 5/quintile 4	1.73	1.71	1.61	1.56	1.76	1.69	1.49	1.60
Quintile 3/quintile 1	2.14	2.00	2.09	2.19	2.38	2.29	2.28	2.08
Quintile 3/quintile 2	1.35	1.32	1.32	1.33	1.37	1.36	1.30	1.31

PER CAPITA CONSUMPTION (yuan)

Quintile 1	4,635	6,350	3,171	3,210	2,505	3,351	1,389	1,265
Quintile 2	6,589	8,542	4,600	4,900	3,153	4,297	1,840	1,480
Quintile 3	8,252	10,319	5,707	6,198	3,743	4,855	2,136	1,758
Quintile 4	10,310	12,573	6,974	7,677	4,761	6,337	2,394	2,110
Quintile 5	16,195	19,575	10,213	11,083	7,385	9,781	3,095	2,916
RATIOS								
Quintile 5/quintile 1	3.49	3.08	3.22	3.45	2.95	2.92	2.23	2.31
Quintile 5/quintile 2	2.46	2.29	2.22	2.26	2.34	2.28	1.68	1.97
Quintile 5/quintile 3	1.96	1.90	1.79	1.79	1.97	2.01	1.45	1.66
Quintile 5/quintile 4	1.57	1.56	1.46	1.44	1.55	1.54	1.29	1.38
Quintile 3/quintile 1	1.78	1.63	1.80	1.93	1.49	1.45	1.54	1.39
Quintile 3/quintile 2	1.25	1.21	1.24	1.26	1.19	1.13	1.16	1.19

Note: For urban households the East excludes Hebei. For rural households the East excludes Hainan, Hebei, Liaoning, Shandong, and Tianjin, the Center includes only Jiangxi, and the West includes only Chongqing, Guangxi, Shaanxi, and Sichuan.

Source: National Bureau of Statistics (2005b).

6.3.1 Alternative estimates of inequality

As observed in Section 6.2, published compilations of the NBS household survey data are probably the most comprehensive, accurate, and readily-available estimates of inequality. However the published estimates are limited in important respects. For example, the lack of data on the distribution of rural income by income group makes it difficult to examine long-term trends in rural distribution and published compilations do not attempt to calculate estimates of nationwide inequality. There are also difficulties involved in combining information from the urban and rural surveys as noted above. The easiest way to remedy these problems is to estimate alternative measures directly from the microdata underlying these surveys. Although the NBS apparently does not make the full data sets available to most researchers, some authors have obtained data which permit more accurate NBS-based estimates than previously possible (e.g., Chen and Wang, 2001; Ravillion and Chen, 2004).

Several studies also use alternative, generally less comprehensive household surveys that have been conducted by the Chinese Academy of Social Sciences (CASS) and the China Health and Nutrition Survey (CHNS), among other sources, to analyze inequality in China. Researchers choose to use these alternative sources first because they have generally found it easier to access the microdata underlying these surveys than the microdata underlying the NBS surveys, facilitating easier compilations of precise estimates from the alternative sources. In addition, the alternative surveys also contain some details not available from the NBS surveys, including more comprehensive definitions of income in some years. The alternative sources are thus useful to illustrate some of the shortcomings of the NBS surveys.

For example, calculations from the CASS surveys by Khan and Riskin (1998, pp. 232–233) for 1995 generate estimates of income that were 46 percent higher than corresponding NBS-based estimates for rural households and 33 percent higher for urban households. For rural households a little over half of the difference resulted from CASS's inclusion of items excluded from the NBS surveys. For urban households, almost all of the difference resulted from inclusion of items excluded from the NBS surveys. Likewise, Benjamin et al (2008) emphasize that the CHNS surveys tend to measure both urban subsidies and non-farm self employment better than the NBS surveys.

Both of these studies give markedly lower estimates of the rural-urban gap than corresponding NBS estimates (c.f., Figure 6.1), with the CHNS-based estimates suggesting particularly large differences.[17] Benjamin et al (2008) also use the CHNS data to show that holding a location's urban-rural status constant for the 1991–2000 period generates smaller and much more constant ratios of urban-to-rural incomes in 1991–2000 than calculations which use the standard NBS practice of allowing changes in an area's urban-rural status over time.[18] In a related calculation, Ravallion and Chen (2004) also show how adjusting for Cost-of-Living (COL) differentials between urban and rural areas greatly reduces urban-rural income differentials and removes any significant upward trend in the differential over time.[19] In marked contrast, a prominent study by China, Development Research Foundation

(2005, pp. 26–27) suggests that failure to account for relatively large subsidies, pensions, unemployment insurance, and minimum living allowances to urban residents resulted in a roughly 20 percent underestimation of the urban-rural gap in 2002 (at current prices) by official data. There is thus substantial disagreement in the literature about the scope of the urban-rural gap and its trend.

Largely because the NBS does not publish estimates of commonly used indices of household distribution such as the Gini coefficient, many studies in this literature have focused on estimating the Gini and other indices of inequality.[20] Moreover, because it is very difficult to generate estimates of national income distribution by combining published urban and rural data from the NBS household surveys, or even by making calculations from underlying microdata, only a few studies have focused on estimating country-wide inequality or comparing inequality in urban and rural areas. Table 6.6 provides a summary of the known studies that provide such estimates, most of which are calculated from underlying microdata.[21] Although these studies use a large number of data sources and compilation methodologies, with some important differences among them, most of this literature reveals a number of similar trends and patterns of importance. For example, the following trends and patterns can be observed from estimates of Gini coefficients assembled in Table 6.6.

1. There has been a long-term trend toward greater inequality nationwide and in urban and rural areas, with the largest increases in the early-1990s and again in the late-1990s and early twenty-first century. This pattern is generally consistent with the officially published data on urban inequality in Table 6.4, though there are no comparable official data on rural or national inequality.

2. Urban inequality has generally been less pronounced than rural inequality. However, urban inequality has increased more rapidly than rural inequality and microdata-based estimates based on the NBS and CASS surveys for 1997–2002 suggest that urban Gini coefficients were only 8–12 percent smaller than corresponding rural coefficients. The CHNS-based estimates suggest that the rural distribution remained somewhat more unequal in 1997 and 2000 (Gini coefficients were 15–17 percent smaller for urban areas), while the calculations of Wu and Perloff (2004) from aggregate NBS data suggest even larger differences remained. The limited comparisons that can be made from Table 6.4 (for 2002 and 2004) also suggest that rural distribution remained more unequal than urban distribution in recent years but that inequality is increasing faster in urban areas.

3. Most estimates suggest that national inequality was generally greater than inequality within rural or urban households, reflecting the influence of increasing urban-rural differentials revealed by most data sets. The CHNS-based estimates from Benjamin et al (2008), which suggest relatively small and constant urban-rural differentials (see above) are a notable exception to this pattern.

4. NBS-based estimates of inequality tend to be somewhat lower than the alternative estimates for rural areas but differences between NBS-based estimates and estimates from alternative sources are much smaller and less consistent

Table 6.6 Some recent estimates of trends in gini coefficients for China (cost of living differential assumed to be zero unless noted)

Sources, region, sample	1987	1988	1990	1991	1993	1995	1996	1997	1998	1999	2000	2001	2002
ESTIMATES BASED ON THE NBS SURVEYS OF URBAN AND RURAL HOUSEHOLDS													
Chen and Wang (2001), national microdata			0.35		0.42	0.42	0.40	0.40	0.40	0.42			
national (cost of living differential = 20%)			0.32		0.39	0.38	0.37	0.37	0.37	0.39			
urban			0.23		0.27	0.28	0.29	0.29	0.30	0.30			
rural			0.30		0.34	0.34	0.33	0.33	0.33	0.34			
Han (2004), national microdata		0.34	0.39			0.39	0.38	0.38	0.39	0.40	0.42		
urban	0.20	0.23	0.23	0.24	0.27	0.28	0.28	0.29	0.30	0.29	0.32		
rural	0.30	0.30	0.31	0.31	0.33	0.34	0.32	0.33	0.34	0.34	0.35		
Ravallion and Chen (2004), national microdata	0.32	0.33	0.35	0.37	0.42	0.42	0.40	0.40	0.40	0.42	0.44	0.45	
national (cost of living differential > 0%)	0.29	0.30	0.32	0.33	0.37	0.37	0.35	0.35	0.35	0.36	0.38	0.39	0.33
urban	0.20	0.21	0.23	0.23	0.27	0.28	0.29	0.29	0.30	0.30	0.32	0.32	
rural	0.29	0.30	0.30	0.31	0.34	0.34	0.33	0.33	0.33	0.34	0.36	0.36	
Wu and Perloff (2004), national aggregates	0.32	0.34	0.33	0.35	0.38	0.38	0.35	0.38	0.38	0.39	0.41	0.42	
urban	0.19	0.20	0.20	0.18	0.22	0.22	0.22	0.23	0.24	0.25	0.26	0.27	
rural	0.28	0.30	0.29	0.32	0.32	0.34	0.32	0.32	0.32	0.33	0.34	0.34	

ESTIMATES BASED ON THE CASS SURVEYS OF URBAN AND RURAL HOUSEHOLDS IN SELECTED PROVINCES (microdata)

China Development Research Foundation (2005)	0.38			0.46
urban	0.23		0.29	0.34
rural	0.30		0.33	0.37
Kahn and Riskin (1998)	0.38	0.45		
urban	0.22	0.33		
rural	0.34	0.42		

ESTIMATES BASED ON THE CHNS SURVEYS OF URBAN AND RURAL HOUSEHOLDS IN SELECTED PROVINCES (microdata)

Benjamin et al (2008), national	0.37	0.42	0.40	0.44
urban	0.29	0.35	0.35	0.38
rural	0.39	0.43	0.41	0.46

for urban areas. Here it should be stressed that differences between NBS-based calculations and the alternatives presented derive both from (a) definitional differences (especially the use of broader definitions of income in alternative sources; see discussion above) and (b) the relatively comprehensive coverage of the NBS surveys, though it is impossible to sort out precisely how these factors contribute to differences in the various estimates.

In short, there is broad agreement that China's income distribution has worsened markedly since the 1990s and that increases in urban inequality have been particularly large. There is also general agreement that urban incomes have been distributed more equally than rural ones and most sources suggest national inequality was greater than inequality within urban and rural areas, reflecting the urban-rural gap. On the other hand, there is substantial disagreement over the size of the urban-rural gap and the degree of inequality.

6.3.2 The Hukou system, migration, and inequality

China's system of collecting household information on the basis of *Hukou*, combined with large rural-to-urban migration and the difficulty of obtaining residence permits for urban areas, complicates data collection for both the national accounts and the official household surveys. Urban residence permits are coveted by migrants because they facilitate access to social benefits not accorded those without permits. However, many urban authorities are hesitant to issue urban residence permits for fear of the budgetary pressure that could result from increases in poor residents eligible for social benefits. As a result, there are now a large number of rural-to-urban migrants who have been unable to acquire urban resident permits and are counted as rural residents or simply ignored. The scale of this problem is large with Hertel and Zhai (2006, p. 77) reporting that 90 million workers or 19 percent of the rural labor force fell into this category in 2001 while Dai's (2005, p. 19) figures suggest that migrant households accounted for between 14 and 25 percent of the urban households in the 13 cities examined in that study.

Because most household surveys and related studies exclude migrant households, actual urban inequality is likely to be greater than generally reported. Recent CASS surveys explicitly include migrants and allow additional perspectives on the size of the problem. For example, Dai (2005) uses the 1999 CASS survey to estimate inequality for Beijing including 100 migrant households and 670 permanent resident households. The resulting Gini coefficient was 0.33, compared to an estimate of 0.20 from official sources. His decomposition analysis further suggests that 53 percent of Beijing's inequality resulted from inequality within migrant households, 46 percent from inequality within permanent residents, but only 1 percent from inequality between migrants and permanent residents. Income inequality was greater among migrants than permanent residents (Gini coefficients of 0.49 and 0.24, respectively), but mean incomes were actually 12 percent higher in migrant households than in permanent resident households.[22]

In addition, to complicating the measurement of inequality, the *Hukou* system also contributes to inequality, especially inequality within urban areas, by withholding social benefits from urban migrants. These aspects of inequality are often not captured in existing measures of income. For example, Démurger, et al (2001) and Liu (2005) highlight how the *Hukou* system is a major contributor to urban-rural gaps and how it denies migrants access to education and formal sector jobs in urban areas. Likewise, other recent studies have highlighted the importance of regional inequalities in education and health care (Hannum and Wang, 2006; Zhang and Kanbur, 2005). Computable general equilibrium simulations by Hertel and Zhai (2006) also suggest that potential reforms in the rural land rent market and the household registration system would increase off-farm mobility and reduce urban-rural income gaps differential dramatically. These and other dimensions of inequality are also important and generally exacerbate income or consumption inequality, if accurately measured.

6.3.3   Decomposition analyses of inequality's sources

Many of the articles in the literature also try to identify sources of inequality. For example, NBS-based estimates by Wu and Perloff (2004) suggest that greater intra-rural and intra-urban inequality as well as increases in the urban-rural gap have been equally responsible for long-term increases in overall inequality, but that the urban-rural gap accounts for an increasing portion of overall inequality in recent years. However, if urban and rural households are reclassified as Benjamin et al (2008) suggest, the urban-rural gap becomes a smaller contributor to overall inequality. Likewise, Ravallion and Chen (2004) argue that economic growth in rural areas and in agriculture was the most important means of national poverty reduction. They also provide evidence that taxation of farmers and inflation hurt the poor; but that external trade had little short-term impact.

Benjamin et al (2008) also emphasize how increased rural inequality between 1987 and 2001 was primarily related to the unequal growth of non-agricultural self-employment income and the slow growth in agricultural income after the mid-1990s, as well as the slow growth in agricultural commodity prices. Likewise, calculations from Khan and Riskin (1998) suggest that differentials in large wage income increases was the most important source of increased inequality in rural areas between 1988 and 1995. Gustafsson and Li (2002) found that most rural inequality in 1995 was spatial and the result of uneven changes in incomes across counties.[23] They also highlight how rural incomes in the East, Center, and West "diverged most forcefully" in 1988–1995 (p. 198). On the other hand, Benjamin et al (2005) found that geography is not the largest cause of rural inequality and that more than half of observed inequality involves neighbors in the same village. Econometric results from Wan (2004) suggest that government support to rural industrial enterprises and education are the two most important sources of inequality in rural areas.

Benjamin et al (2008) also show how increased urban inequality between 1987 or 1991 and 2001 has resulted from reduced subsidies and entitlements, increased wage inequality, and the layoffs. This finding is reinforced by Knight and Song (2003) who highlight the role of increasing wage inequality between 1988 and 1995, and Meng (2004), who emphasizes that increased unemployment played an important role in reducing incomes among poorer households in 1995–1999. In some contrast, Fang et al (2002) suggest that urban inequality began to rise rapidly in 1996–1998 largely because reforms led to a widening gap between urban areas in western China and the rest of the country. Meng (2004) also emphasizes the importance of increased regional disparity in 1988–1995. Meanwhile, Khan and Riskin (1998) report that the rental value of owned housing was the largest contributor to urban inequality in 1995, highlighting the effects of higher land and housing prices. Meng et al (2005) argue that the worsening distribution has led to a rise in urban poverty, which is in turn related to an increase in the relative prices of goods and services that were previously provided free or subsidized by the government (e.g., education, housing and medical care). They also point out that higher saving rates among poor households contribute a lot to greater poverty if measured in terms of expenditure. This is related to Knight and Li's (2006) finding that a large portion of the urban poor have incomes that exceed the poverty line but consumption levels which fall below it.

6.3.4   Convergence among regions

There is now a very large amount of literature on the convergence among China's regions, which is based primarily on estimation of growth models with provincial data. Although this literature does not examine measures of inequality directly, it does reveal whether regional equality tends to increase or decrease over time. Many of these studies have focused on whether real per capita GDP grows faster in poorer provinces and thus converges values in richer provinces or not, or so-called β convergence.

A common way to examine β convergence is to run a regression where the growth of per capita GDP or a related variable (e.g., production per worker) is viewed as a function of the level of the dependent variable at the beginning of the period.[24] If the initial level is the only independent variable, one can examine unconditional convergence or whether convergence is observed when the effects of other factors affecting growth are not controlled for. For example, Makino (2001, p. 37) provides evidence that unconditional β convergence was statistically significant in 1978–1998 but insignificant in earlier periods, while the calculations presented in Sakamoto (2005, p. 11), suggest that estimates of unconditional β convergence were not significant either in 1952–2003 or in 1978–2003.

Another common unconditional measure is to calculate the coefficient of variation in per capita GDP growth, which allows one to examine whether the dispersion of growth rates among regions increases or decreases over a period. If the dispersion decreases the process is called σ convergence. The results of Démurger et al (2001, pp. 148–151) suggest convergence (or at least the lack of divergence) in the initial reform period from 1978 through the 1980s, but divergence in the 1990s, which is particularly pronounced when Beijing, Shanghai, and Tianjin are excluded from their sample. Weeks and Yao (2003) obtain similar results with respect to overall σ convergence in the 1980s and 1990s, while Jia (1998) provides alternative evidence suggesting weak unconditional convergence in 1978–1994.

Although estimates of unconditional convergence are instructive, they can be misleading because they fail to account for the effects of other factors that affect growth. For example, econometric estimates of unconditional β convergence are very likely to be affected by an omitted variable bias. In order to remove these biases it is preferable to estimate convergence in the context of a growth model that includes the initial level of the dependent variable (e.g., GDP per capita) and other factors thought to affect growth as explanatory variables. The most straightforward convergence models are simple cross sections of growth over relatively long periods of time (usually a decade or more) or panels of several five to ten year periods.[25] In recent years, it has also become somewhat common to use annual panels to examine growth determinants, though the use of annual data may be inappropriate in the context of growth models because they are designed to describe changes over longer periods of time.[26] Two striking patterns emerge from these studies. First, almost all the growth studies find evidence of conditional convergence in the early reform period from 1978 through the mid-to-late-1980s or early-1990s. In addition, Gundlach's (1997) calculations from reduced forms that include production function parameters also suggest convergence of output per worker during 1978–1989. Second, the more limited evidence for the late-1980s and the 1990s alone suggests a failure to find convergence or divergence, which is similar to the results for σ convergence noted above.

Some of the panel-based results differ in important respects, however. For example, the results of Weeks and Yao (2003), who use a generalized method of moments estimator, are notably different in that they suggest a "system-wide income divergence during the reform period" (p. 59). These results are similar to those of Pedroni and Yao (2006) who also use a panel of annual data and recently developed nonstationary panel techniques to test whether differences in growth rates among pairs of provinces are stationary so that provincial growth rates are cointegrated, using this as their definition of convergence. Their results also suggest a tendency toward divergence that is pervasive nationally and within various regional and political subgroupings. A Generalized Entropy (GE) decomposition from Bhalla et al. (2003) also indicates that China's provinces tended to form two income clubs in 1952–1997, the rich in the East and the poor in the Central and the West. However, results for subperiods contrasted; there was no clear evidence of club formation in the pre-reform period before, while there was strong evidence of club formation after 1978. Finally, Sakamoto and Islam (2008) also use Markov chains to analyze data for 1952–2003, finding that the distribution of per capita incomes has become bi-modal over this period. However, they also suggest that eventual convergence may result because more provinces moved toward the high end of the distribution during the reform period.

In short, the preponderance of evidence suggests convergence during the early reform period, and the lack of convergence after the late-1980s or early-1990s. However, there are still lots of questions surrounding estimates of convergence. One fundamental problem relates to measurement as indicated by the inconsistency between national and regional GDP estimates and large differences between estimates of regional distribution based on the national accounts and estimates based on the urban and rural surveys. It would thus be helpful to conduct careful analyses of the differences between regional distributions in the national accounts and in the household surveys, in an attempt to sort out the implications of using alternative definitions of regional inequality. Efforts to clarify how alternative statistical methodologies affect estimates of convergence would also be useful. Finally, the issue of timing is also important. If China has indeed been experiencing regional divergence as many studies suggest has occurred in the 1990s, is this only a temporary phenomenon that will eventually give way to convergence? What are the factors that will determine the answer to that question? Unfortunately, the existing literature is probably further away from answering these important questions than is desirable.

6.4   Conclusions

This chapter first examined recent trends in the distribution of income and consumption in China. National accounts data and household survey data from the NBS both indicate a tendency for the incomes to rise faster in the East of the country than in the Center or the West, with particularly large changes in the 1990s. Similar though less pronounced trends are also observed in national accounts' estimates of household consumption. On the other hand, survey estimates indicate a relatively low level of regional inequality in both incomes and consumption, and no trend toward increased regional inequality for consumption. Official surveys also show that urban-rural gaps increased markedly in the early-1990s and then again after 1998, both nationwide and in most regions. They also indicate that incomes grew more rapidly in rich households than in poor households and that this trend accelerated after the late-1990s, both nationwide and within regions. By 2004 per capita income in the richest quintile of households was 5.5 times more than in the poorest quintile in urban areas and 6.9 times more in rural areas. The distribution of income and consumption was generally more equal within regions than nationwide and intra-regional distribution tended to be more equal in the Center and the West than in the East.

The chapter then presented a literature review designed to illustrate how more sophisticated studies have dealt with the problems existing in the published data. Several studies use alternative surveys to address shortcomings in the official survey estimates. They generally indicate that official survey estimates probably underestimate incomes but there is disagreement about the extent of urban-rural gaps. Despite the large adjustments proposed by some studies, most studies suggest generally similar trends in distribution that are broadly similar to the trends observed in official data. Namely, there appears to have been a large increase in

Table 6.A.1 Characteristics of households covered in the urban and rural surveys (number of households and persons per household)

Year	Urban Households			Rural Households		
	Number	Average Size	Average employment	Number	Average size	Average employment
1985	24,338	3.89	2.15	66,642	5.12	2.95
1990	35,660	3.50	1.98	66,960	4.80	2.92
1991	36,730	3.43	1.96	67,410	4.71	2.83
1992	36,290	3.37	1.95	67,490	4.67	2.83
1993	35,390	3.31	1.92	67,570	4.59	2.87
1994	34,940	3.28	1.88	67,420	4.54	2.89
1995	35,520	3.23	1.87	67,340	4.48	2.88
1996	36,370	3.20	1.86	67,610	4.42	2.84
1997	37,890	3.19	1.83	67,680	4.35	2.79
1998	39,080	3.16	1.80	68,300	4.30	2.78
1999	40,044	3.14	1.77	67,430	4.25	2.77
2000	42,220	3.13	1.68	68,116	4.20	2.76
2001	43,840	3.10	1.65	68,190	4.15	2.73
2002	45,317	3.04	1.58	68,190	4.13	2.76
2003	48,028	3.01	1.58	68,190	4.10	2.80
2004	50,430	2.98	1.56	68,190	4.08	2.82

Notes: Until 2001, the urban household survey covered only non-agricultural households; from 2002, it covers all households; for rural households, size refers to the number of permanent residents per household.

Sources: National Bureau of Statistics (various years); State Statistical Bureau (various years).

the late-1980s and early-1990s and then again in the late-1990s and early twenty-first century. The literature review also highlighted how the *Hukou* system and large migration has complicated the measurement of inequality in China, in addition to contributing to the increase of inequality, especially in urban areas. The review then described how alternative sources of income affected inequality in rural and urban areas and concluded with a summary suggesting that per capita GDP in Chinese provinces probably tended to converge in the early reform period but not after the late-1980s or early-1990s. Results regarding the role of regional distribution are varied, however, and there are large differences in alternative measures of regional distribution, which have yet to be analyzed carefully.

The bottom line is that the distributions of income and consumption appears to have become markedly more unequal in many respects during the late-1980s and early-1990s and then again in the late-1990s and the early twenty-first century. However, there is still considerable uncertainty regarding the precise extent to which inequality has risen and the relative importance of inequality's various dimensions.

Acknowledgements

We are very grateful for helpful comments from Ding Lu and Nazrul Islam, and other participants in the Second Workshop of the Project "Recent Economic Growth in China: Performance, Problems, and Prospects," which was held at ICSEAD on 7–8 July, 2006. Nazrul Islam also provided valuable editorial advice. However, we are solely responsible for all opinions expressed and all remaining errors.

Notes

1   A major difference between the revised new series and the old series is that the new series includes larger estimates of GDP in the services industries.
2   Policy makers in China and worldwide are correctly concerned with equality-related issues, though modern economists often have difficulty evaluating these issues or recommending policies toward them. This is because modern economists often define an optimal policy using the Pareto criteria (i.e., a policy should never make one or more members of a society worse off in his or her own eyes). However, realistic solutions to equality-related issues often require one group to sacrifice for the benefit of another and thereby contradict the Pareto criteria.
3   China Development Research Foundation, ed. (2005) and Han (2004) are two other prominent sources that try to analyze recent trends primarily using official data.
4   The distinctions between the East, Center, and West are based primarily on the policy biases accorded each region, though the correlation between policy bias and geography is high. For example, provinces in the Eastern or Coastal region were allowed preferential access to trade and foreign direct investment since the late 1980s, while the West has been given priority in the allocation of development funds and projects in recent years, partially to redress the imbalances resulting from earlier policy biases.
5   These figures refer to precise calculations or the total GDP in a regional group divided by it population. It should be noted that these and all other official calculations cited in this section use population data compiled from residence permits (*Hukou*) to estimate per capita figures. These estimates thus ignore the implications of numerous immigrants who live primarily in urban areas but often do not possess residence permits for the urban area they actually live and work in.
6   Note that these are arithmetic averages across provinces and differ from the precise calculations discussed above. Arithmetic averages are used because precise calculations are impossible using the published survey data. In general, arithmetic averages suggest relatively large interregional differences, but regional patterns and trends in GDP per capita are quite similar whether precise calculations or arithmetic averages are used (Table 6.1).
7   The reluctance to report high incomes and consumption results from fear for potential tax consequences as well as the desire to avoid social stigma attached to the wealthy in a society where the government actively discouraged high incomes and consumption for decades.
8   Note also that provincial authorities have had incentives to over-report GDP and its growth to gain favor with superiors, which suggests that region-based estimates are likely to be overestimates (Movshuk, 2002; Holz, 2004a). On the other hand, it is also likely that incentives for regional authorities to over-report have weakened over time, and probably reduced the size of related overestimation in recent years.
9   Extremely high estimates of fixed investment-GDP ratios in recent years (e.g., 44–46 percent in 2003–2004) suggest that fixed investment may also have been overestimated in the old GDP series, though the implications of this problem for regional distribution are unclear.

10 Holz (2004b) also emphasizes some apparent inconsistencies between publicized procedures for estimating household consumption expenditure and the results of efforts to reconstruct those estimates from underlying household survey data.

11 For example, if arithmetic means are used, the ratio of the East to the national average was 0.17 to 0.26 lower for per capital household consumption than for GDP per capita while ratios for the Center and West were 0.06 to 0.13 higher.

12 Implicit price deflators calculated from these data suggest that inflation was relatively rapid in urban areas compared to rural areas in 1985–1993 (a 2.19-fold versus a 1.80-fold increase), but this was reversed in 1993–2004 (a 1.68-fold increase in urban areas versus 1.88-fold in rural areas).

13 If taken at face value, the fact that consumption-income ratios tended to be lower in rural areas could be interpreted to mean that rural households have more resources available for saving and investment than their urban counterparts. However, estimates of rural incomes include farm-related expenditures on investment goods and intermediate goods, and are thus not directly comparable with estimates of urban incomes.

14 In 1988–1993, incomes grew 2.0 fold in the lowest quintile, 2.1–2.2 fold in the middle quintiles, and 2.3-fold in the top quintile, while consumption grew 1.9-fold in all quintiles.

15 Note that there were particularly large increases in many of these ratios between 2000 and 2002 that may have been related to the expansion of the coverage of the urban surveys to cover agricultural households from 2002.

16 Note that published compilations from these survey data are limited so it is necessary to access underlying microdata in order to correct for many of these problems.

17 Khan and Riskin's 1995 data suggest a current price ratio of 2.47 for 1995, compared to NBS estimates of 2.71 in figure 1. Estimates from Benjamin et al (2005, table 4) show constant (1990) price ratios of 1.80 in 1991, 1.92 in 1993, 1.73 for 1997, and 1.90 for 2000, compared to 2.32, 2.54, 2.46, and 2.74, respectively, if similar (1990 base) calculations are made from the NBS data underlying Figure 6.1.

18 Estimates by Benjamin et al (2008, table 18.4) indicate urban-rural ratios were 1.62 in 1991, 1.68 in 1993, 1.48 in 1997, and 1.53 in 1999, if urban-rural status is fixed for the sample period, while ratios were 1.80, 1.92, 1.73, and 1.90 if urban-rural status is allowed to change over time.

19 According to approximate estimates from figure 3 of Ravallion and Chen (2004), non-adjusted urban-rural ratios rose from about 1.8 in 1988 to 2.5 in 1994 before declining to 2.2 in 1998 and then rising to 2.5 again in 2001. If adjusted by the urban-rural COL differential, the urban-rural ratios fall to about 1.3, 1.8, 1.5, and 1.7, respectively.

20 The Gini coefficient is in many ways less useful indicators of income distribution than the quintile information in Tables 6.4–5 because the same Gini can be associated with very different quintile distributions. However, the Gini is a convenient, single indicator of distribution, which is commonly used.

21 Wu and Perloff (2004) is the only known study that tries to estimate national distributions from published NBS data. All other studies cited in Table 6.6 use microdata from the sources cited.

22 Dai (2005, p. 11) attributes the finding of relatively high incomes among migrants to the fact that this sample of 100 migrant households is "mainly composed of young laborers, and their average household size is smaller than that of the permanent resident households".

23 Wan and Zhou (2005) also highlight the importance of geography as a determinant of regional inequality in their study of representative provinces from the East (Guangdong), Center (Hubei), and West (Yunnan) in 2002.

24 There are several types of methodologies used to examine alternative types of convergence studied and in the literature. See Islam (2003, pp. 313–316) for a comprehensive review.

25   These studies include Bao et al (2002), Brun et al (2002), Chen and Feng (2000), Gao (2004), Gundlach (1997), Jian et al. (1996), Kanbur and Zhang (2005), Wei (1995), Yao and Zhang (2001), Zhang, K. (2001); Zhang, W. (2001), and Zhang et al (2001).
26   Studies including these kinds of analyses are Chen and Fleischer (1996), Démurger (2001), Fu (2004), Pedroni and Yao (2006), and Weeks and Yao (2003).

References

Bao, Shuming, Gene Hsin Chang, Jeffrey D. Sachs, and Wing Thye Woo. 2002. "Geographic Factors and China's Regional Development under Market Reforms, 1978–1998," *China Economic Review*, Vol. 13, No. 1, pp. 89–111.

Benjamin, Dwayne, Loren Brandt, and John Giles. 2005. "The Evolution of Income Inequality in Rural China," *Economic Development and Cultural Change*, Vol. 53, No. 4, pp. 769–824.

Benjamin, Dwayne, Loren Brandt, John Giles, and Sangu Wang. 2008. "Income Inequality during China's Economic Transition," draft prepared for Loren Brandt and Thomas Rawski (eds.), *China's Great Economic Transformation*, Cambridge, UK: Cambridge University Press, pp. 729–775.

Bhalla, Ajit, Shujie Yao, and Zongyi Zhang. 2003. "Regional Economic Performance in China," *Economics of Transition*, Vol. 11, No. 1, pp. 25–39.

Brun, Jean-Francois, Jean-Louis Combes, and Mary-Francoise Renard. 2002. "Are There Spillover Effects between Coastal and Non Coastal Regions in China?" *China Economic Review*, Vol. 13, No. 2–3, pp. 161–169.

Chen, Baizhu and Yi Feng. 2000. "Determinants of Economic Growth in China: Private Enterprise, Education and Openness", *China Economic Review*, Vol. 11, No. 1, pp. 1–15.

Chen, Jian and Belton M. Fleisher. 1996. "Regional Income Inequality and Economic Growth in China", *Journal of Comparative Economics*, Vol. 22, No. 2, pp. 141–164.

Chen, Shaohua and Yang Wang. 2001. China's Growth and Poverty Reduction: Recent Trends between 1990 and 1999, Working Paper, No. 2651, Washington: World Bank, D.C.

China Development Research Foundation, ed. 2005. *China Human Development Report 2005*, Beijing: United Nations Development Program (China Country Office; http://www.undp.org.cn/modules.php?op=modload&name=News&file=article&topic=40&sid=228; downloaded July 2006).

Dai, Erbiao. 2005. "Income Inequality in Urban China: a Case Study of Beijing," Working Paper Series 2005–04, Kitakyushu: International Centre for the Study of East Asian Development.

Démurger, Sylvie, Jeffery D. Sachs, Wing Thye Woo, Shuming Bao, and Gene Chang. 2001. "Geography, Economic Policy, and Regional Development in China," *Asian Economic Papers*, Vol. 1, No. 1, pp. 146–197.

Fang, Cheng, Xiobo Zhang, Shenggen Fan. 2002. "Emergence of Urban Poverty and Inequality in China: Evidence from Household Survey," *China Economic Review*, Vol. 13, No. 4, pp. 430–443.

Fu, Xiaolan. 2004. "Limited Linkages from Growth Engines and Regional Disparities in China," *Journal of Comparative Economics*, Vol. 32, No. 1, pp. 148–164.

Gao, Ting. 2004. Regional Industrial Growth: Evidence from Chinese Industries, *Regional Science and Urban Economics*, Vol. 34, No. 1, pp. 101–124.

Gundlach, Eric. 1997. "Regional Convergence of Output per Worker in China: A Neoclassical Interpretation," *Asian Economic Journal*, Vol. 11, No. 4, pp. 423–442.

Gustafsson, Bjorn and Shi Li. 2002. "Income Inequality within and across Counties in Rural China 1988 and 1995," *Journal of Development Economics*, Vol. 69, No. 1, pp. 179–204.

Han, Wenxiu. 2004. "The Evolution of Income Distribution Disparities in China since the Reform and Opening Up," in Organisation for Economic Co-operation and Development (ed.), *Income Disparities in China: An OECD Perspective*, Paris; Organisation for Economic Co-operation and Development, pp. 9–26.

Hannum, Emily and Meiyan Wang. 2006. "Geography and Educational Inequality in China," *China Economic Review*, Vol. 17, No. 3, pp. 253–265.

Hertel, Thomas and Zhai Fan. 2006. "Labor Market Distortions, Rural Urban Inequality and the Opening of China's Economy," *Economic Modelling*, Vol. 23, No. 1, pp. 76–109.

Holz, Carsten A. 2004a. "China's Statistical System in Transition," *Review of Income and Wealth*, Vol. 50, No. 3, pp. 381–409.

Holz, Carsten A. 2004b. "Deconstructing China's GDP Statistics," *China Economic Review*, Vol. 15, No. 2, pp. 164–202.

Islam, Nazrul. 2003. "What Have We Learnt from the Convergence Debate? A Review of the Convergence Literature," *Journal of Economic Surveys*, Vol. 17, No. 3, pp. 309–362.

Jia, Liqun. 1998. "Regional Catching up and Productivity Growth in Chinese Reform Period," *Journal of Social Economics*, Vol. 25, No. 6/7/8, pp. 1160–1177.

Jian, Tianlun Jeffery D. Sachs, and Andrew M. Warner. 1996. "Trends in Regional Inequality in China," *China Economic Review*, Vol. 7, No. 1, pp. 1–21.

Kanbur, Ravi and Xiaobo Zhang. 2005. "Fifty Years of Regional Inequality in China: a Journey through Central Planning, Reform, and Openness," *Review of Development Economics*, Vol. 9, No. 1, pp. 87–106.

Khan, Azizur Rahman and Carl Riskin. 1998. "Income and Inequality in China: Composition, Distribution and Growth of Household Income, 1988 to 1995," *China Quarterly*, 154, pp. 221–253.

Knight, John and Shi Li. 2006. "Three Poverties in Urban China," *Review of Development Economics*, Vol. 10, No. 3, pp. 367–387.

Knight, John and Lina Song. 2003. "Increasing Urban Wage Inequality in China, Extent, Elements and Evaluation," *The Economics of Transition*, Vol. 11, No. 4, pp. 597–619.

Liu, Zhiqiang. 2005. "Institution and Inequality: the *Hukou* System in China," *Journal of Comparative Economics*, Vol. 33, No. 1, pp. 133–157.

Makino, Matsuyo. 2001. *Kaihatsu Tojou Daikoku Chugoku no Chiiki Kaihatsu – Keizai Seichou, Chiiki Kakusa, Hinkon – [Regional Development in the Developing Giant China – Economic Growth, Regional Disparities, Poverty –]*, Tokyo: Daigaku Kyoiku Shuppan.

Meng, Xin. 2004. "Economic Restructuring and Income Inequality in Urban China," *Review of Income and Wealth*, Vol. 50, No. 3, pp. 357–379.

Meng, Xin, Robert Gregory, and Youjuan Wang. 2005. "Poverty, Inequality, and Growth in Urban China, 1986–2000," *Journal of Comparative Economics*, Vol. 33, No. 4, pp. 710–729.

Movshuk, Oleksandr. 2002. "The Reliability of China's Growth Figures: A Survey of Recent Statistical Controversies," *The Journal of Econometric Study of Northeast Asia*, Vol. 4, No. 1, pp. 31–45.

National Bureau of Statistics. 2000. *Comprehensive Statistical Data and Materials on 50 Years of New China*, and electronic data on accompanying CD-ROM, Beijing: China Statistical Publishing House.

National Bureau of Statistics. 2005a. *China Compendium of Statistics 1949–2004*, Beijing: China Statistics Press.

National Bureau of Statistics. 2005b. *[Province, Region, Municipality Name] Statistical Yearbook 2005* (2005 Statistical yearbooks for China's 31 provinces, autonomous regions, and municipalities), Beijing: China Statistics Press.

National Bureau of Statistics. 2006. "Announcement on Revised Result about Historical Data of China's Gross Domestic Products," 10 January 2006 release downloaded from NBS website (http://www.stats.gov.cn/english/newsandcomingevents/t20060110_402300302.htm).

National Bureau of Statistics. Various years. *China Statistical Yearbook*, 1999–2005 issues and electronic data on accompanying CD-ROMs, Beijing: China Statistics Press.

Pedroni, Peter and James Yudong Yao. 2006. "Regional Income Divergence in China," *Journal of Asian Economics*, Vol. 17, No. 2, pp. 294–315.

Ravallion, Martin and Shaohua Chen. 2004. "China's (Uneven) Progress against Poverty," World Bank Policy Research Working Paper 3408, Washington, D.C.: World Bank.

Sakamoto, Hiroshi. 2005. "Chugoku no Shokan Shotoku Kakusa: Doukou wo Shiru [Income Distribution among China's Provinces: Knowing the Trends]," Working Paper Series 2005–09, Kitakyushu: International Centre for the Study of East Asian Development.

Sakamoto, Hiroshi and Nazrul Islam. 2008. "Convergence across Chinese Provinces: an Analysis Using Markov Transition Matrix," *China Economic Review*, Vol. 19, No. 1, pp. 66–79.

State Statistical Bureau. Various years. *China Statistical Yearbook*, 1987–1998 issues and electronic data on CD-ROMs accompanying 1997–1998 issues, Beijing: China Statistical Publishing House.

Wan, Guanghua. 2004. "Accounting for Income Inequality in Rural China: a Regression-Based Approach," *Journal of Comparative Economics*, Vol. 32, No. 2, pp. 348–363.

Wan, Guanghua and Zhangyue, Zhou. 2005. "Income Inequality in Rural China: Regression-Based Decomposition Using Household Data," *Review of Development Economics*, Vol. 9, No. 1, pp. 107–120.

Weeks, Mevlen and James Yudong Yao. 2003. "Provincial Conditional Income Convergence in China," *Econometric Reviews*, Vol. 22, No. 1, pp. 59–77.

Wei, Shang-Jin. 1995. "The Open Door Policy and China's Rapid Growth: Evidence from City-Level Data," in Takatoshi Ito and Anne O. Krueger (eds.), *Growth Theories in Light of the East Asian Experience*, Chicago: University of Chicago Press, pp. 73–104.

Wu, Ximing and Jeffrey M. Perloff. 2004. "China's Income Distribution over Time: Reasons for Rising Inequality," CUDARE Working Papers, Paper 977, University of California: Berkeley.

Yao, Shujie and Zongyi Zhang. 2001. "On Regional Inequality and Diverging Clubs: a Case Study of Contemporary China," *Journal of Comparative Economics*, Vol. 29, No. 3, pp. 466–484.

Zhang, Kevin Honglin. 2001. "How Does Foreign Direct Investment Affect Economic Growth in China?" *Economics of Transition*, Vol. 9, No. 3, pp. 679–693.

Zhang, Wei. 2001. "Rethinking Regional Disparity in China," *Economics of Planning*, Vol. 34, No. 1–2, pp. 113–138.

Zhang, Xiaobo and Ravi Kanbur. 2005. "Spatial Inequality in Education and Health Care in China," *China Economic Review*, Vol. 16, No. 2, pp. 189–204.

Zhang, Zongyi, Aying Liu, and Shujie Yao. 2001. "Convergence of China's Regional Incomes: 1952–1997, 12(2–3) 243–258," *China Economic Review*, Vol. 13, No. 2–3, pp. 161–169.

7
How Have China's Intra- and Inter-Regional Input-Output Linkages Changed during Reform?

Shiro Hioki and Nobuhiro Okamoto

7.1 Introduction

The Chinese central government has tried to establish the internal division of labor between regions based on their comparative advantages and to deepen the economic interdependency among them. For instance, during the nineth Five Year Plan period, China launched the construction of seven major economic regions. By enhancing various kinds of inter-regional economic cooperation within each area, they tried to accelerate the economic integration of regions. In addition, they also aimed at building rational economic relationships between the areas based on comparative advantages of each area (Fan and Lu, 2001). Subsequently, since the beginning of the Western Development Program, large amounts of investments have been directed to the construction of infrastructures in interior areas. This program is expected to greatly enhance China's inter-regional economic linkages (Huang and Wei, 2001). We can find out from these examples that attaining spatially more integrated market economy and establishing spatial division of labor based on regional comparative advantages have been important policy objectives of the Chinese authorities.

The motivation behind this chapter is to consider the outcomes of the regional policies described above. For this purpose, we will ask the following questions: How have China's spatial economic linkages strengthened during the economic reform? How has China succeeded in deepening the economic interdependencies among its spatial units? How has the pattern of regional interdependencies changed? Quantitative analysis is needed to answer these questions and the input-output analysis is a representative approach for such a purpose. Thus we will make two kinds of input-output analyses in this chapter, namely (a) a multiplier analysis to measure the inter-temporal changes in the strength of spatial input-output linkages and (b) a Qualitative Input-Output Analysis (QIOA) to identify the structural changes in China's spatial linkages. In the first part of the analysis, we compute two kinds of multipliers to measure the linkage effects between sectors located in various regions. In the latter part, some important linkages are extracted and the structures constituted by those linkages are identified by a simple graph-theoretical method. We apply the structural analysis to two time points after the economic reform, namely 1987 and 1997. The inter-temporal comparison of the results is expected to provide new insights into the changes in China's spatial linkages.

The results of our analysis reveal that, compared to the intra-regional linkages, the overall inter-regional linkages among regions, on average, have weakened during the period and that the structure of production linkages has also changed considerably, indicating that the pattern of interdependency between regions has changed with deepening of the economic reform.

The remainder of this paper is organized as follows: Section 7.2 briefly explains the basic data, namely, China's Inter-Regional Input-Output (IRIO) tables; Section 7.3 illustrates the methodology that we use in this chapter; Section 7.4 presents and discusses the main empirical results; Section 7.5 interprets the results; Section 7.6 presents concluding remarks.

7.2   Data

We used two sets of China's IRIO tables as the most basic statistical data for our research. One is the 1997 table (Institute of Developing Economies-JETRO, 2003) and the other is the 1987 table (Ichimura and Wang, 2003).[1]

For the sake of inter-temporal comparison, we set nine sectors and seven regions, namely, agriculture (sector 1), mining (sector 2), light industry (sector 3), energy industry (sector 4), heavy industry (sector 5), construction (sector 6), transport and communication (sector 7), wholesale and retail (sector 8), and other services (sector 9) for sector classification, and the Northeast (NE), North China (NC), East China (EC), South China (SC), Central China (CC), the Northwest (NW) and the Southwest (SW) for regional classification respectively (abbreviation in parenthesis). There is a reasonable comparability between these two IRIO tables even though there are several discrepancies in sectoral and regional classifications between them. The activities included in each sector are listed in Table 7.1, showing that there are some differences in activities contained in the same sector of the tables. The most notable discrepancy among them is that communication services are included in sector 7 in the 1987 table, while they are included in sector 9 in the 1997 table. Next, the provinces included in each region are shown in Table 7.2 and the location of each region is shown in Figure 7.1. There are two discrepancies: one is that Inner Mongolia is included in North China in the 1987 table but in the Northwest in the 1997 table. The other discrepancy is that Chongqing had not been divided from Sichuan in 1987 but was separated as a municipal city in 1997. However this does not cause any problem for our analysis because both Sichuan and Chongqing are aggregated into the same regional unit, namely the Southwest. The discrepancies pointed out thus far can produce some errors in our analysis, but these are not expected to be so large since much of the differences made by the different scheme of regional and/or sectoral aggregation are averaged out when we work with the technical coefficients.

Table 7.1   Comparison of two interregional input-output tables for China

Sector	Ichimura and Wang (2003)	IDE(2003)
	9 sectors	30 sectors
	1 Agriculture	1 Agriculture
	2 Mining	2 Coal mining and processing
		3 Crude petroleum and natural gas products
		4 Metal ore mining
	3 Light industry	5 Non-ferrous mineral mining
		6 Manufacture of food products and tobacco processing
		7 Textile goods
		8 Wearing apparel, leather, furs, down and related products
		9 Sawmills and furniture
		10 Paper and products, printing and record medium reproduction
	4 Energy industry	11 Petroleum processing and coking
		24 Electricity, steam and hot water production and supply
		25 Gas production and supply
		26 Water production and supply
	5 Heavy industry	12 Chemicals
		13 Nonmetal mineral products
		14 Metals smelting and pressing
		15 Metal products
		16 Machinery and equipment
		17 Transport equipment
		18 Electric equipment and machinery
		19 Electric and telecommunication equipment
		20 Instruments, meters, cultural and office machinery
		21 Maintenance and repair of machine and equipment
		22 Other manufacturing products
		23 Scrap and waste
	6 Construction	27 Construction
	7 Transport and communication	28 Transport and warehousing
	8 Trade and restaurant	29 Wholesale and retail trade
	9 Services	30 Services (including communications)

Continued

Table 7.1   Continued

Sector	Ichimura and Wang (2003)		IDE(2003)	
	9 sectors		30 sectors	
Value added	Depreciation of capital	Value added	Depreciation of capital	
	Wages and salaries		Compensation of employee	
	Welfare		Production tax	
	Tax		Operation surplus	
	Others			
Final demand	Household consumption	Final demand	Rural household consumption	
			Urban household consumption	
	Social consumption		Government consumption	
	Fixed capital formation		Fixed capital formation	
	Changes in stocks		Changes in stocks	
	Export		Export	
	Import		Import	
	Discrepancy		Discrepancy	

Source: Prepared by authors from Institute of Developing Ecnomies-JETRO (2003) and Ichimura and Wang (2003).

7.3   Methodology

7.3.1   Multiplier analysis

In the first part of our empirical analysis, we compute two kinds of multipliers, namely the output multiplier and the input multiplier, in order to measure the overall changes in the strength of spatial input-output linkages. Although both the multipliers are derived from the IRIO tables, the models that each multiplier is based on differ from each other. The output multiplier is based on the Leontief demand-driven model,[2] which is the most conventional model in the input-output literature. On the other hand, the input multiplier is based on the Ghosh supply-driven model,[3] which, according to Dietzenbacher (1997), should be conceived as a price model. The output multiplier of sector j is defined as the jth column sum of the Leontief inverse matrix $(I-A)^{-1}$. It shows the amount of gross output in all sectors that is required directly and indirectly for a unit of final demand of sector j. It is a conventional measure of backward linkage effects of an industry since the backward linkage is a concept related to a purchasing industry's dependence on inputs sold by supplier industries. In our IRIO setting, the output multiplier of sector j in region R can be decomposed into two components following $\sum_S \sum_i b_{ij}^{SR} = \sum_i b_{ij}^{RR} + \sum_{S \neq R} \sum_i b_{ij}^{SR}$, where b_{ij}^{SR} (an element of the Leontief inverse matrix) measures the amount of gross output of sector i in region S that is required, directly and indirectly, for a unit of final output of

Table 7.2 Regional correspondance between 1987 and 1997

1987		1997	
Region	Provinces	Region	Provinces
North East	Liaoning, Jilin, Heilongjiang	North East	Liaoning, Jilin, Heilongjiang
North China	Beijing, Tianjin	North Municiparities	Beijing, Tianjin
	Hebei, Shandong Inner Mongolia	North Coast	Hebei, Shandong
East China	Shanghai, Jiangsu, Zhejiang	East Coast	Shanghai, Jiangsu, Zhejiang
South China	Guangdong, Fujian, Hainan	South Coast	Guangdong, Fujian, Hainan
Central China	Shanxi, Henan, Anhui	Central China	Shanxi, Henan, Anhui
	Hubei, Hunan, Jiangxi		Hubei, Hunan, Jiangxi
North West	Shaanxi, Gansu, Ningxia Qinghai, Xinjiang	North West	Shaanxi, Gansu, Ningxia Qinghai, Xinjiang Inner Mongolia
South West	Sichuan, Quizhou, Yunnan	South West	Sichuan, Chongqing, Guizhou
	Guangxi, Tibet		Guangxi, Tibet, Yunnan

Source: Prepared by authors.

sector j in region R. The equation shows that the total output multiplier (i.e., the left side of the equation) can be decomposed into two additive components: the intra-regional portion (i.e., the first term of the right side of the equation) and the inter-regional portion (i.e., the second term). The input multiplier of sector i, on the other hand, is defined as the i-th row sum of the Ghosh inverse matrix $(I-B)^{-1}$. It shows the total increase in the output values of all sectors, due to an initial one Yuan increase in the primary costs of sector i (Dietzenbacher, 2002). A high input multiplier of a sector indicates that the sector sells its output directly or indirectly to many sectors and therefore a small price increase of the sector's product causes considerable price increase of many sectors' products through cost-push processes. The input multiplier is a widely used measure of the forward linkage effects (Beyers, 1976; Jones, 1976; Miller and Blair, 1985; Dietzenbacher, 2002). In our IRIO setting, the input multiplier of sector i in region S can also be decomposed into two components following $\sum_R \sum_j g_{ij}^{SR} = \sum_j g_{ij}^{SS} + \sum_{R \neq S} \sum_j g_{ij}^{SR}$, where g_{ij}^{SR} (an element of the Ghosh inverse matrix) measures the output value increase of sector j in region R that is induced, directly and indirectly, from one Yuan increase of the primary costs of sector i in region S. The equation shows that, as the case of the output multiplier, the total input multiplier can be decomposed into intra- and inter-regional portions.

Figure 7.1   Location of each region

Note: This figure is based on the regional aggregation scheme of 1997. In the regional aggregation scheme of 1987, Inner Mongolia is aggregated into North China, not the Northwest.

Source: Prepared by authors from Institute of Developing Ecnomies-JETRO(2003) and Ichimura and Wang(2003).

7.3.2   Qualitative input-output analysis (QIOA)

We use the methodology of QIOA introduced by Aroche-Reyes (1996) to identify the structure of China's spatial input-output linkages. QIOA is intended to reveal the underlying structure of an input-output table by identifying the intermediate transactions that are important. The overall strategy of our analysis can be explained as follows: (a) Identify "important cells" in the technical coefficient matrix using a mathematical formula; (b) Convert the technical coefficient matrix into a corresponding binary matrix (i.e., adjacency matrix), in which entries of the important cells take value of unity and the unimportant ones, zero. The adjacency matrix shows a structure of important linkages. However, it only shows which sectors are directly linked together through the important linkages; (c) Take indirect linkages into consideration, too. Suppose that there exist important transaction flows from sector j to sector k, and from sector k to sector l. Therefore the linkages from sector j to sector k and from sector k to sector *l* are identified as important. Then suppose that there also exists an important linkage from sector *j* to sector *l* (through sector *k*). We also take into account such indirect linkages using a graph-theoretical method; (d) Obtain a total structure of important linkages by taking both directly and indirectly important linkages into consideration. Compare the structures in different time points to elucidate how the skeleton of spatial input-output linkages has changed during the period of analysis.

We begin with a formula to identify important cells in the technical coefficient matrix *A*. Following Aroche-Reyes (1996), we adopt a formula introduced by Schintke and Stäglin (1988) and Jilek (1971). The formula aims at finding important cells in *A* judging by the impact on the elements of the Leontief inverse matrix when an element in *A* changes in a given proportion. The tolerable limit r_{ij} of change in each technical coefficient a_{ij} is computed by the following equation, so that the output in any related sector varies at most by 1 percent, while final demand remains fixed. The equation is

$$r_{ij} = \frac{100}{a_{ij}[b_{ji} + 100(b_{ii}/\tau_i)\tau_j]}, \tag{7.1}$$

where b_{ij} denotes the corresponding entry in the Leontief inverse matrix, τ_i and τ_j denote the gross output of sector *i* and *j* respectively. If a technical coefficient a_{ij} increases by more than the tolerable limit r_{ij}, then output in a related sector will increase by more than 1 percent. Therefore the less r_{ij} is, the smaller is the change in a_{ij} required to have large effects on the output of related sectors. We identify such entries as important cells (to put it differently, the linkage from sector *i* to sector *j* is regarded to be important). Conventionally an entry in *A* is identified as important when r_{ij} is not greater than 20 percent (Aroche-Reyes 1996, 2002; Ghosh and Roy, 1998).

Next, we turn to the equation

$$(I-A)^{-1} = A^0 + A^1 + A^2 + A^3 \ldots, \tag{7.2}$$

where $A^0 \equiv I$. We convert each matrix layer A^i (*i* = 0, 1, 2, ...) to the corresponding adjacency matrix W^i (*i* = 0, 1, 2, ...). The conversion of *A* into *W* is implemented based on the following equation

$$w_{ij} \begin{cases} = 1, & if \quad r_{ij} < 20 \\ = 0, & if \quad r_{ij} \geq 20, \end{cases} \tag{7.3}$$

where $W = (w_{ij})$ and r_{ij} is the tolerable limit of change for a_{ij} defined by equation (7.1). For the layer of which order is higher than 2, the following equation (7.4) is applied to convert A^k into W^k.

$$W^k = W^1 W^{k-1}, \tag{7.4}$$

The last step is to obtain the qualitative Leontief inverse matrix ψ. The derivation of the matrix is based on the following equation (7.5)

$$\psi = W^0 + W^1 + W^2 + W^3 + \ldots, \tag{7.5}$$

where $W^0 = I$. Note that the matrix multiplications in (7.4) and the summation of W^k in (7.5) should be done in Boolean fashion. An entry ψ_{ij} in ψ will be unity if sectors i and j are connected through a path, regardless of the number of steps needed to go from i to j (Aroche-Reyes, 1996). We regard them as important among all linkages in the following analysis. The resulting structures of important linkages will be shown by directed graphs in the next section.

In some cases, we will want to know about the role of a sector in the structures. For this purpose, we compute Centrality Index (CI) for each sector in each structure. Following Aroche-Reyes (1996), we define the CI of a sector as the ratio of the in-degree to the out-degree of the sector. A sector is categorized as a sink, central, or source if the CI is greater than, equal to, or less than unity. A sink sector has relatively more input linkages than output linkages. It is located at the top of the hierarchy of intermediate transactions between sectors and/or supplies more final goods rather than intermediate goods. A source sector has relatively more output linkages than input linkages. It is important as a supplier of intermediate goods (typically raw materials) to many sectors in the economy. The central sectors have intermediate character between the sink and the source.[4]

It is worthwhile pointing out that we work with the layers derived from *the technical coefficient matrix A*, not with the layers derived from the *intermediate transaction matrix Z*. In other words, we mainly see the technical relationship between production sectors in this present analysis. The latter approach arose from the Minimal Flow Analysis (MFA) introduced by Schnabl (1994), in which the volume and structure of final demands are also taken into consideration. Hioki et al (2005) applied MFA to analyze the structural changes in China's spatial input-output linkages.

7.4   Empirical results

The results of the multiplier analysis show that the IRIO linkages as a whole have generally weakened during the period of our analysis. Figures 7.2.A and B show the output multiplier and the input multiplier of each region.[5] During the period of our analysis, overall backward and forward linkages in all regions have increased considerably, showing that the degree of intermediation has strengthened (this might be a common phenomenon observed in most growing economies). However, as shown in Figures 7.3.A and B, the ratio of the intra-regional linkages to total has increased in many regions, suggesting that industries in a region have mainly intensified their productive relationships with industries within the same region (the Northwest is an exception), leading to a relative weakening of the inter-regional linkages. It follows from these results that China's regional economies have slightly moved toward increased self-sufficiency during the period of our analysis.[6]

Next, let us turn to the QIOA. The results show that some major changes took place in the structure of spatial input-output linkages in China, although there

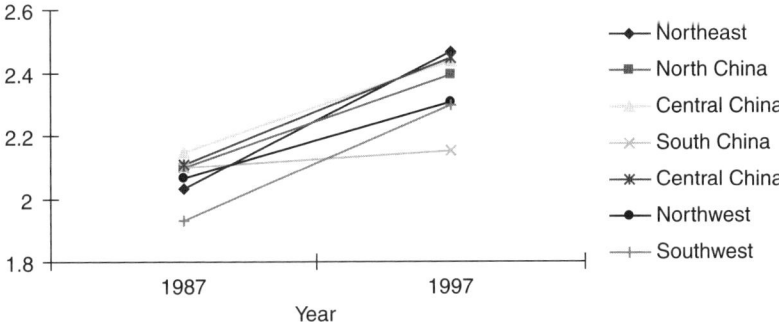

Figure 7.2A　The average output multiplier of each region

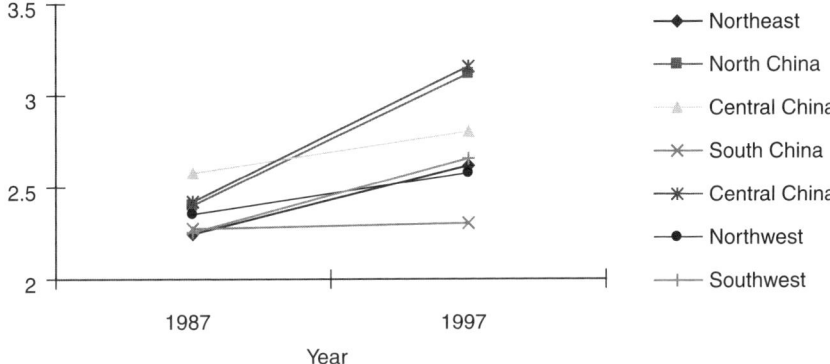

Figure 7.2B　The average input multiplier of each region

are aspects of continuity, too. Figures 7.4 and 7.5.A–D present summary information on the important linkages in both years. Figures 7.6 and 7.7 illustrate the identified structure of the important linkages in both years. (For the abbreviations of sectors and regions, see Section 7.2) For the sake of convenience, we derived Figures 7.8, 7.9, 7.10, and 7.11 from Figures 7.6 and 7.7 to show more clearly the changes and continuity in the structure of spatial input-output linkages. The findings obtained from these tables and figures are summarized as follows:

First, as shown in Figure 7.4, although the numbers of important linkages in both years are almost the same, the proportion of the intra-regional linkages to total has gone up, indicating that the intra-regional linkages have intensified relative to the inter-regional linkages over the period 1987–1997. This is consistent with the fact finding from our multiplier analysis presented earlier. The analysis of the Strongly Connected Components (SCCs) in the structures leads to the same conclusion. A SCC is defined as a set of sectors such that any pair of them is strongly connected.[7] Strongly Connected Components (SCCs) draw our attention especially because two sectors are expected to exercise, directly or indirectly, positive influence on each other if they are strongly connected. In other words, a SCC corresponds to an "industrial complex," in which sectors stimulate

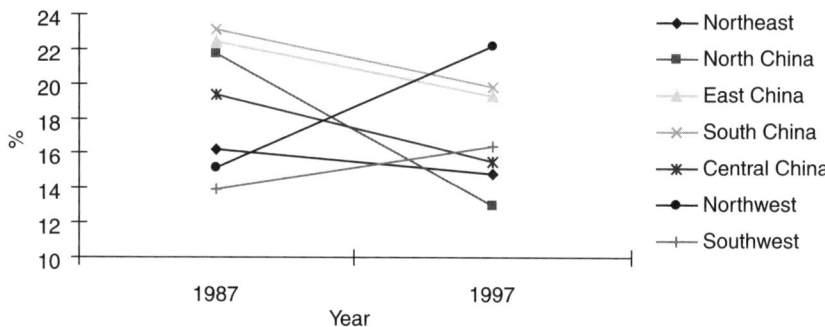

Figure 7.3A   Interregional portion in the output multiplier

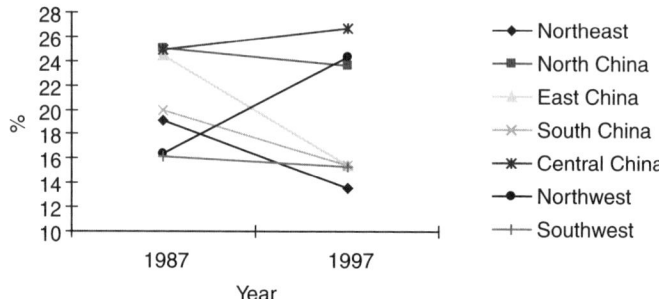

Figure 7.3B   Interregional portion in the input multiplier

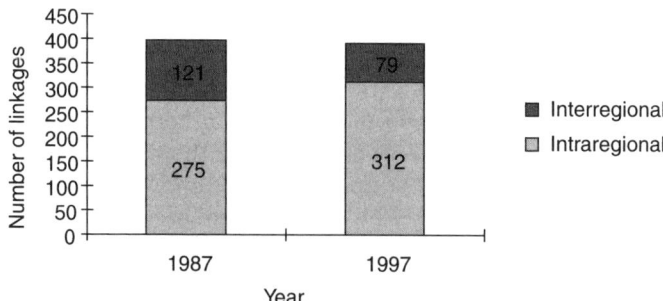

Figure 7.4   Compostion of important linkages

intermediate transactions from each other. The identified SCCs for 1987 and 1997 are listed in Table 7.3, from which we can find that a SCC, namely, SCC No.2 in 1987, consists of many sectors located in four different regions (namely, the Northeast, North China, East China, and Central China), while every SCC in 1997 is only made up of sectors located in a same region. This finding regarding SCCs provides additional evidence to support the finding from multiplier analysis presented earlier.

Table 7.3 Strongly connected components and sectors included in each SCC

	1987		1997
SCC	Sectors included	SCC	Sectors included
1	NE2, NE4, NE7	1	NE1, NE2, NE3, NE4, NE5,
2	NE3, NE5, NE8, NE9,		NE7, NE8, NE9
	NC3, NC5, EC3, EC5,	2	NC1, NC2, NC3, NC4, NC5,
	CC1, CC3, CC5, CC8, CC9		NC6, NC7, NC8, NC9
3	NC2, NC4	3	EC3, EC5, EC8, EC9
4	EC4, EC7	4	EC4, EC7
5	SC1, SC3, SC5	5	SC3, SC5
6	SC4, SC7	6	SC4, SC8, SC9
7	CC2, CC4, CC7	7	CC1, CC2, CC3, CC4, CC5,
8	NW1, NW3, NW5, NW8, NW9		CC7, CC8, CC9
9	NW2, NW4, NW7	8	NW1, NW2, NW3, NW4, NW5,
10	SW2, SW4		NW7, NW8, NW9
11	SW5, SW8, SW9	9	SW1, SW3, SW5, SW8, SW9
		10	SW2, SW4

Note: For abbreviations for regions and sectors, see Section 7.2 of this chapter.

Second, as shown in Figures 7.5.A–D, the number of the intra-regional linkages is distributed more equally across regions in comparison with the number of inter-regional linkages. Besides, Figure 7.8 shows that many intra-regional linkages have been continuously important during the period of our analysis. The structure composed of important intra-regional linkages is very similar in every region. In the structure, mining, energy, transportation and communication in many regions commonly belong to the source sector, while agriculture, light industry, and construction belong to the sink sector. Heavy industry, retail and wholesale trade, and other services in many regions belong to the sink sector, although their characteristics are close to the central sector since their CI is near to one.[8]

In comparison with the case of the intra-regional linkages, considerable changes have occurred in the structure of inter-regional linkages. For the sake of simplicity, we summarize the results for each region.

7.4.1 The Northeast

For the Northeast, a region which has a long history of manufacturing industries, two major changes can be observed. First, many incoming linkages, which used to be important in 1987, have become unimportant by 1997, as shown in Figures 7.5.C and D. From Figure 7.11 we see that most of these weakened linkages go from several industries in North China, East China, and Central China to the heavy industry in the Northeast, indicating that the importance of the heavy industry in the Northeast as a purchaser for the industries located in the surrounding regions has decreased. This change might be attributable to the stagnation of the old heavy industry in the Northeast economy.[9] Second, as Figures 7.5.A and B show, the number of outgoing linkages from the Northeast has almost doubled during the decade. Figure 7.10 clearly shows how this increase has occurred. The most notable change is that the many outgoing linkages from the mining industry in this region to the various industries located in North China and East China have strengthened. In addition, the outgoing linkages from energy, heavy industry, and transportation in this region have changed and become important. This finding indicates that the level of production of various industries, especially the mining industry in the Northeast has become more dependent on the demand from industries of the surrounding regions.[10]

7.4.2   North China and Central China

In North China and Central China, we can observe two common tendencies. First, the number of important outgoing linkages in both regions has decreased considerably as shown in Figures 7.5.A and B. However, we can also find that both regions have strengthened some outgoing linkages to other regions, despite the general tendency toward decreasing such linkages. In the case of North China, the outgoing linkages that changed to be unimportant can be roughly categorized into two groups, namely (a) a set of outgoing linkages from mining, energy, and heavy industry in North China to several industries in Central China and (b) a set of outgoing linkages from several industries in North China to some industries, especially heavy industry, in the Northeast (Figure 7.11). At the same time, we can find out from Figure 7.10 that the outgoing linkages from several industries, especially mining, in North China to various industries in East China have strengthened to be important ones. A similar claim can be made for Central China. Some outgoing linkages from this region to the Northeast and North China, which were originally counted as important linkages, turned out to be unimportant. However some new important linkages going out to East China have been established at the same time (Figures 7.10 and 7.11).

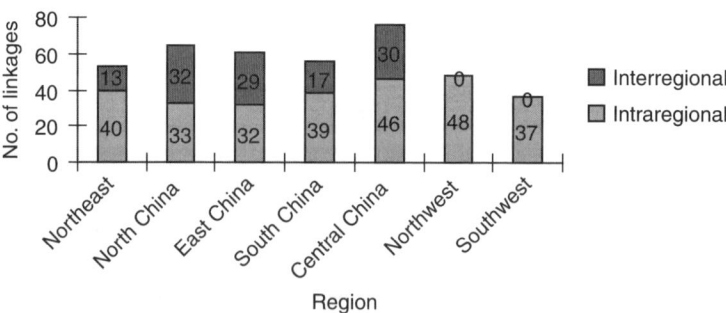

Figure 7.5A   Important outgoing linkages in 1987

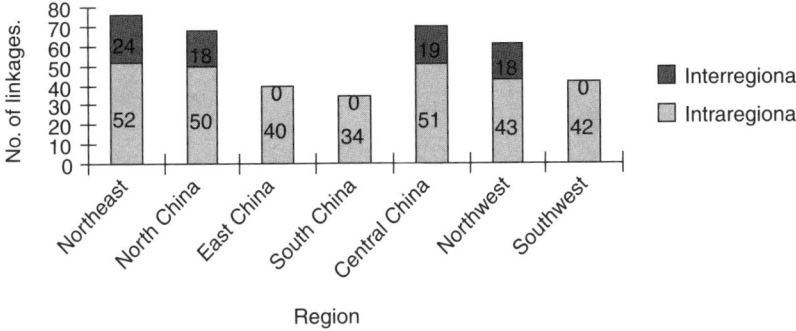

Figure 7.5B Important outgoing linkages in 1997

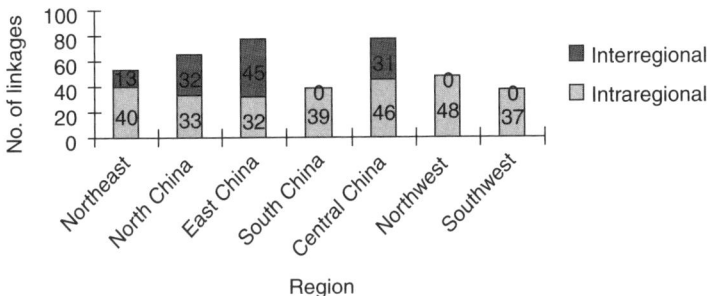

Figure 7.5C Important incoming linkages in 1987

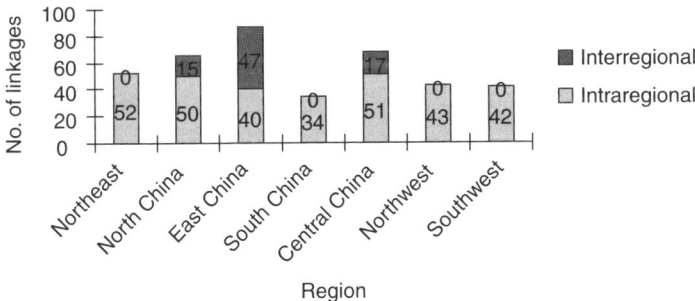

Figure 7.5D Important incoming linkages in 1997

Second, the number of important incoming linkages to North China and Central China has also decreased considerably (see Figures 7.5.C and D), even as these two regions have intensified some other incoming linkages from other regions at the same time. For example, as shown in Figure 7.11, the linkages coming from several industries in the Northeast, East China, and Central China to some industries, especially to heavy industry in North China used to be important in 1987, but they have weakened to be unimportant by 1997. At the same

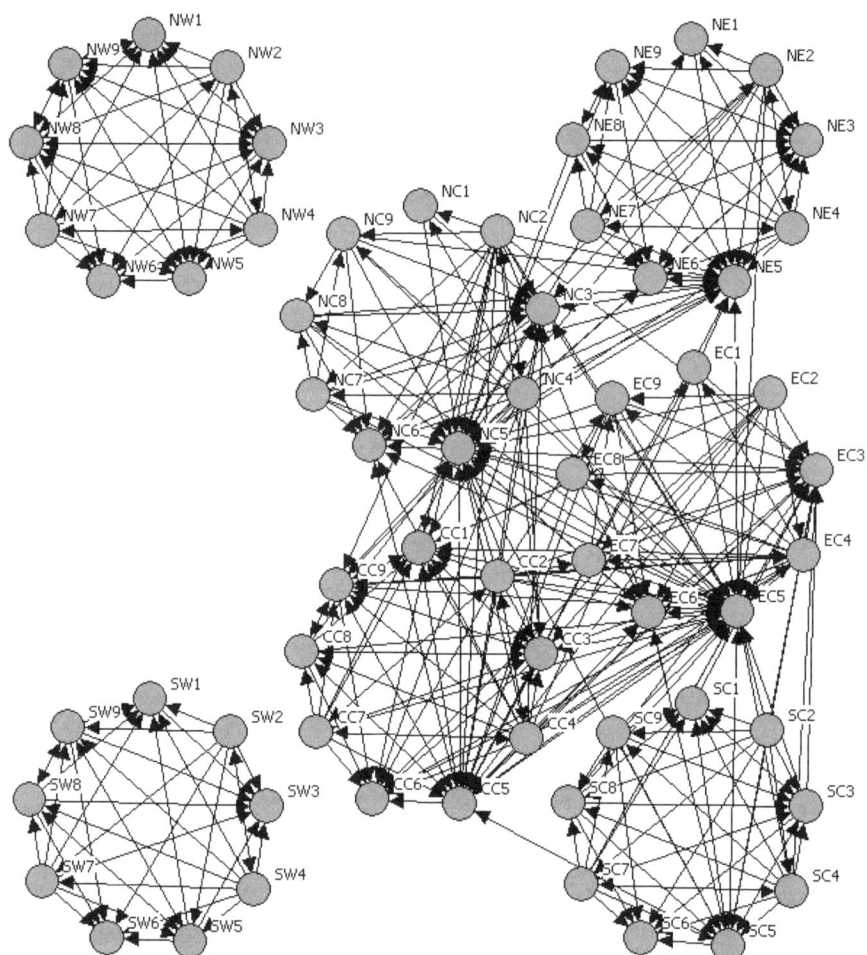

Figure 7.6   Important linkages in 1987

time several linkages coming from the Northeast to this region have changed to become important, as shown in Figure 7.10. As for Central China, the incoming linkages from mining, energy, and heavy industry in North China and East China to many industries in Central China were originally counted as important. However, they have changed to be unimportant, while Central China has newly established some important incoming linkages from industries in the Northwest, as shown in Figure 7.10. This last finding is of interest from the viewpoint of China's regional development policy since it indicates that further development of Central China's industries will stimulate the growth of industries in the Western region through the IRIO linkages between them.

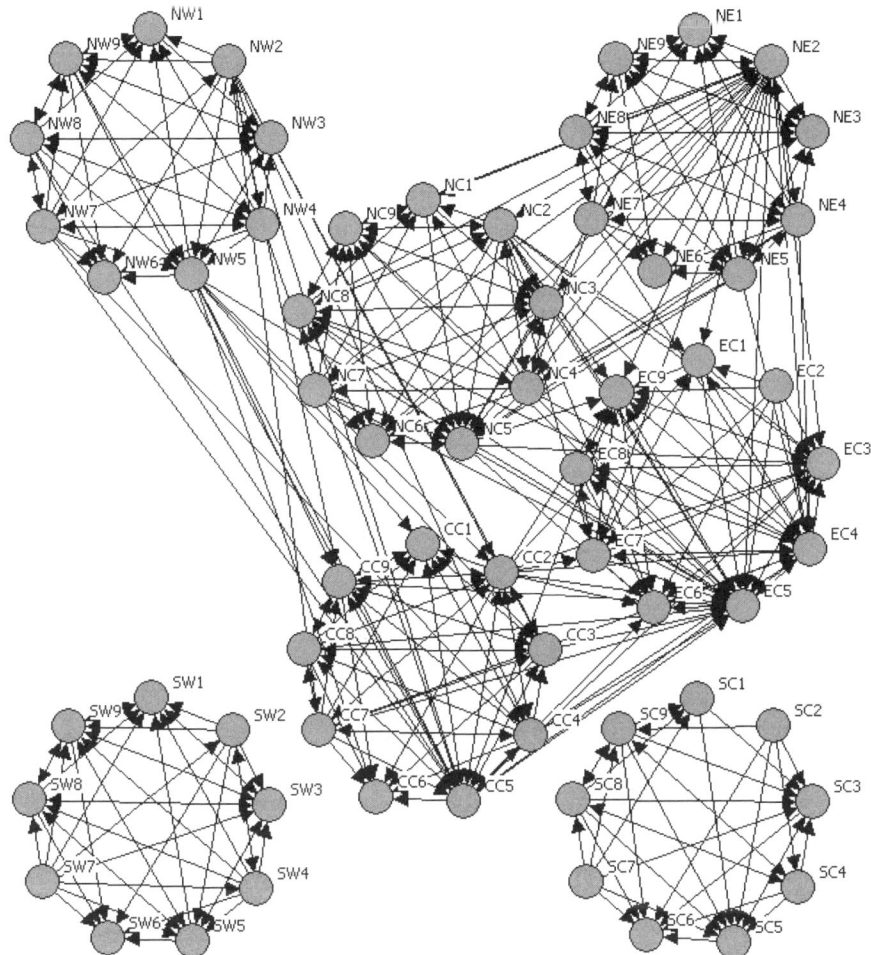

Figure 7.7   Important linkages in 1997

7.4.3   East China and South China

These two regions were expected to become "growth poles" emanating spillovers to surrounding inland regions. Based on a so-called gradient theory (or step-ladder theory), which dominated the thinking of Chinese policymakers for much of the 1980s, Chinese central government's regional development policy put priority on coastal regions, especially South China and granted these regions various kinds of preferential treatments such as the establishment of Special Economic Zones (SEZs). Accordingly public investments were redirected from inland regions to coastal regions (Wang and Hu, 1999). Subsequently at the beginning of the 1990s, Chinese central government proposed a so-called T-character development strategy, which aimed at radiating the spillover effects of East China (more exactly, Yangtze River delta zone)

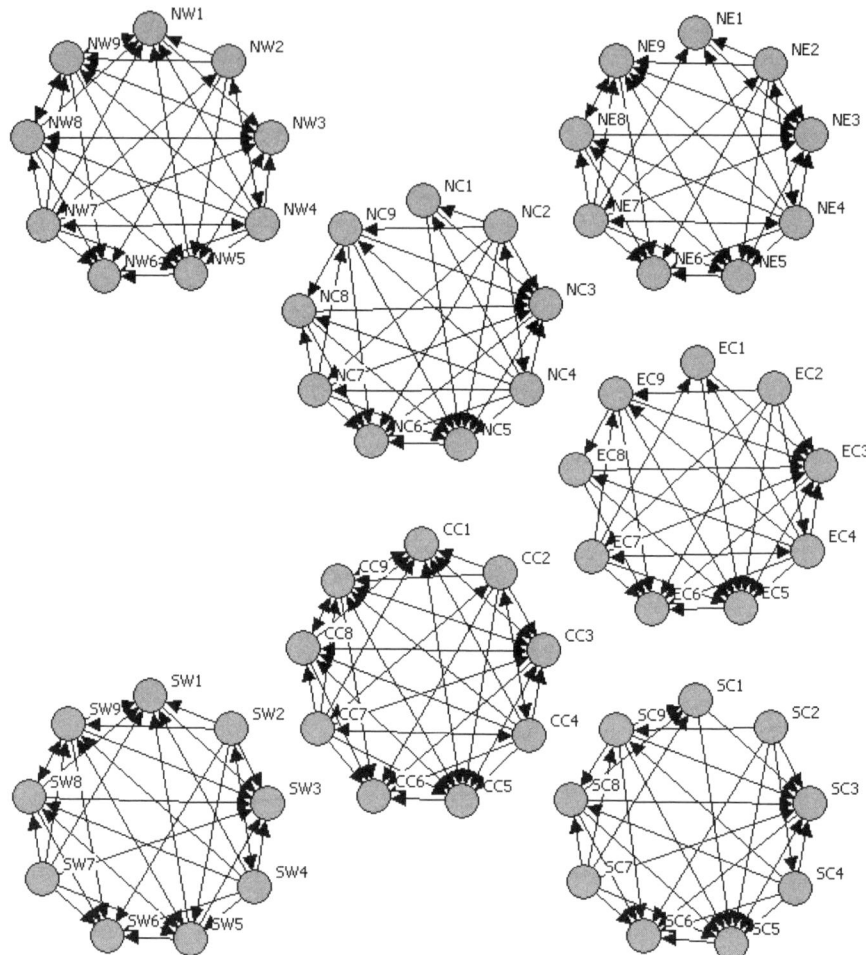

Figure 7.8   Stably important intra-regional linkages

to interior regions up through the Yangtze River (Huang and Wei, 2001). The common view underlying these regional policies was that the fruits of development in the coastal regions would eventually spread to surrounding inland regions.

Our analysis, however, reveals that the two East and South China regions have changed quite differently in terms of linkages with surrounding regions. There used to be a number of important linkages going out from several industries (especially light industry and heavy industry) of both regions to various industries in Central China and North China. All of these outgoing linkages, however, have become unimportant by 1997 (see Figures 7.5.A and B and 7.11), indicating that the importance of these two regions as suppliers of intermediate goods or services to industries in their surrounding regions has decreased. It is also consistent

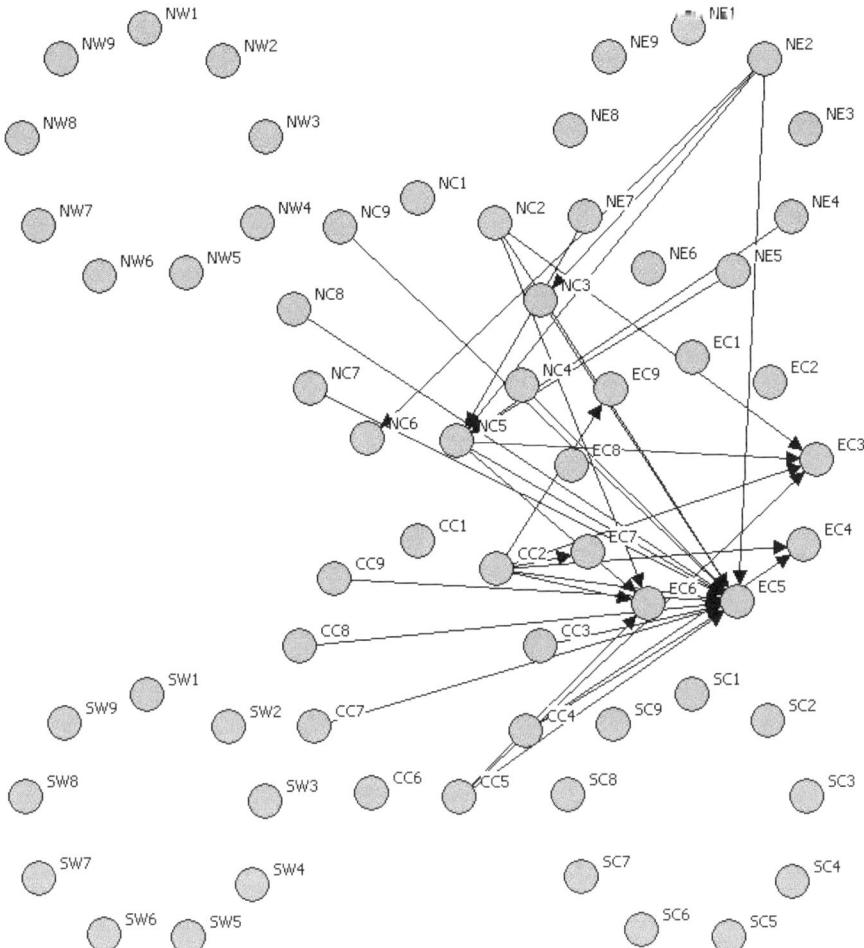

Figure 7.9   Stable important inter-regional linkages

Note: A line from sector i to sector j in this figure means that the linkage from sector i to sector j is important both in 1987 and 1997.

with the fact that inter-regional forward linkage effects of these regions have also declined considerably.

However, East China and South China differ markedly with regard to changes in the incoming linkages from other regions. In the case of East China, the number of important linkages coming from other regions has slightly increased, as shown in Figure 7.5.C and D. Figure 7.9 shows that there are a number of stably important linkages from various industries (especially mining and heavy industry) located in the Northeast, North China and Central China to several

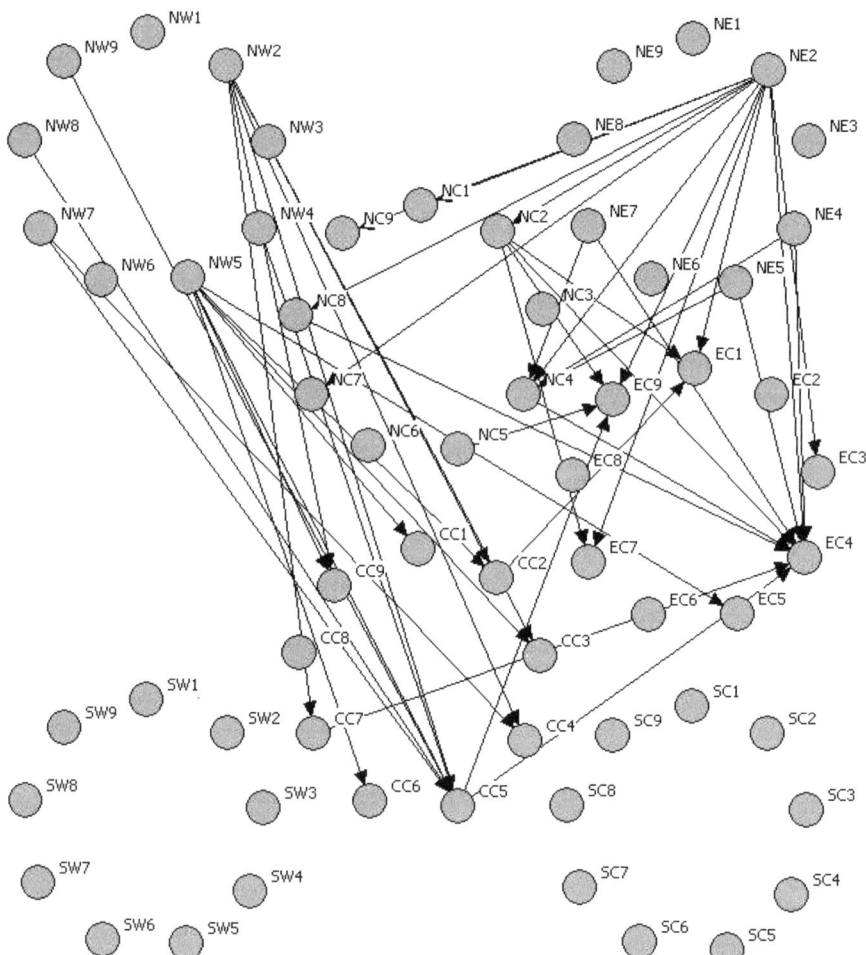

Figure 7.10   Strengthened inter-regional linkages

Note: A line from sector i to sector j in this figure means that the linkage from sector i to sector j was not important in 1987, but changed to be important in 1997.

industries (especially light and heavy industry) in East China. Moreover, Figure 7.10 shows that East China has also increased some important incoming linkages from industries (especially mining and heavy industry) in the Northeast, Central China and North China. These findings show that East China has become more important as an absorber of intermediate goods supplied from surrounding regions. From the standpoint of input-output analysis, it can be concluded that East China is growing up to be a "growth pole" emanating the backward linkage effects on its neighboring regions.

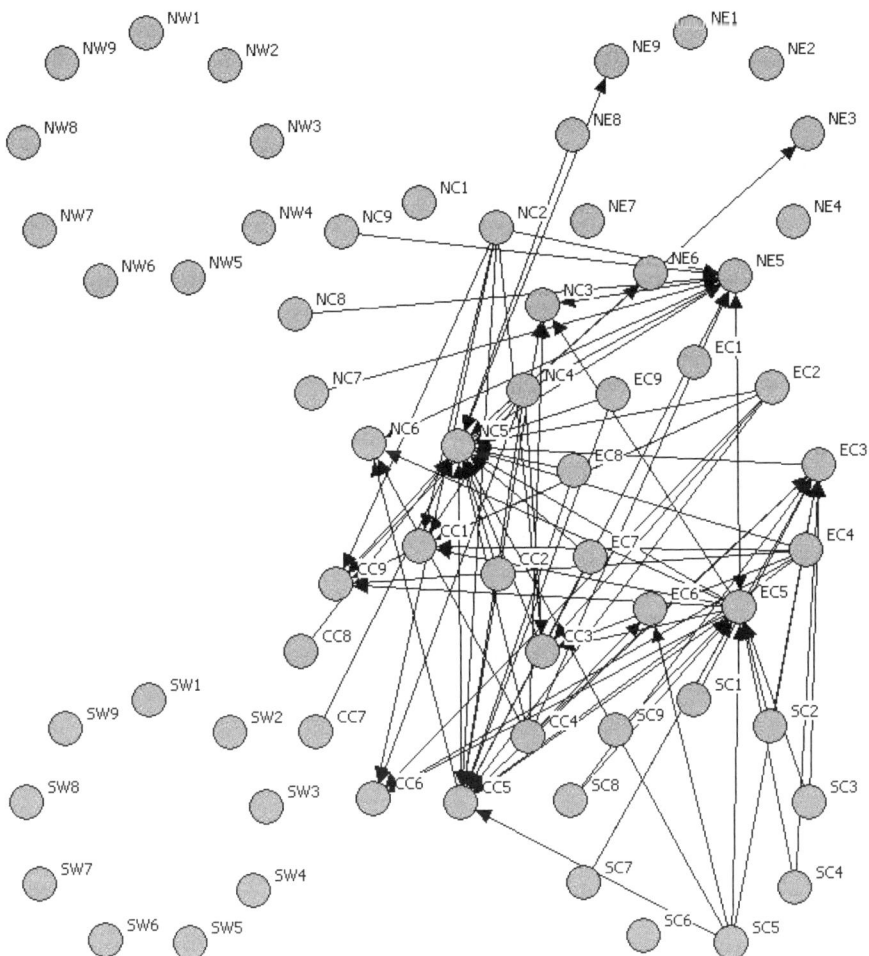

Figure 7.11 Weakened inter-regional linkages

Note: A line from sector i to sector j means that the linkage from sector i to sector j was important in 1987, not in 1997.

In contrast, South China has had no important incoming linkage during the same time period, being isolated from other regions. This finding suggests that the backward linkage effects of South China on surrounding regions have been limited. This may partly be attributed to the fact that rapid industrialization in South China took place largely in the form of processing trade, in which they import most of the raw materials and capital equipments from outside the country and export most of the processed goods to international markets. As a result, the South China economy tends to have close linkages with international markets rather with other regions inside the country.

7.4.4 The Northwest and the Southwest

With the present tolerance limit r_{ij} of 20 percent, we can find no important linkage connecting these two western regions with central or coastal regions in 1987 (see Figure 7.6). As Figure 7.7 shows, the Southwest remained isolated from other regions even in 1997, indicating that the self-sufficient characteristic of the Southwest economy had been persistent during the decade. However, Figure 7.10 shows that the Northwest, on the other hand, has established many important outgoing linkages mainly from its mining and heavy industry to various industries in Central China. This finding suggests that industries in the Northeast have become more dependent on the intermediate demand from Central China. The ongoing Western Development Program is expected to accelerate this tendency of Western economy becoming more integrated with other regions.

7.5 Interpretation of the results

It is beyond the scope of this paper to specify the reasons why China's regional economies have moved toward self-sufficiency with the deepening of the economic reform. Nevertheless it is useful for further research to consider some of the possible reasons briefly. It should be noted in this regard that large investments on infrastructure constructions has enhanced China's transportation capacity and eased the bottlenecks to transportation.[11] Also, some institutional factors that have earlier hindered China's market integration (such as the immaturity of inter-regional payments and settlement mechanisms) have been weakened gradually along with the market-oriented reform. In the light of these changes, the observed tendency toward autarchy seems to be a somewhat unexpected result. The possible causes might be following: (a) the inaccuracy of China's statistical information (b) the substitution of domestic trade by international trade (c) the formation of industrial clusters in coastal areas (d) the influence of the fiefdom economy or the market fragmentation caused by the local protectionism, and (e) the problem associated with the aggregation of regional units. Let us briefly investigate each possible reason below.

7.5.1 Statistical inaccuracy issues

It is possible that the inaccuracy of China's statistical information makes the estimation of inter-regional transactions in the IRIO tables to be understated. According to Zhang (2004), China's transportation statistics are mainly based on the statistical information provided by ministries responsible for the administration of each mode of transportation, with the exception of the pipeline statistics that are directly collected by the National Bureau of Statistics (NBS) from China National Petroleum and Natural Gas Corporation Group and China Petrochemical Corporation Group. For example, the Ministry of Railways and the General Administration of Civil Aviation of China are responsible for the collection of railways transportation statistics and civil aviation transportation statistics, respectively. The Ministry of Transportation bears the responsibility for the collection of highways and waterways transportation statistics. The pipeline, railways and air transportation statistics are, by their nature, thought to have relatively good reliability, and so these can be of less concern. The main problem therefore lies in the quality of highways and waterways transportation statistics.

Let us first consider the problem in terms of China's statistical information system. The most serious problem is that the system has not caught up with the rapid changes taking place in China's transportation sectors. Originally, China's highways and waterways transportation statistics were based on "census" data regularly reported from transportation enterprises, most of which belonged to the state-owned sector. It is known that this kind of statistical reporting system has gradually become unable to give a true picture of China's transportation activities as more and more private enterprises and Township Village Enterprises entered the transportation business, which used to be previously a state monopoly. In order to mitigate this problem, since early 1990s, the NBS and the Ministry of Transportation have tried to construct a new system, in which the data were gathered from both census and sample surveys, covering all registered business units, including household or joint-household business.[12] Zhang (2004) reports that the scheme of road sample surveys has been improved five times so far, so that the system now can give a reasonably accurate picture concerning such basic indicators as the freight traffic, the passenger traffic, the passenger-kilometers, and the freight ton-kilometers at the national level concern, although the same indicators at the sub-regional level (i.e., below province) may be often inaccurate. However, other researchers such as Wang (1997), Yuan and Liu (1997) think that the improvements in the statistical system are still inadequate and do not work very well in reality. In view of this suspected weakness, it is possible that there is considerable understatement in China's highways and waterways freight statistics.

Second, the issue may also be viewed from the point of view of consistency between transportation statistics and other statistics. By showing growing gaps between the growth of transportation and that of fuel use in transportation, Huenemann (2001) claims that China's statistics of road and water freights for 1990s fail to capture a significant portion of the real freights, and that the problem is getting worse. One problem with this argument is that it relies on the accuracy of the fuel consumption statistics. Many observers think that while China's energy statistics were relatively good in the early 1990s, their quality has deteriorated since the mid-1990s. Within energy statistics, the quality of oil production and consumption statistics is thought to be much better than that of coal statistics (Sinton, 2001). We therefore assume that the fuel consumption statistics in transportation can be used to evaluate the extent of errors in highways and waterways transportation statistics. Let us assume that after taking changes in fuel consumption efficiencies for transport sectors into consideration, the remaining gap between the growth of fuel consumption and that of freight volume (ton-km) comes from the statistical errors alone. This would suggest that the official freight volume data might be under-counted by 27.6 percent (we take 1987 as the reference year for this comparison).

Assuming that there is considerable undercount in China's 1997 transportation statistics compared to that of 1987, how does rectification of the error change the results of our analysis? Based on the estimation methods of the 1997 IRIO table, we may expect that results will be affected mainly through the following two different channels. On the one hand, taking into account of previously neglected transportation would cause domestic exports and imports of many sectors in each province to increase to some extent. This would lead to increase in inter-provincial linkages. On the other hand, the rectification of undercounting will also entail changes in the combination ratio of various modes of transportation. Because the errors of omission are believed to come from highways and waterways transportation, the ratio of highways and waterways to whole transportation will go up, whereas the ratio of railways transportation will go down. In general, a relative increase of highways transportation tends to shorten the average transport distance of estimated intra- and inter-regional transactions, since, in China, highways transportation is generally used for hauling cargo over relatively short distances.[13] By contrast, the relative increase of waterways transportation will tend to extend the average distance of transactions. However this effect cannot be overestimated because much of the un-captured waterways freights come mainly from non-state water transportation entities such as private barges, which generally engage themselves in very short distance transportation.[14] Besides, it must be noted that our finding of decreasing inter-regional linkages is obtained in a regional aggregation scheme in which each major region covers a wide area, and hence contains within itself considerably long intra-regional distance. Taking all these things into consideration, our conclusion is that the adjustment to account for possible statistical errors arising from missing highways and waterways transportation will increase inter-regional linkage measures to some extent, but not to the extent that our basic conclusion will be overturned.[15]

7.5.2   Substitution of domestic trade by international trade

Turning to cause (2), there is no doubt that it can partly explain the observed tendency toward relatively weakened inter-regional linkages. This conjecture can be confirmed by examining intermediate goods absorption of each major region. The intermediate goods absorption of a region consists of two parts, namely local goods and non-local goods. The latter in turn can be divided into two parts, namely goods from the rest of China and international goods. We calculate the ratio of international goods to non-local goods in both years to see whether there has been a substitution or not. It is found that the average value of this ratio for seven regions has increased from 8.4 percent in 1987 to 26.3 percent in 1997, indicating that a part of the relative weakening of inter-regional linkages can be explained by the substitution of international trade for domestic trade.

7.5.3   Formation of industrial clusters in coastal areas

So far as cause (3) is concerned, it is likely to be important in coastal areas, since several massive industrial agglomerations have actually taken shape in such coastal regions as the Pearl River Delta Zone in Guangdong and Yangtze River Delta Zone in East China. In a cluster, industries are likely to have denser linkages with related industries within the cluster than with those outside the cluster. The relative importance of intra-regional transactions is therefore likely to be higher in cluster because of the higher degree of intermediation (Wolf, 2000).

7.5.4 Fiefdom

The cause (4) has been highlighted by such authors as Young (2000) and Poncet (2003). In his influential paper, Young (2000) presents an analysis showing that China has evolved into an economy characterized by fragmented domestic market controlled by local governments. By estimating provincial border effects over the 1987–1997 period, Poncet (2003) also comes to a similar conclusion that China's market fragmentation caused by the local protectionism has deteriorated over time. It is possible that artificial market fragmentation had a negative impact on the volume of inter-regional trade in China. Relying solely on this explanation, one would conclude that China's distinctive reform strategy had a very strong influence on the pattern of interactions among its spatial units. In one sense, our finding of relatively weakened inter-regional linkages may be taken as additional empirical evidence to support the Young-Poncet proposition.

However, it is important to note that a growing number of researchers are presenting results that are inconsistent with the Young-Poncet proposition.[16] For example, Li et al (2004) and Development Research Center of State Council (2004) find from a large-scale sample survey that local protectionism has weakened considerably during the decades of reform, even though the problem still exists. They also find that the local protection measures that are most frequently observed are the ones that hinder labor mobility rather than trade, contradicting Poncet (2003).[17] The results show clearly that the view that most Chinese scholars and research institutes have regarding local protectionism contradicts that propounded by Young and Poncet. Second, a good number of studies looking into spatial integration of market of individual commodities have come up with positive conclusions. (See, for example, Wang et al (1997), Yu and Huang(1998) for rice market; Wu (1999) for wheat, maize, and hog market; Park et al (2002) for maize and rice market; Huang et al (2002) for maize, soy bean, and rice market; Li and Sun (2004) for beer market; Sun and Xu (2005) for lumber market). Applying the cointegration approach or the parity bounds model to time series of price data on same commodities obtained from different regions, most of these studies found that there often exists long-term spatial integration in the markets they considered, and that the number of pair of markets integrated to each other has increased with the deepening of the economic reform. These results cast some doubt on the validity of the Young and Poncet's proposition. In light of the arguments above, we are inclined to think that while market fragmentation caused by the local protection is one of the reasons for the weakened inter-regional linkage, it did not have as much of a role as was argued by Young and Poncet.[18]

Table 7.4   Regional structural difference coefficients

	1988	1991	1994	1997
Northeast	0.323	0.336	0.395	0.404
North China	0.230	0.236	0.252	0.296
East China	0.190	0.203	0.229	0.210
South China	0.346	0.341	0.380	0.384
Central China	0.235	0.246	0.262	0.272
Northwest	0.328	0.350	0.396	0.413
Southwest	0.431	0.422	0.472	0.444
Simple average	0.298	0.305	0.341	0.346

Source: National Bureau of Statistics. *China Statistical Yearbook of Industrial Economy* (various years).

7.5.5   Level of aggregation

Finally, it is important to note that the result and its interpretation depend crucially on the level of aggregation used in the analysis. This paper aggregated provincial administrative units into seven major regions. The general finding that intra-regional linkages have intensified relative to inter-regional linkages is therefore contingent on this rather high level of aggregation. Because data on inter-provincial or inter-county trade were not available to the authors, we here just compute how a province has changed the degree of production specialization among provinces belonging to a same major region, in order to indirectly show the direction of changes in inter-provincial linkages within a major region. Table 7.4 shows changes in the regional structural coefficient[19] of each major region over the period from 1988 to 1997. We see that the degree of specialization has gone up during the period. Thus, if we assume that inter-industry trade is the prevailing pattern of inter-provincial trade in present China, then it follows that the degree of market integration within a major region has been reinforced through growing amount of trade between provinces belonging to a same region. Given the present conditions of infrastructure imposing large transaction costs on domestic trades,[20] it may not be unexpected that the spatial integration of the Chinese economy would take place first within relatively small geographical areas such as major economic regions that we analyze in this paper, and would only gradually spread to the whole, national economy.

7.6   Concluding remarks

The purpose of this paper is to explore how economic interdependence among the economies of China's major regions has changed with the deepening of reform. For this purpose, we compute some linkage measures and visualize in the form of graphs the structural changes in the IRIO linkages described on the basis of a QIOA. Our analysis reveals that the interdependence among regions has decreased slightly, indicating that the self-sufficiency of each regional economy has increased in general. We provide a list of possible reasons that may lie behind this finding. Unlike some other researchers, we do not interpret the finding as an evidence of growing market fragmentation. We are rather inclined to think that the finding reflects the specific way in which spatial integration is proceeding in the present Chinese economy. To be more specific, the spatial integration of the Chinese domestic market is initially taking place in relatively small spatial domains, such as regions covering several provinces. With time this spatial integration is likely to extend to the economy as a whole. However, this is a conjecture that only the future course of events can prove. What is more important at this stage is that behind this tendency toward regional self-sufficiency, there have emerged some major changes in the structure of inter-regional linkages.

In the Northeast, the importance of its heavy industry as a purchaser for the industries located in the surrounding regions has decreased, while several industries, especially mining, of this region has become dependent on the purchases from its surrounding regions, reflecting the sluggish growth of this region. North China and Central China have become autarchic as a whole both in terms of forward and backward linkage. However, they have strengthened linkages with several industries of other regions. Both of these two regions have become more dependent on industries in East China in finding outlets for their products. Central China has become more important as a purchaser of intermediate products made in the Northwest. East China and South China has commonly become less important as a supplier of intermediate products to other regions. However, these two regions are contrasted in terms of changes in their spillovers to surrounding regions. East China has become a growth pole to induce spillovers to industries of the surrounding regions, while South China has not. Two western regions are generally isolated from other regions, although the Northwest industries have become dependent on the demands from Central China.

Further research needs to be conducted in order to improve our understanding of the Chinese regional integration process. In the following, we indicate a few lines along which such research can proceed. First, because of lack of reliability of China's statistics, the results of our analysis need to be further checked using different data and methodologies. More comprehensive econometric tests of the market integration should be conducted using time series data on commodity prices in different regions. Second, as our analysis partially showed, the ongoing spatial integration of China's domestic market cannot be separated from its integration with the international market. Future research should therefore include a more detailed analysis of the integration of China's each regional economy with the international economy. Third, the scope of this paper's analysis is limited to the commodity market. It is necessary to broaden the scope of the spatial integration to include factor markets, such as labor and capital markets.

Appendix A

The IRIO table for 1987 was from Ichimura and Wang (2003), which also explains the methodology for construction of the table. On the other hand, the IRIO table for 1997 was constructed by the authors themselves (referenced as Institute of Developing Economies–JETRO, 2003). The details of the methodology for construction of the 1997 IRIO table is provided in Okamoto and Zhang (2003) and Okamoto et al (2005). In this appendix, we provide just the major points of this methodology.

It was impossible for us to construct the IRIO table of China based on the full-survey method, because such an effort requires huge amounts of time, funds and manpower, which were far beyond our capacity. We therefore applied a hybrid compilation methodology which combines mathematical methods and the partial-survey method. This hybrid compilation methodology is a widely accepted technique in the input-output literature (see, for example, Lahr 1993, 2001). We implemented a Multi-Regional Input-Output (MRIO) model and then estimated a tentative IRIO table from the results obtained from the model implementation. Finally, results of a special survey were utilized to ascertain the values of the important cells of the table in order to increase the overall accuracy of the final IRIO table (Jensen, 1980).

Regarding the MRIO model, we would like to note the following. In the usual MRIO settings, the technical structure of production of each region and the inter-regional trade structure of various products are separately built into models. The amount of information necessary to implement MRIO models is therefore much less than in the case of direct estimation of an IRIO table. From many kinds of MRIO models, we chose a so-called column coefficient model (or the Chenery-Moses model) for our estimation, since the accuracy of this model was proved to be relatively good by an empirical test of Japan case (Polenske, 1970).

The fundamental data necessary for implementation of the model are: (a) the technical coefficients for each region (b) some exogenous data, such as total outputs, final demands, and value added for each region, and (c) trade coefficients (or so-called column coefficients), which embody the structure of the intra- and inter-regional commodity flows for each product in a particular way.[21]

In order to obtain data described in items (a) and (b) above, we collected input-output data for each province for 1997 and made some adjustments on the exogenous data, such as final demands and value added, in order to be consistent with national data.

We estimated intra- and inter-regional commodity flows both by a survey and by a spatial interaction model. In order to obtain the necessary information on inter-provincial commodity flows, a survey was conducted in 2001. We selected 549 state-owned enterprises and business groups that are regarded as important in terms of enterprise size and economic activity in China, and questionnaires were distributed to them and collected for the year 2000 (Zhang and Zhao, 2002). Because of limitations regarding the survey scale and response ratio, some sectors (e.g., the service sector) and some regions (e.g., the Northwest) did not have enough data on commodity flows. However the survey provided us with very important information on commodity shipments across regions.

In addition to the survey, a so-called Leontief-Strout Gravity (LSG) model (Leontief and Strout, 1963) was used to estimate the commodity flows. Based on the trade structure of the year 2000 (base year), the inter- and intra-regional trade flows for 1997 were estimated using the LSG model. The trade structure of the year 2000 was obtained from transport Origin Destination (OD) tables for each product.[22] Though the complete OD tables for various products are available for railway transport, they are not fully available for road and water transport. So in the latter cases, we estimated the OD tables (of waterway and highway transport) for each product, using the total outflow of each product from each region and other information, such as the average distance of shipment for each region's every single product. In estimating the OD table, we used a supply constrained gravity model with a condition to make the average distance of the estimated commodity flow close to the known average distance. The estimation above yielded the values of the trade coefficients.

After obtaining regional technical coefficients, trade coefficients, and exogenous data on several variables such as final demands, we implemented the column coefficient model, and a tentative IRIO table was estimated based on the results. The final IRIO table was obtained by revising the tentative IRIO table. The revision was conducted along the following lines. First, comparing the output values obtained from the model to the real data, we found that there were relatively large errors in some sectors and regions. We therefore scrutinized further the sectors with the error ratio over 30 percent. Assuming that these errors came from shortcomings in the estimation of inter-regional commodity flows, we corrected the trade coefficients in accordance with the opinion of experts and the survey results. Second, the sectors with relatively large errors (the error ratio being over 10 percent) were reconciled based on the assumption that the degree of process of goods was different between the related sectors. For example, if the agricultural sector has a positive error and the food sector has a negative error, we consider that agricultural sector includes some processed agricultural products. So we moved some transactions in the agricultural sector to the food sector according to the primary information or specialist opinion. Third, the reconciliation and balancing work was wholly proceeded to the important cells by using the survey result so that "Holistic Accuracy" (Jensen, 1980) of the table could be achieved. However, despite the correction above there still exists relatively large statistical discrepancies in mining, metal processing, electricity, gas and water supply, and service sectors because of data inconsistency between regional and national levels.

Acknowledgements

The authors deeply appreciate the valuable comments by Thomas Rawski, Nazrul Islam, Ding Lu, Katsuzi Nakagane, Kazuhiko Yokota, Erbiao Dai, Eric Ramstetter on earlier drafts of the paper. However, the sole responsibility of this chapter's contents remains with the authors.

Notes

1 The estimation method of the 1997 table is outlined in Appendix A.
2 The basic equation of the Leontief demand-driven model is $X = AX + F$, where X, A, and F denote the output vector, the technical coefficient matrix ($\equiv Z(\hat{X})^{-1}$, where Z and $\hat{X}$ denote the intermediate transaction matrix and the diagonalized matrix of X respectively), and the final demand vector respectively. From this basic equation, we can derive $X = (I-A)^{-1}F$, where I denotes the identity matrix and $(I-A)^{-1}$ is the Leontief inverse matrix.
3 The basic equation of the Ghosh supply-driven model is $X' = X'B + V'$, where B and V' denote the output coefficient matrix ($\equiv(\hat{X})^{-1}Z$) and the value added (or primary costs) row vector respectively. From this basic equation, we can derive $X' = V'(I-B)^{-1}$, where $(I-B)^{-1}$ is a so-called Ghosh inverse matrix.
4 The in-degree and the out-degree of sector i are the i-th column sum and the i-th row sum of the adjacency Leontief inverse matrix respectively.
5 We compute the arithmetic mean of nine sectors in a region in order to conduct the regional comparison. The weighted average, using output vector as a weight, turned out to give almost similar results. Thus we omit the latter results.
6 It should be noted that self-sufficiency here only concerns intermediate transactions among industries.
7 Assume that there is an important linkage from sector i to sector j, or there is no such a linkage but there is a sequence of linkages from sector i to j through other sector(s). It is then said that there is a chain from sector i to sector j. Two sectors are strongly connected if there is a chain from sector i to sector j and a chain from sector j to sector i (Aroche-Reyes, 2001).
8 A list of CIs of all sectors in each year is available from the authors on request.
9 The economy of the Northeast region has experienced sluggish growth, because the state-owned enterprises (mainly in heavy industries), which dominated this region's economy since the first five year plan (1953–1957), could not adapt themselves to the growing market economic environment. The stagnation of the Northeast economy owing to the dominance of old SOEs in the economy is sometimes known as "the Northeast Phenomenon" in China.
10 Note that the increase of outgoing linkages does not necessarily mean that the forward linkage effects of the industries in the Northeast have intensified. In fact, the average forward linkage effect of the Northeast industries on North China, measured by the input multiplier, went down from 0.186 in 1987 to 0.129 in 1997. Why such a seemingly contradicting result? The reason lies in how we identify important cells in the technical coefficient matrix A. The r_{ij} in equation (7.1), by its definition, is supposed to reflect the significance of sector j as a purchasing industry for sector i as a supplier. Thus all that we can say from the observed change is that the purchases by industries in North China and East China have become more important for the industries, especially mining, in the Northeast. This is, however, not the same as the supplies from the industries in the Northeast becoming more important for the purchasing industries in North China and East China.
11 The ratio of investment in capital construction of transportation and communication industries to nominal GDP went up from 16 percent in 1987 to 30 percent in 1997. This indicates that China's transportation bottle-neck might have been mitigated to a certain extent during the period.
12 See "The regulation on the operation of road and water transportation statistics," issued by the Ministry of Transportation and the NBS in 1992.

13 Note that the average transport distance of highway freight is only 54 km, compared to 772 km of railways, 1,696 km of waterways.

14 The average transport distance of private barges was only 56.9 km in 1987 according to Editorial board of Chinese Almanac of Transportation (1991), p. 592.

15 Poncet (2003) assumed a scenario where domestic trade flow data understated real figures by 5, 20 and 40 percent in 1987, 1992, and 1997 respectively and conducted a re-estimation with adjusted data to show that her findings about provincial border effects were not refuted. It would be nice to see whether our own results change if we re-estimated the 1997 IRIO table based on similar hypothetical adjustments as of Poncet. Unfortunately such an exercise was not possible since we did not have access to the data necessary for such re-estimation and re-compilation of the IRIO table.

16 There was a controversy about the tendency of China's market integration. In this debate, some researchers disagreed with Young and Poncet, claiming that with deepening of reform the Chinese market has gradually become integrated (See for example, Xu, 2002; Naughton, 2003; Bai et al., 2004).

17 To take an example from Li et al. (2004), top 5 measures among 42 kinds of protective measures are: (1) "local government demands to give priority to employing local citizens when an enterprise employs people," (2) "it is too expensive for children of employees from outside to study in a local school," (3) "it is difficult for an employee from outside to settle down," (4) "deal a light blow on locally produced imitative commodities," and (5) "because the government's corresponding functions are not perfect, the government can hardly provide pension, medical and unemployment insurance for employees from outside." This list shows that local protection measures are more aimed at the labor markets.

18 Hioki (2003) investigated news reports on the local protectionism in *People's Daily* over the period 1995 to 2002 and found that most of the cases occurred at the county or city level of local districts. Administrative instruments that connect provinces into a regional plan to promote regional autarchy are hardly known.

19 The regional structural coefficient takes values between 0 and 1. The closer the coefficient of a region to 1, the more provinces in the region specialize in terms of production. For the definition of the regional structural coefficient, see World Bank (1994) pp. 16–17. To compute the coefficients, we used values of output for 36 (35 in 1994 and 1997) secondary industrial sectors of all provinces. These data are available in China Statistical Yearbook of Industrial Economy (various years).

20 Chinese transportation infrastructure has been strengthened considerably during the reform decades. Nevertheless, transportation costs in China are still reported to be fairly high. To cite an example from road transportation, the cost to deliver quality truck-hauling services in China is still equal to or up to 15 percent higher than in the United States, owing to very high toll charges and higher deadhead rate, and so on. (See Dai et al., 2005). Li et al. (2004) also reports that "transportation cost is too high" is the second most frequent answer among seven optional answers in their enterprise survey to the question of what prevents enterprises from markets outside their home provinces.

21 The column coefficient model assumes that every sector in a region R purchases a commodity i from other region S at the same fixed ratio given by a column coefficient c_i^{SR}.

22 The omission of air and pipeline shipments may not lower the accuracy of our estimation very much, since relative volume of these shipments is not so large in comparison with those by other transportation modes.

References

Aroche-Reyes, Fidel. 1996. "Important Coefficients and Structural Change: A Multi-layer Approach," *Economic Systems Research*, Vol. 8, No. 3, pp. 235–246.

Aroche-Reyes, Fidel. 2001. "The Question of Identifying Industrial Complexes Revisited: A Qualitative Perspective," in Lahr, Michael L. and Erik Dietzenbacher (eds.), *Input-Output Analysis: Frontiers and Extensions*, Palgrave MacMillan: New York.

Aroche-Reyes, Fidel. 2002. "Structural Transformations and Important Coefficients in the North American Economies," *Economic Systems Research*, Vol. 14, No. 3, pp. 257–273.

Bai, Chong-En, Yingjuan Du, Zhigan Tao, and Sarah Y. Tong. 2004. "Local Protectionism and Regional Specialization: Evidence from China's Industries," *Journal of International Economics*, Vol. 63, pp. 397–417.

Beyers, William B. 1976. "Empirical Identification of Key Sectors: Some Further Evidence," *Environment and Planning A*, Vol. 8, pp. 231–236.

Borgatti, Stephen P., Martin G. Everett, and Linton C. Freeman. 1999. *UCINET 6.0 Version 6.135*. Analytic Technologies: Natick.

Dai, Jim, Yuepeng Li, Xiutian Liu, Yang Wang, Nancy Wong, and Chen Zhou. 2005. *2004 China Road Transportation Enterprise Survey Report*, Mimeo, Georgia Institute of Technology.

Development Research Center of State Council. 2004. "Zhongguo Guonei Difang Baohu de Diaocha Baogao," (A Research Report on China's Domestic Local Protection: A Tentative Analysis Based on Non-Firm Sample Survey). *Jingji Yanjiu Cancao* (Economic Research Reference), No. 1786, pp. 31–38.

Dietzenbacher, Erik. 1997. "In Vindication of the Ghosh Model: A Reinterpretation as a Price Model," *Journal of Regional Science*, Vol. 37, No. 4, pp. 629–651.

Dietzenbacher, Erik. 2002. "Interregional Multipliers: Looking Backward, Looking Forward," *Regional Studies*, Vol. 36, No. 2, pp. 125–136.

Editorial board of Chinese Almanac of Transportation. 1991. *Chinese Almanac of Transportation, 1991*. Zhongguo Jiaotong Nianjianshe: Beijing.

Fan, Jie, and Dadao Lu et al. 2001. *Zhongguo Diqu Jingji Xietiao Fazhan yu Quyu Jingji Hezuo Yanjiu*. (On the Balanced Development of Regional Economies and the Regional Economic Cooperation in China.) Zhongguo Youyi Chuban Gongsi, Beijing.

Ghosh, Santadas and Joyashree Roy. 1998. "Qualitative Input-Output Analysis of the Indian Economic Structure," *Economic Systems Research*, Vol. 10, No. 3, pp. 263–273.

Hioki, Shiro. 2003. "Chugoku no Shijo Bundan: Kizonkenkyu no Ginmi to Genjyo wo Meguru Kousatsu," (On China's Market Fragmentations: a Critical Survey and an Analysis on the Current Situation of the Problem), in Okamoto, Nobuhiro. (ed.) *Interregional Industrial Structure in China – Interregional Input-Output Analysis (II)* (Chugoku no Chiikikan Sangyokouzou – Chiikikan Sangyorenkan Bunseki-[II]), AIO series No. 63, Tokyo, Institute of Developing Economies, pp. 120–165.

Hioki, Shiro, Geoffrey J.D. Hewings, and Nobuhiro Okamoto. 2005. Identifying the Structural Changes of China's Spatial Production Linkages Using a Qualitative Input-Output Analysis. Working Paper, the Regional Economics Applications Laboratory, University of Illinois at Urbana-Champaign.

Huang, Jikun, Scott Rozell, Yuping Xie, and Min Zhang. 2002. "Cong Nongchanpin Jiage Baohu Chengdu he Shichang Zhenghe Kan Rushi dui Zhongguo Nongye de Yingxiang," (The Consideration of the Impact of Entry into WTO upon China's Agriculture: Taken from the Aspect of the Degree of Protecting Produce Price and Market Integration.), *Guanli Shijie*. (Management World) No. 9, pp. 84–94.

Huang, Sujian, and Houkai Wei. 2001. *Xibu Dakaifa yu Dongzhongbu Diqu Fazhan*. (The Western Development Program and the Development of Eastern and Central Areas), Jingji Guanli Chubanshe: Beijing.

Huenemann, Ralph W. 2001. "Are China's Recent Transport Statistics Plausible?" *China Economic Review*, Vol. 12, No. 4, pp. 368–372.

Ichimura, Shinichi, and Hui-Jiong Wang (eds.) 2003. *Interregional Input-Output Analysis of the Chinese Economy*. World Scientific Publishing Co.: New Jersey.

Institute of Developing Economics JETRO. 2003. *Multiregional Input-Output Model for China 2000*. Institute of Developing Economics, Japan External Trade Organization: Chiba.

Jensen, Rodney C. 1980. "The Concept of Accuracy in Regional Input-Output Models," *International Regional Science Review*, Vol. 5, No. 2, pp. 139–154.

Jilek, Jaroslav. 1971. "The Selection of Most Important Input Coefficients," *Economic Bulletin for Europe*, Vol. 23, No. 1, pp. 86–105.

Jones, Leroy P. 1976. "The Measurement of Hirshmanian Linkages," *Quarterly Journal of Economics*, Vol. 90, No. 2, pp. 323–333.

Lahr, Michael L. 1993. "A Review of the Literature Supporting the Hybrid Approach to Constructing Regional Input-Output Models," *Economic Systems Research*, Vol. 5, No. 3, pp. 277–293.

Lahr, Michael L. 2001. "A Strategy for Producing Hybrid Regional Input-Output Tables," in Lahr, Michael.L. and Erik. Dietzenbacher. (eds.), *Input-Output Analysis: Frontiers and Extensions*, Palgrave Macmillan: New York.

Leontief, Wassily, and Alan Strout. 1963. "Multiregional Input-Output Analysis," in Barna,T. (eds.), *Structural Interdependence and Economic Development*, St. Martin's Press: London.

Li, Jie, and Qunyan Sun. 2004. "Cong Pijiu Shichang Zhenghe Kan WTO dui Xiaochu Difang Baohu de Yingxiang," (How Does China's WTO Entry Affect Interregional Protectionism: The Case of Beer Market Integration), *Shijie Jingji* (World Economy), No .6, pp. 37–45.

Li, Shantong, Yongzhi Hou, Yunzhong Liu, and Bo Chen. 2004. "Zhongguo Guonei Difang Baohu Wenti de Diaocha yu Fenxi," (A Research and an Analysis on China's Domestic Local Protectionism), *Jingji Yanjiu* (Economic Research), No. 11, pp. 78–95.

Miller, Ronald E., and Peter D. Blair. 1985. *Input-Output Analysis: Foundations and Extensions*. Prentice-Hall: New Jersey.

National Bureau of Statistics. 1999. *Input-Output Table of China 1997*, China Statistics Press: Beijing.

National Bureau of Statistics. (various years). *China Statistical Yearbook of Industrial Economy*. China Statistics Press: Beijing.

Naughton, Barry. 2003. "How Much Can Regional Integration Do to Unify China's Markets?" In Hope, Nicholas, C., Yang, D.T. and Li, M.Y. (eds.) *How Far Across the River? Chinese Policy Reform at the Millennium*. Stanford University Press: California.

Okamoto, Nobuhiro, and Yaxiong Zhang. 2003. "Compilation Procedure of Multi-regional Input-Output Model for China 2000," in Institute of Developing Economies *Multi-Regional Input-Output Model for China 2000*, Institute of Developing Economies–JETRO: Chiba, pp. 9–20.

Okamoto, Nobuhiro, Yaxiong Zhang, Shiro Hioki, Takaaki Kanazawa and Kun Zhao. 2005. "A Method for Constructing an Interregional Input-Output Model of China 2000," *The Journal of Econometric Study of Northeast Asia*, Vol. 5, No. 2, pp. 23–36.

Park, Albert, Hehui Jin, Scott Rozelle, and Jikun Huang. 2002. "Market Emergence and Transition: Arbitrage, Transaction Costs, and Autarky in China's Grain Market," *American Journal of Agricultural Economics*, Vol. 84, No. 1, pp. 67–82.

Polenske, Karen R. 1970. "An Empirical Test of Interregional Input-Output Models: Estimation of 1963 Japanese Production," *American Economic Review*, Vol. 60, No. 2 LX, pp. 76–82.

Poncet, Sandra. 2003. "Measuring Chinese Domestic and International Integration," *China Economic Review*, Vol. 14, No. 1, pp. 1–21.

Schintke, Joachim, and Reiner Stäglin. 1988. "Important Input Coefficients in Market Transactions Tables and Production Flow Tables," in Ciaschini, Maurizio. (ed.) *Input-Output Analysis, Current Development*, Routledge : London, pp. 43–60.

Schnabl, Hermann. 1994. "The Evolution of Production Structures, Analyzed by a Multi-layer Procedure," *Economic Systems Research*, Vol. 6, No. 1, pp. 51–68.

Sinton, Jonathan E. 2001. "Accuracy and Reliability of China's Energy Statistics," *China Economic Review*, Vol. 12, No. 4, pp. 373–383.

Sun, Dingqiang, and Jintao Xu. 2005. "Cong Shichang Zhenghe Chengdu Kan Zhongguo Mucai Shichang Xiaolu," (The Efficiency of China's Lumber Market Measured by the Degree of Market Integration) *Zhongguo Nongcun Jingji (China Rural Economy)*, No. 6, pp. 37–45.

Wang, Ziyu. 1997. "Dui Xianxing Jiaotong Yunshu Tongji Gaige Wenti de Sikao," (A Thought on the Reform of the Current Transportation Statistics). *Tongji Yanjiu (Statistical Research)*, No. 6 in 1997, pp. 73–74.

Wang, Shaoguang, and Angang Hu. 1999. *The Political Economy of Uneven Development: The Case of China*. M. E. Sharp: New York.

Wang, Guanghua, Zhangyue Zhou, and Liangbiao Chen. 1997. "Woguo Shuidao Shichang Zhenghe Chengdu Yanjiu," (An Analysis on the Degree of Integration of China's Rice Market). *Zhongguo Nongcun Jingji. (China Rural Economy)*, No. 8, pp. 45–51.

Wolf, Holger C. 2000. "Intra-National Home Bias in Trade," *The Review of Economics and Statistics*, Vol. 82, No. 4, pp. 555–563.

World Bank. 1994. *China: Internal Market Development and Regulation*. The World Bank: Washington, DC.

Wu, Laping. 1999. "Woguo Xiaomai, Yumi, he Shengzhu Shougou Shichang Zhenghe Chengdu Yanjiu," (A Research on the Degree of Integration of China's Wheat, Maize and Hog Markets) *Zhongguo Nongcun Guancha (China Rural Survey)*, No. 4, pp. 23–29, 38.

Xu, Xinpeng. 2002. "Have the Chinese Provinces Become Integrated under Reform?" *China Economic Review*, Vol. 13, No. 2–3, pp. 116–133.

Yu, Wen, and Jikun Huang. 1998. "Cong Dami Shichang Zhenghe Chengdu Kan Woguo Liangshi Shichang Gaige" (An analysis on the reform of China's grain market measuring the degree of integration of rice market), *Jingji Yanjiu* No. 3, pp. 50–57.

Young, Alwin. 2000. "The Razor's Edge: Distortions and Incremental Reform in the People's Republic of China," *The Quarterly Journal of Economics*, Vol. 115, No. 4, pp. 1091–1135.

Yuan, Hui, and Zuxiang Liu. 1997. "Qianlun Shuilu Huoyun Tongji Shizhen de Yuanyin he Duice," (A Note on the Cause of False Water Freight Statistics and the Measures for Improvement). *Zhongguo Shuiyun. (China Water Transport)*, No. 4, pp. 21–22.

Zhang, Qi. 2004. "Jiaotong Yunshu Tonji de Xianzhuang yu Fazhan," (The Current Status and the Development of Transportation Statistics). *Zhongguo Tongji (China Statistics)*, No. 4, pp. 10–11.

Zhang, Yaxiong, and Kun Zhao. 2002. "2000 Nian Qiye Shengchan Touu Laiyuan he Chanpin Liuxiang Diaocha Fangfa," (The Methodology of Region of Origin and Destination in Enterprise Activity for 2000), in Okamoto, Nobuhiro. (ed.) *Interregional Industrial Structure: Interregional Input-Output Analysis (I)*, AIO series No. 61, Institute of Developing Economies: China.

8
Regional Competition, Fiscal Federalism, and Economic Structure: Evidence from China

Li Qi

8.1 Introduction

Fiscal decentralization is an important element that fostered the success of China's reforms towards a market economy. If economics is all about incentives, then understanding how fiscal reforms provided incentives for local authorities and economic entities to stimulate economic growth is essential to understanding China's economic success. There is no dispute about the positive impacts of fiscal reforms on China's recent economic growth. However, there are many concerns about the negative impacts of fiscal decentralization, such as corruption and the imbalance of regional development. Among these negative effects, local protectionism seems to be one of the most prominent problems associated with fiscal decentralization and has been widely commented on and studied. General consensus recognizes the seriousness of local protectionism in China and its damaging effect on economic efficiency, but tends to neglect the dynamics of the relationship between local protectionism and market forces.

We will advance the analysis of general views one step further to examine protectionism at both the early stage and the later stage of reforms. In addition to including these stage dynamics horizontally, we also deepen current understanding of local protectionism and its impact on market structure vertically; we investigate the roots of local protectionism and link those issues with the study of industry-wide market concentration ratios of both early and later reform periods. Using a comprehensive and uniquely rich data set that covers a large portion of Chinese industrial firms,[1] we examine industry market concentration ratios and their relationship to tax profit margin and state shares, which are considered to be the primary factors driving local protectionism. We also extend the current study on local protectionism from commodity markets to factor markets with an investigation of capital market integration in early and later reform periods.

Empirical evidence about commodity and factor markets suggests that the initial surge of local protectionism seems to yield to market forces towards the later stage of reforms, a discovery that conforms to the primary prediction of the market-preserving federalism theory. Our empirical findings also contribute to the recent debate on the degree of economic integration in China.

This paper first illustrates the major steps of fiscal reforms in China in Section 8.2. Then we will discuss the positive and negative impacts of fiscal decentralization on economic performance in Section 8.3. Section 8.3 also introduces relevant theories on fiscal reforms and current empirical studies on the economic structure associated with fiscal decentralization. Section 8.4 presents empirical evidence from the commodity market to illustrate the dynamics of local protectionism and market forces. We also provide examples of specific industries that demonstrate such dynamics in this section. Section 8.5 introduces the empirical investigation on factor market structure. Section 8.6 summarizes findings and conclusions.

8.2   Fiscal policy reforms

The history of China's fiscal policy reforms since the establishment of the People's Republic of China in 1949 is intertwined with the theme of centralization-decentralization. Fiscal policies have deep and profound impact on economic development. The study of fiscal policies and their impact deserves special attention, particularly in a party state such as China.

We can divide fiscal policy reforms in China into three periods: the plan period (1949–1978), the market-oriented reforms period featuring the fiscal responsibility system (sometimes referred to as fiscal contracting system) (1979–1993), and the new fiscal policy – the tax sharing system (*fenshuizhi*) since 1994.

In the following section, we will briefly introduce the process of China's fiscal policy reforms. Readers should note that this paper does not intend to offer detailed information on all aspects of fiscal reforms.[2] Rather, we will provide a general description of certain aspects of these reform policies so our readers will be acquainted with the knowledge that is mostly relevant to our analysis in Sections 8.3, 8.4 and 8.5.

8.2.1   The plan period

During the plan period, China went through cycles of centralization and decentralization.

The newly constituted government of the People's Republic viewed the task of restoring the war-damaged economy and rapid industrial development as an essential strategy to strengthen the new country. Indeed, the new government laid out the groundwork for the First Five-Year Plan (1953–1957) and adopted a fiscal policy that would help to achieve its ambitious goals. Facing huge deficits and hyperinflation, the new regime created a highly centralized and unified fiscal system while expanding the tax base. The local governments were left with no power to spend the tax revenues. In 1950, almost all tax revenue came under the uniform allocation of the center. Under this system (unified revenue and unified expenditure – *tongshou tongzhi*),

> the State Planning Commission commanded the authority in determining local revenue and expenditure plans on an annual basis. … Local governments (at province, prefecture, county level and commune level) did not have independent budgets. As to expenditure assignment, the central government was responsible for national defense, economic development (capital spending, R&D, universities and research institutes), industrial policy, and administration of national institutions such as the judicial system. Responsibilities for delivering day-to-day public administration and social services such as education (except universities), public safety, health care, social security, housing, and other local/urban services were delegated to local governments. (Lin, Tao, and Liu, 2003)

Such a policy ensured efficient capital mobilization and allocation, which played a significant role in building a large industrial base and in the ultimate success of the First Five-Year Plan.

Chinese leaders enacted other arrangements of central-provincial fiscal expenditure and revenue relations in addition to total centralization, described above.[3] For example, the contract of "dividing revenue" was in effect from 1951 to 1958. Under this arrangement, both central and local governments have their own respective revenue sources (mostly from enterprise profits) and expenditures. Central and local governments also share other locally collected taxes with the goal of balancing local revenue and expenditure.

These contracts, though different from total centralization, still afforded central government strong control of local production and fiscal performance. As a result, the overall "fiscal management system remained relatively stable from 1950 to 1967, except for the brief fiscal decentralization in 1958"[4] (Oksenberg and Tong, 1991).

The Cultural Revolution (1966–1976), however, not only paralyzed central planning and administrative control, but also brought the economy to the brink of collapse. As the country started to restore order, China continued to experiment with different fiscal regimes to reconcile central and local interests. Many other experimental arrangements were introduced, though all were short lived (none lasted more than three years). However, as the experiment went on, local governments

> acquired increased budgetary authority to arrange the structure of local spending, gained more control over a larger portion of revenues and expenditures than the central government, retained the total shares of year-end budgetary surpluses, secured multi-year revenue-sharing rate adjustments, and earned the power to determine the mode of fiscal relationships with subordinate levels, while the centre also imposed new controls on provincial revenues and expenditures. (Oksenberg and Tong, 1991)

8.2.2   The market-oriented reform period, 1979–1994

Starting in 1978, China has undergone a series of reforms towards a market-oriented system. One of the most important aspects of these reform policies is the central-provincial fiscal relationship, which not only affects economic growth but also becomes affected by the economic development and other structural changes in the larger economic system.

China again experimented with different fiscal arrangements for various provinces in different years.[5] But these complicated multi-arrangements were consolidated into a uniform system in 1983. The new fiscal regime – fiscal responsibility system (also referred to as the fiscal contracting system – *caizheng chengbao zhi*) was implemented from then to 1993. This new policy mainly dealt with the issue of revenue sharing between local and central governments. Local and central governments were engaged in long negotiations to determine the revenue and expenditure sharing structure. As a result, tax revenues were divided into three categories: "central fixed revenue," all of which remitted to the center, "local revenue," all of which remitted to the local governments, and shared revenues.[6] Almost all revenues (except customs duties and a few minor central revenues) were collected by local tax bureaus.

Although the system endured frequent changes due to constant bargaining between central and local governments on sharing formulas,[7] this new system fundamentally changed the previous central-local fiscal relationship from "province-collecting, centre-spending" to self-financing regimes for both the center and the provinces (Zhang, 1999).

The new fiscal contracting system is much less centralized than the previous system before 1979. These new contracting arrangements did provide local governments with great incentives to collect tax revenues and develop local economies, but they also had a potentially negative impact for the central government. For example, provinces collected, owned and spent about 70 percent of budgetary revenue (Zhang, 1999). Bahl and Wallich (1992) point out that local governments have obtained an increased share of fiscal resources because the most important contracts are fixed in nominal terms.

Another consequence of the contracting system is the rapid increase of the extra-budgetary account. "Before the reform, the extra-budgetary revenue was 10 percent of GNP in 1978 compared to the budgetary revenue of 31 percent of GNP. By 1992, the extra-budgetary revenue was up to 16 percent of GNP while the budgetary revenue was down to 14 percent of GNP" (Qian and Weingast, 1996). This significant rise in extra-budgetary revenue is largely due to the fact that the extra-budgetary revenue is not subject to sharing with the central government. Local governments also have the authority to determine the tax rates and fees that would fall under the extra-budgetary revenue category.

Although local governments gained more authority and control from the fiscal contracting system, it would, however, be immature and incomplete to characterize this new fiscal regime as pure decentralization. The whole reform process to establish the fiscal contracting system is far from a consistent linear route to decentralize. In fact, "the central government share of national revenues rebounded from 13.8 percent in 1972 and 14.3 percent in 1979 to over 20 percent in 1982, and more than 30 percent in 1985."[8]

But these periodic increases in the central government's share of revenue did not prevent an overall decline in the budgetary revenue to GDP ratio and the ratio of central government revenue to total revenue. A few reasons lie behind the declines of these two ratios. The contracting system induced local governments to conceal their revenue capacities (as the center tended to revise sharing rules and penalize those provinces with high growing revenues). Meanwhile, reforms in other aspects in the economy weakened tax bases from State-Owned Enterprises (SOEs). Not only were these enterprises allowed to keep some of their business revenues in the process of enterprise autonomy reforms, but their weak performance in competition also rendered less revenues. In an effort to stop the fiscal decline, China introduced a new fiscal regime in 1994: the Tax Sharing System (TSS) – *fenshuizhi*.

8.2.3   The tax sharing system reform since 1994

The Tax Sharing System (TSS) was designed to fundamentally change how central and local governments share revenues. Under the TSS, taxes were assigned either to the central or local governments. Central taxes include customs duties, the consumption tax, Value Added Tax (VAT) revenues collected by customs, income taxes from centrally owned enterprises, turnover taxes on railways, banks, and non-bank financial intermediaries and insurance companies, and resources taxes on offshore oil extraction. Local taxes consist of business taxes (excluding those named above as central taxes), income taxes and profit remittances of locally owned enterprises, urban land-use taxes, personal income taxes, the fixed asset investment orientation tax, the stamp tax, and so on. Initially the only shared tax was to be the VAT, at the fixed rate of 75 percent for the central government and 25 percent for local governments. This was modified by a concession on sharing the growing proceeds from the excise tax. In 1998, the securities trading tax was shifted from a purely local tax to a shared tax, with 88 percent for the central government and 12 percent for the local government (World Bank, 2002).

TSS also clarified the division of spending responsibilities. Central expenditure includes defense, armed police, capital investment, central administration, central-level institutions, and debt services, while the local expenditure items include local administration and local institutions, locally sponsored capital investment and technical renovation, aid to agriculture, urban maintenance and construction, price subsidies, and others.[9]

Another major change in the TSS system was the establishment of the central government's own collection agencies. The center set up National Tax Services (NTSs) in all provinces to collect central taxes and shared taxes. Local tax bureaus can collect only local taxes.

In the meantime, many old elements from the previous regime still remain in effect. For example, the previous transfer mechanisms such as quota subsidies for poor and minority regions, along with most of the old system of special purpose (earmarked) grants are still being carried out. This simultaneous implementation of the two regimes created a complicated and confusing system.

The motivation of introducing TSS stems largely from the center's concern about fiscal decline. In that regard, a major goal of the new TSS system is to restore the center's control and strength. The changes introduced by TSS met with resistance from the provinces. The center reconciled them by offering to return part of the shared revenues to ensure that provincial revenues would not drop below the 1993 level. The resistance subsided, and the system has finally gained prominence since 1996.

TSS did successfully reverse the declines of the two fiscal ratios (revenue to GDP and central revenue share to total revenue). For example, the revenue share for the central government rose from 22 percent in 1993 to 55.7 percent in 1994 (World Bank, 2002). However, the central share has been falling since then, though it still remains higher than its level at the time of the fiscal contracting system. Contributing to this decline is the reality that tax bases for many local taxes (such as the business tax and personal income tax) have grown more quickly than the source for central taxes. The local tax base includes both non-state and some state enterprises, whereas the center relies on business taxes from centrally owned SOEs, which have continued to suffer from weak performance. Meanwhile, VAT, the tax revenue source deemed the most important to the center, experienced a declining share in total tax revenues, whereas many local tax revenue sources (such as business tax, personal income tax, and so on) experienced an increase instead.

The impact of the 1994 TSS system cannot be simplified as re-centralization. This reform showed the center's attempt to regain dominant control over the economy's financial resources, and it increased the center's share of total revenue fairly quickly. The newly established NTSs shifted local provinces' bargaining power as tax collectors to the center. However, the new regime's arrangement also shows considerable reconciliation to local provinces' interest and in fact did provide local governments with strong incentives to enlarge local tax bases by encouraging local business development.

8.3   Impact of fiscal policy reforms on local economic development: theory, reality, and current literature

Although there were clearly times of re-centralization in the history of fiscal reforms in China, the fiscal regimes since China's economic reforms in 1978 have looked more decentralized than previous arrangements in granting local governments more incentives and autonomy. This trend of decentralization created both positive and negative impacts on economic development. Such impacts are predicted and documented by both standard public finance theories (Tiebout, 1956; Oates, 1972) as well as theories inspired to account for China's special circumstances (Qian and Weingast, 1996). This section will introduce the negative and positive impacts of decentralization on local economic development as well as recent theories and literature on local protectionism and its effect on economic structure.

8.3.1   Positive impact of decentralization

Decentralization lived up to its promise of providing great incentives for local governments. Never before had local governments played such a vital role in managing local economies. Not only are the economic incentives tremendous, but the political gain is also critical. Local party officials are evaluated largely based on local economic performance. Complementing the incentive mechanism, local governments possess the authority to set and conduct local economic policies. For example, local authorities have the power to appoint officials to local banks and SOEs, set up tax rates, initialize and implement policies to attract foreign investment, and so on. All of these factors work together to bring unprecedented growth. Local governments not only try to build an investment- and development-friendly environment, they are also heavily involved in handpicking pillar industries and are active in the entire industry establishment process. For example, the Shanghai municipal government provided investment capital, coordinated technology transfer, and lowered the risk of local auto firms to help with the needs of such an "infant industry."

These positive impacts comply with economists' standard view of "decentralization." It is widely believed that induced competition among jurisdictions provides the incentives for local political officials to develop and maintain hospitable environments for markets and economic factors (Tiebout, 1956; Oates, 1972).

Building on existing theories, Qian and Weingast (1996) proposed that "a particular form of decentralization, called market-preserving federalism, Chinese style, provides the critical foundations for market success." This Chinese-style decentralization made regional experiments possible. "Regional experiments also provided demonstration models for persuading people to accept reforms and guided to proceed their own reforms. The demonstration effects of the special economic zones and their associated positive spillovers are overwhelming" (Qian and Weingast, 1996). Decentralization also encouraged and continues to encourage the growth of the non-state sector. "Local governments actively support market-oriented, non-state enterprises because of their incentives to expand their revenue base, and competition between jurisdictions for getting rich first." (Qian and Weingast, 1996) Currently, the non-state sector contributes to more than 60 percent of China's national GDP and has become an indispensable part of China's economy for sustained growth.

8.3.2 Negative impact of decentralization

Like the significant positive impact we have seen from decentralization, the negative effects are equally obvious. The most prominent and most frequently discussed is local protectionism and the resultant segmentation and inefficiency.[10]

In general, local protectionism refers to the act of local governments using political and administrative power to intervene or manipulate markets and set up market entry barriers, which protect local enterprises from fair competition. Several factors induce strong protectionism behavior: lack of proper legislation and weak legal enforcement, central and local tax revenue and expenditure sharing structure, interconnection of SOEs and local governments, evaluation mechanism for local officials, and so on.

The most commonly used policies to protect local industries are:

1. Setting regulations to directly or indirectly ask local enterprises or individuals
   to purchase products or services by local providers only. For example, local

governments may ask businesses to carry only local brands for certain products. Alternately, local governments can indirectly set policies that favor the purchase of local brands.

2. Setting barriers to stop or limit non-local products from entering local markets. For instance, local governments set higher technical standards for out-of-area products, collect additional fees for market entry, or even set up examination posts at major ports, roads, and train stations to stop the flow of non-local products.

3. Abusing administrative power to induce law enforcement to protect local industries, especially those with a high margin of taxes and profits. For example, Chongqing's local government obstructed law enforcement from investigating the production of counterfeit sneakers in a local business because this business was viewed as a success for local business development. Illegal activities were often protected by local officials under the guise of protecting local tax and profit sources.[11]

With the authority of setting local economic policies, many local officials and bureaucracies are engaged in another short-term, rent-seeking behavior: imposing illegal fees – *luanshoufei*. Such corrupt policies create high costs and unnecessary burdens for local business (especially privately owned small and medium-size businesses) and farmers. For example, recent social concerns focus on illegal fees collected by local schools. After extensive investigation, the Vice Minister of Education, Zhang BaoQing, pointed out that the real reason behind illegal schooling fees is that local governments force local schools to collect various fees.[12] In an interview with *China Youth Daily* (*Zhongguo Qingnian Bao*), Wu Kegang, CEO of Yunan Long Liquor Corporation, said that he received multiple illegal bills in one day from the local police department, the local environmental agency, and the local tax bureau for illegal fees or fines.[13] Such stories of private enterprises "besieged" with illegal fees are quite common. It is reported that in an investigation carried by a local tax bureau on taxes and fees, the tax and fees ratio is 1: 1.8. However, the ratio for non-state enterprises is 1: 3.2.[14] Farmers suffer even more from illegal fund raising and fees.

Other negative impacts associated with decentralization include regional inequality and inflation caused by expanded money supply due to local governments' access to too many credits.

8.3.3 Theory and recent empirical literature on local protectionism in China

Many of these negative effects associated with fiscal decentralization impede the establishment of market order and healthy development of local economies. They also create huge inefficiencies. Among these problems, local protectionism and its impact on economic structure and development has become the focus of many academic studies.

Local protectionism fights against the market forces to shield local business from market competition. Indeed, this became a serious problem for China. Academic and media sources detail a range of damaging effects of local protectionism. But a new theory for China, market-preserving federalism, proposed by Montinola., Qian. and Weingast (1995), suggests that such measures of local protectionism to impede market forces will not survive in the long term. Their theory predicts that the competition between regions in a federal system will lead to policy imitation. There may be strong local protectionism in the early stage of reforms. But as local governments with poor economic performance learn from other regions' success, many realize that protectionism does not necessarily bring prosperity. In the later stage of reforms, protectionism may not be as strong as in the early stage.

One of the case studies Montinola., Qian. and Weingast (1995) used illustrates the trend to imitate successful policies from other areas and how that practice changes local policies from market unfriendly to market friendly:

> we discuss Shaanxi's learning from Guangdong's experience in opening trade. The governor of Shaanxi province observed that the reason that Guangdong province achieved fast economic growth was that its markets were open and interregional trade was not blockaded. Shaanxi, in contrast, maintained considerable trade barriers, including large numbers of tax offices across its different counties and prefectures. In 1991, the provincial government released its control over 125 commodity prices and withdrew 12,289 tax offices. The commodity trade soon flourished. In the second half of 1991, the business tax of commerce increased by 20.1 per cent over the same period of 1990. The State Council made copies of Shaanxi government's documents about its reform policy and sent them to other provincial governments. Many provinces, such as Gansu, Yunnan, Sichuan, Henan, Jilin, Ningxia, and Jiangsu, responded earnestly. Before long, Jiangsu established a "market guidance and coordination council"; Guizhou organized a "coordination team for market circulation reform." Many provinces have now incorporated the development of a market system into their socio-economic development plans.

Although the market-preserving federalism theory predicts the decline of local protectionism in the long run, the empirical evidence presented by recent studies investigating whether local protectionism leads to economic segmentation does not reach a consensus. For example, Young (2000) and Poncet (2003 and 2005) argue that China's domestic market is highly fragmented. Xu (2002) also points out that, "although economic integration of the Chinese provinces has progressed under reform, it is by no means complete." However, Bai, Du, Tao, and Tong (2004) find that although local government protection is strong for industries with high tax-plus-profit margins, the overall time trend of regional specialization of China's industries has reversed an early drop in the mid-1980s, registering a significant increase in later years. Park and Du (2005) also demonstrate that regional specialization actually increases, beginning in the early 1980s. Naughton (2003) mentions that "overly simple characterizations of Chinese provinces as quasi-autarchic protected economies simply don't fit the facts." In addition to the ongoing debate over market integration on the commodity and industry side, recent studies also extended the examination to capital market integration. Boyreau-Debray and Wei (2002) study China's provincial savings and investment rates at aggregate level and argue that reforms did not make capital more mobile across provincial borders and have left a fragmented capital market in China.

8.4   Economic structure: empirical evidence from commodity markets

This paper will contribute to the current literature and debates on China's economic structure by providing new evidence from both commodity and factor markets with innovative methodology. We also aim to link the study of economic structure to the roots of local protectionism.

On the commodity market side, we will examine industry market concentration ratios across a period of 20 years (we have data on 1980, 1985, and 1992 to 2004) to detect any change in the trend related to the two stages predicted by "the market-preserving federalism" theory. In addition to this study, which covers industries that constitute a substantial portion of national GDP to reflect the overall economic structure, we also link our investigation of market concentration with core issues at the root of local protectionism. As mentioned in Section 8.3, many argue that local protectionism is most likely to be practiced on industries that yield the highest margin of profits and tax revenues. The interconnection between SOEs and local governments also tends to trigger and exuberate the use of protectionism. Therefore, we trace changes in concentration ratios with industry profitability and state shares in these industries.

8.4.1   Commodity market evidence – sales
Concentration Ratios (CR8)

To examine the degree of China's market concentration, we obtained industry as well as firm-level data to study sales revenue concentration ratios.[15] Our data report firm-level four-digit industry codes, sales revenue, taxes, profits, and ownership in current Yuan for 1980, 1985, 1993, 1996, 2000, 2001, 2002, 2003, and 2004. Although the coverage of micro-level data is extensive, we find that it is not uniform. For example, after 1998, firms outside the state sector with annual sales under RMB5 million (equivalent to US$0.6 million at the 1998 official exchange rate) were excluded. Such data coverage issues lead us to adopt the concentration ratio of the top eight firms with highest sales revenue, because this measure is not sensitive to the exclusion of small firms. We also limit our study of the trend of concentration ratios to the three periods of 1980–1992, 1993–2002, and 2003–2004, because industry codes were changed before 1993 and after 2002, which makes tracing the same industry difficult.

We define concentration ratios *by sector* as the ratio of sales revenue of the top eight firms with the highest sales revenue to the total sales revenue of that industry for the same year. This ratio is denoted as CR8 in our study. We then calculate the average CR8 ratios for all industries for the same year. The CR8 ratios *by sales* are the average of CR8 ratios for all manufacturing sectors weighted by each sector's total manufacturing sales. The adjusted data are the averages of CR8 ratios

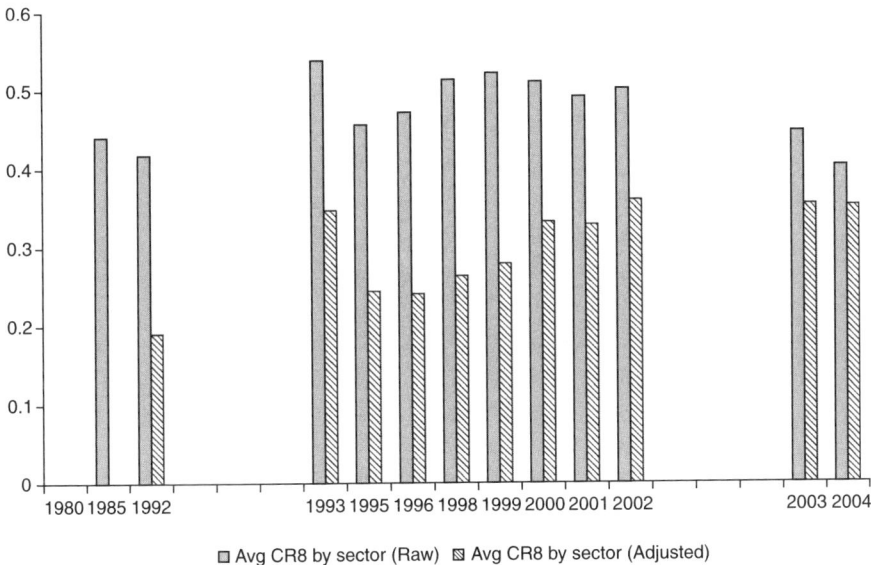

□ Avg CR8 by sector (Raw)   ▨ Avg CR8 by sector (Adjusted)

Figure 8.1   Average CR8 ratios (by sector) for 1980–2004

Note: *Avg CR8 by sector (raw)* is calculated by taking the average of all industries' CR8 ratios for the same year. The adjusted CR8 reflects the coverage of our data set to total industrial output. For example, the ratio of the total revenue from our enterprise microdata set to the total industrial output reported by China Statistical Yearbook is .73 (our coverage ratio) in 1992. Then we multiplied the raw CR8 ratio with the coverage ratio to reflect what the overall concentration ratio might be like given the coverage of our data set.

Source: Author's calculations based on data from *Chinese Industrial Microdata* and Rawski and Fang (2006).

adjusted to reflect the coverage of our data to national GDP.[16] Figures 8.1 and 8.2[17] show the average of CR8 ratios by sector and by sales.

The trends displayed by Figures 8.1 and 8.2 are quite similar. Three periods are shown in these figures. Although we cannot directly compare one period to another due to the industry code changes mentioned above, we can still see the changes in average CR8 ratios within each period. CR8 ratios fell continuously from 1980 to 1992, signaling that segmentation was on the rise. In the period of 1993 to 2002, CR8 ratios continued to fall until 1995, when both adjusted and raw data suggest a reverse in the trend – the continuous rise of concentration ratios. This increase in CR8 ratios slows in 2001 and 2002. In the period covering 2003 and 2004, raw data by sector and sales suggest a drop, while the adjusted data show either no change in CR8 ratios or a slight rise. However, it might be too early to detect a definite trend, with only two years of data for the time after 2002.

Our data indicate that the initial segmentation was reversed and the market became more integrated in the later reform period. This does appear to conform to the predictions of the market-preserving federalism theory, although we should still be cautious in interpreting the reversed trend. Our data are extensive and informative, which show a clear trend of overall industrial CR8 ratios, but examining averages of CR8 ratios does not reflect the idiosyncrasies of each industry.

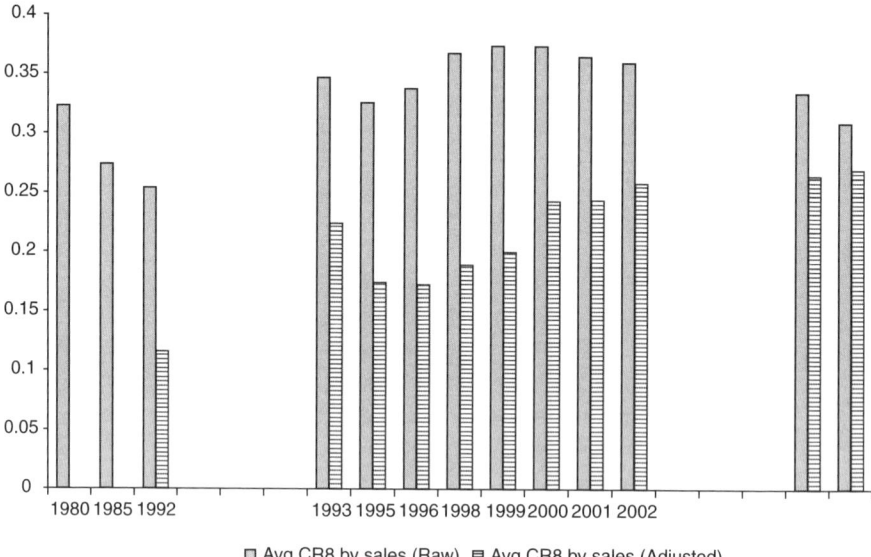

Figure 8.2 Average CR8 ratios (by sales) for 1980–2002

Note: The average CR8 ratio by sales (raw) is calculated using the same technique as the average CR8 ratio by sector (raw) in Figure 8.1, with the additional consideration of industry sizes. When taking the average, each sector's CR8 ratio is weighted by the size of its sales to total sales for the same year in our data set to reflect the size of each industry in the economy. Thus this measure gives more weight to large industries. The adjusted CR8 ratio by sales reflects the coverage ratio as explained in Figure 8.1.

Source: Author's calculations based on data from *Chinese Industrial Microdata* and Rawski and Fang (2006).

For example, changes in CR8 ratios may simply be caused by the natural development process of an industry. Because industries have their own unique structures and idiosyncratic organization, they may experience different stages of development. It is easy to imagine that the early stage of development is dominated by a few early entrants for an infant industry, whereas the more mature and competitive industries might be saturated with many firms. Later on, a large portion of small and inefficient firms will be shaken out in the competition process.

We offer more detailed industry-level account of the Air–Conditioning (AC) and refrigerator sectors as an example to illustrate this development process, and as a complimentary analysis to the macro level CR8 ratio examination we performed so far.

Many sectors of the household electronic appliances industry in China experienced the Klepper's model of development – initial explosive growth period followed by fierce competition that condenses the industry. Table 8.1 shows that the output of refrigerator industry increased nearly 50 times in 14 years (1983–1996). There were only 31 manufacturers in 1986. By 1993, the number of manufacturers had grown to be 193. However, the momentum stopped after mid 1990s. Output growth slowed down after 1996. Meanwhile, the number of manufactures shrank (86 in 2002) to only half of the number at its peak. As the industry became

Table 8.1 Major indicators for the refrigerator sector

Year	Output (Unit in 10,000)	Num. of firms	CR8	TPM
1983	18.85*	–	–	–
1984	54.74*	–	–	–
1985	144.8*	–	–	–
1986	225.5*	31*	–	–
1987	401.3*	44*	–	–
1988	755.45*	49*	–	–
1989	668.05*	51*	–	–
1991	469.94*	59*	–	–
1993	–	193	54.3	0.118
1996	928.22*	128	71.7	0.093
1997	986.09*	–	–	–
1998	1,000.89*	106	80.8	–
1999	1,199.45*	–	–	–
2000	–	96	83.2	0.051
2001	–	96	85.9	0.013
2002	–	86	85.4	0.056

Note: *indicates that data are obtained from China Light Industry Yearbook (1985, 1987, 1989, 1990, 1992, 1997, 1998, 1999, 2000). The yearbook data did not report number of firms and output (by unit) for each year. We do not have CR8 and TPM data either for those years.

Source: Author's calculations based on data from *Chinese Industrial Microdata* and *China Light Industry Yearbook* (various years).

consolidated, CR8 ratios increased steadily (from 54.3 in 1993 to 85.4 in 2002) suggesting a much more concentrated market as the industry matured.

The AC industry in China started to develop a few years later. The China Light Industry Yearbook recorded the output of the AC industry in 1987 for the first time. Table 8.2 demonstrates that the output in 1999 has expanded to over a hundred times more than that of 1987. We observe the same trend in the refrigerator sector when the number of AC manufacturers reduced to only 177 in 2004 from 259 as the CR8 ratios increased. Tables 8.1 and 8.2 not only illustrate the development process and changes in CR8 ratios (in market structures), they further present the timing difference in these two industries' growth experience and how that may affect the average CR8 ratios for separate periods. In fact, according to the China Light Industry Yearbook (1999), while the refrigerator market slowed down, "the markets for AC and microwave that started to grow in the 1990s still have a large room to expand." For example, CR8 ratio steadily increased while the number of manufacturers reduced as the refrigerator industry matured in 1993–2002, while the AC industry was still in the middle of an explosive growth with fluctuating CR8 ratios in the same time period.

Table 8.2   Major indicators for the air conditioning (AC) sector

Year	Output (Unit in 10,000)	Num. of firms	CR8	TPM
1987	12.1*	–	–	–
1988	24.35*	–	–	–
1989	37.39*	–	–	–
1991	63.06*	–	–	–
1993	–	127	53.8	0.087
1996	645.93*	246	65.5	0.083
1997	848.59*	–	–	–
1998	850*	200	57.4	–
1999	1,250*	–	–	–
2000	–	195	45.1	0.096
2001	–	248	49.1	0.065
2002	–	259	50.6	0.087
2003	–	250	66	0.067
2004	–	177	67.2	0.018

Note: *indicates that data are obtained from China Light Industry Yearbook (1985, 1987, 1989, 1990, 1992, 1997, 1998, 1999, 2000). The yearbook data did not report number of firms and output (by unit) for each year. We do not have CR8 and TPM data either for those years.

Source: Author's calculations based on data from *Chinese Industrial Microdata* and *China Light Industry Yearbook* (various years).

Although we should be aware of the links between industries' development process and changes in CR8 ratios, the illustration of such individual cases does not contradict our conclusion on market structure: we are likely to observe the natural competition process and changes in CR8 ratios described above only if market forces prevail; in other words, strong local protectionism measures will interrupt this natural process and lead to a much more severe and long-lasting segmented market.

Another limitation of the CR8 ratio analysis is its ambiguity on the issue of spatial allocation.[18] The CR8 ratio does not address market concentration from the perspective of geographic location. The top eight firms located in one province are treated the same as the case of the eight firms spread out in different provinces.

8.4.2   Local protectionism: CR8 ratios and Tax-Profit-Margins (TPMs)

The empirical evidence provided in Section 8.4.1 demonstrates the changes in China's industrial market structure. In this section, we will advance our examination to determine whether changes in the concentration ratios are linked to the roots of local protectionism. We calculated two more measures: the TPM as the ratio of taxes plus profits for all firms in the same industry to the total sales revenue of the same industry;[19] the state share of each industry is the ratio of the output of all SOEs to the total output of all firms in the same industry using current value.

The general theory of local protectionism would predict that local governments will protect industries that yield the highest TPMs in order to maximize sources of taxes and revenues. In China, such incidences have been abundant. For example, tobacco industries often yield the highest TPMs – about 46 percent for the period we examined. Naturally, local governments often exercise administrative powers to protect such profitable local manufacturers. Hence the market structure of the tobacco industry tends to be much more segmented than others. It is reported that over 140 enterprises produce cigarettes and tobacco-related products in China. The market share of the largest enterprise is about 6.5 percent, and the market share of the four largest enterprises is 17.5 percent. This four-firm concentration ratio is much lower in comparison to the market of the United States (97.5 percent), England (52.25 percent), and Japan (91.5 percent).[20] The beverage industry is another target of local protectionism. For example, the Xinjiang local administration established a policy of asking local vendors in certain districts of Urumqi (the capitol of the Xinjiang province) to carry only the beer produced by Xinpi Corporation (*Xinpi Jituan*) (Tan, Yu, and Zhang, 1996).

If local governments interfere with market order and competition in an effort to protect industries with high TPMs, we will expect to see a negative correlation between CR8 ratios and industry TPMs; that is, the higher the TPMs, the lower the CR8 ratio, since local governments' strong interference is likely to produce a more segmented market not dominated by a few giants. However, our data did not completely support this prediction.

We examine industry-level TPMs for 1993 and 2002, the longest period with consistent data measures in our data set.[21] TPM average for both years is .09. In fact, during the ten years from 1993 to 2002, the TPM average does not exhibit a drastic annual change, although each industry might experience its own ups and downs. Figure 8.3 demonstrates the relationship between CR8 ratios and TPM. For each year, we rank industries with their TPM figures and plot two different indicators: the average CR8 ratio for the 10 percent of the industries with the highest TPMs, and the average CR8 ratio for the 10 percent of the industries with the lowest TPMs. Readers can see that we are examining the CR8 ratios for the most profitable and the least profitable industries in Figure 8.3. Surprisingly, Figure 8.3 does not demonstrate the expected decrease in CR8 ratio for the most profitable industries, as mentioned earlier as the general theory's prediction. On the contrary, the market for industries with the highest TPMs became more concentrated, with the CR8 ratio rising from .63 to .66.

Naturally, we would expect that market forces are probably more prevalent for industries with low TPMs, leading, therefore, to a higher CR8 ratio. This turns out to be the case for the 10 percent of the industries with the lowest TPM. The average CR8 ratio for these industries is .68 for 1993, much higher than that of the industries (.63) with the highest TPM. Interestingly, we find that the CR8 ratio for the least profitable industries experienced a slight drop from .68 to .62 in 2002. This observation leads us to speculate other explanations (such as idiosyncratic characteristics of various industries and their development process) than local protectionism since local protectionism is expected to be exercised

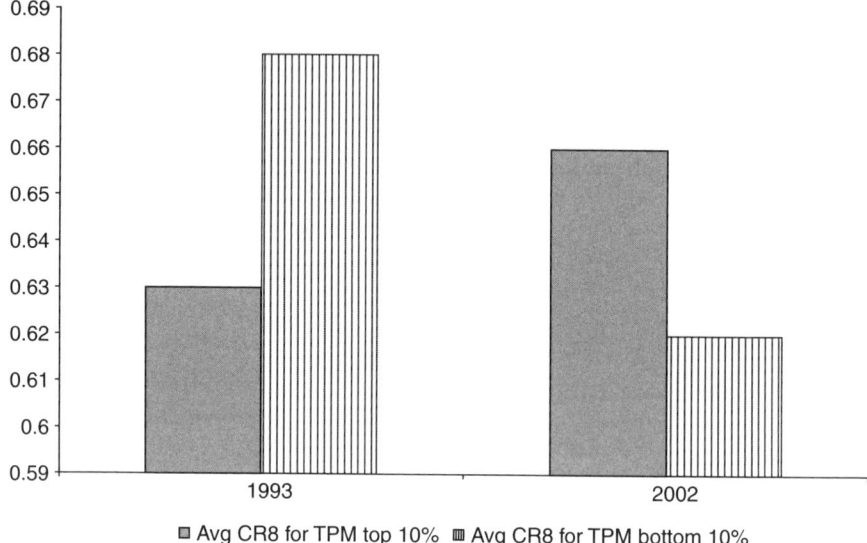

Figure 8.3   Average CR8 ratios and TPM for 1993 and 2002

Source: Author's calculations based on data from *Chinese Industrial Microdata*.

on more profitable industries. In any case, without further industry-by-industry-level analysis, we won't be able to determine the particular cause for this rise in the CR8 ratio for these least profitable industries.

However, Figure 8.3 clearly demonstrates one thing: whatever the true cause for the changes in the trend of these CR8 ratios for the most and least profitable industries, the prediction of the general theory on local protectionism and TPM is not fully supported by our data comparison of 1993 and 2002. The most distinguished feature of Figure 8.3 is that we do not see the expected high TPM/low CR8 ratio relationship. Although we cannot single out the particular effects of protectionism from the other possible idiosyncratic features of each industry, Figure 8.3 illustrates that protectionism may not be as strong now as it was 10 or 15 years ago at the early stage of reforms. Further, protectionism based on TPMs clearly is not the ultimate driving force of the current economic structure.

8.4.3   Local protectionism: CR8 ratios and state shares of local economy

We then turn to examine the empirical evidence for another theory at the core of local protectionism, particularly for China: the theory relating to the relationship between protectionism and SOEs. We calculate the state share of each industry as the ratio of the output of all SOEs to the total output of all firms in the same industry using current value for the years 2000 to 2003. In general, theory would predict that the higher the state share, the lower the CR8 ratio. Tan, Yu, and Zhang (2006) point out that SOEs' corporate reforms lag behind, and low efficiency levels disadvantage them in market competition. Hence, many SOEs are still used to seeking protection from local governments. Local governments

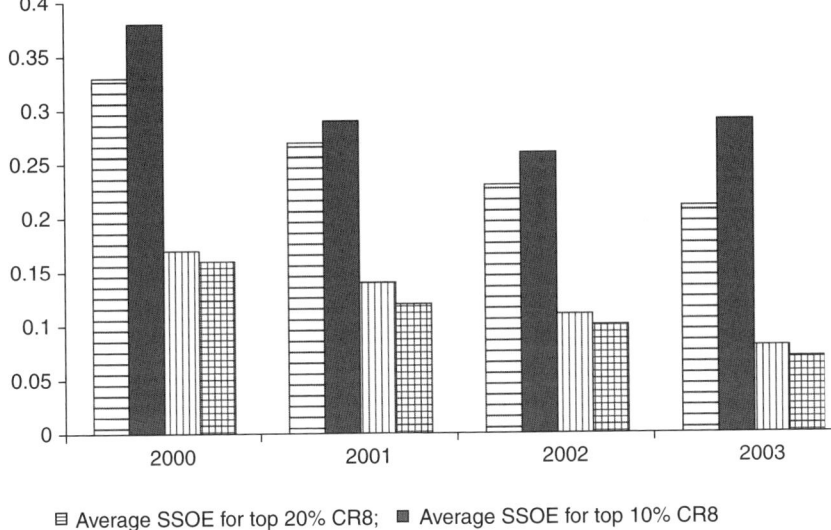

☐ Average SSOE for top 20% CR8; ■ Average SSOE for top 10% CR8
▥ Average SSOE for bottom 20% CR8; ▦ Average SSOE for bottom 10% CR8

Figure 8.4 State share average and CR8 ratios for 2000 to 2003
Source: Author's calculations based on data from *Chinese Industrial Microdata*.

also have incentives to protect SOEs for various reasons, such as employment, tax revenues, and so on.

There is no doubt that protectionism does exist with fiscal decentralization in China. But is state share still at the center of local protectionism at the later stage of reforms? Figure 8.4 does not fully support this view. We present the average of state share and CR8 ratios for 2000 to 2003 in Figure 8.4. We rank all industries based on CR8 ratios and calculate the average state shares for the industries that are in the top 10 percent and 20 percent, and bottom 10 percent and 20 percent of the CR8 ratios. If state share is one of the core factors leading to strong protectionism, we would expect to see that the lower the CR8 ratio, the higher the state share is for an industry. However, we find a lot more SOEs in the top 10 percent and 20 percent of the CR8 ratio levels than in the bottom 10 percent and 20 percent of CR8 ratio levels. It seems that a higher share of SOEs does not prevent the market from becoming more concentrated.

Another obvious trend in Figure 8.4 is the continuous decrease of state shares over this four-year period. This is not surprising considering the overall decline of state shares in China's economy since reforms started in 1978. Overall, Figure 8.4 does not demonstrate strong evidence to support the premise that at the later stage of reforms, state share is still the core reason leading towards strong protectionism.

Our examination of market concentration ratios and their link to TPMs and state shares for various periods in China suggests that protectionism associated with fiscal reforms seems to be much stronger in the early stage of reforms than the later stage, which generally conforms to the market-preserving federalism theory.

8.5 Economic structure: empirical evidence from factor markets

The competition among local governments also extends very much to the competition for production factors. We therefore continue to examine factor market structure in China.

8.5.1 Labor market

On the front of labor mobility it appears that, even though Chinese residents have been largely confined to the place of their births by the household registration system (*houkou* system[22]), it is well known that labor migration has been enormous. Official migration rates might be low for the 1980s and 1990s, but the evidence of labor migration is striking. "Despite its illegality, there appears to be migration in China. The numbers are not official but China's so-called floating population has been estimated to be as large as 100 million workers" (Bahl and Martinez-Vazquez, 2003). As expected, most labor migrants go to areas with higher wages and more urban employment opportunities. Thus, it is not surprising that many coastal provinces with rapid economic growth and more foreign investment see a higher rate of migration workers.

In addition to the self-motivated labor migration, Montinola., Qian. and Weingast (1995) also reported cases of organized labor export.

> Labor moves from areas of surplus to areas of need. An interesting story concerns labor export from Sichuan province. Total labor exported from this province has reached 3 million per year. Remittances from migrants have totaled as much as 3–5 billion yuan annually, accounting for ten percent of net farmer income in the province. Provincial authorities have attached great importance to labor export. The vice governor of Sichuan province pointed out that labor export has become an important means of developing backward local economies. It requires less capital and yields quick and high returns. Individuals leave with nothing and return with what is, by local standards, a fortune. Their annual incomes are largely higher than 1000 yuan, and some have assets over 1 million. They bring back capital to invest in the local economies, promoting the local economy and township village enterprises. To foster the process of labor export and capital import, the Sichuan provincial government established a labor development office headed by the vice governor. Different levels of local government authorities established organizations that are responsible for managing labor exports and the provision of training to improve skills.

In summary, there are existing barriers (such as the *Houkou* system) for migration, but labor does not seem to be a highly immobile production factor due to local protectionism or competition among different jurisdictions.

8.5.2 Capital market

However, the picture is not as clear when it comes to another important production factor, capital. In fact, many recent studies seem to converge to a consensus that China's capital markets are highly fragmented and capital lacks mobility. The most common method used to test capital market integration and capital mobility is the Feldstein and Horioka model (1980), which estimates the relationship between national savings and investment rates. Under the hypothesis of perfect capital mobility, the correlation between one country's savings and investment rates should be very low. Although their paper generated a debate on the validity of their test on international capital mobility,[23] it has been widely agreed that their method serves as a reasonable indicator of capital mobility across different regions within a country.[24] Applying the same method, both Boyreau-Debray and Wei (2002) and Zhao (1998) find that the correlation between China's provincial savings and investments is exceptionally high (around 0.5).[25] This result leads the conclusion that China's capital market is highly fragmented.

In addition to these empirical studies documenting capital market fragmentation, some also argue the existence of a direct link between fiscal policies and capital immobility. Dayal-Gulati and Husain (2002) suggest that the profit retention system in the early 1980s discouraged capital mobility because retained profits were part of local government revenues; thus, local governments discouraged the transfer of enterprises to other locations.

However, if we decompose total provincial savings and investment data to investigate savings and investment flows that fall under the "official" sector and "commercial" sector separately, such strong correlation disappears, at least where the commercial sector is concerned. Qi (2006) estimates the provincial savings and investment rates for the substantial commercial sector in China in the later stage of reforms (from 1995 to 2000) and finds that the coefficient moves further from fragmentation and closer to integration as the officially influenced capital flows are peeled away.[26] This demonstrates evidence that the commercial sector's behavior is different from the aggregate layer and is probably more integrated than we thought.

Qi (2006) also documents domestic policies and channels made available for improving capital market integration. For example, in the meetings of the 16th Central Committee of the Communist Party of China held in 2002, Beijing made it clear that its goal is to break regional and industrial blockages to promote the mobility of commodities and factors of production in the national market. In the survey on local protectionism conducted by the Development Research Center of the State Council (Li, Hou, Liu, and Chen, 2003), most surveyed enterprises report that local protectionism declined tremendously in the past two decades, and local governments' interference with funds transfer is not extensive, either. In addition, the survey also finds that as the scale of enterprises becomes larger, the percentage of local sales declines.[27]

The establishment of two stock markets in Shenzhen and Shanghai (in the early 1990s) and a nationwide stock brokerage, the launch of an inter-bank market for short-term funds transfers, the establishment of Trust and Investment Companies (TICs) – which have chosen borrowers and projects outside the state's Credit Plan – and the development of a commercial paper market all help to facilitate inter-regional funds transfers tremendously. In addition, Dayal-Gulati and

Husain (2002) also argue that changes in tax policies in the late 1980s and 1990s led to increased inter-regional capital mobility. Local authorities often offer fiscal incentives (such as tax holidays) to attract outside investment.

Other than the empirical support from rigorous analysis on provincial-level data (as presented in Qi [2006]), numerous anecdotal evidence shows that the production factor, capital, does move across provincial borders. The flows of commodities are accompanied by increased flows of private investment.

The trend for these private entrepreneurs to "go out" has already seen 7.62 billion yuan (US $910 million) invested in the Northeast, creating employment and at the same time injecting an enterprising spirit. More than 500 private enterprises from Zhejiang are due to take part in the annual Harbin Business and Trade Symposium, to be held on June 15–19, and co-sponsored by the governments of Heilongjiang and Zhejiang provinces.[28]

On April 20, 2004, *China Daily* stated that

economic cooperation between South China's Guangdong Province and Central China's Hunan Province was stepped up yesterday as some 98 contracts were signed involving a total investment of 35.83 billion yuan (US$4.3 billion). Guangdong's investment in Hunan is 24.1 billion yuan (US $2.9 billion), and the remaining 11.73 billion yuan (US $1.4 billion) consists of Guangdong's capital inflow by its business partners in Hunan.[29]

Local protectionism does not seem to stop commercial capital flows from moving across local borders to seek higher returns. Two decades of reforms did create a large commercial sector with market characteristics within China's financial system that displays important elements of market integration. Similar to the empirical evidence from the commodity market, we find that the integration in the factor market is also improving.

8.6 Conclusions

Our paper illustrates the major steps in fiscal reforms and discusses their impacts on China's economic structure. We focus on local protectionism, a phenomenon linked with fiscal decentralization, and its positive and negative effects on economic performance. General views recognize the inefficiencies and segmentation caused by local protectionism. Our analysis, however, advances these general views one step further to show that local protectionism tends to yield to market forces in the later stage of reforms. We find that both commodity and factor markets suggest a significant improvement in economic integration.

The evidence presented by this paper provides further insights in evaluating China's fiscal policy reforms on economic structure. The fiscal regime in China since the 1978 reforms offers provincial governments strong incentives to develop local economies. Though still problematic in regard to central-local fiscal relations and far from perfect, the reformed fiscal arrangements and jurisdiction competition seem to yield to market forces in the later stage of reforms. This process helps to build market order and competition in China's economic system, a theory supported by our macro level analysis in the paper.

In the future, a study focused on specific industries as case studies will complement the present research with detailed micro-level analysis on fiscal policies' impact on business development and industry structure. Such a study will also allow us to consider the forces of technical changes and institutional differences that are industry-idiosyncratic in understanding economic structure.

Acknowledgements

The author would like to thank Nazrul Islam, Tom Rawski, Shiro Hioki, Nobuhiro Okamoto, and Eric Ramstetter for their helpful comments on initial drafts of the paper. Special thanks to Tom Rawski and Ying Fang for generous assistance with data.

Notes

1 The data set, Chinese Industrial Microdata, was compiled by National Bureau of Statistics. Readers can find the description of this data set in the section ANNEX 2.A2 in OECD Economic Survey of China 2005. Web Site: available at http://www.oecd. org/docum ent/21/0,2340,en_2649_201185_35331797_1_1_1_1,00.html and www.bergamo.cisl.it/repository/edtlte/files/OBJ0000840.pdf. accessed on June 25, 2008.

2 Readers can find more detailed documentation of fiscal reforms in China in Bahl and Wallich (1992), Lin, Tao, and Liu (2003), Qian and Weingast (1996), World Bank report (2002), Oksenberg and Tong (1991), Zhang Le-yin (1999), and Wong (1991).

3 The other arrangements are: dividing revenue, sharing total revenue, decoupling expenditure from revenue, and lump-sum transfer. Oksenberg and Tong (1991) described the details of these arrangements and the duration of these different contracts in their study.

4 In addition to balancing central control and local autonomy, some argue that Mao's inclination to decentralization is the reason for such a switch. For example, Qian and Weingast (1996) mention that "From the beginning, Mao Zedong did not like the Soviet type planning system because he felt that over centralization depressed people's incentives. Mao believed in people's initiatives and incentives, although he emphasized incentives from autonomy and political consciousness, not profits or materials." Others point out that the decision to reverse is due to the complication of managing and monitoring such a large economy under a complete centralized system. "The classical problem of control and monitoring under information asymmetry emerged soon after the planned system was set up. As the economy grew larger with more projects initiated and enterprises started, the plan system became increasingly unmanageable" (Lin, Tao, and Liu, 2003).

5 Details of these experiments are available in Oksenberg and Tong (1991).

6 About 80 percent of the shared revenues were remitted to the central government, and 20 percent were retained by local governments.

7 For example, from 1980 to 1984, wealthy provinces accumulated a large amount of surpluses based on the uniform sharing formula, whereas poor provinces ended up with large deficits. In 1985, the State Council adopted different sharing arrangements for different provinces based on local governments' budget balances in previous years.

However, this new sharing formula lowered the revenue growth of wealthy regions. So in 1998, the State Council started a new system with six different sharing schemes for different provinces. They are: (1) "Fixed sharing," whereby a fixed proportion is remitted to the center (applied to three provinces/cities); (2) "Incremental sharing," whereby a certain proportion is retained up to a quota and then a higher proportion is retained in excess of the quota (applied to three provinces/cities); (3) "Sharing up to a limit with growth adjustment," whereby the localities retain a specified proportion that is within a specific percentage of revenue from the previous year and then retain all revenues above that quota (applied to ten provinces/cities); (4) "Fixed quota delivery," whereby a specified, nominal amount is remitted to the center (applied to three provinces/cities); (5) "Fixed quota with growth adjustment," whereby the fixed amount remitted to the center is increased at a contracted rate (applied to two provinces/cities); and (6) "Fixed subsidies" (applied to 14 provinces/cities). See Bahl and Wallich (1992).

8 See Yinong, Tian et al. (1985) "On Reforms of the Fiscal Management Structure," *Economic Almanac*, IV–12, pp. 90.

9 See details from Zhang, 1999.

10 For example, Qian and Weingast point out in their market-preserving theory that "some areas have used their freedom and authority to maintain considerable trade barriers" (World Bank, 1993).

11 Source: research paper published on the Web site of the National Development and Reform Commission. Also available at http://www.sdpc.gov.cn/tzgg/zhdt/t20051207_52696.htm. accessed on June 25, 2008.

12 Source: Information Times. Also available at: http://informationtimes.dayoo.com/gb/content/2005-09/06/content_2210071.htm. accessed on June 25, 2008.

13 Source: China Youth Daily. Also available at: http://finance.sina.com.cn/leadership/jygl/20060110/07192262020.shtml. accessed on June 25, 2008.

14 Source: Guangming Daily, May 11, 1998. Also available at: http://www.gmw.cn/01gmrb/1998-05/11/GB/17689%5EGM5-1112.htm. accessed on June 25, 2008.

15 There are various indicators to measure economic structure. For example, HHI (Herfindahl-Hirschman Index) is another commonly accepted measure of market concentration. It is calculated by squaring the market share of each firm competing in the market and then summing the resulting numbers.

16 For example, our data for 1993 cover about 64.5 percent of total industrial output in China. The adjusted average CR8 is (raw average CR8)*(64.5 percent).

17 Note: data before 1992 presented in Figures 8.1 and 8.2 are based on unpublished calculations by Tom, Rawski and Ying, Fang (2006), University of Pittsburgh.

18 Readers can obtain more information on spatial input-output linkages among different provinces in China from the study by Hioki and Okamoto (Chapter 7 in this volume).

19 Bai, Du, Tao, and Tong (2004) adopted the same definition of TPM.

20 Source: Li, Baojiang (2001). "Yingxiang Woguo Yancao Hangye Fazhan de Beijing Tiaojian Fenxi," *Zhongguo Gongye Jingji*, No. 6. Also available at: http://www.usc.cuhk.edu.hk/wk_wzdetails.asp?id=3793. accessed on June 25, 2008.

21 We also have the data for 1992, 2003, and 2004. However, due to the changed industry codes mentioned above, we cannot compare the results of these years with the ten-year period from 1993 to 2002.

22 The *Hukou* system was

> re-adopted by PRC from long standing Chinese tradition, households were designated as rural or urban. The designation, which went beyond mobility issues, was openly unfair towards rural households. In effect, Hukou meant that only designated urban households were allowed to reside in cities and towns employed by state enterprises and with access to subsidized foods and other benefits. (Bahl and Martinez-Vazquez, 2003)

23 For example, Robert, Murphy (1984) points out that in citing the positive correlation between savings and investment as the evidence to demonstrate the immobility of the

capital, Feldstein and Horioka "appear to have confused two assumptions frequently employed together in international macroeconomic modeling: namely, the assumption of perfect capital mobility and the assumption of a small country." Further, Murphy states that "even when potential econometric problems are left aside, their test is not a test of capital mobility alone, but a joint test of capital mobility and country size." Linda, Tesar (1991) provides a comprehensive survey of the theory and evidence on the relationship between savings and investment.

24   See the logic and reasoning provided by Boyreau-Debray and Shang Jin Wei (2002). John, F Helliwell. and Ross, McKitrick. (1998) also show that the "savings retention disappears if the region of study is a province within Canada rather than the nation as a whole."

25   This figure is high compared to estimates obtained for other advanced economies whose domestic financial markets are generally presumed to be highly integrated. For example, Boyreay-Debray and Wei (2002) report that the coefficients on provincial/ state savings and investment rates for Japan, the United States, Canada, and Germany are close to zero or even negative.

26   In some cases, the coefficient even looks like those in advanced nations.

27   For example, "21 percent of the small-size enterprises' local sales figures are less than 10 percent of their total sales, 27 percent of the large-size enterprises' local sales figures are less than 10 percent of their total sales."

28   Shao, Ziaoyi. 2004. "Zhejiang Enterprises Strive to Go Outside," *China Business Weekly*, May 17–23, pp. 17.

29   Liu, Weifeng. 2004. "Guangdong, Hunan Strengthen Co-operation," *China Daily*, April 20, pp. 10.

Bibliography

Bahl, Roy and Christine Wallich. 1992. "Intergovernmental Fiscal Relations in China," PRE Working Paper 863 (February). Washington, D.C.: The World Bank, Policy Research Department.

Bahl, Roy and Jorge Martinez-Vazquez. 2003. "Fiscal Federalism and Economic Reform in China," Georgia State University Andrew Young School of Policy Studies working paper 03–13.

Bai, Cong-En, Yingjuan Du, Zhigang Tao, and Sarah, Y. Tong. 2004. "Local Protectionism and Regional Specialization: Evidence from China's Industries," *Journal of International Economics*, Vol. 63, pp. 397–417.

Boyreau-Debray, G. and ShangJin, Wei. 2002. "Can China Grow Faster? A Diagnosis of the Fragmentation of Its Domestic Capital Market," IMF Working Paper No. 04/76. IMF: Washington, D.C.

China Light Industry Yearbook. *China Light Industry Yearbook* (various years). Beijing, China: China Light Industry Yearbook Press.

Dayal-Gulati, Anuradha and Aasim, M. Husain. 2002. "Centripetal Forces in China's Economic Takeoff," IMF staff paper Vol. 49, No. 3.

Helliwell, John F. and Ross McKitrick. 1999. "Comparing Capital Mobility Across Provincial and National Borders," *The Canadian Journal of Economics*, Vol. 32, No. 5, pp. 1164–1173.

Li, Shantong, Yongzhi Hou, Yunzhong Liu and Bo Chen. 2003. "Survey Report on China's Domestic Local Protectionism," Development Research Centre of the State Council, Vol. 65, October, 2003, Beijing, P. R. C.

Lin, Justin Yifu, Ran Tao, and Mingxing Liu. 2003. "Decentralization and Local Governance in China's Economic Transition," Paper prepared for the conference *The Rise of Local Governments in Developing Countries*, London School of Economics, May 2003.

Ma, Jun and Norregaard John. 1998. "China's Fiscal Decentralization," Research Paper listed for the China Project at Chatham House, Web Site available at http://unjobs.org/authors/jun-ma

McKitrick, J. 1998. "Comparing Capital Mobility across Provincial and National Borders," NBER Working Paper 6624.

Montinola, Gabriella, Yingyi Qian and Barry R. Weingast. 1995. "Federalism, Chinese Style: The Political Basis for Economic Success in China," *World Politics*, Vol. 48, No. 1, pp. 50–81.

Murphy, Robert G. 1984. "Capital Mobility and the Relationship between Saving and Investment Rates in OECD Countries," *Journal of International Money and Finance*, Vol. 3, pp. 327–342.

Naughton, Barry. 2003. "How Much Can Regional Integration Do to Unify China's Markets?" In Nicholas, Hope, Dennis, Yang and Mu, Yang Li. (eds.) *How Far Across the River? Chinese Policy Reform at the Millennium*, Stanford: Stanford University Press, pp. 204–232.

Oates, Wallace. 1972. *Fiscal Federalism*, New York: Harcourt Brace Jovanovich.

Oksenberg, Michel and Tong James. 1991. "The Evolution of Central-Provincial Fiscal Relations in China, 1971–1984: The Formal System," *The China Quarterly*, Vol. 125, pp. 1–32.

Park, Albert and Yang Du. 2005. "Blunting the Razor's Edge: Regional Development in Reform China," *Jingji Xuebao (China Journal of Economics)*, Vol. 1, No. 2, pp. 149–159.

Poncet, Sandra. 2003. "Measuring Chinese Domestic and International Integration," *China Economic Review*, No. 14, pp. 1–21.

Poncet, Sandra. 2005. "A Fragmented China: Measure and Determinants of Chinese Domestic Market Disintegration," *Review of International Economics*, Vol. 13, No. 3, pp. 409–430.

Qi, Li. 2006. Capital Flows and Domestic Market Integration in China. Unpublished dissertation, University of Pittsburgh.

Qian, Yingyi and Barry R. Weingast. 1996. "China's Transition to Markets: Market-Preserving Federalism, Chinese Style," *Journal of Policy Reform*, No. 1, pp. 149–185.

Rawski, Tom and Ying Fang. 2006. Unpublished analysis of enterprise-level data from China Industrial Microdata. University of Pittsburgh.

Tan, Xiaoying, Yu Kongju and Zhang Tai. 2006. "Difang Baohu Zhuyi de Chengyi, Weihai ji DuiCe," National Development and Reform Committee Web site, available at http://www.sdpc.gov.cn/tzgg/zhdt/t20051207_52696.htm. Accessed on June 26, 2008.

Tesar, Linda L. 1991. "Savings, Investment and International Capital Flows," *Journal of International Economics*, Vol. 31, pp. 55–78.

Tiebout, Charles. 1956. "A Pure Theory of Local Expenditure," *Journal of Political Economy*, Vol. 64, pp. 416–424.

Wong, Christine P. W. 1991. "Central-Local Relations in an Era of Fiscal Decline: the Paradox of Fiscal Decentralization in Post-Mao China," *The China Quarterly*, Vol. 128, pp. 691–715.

World Bank. 1993. "China: Internal Market Development and Regulation," Country Operation Division, China and Mongolia Department. November 24, 1993.

World Bank. 2002. "China: National Development and Subnational Finance, a Review of Provincial Expenditures," April 2002. Report No. 22951-CHA.

Xu, Xinpeng. 2002. "Have the Chinese Provinces Become Integrated under Reform?" *China Economic Review*, Vol. 13, pp. 116–133.

Young, Alwin. 2000. "The Razor's Edge: Distortions and Incremental Reform in the People's Republic of China," *The Quarterly Journal of Economics*, Vol. 115, No. 4, pp. 1091–1135.

Zhang, Le-yin. 1999. "Chinese Central-Provincial Fiscal Relationships, Budgetary Decline and the Impact of the 1994 Fiscal Reform: An Evaluation," *The China Quarterly*, Vol. 157, pp. 115–141.

Zhao, Rui. 1998. "Capital Mobility and Regional Integration in China," (mimeo) International Monetary Fund.

9
Exploring the Persistence of State Corporate Ownership in China

Ken Imai

9.1   Introduction

After more than a quarter of a century of the transition process beginning in the late 1970s, China is now probably one of the most competitive market economies in the world. In many industries in the country, you can witness an overwhelming number of firms engaging in throat-cutting types of competition. Growth in demand invites building-up of new capacities and almost endless new entries, which often lead profitability down to extreme lows. While the government occasionally tries in vain to control new investment in or entries into those sectors, this "excessive" competition as is often alleged, eventually turns out to be the very driving force of the industrial development.

You may reasonably expect that this apparent progress in transition to a market economy should accompany an ever-dwindling share of State-Owned Enterprises (SOEs) and massive privatization. It surely does, at least in many industrial subsectors where market entry is relatively easy. But in terms of the share of broadly defined SOE that includes corporations in which the state retains dominant equities, the presence of state-ownership has not shown a clear sign of decline in recent years. At the same time, even in some of the competitive sub-sectors like consumer products there remains a handful of state-owned firms successfully surviving harsh competition. Thus state corporate ownership still persists in China.

The main motivation of this chapter is to show that, behind these seemingly paradoxical phenomena, there is significant evolution in the nature of state-ownership in response to diversified market environments. It also highlights several dilemmas that China faces in restructuring SOEs, especially those of which the scale is so large that their fates are likely to incur significant influence on the regional economies where they are located, industrial sub-sectors to which they belong, or even the national economy as a whole.

The following sections are organized as follows. Section 9.2 roughly sketches the progress of the reform of SOEs in China so far as background information, focusing mainly on the tide of privatization of small and medium SOEs and corporatization of large enterprises that has accelerated since the second half of the 1990s. The section then proceeds to provide the data that illuminate the persistence of state-ownership. Sections 9.3 and 9.4 focus on two distinctive types of large SOEs and explore the nature of state-ownership and dilemmas they face in restructuring themselves in the process of marketization. Section 9.5 concludes the chapter with presenting some prospects of the reform.

9.2   China's SOE reform: progress so far

During the first decade, beginning in the early 1980s, reform of SOEs had focused almost solely on enhancing the managerial autonomy, which means delegation of managerial decision-making rights from supervisory government bureaus (either central or local, depending on the original affiliation of the SOE in question) to the management. This early stage of SOE reform, along with increasing pressure from newly emerging competitors such as township and village enterprises (TVEs), undoubtedly promoted more market-oriented behavior of SOEs. Econometric studies that measure productivity growth in China's industrial sector show that in this period SOEs as a whole experienced improvement in efficiency, while the margin of improvement was slim in comparison with non-SOEs, especially TVEs.[1]

Along with the efficiency improvement of more or less limited scale, the reform that focused on managerial autonomy also produced a new dilemma, that is the balance between the autonomy of management and control rights of the state as the single largest shareholder of SOEs. Government bureaus in charge of supervising SOEs were obliged to monitor the management to prevent managerial slack or embezzlement of state-owned assets by the management. At the same time, excess intervention was apt to affect efficiency, which in turn would result in instant deterioration of financial performance under the increasingly competitive market environment. It was always almost impossible to draw the line between legitimate monitoring as the state-shareholder and inefficient government intervention. These limitations in the first stage of the reform led to the second stage of reform in China: privatization of small and medium firms and corporatization of large firms.

9.2.1   Upsurge of privatization

The first turning point came in the early 1990s, when the Communist Party of China (hereafter "the Party") declared that the goal of the economic reform is the realization of a so-called "socialist market economy." which virtually means a full transition to a standard market economy, with the state keeping control by way of state ownership in "key sectors" (although exactly what "key sectors" means has never been clearly stated to date[2]). With regard to enterprise reform, the Party Communiqué in 1993 authorized local governments to experiment with "various measures" including straightforward sellout of small SOEs.

This political sea change came at the moment when local governments saw financial performance of small and medium SOEs under their jurisdiction deteriorate seriously owing mainly to ever-increasing competition with TVEs and private enterprises. This triggered acute budgetary crises especially in county- or ward-level governments, which used to depend on tax from SOEs for much of their revenue. As the new policy had become more firmly confirmed through the second half of the 1990s, a growing number of local governments, with a view to shedding off financial burden, set out to sell off small and medium SOEs that were mostly losing money.[3]

Despite the fact that the process has been underway for more than a decade, we can not accurately assess the progress of privatization so far due to unavailability of reliable data. The Party and the central government still refrain from officially endorsing privatization in order to avoid ideological disputes that may disturb further progress of the reform. Privatization is, together with other forms of reform such as corporatization (which does not necessary involve change of ownership) or merger (which may be a merger with another SOE), labeled rather ambiguously as "property-rights restructuring (*chanquan gaige* or *gaizhi*)." Aside from sample surveys conducted sporadically, no official data is published as to the progress of privatization or even "property-rights restructuring". Thus, we need to call upon some proxy measures that are likely to approximate the trend best of all.

Table 9.1 shows the number of SOEs published annually from Ministry of Finance (later from State-owned Assets Supervision and Administration Commission). It is important to note that these statistics covers not only traditional SOEs which are wholly owned by the state (*guoyou qiye* or *guoyou duzi qiye*: WSOEs, or wholly-state-owned enterprises), but also corporations of which majority equities are still in the hand of the state. The latter type of firms is designated "state-equities-controlled enterprises" (*guoyou konggu qiye*: SCEs)

Table 9.1   The number of SOEs (excluding the financial sector)

	1995	2000	2001	2002	2003	2004	2005	1995–2005 change
Broadly-defined SOEs	253,525	190,508	173,504	158,712	146,000	137,753	127,067	−49.9%
Large	8,442	9,283	9,453	9,436	n.a.	n.a.	2,761	−67.3%
Medium	38,413	27,672	27,527	27,886	n.a.	n.a.	12,764	−66.8%
Small	206,670	153,553	136,524	121,390	n.a.	n.a.	111,542	−46.0%
WSOEs	218,582	144,406	n.a.	n.a.	n.a.	n.a.	72,640	−33.9%
SCEs	14,283	32,146	n.a.	n.a.	n.a.	n.a.	44,138	125.1%

Notes:
1) The criteria for scale classification lack continuity between 2002 and 2005 (see footnote 9 in the text).
2) In 2005 the number of WSOEs and SCEs is less than the total SOE since the total includes 10,289 independent public business agencies that are classified into neither WSOEs or SCEs.

Source: 1995–2003: Ministry of Finance. 2004 and 2005: State-owned Assets Supervision and Administration Commission.

in official statistics.[4] The two categories combined together compose "broadly defined SOEs". Hereafter in this chapter we call them just "SOEs" for simplicity and in accordance with the now prevalent wording in China.

The data indicate that the number of SOEs declined drastically from 1995 to 2005. Within 11 years the number of SOEs was nearly halved. Despite the discontinuity of disaggregated data, it is apparent that the overwhelming majority of the decline is attributable to small- and medium-scale firms, most of which fall under the jurisdiction of municipal, county, and ward governments. The disproportionate decrease of large and medium SOEs between 2002 and 2005 may likely be explained by the upward revision of criteria for scale classification of industrial enterprises. Statistics of SOE bankruptcy cases filed to the courts, which are mostly of small and medium SOEs, indicates that bankruptcy roughly accounts for only one third of the decline in the number of SOEs.[5] Thus we can assume that the remaining two thirds of the decline resulted from non-bankruptcy property-rights restructuring including privatization, liquidation, and mergers.[6]

The fact that as late as 2005 there still remained more than a 100,000 small and medium SOEs nationwide suggests that, in spite of prevailing enthusiasm on the side of local governments for promoting privatization, full privatization or liquidation of smal and medium SOEs may take more time than conventional wisdom predicts,[7] There are a number of factors that may deter smooth transition.

Surveys show that in many cases privatization of small and medium SOEs take place by way of buyout by incumbent managers (Management Buyout: MBO) or employees including managers (Management-Employee Buyout: MEBO).[8] Privatization by outsiders such as acquisition by private enterprises, though increasing in numbers, still remains in a minority, due probably to factors such as serious information asymmetry between insiders and outsiders, aversion by insiders, or just sheer lack of investment value. Whichever way of privatization is to be chosen, pricing of state-owned equity is always a controversial issue. Managers or outside investors are often alleged to have acquired state equity at "unfair" prices, which usually mean significantly lower than the book value (We will return to the pricing issue in Section 9.4). Privatization also frequently invites labor disputes. In some cases, employees are forced to buy state equities in return for job guarantees.

These frictions in the process of privatization invite occasional interventions by the central government aiming at "institutionalizing" the tide of privatization of small and medium SOEs. Nevertheless, both central and local governments have been convinced that in the long run leaving those small and medium firms owned by the state, most of which have been losing money for years, costs much more than letting them be privatized or liquidated by whichever way that is feasible. Thus there is virtually no chance that the current trend of sweeping privatization will be reversed.

At the same time, it is noteworthy that the number of firms designated as "large", which usually employ more than thousands of workers, showed little sign of decline at least up to 2002. Did the drastic decline in the number of large

SOEs thereafter lead to a shrinking share of SOEs in China's economy? We examine this issue in the next subsection.

9.2.2 Persistence of state-ownership

First we check the industrial sector, of which most systematic data is available. Table 9.2 presents the number of industrial SOEs and their share in the sector in terms of value-added. Because of the unavailability of output data that covers all industrial firms, we use value-added of the industrial sector in the national income statistics (i.e., the industrial sector's component of GDP), which covers value-added produced by all industrial enterprises at least in theory, as denominator.[9]

So far as the number of firms is concerned, the data show a much similar trend as is indicated in the previous all-sector data in Table 9.1. Rather, the decline in the number of SOEs is far more outstanding than in the case of the all-industry data. WSOEs almost solely account for the decline. It had also been accompanied by a sharp reduction in the share of the output of WSOEs in the industrial sector at least up to 2003, the latest year of which relevant data is available.

It should be noted, however, that the share of broadly defined SOEs in the sector had shown no apparent sign of decline since the late 1990s up to 2004. It had been more or less stable around 34 to 36 percent until 2004–2005, after which a

Table 9.2 The number and share of SOEs in the industrial sector

	Number of firms			Share (%) of SOEs in the sector value-added[1]		
	All SOEs	WSOEs	SCEs[2]	All SOEs (%)	WSOEs (%)	SCEs[2] (%)
1993	n.a.	80,586	n.a.	n.a.	51.5	n.a.
1994	87,084	79,731	7,353	n.a.	40.8	n.a.
1995	n.a.	87,905	n.a.	n.a.	33.6	n.a.
1996	n.a.	86,982	n.a.	n.a.	30.1	n.a.
1997	84,397	74,388	10,009	34.0	28.4	5.6
1998	64,737	n.a.	n.a.	33.2	n.a.	n.a.
1999	61,301	50,651	10,650	34.6	23.4	11.2
2000	53,489	42,426	11,063	35.3	18.5	16.8
2001	46,767	34,530	12,237	35.7	14.6	21.0
2002	41,125	29,499	11,626	34.2	14.1	20.2
2003	34,280	23,228	11,052	35.5	13.5	22.0
2004	31,750	n.a.	n.a.	37.0	n.a.	n.a.
2005	29,229	n.a.	n.a.	34.2	n.a.	n.a.
2006	24,961	14,555	10,406	31.4	n.a.	n.a.

Notes:
1) Value-added of SOEs divided by GDP produced by the industrial sector. All GDP data before the year 2005 are figures prior to the upward revision announced in 2005.
2) SCEs in this table include limited liability companies owned wholly by the State.

Source: National Bureau of Statistics and the author's calculation.

Table 9.3   Ratio (%) of SOE sales to GDP (2003–2006)

	All SOEs	Centrally-monitored SOEs
2003	79.0	32.9
2004	77.0	34.7
2005	76.8	36.6
2006	76.9	39.4

Note: Excluding the financial sector.

Source: Compiled by the author based on press release from SASAC.

clear sign of decline came to the fore. While the data is patchy due to frequent changes of format in original sources, it is highly likely that this seemingly paradoxical stability of the share of SOEs is attributable to the growing share of SCEs that compensates the steep decline of the WSOEs share.

To buttress the point we return to all-sector statistics again. Table 9.3 shows the ratio of sales by SOEs to GDP since 2003 to 2006, the only period for which consistent data is available. It indicates that sales by SOEs in relation to GDP has been barely declining (we will refer to more detail of the data later). In spite of the conceptual limitation (sales is not directly comparable with value-added), the data in Table 9.3 combined with Table 9.1 supports our presumption that growth of SCEs in terms of production explains the "persistence of state-ownership" in China's economy.

The most important contributors to the growth of SCEs are listed companies of which the state remains the single largest shareholder. After a government-driven campaign of corporatization and stock listing since the late 1990s, most of the largest SOEs nowadays had reorganized their core business as corporations and had them listed on domestic or overseas stock exchanges so that they can cash in on the drastic growth of China's capital market. About 60 percent of companies listed on the Shanghai and Shenzhen Stock Exchanges are SCEs, controlled by so-called state-shareholders, that is the central government, local governments, or SOEs which are entrusted with the state-owned shares (*guoyougu*).[10] Table 9.4 shows that in the Shanghai Stock Exchange around 50 percent of shares issued are classified as state-owned shares. Thus, in spite of a growing number of stock listings and acquisitions of listed companies by private firms, the dominance of state-shareholders remains basically intact to date.

China's large SOEs today are very much diversified. In the following two sections we focus on two distinctive cases, in which SOEs remain viable under sharply contrasting market environments. In industries where minimum capital requirement is significantly large or increasing return to scale works, SOEs' dominance has not been seriously challenged yet. SOEs still take hold of their established

Table 9.4 Composition of shares (percent of the total) issued by companies listed on Shanghai stock exchange

	2001	2002	2003	2004	2005	2006	June 2007
State-owned shares	50.3	52.3	57.7	57.6	57.3	44.7	52.3
Legal persons' shares	12.7	10.8	8.6	8.2	8.1	6.4	10.0
Other shares with trade listriction	0.0	0.0	0.5	0.8	0.6	26.4	8.9
Tradable shares	37.0	36.8	33.2	33.4	34.0	22.5	28.8

Source: Shanghai Stock Exchange Statistics.

positions in these industries largely on account of the oligopolistic nature of the market (we call them "Oligopolistic type" SOEs). On the other hand, even in highly competitive industries, there exists a handful of SOEs that are successfully surviving harsh competition and remain leading companies in the industries. Their survival and growth under an adverse market environment depends on ingenious entrepreneurship of managers *par excellence* ("Entrepreneurial type" SOEs).

In reality, the dichotomy cannot be rigorously applied. The majority of SOEs lie somewhere between the two "polar" types. We focus on the two types in this chapter, however, because by comparing the "polar" types we can illustrate how the difference in market condition affects the allocation of control rights between the state and managers. The two types also highlights issues large SOEs face in promoting further reform, which are interconnected with the issue of control rights. In the following two sections, we examine the oligopolistic type and the entrepreneurial type respectively based mainly on case studies of two SOEs.

9.3 Oligopolistic type

Corporate ownership structure differs widely across industries in China. As far as the industrial sector is concerned, SOEs have retained their dominance in heavy industries above all, where entry barriers are higher due to large minimum requirement for fixed investment.[11]

Figure 9.1 illustrates the point by showing relationship between average capital/labor ratio and the share of broadly defined SOEs in 34 industrial sub-sectors. It indicates that, mainly on account of the continuous decline of SOEs' share in less capital-intensive industries, capital intensity and the share of SOEs has become more strongly correlated. The dominance of SOEs still remains more or less intact in industrial sub-sectors such as mining, petrochemicals, ferrous and non-ferrous metals, and transportation equipment.[12] Competition does exists in these industries too. Aside from increasing competition among SOEs and with foreign-invested companies, a handful of private companies are growing so vigorously that they have started to pose serious threats to the incumbents, which

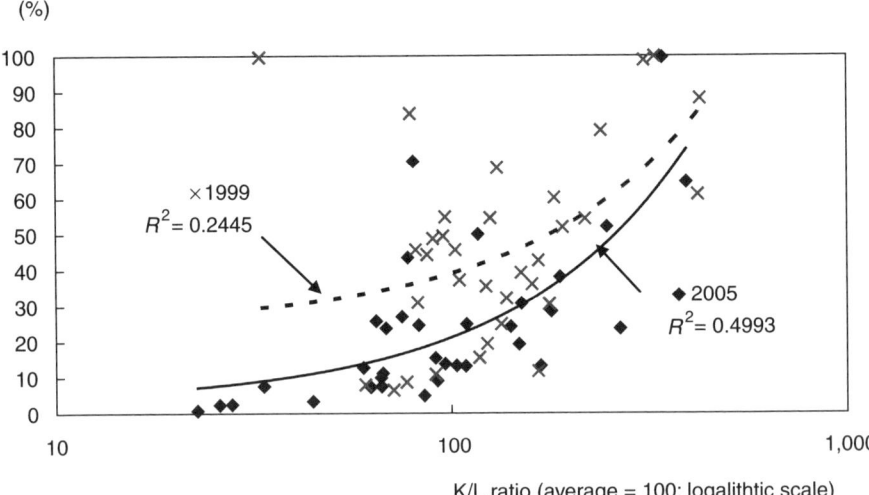

(%)

K/L ratio (average = 100; logalithtic scale)

Figure 9.1   Relationship between K/L ratio and the share of SOEs by industrial sub-sector (excluding public utilities) in 1999 and 2005

Notes:

1) K/L ratio is calculated by dividing nominal fixed assets net of depreciation by the number of employees.
2) The petroleum and natural gas extraction industry is excluded because of the exceptionally high K/L ratio.
3) The shares of SOEs are biased upward because of the coverage problem of industrial statistics (see footnote 9 in the text).

Source: Calculated by the author based on *Statistical Yearbook of China*, various years.

makes them act more in accordance with market principles. However, as long as the scales of the incumbents, which are mostly state-owned, are overwhelmingly larger than the newcomers, markets remain to be oligopolistic by the standard of China's highly competitive environment.[13] Statistical data in connection with ownership attributes is rather scarce outside the industrial sector; but it is apparent that in some highly capital-intensive and still highly regulated service sectors such as telecommunication, transportation, and finance, the dominance of SOEs is much more confirmed.[14]

Many of SOEs in these sub-sectors are traditional large SOEs. They are "traditional" in the sense that they are usually under more stringent control by government ministries and at the same time are still heavily burdened with the legacy of the planned economy, such as redundant workforce, underperforming assets, and money-losing business units.

The largest ones among the large SOEs in these industries, which typically employ hundreds of thousands of workers, are supervised directly by the State-owned Assets Supervision and Administration Commission (*Guoyou zichan jiandu guanli weiyuanhui*: SASAC) of the central government, which was established in 2003 as a result of the reshuffling of two organizations: the former

State Economic and Trade Commission of the State Council and the Central Enterprise Work Commission of the Party.[15] Below we look into the case of SINOPEC Group as one of the most representative of traditional large SOEs in oligopolistic industries.

9.3.1 SINOPEC Group

China Petrochemical Corporation (*Zhongguo Shihua Jituan Gongsi or* SINOPEC: hereafter "SINOPEC Group") is the largest company in China by sales as of 2006, according to China Enterprise Confederation. SINOPEC Group was established as a result of sweeping reorganization of the petroleum and petrochemical industries led by the government in 1998. Before the reorganization, while old SINOPEC had been defined as a business entity since the early 1980s, in fact it had been a semi-ministerial organization responsible also for the administrative control of the petrochemical industry. The reorganization in 1998, aimed at introducing competition into the industries, produced two gigantic state-owned corporations that integrate development, drilling, and refining of petroleum and production of petrochemical products: SINOPEC, and China Natural Gas and Petroleum Group Company (CNPC Group). These two and China National Offshore Oil Corporation (CNOOC), which is also a WSOE established earlier, are by far the three largest competitors in China's petroleum, natural gas, and petrochemical markets. All of the three companies fall under the jurisdiction of SASAC.

In 2000 SINOPEC Group separated its core business and reorganized it into China Petroleum and Chemical Corporation (SINOPEC Corp.), a Joint Stock Company (hereafter "JSC") of which state-owned shares are entrusted with the group (Figure 9.2). SINOPEC Corp. had its shares listed on Hong Kong, New York, London, and Shanghai stock exchanges and successfully raised close to US$5 billion. SINOPEC Group remains to be wholly state-owned. CNPC and CNOOC carried out schemes of reorganization and stock listing almost simultaneously.

Legally speaking, the relationship between SINOPEC Group and SINOPEC Corp. is a shareholding company and its subsidiary listed company. However, as is illustrated by the fact that the Chairman of SINOPEC Corp. serves also as Chief Executive Officer of the group company, in actuality the operation of the two companies is by no means strictly separated.[16]

Since most unprofitable business units and non-business auxiliary service units have been left to SINOPEC Group, it is losing money if the profit of SINOPEC Corp. is excluded (Table 9.5). Still, it employs as many as 340,000 workers.

Since 2005, due primarily to the historical surge in oil price, SINOPEC Corp. saw its net profit grow by more than 20 percent on a year-on-year basis. Nonetheless, in the long run, dividends from SINOPEC Corp. do not sufficiently provide for more than 300,000 workers of SINOPEC Group at the same time as repaying interests and principals of debts outstanding that amount to two thirds of the company's total assets (net of SINOPEC Corp.). It is reported that more than half of SINOPEC Group's employees are in non-core business or auxiliary service units, most of which are losing money and need to be separated out from the group.[17]

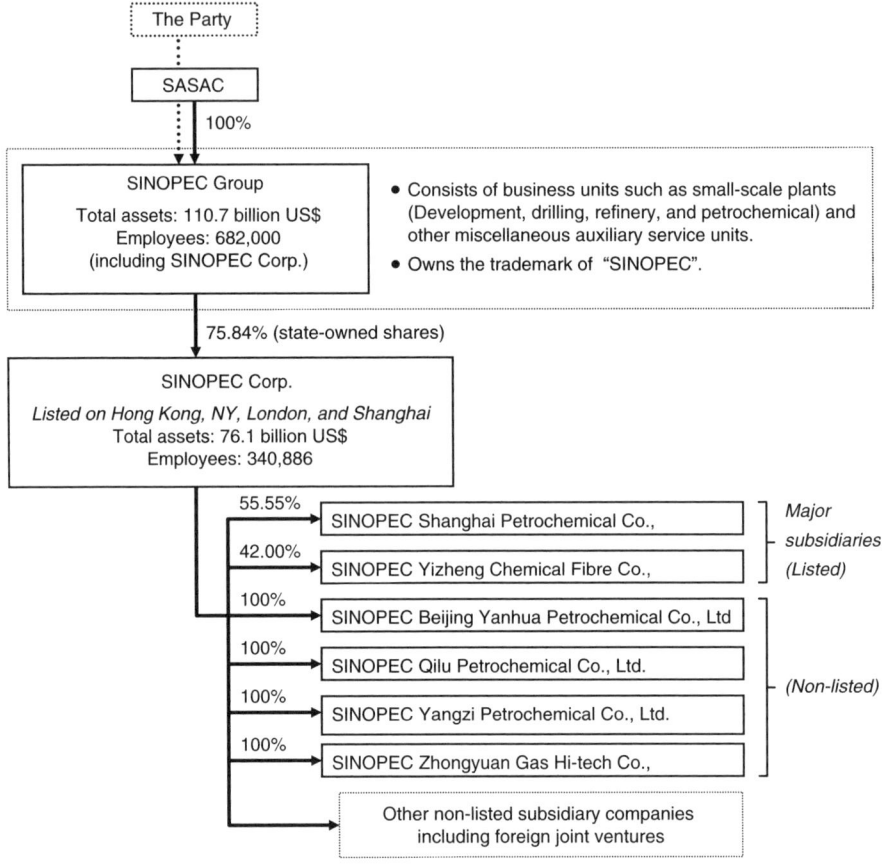

Figure 9.2   Corporate structure of SINOPEC Group (as of the end of FY 2006)

Note: Four non-listed major subsidiaries, which had been stock listed, were privatized by SINOPEC Corp. in 2005 as part of the plan to further consolidate its business that used to be excessively decentralized.

Source: Compiled by the author based on the prospectus and annual reports of SINOPEC Corp. and various sources.

Table 9.5   Financial performance of SINOPEC Group

	Net profit (Million US$)		
	2004	2005	2006
SINOPEC Group [consolidated]	1,269	2,668	3,781
[Excluding SINOPEC Corp]	–2,631	–2,159	–2,707
SINOPEC Corp	3,900	4,828	6,488

Source: Annual reports.

The cost of restructuring of labor, asset and debt is roughly estimated to be US$5 billion.[18] The group company has to promote the restructuring without inflicting social disputes.[19]

Apparently, the most feasible way to finance the large-scale restructuring is divesting a part of the state shares of SINOPEC Corp, as the group company itself recognizes.[20] But hasty divestiture entails a great risk of drastic disruption in the stock price and/or destabilization in corporate management, since China still lacks qualified investors that have financial resources and managerial capability to lead the corporate governance of huge public companies such as SINOPEC Corp.. Thus it is highly likely that SINOPEC Corp. will remain dominated by the state capital for the foreseeable future.

Being a large wholly state-owned corporation of strategic importance, SINOPEC Group, along with CNPC and CNOOC, is supervised by SASAC, which acts as the state-shareholder. The officially claimed mission of SASAC is the maximization of corporate value of companies under its supervision including SINOPEC Group. Recently SASAC is inclined to favor the idea that it will follow the model of Temasek, the largest Singaporean state investment company which has a high international reputation as a successful institutional investor. However, at present the role of SASAC seems to be more promotion of industrial policy than maximization of corporate value, reflecting its previous organizational background.

The sheer size of the companies under its jurisdiction – 147 large SOEs covering almost all industrial and services sectors with assets exceeding one trillion US dollars and more than nine million employees – also rules out a quick shift of SASAC to the value-maximizing investment model a la Temasek. On top of that, it is reported that the Party retains the appointment power of the top management of 53 ultra-large SOEs including SINOPEC Group.[21] There is also close interconnection in terms of personnel between party cadres and bureaucrats on the one side and strategically important industries such as petroleum and petrochemical. Many of the senior party cadres and ministers have job experience in large SOEs and many of the large SOE managers have served as (mainly local) party cadres or bureaucrats. Table 9.6 summarizes job careers of senior cadres and ministers who had worked in SINOPEC and top executives of SINOPEC who had served as bureaucrats. The interrelated tie between politics and business, or "State corporate nexus," makes "politicization" (Qian, 1995) of those companies' management inevitable.

While the scale of SINOPEC is exceptionally large, its corporate structure and the circumstances the company faces represent to a great extent those of large SOEs in capital-intensive industries, where the market still remains more or less oligopolistic. Many such companies have separated their profitable business and reorganized them into JSCs, then had their shares listed. This surely is an important step towards full commercialization of SOEs, as the newly born JSCs are (at least in theory) by and large free from the burden of the legacy of the planned economy and exposed to monitoring by non-state shareholders. The organizational restructuring, along with growing competitive pressure from other SOEs

Table 9.6   Personel relationship between the state and SINOPEC

	Name	Current position	Past major job career
I. Senior party cadres and ministers	Wu Yi	* Central Politobureau Member, CPC * Vice Minister	* Vice President and Party Secretary, Beijing Yanshan Petrochemical Company (SINOPEC Group) (1983–1988)
	Li Yizhong	* Central Committee Member, CPC * Director, State Administration of Work Safty	* Vice President, SINOPEC Group (1987–1997) * President and Party Secretary, SINOPEC Group (1998–2000), and CEO (2000–2003) * Paty Secretary and Vice Director, SASAC (2003–2005)
II. SINOPEC executives	Chen Tonghai	* President and Party Secretary, SINOPEC Group and CEO, SINOPEC Corp.(-June 2007)[1]	* Senior Dupity Mayor, Ningbo Municipality Government (1986–1989) * Senior Vice Director, Planning Comission, Zhejiang Province Government (1989–1991) * Mayor, Ningbo Municipality Government (1991–1994) * Senior Vice Director, State Planning Comission (1994–1998)
	Su Shulin	* President and Party Secretary, SINOPEC Group and CEO, SINOPEC Corp. (June 2007–) * Alternate Member of Central Committee, CPC	* Vice President, CNPC Group (–June 2006) * Senior party cadre, Party Committee of Liaoning Province (June 2006–June 2007)
	Zhou Yuan	* Vice President, SINOPEC Group, and Vice CEO, SINOPEC Corp.(June 2007-)	* Senior party cadre, Xinjiang Uighur Autonomous Region (1994–2002)

Note: All positions are as of July 2007. Chen Tonghai was dismissed by SINOPEC on June 2007 reportedly due to suspicion of bribery.

Source: Compiled by the author based on Zhonggong Zhongyang Zuzhibu he Zhonggong Zhongyang Dangshi Yanjiushi (eds.) (2004), annual reports of SINOPEC Corp., and *Finance* (Caijing), June 9, 2007.

(CNPC and CNOOC in the case of SINOPEC) and other newcomers such as private enterprises or foreign-invested companies, have made their behavioral patterns more in accordance with market principles. Still, as long as the ultimate control right of the companies lies in the hand of the state by means of both ownership and personnel ties, politics will remain at least one of the key factors that affect their strategic managerial decisions.[22]

9.4. Entrepreneurial type

In the previous section we referred to the fact that SOEs today are increasingly concentrated in heavy industries that remain to be relatively oligopolistic. In contrast, as can be seen from Figure 9.1, in most of the less capital-intensive industries the share of SOEs is much lower. Especially in the least capital-intensive light industries such as apparel and footwear manufacturing, SOEs' share is already becoming insignificant.

It is noteworthy, however, that even in the industries where the dominance of SOEs has long gone, there still are a handful of SOEs which survive competition and remain viable. They are surely anomalies in the sense that they account for a tiny fraction of SOEs. But within the industries these "atypical" SOEs are often quite influential players. Below we focus on the case of Doublestar Group Corporation, one of the largest domestic brand makers of rubber-soled shoes.[23]

9.4.1 Doublestar Group Corporation

The shoemaking industry is, in line with other light industries, probably one of the most competitive and "privatized" industries in China. The domestic market of rubber-soled shoes is packed with a huge number of domestic manufacturers, mostly private firms, Taiwanese contract manufacturers, and major foreign brands such as Nike and Adidas.

Doublestar Group Corporation (*Shuangxing Jituan Gongsi*: hereafter "the corporation") is almost the only SOE that remains competitive in the industry. According to the first economic census conducted in 2004, only 39 out of 636 rubber-soled shoes makers surveyed were SOEs (Guowuyuan Diyici Quanguo Jingji Pucha Lingdao Xiaozu Bangongshi [ed.], 2004). They account for about 20 percent of the national total by sales, more than half of which is attributable to Doublestar.

Figure 9.3 summarizes present organizational structure of Doublestar. Its predecessor was a medium-scale factory subordinate to Qingdao Municipality Government.[24] The factory used to produce the cheapest type of rubber-soled shoes until the mid-1980s, when the factory faced rapid piling-up of inventory due to an abrupt decrease in the demand of the product as a result of income growth. Being an unimportant factory in a non-strategic sector, the factory could enjoy little support from the local government, let alone the central government. In consequence the factory's financial position deteriorated seriously.

The major reason why the factory could survive the crisis and increasingly harsh market competition thereafter is that it swiftly adjusted its product lineup and built a marketing network of its own, making it possible to circumvent the traditional inefficient channel of state-owned distributors. Along with putting great emphasis on improving product quality, the factory created its own brand "Doublestar" and successfully promoted the brand to the growing market, becoming the largest domestic manufacturer of rubber-soled shoes. In 1992 it changed its company name after the brand name and reorganized itself as "Doublestar Group Corporation," a wholly state-owned limited liabilities company under the direct supervision of Qingdao Municipality Government.[25]

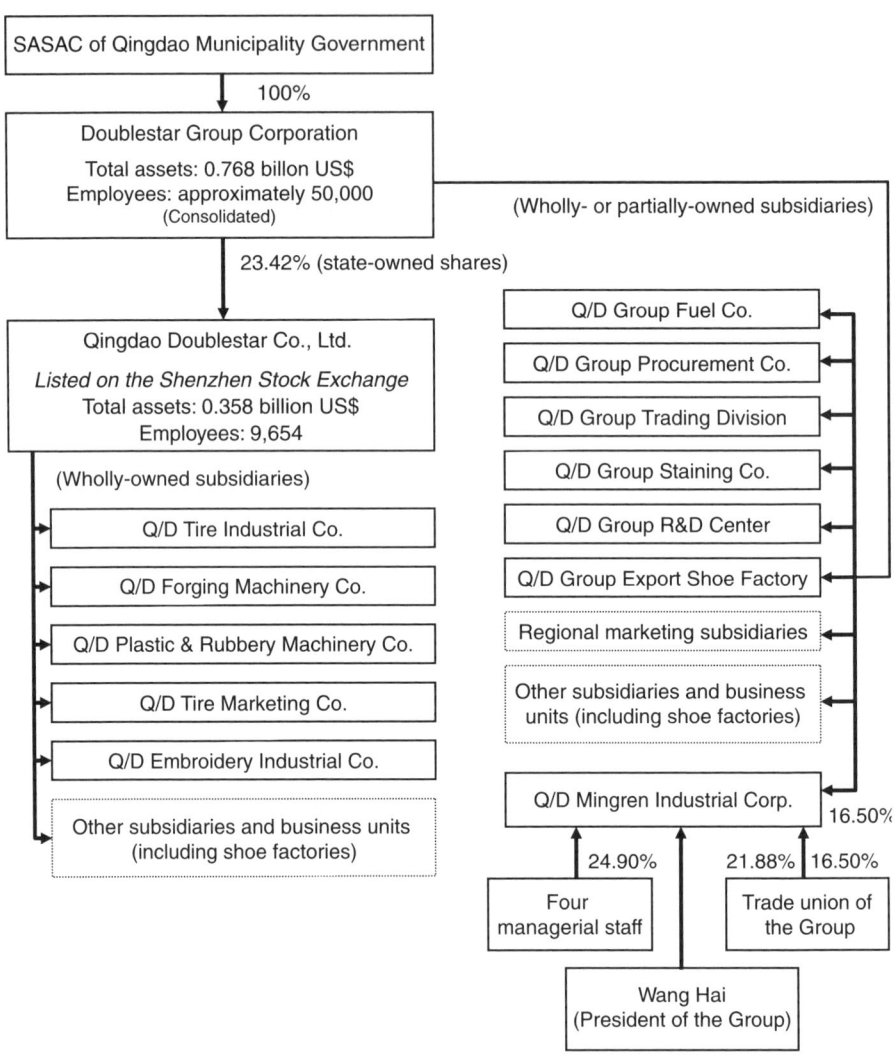

Figure 9.3   Corporate structure of Doublestar Group (as of the end of FY 2006)

Note: *"Q/D" stands for "Qingdao Doublestar".

Source: Annual reports of Qingdao Doublestar, Doublestar Group corporate website and interview with the company (October 28, 2005). Ownership structure of Qingdao Mingren Industrial Corp. is based on an announcement by Qingdao Doublestar Co., Ltd. (April 24, 2006).

The corporation soon established a JSC consisting of a part of its shoemaking business and listed it on the Shenzhen Stock Exchange in 1996. However, a large part of the original business including the production of low-end rubber-soled shoes has remained as business units within the corporation. The listed company has been diversifying into the tire industry by acquiring several tire manufacturers in recent years (Figure 9.3).

The corporation is one of the few SOEs in Qingdao that have successfully adapted to the ever-changing market environment of the transition period. It is widely acknowledged that the success of the corporation is to a great extent attributable to President Wang Hai, an army veteran who was appointed as Party Secretary of the factory in 1983 and has been in commanding control of management since then (after the reorganization he doubled as president of the corporation and CEO of the listed company). While the corporation itself still remains a WSOE supervised by the Qingdao Municipality Government, the local government rarely intervenes in the management of the corporation. The management control of the corporation is so centralized that any nonrecurring expenditure exceeding two thousand RMB (about US$260) requires approval by the president.[26] In principle a manager of a SOE has to retire at the age of 60 but the municipality government decided in 2005 to grant three CEOs of two SOEs and one urban collective enterprise, including Wang Hai, who was already 63 at that time, three years' special term extension.[27] The behavior of the Qingdao Municipality Government to a large extent reflects the market- oriented nature of local governments in China, which is particularly evident in the coastal region where merciless market competition prevails.

The management of the corporation is so personalized that it looks almost like a private enterprise. As a result of rapid expansion the majority of the workforce are migrant workers from rural areas, making the corporation capable of flexibly adjusting labor in response to the market. The dilemma is, however, as long as it remains wholly owned by the state, the municipality government retains the ultimate control right of the corporation. The president has no legal claim to the net assets of the corporation, although there is no doubt that as a virtual entrepreneur he has made an essential contribution for creating it.

The solution to this dilemma is obvious: privatization. But the central government still takes a strongly negative stance against privatizing large SOEs. It strictly prohibits giving-out or "underpriced" selling of state shares of large SOEs to managers by local governments. Besides, it is extremely difficult to sort out exactly what amount of equity the president can justifiably claim. Notwithstanding these constraints, the corporation seems to be already preparing for promoting privatization by a more or less covert way probably with tacit approval from the municipality government. It established Qingdao Doublestar Mingren Industrial Co., Ltd. (Mingren Industrial), a JSC with its shares jointly owned by the corporation and a group of senior managerial staff including Wang Hai, the latter of which holds controlling shares (Figure 9.3). The corporation has begun to use the brand name of "Doublestar Mingren" interchangeably with the original "Doublestar" brand, which suggests that Mingren Industrial will become the future platform for privatization of the corporation.[28]

There are a handful of SOEs such as Doublestar that have survived the challenge of transition to a market economy and realized spectacular growth under the initiative of managers who functioned as entrepreneurs, whereas they are minority distinctive from the majority of SOEs in China that failed to adapt to the drastic change of business environment. In these "entrepreneurial" SOEs control rights of management has shifted significantly from the state to the managers. They face the similar dilemma as Doublestar does.[29] Generally speaking, local governments in charge of supervising them are inclined to "let them go off" by granting managers state equities at prices lower than book value or just without charge, or allowing (explicitly or tacitly) them to operate indirect privatization via a sort of special purpose companies (such as Mingren Industrial in the case of Doublestar). On the other hand, however, the central government puts stringent restrictions on MBO (or MEBO) of large SOEs as it has a strong interest in securing the source of financing for SOE restructuring, and filling the serious shortage of pension funds due to the painstaking transition from the pay-as-you-go system to the fully funded system. The central government and the Party also worry that once the restrictions are relaxed local government are apt to rush for wholesale selling of SOEs with generous discounts, which may arouse the discontent of workers or the general public, as the ongoing experience of the privatization of small and medium SOEs illustrates.

9.5   Conclusion

In recent years there has been a growing number of econometric studies focusing on assessing the effects of corporate ownership on efficiency in China.[30] Despite wide divergences in methods applied and specific conclusions, most of the studies agree that state-ownership is detrimental to efficiency. Privatization or at least dilution of state-ownership is the key for efficient corporate governance.

The Party and the central government have long recognized that corporatization and diversification of ownership of large SOEs are necessary both for efficient management and effective governance. From the late 1990s to the beginning of this century they have further conceded a gradual exit of state investment from "non-strategic sectors", which are rather vaguely defined as sectors in which market mechanism function works sufficiently and that are not concerned with fundamental development of the economy and national security. They have also acknowledged that the dominance of state investment in listed SCEs needs to be decreased regardless of which industry they belong to.[31]

In spite of the progress in the political arena, figures quoted in Section 9.2 indicate that the presence of broadly defined SOEs in the economy has barely changed since the late 1990s, at least up to 2005. The preceding two sections focused on two distinctive types of large SOEs that remain viable: oligopolistic type and entrepreneurial type. They contrast starkly with each other, in the sense that their survival and success in the markets depends respectively on oligopolistic position and improvisational entrepreneurship. The two cases show how allocation of control rights under state corporate ownership varies in response to market environment. At the same time, they illustrate several important factors constraining further progress of reform such as financing the costs of restructuring, redefining the role of the state as the single dominant shareholder, and balancing the interests of the state and managers as entrepreneurs.

In 2005 the government introduced a comprehensive scheme of step-by-step conversion of state-owned shares and non-state-owned legal persons' shares, both of which were previously defined as non tradable shares, into tradable shares, that is shares that can be freely traded on the stock exchanges. No doubt the conversion, now underway at an unprecedented pace, will be a big step towards establishing a well-functioning market of corporate ownership. But how far the reform will reshape the current ownership structure of large corporations in China in coming years remains an open question.

Apparently, foreign capital and private enterprises are the major candidates that will replace the state as the dominant shareholder of large corporations. Acquisitions of large SOEs or a part of their equity by foreign capital have been surely increasing; on the other hand, at least at present, they are by and large concentrated in a limited number of industries where regulations and/or existing network in the domestic market induce foreign investors favor acquiring incumbent Chinese companies (e.g., the banking industry and the beer industry). Recently the government seems more inclined to restrict acquisition of major SOEs (or domestic companies in general) in "strategic sectors," which are, again, very vaguely defined.

Private enterprises are growing rapidly, not a few of which have the financial capability to acquire a number of large SOEs. However, it is often the case that those emerging companies by themselves, having grown out of nothing within a very short period of time, lack internal stability to be capable of managing large complex organizations such as China's SOEs.[32] Thus, the most likely picture of corporate ownership structure in China will be a combination of the state, foreign investors, and private capitals, in which the state keeps dominance in the foreseeable future though it is likely to be gradually eclipsed.

Recent international comparative studies on ownership structure of large corporations show that, except for a small number of industrialized countries such as the United States, Japan, Germany and the United Kingdom, concentration of ownership is the rule rather than the exception. Especially in developing countries, large corporations tend to be controlled by three types of entities: private business concerns owned by rich families, foreign investors, and the state (La Porta et al., 1998; Claessens, Djankov and Lang, 1999). In this sense we may say that we are witnessing a trend of gradual conversion of China's corporate ownership pattern to the tripolar structure prevalent in many developing countries. However, there remains (and will remain for the foreseeable future) an outstanding combination of characteristics that distinctively separate China from other developing countries: the increasingly competitive market environment SOEs face on the one hand and, the persistence of the state-ownership on the other hand, the latter of which we focused on in the preceding sections.[33] At the basis of this seemingly puzzling combination are the decentralized nature of economic policy jurisdictions that promotes competition as is designated as "market-preserving federalism, Chinese style" by Montinola, Qian and Weingast (1995) and the State's strong orientation for economic development.

Then emerges our last question: what kind of consequences will the persistence of state-ownership have on China's economy? On the surface, with the aggregated saving rate being close to 40 percent, the momentum of the growth does not seem to be seriously affected by inefficiency in resource allocation associated with state-ownership.[34] Besides, competition in the product markets will continue to exercise pressure on surviving SOEs to improve efficiency, so as to make them converge to the behavior model of private enterprises.

At the same time, however, in view of China's policy emphasis on pursuing high speed growth (especially with regard to local governments) and underdevelopment of monitoring by outside investors, it is highly likely that state-ownership will remain an important source of macroeconomic instability by encouraging excessive investment.[35] Furthermore, in the long run, in order to sustain growth momentum China needs industrial upgrading, which is to be supported by evolution of corporate organization. Weakness inherent in corporate governance under state-ownership will be one of the central issues that must be addressed in the process.

Acknowledgements

I would like to thank Dai Erbiao, Han Chaohua, Huang Xiaochun, Nazrul Islam, Koh Yong Soo, Reiitsu Kojima, Thomas G. Rawski, Masahiro Shimotani, and Zhang Wenkui for their helpful comments and discussions. All remaining errors are however mine.

Notes

1 See Otsuka, Liu and Murakami (1998) and Jefferson and Singh (eds.) (1999). Studies focus on later periods show largely similar patterns of efficiency gain in different types of enterprises (Zhang Anming et al. [2002] and Zhang Jinghai et al. [2003]).

2 We return to this issue in the last section.

3 For documentation and analysis of privatization of small and medium SOEs, see Tenev et al. (2002), chapter 2 of Imai (ed.) (2003), Song et al. (2005) and Zhang (2007).

4 According to the official definition, the following three types of firms are classified as "state-controlled enterprises." (1) Firms of which more than 50 percent of the equities are owned by the state. (2) Firms of which the state owns less than 50 percent of the equities but still is the largest shareholder. (3) Firms in which the state is not the largest shareholder but effectively controls the management by means of agreement with other shareholders.

5 See *Law Yearbook of China*, various issues.

6 Note that mergers and acquisitions between SOEs, which take place increasingly frequently, also cause the decline in the number of SOEs. How much M&A activities in the state-owned sector account for the decrease in the number remains uncertain.

7 A caution is due here that part of privatized ex-SOEs may remain registered as SOEs for various reasons. Dollar and Wei (2007) points out such ex-SOEs account for about 15 percent of their sample of registry base SOEs.

8 In recent years MBO rather than MEBO has become prevailing because the former is generally superior to the latter in terms of efficiency in decision making and incentive structure. See Tenev et al. (2002), chapter 2 of Imai (ed.) (2003), and Zhang (2005, 2007). As we will discuss in Section 9.4, MBO is increasingly adapted (or comes close to be adapted) by larger SOEs.

9 From 1997 onward, China's industrial statistical reporting system has revised so that it covers only (a) all SOEs (broadly defined) and (b) non-SOEs of which annual sales are no less than five million Renminbi (RMB). As a result, the majority of non-state-owned small enterprises are excluded from the statistics. According to the economic

census in 2004, out of 1,375,263 industrial enterprises surveyed by the census, only 276,474 were covered by the reporting system, while they account for 90 percent of the annual gross industrial output of the year (Guowuyuan Diyici Quanguo Jingji Pucha Lingdao Xiaozu Bangongshi [ed.] [2004]).When compiling national income statistics, the National Bureau of Statistics makes up for this lack of coverage by means of estimation based on sample surveys (Xu, 2000, p. 26).

10 In a press conference held in October 2006, Li Rongrong, Director of SASAC, remarked that among 1,375 companies listed on the Shanghai and Shenzhen stock exchanges, 837 companies are controlled by state-shareholders (www.people.com, October 10, 2006).

11 Except for the tobacco industry, where private capitals are basically barred in consideration for preserving the tax base, the great majority of mining and manufacturing industries are basically open to entries by private capitals. Although there still remain explicit or tacit restrictions, they tend to be circumvented and finally abolished.

12 In some industries such as the automotive and shipbuilding industries, regulations that limit the equity share of foreign capitals below 50 percent helps keep the dominance of SOEs.

13 The automobile and iron and steel industries are the most significant cases in which the dominance by SOEs has come to be seriously challenged by private newcomers. I will examine the case of the iron and steel industry in my forthcoming paper (Imai forthcoming).

14 The most typical example is mobile telecommunication, which is exclusively monopolized by two giant SCEs, China Mobile and China Unicom. Both of the two companies (plus other four telecom service providers) are ultimately controlled by SASAC through their parent WSOEs.

15 Later provincial governments (including four municipalities and five autonomous regions) also established their own SASAC that monitor large SOEs under their jurisdiction.

16 For example, although SINOPEC Shanghai Petrochemical Co., Ltd. is a subsidiary of SINOPEC Corp., the company's auxiliary and non-business units are under the direct control of the group company (Interview with SINOPEC Group, October 30, 2005).

17 In 2004 the central government designated three largest state-owned corporate groups, SINOPEC, CNPC and Dongfeng Motor Corporation as first test cases of comprehensive restructuring focused on separation of non-core business units.

18 *China Business Post* (*Caijing Ribao*), August 21, 2004.

19 In 2002, tens of thousands of laid-off workers of Daqing Oilfield, which is a subsidiary of CNPC Group, demonstrated on the streets in protest of scantiness of compensation.

20 *China Business Post* (*Caijing Ribao*), August 21, 2004.

21 *Finance* (*Caijing*), February 21, 2005.

22 Many large SOEs in oligopolistic industries are affiliated with local governments for historical reasons. For example, out of the five largest steel companies, two are affiliated with provincial or municipal governments (Shougang Steel with Beijing Municipality and Tangshan Steel with Hebei Province), while the other three are subordinate to SASAC of the central government. Those large local SOEs face basically similar problems as central SOEs do.

23 Description of the corporation is based on two interviews with the company on September 20, 1996 and October 28, 2005, annual reports of Qingdao Doublestar Co., Ltd. and various materials.

24 The factory had been under jurisdiction of Ministry of the Chemical Industry of the central government before it was transferred to Qingdao Municipality Government amid decentralization during the Great Cultural Revolution in the 1960s.

25 Before the corporatization the factory had been supervised by Bureau of the Chemical Industry of the municipality government. The bureau was later abolished together with other industrial bureaus.

26   Interview with managerial staff of the corporation (October 28, 2005). However, how exactly this rule is obeyed is questionable.

27   The other two are CEOs of Haier and Tsingtao Beer, both of which are widely known as successful survivors among public enterprises in extremely competitive industries.

28   In May 2006 Qingdao Doublestar Co., Ltd. announced that the company decided to sell its shoe making business to Mingren Industrial (*21st Century Herald (21 Shiji Jingji Baodao)*, June 2, 2006), which seems to be a further step towards indirect privatization of the group business.

29   Huang (2003) explores the failed case of privatization of Mailyard Group, once the largest OEM manufacturer of men's suits for the Japanese market, which was also a typical case of entrepreneurial type of SOEs.

30   For example see Tian (2001) and Liu et al (2003).

31   The Party still emphasizes keeping control of the most important large SOEs. To what extent the Party will concede diversification of corporate ownership of these companies is a very political issue, which we cannot afford to discuss further here.

32   D'Long Group (*Delong Jituan*)'s rise and fall is the case in point. D'Long, established as a small business concern by the Tang brothers and grew mainly through stock market speculation, acquired four stock-stock listed SOEs in succession within several years beginning in the late 1990s. The group, however, fell dramatically due to excessive debt burden and the sudden tightening of monetary policy in early 2004, leaving debts as much as ten billon RMB approximately.

33   Zhang Xindong et al (2002) compares distribution of control rights of stock-listed companies in European countries and East Asian countries including China. Their comparison shows that while state-controlled companies account for a relatively large fraction in some countries such as Singapore (more than 20 percent), Malaysia, Austria, Finland, Italy and Norway (more than 10 percent), they are no match for Chinese counterparts that account for more than 60 percent of listed companies.

34   Dollar and Wei (2007) measures the extent of efficiency in allocation of financial resource due to state ownership.

35   Ironically, however, in many cases seemingly excessive investment initiated by SOEs eventually leads to further increase in competitive pressure and reshuffling of the industry that enhances efficiency.

References

English

Claessens, Stijin, Simeon Djankov and Larry H. P. Lang . 1999. "Who Controls East Asian Corporations?" *Policy Research Working Paper*, 2054, Washington, D.C.: The World Bank.

Dollar, David and Shang-Jin Wei. 2007. "Das (Wasted) Kapital: Firm Ownership and Investment Efficiency in China," NBER Working Paper Series, 13103 (http://www.nber.org/papers/w13103), accessed on October 7, 2007.

Huang, Xiaochun. 2003. "Privatization of Newly-Emerging State-Owned Enterprises: the Case of Mailyard Group," in chapter 3, Imai (ed.) (2003).

Imai, Ken. (ed.) 2003. *Beyond Market Socialism: Privatization of State-owned and Collective Enterprises in China*, Chiba: The Institute of Developing Economies: (http://www.ide.go.jp/Japanese/Publish/Spot/25.html), accessed on October 7, 2007.

Imai, Ken (forthcoming). "State Corporate Nexus and Industrial Growth in China," *IDE Discussion Paper Series*.

Jefferson, Gary H. and Inderjit Singh. (eds.) 1999. *Enterprise Reform in China: Ownership, Transition, and Performance*, New York: Oxford University Press.

La Porta Rafael, et al. 1998. "Corporate Governance around the World," *NBER Working Paper*, No. 6625, June. National Bureau of Economic Research: Stanford.

Montinola, Gabriella, Yingyi Qian and Barry R. Weingast. 1995 "Federalism, Chinese Style: the Political Basis of Economic Success in China," *World Politics*, Vol. 48, No. 1, October, pp. 50–81.

Otsuka, Keijiro, Deqiang Liu and Naoki Murakami. 1998. *Industrial Reform in China: Past Performance and Future Prospects*, Oxford: Clarendon Press.

Qian, Yingyi. 1995. "Reforming Corporate Governance and Finance in China," in Masahiko Aoki and Hyung-Ki Kim. (eds.) *Corporate Governance in Transition Economies: Insider Control and the Role of Banks*, Washington, D.C.: The World Bank, pp. 215–252.

Song, Ligang, Stoyan Tenev, Yang Yao, and Ross Garnaut. 2005. *China's Ownership Transformation: Process, Outcomes, Prospects*, Washington, D.C.: The World Bank.

Tenev, Stoyan, Chunlin Zhang, and Loup Brefort. 2002. *Corporate Governance and Enterprise Reform in China: Building the Institutions of Modern Markets*, Washington, D.C.: World Bank and the International Finance Corporation.

Tian, Lihui. 2001. "Government Shareholding and the Value of China's Modern Firms," *William Davidson Institute Working Paper*, No. 395, April (http://wdi.umich.edu/Publications/WorkingPapers/WP301to400), accessed on October 7, 2007.

Zhang, Anming et al. 2002. "Profitability and Productivity of Chinese Industrial Firms: Measurement and Ownership Implications," *China Economic Review*, Vol. 13, No. 1, pp. 65–88.

Zheng, Jinghai et al. 2003. "Efficiency, Technical Progress, and Best Practice in Chinese State Enterprises (1980–1994)," *Journal of Comparative Economics*, Vol. 31, No. 1, pp. 134–152.

Chinese

Guowuyuan Diyici Quanguo Jingji Pucha Lingdao Xiaozu Bangongshi. (ed.) 2004. *Zhongguo Jingji Pucha Nianjian 2004: Di-er Chanye Juan/Shangce* (China Economic Census Yearbook 2004), Beijing: Zhongguo Tongji Chubanshe.

Liu, Shaojia, Pei Sun and Naiquan Liu. 2003. "Zhongji Chanquan, Guquan Jiegou, Ji Gongsi Jixiao," (A Theory of Ultimate Property Rights, Equity Ownership Structure, and Corporate Performance), *Jingji Yanjiu*, No. 4, pp. 51–62.

Xu, Xianchun (ed.). 2000. *Zhongguo Guonei Shengchan Zongzhi Hesuan* (China's Accounting System of Gross Domestic Product), Beijing: Beijing Daxue Chubanshe.

Zhang, Wenkui. 2005. "Gaige Shi Yilianchuangde Shijian: Guoqi Gaizhi Diaocha Baogao,"(Reform as a Consequential Process: a Survey on SOE Restructuring), *21 Shiji Jingji Baodao*, October 15.

Zhang, Wenkui. 2007. *Zhongguo Guoyou Qiye Chanquan Gaige Yu Gongsi Zhili Zhuanxing* (China's State-owned Enterprise Property-rights Reform and Corporate Governance Transition), Beijing: Jingji Fazhan Chubanshe.

Zhang, Xindong et al. 2002. "Jiazugu: Zhongwai Jiazu Kongzhi Shangshi Gongsi Bijiao," (Family Ownership of Shares: a Comparative Study of Family Controlled Listed Companies in China and Foreign Countries), *Xincaifu*, No. 8, pp. 28–35.

Zhonggong Zhongyang Zuzhibu he Zhonggong Zhongyang Dangshi Yanjiushi (eds.) 2004. *Zhongguo Gongchandang Lijie Zhongyang Weiyuanhui Dacidian (1921–2003)* (Biographical Dictionary of the Central Committee of the Chinese Communist Party 1921–2003), Beijing: Dangshi Chubanshe.

10
Banking and Financial Sector Reforms in China: Experience and Prospects for the Future

Ding Lu

10.1   Introduction

Since the launch of market-oriented reforms in 1979, in a range of a quarter of a century, China has successfully completed two transitions: One is the transition from a low-income under-developed economy featured by poverty and isolation to a middle-income, newly industrialized, and booming economic giant that has changed world economic landscape. The other transition is institutional: the economic system has evolved from an inward-looking, centrally planned socialist command economy to a predominantly market-based one with considerable openness to trade and foreign investment.

In these transitions, the country's banking and financial sector has experienced fundamental changes and played an indispensable role in the process of modernization and economic growth. A major driving force of China's hyper economic growth in the past 25 years has been a high rate of capital formation sustained and backed by a saving rate that is astonishingly high by international comparison. China's gross saving rate has been above 35 percent of GDP in most years since the mid-1980s and climbed to above 40 percent in most part of the 1990s and early 2000s. According to the World Bank (1997), apart from the effects of rising income and changing demographics, the banking sector's systemic efforts to attract deposits and mobilize savings were one of the most important institutional factors that contributed to this phenomenon.

The economy's transition to a market-based system has been mirrored in its monetization. The process is remarkable for a transition economy since it indicates the extent of monetary transaction and financial deepening. In this regard, China's experience contrasts sharply with Russia's. Despite the big-bang approach of privatization implemented in the Russian economy at the beginning of the transition, barter arrangements and use of quasi-monies were widely practised through the 1990s. While most market economies have a M2 to GDP ratio of 60 percent or higher, the same ratio in Russia was never close to 20 percent in the decade after transition and fell below 10 percent in 1999 (Sutela, 1999). In contrast, this ratio in China surpassed the 60 percent threshold in the late 1980s and has been well over 100 percent of GDP since the mid-1990s. By 2004 the ratio had risen to 185 percent. The financial sector has expanded in parallel with the country's GDP growth for over two decades. Banking-sector assets rose by about 35 percent per year, reaching 37.5 trillion *yuan* (USD4.7 trillion) by the end of 2005.[1] The capitalization of the domestic equity market rose from virtually zero in 1990 to 4.6 trillion *yuan* (USD31 billion), or 53 percent of GDP, at the end of 2000.[2]

How has China gone through the transition of its financial system? What problems and difficulties China has faced in the process of financial deepening? What are the prospects of China's banking and financial sector development? This chapter attempts to address these questions. The next section reviews the key reforms that transformed the sector from a mono-banking system to a central banking system based on fractional reserves. We then, in the third section, examine the main problems and challenges facing the sector in recent years, in particular the non-performing loan crisis since the late 1990s. In Section 10.4, we discuss recent reforms in answering these challenges in the context of the imminent opening up of the sector to foreign banks five years after China joined the World Trade Organization (WTO). Prospects of future reforms are discussed in the fifth section and the final section concludes the chapter.

10.2 Market-oriented reforms

In the pre-reform years (from the early 1950s to end of the 1970s), China's domestic banking business was operated by the People's Bank of China (PBOC), which was in essence an accounting subsidiary of the Ministry of Finance (MOF). There was no division of roles between a central bank and commercial banks in the system. The PBOC simply functioned as a mono-bank to provide financial assistance for the fulfillment of the state physical production plan. It centralized deposits, allotted credits to production units for their partial working capital needs (mainly wage payments), and issued currency primarily to fill the mismatch between deposits and loans.[3] Such a mono-bank system corresponded well to the centrally planned economic system with the following features:

- Enterprises in manufactures and services were mostly nationalized (or state-owned) and all farmers were collectivized.
- The state set a physical production plan for all production agents and directly allocated material resources.
- Enterprises were required to turn in almost all earnings to the state, while their capital investment and working capital were financed by government's budget.
- Apart from being exchange media for retail sales, wage payments, and procurement of agricultural goods, money played very limited roles in the economy. Commodity prices, interest rates, and exchange rates were all under tight control of the state. Housing and most consumer goods were rationed. With no link to relative resource scarcity, prices served merely as accounting units in the central planning process.

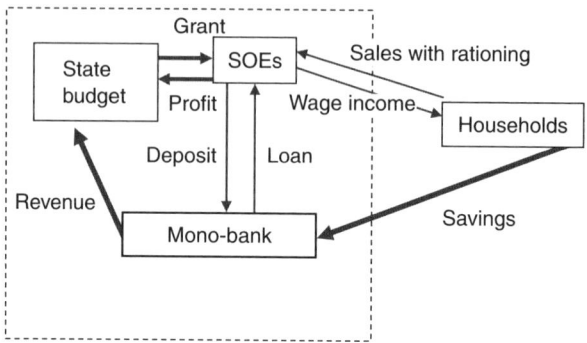

Figure 10.1 Circular flow of funds in the pre-reform economy
Source: CBRC.

The circular flow of funds in this system is illustrated in Figure 10.1.

Through the 1980s, market-oriented reforms liberalized price determination and altered the means of resource allocation. Greater autonomy was granted to enterprises and local governments, which were motivated to seek profits or local revenues. The growth of the non-state sectors was also at first allowed and later encouraged. Propelled by these developments, monetary transactions and market exchanges gradually permeated all walks of life.

Two major reforms were introduced in 1983 and 1984. One was the so-called *"li gai shui* (利改税*)"* (taxes-for-profits), which sought to dismantle the system where all profits after subtracting a small retained portion for the enterprise were simply returned to the state. The reform aimed to adopt a corporate tax that would allow substantial retained earnings. By 1986, almost all enterprise profits were taxed, instead of being remitted to the government. The other reform was the so-called *"bo gai dai* (拨改贷*)"* (loans-for-grants), which strove to move away from the provision of investment funds on a grant basis from the state budget toward the allocation of working capital and investment funds through the banking system.

The PBOC was reconstituted into a central bank in 1984. Meanwhile four big state "specialized banks" were reorganized or established to take over regular banking businesses in the period of 1979–1984. These banks include the Bank of China (BOC, reorganized in 1979), the Agricultural Bank of China (ABC, reorganized in 1979), the China Construction Bank (CCB, reorganized in 1981), and the Industrial & Commercial Bank of China (ICBC, reorganized in 1984).

Through the mid-1980s to the mid-1990s, despite the separation of the PBOC as a central bank from the regular banking businesses which were conducted by the state-owned "specialized banks," the banking sector continued to operate in a central planning manner (Lu and Yu, 1998). To achieve the government's annual money supply target, the PBOC carried on national credit planning and imposed an overall credit ceiling on all banks and financial institutions. The national credit plan matched annual fund usage (loans) with fund sources (deposits) and decided the volume of new currency issued to balance the gap between fund uses and sources. The PBOC combined all banks' fund sources and uses, which were aggregated from the banks' regional branches. The national credit plan controlled credit uses both quantitatively and qualitatively through specifying mandatory annual credit targets. The central allocation of credit quotas was supplemented by the PBOC's mandatory control of the deposit and lending interest rates to ensure the fulfillment of the credit-plan goals.

During this credit planning period, the PBOC started to experiment with the more conventional central banking instruments. One was the central bank's lending (with the primary lending interest rate) to the specialized banks, which affected about one third of fund sources for banks by the mid-1990s. Another was the adjustment of required reserve ratio for banks. Meanwhile, credit control was often reinforced by government's direct administrative interventions. Those include issuance of ad hoc administrative decrees to direct financial activities and dispatch of inspection teams to check the enforcement of government orders in the banks.

China's market-oriented reform was accelerated after the Communist Party leadership reached a consensus in the Party's national congress in October 1992 to establish the "socialist market economic system" as the goal of the reform. In November of the following year, the Party's Central Committee passed a 50-article "Decision" on the strategies of further reforms, which led to a series of centrally initiated reforms in the 1990s to build the bedrock of a modern market economy.

The events in 1992–1993 immediately accelerated reforms in all fronts, including the banking and financial sector. China's two stock exchanges in Shanghai and Shenzhen, launched on an experimental basis around 1990, started to grow by leaps and bounds after the establishment of the State Council Securities Committee (SCSC) and the China Securities Regulatory Commission (CSRC) in October 1992. From October 1992 to mid-1998, the SCSC was the immediate supervisory body over the CSRC, which was set up as a specialized independent regulatory body in charge of day-to-day monitoring of the securities market and market participants. When the SCSC was dissolved in 1998, the CSRC was upgraded to the equivalent rank of a ministry with extensive authorities, including the supervisory role over brokerage houses and stock exchanges in Shanghai and Shenzhen. China's first Securities Law, which took effect in July 1999, further strengthened the CSRC's supervisory power.

The promulgation of a central bank law and a commercial bank law in 1995 marked a watershed between a centrally planned mono-bank system and a post-reform modern central banking system based on fractional reserves. Guided by these laws, the four major state-owned "specialized banks" were restructured and incorporated, with their burdens of providing "policy loans" taken over by three policy-loan banks created in 1994.[4] Within the state banks, the "asset-liability management method" was introduced into the accounting system to consolidate their financial independence and business autonomy. A nationwide inter-bank market started operation in 1996.

The legal framework of a modern central banking system has allowed the emergence and development of some second-tier commercial banks and many non-bank financial institutions. Some of the non-bank institutions, such as the Rural Credit Cooperatives (RCCs), had existed in the pre-reform era but have been restructured since then to adapt to the new business environment. Many of the Urban Credit Cooperatives (UCCs) have been merged into urban commercial banks since the mid-1990s. Since the restructure of the Bank of Communications (BoCom) into a commercial bank in 1988, a number of second-tier commercial banks have emerged. The largest second-tier commercial banks include the BoCom, CITIC Industrial Bank, China Everbright Bank, Hua Xia Bank, Minsheng Banking Corporation, Guangdong Development Bank, Shenzhen Development Bank, China Merchants Bank, Shanghai Pudong Development Bank, and Fujian Industrial Bank. Most of these banks are organized on a shareholding basis and owned by local governments, various state departments, and/or large enterprises. At least one of them, Minsheng Banking Corporation, was founded by private businesses.[5] In the past few years, most of these banks became public listing companies in domestic and/or overseas stock markets.

From the late 1980s through the 1990s, local provincial authorities and various government agencies established many financial institutions that engaged in various forms of merchant and investment banking activities. These include the Trust and Investment Corporations (TICs), Financial Companies (FCs), and Financial Leasing Companies (FLCs), etc. The TICs, of which the number once reached over 240 in the late 1990s, experienced severe liquidity problems after the bankruptcy of the Guangdong International Trust and Investment Corporation (GITIC) in late 1998. The largest surviving TIC is China International Trust and Investment Corporation (CITIC), the parent of the CITIC Industrial Bank. Since the launch of the first Sino-foreign joint-venture investment bank, China International Capital Corporation (CICC), in 1995,[6] foreign capital has entered in investment banking business. The phenomenal rise of these banks and financial institutions in the past two decades has remarkably diversified China's financial structure and substantially reduced the four major State-Owned Commercial Banks' (SCBs) share of total bank credits from over 75 percent in the early 1990s to below 60 percent in recent years, as can be seen in Figure 10.2.[7]

By the last quarter of 2005, there were over 30,000 financial institutions in the banking sector. These include: 3 policy banks, 4 major SCBs, 13 shareholding commercial banks, 115 urban commercial banks, 57 rural coop banks, 626 UCCs, 30,438 RCCs, 238 foreign banking institutions, 4 state asset-management companies, 59 TICs, 74 business group FCs, 12 FLCs, 5 automobile finance companies, and a nationwide postal saving network (CBRC [2005]). As shown in Table 10.1, the major state-owned banks' share of total banking assets has continued the declining trend in recent years while the shares of the shareholding banks and other financial institutions have risen to above 15 percent and 26 percent respectively. However, the weight of state ownership in the banking sector is still dominant. According to the estimates by Farrell et al (2006), 83 percent of total bank assets was still state-owned by 2004.

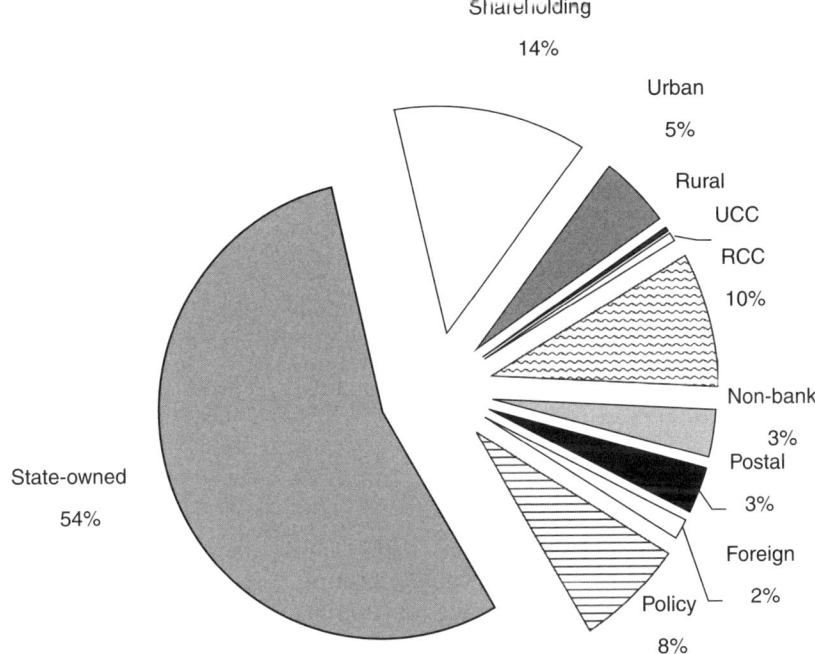

Figure 10.2   Share of bank assets (end of 2003)
Source: CBRC.

Table 10.1   Composition of banking sector assets (unit: trillion *yuan*)

	2003		2004		2005	
	Value	%	Value	%	Value	%
State-owned banks	15.22	54.9	16.92	53.7	19.66	52.5
Shareholding banks	3.85	13.9	4.70	14.9	5.81	15.5
Urban commercial banks	1.47	5.3	1.71	5.4	2.04	5.4
Other institutions	7.19	25.9	8.17	25.9	9.96	26.6
Total	27.72	100.0	31.50	100.0	37.47	100.0

Source: CBRC.

Starting in 1998, the PBOC abandoned the credit-quota plan to allow SCBs to make their own lending decisions. A loan risk classification system was subsequently introduced at the end of 1998 to help banks better manage lending risks. Under this system, banking loans are evaluated with a five-grade classification scheme, according to their financial risks (ref. Appendix 1). To ameliorate provincial governments' interference in bank lending, the PBOC consolidated its 30 provincial branches into nine regional centers, which are supposed to operate more independently (Zeng et al., 1999; Standard Chartered, 2001). In 2000, PBOC began to liberalize interest rates by lifting the control on foreign currency rates for deposits larger than US$3million. All foreign currency and Chinese *yuan* interest rates were scheduled to be deregulated over the following few years (Deutsche Bank, 2001).

The creation of a central regulator, the China Banking Regulatory Commission (CBRC), in April 2003 was another milestone of the transition. After the birth of CBRC, the central bank PBOC has focused its responsibility on formulating and implementing monetary policy as well as enacting safeguards to ensure financial stability. The CBRC, the main regulator of the banking sector, is responsible for formulating and enforcing the supervisory rules and regulations governing bank institutions. It monitors and ensures that all banks and depository institutions classify their loans consistently and accurately, prepare sufficient provisions, keep their balance sheets by accounting standards, and meet the global standard (Basel I) of capital ratio.

10.3 Problems and challenges

Despite the series of reforms, in the late 1990s China's banking sector was mired in an unprecedented piling up of Non-Performing Loans (NPLs).[8] With the NPL ratio officially amounting to over one-fourth of bank loans, the four major state banks, namely, the BOC, the ABC, the CCB, and the ICBC, became technically insolvent (Xu, 1998 and Lardy, 1998). The Citigroup estimated that the NPL ratio at the four biggest SCBs was about 35 percent at the beginning of 2002, and that the average capital-adequacy ratio of these four banks was only 5 percent.[9] Compared to the big-four state-owned banks, the second-tier banks have been generally healthier in terms of asset quality and profitability and have had much lower non-performing loan ratios.

The NPL crisis of the late 1990s could be attributed to various causes. First, such a crisis is not unique to China but a common problem for transition economies. In a centrally planned economy, all that State-Owned Enterprises (SOEs) cared about was to meet the government-designated production quota and all their capital needs were financed by fiscal grants and subsidies from the state budget (Figure 10.1). As the economy started shifting toward market-orientation, such a direct link to state budget was severed. In the post-reform economy, the state budget no longer finances SOEs' capital needs. Instead, the state-owned banks now had to take over the role to meet the SOEs' financial needs through lending credits (Figure 10.3).

However, profitability and liquidity of many SOEs suffered due to their inability to adapt to the post-reform business environment dominated by consumer sovereignty. Meanwhile, these enterprises were also troubled by non-paying or delinquent loans incurred among SOEs that have now become financially independent from state budget. Facing the competition from non-state firms, most SOEs had been disadvantaged (until the recent years) by carrying the burdens of their over-employed staff and the duties to provide various welfare benefits to their employees.

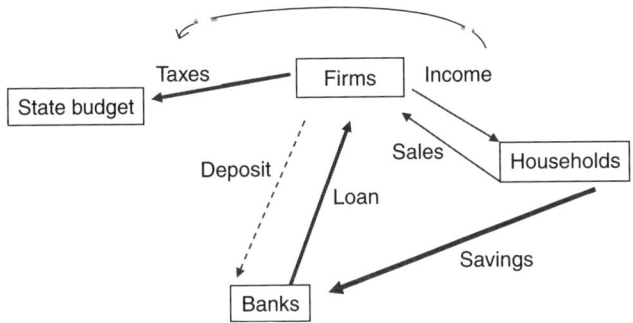

Figure 10.3 Circular flow of funds in the post-reform economy

Source: Compiled by the author.

Thus the reckless lending of state banks could be a result of government's *ex ante* intervention in banking business, in the form of pressure on the banks to issue loans (to SOEs and government-sponsored projects). Fearing social unrest due to mass unemployment and mass SOE failures, authorities at various government levels have pressed or influenced the state-owned banks to extend credits to keep many loss-making SOEs afloat. Political considerations have also propelled local authorities to compel the banks to finance commercially nonviable construction projects or unprofitable enterprises backed by the government. Many of these projects were under-funded by government budget and banks were called upon to make up for the undercapitalization (Li and Mehta, 2001).

Until 1994, the Chinese banks were obliged to make policyloans, which were granted out of policy or political considerations. Chinese Academy of Social Sciences (CASS, 1998) estimated that policy loans accounted for 35 percent of total loans made by the state banks in the first half of the 1990s, and policy loans are well known for their poor returns and high risks compared to commercial loans (CASS, 1999; Xu and Lu, 2001). Due to its discretionary nature, *ex ante* government intervention would make it difficult to measure the banks' performance. As a result, the Chinese state banks could easily use policy lending as an excuse for their poor record of lending decisions (Xie, 1994).

The piling up of NPLs could be a direct consequence of the "macroeconomic adjustment" in 1993–1994 when the government ordered a total credit freeze that forced termination of thousands of projects. The government campaign in the mid-1990s to clear up the widespread inter-firm arrears (the so-called "*san-jiao zhai* (三角债")" among many SOEs was partially achieved through injecting bank loans to the debt-ridden SOEs. It is also plausible that, in the late 1990s, the SCBs did not enjoy real business autonomy and continued to be pressed by authorities at various government levels to extend low-quality loans to unprofitable projects and firms.

Since the late 1990s, the Chinese government has also intervened in the credit market *ex post* by bailing out troubled SOEs or state-owned financial institutions (including banks). After bad lending has occurred, the government *ex post* bailout can take various forms, such as injecting funds to restructure the ailing SOEs, the takeover of NPLs, and deliberately delaying the closure of insolvent financial institutions. The bailout may also be in the form of government's implicit guarantee of loan security. Such bailout activities may reduce the banks' incentive to improve lending efficiency, leading to moral-hazard type of risky lending (Xie, 2001; Xu and Lu, 2001). According to Mitchell (1997) and Roland (2000), in expecting repeated bailouts, banks may "gamble for resurrection" by lending even more recklessly to government-sponsored borrowers. This kind of behaviour may occur even when banks have full business autonomy and are able to make lending decisions on their own, based on commercial considerations. The study by Lu et al (2005) lends strong support to the hypothesis of moral-hazard behaviour as a major cause of China's NPL piling up in recent years.

The NPL crisis of the late 1990s coincided with the government's bolstered efforts to restructure the SOEs. When he was designated Premier in 1997, Zhu Rongji vowed to solve the SOE problem in three years. Under his leadership, great efforts were made to harden budget constraints of SOEs in 1997–2000, highlighted by official policies of "encouraging mergers and consolidation, standardizing and streamlining bankruptcy procedures, downsizing SOEs to raise efficiency, replacement and reemployment projects for laid-off workers." The number of laid-off SOE employees amounted to 6.10 million in 1998 and nearly doubled to 11.74 million in 1999 (Zeng et al., 1999, 2000).

To give the restructured SOEs and the SCBs a fresh start, the government acted to remove the financial burdens of bad debts from the SOEs and bad loans from the banks. In 1998, the MOF issued bank restructuring bonds worth 270 billion *yuan* (US$33billion) to re-capitalize the big-four state-owned banks by doubling their capital base. A year later, the government established four state-sponsored asset-management companies to take over 1.4 trillion *yuan* (US$169billion) of bad debts from the banks' balance sheets.[10] This scheme of *zhai-zhuan-gu* (债转股, debt-for-equity) swap transferred the debt owed by the SOEs to the bank into the equity rights held by the asset management company, which would seek to recover the principal either by an initial public offering or by transferring the ownership. Despite these rescue efforts, by end of 2003, the NPLs of these big-four banks still amounted to 2.6 trillion *yuan* (US$300billion) or 23.7 percent of total loans, according to official estimates. Some independent estimates put the level of bad loans at around 3.5 trillion *yuan* (US$420billion), or nearly 40 percent of gross domestic product.[11] In January 2004, the PBOC injected another US$45billion from China's foreign reserves, equivalent to 1/10 of the total reserves, to boost the capital-adequacy ratios of CCB and BOC, two of the four big SCBs. In 2005, the authorities approved and started a restructuring plan for the ICBC, which costs over US$80billion, including another US$15billion capital injection from foreign exchange reserves and writing off of 170 billion *yuan* of MOF's equity in the bank.[12] These "indirect bailout" plans aim to refresh the banks' balance sheet with the injected funds so that they could soon list their shares on the stock market and be able to make new, supposedly more profitable, lending.

As for the equity market, its institution-building process has been heavily influenced by the political-economic dynamism in the country. As observed by Walter and Howie (2001), there had been a continuous power struggle among the PBOC, the MOF and other bureaucracies over the control of the securities industry. So despite the organizational restructure, the regulatory framework still remains fragmented. What makes things worse is the conflicting policy missions assigned to the CSRC. As noted by Heilmann (2002), the agency's policy mission to provide preferential capital access for SOEs and to increase the value of state assets constantly conflicts its role of being an impartial supervisory and regulatory authority. Under the so-called "split share structure", about two-thirds of the shares, held and owned by the government or state-owned agencies, were non-tradable until recently. This system severely undermined the stock market's ability to effectively discipline management of many mainly state-owned listed companies. Since its launch, China's stock market has won the reputation as a vehicle for the government to unload the financial burdens of keeping those mammoth SOEs to the retail investors. The poor accounting standards, weak corporate governance, lack of transparency, and scandals of insider trading have further marred the public confidence in this emerging market. At the turn of the century, the market started a slump, sharply contrasting the economic boom after China joined the WTO (Figure 10.4). Thanks to the slump, China's market capitalization ratio, once peaked at 53 percent of GDP in 2000, declined to under 20 percent of GDP in 2005 (Figure 10.5).

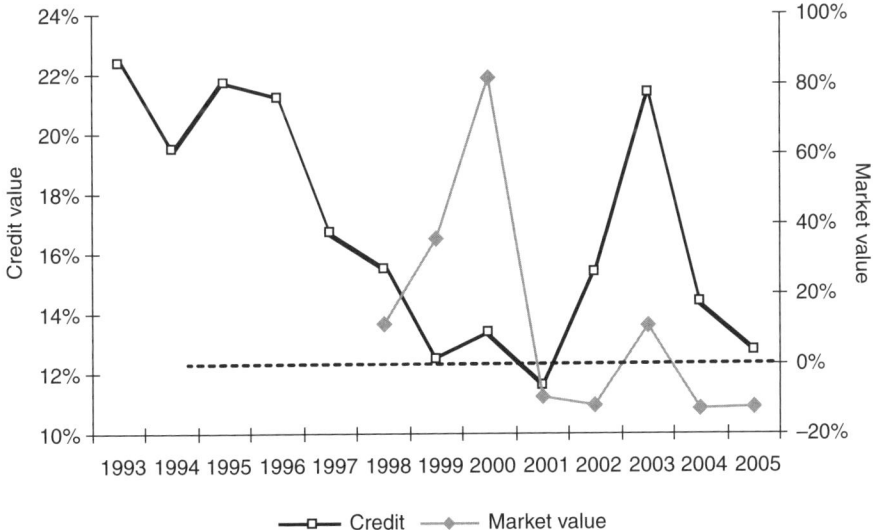

Figure 10.4 Growth rates of all financial institutions' year-end credit balance and domestic stock market capitalization year-end value (1993–2004)

Sources: NBSC, People's Bank of China.

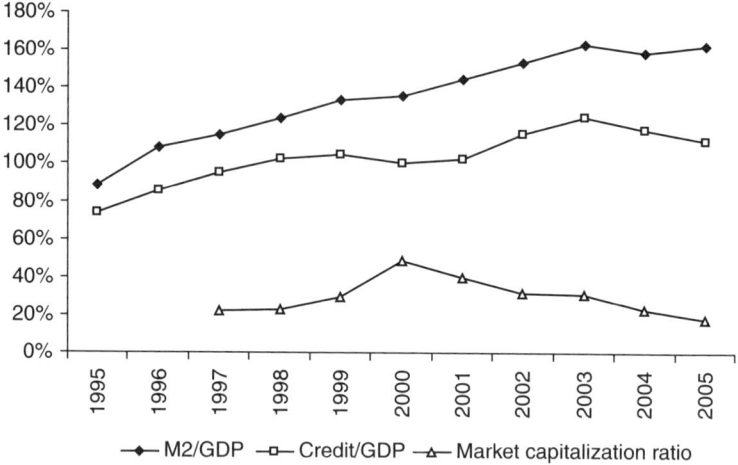

Figure 10.5   Indices of monetization and market capitalization (1995–2005)

Note: The GDP statistics are based on the adjusted values in NBSC (2006a).

Sources: NBSC, People's Bank of China.

The marginalization of equity market coincided with a recent wave of credit expansion in the banking sector in 2002–2004 (Figures 10.4 and 10.5). The speed of credit expansion in this period has been the fastest since 1993, the previous overheating boom that caused the piling up of NPLs in the late 1990s. With one of the world's highest domestic saving rate of nearly 50 percent of GDP, the banks have been flooded with deposit money that cannot find trustworthy investment opportunities in the dismal stock market. The Chinese currency's rigid exchange rate regime has certainly not been helpful in checking this colossal macroeconomic imbalance. Till July 2005, Chinese *yuan* had maintained a de facto peg to the US dollar for over a decade at a rate widely believed in its later years to have substantially undervalued the currency. Exchange rate rigidity has been one of the factors behind China's rising current-account surplus and net national savings, which are mirrored in the drastic growth of foreign exchange reserves by over 4.5 times between 2001 and 2006 to above US$900 billion. Betting on the *yuan*'s revaluation since China joined the WTO has in the past few years fuelled a huge inflow of hot money, leading to surging speculative investment in domestic assets and pressing the PBOC to sterilize the excessive liquidity by issuing treasury bills.[13]

To utilize the domestic saving glut, Chinese banks have in recent years substantially increased their business in consumer credit and housing loans, amidst the emergence of a property market bubble.[14] Meanwhile, the PBOC, the central bank, ordered the major SCBs to lower their NPL ratio by 3–5 percentage points per year from around 25 percent level in 2001 down to below 15 percent by 2005, the year that the PBOC targeted to list the major state banks on the stock market.[15] To meet this requirement, the banks "went on a lending binge between 2003 and 2004, partly to 'grow out of' their bad loan problem", observed *The Economist*.[16] The banks' urge to expand their lending has met well the demand for fresh investment funds to support various development projects sanctioned by the local governments. In particular, many urban development projects have involved illicit expropriation of farm or residential lands and thus been highly lucrative and become a hotbed for bureaucratic corruption and rent seeking. A survey of 16 cities by the Ministry of Land and Resources in 2005 showed that nearly 50 percent of the new land under development was acquired illegally with the support by local officials. The figure was as high as 90 percent in some cities. Such development projects have been a leading cause of the recent years' wave of runaway investment.[17]

Consequently, China has experienced a new capital formation boom in recent years. The quality of China's bank-dominated investment boom is questionable. For economies experiencing fast industrialization, infrastructure building and fast capital accumulation may lead to a relatively high Incremental Capital to Output Ratio (ICOR). It is, however, rather worrying that China's ICOR has gone up substantially in recent years and is clearly higher than those of Japan, South Korea, and Taiwan during latter's high-growth periods, and even that of India in recent years (Table 10.2). As shown in Figure 10.6, China's ICOR has exhibited a worrying rising trend since the early 1990s.[18] These figures indicate that (a) China's economic growth has been much more costly than that of Japan, South Korea, and Taiwan; and (b) China's growth efficiency has deteriorated over the last 15 years: it now takes much more investment to generate the same value of wealth than it used to be in the early 1990s. The trend raises doubts about the sustainability of China's hyper economic growth.

Table 10.2 Incremental Capital to Output Ratio (ICOR): China compared to Japan, South Korea, Taiwan, and India

	Period	Investment share of GDP		GDP growth rate		ICOR	
China[a]	1991–1995	33.2	*32.6*	12.0	*12.2*	2.8	*2.7*
	1996–2000	35.1	*32.6*	8.3	*8.6*	4.3	*3.8*
	2001–2005	45.1	*40.4*	8.7	*9.5*	5.1	*4.3*
Japan[b]	1961–1970	32.6	–	10.2		3.2	–
S. Korea[b]	1981–1990	29.6	–	9.2		3.2	–
Taiwan[b]	1981–1990	21.9	–	8.0		2.7	–
India[c]	1995–2004	21.2	–	5.6		4.1	–

Note: Numbers in italics are based on adjusted GDP statistics in NBSC (2006a).

Sources: [a]compiled from NBSC (varies issues) and NBSC (2006a); [b]Kwan (2004); [c]Farrell et al (2006).

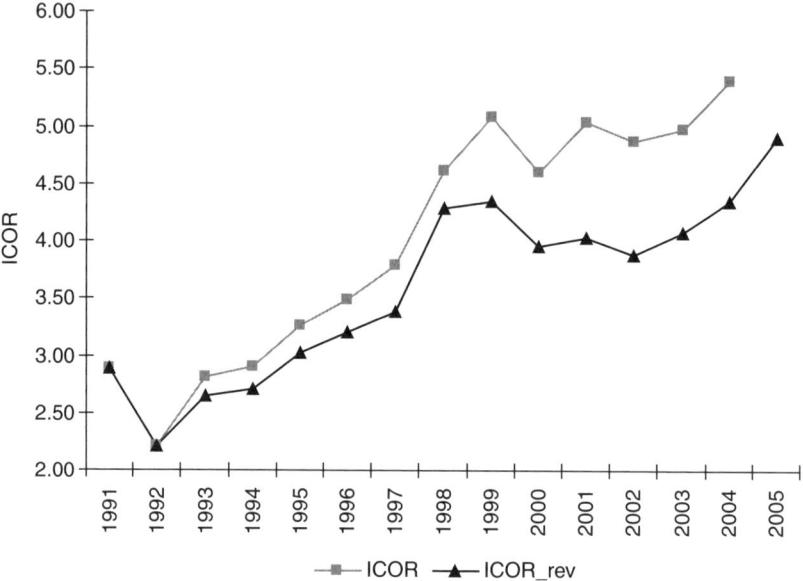

Figure 10.6   Incremental capital-output ratio (1991–2005)

Note: ICOR is the ratio between fixed capital investment to GDP ratio and real GDP growth rate. ICOR_rev is based on the adjusted values in NBSC (2006a).

Source: NBSC.

An immediate outcome of this round of bank lending and investment boom is the macroeconomic overheating in 2004–2006, which has signalled more problematic loans ahead. As pointed out by Hale (2005):

> China's lending boom of 2003 and 2004 could lead to another wave of defaults this year and next. In 2004, the investment share of GDP rose to 45% – one of the highest levels in recorded financial history – as banks financed a huge expansion of property development and manufacturing capacity. Now, the largest banks are claiming significant increases in non-performing property loans, while the glut of new industrial capacity implies that some firms may not have adequate profits to service their debts.

10.4   Overhauling the banks

The need of overhauling the banking sector has become more urgent in light of China's WTO-bound commitment to accelerate the opening up of this sector. In December 2001, China joined the WTO as its 143rd member. In exchange for WTO membership, China has made a wide range of concessions and commitments to further open up its domestic industries to foreign imports and investment. Most of these market opening conditions are more stringent than those imposed on other developing countries by the WTO or its predecessor General

Agreement of Tariffs and Trade (GATT). The willingness of China to make these concessions is based on rational calculations. One is institutional, which reflects "an attempt by reformers to lock economic policies on to a course for further marketization and internationalization that is costly to reverse." (Woo, 2001) In other words, accession to the WTO is China's public recognition of marketization and internationalization as the primary sources of its rapid growth since the 1980s. The other consideration relates to China's strong desire to secure access to its major export markets. Without WTO membership, for instance, the continuity of China's normal trading relationship with the United States was subject to annual reviews by Congress, leaving China's export trade vulnerable to the vagaries of American domestic politics. WTO membership guarantees that this engine of growth would no longer be unilaterally shut off by the United States without this being a major violation of Washington's international commitments (Sachs and Woo, 2002). As part of China's WTO-bound commitments, China has to open up its banking sector to foreign banks according to the following agenda:[19]

- For foreign currency business, foreign financial institutions should be permitted to provide services in China without restriction as to clients or geographical areas upon accession.
- Geographical restrictions on foreign banks on Chinese currency (*yuan*) businesses are to be phased out by opening up four cities (Shanghai, Shenzhen, Tianjin, and Dalian) upon accession and a few more cities every subsequent year. Within the fifth year after accession, all geographical restrictions should be removed.
- For local currency business, within two years after accession (before the end of 2003), foreign financial institutions should be permitted to provide services to Chinese enterprises. Within five years after accession (before the end of 2006), foreign financial institutions should be permitted to provide services to both enterprise- and household-clients. Foreign financial institutions licensed for local currency business in one region of China may service clients in any other region that has been opened for such business.
- Criteria for authorization to deal in China's financial services sector should be solely prudential (i.e., contain no economic needs test or quantitative limits on licenses). Within five years after accession (before end of 2006), any existing non-prudential measures restricting ownership, operation, and judicial form of foreign financial institutions, including on internal branching and licenses, should be eliminated. In other words, foreign banks shall receive national treatment in banking regulations.

By the third quarter of 2005, there had been 138 foreign banks approved for conducting RMB-related businesses.[20] Their assets amounted to US$84.5billion, equivalent to 2 percent of total assets in China's domestic banking sector. Their share of China's foreign exchange loan market, however, had exceeded 20 percent. In Shanghai, the city pioneering financial opening, foreign banks have achieved a share of total banking assets as high as 12.4 percent and a share of the foreign exchange loan market up to 54.5 percent (CBRC, 2005).

In wake of the imminent foreign banks' competition, the Chinese government has taken a series of measures to prepare the banking sector for the post-WTO opening:

The first measure is improving banking sectors' asset quality. As mentioned above, since 1998, the government has injected a huge amount of money to facilitate debt-for-equity restructure of the commercial banks and deposit institutions. The rationale for doing so is to help these banks and institutions offload the NPL burdens incurred in the early stage of transition so that they could have a fresh start of business and better prepare themselves for the environment after the banking sector opens up to foreign competition by end of 2006. Apart from injection of funds into the big-four SCBs, the CBRC has coordinated with various levels of local governments since January 2005 to implement debt-for-equity restructure of local deposit institutions, write off their bad loans, and close down some insolvent credit coops and local banks. A total amount of 23.3 billion *yuan* has been injected by local governments in seven provinces to carry out debt-for-equity restructuring of 28 city commercial banks (CBRC, 2005).

Liberalizing interest rates is another important step to allow commercial banks to stand on their own and to do business more in line with commercial norms. In July 2004, the PBOC increased the allowed range of lending rate float from the originally 0.9 to 1.3 times of the official benchmark rate (5.31 percent for one-year corporate lending in 2004) to 0.9 to 1.7 times.[21] Another move was a pilot scheme jointly promulgated by the PBOC, CBRC and CSRC in early 2005 to allow a limited number of commercial banks to enter into the fund management business on a *"shidian (试点)"* (trial) basis.[22] The rationale of this scheme is twofold. One is to diversify banks' sources of revenue beyond interest income, which now accounts for more than 90 percent of revenue for most banks. The other is to facilitate the growth of capital market and financial deepening process. By diversifying commercial banks' businesses, the move was not only meant to reduce banks' operation risks but also to give a boost to the development of equity financing market.

The second measure is beefing up supervision over the commercial banks and deposit institutions. This has been mainly conducted by the CBRC, founded in April 2003. The functions of the CBRC are to monitor and ensure that all banks and depository institutions would (a) classify their loans consistently and accurately according to a five-category scale of loan quality (b) prepare sufficient provisions (c) keep their balance sheets by accounting standards, and (d) meet the capital ratio of 8 percent of risk-weighted assets as decreed by Basel I, a global standard.

To achieve these goals, the CBRC has set up 36 bank regulatory bureaus, 296 branch bureaus, 1,753 regulatory branch offices. The banking institutions under its supervision number to 34,000, with total assets worth 31.6 trillion *yuan*, or over 90 percent of total assets of all financial institutions. Since its creation, the CBRC has promulgated over 200 regulations and sets of rules (CBRC, 2005, 2006). Its 23,000 staff constantly visit and check the banks and deposit institutions to ensure compliance. For instance, in 2004, the CBRC staff made 16,700 visits to 36 percent of all banks and deposit institutions to conduct on-site checks on lending records. These visits revealed illicit lending practices involving 2,202 institutions and 584 billion *yuan* of loans.[23] The CBRC required all the commercial

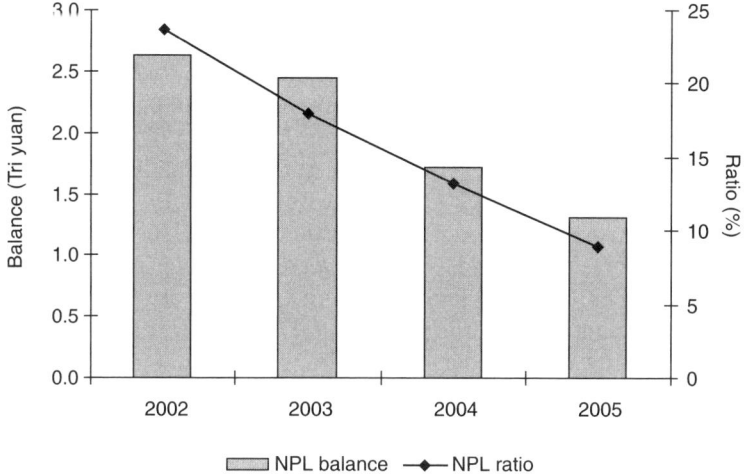

Figure 10.7   The "double declines" of NPL balance and NPL ratio

Note: Year-end figures.

Sources: CBRC, National Bureau of Statistics of China (NBSC).

Table 10.3   Financial status of China's banking sector

	Loan increase %	NPL Trillion yuan	NPL ratio %	Pre-tax profit Billion yuan	Provision fund ratio %	Banks with capital-adequacy ratio ≥ 8%	
						Number of banks	Share of bank assets
2002	15	2.63	23.7	–	–	–	0.5
2003	21	2.44	17.9	11.5		<8	0.6
2004	14	1.72	13.2	63.5	20	–	47.5
2005	13	1.31	8.6	185.0	33	53	75.0

Source: CBRC and NBSC.

banks to meet the Basel I capital ratio by January 2007 or face severe sanctions, including the removal of senior management.[24] The extent of regulator's supervision is pervasive. "At every board meeting, the CBRC guy is right there taking notes and pounding the table," observed a foreign independent director at Hangzhou City Commercial Bank.[25]

Thanks to a combination of public fund injection, offloading bad loans through debt-for-equity process, expansion of lending scale, and perhaps some improvement in management, China's banking sector has achieved the so-called "double declines" of both NPL balance and NPL ratios for the fourth year since 2002. By end of 2005, all commercial banks' NPL balance has been lowered to 1.3 trillion *yuan* and the NPL ratio dropped for the first time to below 10 percent, reaching 8.6 percent (Figure 10.7).[26] On top of that, the number of banks that have met Basel I capital-adequacy ratio reached 53, accounting for 75 percent of total banking sector's assets, compared to fewer than eight banks in 2003 (0.54 percent of total bank assets) at the end of 2002. Meanwhile, banks also have substantially increased their pre-tax profits from 2002 to 2005 (Table 10.3).

China's regulators understand well that regulatory supervision alone is not enough to change banks' behaviour. Therefore a third measure is being taken to bring in more fundamental changes to the banking sector, that is, incorporating SCBs and pluralizing their ownership. In the words of Liu Mingkang, head of CBRC:

> A very important issue of reforming the state-owned banks is to fundamentally change these banks' sole ownership by the state through pluralizing the ownership structure. Only when the shareholding and stake-holding are pluralized, it will not be possible for the state budget to "pay the bill" for the losses made by the state-owned commercial banks in violation of the market principle of fair competition. This reform will not only eliminate the institutional cause of moral-hazard behaviour in business operation of these banks but also motivate them to be innovative and market-oriented, stand on their own, and improve management and organizations.[27]

As shown in Figure 10.8, the NPL ratio for the shareholding banks has been much lower than that of the SCBs (the big-four) and the urban commercial banks (mainly owned by local city/municipal governments). Among all commercial banks, the foreign ones have had the lowest NPL ratio.

In 2004, the government started to incorporate the "better two" of the big-four SCBs , the CCB and the BOC. For this purpose, the government established a new agency, Central Huijin Investment Company, to manage and re-capitalize the big state-owned banks before they go for Initial Public Offering (IPO) In 2005, the third member of the "big-four," the China Industrial and Commercial Bank also underwent incorporation. By Fall 2005, Huijin had injected US$60 billion of China's foreign exchange reserves into the three banks. One year after it was set up in September 2004, the CCB Co. Ltd. successfully launched its IPO in the Hong Kong stock exchange on 27 October 2005, raising US$8billion from foreign investors for 12 percent of its shares. On 24 May 2006, the BOC raised US$9.7billion (for 10.5 percent of its shares) via its IPO in Hong Kong market.

To facilitate the ownership restructure, the government has encouraged Chinese banks to sell their shares to "strategic investors" from abroad. To foreign banks, becoming a major strategic investor of a Chinese bank means immediate access to the latter's domestic banking network and customer base. To the Chinese, selling the stakes not only pluralizes the ownership of these banks but also opens a short-cut to introducing foreign management, technology, and financial products. To

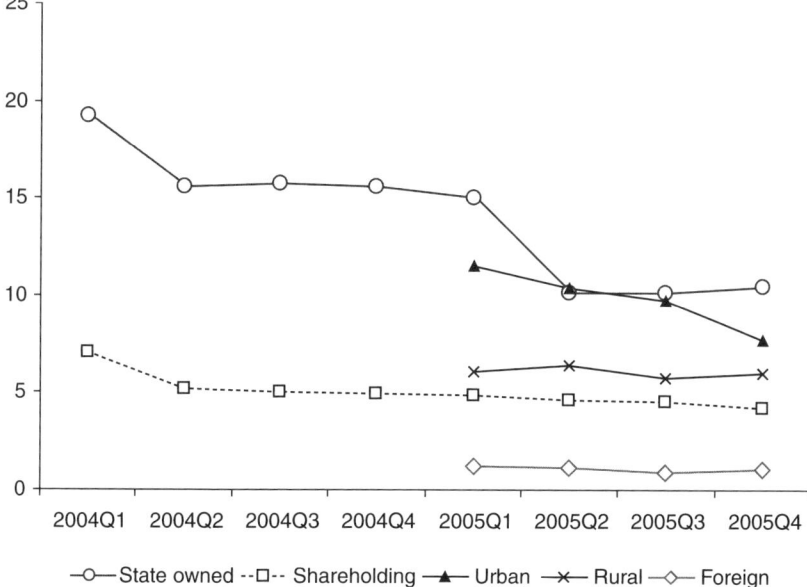

Figure 10.8   NPL ratios of commercial banks by category
Note: Quarter-end figures.
Source: CBRC.

ensure that the move meets these objectives, the government has set five requirements for such partnerships:

(a) The foreign investor's holding stake should not be lower than 5 percent but
     not to exceed 20 percent (or in the case of multiple foreign strategic investors,
     25 percent).
(b) The holding should not be for less than 3 years.
(c) The strategic investor must send personnel to join the Chinese bank's board
     of directors to participate in management and decision making; participation
     in senior management is also encouraged.
(d) The strategic investor must have a strong background in banking business.
(e) Each foreign strategic investor may not invest in more than two Chinese
     banks.[28]

These measures to overhaul the banking sector have made significant achievements so far. Foreign strategic investors have lined up to take advantage of China's
red carpet rolled out for them (Table 10.4). By the end of October 2005, there had
been a total of 17 domestic commercial banks that had partnered with foreign
strategic investors, including CCB, BOC, Bank of Communications (BoCom),
five of the 13 shareholding commercial banks, and seven city commercial banks

Table 10.4   Major deals with foreign strategic investors (till March 2006)

Bank	Investor	Amount $ billion	% of stake	Deal date	IPO value and date
BoCom	HSBC (HK)	1.70	19.9	August 2004	$1.9 billion in June 2005, Hong Kong
CCB	Bank of America (US)	3.00	10.0	June 2005	$8 billion in October 2005
	Temasek (Singapore)	1.40	5.1	August 2005	Hong Kong
BOC	Royal Bank of Scotland (UK), Merrill Lynch (US), Li KS Foundation (HK)	3.10	10.0	August 2005	$9.7 billion in May 2006, Hong Kong
	Temasek (Singapore)**	1.55	5.0	February 2006	–
	UBS (Switzerland)	0.50	1.6	August 2005	–
	Asian Development Bank	0.075	0.24	September 2005	–
	Bank of Tokyo Mitsubushi – UFJ (Japan)	0.30	1.0	Bid in January 2006	–
ICBC	Goldman Sachs (US), Allianz (Germany), American Express (US)	3.78	9.9	January 2006	$19.1 billion and 36.3 billion *yuan* in October 2006, Hong Kong and Shanghai
GDB*	A Citigroup-led consortium	3.00	85.0	Bid in January 2006	–
China CITIC Bank	CITIC (HK)	0.70	19.9	March 2006	–

Notes:
* Guangdong Development Bank. Since the deal exceeds the 25 percent stake limit for foreign institutions, it had been pending on CBRC's approval by November 2006.
** BOC' state-owned parent, China Huijin Investment Co, rejected the original deal in August 2005 of selling 10 percent of BOC stake to Temasek due to concerns that Temasek had already secured 5.1 percent of CCB stake. The deal finalized in February 2006 by halving the original sale.

Source: Kwan (2006) and other media reports.

(CBRC, 2005). The total investment pledged by these investors amounts to US$16.5billion.[29] The first big deal to engage foreign strategic investors was the US$1.7billion The Hongkong and Shanghai Banking Corporation (HSBC) paid for a 19.9 percent stake in BoCom, the fifth largest bank in China in August 2004. BoCom has also been successfully listed on overseas stock markets. Before its IPO, the CCB pocketed US$4 billion by selling 9 percent of shares to Bank of America and 5.1 percent to Temasek Holdings, a Singapore government investment agency. Apart from the BoCom and CCB deals, the Royal Bank of Scotland led an investment consortium to invest US$3.1 billion in the BOC and the consortium of Goldman & Sachs (United States), Allianz (Germany) and American Express (United States) closed a deal to acquire a 9.9 percent stake in the ICBC for a similar sum.[30]

10.5 Prospects of future reforms

China's banking and financial sector has gone through substantial transitions in the country's two-and-half-decade long gradualist reform process. With imminent full-scale opening to foreign bank competition, the banking and financial sector has now come to a critical stage of further transition. Given the momentum of recent reforms, we can expect that further pluralization of banking ownership will be a major form of foreign bank entry and the main driving force behind banking restructuring in the coming years.

To fulfill WTO-ruled opening agenda for the banking-financial sector, a number of reforms are being carried out or planned for many fronts in the financial sector. Rules and regulations have been amended to open up banking businesses to foreign banks and financial institutions, presumably in accordance with the WTO National Treatment principle. Corporate bankruptcy law is to be revised and a credit bureau will be established. Lending floor rate is to be removed gradually between 2006 and 2009 while deposit ceiling rate is to be removed gradually from 2008 to 2010.

For capital market reforms, it is worth noting that China made a legislative overhaul of its two laws in October 2005. One is the Law of Financial Securities and the other is the Law of Corporations. The former provides greater investor protection by, for instance, granting CSRC more power to supervise the market and requiring investors' cash to be deposited into their personal accounts rather than the accounts of the securities companies. The Law of Corporation now has lowered the minimum registered capital to start a business for all industries and allows up to 70 percent of the registered capital to be non-cash contributions. The new versions of the two laws took effect at the beginning of 2006. On top of that, a crucial reform was launched in April 2005 to make all the non-tradable shares held by state agencies to be converted into tradable ones.[31] By mid-2006, this reform had achieved remarkable success as 1,092 companies (out of a total of 1,300 plus listed companies) had already completed the reform or had been going through the reform procedures. These companies accounted for 81.25 percent of all listed companies' market value.[32] The supposed roles of these reforms to improve corporate governance and recover public confidence in China's capital market will be tested in the coming few years, which are a critical period of the country's financial development.

In the banking sector, it is undeniable that there have been profound changes in the composition of bank lending. Lending to consumers started only in 1997 but has increased 123 times from the first-year level to more than 2 trillion *yuan* (US$250 billion) in seven years. Mortgages, car and education loans made up 11 percent of the total and 26 percent of new lending in 2005, up from 1.5 percent of the total in 1999, when these loans were first provided.[33]

It is, however, still a question whether the SCBs have changed their corporate-loan lending habit that favors the SOEs. A study by CASS (1998) shows that SOEs contributed only one third of GDP but accounted for two-thirds of the total domestic loans in the mid-1990s. A recent count by Farrell et al (2006) reveals that the wholly and partially state-owned companies continue to absorb most of the funding from the financial system. In 2003, wholly state-owned companies received 35 percent of bank credit and accounted for all equity and bond issues, despite the fact that they only contributed to 23 percent of GDP. The many shareholding enterprises that are partially state-owned and the collective enterprises took up another 38 percent of credit, although producing only 25 percent of output. Private and foreign enterprises, being the engine of China's growth and producing 52 percent of GDP, received only 27 percent of bank loans. Meanwhile, The small and medium-sized enterprises (SMEs),[34] which provide 75 percent of jobs and create 55 percent of GDP, receive merely 16 percent of total bank loans in recent years.

Banks were also more risk-taking (or less cautious in dealing with risks) when giving loans to SOE borrowers. Lu et al (2005) used a sample of 268 public listing companies in China for the period 1994–1999 to test the relation between firms' bank borrowing and their loan default risks. The study shows that, at all default risk levels, firms with higher state-owned share ownership ratios tend to get more loan credits than those with lower ones. In particular, the SOEs with higher risks also tend to get more money from the banks after controlling other factors that affect borrowing/lending decisions. Podpiera (2006) examined data from 1997 through 2004 and found that the large SCBs have slowed down credit expansion, but that the pricing of credit risk remains undifferentiated and banks do not appear to take enterprise profitability into account when making lending decisions. Farrell et al (2006) identifies several operational weaknesses prevailing in many Chinese banks, including lack of good internal credit-assessment, lack of external information on credit histories and the financial conditions of potential borrowers, and ineffective performance-management systems.

The inability of the formal financial system to meet the financial needs of the SMEs and private businesses force the latter to turn to informal/underground finance. The rising importance of such finance in filling up the gap left by the formal system has drawn research interests in recently years (ref. Tsai, 2001; Guo and Liu, 2002; Mao, 2005 and Gonzalez 2006). These studies show that the booming private businesses in China have for years relied primarily on informal finance (the so-called "curb market") for their start-up and working capital needs. The informal financing mechanisms range from loans between friends and relatives to sophisticated financing arrangements that circumvent national banking laws in creative ways. Underground lending organizations operate actively in the coastal regions, functioning like deposit institutions and granting loans to local entrepreneurs at interest rates as high as 15–20 percent. It is estimated by some researchers that lending from these institutions amounts to 800 billion *yuan* (3 percent of total bank deposits), providing 6 percent of corporate loans. On top of that, lending based on personal arrangements (among family members and friends) could be as high as one-fourth of the bank deposits (Farrell et al., 2006). The prevalence of the high-cost informal finance highlights the potentials for improving the efficiency of China's financial system.

The outlook of efficiency improvement in the formal banking sector, however, remains uncertain. Despite recent efforts to engage foreign strategic investors, it is clear that the government is not yet prepared to relinquish its grip on the SCBs that dominate the banking business. So far there has not yet been a case of foreign takeovers of even the non-state financial institutions. As strategic partners with limited stake-holding, the foreign banks may be more interested in sharing the privilege and market power of the major state-owned banks than seriously helping the latter improve their management and change the way of doing business. Meanwhile, since state-owned banks' low-quality lending has been driven by the demand for funding the government-linked companies and projects, involving foreign banks as strategic partners will not be a panacea for the problem of deteriorating capital finance and growth quality (as evident in the rising ICOR in recent years).

While interest rate liberalization is yet to be fully accomplished, the consequence of the banks' "lending binge" between 2003 and 2004 to grow out of their bad loan problem remains a serious concern in the coming years. As estimated by Farrell et al (2006), of the substantial reduction of NPLs of the big-four state-owned banks between 2001 and 2005, about 59 percent was due to the transfer of bad loans to asset-management companies. The remaining reduction came from NPL resolution and dilution due to growth in new loans. That is why the CBRC has taken a very stern position to require that every bank must meet Basel I capital-adequacy ratio by January 2007. It has also set up a nationwide reporting network to monitor every loan worth more than 100 million *yuan*. It constantly checks every bank's classification of the 5-category scales of loans, traces changing trends of loan quality composition, and informs banks of their performance ranking.[35] At the beginning of 2006, CBRC introduced the CAMEL rating system, an international standard, to beef up its supervision of commercial banks.[36] Even so, the average capital-adequacy ratio of China's banks (7.8 percent) is still much lower than those of other major Asian economies, including India (12.9 percent), Indonesia (19.9 percent), and Thailand (12.7 percent). China's rate of return on bank assets is also the lowest compared to those of the major Asian economies.[37] It remains to be seen whether the measures taken by CBRC are sufficient to prevent a re-bounce of NPLs.

In the longer run, China has to restructure its highly unbalanced financial infrastructure built almost solely upon an inefficient banking sector. In the past, China's economic growth has been fuelled by an extraordinary high fixed capital investment rate, mainly financed (indirectly) through the banking sector, which intermediates nearly 75 percent of the capital in the economy. This ratio is glaringly high with those in other Asian countries (43 percent in India, 35 percent in Japan, and 33 percent in South Korea) and the United States (19 percent). Excluding the value of non-tradable equity shares,[38] China's equity market capitalization was only 17 percent of GDP by 2004, much lower than in many developed and developing countries (29 percent in Poland, 56 percent in India, 63 percent in South Korea, 79 percent in Japan, 139 percent in the United States). China's net corporate debt was only about 1 percent of GDP,[39] one of the lowest in the world (Farrell et al., 2006). Direct finance (by share holding or bond issuing) only accounts for less than 10 percent of business finance in today's China and there are only about 1,400 listed companies out of the several millions of enterprises.[40] In 2004, for instance, roughly 93.6 percent (or US$300billion) of firms' formal finance came from the banking system, only about 1.4 percent (US$4.5 billion) from the bond market and 5 percent (US$16 billion) from the sale of shares on domestic exchanges.[41] By end of 2005, bank lending stood near 113 percent of GDP and bank deposit base was a bit under 158 percent of GDP. By comparison, bond market capitalization and equity market capitalization were only about 15 percent and 8 percent of GDP, respectively (Setser, 2006). Thanks to capital account control and under-developed corporate capital-bond market, the banking sector has been able to absorb almost the entire pool of household savings (despite the suppressed interest rates) and provide them as low-cost capital (thanks to the suppressed interest rates) to support the investment-driven growth in the past two decades. High concentration of corporate finance in an inefficient banking sector not only increases overall financial risks for both the lender and the borrower but also constrains business opportunities for entrepreneurs.

This model of capital misallocation and high-cost growth will face increasing challenges in future as the Chinese economy becomes more mature and open. The worrying trend of rising ICOR displayed in Figure 10.6 reveals an increasingly unsustainable growth path. Further financial reforms are essential to China's future growth efficiency. Farrell et al (2006) estimate that reforms to improve banking efficiency, modernize the payments system, and diversify the mix of financing vehicles available to companies could save US$62 billion per year, which nearly equals to the amount of foreign direct investment that China receives each year, or 3.2 percent of GDP. On top of that, reforms that enabled a larger share of funding to go to the more productive private enterprises would, over time, increase investment efficiency and raise GDP by up to 13 percent.

Such huge potential gains to the economy will certainly be appealing enough to the Communist ruling elites, who rely on their role in "delivering" economic growth and prosperity to justify the legitimacy of the Party's governance. The booming business of informal finance signifies the vitality of the private sector and the strong market demand for financial services that are friendly to private businesses. To the foreign financial investors, the rapid rise of China's economy offers an optimistic prospect for business opportunities. For instance, the financial consulting agency Goldman & Sachs forecasts that China's total banking assets in 2010 will be twice what they were in 2004, the market for insurance will almost triple, and assets under (fund) management will increase six-fold.[42] The highly unbalanced financial structure suggests great potentials for growth in capital market and business finance beyond the banking sector only if the existing institutional constraints are removed. All these factors promise a continuing momentum of reforms.

10.6 Concluding remarks

This chapter reviews the key reforms that China has undertaken to transform its banking-financial sector from an instrument of central planning in a command economy to a dynamic sector increasingly capable of serving the financial needs of a market-based economy. However, we have observed that some transitional features of the banking sector, such as the dominance of state ownership, the lending habit that favours government-linked borrowers or projects, and the poor management, have led to reckless credit expansion that undermines investment efficiency and growth quality. These defects have also contributed to the sector's failure to meet the financial needs of the SMEs and private businesses, the most vigorous and productive segment of the economy. Huge potential economic gains can be harvested through rectifying these defects. Thus a major policy implication of our analysis is to keep the momentum of recent-year reforms to fulfil China's post-WTO financial market opening commitments and to further pluralize the banking sector's ownership structure.

To address the issue of China's highly unbalanced financial structure that relies almost solely on bank financing, fundamental reforms are necessary to promote the development of the equity market and bond market – another policy implication of this chapter. Due to the length limit of the current chapter, we have focused on the banking sector reforms only. Future studies should be directed to equity-bond market development and its integrated role in further financial deepening of the Chinese economy.[43]

Appendices

A1 Classifications of non-performing loans

Before 1998, China's banking sector monitored and recorded NPLs following an accounting standard set by the MOF in 1988. According to this standard, a loan would be classified as "*yu qi* (逾期)" (overdue) if the borrower has defaulted payment of the principal and interest over 180 days. If the default has been longer than three years, the loan would be classified as "*dai zhi* (呆滞)" (inactive). If the borrower cannot be located or is dead or the loan is approved to be classified as by the Ministry, the loan would be classified as a "dai zhang (呆账)" (dead loan).[44]

In August 1996, the PBOC promulgated *General Rules of Loans*,[45] which defines "non-performing loans" as those include "dead loans", "inactive loans", and "overdue loans". The definitions of "dead loans" and "inactive loans" follow that of the MOF while the "overdue loans" include all loans unpaid after the due date. The criterion, dubbed as the "yi yu liang dai (一逾两呆)" (overdue-inactive-dead) standard, was only a bit more stringent than before but still not consistent with international standards.

In 1997, China's cabinet, the State Council, decided to try the five-category scale for classifying loan quality recommended by the World Bank. The new criterion was first applied on a trial basis in Guangdong province in 1998. In the following few years till 2001, the "overdue-inactive-dead" standard continued to dominate NPL reporting rules while the major Chinese banks started to report loan quality in compliance of the five-category scale. In September 2000, the PBOC issued the *Scheme of Identifying Non-performing Loans*, which required reports of NPLs according to a four-stage overdue yardstick: 3-month overdue, 6-month overdue, one-year overdue, and over-one-year overdue.[46]

To meet China's post-WTO agenda of financial sector opening, the PBOC promulgated the *Guidelines of Loan Risk Classification* on December 25, 2001 and decided to implement the guideline to most banks and lending institutions while continued to require reports of overdue loans by the four-stage overdue standard.[47]

According to the *Guidelines of Loan Risk Classification,*[48] loans are classified into five categories, namely "passed", "special mention", "substandard", "doubtful", and "loss", according to their financial risks. Under the "passed" category, the borrower fulfills the loan contract and there is no sufficient reason to doubt the borrower's ability to pay principal and interest in time. The "special mention" category refers to the case where there exist some factors that may negatively affect payment despite that the borrower is still able to pay the principal and interest. When there emerge apparent problems regarding the borrower's ability to pay, the case would be treated as "substandard". In such a case, the borrower may not rely on normal business revenue to fulfill payment commitment so some losses may occur to the bank even with collaterals. Under the "doubtful" case, the borrower is unable to pay the principal and interests and the bank is sure to suffer major losses even by taking the collaterals. The "loss" category refers to the case that the bank cannot get back all or most values of the principal and interest after taking all possible measures and necessary legal procedures to recover the loss. The definition of NPLs refers to those loans classified as "substandard", "doubtful", and "loss".

The early trial in Guangdong Province in 1998 suggested that the five-category risk scale classification reported a non-performing loan ratio 20 percentage points higher than the "overdue-inactive-dead" (1996) standard.[49] From 2002 to 2003, the banking sector was in a transition from the "overdue" standard to the five-category scale. The *China Financial Yearbook* started to publish major state banks' non-performing loan data from 2002, which has been based mainly on the five-category scale. Shi (2006) estimated that, for the state commercial banks, the NPL ratio based on the four-stage overdue standard was 25.7 percent in 2002, 4.1 percentage points lower than the 29.8 percent NPL ratio based on the five-category risk scale.

A2   Administrative structure that oversees the banking-financial sector

In China, the ruling status of the Communist Party is defined by the Constitution as a prime feature of the People's Republic. The Party's Central Committee and its Political Bureau make the major decisions for the government. In financial and

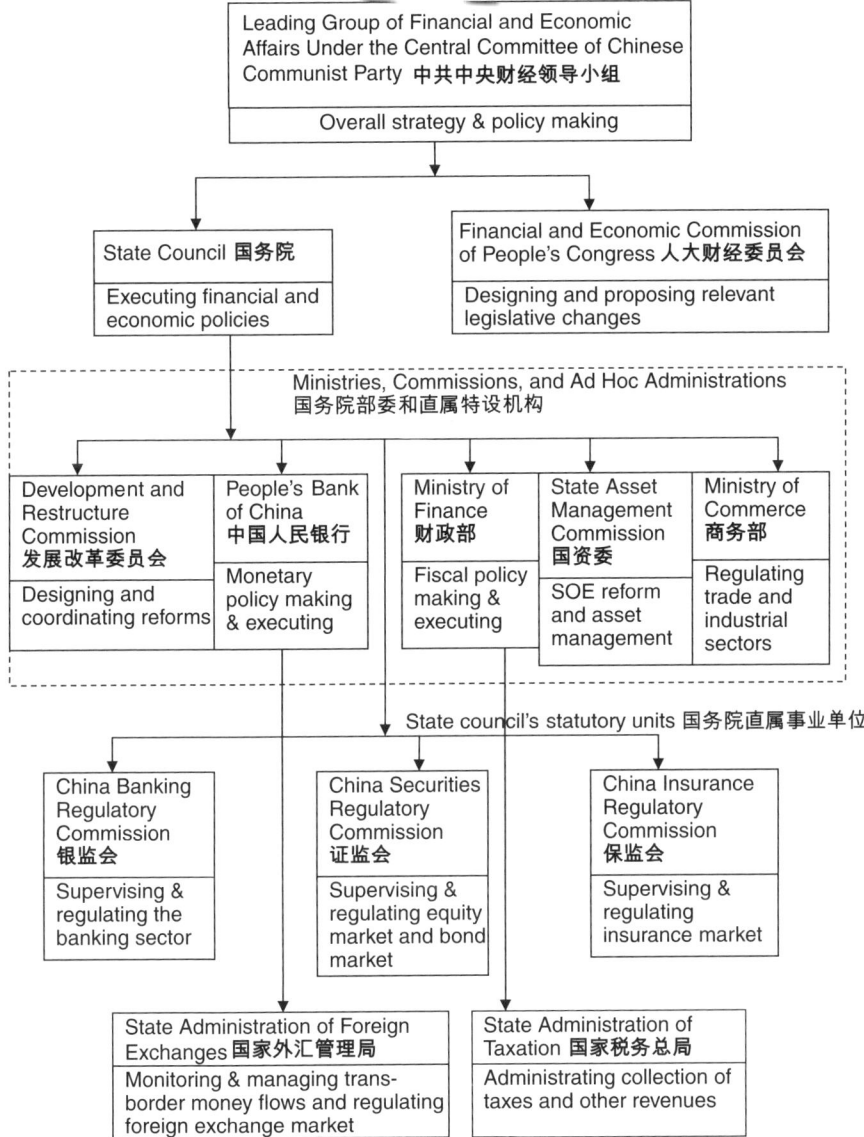

Figure 10.9   Administrative bodies that oversee the banking-financial sector

Source: Compiled by the author.

economic policy making, key decisions are made by the Leading Group of Financial and Economic Affairs of the Party.[50] All legislative changes about financial and economic affairs are to be voted into law by the People's Congress, the legislative branch of the government, after these changes are drafted and proposed by the Congress' Financial and Economic Commission. The State Council, the executive branch of the government, oversees implementation of the policies made by the Party. Under the State Council, the ministry-level units directly involved in financial and economic affairs include the Development and Restructure Commission, the PBOC (the Central Bank), the MOF, the Ministry of Commerce, and the State Asset-Management Commission. The State Administration of Foreign Exchanges, under the Central Bank, oversees foreign exchange market and cross-border money flows. The State Administration of Taxation, under the MOF, takes care of collection of taxes and other fiscal revenues. The three regulatory bodies, the CBRC, the CSRC, and the China Insurance Regulatory Commission, supervise and regulate the banking sector, equity and bond markets, and insurance sector, respectively (Figure 10.9).

Acknowledgements

The author deeply thanks Ken Imai, Nazrul Islam, Reeitsu Kojima, Kazuyuki Motahashi, Xizhe Peng, Thomas Rawski, Kazuhiko Yokota, and other conference participants for their valuable views and comments on the earlier drafts of this paper.

Notes

1   Statistics in this paragraph are cited from China State Statistical Bureau, various years. A factor that may overstate China's financial depth is a very high level of corporate deposits (accounting for ¼ of total deposits) since firms are obliged to keep them as collaterals. Excluding that, China's financial depth is still relatively high for its per capita income, reflecting China's financial system's unequivocally successful in mobilizing savings [See Farrell et al (2006) for more detailed discussions].
2   The capitalization of equity market refers to market values of all shares (including tradable and non-tradable shares (see endnote 31).
3   For a more detailed discussion of the pre-reform monetary system in China's centrally planned economy, see Peebles (1991).
4   The three policy-loan banks are: the State Development Bank, the Agriculture Development Bank of China, and the Export & Import Bank of China.
5   For Minsheng Bank, however, there is a question about "the extent to which it is truly private" (Gonzalez, 2006).
6   Reuter, *Straits Times* (Singapore), May 23, 1995.
7   CCER (2000, p. 12) and remarks by Liu Mingkang, BOC governor, at a news conference on December 1, 2003 (xinhuanet.com, December 2, 2003).
8   See Appendix for evolution of NPL classifications.
9   Citigroup, *Greater China Insights*, June 14, 2002.
10   "NPL Reduction Move on the Way", *China Daily*, December 2, 2003.
11   "Don't Bank on a Bail-Out", *The Economist*, December 4, 2003; "China's Banks: Beyond a Bail-out", *The Economist*, January 10, 2004.
12   "Recapitalising China's Banks", *The Economist*, January 8, 2004; Podpiera (2006); Setser (2006).
13   For a more detailed discussion on exchange rate rigidity and excessive liquidity in the domestic economy, see Goodfriend and Prasad (2006).
14   The investment in real estate development increased by 29.7 percent and 28.1 percent in 2003 and 2004 respectively (China State Statistical Bureau).

15 "NPL is the Main Barrier to the Big Four State Banks' Public Listing", *Lianhe Zaobao (United Mornings, Singapore)*, January 27, 2003.

16 "A Great Big Banking Gamble", *The Economist*, October 29, 2005.

17 "China Tightens Land Supply to Curb Economic Overheating", *People's Daily*, September 6, 2006.

18 China carried out a nationwide census on its secondary and tertiary industries in 2004. Based on the survey results, the National Bureau of Statistics of China adjusted up the country's GDP in 2004 by 16.8 percent and recalculated GDP statistics for years back to 1993 (NBSC, 2006a).

19 WTO, *Report of the Working Party on the Accession of China*, Addendum, Schedule CLII, November 10, 2001.

20 By the WTO rules, these banks' entry into RMB-related businesses does not require Chinese-bank partnership.

21 "PBOC Governor: Speeding Up Interest Rate Reform", *Lianhe Zaobao (United Mornings, Singapore)*, July 9, 2004.

22 "Officials of PBOC, CBRC, and CSRC answered media questions about the pilot scheme on commercial banks' operation of fund management business", www.cbrc.gov.cn, February 20, 2005.

23 "Achievements of CBRC on-site checks in 2004", www.cbrc.gov.cn, January 17, 2005.

24 "Liu Mingkang at Media Conference", www.cbrc.gov.cn, December 1, 2004.

25 "A Great Big Banking Gamble", *The Economist*, October 29, 2005.

26 The official statistics of achieving "double declines" in NPL are not free of controversy. For instance, in May 2006, Ernst & Young published an analytical report claiming that China's stock of NPLs was more than five-and-a-half times the latest government estimate and size of bad loans carried by the big-four state-owned banks was almost three times of the official tally. After the PBOC's rebuttal, however, Ernst & Young withdrew the report and admitted the report being "factually erroneous" ("A Muffled Report", *The Economist*, May 18, 2006).

27 "Liu Mingkang's answers to correspondents", www.cbrc.gov.cn, December 5, 2005.

28 "Liu Mingkang's answers to correspondents", ibid.

29 "A Chinese Coup", *The Economist*, January 5, 2006.

30 AFP, "Bank of China sells 5% Stake to Temasek for US$1.55b", February 17, 2006, www.channelnewsasia.com.

31 Before the reform of 2005, about two-thirds of shares of listed companies (mostly state-owned before their incorporation and listing) represented state-owned assets and were held by the government (the State) through its organs or agencies (i.e., "legal persons"). These shares were not allowed to be traded in open market till the 2005 reform and their non-tradability was a major obstacle to capital market development.

32 *Xinhuanet News*, July 3, 2006.

33 "A Great Big Banking Gamble". *The Economist*, October 29, 2005.

34 SMEs are defined in China as enterprises with between 8 and 2,000 employees, less than US $50 million assets, and less than US $37 million sales (which varies depending on sector). About 80 percent of SMEs were estimated to be private by Citibank in 2001.

35 "Liu Mingkang's answers to correspondents", www.cbrc.gov.cn, December 5, 2005.

36 "CRBC unifies the bank rating system", www.cbrc.gov.cn, January 12, 2006.

37 "A Great Big Banking Gamble", *The Economist*, October 29, 2005.

38 Even after the 2005 reform, the former non-tradable shares will only be allowed to be sold to the open market by their holders by phases over three years lest their sales would cause a slump in share prices.

39 In 2004, total corporate debt accounted for 11 percent of GDP. More than 90 percent of the outstanding amount corresponds to bonds that was issued by policy banks exclusively for the inter-bank market; most of the remaining 1 percent of GDP was issued by large state-owned enterprises.

40 "China Allows Local Governments to Issue Bonds", *Lianhe Zaobao (United Mornings, Singapore)*, September 24, 2005.
41 McGregor, R. "China Looks to Banks for 99% of All Financing", *Financial Times*, May 29, 2005.
42 Cottrel, R. "Thinking Big: A Survey of International Banking", *The Economist*, May 20, 2006.
43 Readers interested in equity market development may be referred to Lu and Li (2006).
44 "10-Year Reform of Loan Classification System", *Zhongguo Caijinbao (China Financial News)*, September 9, 2003.
45 *PBOC Gazette* (1997), no. 173.
46 "10-Year Reform of Loan Classification System", *Zhongguo Caijinbao (China Financial News)*, September 9, 2003.
47 *PBOC Gazette* (2001), no. 416.
48 Xinhua News Agency, December 25, 2001.
49 "10-Year Reform of Loan Classification System", *Zhongguo Caijinbao (China Financial News)*, September 9, 2003.
50 The current head of this group is Wen Jiabao, the Premier and the No. 2 Party leader after the General Secretary, Hu Jintao.

References

Chinese Academy of Social Sciences (CASS). 1998. "Macro Situations, Financial Risk and External Shock," *Economics Research Journal (Jin Ji Yan Jiu)*, Vol. 3, pp. 3–14.
Chinese Academy of Social Sciences (CASS). 1999. "Investment, Cyclic Fluctuation and Institutional Retrenchment Effect," *Economic Research Journal (Jin Ji Yan Jiu)*, Vol. **3**, pp. 16–25.
China, Banking Regulatory Commission (CBRC). 2005. "New Progress of Reform, Opening, and Regulation of China's Banking Sector," http://www.cbrc.gov.cn/ (accessed on December 15, 2005).
China, Banking Regulatory Commission (CBRC). 2006. "Regulation of China's Banking Sector Has Made Historical Breakthrough," http://www.cbrc.gov.cn/ (accessed on January 26, 2006).
China, Center for Economic Research (CCER). 2000. "China's Financial System Reform: Retrospect and Prospect," CCER Working Paper Series, No. C2000005.
Deutsche Bank. 2001. "China's Financial Liberalization Agenda," *Global Market Research*, May 2001. Deutsche Bank.
Farrell, Diana, Susan Lund, Jaeson Rosenfeld, Fabrice Morin, Niyati Gupta, and Ezra Greenberg. 2006. *Putting China's Capital to Work: The Value of Financial System Reform*, San Francisco: McKinsey Global Institute.
Gonzalez, Michael. 2006. Chapter 4, Informal Finance: Encouraging the Entrepreneurial Spirit in Post-Mao China, in *2006 Index of Economic Freedom*, Washington, D.C.: Heritage Foundation.
Goodfriend, Marvin and Eswar Prasad. 2006. A Framework for Independent Monetary Policy in China. *IMF Working Paper*, WP/06/111, available at www.imf.org/external/pubs/ft/wp/2006/wp06111.pdf (accessed on June 28, 2008).
Guo, Bin and Liu Manlu. 2002. Private Finance and Development of Small-&-Medium-Sized Enterprises: An Empirical Study on Wenzhou City. *Jingji Yanjiu (Journal of Economic Research)*, Vol. 413, No. 10, pp. 40–46.
Hale, David. 2005. China's Banking Revolution. www.project-syndicate.org (accessed on September 1, 2005).
Heilmann, Sebanstian. 2002. The Chinese Stock Market: Pitfalls of a Policy-Drive Market. Working Paper, Center for East Asian and Pacific Studies, Germany: Trier University.
Kwan, Chi Hung. 2004. Why China's Investment Efficiency is Low – Financial Reforms are Lagging Behind, www.rieti.go.jp/users/kan-si-yu/ (accessed on June 18, 2004).

Kwan, Chi Hung. 2006. Capital Participation of Foreign Investors in China's State-Owned Commercial Banks – A Win-Win Game. Available at www.rieti.go.jp/en/china/06021501. html (accessed on October 2, 2006)

Li, Bing-xiang and Dileep Mehta. 2001. "Restructuring of Chinese Banking Industry," *China & World Economy*, 3, available at http://www.iwep.org.cn/ (accessed on October 2, 2006).

Lu, Ding, and Li Ning. 2006. China's Capital Market Reform: Problems and Prospects, paper presented at International Conference on "China's Surging Economy: Adjusting for More Balanced Development," August 17–18, 2006, Singapore.

Lu, Ding, Shandre M. Thangavelu and Qing Hu. 2005, "Biased Lending and Non-Performing Loans in China's Banking Sector," *Journal of Development Studies*, Vol. 41, No. 6, pp. 1071–1091.

Lu, Ding and Qiao Yu. 1998. "Bank Credit-Quota Plan as a Macroeconomic Policy Instrument in China: Effectiveness and Costs," *Economic Systems*, Vol. 22, No. 2, pp. 147–174.

Mao, Jinmin. 2005. On Private Financial Market: A Survey and Analysis on the Cases of Private Finance in Shanxi Province, Jinrong Yanjiu, No. 1 available at www.cnki.com.cn/ Article/CJFDTotal-JRYJ200501016.htm (accessed on June 28, 2008).

Mitchell, Janet. 1997. Strategic Creditor Passivity, Regulation, and Bank Bailouts. *LSE/Center for Economic Performance Discussion Paper* 1780, London: London School of Economics.

National Bureau of Statistics of China (NBSC) various years. *Statistical Communiqué of National Economic and Social Development.* Beijing: NBSC.

National Bureau of Statistics of China. 2006a. Announcement of Adjustments to Historical Statistics of China's GDP. January 9, 2006, available at www.stats.gov.cn (accessed on October 2, 2006).

National Bureau of Statistics of China. 2006b. The National Economy Kept Steady and Fast Growth in 2005. January 25, 2006, available at www.stats.gov.cn (accessed on October 2, 2006).

Peebles, Gavin. 1991. *Money in the People's Republic of China: A Comparative Perspective*, Sydney: Allen & Unwin.

Podpiera, Richard. 2006. Progress in China's Banking Sector Reform: Has Bank Behavior Changed? *IMF Working Paper*, WP/06/71, available at www.imf.org/external/pubs/ft/ wp/2006/wp0671.pdf (accessed on June 28, 2008).

Roland, Gerald. 2000. *Transition and Economics: Politics, Markets, and Reforms*, Cambridge, MA: The MIT Press.

Sachs, Jeffery and Wing T. Woo. 2002. "China's Economic Growth after WTO Membership," *Journal of Chinese Economic and Business Studies*, Vol. 1, No. 1, pp. 1–32.

Sutela, Pekka. 1999. "Russia: Rise of a Dual Economy," *Transition*, Vol. 10, No. 5, pp. 20–22.

Setser, Brad. 2006. "The Chinese Conundrum: External Financial Strength, Domestic Financial Weakness," Paper Produced for CESifo Conference "Understanding the Chinese Economy," April 2006.

Shi, Huaqiang. 2006. State-Owned Commercial Banks' Non-Performing Loan Records: Re-Estimation of Its Severity: 1994–2004 (in Chinese). *Jinrong Yanjiu* (Finance Studies), February 2006, available at www.21our.com/readnews/757/757825.html (accessed on October 2, 2006).

Standard Chartered. 2001. China's Banking System in Transition, Business Intelligence No. 6 – China, available at www.tdctrade.com/econforum(accessed on October 2, 2006).

Tsai, Kellee. 2001. Beyond Banks: The Local Logic of Informal Finance and Private Sector Development in China. Paper prepared for the conference on Financial Sector Reform in China, co-sponsored by the China Public Policy Program at the Kennedy School of Government, Harvard Business School, and Massachusetts Institute of Technology, Cambridge, MA, September 11–13, 2001.

Walter, Carl E., and Howie, Fraser J. T. 2001. *To Get Rich is Glorious: China's Stock Markets in the 80s and 90s,* London: Palgrave Press.

Woo, Wing Thye. 2001. "Recent Claims of China's Economic Exceptionalism: Reflections Inspired by WTO Accession," *China Economic Review*, Vol. 12, No. 2/3, pp. 107–136.

World Bank. 1997. *China 2020*, Washington, D.C.: World Bank.

Xie, Ping. 1994. "On State Specialized Banks Reform," *Economic Research Journal (Jing Rong Yan Jiu)*, February 1994, pp. 1–8.

Xie, Ping. 2001. "The Debate on the Reform of China's Rural Credit Cooperatives System," *Journal of Financial Research (Jin Rong Yan Jiu)*, Vol. 1, pp. 1–13.

Xu, Guoping and Lei Lu. 2001. "Incomplete Contract and Moral Hazard: China's Financial Reform in 1990s," *Journal of Financial Research (Jin Rong Yan Jiu)*, Vol. 2, pp. 28–41.

Zeng, Peiyan et al. eds. 1999. *Report on China's National Economic and Social Development for 1998*, Beijing: China Planning Publisher.

Zeng, Peiyan et al. eds. 2000. *Report on China's National Economic and Social Development for 1999*, Beijing: China Planning Publisher.

11
Alternative Estimates of TFP Growth in China: Evidence from Application of the Dual Approach

Nazrul Islam and Erbiao Dai

11.1 Introduction

Whether or not Total Factor Productivity (TFP) growth is playing a significant role in China's recent economic growth is an important issue from several points of view. The first concerns sustainability of growth. As emphasized by Young (1995), Krugman (1994), and others, growth driven by input accumulation may soon hit the limits of diminishing returns and prove not sustainable. By contrast, growth driven primarily by productivity growth may be more sustainable. Second, findings regarding relative contribution of input accumulation and productivity can be useful in formulating policies necessary to confront rising regional inequality that has now become a well recognized problem in China. A finding showing the importance of TFP growth may indicate that mere channeling of investment into lagging provinces may not ensure their faster growth unless the investment is associated with productivity growth.

In view of the above, it is not surprising that issues concerning China's TFP have drawn considerable research, revolving generally around the following two questions: (a) How significant has TFP's role been in China's recent growth? (b) Has TFP Growth Rate (TFPGR) slowed down in recent years? Not unexpectedly, researchers have furnished to these questions varied answers, among which the following two broad trends may be distinguished. At one end are those who have provided very upbeat assessments of TFP's contribution to Chinese growth, and many of whom have also suggested that the Chinese TFP is *accelerating* with further reforms. Researchers belonging to this trend include Nogami and Li (1995), Hu and Khan (1997a, b), Ezaki and Sun (1999) and Wang and Yao (2001). At the other end are researchers who have discounted the importance of TFP in China's growth, and many of whom have also suggested that the Chinese TFP was *decelerating*. Scholars belonging to this trend include Young (2000) and Sachs and Woo (2000).

In their research on China's TFP, scholars have generally followed, what is known as the *primal approach* to growth accounting, an approach that relies almost exclusively on National Income Accounts (NIA) data. Unfortunately, despite attempts to rectify them, Chinese NIA data continue to suffer from many problems, which therefore cannot but affect the results obtained from the primal approach. Problems with NIA data are however not uncommon, and in view of similar problems with Singapore's NIA data, Hsieh (2002) earlier used what is known as the *dual approach* to growth accounting to examine issues concerning TFPGR in Singapore and South Korea. The advantage of the dual approach is that it does not have to depend on NIA data, and instead can make use of independent information on factor prices.

Application of the dual approach to China however has its own problems, because factor price information is not easy to obtain. This is particularly true for the rate of return to capital, because China did not have organized capital markets in the past, and the scope and coverage of her current capital markets remain limited. At the same time, China's banking sector is still very much government controlled, so that the bank deposit and lending rates are to a large extent determined by administrative decisions rather than through market clearing. Thus, readily observable rates of return to capital are not available and need to be computed from more primary information on capital stock (the denominator) and profits (the numerator).

Fortunately, some data on profits and taxes for the manufacturing sector are available in the Chinese Industry Economy Statistical Yearbook (CIESY), and these data, together with other data necessary for estimation of the capital stock, can be used to compute the rate of return to capital in the manufacturing sector (r_M). Unfortunately, analogous data are not available for computation of r_O, the rate of return to capital in the "Other" (non-manufacturing) sector, comprising mostly of the "agriculture" and "services."

In view of the problem, this study presents three alternative routes to computing r_O. The first is referred to as the "CIESY route," because it involves substitution of r_O by r_{NSE}, the rate of return to capital in the "Non State-Owned Enterprises (NSE)" part of the manufacturing sector, as obtained from the CIESY data. Estimates following this route show relatively low TFPGR for China, because r_{NSE}, being the rate of return to capital in the manufacturing sector, witnessed a sharper decline, reflecting considerable capital accumulation in this sub-sector. The second route is referred to as the "Hybrid route", because it involves computation of r_O in a residual manner using data from both CIESY and NIA. TFPGR estimates obtained following the Hybrid route prove to be relatively high, because r_O obtained from this route has, by construction, a tendency to rise. This is because r_{NIA}, the economy-wide rate of return to capital obtained from NIA, displays a tendency to remain stable. The r_O obtained as a residual therefore has to rise to offset the declining r_M and ensure a stable r_{NIA}. Apart from the upward bias imparted to TFPGR estimates, another weakness of the Hybrid route lies in the fact that in order to compute r_O it falls back, albeit partially, on NIA data that the dual approach strives to avoid.

In view of the above limitations of the "CIESY route" and "Hybrid route," this study advocates a "Neutral route" that does not impose either a declining or a rising trend on r_0 and instead lets it to remain stable. Estimates obtained from this route show that China's TFPGR for the entire 1978–2002 period was 2.26 percent per annum. However, the rate for the initial 1978–1984 sub-period was much higher, 4.59 percent per annum, and it declined to 3.21 percent during 1991–2002.[1] These findings show that China did enjoy high TFPGR during the initial years of reform, and this rate still remains significant. However, there has been a significant slowdown in TFPGR during recent years. This finding regarding productivity deceleration agrees with the finding of rising Incremental Capital-Output Ratio (ICOR) reported in Chapter 10 of this volume and should be of concern for Chinese policy makers as it raises the question of sustainability of China's growth.

The discussion of the chapter is organized as follows. Section 11.2 provides the background by reviewing the growth accounting exercises that have been conducted for China so far. It also discusses the problems of Chinese NIA data. Section 11.3 presents the theory of the dual approach to growth accounting. Section 11.4 presents the implementation of the dual approach for China and discusses the results. Section 11.5 concludes.

11.2 Background

11.2.1 Previous findings regarding TFP in China

Research on sources of Chinese growth has by now led to a sizable literature. One of the initial studies on this topic is by Chow (1993), who focuses on the period of 1952–1980. Chow's main finding for this pre-reform period is that growth was almost entirely driven by capital accumulation, and there was no TFP growth. Based on both graphical presentation and estimation of aggregate production functions, Chow concludes that "technological change was absent in the growth of the Chinese economy from 1952 to 1980 (p. 841)".

Chow and Li (2002) return to this issue, following a similar methodology as of Chow (1993), but updating the analysis to the more recent year of 1998. They find that in contrast to the pre-reform period, growth during the reform period was driven to a considerable degree by TFP growth.[2] According to their estimated results, "there is an average increase in TFP of about 2.6 percent per year from 1978 to 1998 (p. 249)".

Borensztein and Ostry (1996) offer a starker contrast of the pre-reform and reform periods. According to their computation, while TFPGR was negative 0.7 percent during 1953–1978, it was positive 3.8 percent during 1979–1994. Hu and Khan (1997a, b) provide an even more upbeat assessment of the role of TFP growth in the reform period. They compute a translog productivity index taking the directly observed capital and labor income shares as respective elasticities. According to their results, the TFPGR for the pre-reform, 1953–1978 period was 1.1 percent, while it rose to 3.9 percent during 1979–1994.[3]

There is not much debate about the relative absence of TFP growth in the pre-reform Chinese economy. Similarly there is not much debate that TFP growth played an important role in growth during the reform period. The debate rather concerns the following two questions: (a) *How important* has TFP's role been in China's growth since reforms started? (b) Has China's TFPGR *slowed down* in recent years?

With regard to the second question, Hu and Khan (1997a, b), for example, think that China's TFP is rather *accelerating*. According to their computation, TFPGR for 1990–1994, the last few years of their sample period, was as high as 5.8 percent, and during this sub-period TFP growth surpassed growth in capital stock as a source of output growth. The authors attribute the higher TFPGR of more recent years to further deepening of economic reforms.[4] Nogami and Li (1995) reach similar conclusions. Confining their analysis to the industrial sector, these authors divide the post-reform period into the following three sub-periods: 1977–1984, 1984–1988, and 1989–1992. According to their computation, TFPGR for these sub-periods was 2.06, 2.14, and 5.14 percent, contributing 24.8, 19.6, and 44.2 percent of the overall growth, respectively.[5] Ezaki and Sun (1999) also agree with a rising trend in TFPGR. Based on their analysis, these authors conclude that "the TFP growth has been fairly high at from 3 to 4 percent *with a slight tendency to increase* (italics added), and its contribution to GDP growth is around 40 percent" (p. 49).

Not everybody however shares such upbeat assessments of the role of TFP growth in China's recent growth. Skepticisms have been voiced with regard to both the role of TFP and the claimed acceleration of productivity. Woo (1998), for example, suggests that Chinese TFPGR are not only lower in general, they are also declining with time. According to his computation, net TFPGR for 1979–1993 ranges from only 1.1 to 1.3 percent per year.[6] He divides the reform period into two sub-periods, namely 1979–1984 and 1985–1993, and shows that while TFPGR ranges between 2.76 and 3.76 percent per annum (depending on the chosen value of labor share in income) during the first sub-period, it ranges between –0.11 and 1.58 per annum only during the second sub period.[7] Woo interprets this slowdown as evidence that "the TFP growth unleashed by the 1978 reforms was a *one-time recovery in efficiency* (italics added) from the decade-long Cultural Revolution and from the overregulation of the economy by central planning" (p. 10).[8]

Young (2003) also contends that China's TFPGR has been over reported. He adopts a skeptical view of the Chinese official data, and undertakes a laborious effort to reconstruct these data using information from both Chinese NIA and non-NIA sources. Young focuses on the 1978–1998 period and considers only the industrial sector. He substitutes the official industrial output deflator by ex-factory price index.[9] He also uses the national income identity to derive a deflator for the investment series in a residual manner. Young conducts a meticulous analysis of the demographic and labor force participation data to derive the labor force growth rate to be 2.2 percent per annum.

A major advance in Chinese growth accounting that Young accomplishes in his paper is incorporation of labor quality into the analysis. In this regard, he uses the Jorgenson et al. (1987) approach of using the income earned by a particular category of labor as indicator of its productivity. He uses various surveys to get data on income of labor of different categories. Based on the exercise, he finds "the growth of human capital in the non-agricultural sector of the Chinese economy (to be) between 1978 and 1998 to be 1.1 percent per annum" (p. 31).[10]

On the basis of reconstructed data along the above lines Young (2003) finds that TFPGR in the Chinese economy for the 1978–1998 period was 1.4 percent per annum.[11] He comments that this is "a respectable performance, but by no means extraordinary." Young does not consider explicitly the issue of slowdown of Chinese TFPGR, but the spirit of his analysis suggests that he would support the slowdown view.

Wang and Yao (2001) also allow for improvement in labor quality in growth accounting for China. However, they voice doubts regarding Young's (2003) data on income for specific categories of labor, and instead use the number of schooling years as indicative of labor quality. They follow the Barro and Lee (1997) approach of using enrolment rates in a perpetual inventory framework to derive the number of people belonging to different education categories. Changes in these numbers are taken to reflect changes in the quality of labor. On the basis of this exercise, Wang and Yao find significant improvement in the quality of Chinese labor. However, they find that even after taking into account the role of labor quality improvement, the contribution of TFP remains high.[12] Wang and Yao offer results with alternative assumptions regarding labor share in income. For example, for the pre-reform period of 1953–1977, they assume the labor share to be 0.40 and find output, physical capital, labor quantity, human capital stock, and TFP to grow at an annual rate of 6.46, 6.11, 2.63, 5.30, and −0.57 percent, respectively, and the contribution to output growth of physical capital, labor, human capital, and TFP to be 56.8, 16.3, 32.8, and −5.9 percent, respectively. For the reform period of 1978–1999, they assume a labor share of income of 0.50, and find output, physical capital, labor quantity, human capital stock, and TFP to grow at an annual rate of 9.72, 9.39, 2.73, 2.69, and 2.32 percent, respectively, and the contribution to output growth of physical capital, labor, human capital, and TFP to be 48.3, 14.0, 13.8, and 23.9 percent, respectively.[13] Thus, while in the pre-reform period TFPGR is negative 0.57 percent, during the reform period it is 2.32 percent. These results regarding TFP of Wang and Yao are somewhere in between the very high estimates of 4 to 5 percent per annum offered by Hu and Khan, Nogami and Li, and others and the very low estimates of 1.1 to 1.4 percent of Woo and Young.[14]

This brief survey shows that findings vary widely with regard to both the importance of TFP in China's growth and whether or not China is witnessing productivity slowdown. We next consider the role that Chinese NIA data problems have in producing these varied results.

11.2.2 Problems with Chinese National Income Accounts (NIA) data

Many factors contribute to the differences in results concerning China's TFP. Among them are differences in coverage of sectors, sample period, specification of production function, choice of estimation method, etc.[15] However, a particular role in this regard belongs to the problems that persist in the Chinese NIA data and different ways in which researchers try to overcome them.

It may be noted that there are quite contrasting views regarding the merit of the Chinese NIA statistics. At one extreme is probably Chow (1993, p. 810), who relies entirely on Chinese official statistics, viewing that these are by and large "internally consistent and accurate enough for empirical work." He also adds that "official statistical reporting in China is by and large honest." Young (2003) probably represents the other extreme, noting that under the Chinese system, there are inbuilt tendencies for local officials to "overstate the growth of output, while understating investment and births."[16] Young sarcastically comments that "while the Chinese government has conducted laudable campaigns against statistical misrepresentation, recording no less than 70,000 such cases in 1994 and 60,000 cases in 1997, this information has difficulty in finding its way into revisions of the GDP estimates."

Apart from the problems of honest reporting, Chinese national accounts data are also affected by several methodological problems. During the pre-reform period, China was following the Material Product System (MPS), under which output of many service sectors was not included in the measured national product. From 1985, China began its shift to the international System of National Accounts (SNA) and completed it in 1992. Despite the shift, Wang and Yao (2001), for example, note the following three problems. The first concerns compatibility of national income (GDP) measure before and after the reform. The second is the problem of absence of deflator for national income of the pre-reform period of 1952–1977, and the third is the problem of absence of investment deflator for the period of 1952–1990.[17] Attempts have been made to correct these statistical problems, including a significant contribution by Hsueh and Li (1999).[18] Using historical data, these authors try to fill up for the missing service sector output in the national income data for the pre-reform period of 1952–1977. As a result, these data are now more comparable with those of the reform period of 1978–1995. Hsueh and Li also provide deflators for both GDP and investment, so that real values of these variables are now available for the entire period of 1952–1995.

Some researchers, such as Wang and Yao (2001), are very upbeat about the contribution of Hsueh and Li (1999) and think that with their work all major methodological problems of the Chinese NIA data have been resolved.[19] Others have however voiced doubts. For example, Young (2003) notes that the way missing service sector output was incorporated in the GDP is not proper, because it assumes that most of the service sector activities sprang up only during the post-reform period and almost nothing existed during the earlier years.

Young also has serious reservations about the deflators. He thinks that "despite...riders and exceptions, it is fair to say that overall the SSB (State Statistical Board) remains heavily dependent upon enterprise-provided output-based implicit deflators to deflate nominal value added." Echoing views expressed earlier by Ruoen (1995) and Woo (1998), Young (2003) also thinks that "implicit deflators provided by Chinese enterprises are systematically biased." He formulates and estimates a sophisticated bi-factor latent variable model to prove this systematic bias. Young laments that SSB uses implicit deflators provided by enterprises themselves instead of using "independent price indices," on which it does collect data. This choice of deflator leads to the much discussed problem of *underdeflation* of the industrial output, particularly of the output of TVEs. It is in view of this bias that Young uses for this own analysis the ex-factory price index as the deflator instead of the one provided by the national accounts data.

Young (2003) is similarly unhappy with the official deflator for Gross Fixed Capital Formation (GFCF). He thinks that the official deflator for GFCF may not be an appropriate choice, because it too relies upon enterprise output deflators and is therefore likely to be characterized by the same understatement of inflation that plagues China's production estimates. As mentioned above, Young therefore resorts to an elaborate exercise to derive an investment deflator via the income expenditure identity.

The above discussion shows that the Chinese NIA data continue to have problems, despite efforts to overcome them. The revision in 2005 (December) of the Chinese GDP upwards by about 17 percent (mainly on account of previous undercounting of service sector output) once again pointed to these problems. Growth accounting exercises using the *primal approach* cannot but be affected by these problems. This creates a scope for the *dual approach*, which does not have to depend on NIA data, to play a useful role in resolving the controversies regarding sources of growth and the role of TFP in China. Earlier, Islam, Dai, and Sakamoto (2006) presented an application of the dual approach to growth accounting for China. The current study builds on that study and extends it further.

11.3   The dual approach to growth accounting

The dual approach to growth accounting was proposed earlier by Jorgenson and Griliches (1967). Presenting the expressions for TFPGR from the primal and dual approaches, they noted that "these two definitions of TFP are dual to each other and are equivalent. In general, any index of TFP can be computed either from indexes of the quantity of total output and input or from the corresponding price indexes." (p. 252) There are many different ways in which the dual approach may be presented. A rather simple way is to proceed from the following national income accounting identity:

$$Y = rK + wL, \tag{11.1}$$

where Y is the aggregate output (or aggregate income), r is the rate of return to capital, w is the real wage, L is labor, and K is capital.[20] Upon differentiation with respect to time and dividing by Y, we get

$$\hat{Y} = s_K(\hat{r} + \hat{K}) + s_L(\hat{w} + \hat{L}), \tag{11.2}$$

where $s_k = rK/Y$ and $s_L = wL/Y$ are factor income shares, and variables with "^" on top are corresponding growth rates, so that $\hat{Y} = (dY/dt)/Y$, $\hat{r} = (dr/dt)/r$, and $\hat{w} = (dw/dt)/w$. Rearranging equation (11.2), we get

$$\hat{Y} - s_K\hat{K} - s_L\hat{L} = s_K\hat{r} + s_L\hat{w}. \tag{11.3}$$

The left hand side of the equation (11.3) represents the usual, primal representation of TFPGR, or the Solow residual, so that we can write

$$TFPGR_p = SR_{primal} = \hat{Y} - s_K \hat{K} - s_L \hat{L}. \tag{11.4}$$

However, equation (11.3) also shows that this is equal to the right hand side, which gives the dual representation of TFPGR or the Solow residual in terms of the share-weighted growth in factor prices, so that we can write

$$TFPGR_d = SR_{dual} = s_K \hat{r} + s_L \hat{w}. \tag{11.5}$$

Note that this equality between SR_{primal} and SR_{dual} proceeds entirely from the national income identity and does not require any additional assumption regarding the form of the aggregate production function or equality between marginal product and factor return.

Just as the SR_{primal} can be interpreted as a measure of shift in the production frontier, provided the efficiency parameter is Hicks neutral and equality between marginal products and factor returns hold, SR_{dual} can also be interpreted under these assumptions as a measure of shift in the corresponding factor price frontier.[21]

The equality shown by equation (11.3) also makes it clear that if one computes the SR_{dual} using r and w obtained from capital and wage income data provided by NIA, SR_{dual} should be exactly equal to SR_{primal}. Such an exercise would therefore be redundant. However, the usefulness of SR_{dual} lies in the fact that it can be computed based on factor price information from alternative, independent sources, and $TFPGR_d$ estimates computed on the basis of such information can provide a useful check on the validity of $TFPGR_p$ estimates and/or the validity of the NIA data.

Both the primal and the dual version of the Solow residual, as given by equations (11.4) and (11.5) above, are growth rates of continuous time, Divisia-type indices. In order to compute Solow residual using discrete time data, Jorgenson and Griliches (1967) introduce a discrete time approximation to the Divisia index derived from Tornqvist index. Under this approximation, the $TFPGR_d$ between time $t-1$ and t, as measured by SR_{dual} is given by:

$$TFPGR_{dt} = SR_{dual} = S_{L\tau} \cdot \hat{w}_t + S_{K\tau} \cdot \hat{r}_t, \tag{11.5'}$$

where $\hat{w}_t$ and $\hat{r}_t$ are growth rates of w and r, respectively, between $t-1$ and t, and

$$S_{L\tau} = \frac{1}{2}\left[s_{L,t-1} + s_{Lt} \right], \tag{11.6.a}$$

$$S_{K\tau} = \frac{1}{2}\left[s_{K,t-1} + s_{Kt} \right]. \tag{11.6.b}$$

In other words, continuous time (exponential) growth rates are replaced by growth rates between discrete time periods $t-1$ and t, and the continuous time shares (s) are replaced by averages of the shares of $t-1$ and t.[22]

Just as is the case with the primal approach, the dual approach to growth accounting can also be extended to take into account improvements in the quality of inputs. This is usually done by allowing for different types of labor and capital.[23] The Divisia index framework facilitates the task. For example, assuming that there are m different types of labor, the overall wage growth rate, $\hat{w}$, can be derived as a share-weighted average of growth rates of wages of individual labor types, using the following formula:

$$\hat{w} = \sum_{j=1}^{m} s_{L_j} \hat{w}_j, \tag{11.7}$$

where $\hat{w}_j$ is the growth rate of the wage of a worker of type j, and S_{Lj} is the share of wage-payments to workers of type j in total wage payments. Similarly, if there are n different types of capital, the overall rate of change in the rate of return to capital can be obtained as a weighted average of the rate of changes in the rate of return of these different types of capital, using the formula:

$$\hat{r} = \sum_{i=1}^{n} s_{k_i} \hat{r}_i, \tag{11.8}$$

where $\hat{r}_i$ is the rate of change of the rate of return to capital of type i, and S_{ki} is the share of payments to capital type i in total payments to capital. This property of the Divisia index can be used to compute $\hat{w}_j$ and $\hat{r}_i$ based on sub-types into which labor of type j and capital of type i can be further disaggregated. In all cases, the Tornqvist approximation helps in estimating the Divisia growth rates using discrete data.

It is important to account for input quality improvements while computing TFP, because it represents the *costless* part of the growth in output (in the primal approach) and returns to factors (in the dual approach).[24] For example, high educational attainment is widely known to have been a key characteristic of East Asian growth, and East Asian economies had to make substantial investments (incur costs) in order to achieve the educational attainment. Unless improvement in the quality of labor arising from higher educational levels is accounted for (instead of measuring the labor input only by the number of bodies or even hours), the *TFPGR* will be overestimated. From the dual point of view, wage growth achieved by having more people with higher education than before should not count as TFP growth. Only wage growth with unchanged labor quality (education) can be taken as reflective of TFP growth. Equation (11.7) allows us to capture that costless part of wage growth. If wages for workers of given levels of education do not increase, the value of $\hat{w}$ will be zero, even though the unweighted growth rate is positive. Similarly, the aggregate rate of return to capital may be higher because of relatively more productive capital goods being in place than before. However, societies usually have to incur costs to bring about such improvements in the composition of its capital stock. Equation (11.8) allows us to capture the change in the rate of return to capital of a constant quality (composition). Thus, unless there are changes in the rate of return to capital of a given quality, the value of $\hat{r}$ computed using equation (11.8) will be zero, even though the unweighted average rate of return to capital may change.[25]

Though in terms of algebra the above framework is symmetric with respect to labor and capital, it differs in terms of actual capability to capture their quality changes. The difference owes to the fact that while there are independent physical measures of both quantity and quality of the labor input, such measures are generally absent for capital. For example, the quantity aspect of the labor input can be measured by the number of bodies or hours, and the quality aspect of the labor input can be measured by the number of schooling years. By contrast, given the heterogeneity of capital goods, there is no physical measure of the quantity of capital, either at the national, sectoral, or even plant level. Similarly, there is no physical measure of the quality that can apply to different types of capital goods. The Jorgenson-Griliches approach of taking the rate of return earned by a particular type of capital as a measure of its quality can in principle provide a way around the problem. However, data on such rates of return are often difficult to obtain. More importantly, this does not obviate the problem of absence of a physical measure of the quantity of capital. These problems are of general nature, and they are encountered in growth accounting for China too.

In recent years, there have been several prominent applications of the dual approach to growth accounting. For example, Shapiro (1987) uses this approach to show that TFP movements are not caused by demand side shocks. As already mentioned, Hsieh (1999, 2002) applies the dual approach to respond to Young's (1992, 1995) earlier work showing that Singapore experienced negative TFP growth. Hsieh notes that constant capital share and spectacular capital deepening suggested by Young's data obtained from Singapore's NIA would imply a significant fall in the rate of return to capital. However, such a fall is unlikely given the openness of the Singaporean economy to cross border capital mobility and given the already low level of the rate of return to capital at the beginning of the period.[26] Independent information on rates of return to capital in Singapore also does not support such a fall. This anomaly points to problems in investment data in the Singaporean NIA, so that capital stock estimated by Young on the basis of these data might have suffered from over estimation.[27] In view of the problem, Hsieh conducts a dual approach growth accounting for the East Asian Tigers, namely Hong Kong, South Korea, Singapore, and Taiwan, and shows that while for South Korea and Hong Kong the dual estimates of TFP growth are similar to the primal estimates, for Singapore they exceed the primal estimates by more than 2 percentage points.

One can see a parallel between China and Singapore, in that NIA of both have problems, though the nature of the problems may be different. The dual approach can therefore be of help in answering questions about TFP in China, just as it did in the case of Singapore.

11.4 Growth accounting for China using the dual approach

A question that is sometimes asked is whether actual conditions of developing economies, such as China, satisfy the neoclassical assumptions of competition and equality between factor prices and their marginal value products so as to justify application of the growth accounting methodology for them. While most authors of Chinese growth accounting studies do not address this question explicitly, some do. For example, Nogami and Li (1995, p. 1) note that "it has been a long controversy whether or not neoclassical model is applicable for the Chinese economy." They offer a positive conclusion referring to Rawski and Zheng (1993), who argue that perfect market economy exists nowhere, China has been changing into a market economy, and experience has shown that data handling is more important than the model used.[28]

What is more important in this regard is to note that the equality of prices with marginal products is required for the *interpretation* of the Solow residual as shifts of the production frontier (in the primary approach) and of the factor price frontier (in the dual approach). Even if this interpretation does not hold exactly because of departures from competitive equilibrium conditions, it is still possible to compute Solow residual and treat it as the *measured* productivity growth. As noted earlier, the derivation of the formula for TFPGR given by equations (11.4), (11.5), and (11.5′) does not depend on specification of the aggregate production function and equality of marginal products of factors with their returns. Finally, the focus of this study is entirely on the reform period of 1978–2002, during which China has embraced increasingly the market mechanism so that the conditions of competitive equilibrium are likely to be satisfied to a greater extent than is the case for the pre-reform period.

11.4.1 Measuring wage growth

We first focus on the wage growth part, $S_L \hat{w}$, of SR_{dual}, using equation (11.7) to compute $\hat{w}$ taking into account different types of labor. Labor is disaggregated in terms of both education level and residence (urban and rural). The disaggregation along these two lines turns out to be intertwined for China. As observed earlier, very few studies on China's TFP have attempted to incorporate changes in the quality of labor, with Young (2003) and Wang and Yao (2001) being exceptions. Both these studies have however used the primary approach to growth accounting that required construction of a *quantity index* of the labor input. In the dual approach, the quantity index is not required. What is needed instead is a measure of wage growth that is net of the impact of improvements in labor quality, as measured by the level of education. For that however we need data on wages differentiated by quality types (education categories) and also the distribution of the labor force among these quality types.

11.4.1.1 Distribution of labor among different education types

The distribution of educational attainment by levels of schooling in total Chinese population and labor force is available only in three recent censuses (1982, 1990, and 2000) and in several small sample-based "Surveys on Population Change" conducted in recent years. In order to get the distribution for all the years of the sample period, we proceed from the 1990 distribution (obtained from the census) and extrapolate forward and backward using the perpetual inventory method introduced by Barro and Lee (1997, 2000) and implemented recently for China by Wang and Yao (2001). There are two reasons why we anchor our data construction on the 1990 census. First is that 1990 is the midpoint of our sample period of 1978–2002. Extrapolation (forward and backward) from the midpoint is likely to be less biased than when it is done on the basis of census of either 1982 or 2000, which are close to the endpoints of the sample period. Second, the published census data for 1982 do not provide the details that are necessary for our data construction, so that extrapolation on the basis of 1982 census is not a feasible option. The extrapolation however requires the knowledge of year specific enrolment (annual graduation flow data) and mortality rates. These rates are obtained from "Comprehensive Statistical Data and Materials on 50 Years of New China, 1949–98" and China Statistical Yearbook (CSY) for various years. The formulas for the perpetual inventory computation are as follows:

$$SP_{0,t} = (1-d_t)SP_{0,t-1} + (PRI\_ENROLLED_{0,t}-PRI\_GRADUATED_{0,t+6}), \quad (11.9)$$

$$SP_{1,t} = (1-d_t)SP_{1,t-1} + (PRI_t-JUNIOR_{t+3}), \quad (11.10)$$

$$SP_{2,t} = (1-d_t)SP_{2,t-1} + (JUNIOR_t-SENIOR_{t+3}-SPECIAL_{t+3}), \quad (11.11)$$

$$SP_{3,t} = (1-d_t)SP_{3,t-1} + (SENIOR_t-HIGHER_{t+3.5}), \quad (11.12)$$

$$SP_{4,t} = (1-d_t)SP_{4,t-1} + SPECIAL_t, \text{ and} \quad (11.13)$$

$$SP_{5,t} = (1-d_t)SP_{5,t-1} + HIGHER_t, \quad (11.14)$$

where $SP_{j,t}$ is the number of persons in the population for whom j is the highest level of schooling attained, with $j = 0$ for incomplete primary, 1 for primary, 2 for junior secondary school, 3 for senior secondary school, 4 for specialized secondary school, and 5 for higher education.[29] If a person cannot complete the enrolled education level, we take that person as belonging to the schooling level he had before. The variable d_t is the annual mortality rate in the population.

Although these equations are broadly similar to those of Wang and Yao (2001), there are a few differences. First, we allow for a separate category of "incomplete primary education." In the classification of Wang and Yao, people with incomplete primary education are lumped with people with no schooling at all. Second, we take the number of years required to complete "specialized secondary school" to be three, instead of two, as assumed (incorrectly, in our view) by Wang and Yao.

The perpetual inventory exercise described above allows us to distinguish six different categories of education, but the corresponding data on wages are difficult to get, as noted earlier by Young (2003) and Wang and Yao (2001). In view of this difficulty, we collapse the education categories into three broad categories, namely "junior secondary school and below (Type *E1*)", "high secondary school (including specialized secondary school and vocational school) (Type *E2*)", and "higher education" (Type *E3*). Let *P1*, *P2*, and *P3* denote the number of persons in the *population* belonging to the three education types *E1*, *E2*, and *E3*, respectively.

The constructed values of *P1*, *P2*, and *P3* can be seen in Table 11.1. As a check, we compare the values for 2000 with their actual values obtained from the census of that year, and find them to be very similar, suggesting that the constructed values are close to actual values of other years too.[30]

Having obtained the education distribution in *population*, we next compute the education distribution in *labor force*. The first step is to get the total labor force data. In view of absence of any other more reliable source, we depend in this regard on the CSY. However, we make a few adjustments to the pre-1990 labor force data. Based on the results of the 2000 Population Census, the Chinese statistical authority has revised labor data for 1990–2000 significantly upwards, creating a huge jump (of 94.2 million) between the labor force figures of 1989 and 1990. Such a large increase in labor force in one year is unlikely. We therefore smooth out this jump by taking new 1990 labor data as the base and calculating backwards the labor force figures for 1978–1990 using the labor growth rates calculated from old data series for this period. This adjustment is made to all labor figures, namely total, urban, and rural.

Next we compute *L1*, *L2*, and *L3*, which denote number of persons in the *labor force* belonging to education type *E1*, *E2*, and *E3*, respectively. To obtain *L3* from *P3*, we use the formula:

$$L3 = P3\,(1-b), \tag{11.15}$$

where *b* is the proportion of *P3* who are over 65 years of age and therefore do not belong to the labor force, at least officially. To obtain year specific values of *b*, we rely on the census data for 1990 and 2000, for which the value of *b* proves to be 2.40 and 1.67 percent respectively, reflecting the fact that in the intervening years the rate at which people reached education level *E3* surpassed the rate at which the people of this education group were aging (crossing 65 years of age). The yearly rate of change of this percentage proves to be −0.036 for the period of 1990–2000. We use this rate to extrapolate and obtain year specific values of *b* and use them in equation (11.15).[31]

To obtain values of *L2*, we use equation (11.16):

$$L2 = P2\,(1-a). \tag{11.16}$$

Unlike *b* of equation (11.15), the value of *a* in equation (11.16) depends on two factors. The first is the proportion of *P2* who are over 65 years of age and hence are out of the labor force. We denote this part by a_1. The second is the proportion

Table 11.1   Labor stock by education level (10,000 persons)

(1)	(2)	(3)	(4)	(5)	(6)	(7)	(8)	(9)	(10)
	Total popu-	Educated population				Labor by education level			
Year	lation	P1	P2	P3	Total P	L1	L2	L3	Total L
1978	95,617	42,177	4,322	502	47,001	41,101	4,235	483	45,820
1979	96,901	45,542	4,965	515	51,021	41,461	4,857	496	46,815
1980	98,124	48,213	5,539	540	54,291	42,409	5,411	521	48,340
1981	99,389	51,207	6,003	563	57,772	43,500	5,853	544	49,897
1982	100,863	53,783	6,264	646	60,693	44,967	6,096	625	51,689
1983	102,331	56,095	6,427	705	63,227	46,065	6,243	683	52,991
1984	103,683	58,482	6,535	755	65,771	47,934	6,334	732	55,000
1985	105,104	60,637	6,665	810	68,112	49,681	6,445	786	56,913
1986	106,679	62,697	6,842	879	70,418	51,066	6,600	854	58,521
1987	108,404	64,645	7,059	974	72,678	52,495	6,791	948	60,233
1988	110,163	66,568	7,285	1,073	74,926	53,970	6,988	1,045	62,003
1989	112,704	68,311	7,520	1,173	77,004	54,805	7,190	1,144	63,139
1990	114,333	69,895	7,753	1,275	78,924	56,116	7,388	1,245	64,749
1991	115,823	71,268	7,965	1,391	80,625	56,569	7,564	1,359	65,491
1992	117,171	72,519	8,157	1,494	82,170	56,976	7,716	1,460	66,152
1993	118,517	73,541	8,344	1,585	83,470	57,398	7,859	1,551	66,808
1994	119,850	74,409	8,511	1,684	84,604	57,826	7,980	1,649	67,455
1995	121,121	75,175	8,695	1,817	85,687	58,171	8,113	1,781	68,065
1996	122,389	75,856	8,903	1,966	86,725	58,758	8,264	1,928	68,950
1997	123,626	76,641	9,141	2,125	87,907	59,298	8,436	2,086	69,820
1998	124,761	77,542	9,401	2,277	89,220	59,777	8,624	2,236	70,637
1999	125,786	78,440	9,786	2,436	90,662	60,083	8,918	2,394	71,394
2000	126,743	82,078	10,351	2,608	95,038	60,155	9,366	2,565	72,085
2001	127,627	85,789	10,942	2,788	99,520	60,458	9,824	2,743	73,025
2002	128,453	89,644	11,545	3,022	104,211	60,486	10,279	2,975	73,740

Notes:
1. $P1 = SP0 + SP1 + SP2$; $P2 = SP3 + SP4$; $P3 = SP5$. $SP5$, $SP4$, $SP3$, $SP2$, $SP1$, $SP0$ are the numbers of persons in the *population* for whom the highest level of schooling is higher education (university and college), special secondary, senior secondary, junior secondary, primary, and incompletely primary, respectively.
2. L is the size of the total labor force; $L1$ is the number of persons in the labor force who received education lower than senior secondary school; $L2$ is the analogous number of persons who completed senior secondary school education; $L3$ is the analogous number of persons who completed higher education.
3. $L2 = P2 (1 - a)$; $L3 = P3 (1 - b)$; $L1 = (L - L2 - L3)$. As explained in the text, a and b are respectively proportions of $P2$ and $P3$ who do not belong to the labor force. We calculate the values of a and b for each year by interpolation based on census data for 1990, 2000, and 1982.

Sources: *China Labour Statistical Yearbook* (various years), *China Statistical Yearbook* (*CSY*) (various years), and the authors' calculations.

of *P2* who enroll for higher education and hence are not in the labor force. We denote this part by a_2. In actual data, the value of a is dominated by that of a_2. For example, for 1990 (according to census data), the values of a_1 and a_2 prove to be 0.9 and 3.8 percent respectively, yielding a value of 4.7 for a. The value of a (from census data) for 2000 proves to be 9.52, indicating that a much higher proportion of *P2* got enrolled for higher education in 2000 than in 1990. This reflects the general spread of higher education in China over the years. These values of a for 1990 and 2000 suggest an annual rate of increase by 0.073 percentage points. We use this rate to extrapolate and get year specific values of a for the remaining years of the sample. These values of a are then used in equation (11.16) to obtain the year specific values of *L2*. Once the values of *L3* and *L2* are available, the value of *L1* can be computed easily because $L1 = (L - L2 - L3)$. The results of the above perpetual inventory calculation can be seen in Table 11.1.

11.4.1.2 Wages of urban labor

We now need information on wages of labor belonging to different education types. There are some urban wage data by education level (for 1993–2001) reported in post 1994 issues of China Labor Statistical Yearbook (CLSY). However, these wage data are based on small sample surveys, covering usually only four to five cities. Examination shows that these wage data are difficult to explain and far from being reliable. For example, according to these data, average wage rates for all education types are lower in 1995 than in 1994. The probable reason for this unlikely finding is that while the 1994 survey included more coastal cities, the 1995 survey included more inland cities.

Since CLSY data on wages are problem-ridden, we use CSY data to get education specific labor incomes. Considering *urban* labor first, let w_{L1}, w_{L2}, and w_{L3} denote wage rates of urban labor of education type *E1*, *E2*, and *E3*, respectively. To the extent that *E3* represents higher education, we take w_{L3} to be equal to the average wage rate (salary) in science and technology research sector institutes and enterprises (in both state-owned and private sector). Such institutes and enterprises usually have the highest share of labor with completed higher education. By analogous reasoning, we take w_{L2} to be equal to the average wage in the manufacturing sector, including both state owned and non-state owned enterprises.[32] Finally, we use the average wage of Collectively Owned Enterprises (COE) as w_{L1}. In China's statistical system, COE is a type of small scale cooperatively owned enterprises, which (particularly the ones in the service sector) generally employ less educated urban labor and some migrant rural labor. Information on urban wages obtained as above is provided in Table 11.2.

11.4.1.3 Rural labor and its wage

In principle, both urban and rural population and labor may fall into different education categories. However, data from Surveys on Population Change (CLSY, 2003) show that less than five percent of rural labor has completed senior secondary school or above. This would put 95 percent of the rural labor into education

Table 11.2　Urban labor and wage by education level

(1)	(2)	(3)	(4)	(5)	(6)	(7)	(8)	(9)	(10)	(11)
	Nominal wage rate (Yuan)			Composition of urban labor (10,000)				Real wage rate (Yuan)		Total real wage (100 MY)
Year	w_{L1}	w_{L2}	w_{L3}	$L1_u$	$L2_u$	$L3_u$	w_{L1}	w_{L2}	w_{L3}	
1978	506	597	669	6,308	4,235	483	506	597	669	604.3
1979	542	654	717	6,228	4,857	496	532	642	704	677.9
1980	623	752	851	6,255	5,411	521	569	686	777	767.6
1981	642	757	850	6,396	5,853	544	572	674	757	801.5
1982	671	769	857	6,506	6,096	625	586	671	748	837.3
1983	698	789	990	6,670	6,243	683	598	675	847	878.1
1984	811	955	1,072	7,087	6,334	732	676	796	894	1,048.7
1985	967	1,112	1,272	7,589	6,445	786	737	848	970	1,182.5
1986	1,092	1,275	1,492	7,924	6,600	854	782	913	1,068	1,313.4
1987	1,207	1,418	1,620	8,205	6,791	948	805	946	1,081	1,406.0
1988	1,426	1,710	1,931	8,469	6,988	1,045	801	961	1,085	1,463.0
1989	1,557	1,900	2,118	8,313	7,190	1,144	741	904	1,008	1,381.9
1990	1,681	2,073	2,403	8,408	7,388	1,245	776	957	1,110	1,497.9
1991	1,866	2,289	2,573	8,543	7,564	1,359	833	1,022	1,149	1,641.1
1992	2,109	2,635	3,115	8,685	7,716	1,460	885	1,106	1,307	1,812.9
1993	2,592	3,348	3,904	8,852	7,859	1,551	948	1,225	1,429	2,023.9
1994	3,245	4,283	6,162	9,024	7,980	1,649	957	1,263	1,817	2,170.7

Year										
1995	3,931	5,169	6,846	9,146	8,113	1,781	990	1,302	1,724	2,268.2
1996	4,302	5,642	8,048	9,730	8,264	1,928	1,000	1,312	1,871	2,418.0
1997	4,512	5,933	9,049	10,259	8,436	2,086	1,020	1,342	2,047	2,605.7
1998	5,331	7,064	10,241	10,756	8,624	2,236	1,215	1,610	2,335	3,218.3
1999	5,774	7,794	11,601	11,101	8,918	2,394	1,335	1,802	2,682	3,731.2
2000	6,262	8,750	13,620	11,221	9,366	2,565	1,442	2,015	3,137	4,310.0
2001	6,867	9,774	16,437	11,373	9,824	2,743	1,570	2,235	3,759	5,013.3
2002	7,667	11,001	19,113	11,526	10,279	2,975	1,768	2,536	4,406	5,955.2

Notes:

1. $L1 = L1_u + L_R$ (Total rural labor). Thus, $L1_u = L1 - L_R$; $L2u = L2$; $L3u = L3$.
2. w_{L1} is the average wage of $L1_u$. The average wage for laborers of urban Collectively Owned Enterprises (COE) is used as proxy of w_{L1}.
3. w_{L2} is the average wage of $L2$. The average wage for laborers of urban manufacturing sector enterprises (both state- owned and non-state owned) is used as proxy of w_{L2}.
4. w_{L3} is the average wage of $L3$. The average wage for laborers of urban science and research sector enterprises (both sate owned and non-state owned) is used as proxy of w_{L3}.
5. *MY* refers to Million Yuan.
6. Total real wage for year $i = L1_i*W_{L1i} + L2_i*W_{L2i} + L3_i*W_{L3i}$.

Sources: China Labor Statistical Yearbook (various years) and authors' calculations.

type *E1*. Furthermore, the quality of high school education in rural areas is much lower than that in urban areas, so that rural labor nominally belonging to type *E2* does actually belong to type *E1*, when quality of school education is taken into consideration. The wage data for rural labor also validates this observation, as we shall soon see. Also, though there are some official sample surveys on rural labor in China, none of these provide wage data distinguished by education categories. Thus even if we wanted to distinguish education types *E2* and *E3* in rural labor, we would not have corresponding data on wages. In view of this situation, we classify the entire rural labor (L_R) into education type *E1*.

Relevant information on rural labor and wages is presented in Table 11.3. It gives total nominal rural wage, rural labor, nominal rural wage, and national Consumer Price Index (CPI).[33] It would seem proper to deflate nominal rural wage using rural CPI. Unfortunately, the rural CPI is generally regarded as very problematic, so that the use of the national CPI is preferred for this purpose. These average real rural wages (at 1978 prices), denoted by w_R, and their year-to-year growth rates, denoted by $\hat{w}_R$, are presented in Table 11.3. A comparison between w_R and w_{L1}, the urban wage of labor of education type *E1* (shown in Table 11.2) shows that the former is indeed much lower than the latter, supporting our earlier observation about the inferior quality of rural education and hence the decision to classify all rural labor into education type *E1*.

11.4.1.4   Aggregation of wage growth

Subtracting L_R from *L1*, the total labor of education type *E1*, we get $L1_U$, the urban labor belonging to education type *E1* and is shown in Table 11.2. The rest of the computation of the urban wage growth rate is shown in Table 11.4, and is carried out using the following equation:

$$\hat{w}_U = s_{L1} \cdot \hat{w}_{L1} + s_{L2} \cdot \hat{w}_{L2} + s_{L3} \cdot \hat{w}_{L3}, \tag{11.17}$$

where $\hat{w}_{L1}$, $\hat{w}_{L2}$, and $\hat{w}_{L3}$ are the growth rates of w_{L1}, w_{L2}, and w_{L3}, respectively, and s_{L1}, s_{L2}, and s_{L3} are shares of wage payments made to *E1*, *E2*, and *E3* type labor in the total urban wage-payments, respectively.[34]

The weighted average of the wage growth rate for the economy as a whole ($\hat{w}$) can now be computed using the formula:

$$\hat{w} = s_U \hat{w}_U + s_R \hat{w}_R. \tag{11.18}$$

The results are shown in Table 11.5. The values of s_U and s_R, presented in this table show the secular rise in s_U and decline in s_R, reflecting China's urbanization process. It may be noted that by 2000 more income was accruing to urban residents than to rural residents.

A comparison between weighted wage growth rates ($\hat{w}$) with corresponding unweighted growth rates ($\hat{w}^{UN}$), also presented in Table 11.5 (and a similar comparison between the weighted urban wage growth rates and corresponding unweighted urban growth rates presented in Table 11.4) shows that the former are

Table 11.3 Rural wage growth rate

(1)	(2)	(3)	(4)	(5)	(6)	(7)	(8)
Year	Total rural nominal wage (100 MY)	Rural labor (10,000)	Nominal wage rate (Yuan)	CPI (1978 = 100)	Total rural real wage (100 MY)	Real wage rate (Yuan)	Real wage growth rate $\hat{w}_R$ (%)
1978	1,055.4	34,793.6	303.3	100.0	1,055.4	303.3	–
1979	1,266.1	35,233.1	359.3	101.9	1,242.5	352.6	16.26
1980	1,522.3	36,154.1	421.1	109.5	1,389.7	384.4	9.00
1981	1,785.3	37,103.4	481.2	112.3	1,590.0	428.5	11.49
1982	2,165.6	38,460.5	563.1	114.5	1,890.9	491.6	14.73
1983	2,500.9	39,395.2	634.8	116.8	2,140.9	543.4	10.53
1984	2,854.7	40,846.5	698.9	120.0	2,379.5	582.5	7.20
1985	3,210.9	42,092.3	762.8	131.1	2,448.7	581.7	−0.14
1986	3,438.4	43,142.7	797.0	139.7	2,462.1	570.7	−1.90
1987	3,775.6	44,289.7	852.5	149.8	2,519.7	568.9	−0.31
1988	4,488.4	45,501.5	986.4	178.0	2,521.3	554.1	−2.60
1989	5,002.4	46,491.7	1,076.0	210.1	2,381.4	512.2	−7.56
1990	5,774.5	47,708.0	1,210.4	216.6	2,666.3	558.9	9.11
1991	5,995.8	48,026.0	1,248.4	223.9	2,677.4	557.5	−0.25
1992	6,663.6	48,291.0	1,379.9	238.3	2,796.7	579.1	3.88
1993	7,865.5	48,546.0	1,620.2	273.3	2,878.0	592.8	2.37
1994	10,461.5	48,802.0	2,143.7	339.2	3,084.5	632.1	6.61
1995	13,560.2	49,025.0	2,766.0	397.2	3,414.3	696.5	10.19
1996	16,388.0	49,028.0	3,342.6	430.1	3,810.1	777.1	11.58
1997	17,594.1	49,039.0	3,587.8	442.2	3,979.1	811.4	4.41
1998	17,977.5	49,021.0	3,667.3	438.6	4,098.6	836.1	3.04
1999	18,133.2	48,982.0	3,702.0	432.5	4,192.8	856.0	2.38
2000	18,216.0	48,934.0	3,722.6	434.2	4,195.2	857.3	0.15
2001	18,827.8	49,085.0	3,835.8	437.3	4,305.9	877.2	2.32
2002	19,369.6	48,960.0	3,956.2	433.8	4,465.6	912.1	3.97

Note: Total nominal rural wage = (Rural population) × (Per capita income of rural population). MY refers to Million Yuan. Data in columns (6) and (7) are calculated using CPI.

Sources: *China statistical Yearbook* (CSY) (various years) for rural population, per capita income of rural population, rural labor, CPI, and rural CPI. Results in other columns are from authors' calculations.

lower than the latter, a result that is expected. However, differences between the two are small, indicating that much of wage growth during the period has been a result of TFP growth and not of a rise in education level. This is an interesting finding, which however requires further probing based on more detailed breakdown of labor in terms of quality and more accurate information on labor quality specific wages.

Table 11.4   Urban wage growth rate

(1)	(2)	(3)	(4)	(5)	(6)	(7)	(8)	(9)
	Growth rate by education			Share in total wage			Urban growth rate	
Year	$\hat{w}_{L1}$ (%)	$\hat{w}_{L2}$ (%)	$\hat{w}_{L3}$ (%)	S_{L1}	S_{L2}	S_{L3}	$\hat{w}_U$ (%)	$\hat{w}_U^{UN}$ (%)
1978	–	–	–	0.53	0.42	0.05	–	–
1979	5.12	7.51	5.18	0.49	0.46	0.05	6.17	6.80
1980	6.93	6.96	10.41	0.46	0.48	0.05	7.12	7.61
1981	0.54	−1.79	−2.55	0.46	0.49	0.05	−0.76	−0.54
1982	2.47	−0.41	−1.15	0.46	0.49	0.06	0.86	1.04
1983	1.98	0.59	13.25	0.45	0.48	0.07	1.99	2.03
1984	13.13	17.86	5.44	0.46	0.48	0.06	14.91	14.73
1985	9.09	6.53	8.56	0.47	0.46	0.06	7.85	7.68
1986	6.03	7.66	10.14	0.47	0.46	0.07	7.06	7.05
1987	3.01	3.65	1.19	0.47	0.46	0.07	3.17	3.25
1988	−0.55	1.51	0.33	0.46	0.46	0.08	0.46	0.53
1989	−7.47	−5.84	−7.05	0.45	0.47	0.08	−6.68	−6.37
1990	4.72	5.82	10.04	0.44	0.47	0.09	5.71	5.89
1991	7.36	6.79	3.55	0.43	0.47	0.10	6.73	6.90
1992	6.22	8.19	13.78	0.42	0.47	0.11	7.91	8.02
1993	7.15	10.77	9.27	0.41	0.48	0.11	9.09	9.18
1994	0.88	3.08	27.19	0.40	0.46	0.14	5.17	5.01
1995	3.45	3.06	−5.12	0.40	0.47	0.14	2.10	2.36
1996	1.05	0.79	8.55	0.40	0.45	0.15	2.00	1.89
1997	2.02	2.29	9.38	0.40	0.43	0.16	3.29	3.31
1998	19.10	20.02	14.09	0.41	0.43	0.16	18.68	18.74
1999	9.85	11.90	14.89	0.40	0.43	0.17	11.58	11.82
2000	8.02	11.82	16.94	0.38	0.44	0.19	11.27	11.82
2001	8.90	10.93	19.84	0.36	0.44	0.21	11.93	12.49
2002	12.55	13.46	17.22	0.34	0.44	0.22	13.94	14.76
1978–2002	5.35	6.21	8.17	0.43	0.46	0.11	6.05	6.35
1978–1984	4.95	4.91	4.94	0.47	0.47	0.06	4.93	5.15
1984–1991	3.03	3.64	3.66	0.46	0.47	0.08	3.36	3.45
1991–2002	7.08	8.61	13.00	0.40	0.45	0.15	8.68	8.91

Notes:
1 $\hat{w}_{L1}$, $\hat{w}_{L2}$, and $\hat{w}_{L3}$ are wage growth rates of labor categories, $L1_u$, $L2$, and $L3$, respectively. $\hat{w}_u$ is the weighted urban overall wage growth rate, while $\hat{w}_u^{UN}$ is an unweighted rate, which is calculated from the data of total urban labor and total real urban wage (column [11] of Table 11.2).
2 Average growth rates for 1978–2002, 1978–1984, 1984–1991, and 1991–2002 in this table and all other tables of this paper are compound averages, calculated as using the formula: Growth rate = $(X_t/X_1)^{(1/(t-1))} - 1$, where, X_1 and X_t are the values of item for period's first year and last year, respectively, while $(t - 1)$ is the length of the period.

Source: Authors' calculations

Table 11.5 Overall wage growth rate

(1)	(2)	(3)	(4)	(5)	(6)	(7)	(8)	(9)
	Total wage (100 MY)	Wage rate (Yuan)	$\hat{w}^{UN}$ (%)	s_U	$\hat{w}_U$ (%)	s_R	$\hat{w}_R$ (%)	$\hat{w}$ (%)
1978	1,660	362	–	0.36	–	0.64	–	–
1979	1,920	410	13.25	0.35	6.17	0.65	16.26	12.64
1980	2,157	446	8.79	0.36	7.12	0.64	9.00	8.33
1981	2,392	479	7.40	0.34	−0.76	0.66	11.49	7.26
1982	2,728	528	10.12	0.31	0.86	0.69	14.73	10.28
1983	3,019	570	7.94	0.29	1.99	0.71	10.53	7.98
1984	3,428	623	9.41	0.31	14.91	0.69	7.20	9.50
1985	3,631	638	2.36	0.33	7.85	0.67	−0.14	2.38
1986	3,776	645	1.12	0.35	7.06	0.65	−1.90	1.12
1987	3,926	652	1.02	0.36	3.17	0.64	−0.31	0.92
1988	3,984	643	−1.40	0.37	0.46	0.63	−2.60	−1.49
1989	3,763	596	−7.25	0.37	−6.68	0.63	−7.56	−7.24
1990	4,164	643	7.90	0.36	5.71	0.64	9.11	7.87
1991	4,319	659	2.53	0.38	6.73	0.62	−0.25	2.33
1992	4,610	697	5.67	0.39	7.91	0.61	3.88	5.44
1993	4,902	734	5.30	0.41	9.09	0.59	2.37	5.08
1994	5,255	779	6.18	0.41	5.17	0.59	6.61	6.02
1995	5,683	835	7.16	0.40	2.10	0.60	10.19	6.90
1996	6,228	903	8.19	0.39	2.00	0.61	11.58	7.81
1997	6,585	943	4.41	0.40	3.29	0.60	4.41	3.97
1998	7,317	1,036	9.83	0.44	18.68	0.56	3.04	9.58
1999	7,924	1,110	7.15	0.47	11.58	0.53	2.38	6.57
2000	8,505	1,180	6.30	0.51	11.27	0.49	0.15	5.59
2001	9,319	1,276	8.16	0.54	11.93	0.46	2.32	7.34
2002	10,421	1,413	10.74	0.57	13.94	0.43	3.97	9.50
1978–2002			5.84	0.39	6.05	0.61	4.69	5.22
1978–1984			9.47	0.33	4.93	0.67	11.49	9.32
1984–1991			0.81	0.35	3.36	0.65	−0.63	0.78
1991–2002			7.18	0.44	8.68	0.56	4.58	6.39

Notes:
1 Total wage is the sum of total urban real wage (column [11] in Table 11.2) and total rural real wage (column [6] in Table 11.3).
2 The data in column (9) show weighted overall wage growth rate, while the data in column (4) show unweighted rate.
3 The values of $\hat{w}_U$ and $\hat{w}_R$ are from previous tables. The average values of s_U and s_R for different periods shown in the bottom panel are arithmetic average of respective yearly values, while the average values of all wage growth rates are compound averages, as explained in Note 2 of Table 11.4.

Source: Authors' calculations.

11.4.2 Rate of return to capital in China

In view of the absence of readily available and acceptable rates of return to capital in China, these need to be computed on the basis of more primary data on capital stock (denominator) and profits (numerator).

11.4.2.1 China's capital stock

We use the perpetual inventory method based on annual investment data in order to compute China's capital stock. The exercise is presented in Table 11.6. It begins with the gross investment series in current prices, and their conversion, using the GDP deflator, to constant 1978 price values, which are then fed into the following familiar equation:

$$K_t = (1-\delta)K_{t-1} + I_t, \qquad (11.19)$$

where K stands for capital, I for investment, and δ for the depreciation rate. The capital stock for the initial year, K_0, is computed using the formula: $K_0 = I_0/[g_0 + \delta_0]$, where I_0 and δ_0 are the investment and depreciation rate, respectively, for the initial period, and g_0 is ideally the rate of growth of capital around the initial year.[35] We take 1957 as the initial year, and g_0 to be 0.13, the average growth rate of investment during 1952–1957. As per Chinese official documents, the depreciation rate ranges between 0.02 and 0.04. We therefore take δ_0 to be equal to 0.03, the midpoint of this range. Since the period analyzed in this paper is 1978–2002, the assumptions made in computing the initial capital stock for 1957 will not have much influence on the capital stock data actually used.

Table 11.6 Estimation of China's capital stock (in hundred million yuan and in 1978 price, unless otherwise indicated)

(1)	(2)	(3)	(4)	(5)	(6)	(7)	(8)
					Comparison with other estimations		
	Gross fixed investment (current prices)	GDP deflator (1978 = 100)	Gross fixed invest- ment	Capital stock[1]	Hu and Khan (1997b)[2]	Ezaki and Sun (1999)[3]	Chow and Li (2002)[4]
1978	1,377.9	100.0	1377.9	12,289.7	8,239.0	–	14112.0
1979	1,474.2	103.6	1423.6	13,221.7	8,850.0	–	1,5273.0
1980	1,590.0	107.5	1479.5	14,172.3	9,489.0	8,324.6	1,6438.0
1981	1,581.0	109.9	1,438.8	15,044.2	9,993.0	8,948.3	1,7268.0
1982	1,760.2	109.8	1,603.6	16,046.1	10,699.0	9,680.6	1,8297.0
1983	2,005.0	110.9	1,807.2	17,211.5	11,525.0	10,606.2	1,9515.0
1984	2,468.6	116.4	2,120.9	18,643.9	12,629.0	11,752.6	2,0928.0

Continued

Table 11.6 Continued

(1)	(2)	(3)	(4)	(5)	(6)	(7)	(8)
					Comparison of several estimations		
	Gross fixed investment (current prices)	GDP deflator (1978 = 100)	Gross fixed invest-ment	Capital stock[1]	Hu and Khan (1997b)[2]	Ezaki and Sun (1999)[3]	Chow and Li (2002)[4]
1985	3,386.0	128.2	2,640.6	20,538.7	13,984.0	13,252.6	2,2755.0
1986	3,846.0	134.1	2,869.0	22,586.2	15,321.0	15,079.4	2,4822.0
1987	4,322.0	140.9	3,067.9	24,750.6	16,847.0	17,154.8	2,7123.0
1988	5,495.0	158.0	3,477.8	27,238.3	18,502.0	19,466.2	3,0085.0
1989	6,095.0	172.0	3,544.1	29,692.9	19,423.0	21,507.1	3,3445.0
1990	6,444.0	181.7	3,546.9	32,052.0	20,445.0	23,090.2	3,6565.0
1991	7,517.0	193.9	3,876.3	34,646.3	21,718.0	24,725.8	3,9776.0
1992	9,636.0	209.2	4,606.8	37,867.2	23,311.0	26,823.1	4,3589.0
1993	14,998.0	239.6	6,258.7	42,232.5	25,532.0	29,700.0	4,8994.0
1994	19,260.6	287.2	6,707.1	46,828.0	28,297.0	33,372.6	5,5006.0
1995	23,877.0	325.0	7,346.9	51,833.5	–	37,593.8	6,1856.0
1996	26,867.2	344.3	7,804.2	57,046.1	–	–	6,9304.0
1997	28,457.6	347.0	8,202.2	62,395.9	–	–	7,7218.0
1998	29,545.9	338.6	8,726.6	68,002.8	–	–	8,5692.0
1999	30,701.6	331.0	9,274.9	73,877.5	–	–	–
2000	32,499.8	334.1	9,726.1	79,909.8	–	–	–
2001	37,460.8	338.1	11,079.7	86,994.0	–	–	–
2002	42,355.4	337.2	12,559.4	95,203.7	–	–	–

Notes:

1 The values shown in this column are from authors' own calculations. The gross fixed investment series is used to compute the capital stock using the perpetual inventory method, $K_t = (1 - \delta) K_{t-1} + I_t$. The capital stock for the initial year (1957), K_0, is computed using the formula $K_0 = I_0 / (g_0 + \delta_0)$, where I_0 is the investment for the initial period, and δ_0 is the rate of depreciation applicable for the initial year, and g_0 is ideally the rate of growth of capital around the initial year. In this study, g_0 is taken as 0.13, which is the average growth rate of investment during 1952–1957, and δ_0 is 0.03, which is the average value of rate of depreciation usually used by China government. After 1978, δ is taken as 0.04 for 1978–1992, and 0.05 for 1993–2002.

2 Hu and Khan (1997b) take depreciation rate to be 0.036 for 1978–1994. Investment deflator they used are not shown in their paper, but seem to be obviously higher than those used in Ezaki and Sun (1999) and Chow and Li (2002).

3 Ezaki and Sun (1999) take depreciation rate to be 0.049 for 1980–1995. For comparison, we converted the Ezaki and Sun's values, which are in 1995 prices, into those of 1978 prices.

4 Chow and Li (2002) take depreciation rate to be 0.04 for 1978–1998. Land is included in their esti-mated capital stock.

Source: *The Gross Domestic Product of China 1952–1995 (SSB,1997)*, *China Statistical Yearbook* (CSY) (NBSC, various issues), and authors' calculations.

Over the years, the composition of the Chinese capital stock changed considerably, with the share of "machinery and equipment", which depreciate faster, increasing relative to the share of "buildings and structures", which depreciate at a slower pace. This implies that the depreciation rate of the aggregate Chinese capital stock has increased over time. To reflect this process, we take the depreciation rate to be 0.03 for 1952–1978, 0.04 for 1979–1992, and 0.05 for 1993–2002. The rates assumed for the first two sub-periods are based on Chinese statistical authorities. The assumed rate for the more recent sub-period is based on studies by Ezaki and Sun (1999) and Hu and Khan (1997b).

Clearly, assumptions concerning deflators, initial capital stock, and depreciation rates influence the estimated values of capital stock. Table 11.6 therefore offers a comparison of our estimated values of capital stock with those presented recently by other researchers. The comparison shows our capital stock figures to be larger than those of Hu and Khan (1997b) and Ezaki and Sun (1999). However, they prove smaller than those of Chow and Li (2002), who include land in their capital stock.

11.4.2.2   Rate of return to capital according to NIA data

It is instructive to note first the rate of return to capital implied by NIA data. This exercise is shown in Table 11.7 that presents data on "Net Taxes" and "Operation Surplus", which together comprise the return to capital, net of depreciation. In Chinese national accounts, such data are available only at the provincial level, so that the national level figures presented in Table 11.7 are from aggregation of the provincial data.[36] After converting into constant 1978 values, the aggregate returns are divided by the capital stock data to obtain the rate of return to capital. This rate of return is denoted by r_{NIA} to indicate that it is obtained from NIA data. The year-to-year changes in r_{NIA} (as percentages of the base years' values) are denoted by $\hat{r}_{NIA}$. The compound average rates of $\hat{r}_{NIA}$ for different sub-periods of interest are presented in the bottom panel of the Table 11.7.

What is striking about these results is the relative constancy of r_{NIA}, whose value hovers around 11 to 12 percent during the entire period of 1978–2002. Such relative constancy contradicts the general expectation that capital deepening will pull the rate of return down as a result of diminishing returns to capital. As data in Table 11.6 show, between 1978 and 2002, the aggregate capital stock has increased 7.8 fold, and per worker capital stock has increased by 4.8 fold. In view of this manifold increase in capital stock, it is remarkable that the rate of return to capital, according to the NIA data, has remained relatively unchanged.

Hsieh (2002) argues in the context of Singapore that such an outcome is untenable if capital-output ratio has increased and the share of capital in national income has remained unchanged.[37] However, unlike for Singapore, the data for China do not show any significant rise in the capital-output ratio. Based on our capital stock estimates, the capital-output ratio (K/Y) for 1978 and 2002 are 3.39 and 3.06 respectively. Thus, instead of increasing, the capital-output ratio has declined somewhat, at least up to 2002.[38] Similarly, based on national accounts data, the value of capital share in income, β, has also remained almost constant. This would suggest that marginal product of capital, MP_K, has also remained

Table 11.7 Return to capital according to national income accounts (NIA) data (in hundred million yuan, unless otherwise indicated)

(1)	(2)	(3)	(4)	(5)	(6)	(7)
Year	Net taxes (current prices)	Operation surplus (current prices)	Return to capital (current prices)	Return to capital (1978 prices)	Rate of return to capital (%)	Year to year change (%)
1978	464.3	1,008.4	1,472.7	1,472.7	11.98	—
1979	493.4	1,081.6	1,575.0	1,520.9	11.50	−4.01
1980	547.9	1,215.6	1,763.5	1,641.0	11.58	0.66
1981	578.9	1,237.0	1,815.8	1,652.5	10.98	−5.13
1982	615.3	1,312.8	1,928.2	1,756.6	10.95	−0.34
1983	687.6	1,468.6	2,156.1	1,943.5	11.29	3.15
1984	844.0	1,754.4	2,598.4	2,232.4	11.97	6.04
1985	1,080.3	2,249.9	3,330.2	2,597.0	12.64	5.60
1986	1,276.1	2,467.0	3,743.1	2,792.3	12.36	−2.23
1987	1,492.9	2,960.8	4,453.7	3,161.3	12.77	3.32
1988	1,949.9	3,664.2	5,614.1	3,553.1	13.04	2.13
1989	2,247.0	4,039.8	6,286.8	3,655.6	12.31	−5.62
1990	2,421.8	4,052.8	6,474.7	3,563.8	11.12	−9.69
1991	2,868.4	4,808.8	7,677.2	3,958.9	11.43	2.77
1992	3,562.6	6,303.6	9,866.3	4,716.8	12.46	9.01
1993	4,792.5	8,266.0	13,058.5	5,449.3	12.90	3.59
1994	6,372.2	10,907.1	17,279.4	6,017.2	12.85	−0.41
1995	7,515.9	12,841.0	20,356.9	6,263.8	12.08	−5.95
1996	8,533.9	14,410.3	22,944.2	6,664.7	11.68	−3.32
1997	9,796.9	15,207.6	25,004.5	7,206.9	11.55	−1.14
1998	10,498.1	14,875.6	25,373.7	7,494.3	11.02	−4.59
1999	11,111.5	15,600.3	26,711.8	8,069.6	10.92	−0.89
2000	12,664.5	17,053.1	29,717.6	8,893.5	11.13	1.89
2001	13,697.1	18,252.3	31,949.3	9,449.6	10.86	−2.40
2002	14,715.3	20,292.6	35,007.9	10,380.7	10.90	0.38
1978–2002						−0.39
1978–1984						−0.01
1984–1991						−0.67
1991–2002						−0.42

Note: "Net taxes" and "Operation surplus" are aggregated from provincial data provided in tables of National Income Account. "Return to capital" (net of depreciation) at current price = Net taxes (current price) + Operation surplus (current price). It can also be calculated as follows: "Return to capital" (net of depreciation) at current price = GDP (current price)–payments to wages (current price)–depreciation of fixed assets (current price). "Rate of return to capital" is calculated as "Return to capital" (in 1978 price)/"Capital stock" (in 1978 price).

Sources: *The Gross Domestic Product of China 1952–1995* (SSB, 1997), *China Statistical Yearbook (CSY)* (NBSC, various issues), and authors' calculations.

constant. Thus unlike that of Singapore, the NIA data for China does not suggest any decline in the rate of return to capital.

11.4.2.3   Rate of return to capital in manufacturing

The advantage of the dual approach is that it does not have to depend on the rate of return to capital implied by the NIA data and instead can use information from non-NIA sources. Fortunately, the "China Industry Economy Statistical Yearbook (CIESY)" provides an alternative source of information on rate of return to capital in China's manufacturing sector. It also furnishes information allowing disaggregation into the "State-Owned Enterprises (SOE)" and "Non State-owned Enterprises (NSE)" parts of the manufacturing sector. Since 1978 the Chinese economy has been undergoing a radical transformation of ownership, particularly in its manufacturing sector where the share of state-ownership has fallen, while the share of private and cooperative ownership has risen. In addition, there is now considerable intrusion of foreign ownership in various forms. It is often maintained that capital under these various types of ownership differ in quality, and consequently in the rate of return they earn. The disaggregation in terms of ownership may therefore help to net out the impact of quality improvements in capital to the extent that these improvements correspond to the changes in ownership.

Table 11.8 shows the computation of r_M, the rate of return to capital in the manufacturing sector, using CIESY data on "profit plus taxes paid" as the numerator and the value of the fixed assets as the denominator. We see that r_M displays a declining trend, decreasing from about 26 percent in 1978 to about 13 percent in 2002. The decline is sharper for r_{NSE}, the rate of return of capital in the NSE part, which falls from 44 percent in 1978 to about 18 percent in 2002.[39] By comparison, the rate of return for the SOE part, denoted by r_{SOE}, declines from 25 percent in 1978 to 10 percent in 2002. The year-to-year changes in r_{SOE} and r_{NSE}, denoted by $\hat{r}_{SOE}$ and $\hat{r}_{NSE}$, respectively, and computed as percentage of their base year values, are also shown in Table 11.8. Using the SOE and NSE shares in the total manufacturing capital income, denoted by s_{SOE} and s_{NSE}, respectively, the weighted change in r_M, denoted by $\hat{r}_M$, is computed using the following formula:

$$\hat{r}_{Mt} = s_{SOE,\tau} \cdot \hat{r}_{SOE,t} + s_{NSE,\tau} \cdot \hat{r}_{NSE,t}. \tag{11.20}$$

The data on s_{SOE} and s_{NSE}, presented in Table 11.8, confirm significant changes that have occurred in the ownership of capital, with s_{SOE} decreasing from 92 percent in 1978 to 69 percent in 2002, and s_{NSE} increasing from 8 to 31 percent over the same period. As explained earlier, $\hat{r}_M$ shows the change in r_M, controlling for changes in the composition of capital in terms of ownership. Table 11.8 also shows $\hat{r}_M^{UN}$, the unweighted change in r_M. A comparison between $\hat{r}_M$ and $\hat{r}_M^{UN}$ shows the former to be (algebraically) lower than the latter (−3.60 vs. −2.96 percent for the entire sample), indicating that the capital quality changes, as reflected in ownership changes, have counteracted the forces of diminishing returns to a certain extent.

Table 11.8 Rate of return to capital in the manufacturing sector

(1)	(2)	(3)	(4)	(5)	(6)	(7)	(8)	(9)	(10)
	By ownership type (in manufacturing sector)							Overall change rate (%) (Manufacturing sector)	
	Rate of return (%)			Year-to-year change (%)		Capital share			
Year	r_M	r_{SOE}	r_{NSE}	$\hat{r}_{SOE}$	$\hat{r}_{NSE}$	S_{SOE}	S_{NSE}	$\hat{r}_M$	$\hat{r}_M^{UN}$
1978	26.34	24.76	44.09	–	–	0.92	0.08	–	–
1979	26.13	24.93	38.48	0.70	–12.73	0.91	0.09	–0.44	–0.78
1980	25.66	24.32	38.05	–2.47	–1.09	0.90	0.10	–2.34	–1.81
1981	23.99	22.90	33.24	–5.84	–12.65	0.89	0.11	–6.53	–6.52
1982	23.17	22.22	30.69	–2.94	–7.69	0.89	0.11	–3.46	–3.40
1983	22.89	21.66	32.17	–2.53	4.84	0.88	0.12	–1.69	–1.21
1984	23.43	22.30	31.30	2.94	–2.71	0.87	0.13	2.25	2.37
1985	24.89	22.40	45.21	0.45	44.44	0.89	0.11	5.63	6.21
1986	21.02	19.89	27.51	–11.21	–39.15	0.85	0.15	–14.81	–15.54
1987	20.67	19.72	25.62	–0.84	–6.86	0.84	0.16	–1.78	–1.65
1988	21.51	20.18	27.84	2.33	8.65	0.83	0.17	3.39	4.04
1989	18.24	17.45	21.72	–13.53	–21.99	0.81	0.19	–15.05	–15.19
1990	13.52	12.95	15.93	–25.81	–26.65	0.81	0.19	–25.97	–25.87
1991	13.02	12.25	15.89	–5.35	–0.23	0.79	0.21	–4.32	–3.74
1992	14.03	12.38	20.08	1.06	26.31	0.79	0.21	6.40	7.75
1993	15.20	12.87	21.76	3.97	8.37	0.74	0.26	5.02	8.35
1994	14.76	12.45	19.91	–3.29	–8.47	0.69	0.31	–4.77	–2.89
1995	11.23	9.29	15.48	–25.38	–22.24	0.69	0.31	–24.40	–23.93
1996	9.89	7.87	13.96	–15.26	–9.83	0.67	0.33	–13.51	–11.87
1997	9.64	7.58	13.35	–3.72	–4.36	0.64	0.36	–3.94	–2.60
1998	8.52	7.04	12.71	–7.19	–4.79	0.74	0.26	–6.45	–11.62
1999	9.33	7.68	14.03	9.09	10.32	0.74	0.26	9.41	9.52
2000	12.10	10.26	17.02	33.69	21.35	0.73	0.27	30.41	29.67
2001	11.94	9.79	17.37	–4.60	2.06	0.72	0.28	–2.75	–1.27
2002	12.80	10.25	18.41	4.74	5.99	0.69	0.31	5.11	7.22
1978–2002	–	–	–3.61	–3.57	0.80	0.20	–3.60	–2.96	
1978–1984	–	–	–1.73	–5.55	0.90	0.10	–2.13	–1.93	
1984–1991	–	–	–8.20	–9.23	0.84	0.16	–8.37	–8.06	
1991–2002	–	–	–1.61	1.35	0.72	0.28	–0.77	–0.15	

Notes:

1. The fixed asset for NSEs equals gross fixed asset of the Manufacturing sector minus that of SOEs, while profit and tax for NSEs equals to gross profit and tax of the Manufacturing sector minus that of SOEs. $\hat{r}_M^{UN}$ is the unweighted growth rate of return rate to capital for two kinds of enterprises in Manufacturing sector, SOEs and NSEs, and $\hat{r}_M$ is the weighted growth rate.

2. Average growth rates for 1978–2002, 1978–1984, 1984–1991, and 1991–2002 shown in the bottom panel in columns (5) and (6) are compound averages, calculated as using the formula: Growth rate = $(X_t / X_1)^{(1/(t-1))} - 1$, where, X_1 and X_t are the values of the item for the period's first year and last year, respectively, while $(t-1)$ is the length of the period.

Sources: National Bureau of Statistics of China, *China Industry Economy Statistical Yearbook (CIESY)* (2003) and authors' calculations.

11.4.2.4   Three routes to the rate of return to capital in "other" sector

Unfortunately, alternative sources of information (analogous to CIESY) are lacking for computation of r_O, the rate of return to capital in the non-manufacturing, "Other" sector. In view of this absence, this study offers three indirect routes to arriving at an estimated values of r_O. These are:

(a) CIESY route
(b) Hybrid route, and
(c) Neutral route.

CIESY Route: The CIESY route is based on the assumption that the rate of return to capital in the "Other" sector is similar to that in the NSE part of the manufacturing sector. The rationale behind this assumption is that the "Other" sector comprises mainly of agriculture and services (including very small scale manufacturing), which are mostly under non-state ownership. This similarity in ownership may imply a similarity in the rate of return to capital in these two parts of the Chinese economy, suggesting that r_{OC}, the value of r_O computed via the CIESY route, is equal to r_{NSE}. Table 11.9 presents the values of r_{OC} and changes in r_{OC}, denoted by $\hat{r}_{OC}$, which are the same as of r_{NSE} and $\hat{r}_{NSE}$ as presented in Table 11.8. An appealing feature of the CIESY route is its independence of the NIA data.

The direction in which the CIESY route will influence the results is clear. As already noted, r_{NSE} experienced a steep decline over the sample period as a whole. Assuming $r_{OC} = r_{NSE}$, as per the CIESY route, therefore extends this steep decline to a much wider swathe of the Chinese economy. As can be seen from Table 11.10, the share of the "Other" sector in total capital income is more than 70 percent. As a result, the "CIESY route" should cause the rate of return to capital for the entire economy to undergo a sharp decline. When computed following the "CIESY route", the TFPGR should therefore prove to be low, yielding, most likely, a lower bound of this rate.

The weakness of the "CIESY route" lies in the fact that the NSE part of the manufacturing sector and the "Other" sector, despite their similarity in terms of ownership, are dissimilar in other respects, including technological composition of capital, organization of the firm, etc. For example, the NSE part of manufacturing employs industrial technology, is formally organized, and usually has a higher capital-labor ratio. In contrast, Chinese agriculture, which is the largest component of the "Other" sector, still employs pre-industrial technology widely, has low capital-labor ratio, and does not have formal organization. The same may be said about the service and other small scale manufacturing (handicrafts and artisan production) enterprises which comprise an important part of the "Other" sector. These dissimilarities probably outweigh in importance the similarity in terms of ownership. More importantly, it may be argued that the "Other" sector did not witness the kind of capital deepening that the manufacturing sector did, so that the rate of return to capital in the "Other" sector would not undergo the kind of steep decline that we observe in the CIESY data for the manufacturing

Table 11.9 Rate of return to capital in the non-manufacturing sector and growth rate of TFP estimated by the primal approach

(1)	(2)	(3)	(4)	(5)	(6)	(7)	(8)	(9)	(10)
	Rate of return to capital in non-manufacturing (other) sector		Growth rate (%)					Labor share	TFP growth rate (%)
Year	r_{OC}	r_{OH}	$\hat{r}_{OC}$	$\hat{r}_{OH}$	GDP	Labor	Capital	S_L	$TFPGR_p$
1978	44.09	6.32	–	–	–	–	–	0.50	–
1979	38.48	5.88	–12.73	–7.01	7.60	2.17	7.58	0.51	2.75
1980	38.05	6.33	–1.09	7.79	7.81	3.26	7.19	0.51	2.63
1981	33.24	6.11	–12.65	–3.50	5.26	3.22	6.15	0.53	0.63
1982	30.69	6.20	–7.69	1.45	9.01	3.59	6.66	0.54	3.98
1983	32.17	6.72	4.84	8.36	10.89	2.52	7.26	0.54	6.17
1984	31.30	7.68	–2.71	14.30	15.18	3.79	8.32	0.54	9.28
1985	45.21	8.48	44.44	10.41	13.47	3.48	10.16	0.53	6.87
1986	27.51	9.30	–39.15	9.63	8.86	2.83	9.97	0.53	2.67
1987	25.62	9.96	–6.86	7.13	11.57	2.93	9.58	0.52	5.48
1988	27.84	10.26	8.65	3.07	11.27	2.94	10.05	0.52	4.91
1989	21.72	10.39	–21.99	1.27	4.07	1.83	9.01	0.52	–1.24
1990	15.93	10.33	–26.65	–0.62	3.83	2.55	7.95	0.53	–1.28
1991	15.89	10.88	–0.23	5.34	9.19	1.15	8.09	0.52	4.77
1992	20.08	11.93	26.31	9.61	14.24	1.01	9.30	0.50	9.18
1993	21.76	12.12	8.37	1.59	13.49	0.99	11.53	0.51	7.27
1994	19.91	12.22	–8.47	0.83	12.66	0.97	10.88	0.51	6.83
1995	15.48	12.40	–22.24	1.47	10.51	0.90	10.69	0.53	4.91

Continued

317

Table 11.9 Continued

(1)	(2)	(3)	(4)	(5)	(6)	(7)	(8)	(9)	(10)
	Rate of return to capital		Growth rate (%)					Labor share	TFP growth rate (%)
Year	r_{OC} (Non-manufacturing sector)	r_{OH} (Non-manufacturing sector)	$\hat{r}_{OC}$	$\hat{r}_{OH}$	GDP	Labor	Capital	S_L	$TFPGR_p$
1996	13.96	12.33	−9.83	−0.56	9.59	1.30	10.06	0.53	4.18
1997	13.35	12.28	−4.36	−0.42	8.84	1.26	9.38	0.53	3.77
1998	12.71	12.00	−4.79	−2.24	7.82	1.17	8.99	0.53	2.97
1999	14.03	11.59	10.32	−3.46	7.14	1.07	8.64	0.52	2.50
2000	17.02	10.73	21.35	−7.43	8.00	0.97	8.17	0.51	3.56
2001	17.37	10.41	2.06	−2.91	7.50	1.30	8.87	0.51	2.52
2002	18.41	10.12	5.99	−2.84	7.96	0.98	9.44	0.51	2.85
1978–2002			−3.57	1.98	9.37	2.00	8.90	0.52	4.06
1978–1984			−5.55	3.31	9.25	3.09	7.19	0.52	4.20
1984–1991			−9.23	5.11	8.84	2.53	9.26	0.53	3.12
1991–2002			1.35	−0.66	9.77	1.08	9.62	0.52	4.57

*Notes:*p

1. Rate of return to capital for the Non-manufacturing sector is calculated /estimated using three methods. r_{OH} = (gross profit and tax)/(fixed asset). It is calculated using both CIESY and NIA data. The value of fixed asset for the Non-manufacturing sector equals to gross capital stock minus fixed asset of the Manufacturing sector, while the value of profit and tax for the Non-manufacturing sector equals to gross capital income minus profit and tax of the Manufacturing sector; r_{OC} is look ed as equal to r_{NSE} in the column 4 of Table 11.8; r_{ON}, which is not shown in this table, is regarded as constant.

2. $TFPGR_p$ is estimated by the primal approach.

3. The average values of labor share for different periods shown in the bottom panel of column (9) are arithmetic averages of respective yearly values.

Sources: National Bureau of Statistics of China, *China Industry Economy Statistical Yearbook* (2003), and authors' calculations.

Table 11.10 Growth rate of TFP estimated by the dual approach

(1)	(2)	(3)	(4)	(5)	(6)	(7)	(8)	(9)	(10)	(11)
	Capital share by sector			Growth rate (%)			Labor share	TFP growth rate (%)		
Year	S_M	S_O	$\hat{w}$	$\hat{r}_C$	$\hat{r}_H$	$\hat{r}_N$	S_L	$TFPGR_{d,C}$	$TFPGR_{d,H}$	$TFPGR_{d,N}$
1978	0.28	0.72	–	–	–	–	0.50	–	–	–
1979	0.28	0.72	12.64	-9.29	-5.17	-0.12	0.51	1.79	3.83	6.32
1980	0.27	0.73	8.33	-1.44	5.01	-0.64	0.51	3.57	6.71	3.96
1981	0.27	0.73	7.26	-10.98	-4.32	-1.78	0.53	-1.51	1.69	2.91
1982	0.28	0.72	10.28	-6.52	0.10	-0.95	0.54	2.40	5.50	5.01
1983	0.28	0.72	7.98	3.00	5.54	-0.47	0.54	5.67	6.85	4.05
1984	0.27	0.73	9.50	-1.33	10.95	0.62	0.54	4.47	10.17	5.38
1985	0.25	0.75	2.38	34.22	9.15	1.48	0.53	17.27	5.55	1.96
1986	0.26	0.74	1.12	-32.87	3.33	-3.82	0.53	-14.91	2.16	-1.21
1987	0.26	0.74	0.92	-5.53	4.80	-0.47	0.52	-2.15	2.76	0.26
1988	0.25	0.75	-1.49	7.31	3.16	0.86	0.52	2.75	0.75	-0.36
1989	0.24	0.76	-7.24	-20.28	-2.74	-3.70	0.52	-13.55	-5.06	-5.52
1990	0.25	0.75	7.87	-26.49	-6.85	-6.38	0.53	-8.46	0.87	1.10
1991	0.26	0.74	2.33	-1.25	2.91	-1.08	0.52	0.64	2.61	0.72
1992	0.25	0.75	5.44	21.26	8.80	1.62	0.50	13.17	7.08	3.57
1993	0.26	0.74	5.08	7.52	2.46	1.27	0.51	6.29	3.78	3.19
1994	0.25	0.75	6.02	-7.54	-0.58	-1.20	0.51	-0.63	2.78	2.48
1995	0.27	0.73	6.90	-22.80	-5.20	-6.29	0.53	-7.35	1.09	0.57
1996	0.26	0.74	7.81	-10.81	-4.01	-3.59	0.53	-0.92	2.27	2.46

Continued

319

Table 11.10 Continued

(1)	(2)	(3)	(4)	(5)	(6)	(7)	(8)	(9)	(10)	(11)
	Capital share by sector		Growth rate (%)				Labor share	TFP growth rate (%)		
Year	S_M	S_O	$\hat{w}$	$\hat{r}_C$	$\hat{r}_H$	$\hat{r}_N$	S_L	$TFPGR_{d,C}$	$TFPGR_{d,H}$	$TFPGR_{d,N}$
1997	0.28	0.72	3.97	-4.25	-1.37	-1.06	0.53	0.12	1.47	1.61
1998	0.28	0.72	9.58	-5.25	-3.41	-1.80	0.53	2.60	3.47	4.23
1999	0.29	0.71	6.57	10.06	0.24	2.71	0.52	8.22	3.58	4.74
2000	0.29	0.71	5.59	24.02	3.70	8.95	0.51	14.45	4.68	7.20
2001	0.29	0.71	7.34	0.65	-2.86	-0.81	0.51	4.09	2.39	3.38
2002	0.29	0.71	9.50	5.74	-0.51	1.50	0.51	7.66	4.61	5.60
1978–2002	0.27	0.73	5.22	-3.58	0.48	-0.97	0.52	1.01	2.95	2.26
1978–1984	0.28	0.72	9.32	-4.60	1.80	-0.59	0.52	2.67	5.73	4.59
1984–1991	0.26	0.74	0.78	-9.01	1.66	-2.14	0.53	-3.87	1.20	-0.61
1991–2002	0.27	0.73	6.39	0.77	-0.69	-0.21	0.52	3.68	2.98	3.21

Notes:

1. The values of $\hat{w}$ are from Table 11.5. The values of $\hat{r}$ in columns (5) (6), and (7) are the weighted growth rate of return rate to capital for the economy comprising of both the Manufacturing and the Non- manufacturing sector, which are calculated from three methods.

2. Average growth rates for 1978–2002, 1978–1984, 1984–1991, and 1991–2002 shown in the bottom panel in columns (4) (5) (6) and (7) are compound averages, calculated as using the formula: Growth rate = $(X_t/X_1)^{1/(t-1)} - 1$, where, X_1 and X_t are the values of item for periodl's first year and last year, respectively, while $(t-1)$ is the length of the period. The average values of S_{SOE}, S_{NSE} and S_L for different periods shown in the bottom panel of columns (2) (3), and (8) are arithmetic average of respective yearly values.

3. $TFPGR_{d,C}$, $TFPGR_{d,H}$, $TFPGR_{d,N}$ which are calculated by the dual approach, are based on weighted wage growth rate in column (4) and weighted growth rate of capital return rate in columns (5) (6), and (7), respectively,

Source: Authors' calculations.

320

sector. These various factors undercut the appeal of the CIESY route, despite its merit as being independent of the NIA data.

Hybrid route: The Hybrid route is called so because it involves use of data from both CIESY and NIA to compute r_O. More concretely, r_{OH}, the rate of return to capital in the "Other" sector following the Hybrid route, is obtained by subtracting relevant data for the manufacturing sector obtained from CIESY from corresponding data for the entire economy obtained from NIA.[40] Thus, the value of fixed assets for the "Other" sector is obtained by subtracting the value of fixed assets of the Manufacturing sector (obtained from CIESY) from the total capital stock of the economy, computed earlier through the perpetual inventory method using investment data and shown in Table 11.6. Similarly, the value of profit and taxes for the "Other" sector is obtained by subtracting the profit and tax of the Manufacturing sector (obtained from CIESY) from the total value of profit and tax in the economy obtained from NIA. Taking the latter as the numerator and the former as the denominator, we obtain r_{OH}, the hybrid variant of r_O.

The direction in which the "Hybrid route" will influence the results is not too difficult to predict. We know that r_{NIA} does not decline much, while r_M, according to CIESY data, experiences a steep decline. When r_O is derived as a residual, it has to have, by construction, an upward movement offsetting the declining trend of r_M so as to ensure a stable r_{NIA}. This is confirmed by results shown in Table 11.9, where we see that r_{OH} increases from 6.32 percent in 1978 to 10.12 in 2002, implying a compound average rate of *increase* by 1.98 percent per annum. The "Hybrid route" is therefore likely to yield an upper bound of the TFPGR. Apart from the upward bias that it imparts to the TFPGR estimates, the other unappealing feature of the Hybrid route is that it requires use of NIA data, which the dual approach strives to avoid.

Neutral route: The weaknesses of both the "CIESY route" and the "Hybrid route" create the rationale for the "Neutral route", which aims at avoiding both the downward bias (of the CIESY route) and the upward bias (of the Hybrid route) by not making any sharp assumption regarding the trend of the rate of return to capital in the "Other" sector. The main argument for this assumption is that major components of the "Other" sector, namely agriculture and services, did not experience the kind of capital deepening that China's manufacturing sector did. There are in fact complaints that productivity in the Chinese agriculture has stagnated due to lack of investment.[41] Similarly, though there is a capital intensive high end of the service sector, much of it in China is still low capital intensive operations carried out by informal groups of people. Also, there is the possibility of engaging labor of better quality (in the form of workers with higher educational qualifications), which may offset the downward pull on the rate of return to capital of any capital accumulation that might have occurred. In view of the above considerations, r_{ON}, the rate of return to capital in the "Other" sector, is assumed under the Neutral route to have remained unchanged, so that $\hat{r}_{ON}$, the rate of change in r_{ON} is zero. In a sense, this is an agnostic position, which may lead to some overestimation of the TFPGR by ruling out any declining trend in the rate of return to capital in the "Other" sector. However, in terms of the order of magnitude, the possible error involved with the Neutral route is likely to be much less than that involved with either the CIESY route or the Hybrid route, and hence under the circumstances the Neutral route seems to be the safest one to take.

11.4.2.5 Computation of the economy-wide rate of return to capital

Given the three routes producing three different series for r_O, it is possible to produce three different sets of results with regard to the rate of return to capital in the entire economy and consequently of the TFPGR.[42] The present study therefore provides a broader basis for drawing conclusions about the magnitude of TFPGR and the direction of its dynamics.

Table 11.10 presents the results. It first shows the values of s_M and s_O, the shares of the "Manufacturing" and "Other" sector in the total capital income. These shares are used to compute $\hat{r}$, the economy wide (weighted) rate of change in the rate of return to capital, using the formula:

$$\hat{r} = s_M \cdot \hat{r}_M + s_O \cdot \hat{r}_O. \tag{11.21}$$

Use of three variants of $\hat{r}_O$, namely $\hat{r}_{OC}$, $\hat{r}_{OH}$, and $\hat{r}_{ON}$, yields three variants of $\hat{r}$, namely $\hat{r}_C$, $\hat{r}_N$, and $\hat{r}_H$, respectively. The results shown in Table 11.10 confirm the predictions made earlier. We see that the economy-wide rate of return to capital according to the "CIESY route" declines at a compound average rate of 3.58 percent per annum for the entire period of 1978–2002. This is a very different picture than what we get on the basis of NIA data, according to which the rate of return to capital (r_{NIA}) remained roughly constant, or more accurately, declined by only 0.39 percentage point per annum on average during the 1978–2002 period.[43] Looking at $\hat{r}_H$ values, we see an opposite picture, with rate of return to capital rising at a compound average rate of 0.48 percent per annum for the entire sample period. The computed values of $\hat{r}_N$ avoid these extremes and suggest that the economy-wide rate of return to capital declined at a compound average rate of 0.97 percent. It may be noted that r_N is also different from r_{NIA}, so that results regarding $\hat{r}_N$ also differ from results regarding $\hat{r}_{NIA}$.

11.4.3 Alternative estimates of TFPGR using the dual approach

We may now collect the results obtained in the above sections in order to compute $TFPGR_d$, or SR_{dual}. To establish a benchmark for comparison, we first present in Table 11.9 the values of $TFPGR_p$ or SR_{primal}. The table shows year-to-year growth rates of GDP, labor, capital, and also values of s_L, the share of labor income in GDP as per NIA data. The values of s_K, the share of capital, can be obtained as $(1 - s_L)$. These values are fed into equation (11.4) to produce the primal, $TFPGR_p$, whose values are shown in Table 11.9. The lower panel of the table shows that the (compound) average of $TFPGR_p$ for the entire 1978–2002 period equals 4.06 percent. This would suggest that about 43 percent of growth was the result of TFP growth. For the initial 1978–1984 period of reform, the average TFPGR proves to be 4.20 percent, whereas for the more recent 1992–2002 period this average equals 4.57 percent. So according to the primal approach, the TFPGR is not only high (exceeding 4 percent per annum), but has also witnessed some increase in the more recent period. We may now turn to the results obtained from the dual approach.

All the ingredients for computation of $TFPGR_d$ are shown in Table 11.10, including $\hat{w}$, the weighted growth rate of wage, and $\hat{r}_C$, $\hat{r}_N$, and $\hat{r}_H$, the three alternative values of $\hat{r}$ obtained from following the CIESY, Hybrid, and Neutral route, respectively. These values, together with the values of s_L and s_K, are fed into equation (11.5') to produce the three variants of TFPGR, denoted by $TFPGR_{dC}$, $TFPGR_{dH}$, and $TFPGR_{dN}$, corresponding to the CIESY, Hybrid, and Neutral routes, respectively.

The lower panel of Table 11.10 presents the average values of $TFPGR_d$ over relevant periods of interest. We notice that, for the entire sample period of 1978–2002, the annual (compound) average value of $TFPGR_d$ proves to be 1.01, 2.95, and 2.26 percent following the CIESY, Hybrid, and Neutral routes respectively. This confirms our prediction that CIESY and Hybrid routes are likely to produce some kind of lower and upper bounds of the $TFPGR_d$. Comparing these values with the analogous $TFPGR_p$ value (4.06 percent), we notice that the dual approach produces much lower values of TFPGR for China, no matter which particular route is chosen to compute r_0. Given that China's GDP grew at an average rate of 9.37 (see Table 11.9) percent during 1978–2002, a TFPGR value of 2.26 (as suggested by the Neutral route) implies that about a quarter of this growth was derived from productivity growth.

The second point of note is that the average $TFPGR_d$ values (2.98 and 3.21, respectively) for the more recent 1991–2002 period produced by both the Hybrid and Neutral approaches prove to be lower than its values (5.73 and 4.59, respectively) for the initial 1978–1984 period. This result points to *deceleration* of China's productivity, and provide a contrast with the result obtained from the primal approach suggesting acceleration.[44]

In making these comparisons, it needs to be remembered that the $TFPGR_p$ values presented in Table 11.9 are obtained without controlling for changes in quality (or composition) of the inputs and are therefore likely to be higher than if were obtained upon accounting for these changes. From this viewpoint, $TFPGR_p$ values of Table 11.9 are not exactly comparable with the $TFPGR_d$ values (presented in Table 11.10) that have been computed taking into account quality (composition) changes in labor and capital, to the extent was possible given the data limitations. However, our results also show that accounting for quality improvement does not affect the results regarding $TFPGR_d$ radically, suggesting that the comparison between $TFPGR_p$ and $TFPGR_d$, as offered above, would still hold in broad terms if the $TFPGR_d$ were computed without accounting for input (quality) composition changes.

11.5 Concluding remarks

How important productivity has been in China's recent growth and whether productivity is slowing down are important questions for both researchers and policy makers. Most of the answers to these questions provided so far were obtained using the primal approach to growth accounting that relies almost exclusively on national income accounting data. This is problematic in view of the many issues that persist with Chinese NIA data despite recent efforts to overcome them. This study therefore uses the dual approach to growth accounting that does not have to rely exclusively on NIA data. The results show that China's productivity growth, after playing an important role in China's growth, has now slowed down. This finding matches with recent data showing rising ICOR.

The TFPGR slowdown reported in this study is not exactly the same as reported by several previous studies, which were comparing the 1978–1984 period with post-1984 periods, inclusive of 1988–1991 years. These latter years were when China's growth as a whole slowed down, not only her productivity. As our results also show, $TFPGR_{dN}$ (i.e., TFPGR following the Neutral route) averaged to negative 0.61 during 1984–1991. However, both GDP and productivity growth bounced in China after 1991, and that is why researchers comparing 1978–1984 period with post 1991 sub-periods often observed productivity acceleration. However, their samples in many cases ended with late 1990s (say 1997 or 1998), and therefore did not capture the more recent dynamics. The productivity slowdown reported in this study is from a comparison of the earlier 1978–1984 period with a more recent period of 1991–2002, leaving out the intervening years of 1988–1991.

The above shows that choice of periods for comparison is important for the results and interpretation.[45] While the productivity slowdown of the 1988–1991 period was associated with a general slowdown and political turmoil, the more recent phase of slowdown reported in this study is occurring when the economy is still growing fast and there is no political turmoil. The current combination of fast GDP growth and productivity deceleration is made possible by extraordinarily high rates of investment. However, these high rates of investment are already causing macroeconomic imbalances, and thus high GDP growth rate along with deceleration of productivity may not be sustainable for too long.

There is a consensus that high TFPGR of the initial years was to a large extent the result of institutional changes introduced in agriculture. To the extent that reforms later moved to industry, where institutional changes alone were not always sufficient for output increase, instead deployment of capital and hired labor was necessary, the role of productivity in output growth was expected to decrease. However, as a follower-industrializing country, there remains much for China to gain from technological diffusion. Many have argued that as a country develops, her capability to benefit from technological diffusion increases, and this increased capability may outweigh the negative effect of narrowing of the technological gap. Based on this and similar other arguments, many researchers had indeed predicted an acceleration of productivity in China with time. Against this backdrop, a deceleration in Chinese productivity seems quite unwarranted. Discussions of previous chapters (particularly Chapter 9 and 10) show that productivity slowdown is a concentrated manifestation of several different problems faced by the contemporary Chinese economy.

To complete the process of industrialization and successful transformation of the entire economy, China needs to continue her growth momentum for a considerable period into the future, and for that she needs to continue to have productivity growth. It may therefore be hoped that the Chinese policy makers will pay more attention to the problem of productivity slowdown, delve into its causes, and then take appropriate steps to arrest and reverse it.

Acknowledgments

The authors would like to thank the participants of ICSEAD's China Growth Project and its two workshops for their helpful comments on earlier drafts of the paper. They are however not responsible for remaining errors and shortcomings. The views expressed in this chapter are authors' personal and should not be ascribed to institutions with which they are associated.

Notes

1 The overall average, 2.26 percent is lower than the average rate for both the initial and recent sub-periods, because during the intervening period of 1984–1991 that include the years of political turmoil involving the Tiananmen incident, the TFP growth rate fell to –0.61 percent.

2 Since China's reform is still continuing, we refrain from using the expression "post-reform," and instead use the expression "reform period" to refer to post-1978 years.

3 This also implies that while TFP contributed only 18 percent of the pre-reform growth, its contribution to the growth during 1979 –1994 was 41.6 percent.

4 In their words, "Instead of slowing down (as one might have expected), productivity growth reached stunning new highs as China moved forward on the reform path, albeit at an uneven pace." (Hu and Khan, 1997b, p. 124) They further add the following commentary in this regard:

> Therefore, the evidence from this study points to a somewhat different conclusion from that reached by Sachs and Woo (2000). Even though the efficiency gains brought about by earlier agricultural reforms may have dissipated, the sharp growth in rural industry, the surge in foreign direct investment, the export boom, the further dismantling of the central planning system, and the increasing market orientation in the state-owned sector have combined to boost aggregate productivity growth in the 1985–94 period, and even more so during 1990–94. (Hu and Khan, 1997b, p. 124)

5 According to their computation, the average growth rate of TFP for the whole period of 1977–1992 is 2.40 percent, accounting for 25.6 percent of the output growth.

6 Woo (1998) adds that inclusive of labor reallocation (from agriculture to industry) effect, TFPGR for this period would range from 2.2 to 2.4 percent per annum.

7 The choice of sub-periods is important for comparison. Woo (1998) provides the following reasoning for the choice of the sub periods:

> The delineation of the sub-periods corresponds, one, to the policy regime change toward accelerating reforms in the non-agricultural sectors, and two, to the emergence of industry as the undisputed primary engine of growth. The growth performance of the 1985–93 subperiod may be a better guide (than that of the entire period) to understanding the future growth prospects of China. This is because future Chinese growth is likely to be led by the (non) agricultural sectors as in 1985–93 period.

8   Woo (1998) informs that "The agricultural reforms may have accounted for a large part of the initial high net TFP growth."

9   Young (2003) notes that the use of this alternative deflator brings down the growth of real GDP between 1978 and 1998 from the official 9.1 percent to 7.4 percent for the aggregate and from 10.6 to 8.1 for the non-agricultural sector.

10 Young (2003) recognizes that "... both slightly lower and moderately higher estimates are plausible, but all estimates are tolerably concentrated around a value of 1.1 percent."

11 So far as factor shares are concerned, Young (2003) accepts what is there in the official data, viewing that "...there is no reason to modify the reported Chinese estimates of the share of labor...In this paper I use the average share of labor reported in the Chinese national accounts, in preference over the more volatile figures of the input output tables."

12 We found that, first, the accumulation of human capital was quite rapid and it contributes significantly to growth and welfare. Second, after incorporating human capital, the growth of TFP still plays a positive and significant role during the reform period 1978–1999. In contrast, productivity growth was negative in the pre-reform period. Results are robust to changes in labor shares in GDP. (Wang and Yao 2001, p. 3)

13 See Wang and Yao 2001, Table 1, p. 15.

14 In fact that is exactly how they themselves view their results. They think that "Regarding the on-going debate, this paper proposes a middle-road answer to the sources of growth, and that is, both productivity growth and factor accumulation are very significant in accounting for China's growth performance during the reform period." (Wang and Yao, 2001, p. 3) One thing that needs to be noted is that the contrast between the upbeat TFP growth rates of Hu and Khan and those of Young, Woo, and Wang and Yao may not be as great as it appears. This is because Hu and Khan's analysis does not take into account quality improvements of labor. Hence their estimates of TFP are inclusive of the contribution of human capital growth. On the other hand, both Young and Wang and Yao account for quality improvements in labor, and hence their TFP growth rates do not include the contribution of quality improvements in labor. As we can see from the results of Wang and Yao, presented above, the total of human capital growth and TFP growth rates prove to 5.01 for the reform period. (Analogous total for the pre-reform period proves to be 4.73 percent per annum) This is higher than the TFPGR reported by even Hu and Khan! Similarly, Young finds that while output per worker increases in the post-reform period by 3.6 percent, output per effective worker increases by 2.6 percent, suggesting a growth rate of human capital of about 1 percent. Adding this to his TFP growth rate would raise it to 2.4 percent, much higher than the measly 1.4 percent!

15 Referring to the wide range of TFP estimates, Sachs and Woo (2000, p. 21) offer the following observation:

> The wide range of TFP estimates in the literature could be caused by a wide array of factors which include the choice of data set (e.g., geographical and sectoral representation, time period), the specification of the production function (e.g., Cobb-Douglas, Griliches-type), the assumption of technical change (e.g., Hicks-neutral, labor-augmenting), the estimation method (e.g., OLS, stochastic frontier), the selection of deflators for outputs and inputs, and ad hoc exclusion of observations.

This is quite an apt description, and there is not much to add to this statement. See Islam (1999, 2003) for discussions of different methodological approaches to computation of TFP.

16 Young (2003) observes that "Following a nationwide audit of statistical reports, the 1994 gross industrial output estimates were revised downwards by about 9 percent, with most of the adjustment falling on township and village enterprises, whose output was deemed to have been exaggerated by about a third."

17 State Statistical Bureau (SSB) of China (i.e., National Bureau of Statistics of China after 1998) began constructing fixed asset investment price index only in 1991.

18 For example, a Census of Services was conducted in 1991–1992 in order to gather data on the service sector, "which produced a dramatic revision of the national accounts." (Young, 2003)

19 "With the support and cooperation of the SSB, Hsueh and Li (1999) have made significant progresses and published the most complete set of Chinese national income from 1952 to 1995 based on SNA in 1999 both at the national and provincial level." (Wang and Yao, 2001, p. 5)

20 The presentation here follows Hsieh (2002).

21 Samuelson (1962) provides an elaborate discussion of the relationship between the production frontier and factor price frontier. Diamond (1965) and Phelps and Phelps (1966) in fact use factor price frontier in defining changes in total factor productivity. As Hsieh (2002, p. 503) notes,

> In a simple model with two factors, say capital and labor, the outward shift of the factor price frontier is simply a share-weighted average of the growth rate of real wages and the rental rate of capital. According to the dual growth accounting formula, if real wage growth is entirely due to capital accumulation, the return to capital must fall by the same magnitude as the rate of real wage growth.

22 It is also known that the Tornqvist indices are not only a good approximation of the corresponding Divisia indices. They are also the exact indices if the underlying production function has the translog specification. To the extent that translog function can serve as the second order approximation to any other production function, the validity of the Tornqvist index is quite general. See Hulten (2001) for an excellent recent discussion of various issues regarding the theory and computation of TFP.

23 See Jorgenson et al (1987, p. 2) for further elaboration of these issues.

24 See Abramovitz (1962, p. 764), Griliches and Jorgenson (1967, pp. 250–251), and Hulten (2001) for further elaboration of this point.

25 See Hsieh (2002, p. 506) for further discussion of these issues.

26 Actually, Hsieh's figure 2 makes it clear that r did not have any further room to fall in Singapore. In 1962, r, as given by "Average lending rate," was already at the level of around 6–7 percent. In contrast, Hsieh's figure 1 shows that r in Korea, as measured by curb loan rate was at the level of around 16–17 percent, and so there was considerable room to fall.

27 "This evidence suggests that while the data on investment expenditures in the Korean national accounts are reasonable accurate, Singapore's national accounts significantly overstate the amount of investment spending." (Hsieh, 2002, p. 503)

28   The absolutely complete market economy doesn't exist in reality…. It cannot be obstructed that we describe the basic trends of the Chinese economy with the simple theory model. The practice proves that the Chinese economy which is changing into a market economy can be described with such simple theory model to some extent, and the results are basically fitted the reality…. and the practice also proved that the result is more sensitive to different data than to different methods. So we should pay more attention to data handling. Rawski and Zheng (1993, pp. 320–321).

29 In order to conform to the definitions used in the censuses, the flow data for higher education include graduates from Adult Education Schools. This results in higher numbers of people belonging to $E3$ than would be the case if these graduates were excluded and only those who graduated from regular schools were counted.

30 Unfortunately, as already mentioned, census data for 1982 do not provide necessary details for such a comparison.

31 It may be said that some of $P3$ who are over 65 continue to work and be in the labor force. However, conversely it is also true that some of $P3$ who are less than 65 do not participate in the labor market and hence remain out of the labor force. These two opposing influences may largely cancel each other out.

32   Since the end of the 1970s, labor growth in SOEs has been very slow. Usually only persons with completed senior secondary or special secondary education find employment in SOEs. On the other hand, SOEs do not attract and employ persons with completed higher education, except in some selected professional fields. Thus, employees of SOEs can be regarded as representing labor of education type *E2*. The same seems to be true with NSEs of the formal sector. We did the computation taking w_{L2} to be equal to average wage of the SOEs only. However, the results did not differ that much. The same was the case with w_{L3}. The results do not differ that much when w_{L3} is taken to be equal to the average wage of scientific and research enterprises in the state sector only instead of taking it to be equal to the average wage of such enterprises belonging to both state- owned and non-state owned sectors.

33   The rural nominal *wage* is computed from data on rural nominal *income*. It is true that not all of rural income may fall under the category of wages. However, capital intensity of the Chinese agriculture is still very low. Also, Chinese farmers have the land basically for free and do not have to pay for the use of land. These two circumstances together may justify taking income as a proxy for wages. Finally, even if one was skeptical about the above two arguments, there are no available data that would allow us to separate out capital income from wage in the rural income. This makes the assumption of equality between rural income and rural wage almost unavoidable. No wonder therefore that almost all related studies make this assumption.

34   The shares are computed following equations (6a) and (6b).

35   To the extent that the value of capital stock is unknown, various proxies are used. For example, in computing initial capital stock for 1960, Hall and Jones (1999, p. 89, ff. 5) takes g_o to be "the average geometric growth rate from 1960 to 1970 of the investment series."

36   This data series from 1978 are available in "The Gross Domestic Product of China 1952–1995" and "China Statistical Yearbook" (various years)

37   This can be clearly seen from the following expression of capital share, $\beta = MP_K * \left(\frac{K}{Y} \right)$. Clearly, if (K/Y) goes up while β remains unchanged, MP_K has to fall.

38   This finding regarding lack of capital deepening is not new. Earlier researchers have also been struck by this. For example, Hu and Khan (1997a, p. 3) make the following comment in this regard:

> although the capital stock grew by nearly 7 percent a year over 1979–94, the capital-output ratio has hardly budged. In other words, despite a huge expenditure on capital, production of goods and services per unit of capital remained about the same. This pronounced lack of capital deepening suggests a constrained role for capital.

However, this constancy (or decline) of capital-output ratio contradicts rising ICOR reported by many researchers. This apparent contradiction may be the result of the fact that the rise on ICOR is too recent a phenomenon to affect the average capital-output ratio appreciably. However, more research is necessary to shed light on this and related issues.

39   The capital stock (value of fixed assets) of NSEs is calculated by subtracting the value of fixed assets of SOEs from the value of total fixed assets of the Manufacturing sector as a whole. Similarly, the profit-plus-tax of NSEs is computed by subtracting the profit-plus-tax of SOEs from the corresponding total for the Manufacturing sector as a whole.

40   The TFPGR results presented in Islam, Dai, and Sakamoto (2006) were obtained following the Hybird route.

41   Some observers point to the lack of ownership over land as one reason why requisite investments in agriculture are not forthcoming.

42   Needless to say, lack of data prevents us from disaggregation of the "Other" sector into SOE and NSE parts. However, given that most of the "Other" sector belongs to the NSE part of the economy, this may not matter much.

43   The following observations by Hu and Khan (1997b) may help understand the reasons

causing the differences in rate of return to capital obtained from NIA and CIESY sources:

> The Chinese authorities regularly undertake fixed asset surveys for the state-owned sector, obtaining information on (1) gross stock of fixed assets valued at the original acquisition prices of the respective assets; and (2) the stock of fixed assets valued at current prices in the survey years, net of depreciation. In comparing the net stock value series, as reported by the official asset surveys, with the capital stock estimated using cumulated investment flows and the official depreciation table for the state-owned sector, large discrepancies emerge. One possible explanation is that the state owned enterprises (SOEs) and other state entities fail to use consistent price deflators for those asset surveys. Another possible reason is that official surveys suffer from serious reporting errors and omissions. In any event such official surveys are not conducted for urban collective and rural agricultural sectors, and thus do not cover the economy as a whole. (p. 110)

This difficulty was also mentioned in the shorter version of Hu and Khan (1997a, p. 8): "Chinese asset surveys do not produce capital stock estimates consistent with the investment data in the national accounts. The difficulties of bridging this gap are considerable."

44 However, it needs to be noted that under the CIESY approach the average $TFPGR_d$ value (3.68 percent) for 1991–2002 period proves to be higher than its value (2.67) for the 1978–1984 period, showing that the dual approach *per se* is not the reason for reversal of the acceleration result.

45 This shows that choice of sub-periods for comparison is important. That is also why we present all the yearly growth rates, so that readers can choose for comparison any other sub-period that they may be interested in.

References

Abramovitz, Moses. 1962. "Economic Growth in the United States," *American Economic Review*, Vol. 52, No. 4 (September), pp. 762–782.

Barro, Robert and Jong-Wha Lee. 1997. "International Measures of Schooling Years and Schooling Quality," *American Economic Review*, Papers and Proceedings, Vol. 86, No. 2, pp. 218–223.

Barro, Robert and Jong-Wha Lee. 2000. International Data on Educational Attainment: Updates and Implications, CID Working Paper, No. 42, Harvard, April.

Borensztein, Eduardo and Jonathan D. Ostry. 1996. "Accounting for China's Growth Performance," *American Economic Review*, Papers and Proceedings, Vol. 86, No. 2, pp. 224–228.

Chow, Gregory C. 1993. "Capital Formation and Economic Growth in China," *Quarterly Journal of Economics*, Vol. 3, No. 3, pp. 809–842.

Chow, Gregory C. and Kui-Wai Li. 2002. "China's Economic Growth: 1952–2010," *Economic Development and Cultural Change*, Vol. 51, No.1, pp. 247–256.

Diamond, Peter A. 1965. "Technical Change and the Measurement of Capital and Output," *Review of Economic Studies*, Vol. 32, No. 4, 92 (October), pp. 289–298.

Ezaki, Mitsuo and Lin Sun. 1999. "Growth Accounting in China for National, Regional, and Provincial Economies: 1981–1995," *Asian Economic Journal*, Vol. 13, No. 1, pp. 39–73.

Griliches, Zvi and Dale W. Jorgenson. 1967. "The Explanation of Productivity Change," *Review of Economic Studies*, Vol. 34, No. 99 (July), pp. 249–283.

Hall, Robert E., and Charles I. Jones. 1999. "Why Do Some Countries Produce So Much More Output than Others?", *Quarterly Journal of Economics*, Vol. 114, pp. 83–116.

Hsieh, Chang-Tai. 1999. "Productivity Growth and Factor Prices in East Asia," *American Economic Review (Papers and Proceedings)*, Vol. 89, No. 2 (May), pp. 133–138.

Hsieh, Chang-Tai. 2002. "What Explains the Industrial Revolution in East Asia? Evidence from Factor Markets," *American Economic Review*, Vol. 92, No. 3 (June), pp. 502–526.

Hsueh, Tien-Tung and Qiang Li (eds.) 1999. *China's National Income: 1952–1995*, Boulder: Westview Press.

Hulten, Charles R. 2000. Total Factor Productivity: a Short Biography, NBER Working Paper, No. 7471.

Hu, Zuliu and Mohsin Khan. 1997a. "Why is China is Growing So Fast?" *Economic Issues*, No. 8, pp. 1–10. Washington, D.C.: International Monetary Fund.

Hu, Zuliu and Mohsin Khan. 1997b. "Why is China Growing So Fast? *IMF Staff Papers*," Vol. 44, No. 1, pp. 103–131. Washington, D.C.: The International Monetary Fund.

Islam, Nazrul. 1999. "International Comparison of Total Factor Productivity: A Review," *Review of Income and Wealth*, Series 45, No. 4 (December), pp. 493–518.

Islam, Nazrul. 2003. "Productivity Dynamics in a Large Sample of Countries," *Review of Income and Wealth*, Series 49, No. 2 (June), pp. 247–273.

Islam, Nazrul, Erbiao Dai and Hiroshi Sakamoto. 2006. "Role of TFP in China's Growth," *Asian Economic Journal*, Vol. 20, No. 2 (June), pp. 127–159.

Jin, Hehui, Yingyi Qian and Barry R. Weingast. 2005. "Regional Decentralization, and Fiscal Incentives: Federalism, Chinese Style," *Journal of Public Economics*, Vol. 89, pp. 1719–1742.

Jorgenson, Dale W. and Zvi Griliches. 1967. "The Explanation of Productivity Change," *Review of Economic Studies*, Vol. 34, pp. 349–383.

Jorgenson, Dale W., Frank Gollop and Barbara Fraumeni. 1987. *Productivity and US Economic Growth*, Cambridge: Harvard University Press.

Krugman, Paul. 1994. "The Myth of Asia's Miracle," *Foreign Affairs*, Vol. 73, No. 6, pp. 62–78.

Li, Hongin and Li-An Zhou. 2005. "Political Turnover and Economic Performance: The Incentive Role of Personnel Control in China," *Journal of Public Economics*, Vol. 89, pp. 1743–1762.

National Bureau of Statistics of China. 2003. *China Industry Economy Statistical Yearbook (CIESY)*, Beijing: China Statistics Press.

National Bureau of Statistics of China. Various years. *China Labour Statistical Yearbook (CLSY)*, Beijing: China Statistics Press.

National Bureau of Statistics of China. Various years. *China Statistical Yearbook (CSY)*, Beijing: China Statistics Press.

National Bureau of Statistics of China. 1999. *Comprehensive Statistical Data and Materials on 50 Years of New China, 1949–98*, Beijing: China Statistics Press.

National Bureau of Statistics of China. 1997. *The Gross Domestic Product of China 1952–1995*, Beijing: China Statistics Press.

Nogami, K. and Li K. 1995. An Analysis of China's Economic Growth: Estimation of TFP in the Chinese Industrial Sector, ICSEAD (International Centre of Study for East Asian Development) Working Paper 95–1, Kitakyushu.

Phelps, Edmund S. and Charlotte Phelps. 1966. "Factor Price Frontier Estimation of a Vintage Production Model," *Review of Economics and Statistics*, Vol. 48, No. 3 (August), pp. 261–265.

Population Census Office (PCO) under the State Council & Department of Population, Social, Science and Technology Statistics (DPSSTS) of National Bureau of Statistics of China. 2002. *Tabulation on the 2000 Population Census of the People's Republic of China*, Beijing: China Statistics Press.

Population Census Office (PCO) under the State Council & Department of Population Statistics (DPS) of State Statistical Bureau. 1993. *Tabulation on the 1990 Population Census of the People's Republic of China*, Beijing: China Statistics Press.

Population Census Office (PCO) under the State Council & Department of Population Statistics (DPS) of State Statistical Bureau. 1985. *Tabulation on the 1982 Population Census of the People's Republic of China*, Beijing: China Statistics Press.

Rawski, Thomas G., and Yuxin Zheng (eds.) 1993 *Productivity and Reform in Chinese Industry*, Beijing: Social Science Doc. Publishing Co.

Ren, Rouen. 1995. China's Economic Performance in International Perspective, OECD Development Centre manuscript. Paris: OECD Development Centre.

Sachs, Jeffrey D., and Wing-Thye Woo. 2000. "Understanding China's Economic Performance," *Journal of Policy Reform*, Vol. 4, No. 1, pp. 1–50.

Samuelson, Paul A. 1962. "Parable and Realism in Capital Theory: The Surrogate Production Function," *Review of Economic Studies*, Vol. 29, No. 3, 80 (June), pp. 193–206.

Siegel, Irving H. 1952. *Concepts and Measurement of Production and Productivity*, Washington: US Bureau of Labor Statistics.

Shapiro, Matthew D. 1987. "Are Cyclical Fluctuation in Productivity Due More to Supply Shocks or Demand Shocks?" *American Economic Review*, Papers and Proceedings, Vol. 77, No. 2 (May), pp. 118–124.

State Statistical Bureau (SSB). 1997. *The Gross Domestic Product of China 1952–1995*, Dalian: Dongbei University of Finance and Economics Press.

Wang, Yan and Yudong Yao. 2001. Sources of China's Economic Growth: 1952–99: Incorporating Human Capital Accumulation, Policy Research Working Paper 2650. Washington, D.C.: World Bank, Development Research Group.

Woo, Wing-Thye. 1998. "Chinese Economic Growth: Sources and Prospects," in Michel Fouquin and Francoise, Lemoine. (ed.), *The Chinese Economy*, London: Economica.

Young, Alwyn. 1992. Tale of Two Cities: Factor Accumulation and Technical Change in Hong Kong and Singapore, NBER Macroeconomics Annual 1992, Cambridge, MA; and London: MIT Press.

Young, Alwyn. 1995. "The Tyranny of Numbers: Confronting the Statistical Realities of the East Asian Growth Experience," *Quarterly Journal of Economics*, Vol. 110, No. 3 (August), pp. 641–680.

Young, Alwyn. 2003. "Gold into Base Metals: Productivity Growth in the People's Republic of China during the Reform Period," *Journal of Political Economy*, Vol. 111, No. 6 pp. 1220–1261.

12
Environmental and Resource Implications of Chinese Growth: Current Trends and Future Prospects

Xizhe Peng, Kexi Pan, and Juan Yu

12.1   Introduction

China is a country rich in natural resources. However, due to its large population size, the per capita availability of many essential natural resources is much less than the corresponding world average. For instance, China's per capita availability of water, arable land, and mineral resources is only 28, 32, and 50 percent of the corresponding global levels. As the result of her remarkable economic growth, China's consumption of natural resources has increased very rapidly over the last few decades. Among 45 major natural resources that are essential for industrial development, one quarter has already been in shortage of supply. The shortage of key natural resources is viewed as one of the critical constraints on China's future economic growth.

China supports approximately 20 percent of the world's population but has only 7 percent of the world's arable land. In 2003 China had 123.39 million hectares of cultivated land, implying per capita arable land availability of only 0.095 hectare, which was much lower than the corresponding world average. Not only are opportunities for expanding cultivated area limited, but as a result of rapid economic development, population growth, agricultural restructuring and urbanization, China is actually experiencing a decline in cultivated area. It was reported that the net reduction of cultivated land in 2003 was 2.5374 million hectares.[1] By contrast, land for residential, industrial and mining has grown continuously. This trend is likely to cause a decline in agricultural production. Partly as a result of shrinking cultivated area, grain production in China has dropped from the recent peak of 512 million tones in 1998 to 457 million tones in 2002. To produce sufficient food to feed the increasing population remains a hard task of the Chinese government. A series of strict measures have been promulgated for protection of cultivated land. Both institutional and technological innovations and efficient resource allocation will be necessary to meet this development need.

During the past few decades, China has experienced many changes in her energy consumption patterns in both quantitative and qualitative terms. For the first time in 2003, China has become the second largest energy consumer, after the United States and surpassing Japan. This change has been brought about mainly by two factors. The first is population growth and demographic changes, including changes in age composition and household size. The second is increase in the level and intensity of economic activity. Energy consumption will continue to increase in the next few decades and there will be an increasing demand on external sources of energy.

At present, coal meets 65 percent of China's primary energy consumption. While coal's share of China's energy consumption is projected to fall, coal consumption will increase in absolute terms. The demand for oil, currently at 5.56 million barrels per day, is increasing rapidly, and is projected to reach 12.8 million barrels per day by 2025.

Caused by economic growth and rise in per capita income, household energy consumption is expected to increase throughout mainland China. In the backward areas of China, households still rely largely on non-commercial energy, particularly on bio-fuels, such as wood-fuel, crop and livestock residues, and charcoal.

As already mentioned, per capita water availability in China is only about one quarter of the world average and is projected to further decline. Per capita water availability in 1995 was 2,295 cubic meters, and is likely to decline by 2030 to only 1,700 cubic meters, a generally acknowledged danger limit. To make matter worse, water resources in China are distributed unevenly. Most of the surface water (77 percent) comes from the 7 major river systems, and 90 percent of the population is concentrated in the basins of these rivers. According to government reports, China consumed 549.7 billion cubic meters of water in 2002. Of this total, urban residents used 5.8 percent, rural farmers 5.4 percent, industries 20.8 percent, and agriculture and other primary productions used 68 percent. In 2002, China's urban residents used 219 liters per capita per day, while rural farmers consumed an average of 94 liters per capita per day. The urbanization process, together with population growth, will therefore increase the demand for water, worsening the already severe shortage of water in the north and northwest parts of China.

This chapter examines the issue of environmental and resource constraints on Chinese growth. There is an apprehension that China's rapid growth is leading to resource shortages at the global level. To examine the question, this chapter uses the concept of "ecological footprint", which is an index of how much land and water resource is required for the population to produce what it consumes and to absorb its wastes, under the prevailing technology.[2] The chapter shows that, by this measure, China is already running "ecological deficit," which may get more serious over time. The chapter also points to the marked variation in this regard across Chinese provinces. In order to address the issue of resource constraints, the chapter next examines in some detail China's demand and supply of several key resources. Meeting China's future energy and resource requirements in a peaceful way is one of most important issues facing China in the near future.

12.2   Ecological footprints[3]

Ecological footprint is a framework developed by Mathis Wackernagel and his colleagues to examine the relationship between population, development and resources.[4] The ecological footprint is also a resource management tool designed to generate aggregate information on a population's past and present demand on nature.

The time series of ecological footprint and biocapacity have been calculated for the period between 1961 and 2001 and presented in Figure 12.1. It demonstrates a sharp rise of mainland China's total ecological footprint and a much slower rise of its biocapacity, together leading to an ecological deficit around 1979. In 2001, China's total ecological footprint ranked 75th in the world, a figure well below the world average. However, due to its huge population size, causing low per capita biocapacity, its ecological deficit is much higher than the world average. Mainland China is using natural resource by 43 percent more than the regenerate capacity of its ecosystem. A large population and rapid economic growth will worsen the situation.

The changes in ecological footprint and biocapacity are the results of multi-dimensional influence of population, consumption, and technology. A further analysis reveals the relationship between the economic development, population growth and ecosystem balance in different phases, and demonstrates the influence that economic and population policies can exert.

Figure 12.2 compares China's production footprint and consumption footprint with her per capita biocapacity. It shows that per capita biocapacity fell with time, while the average ecological footprint rose, leading to an increasing gap, which peaked in 1996. The decomposition exercise shows that population growth and

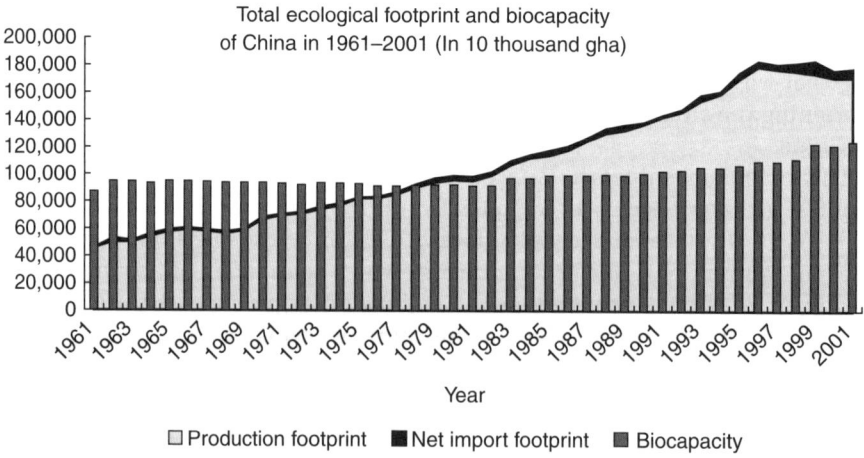

Figure 12.1   Total production footprints, net-import footprints, biocapacity of Mainland China in different years

Source: Liu Yuhui & Peng Xizhe (2004), *Acta Ecologica Sinica*, 10

consumption change contributed to 56 and 11 percent of the rise of ecological footprint, while technological development offset 21 percent of this rise.

Similar analysis has been carried out at the provincial level. By comparing the biocapacity and production footprint, a basic sustainability assessment across China's provinces can be made (Figure 12.3). The analysis reveals that the production footprint of most provinces exceeds their biocapacity. In other words, most provinces are in a situation of "ecological overshooting."

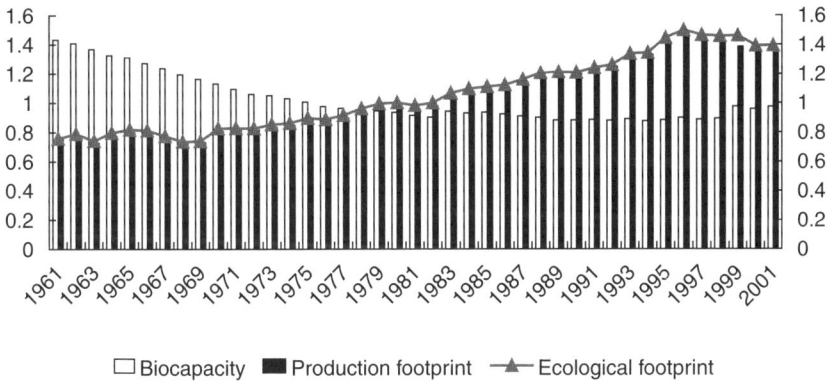

Figure 12.2 Per capita production footprint, ecological footprint, biological capacity of Mainland China in different years

Source: Liu Yuhui & Peng Xizhe (2004), *Acta Ecologica Sinica*, 10

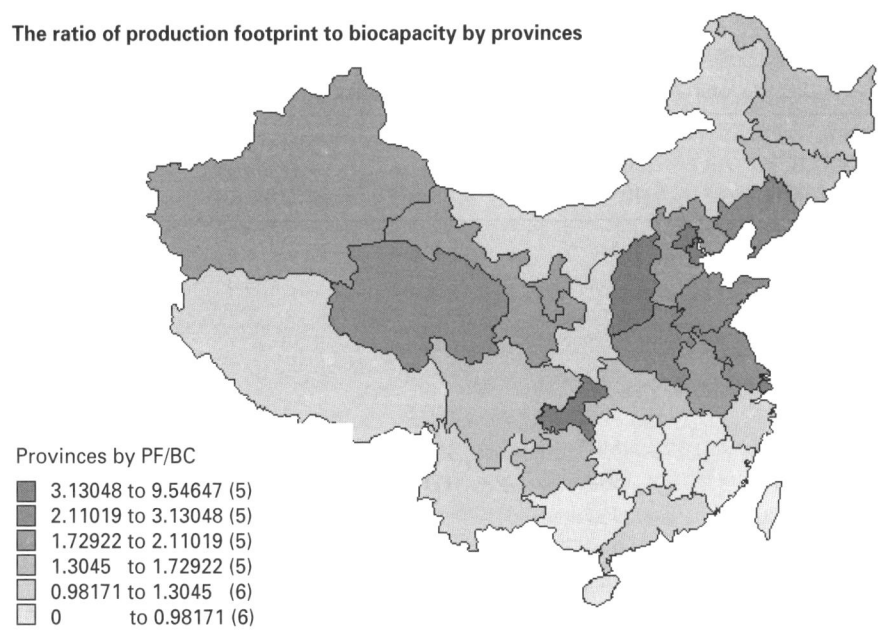

Figure 12.3 The ratio of production footprint to biocapacity

Source: Liu Yuhui & Peng Xizhe (2004), Acta Ecologica Sinica, 10

There are however remarkable regional and rural-urban variation in this regard. It may be observed that the population of wealthy urban centers extend their eco-footprints deep into backward rural areas. People in rich areas and high income groups contribute disproportionately to the ecological deficit. The ecological footprint of a low-income household is much less than that of a wealthier one. In 2004, the average income of urban residents in China was 3.23 times that of rural residents, causing rural and urban consumption patterns to differ markedly. It is reported that consumption in six major Chinese cities, including Beijing and Shanghai, accounted for one fifth of China's total annual consumption in 2004. It is therefore clear that as China urbanizes, her ecological footprint and deficit is likely to grow even faster in the near future.

12.3   Water resource and consumption

Water resource includes both surface water and groundwater, with precipitation being the main source of recharge. With 2711.5 billion cubic meters of annual river runoff, 828.8 billion cubic meters of annual groundwater resources, and 727.9 billion cubic meters of overlapping volume between them, the volume of total water resources in China is 2812.4 billion cubic meters. The five northern river basins in total have 535.8 billion cubic meters of annual total water resources, accounting for 19 percent of the national total, and the four southern river basins provide 2276.6 billion cubic meters, 81 percent of the national total. Table 12.1 shows the annual total water resources by river basin. It can be seen that the status of water resources varies greatly across river basins, resulting in

Table 12.1   Annual total water resource by river basin

River basin	Surface water resource (10^9 m^3)	Groundwater resource (10^9 m^3)	Total water resource (10^9 m^3)	Water yield module (10^9 m^3/km^3)
China	2711.5	828.8	2812.4	294.6
Songhua-Liao River	165.3	62.5	192.8	155.6
Haihe River	28.8	26.5	42.1	132.4
Huaihe River	74.1	39.3	96.1	289.5
Yellow River	66.1	40.6	74.4	93
Yangtze River	951.3	246.4	961.3	534.4
Pearl River	468.5	111.6	470.8	816
Southeast Rivers	255.7	61.3	259.2	1080.8
Southwest Rivers	585.3	154.4	583.3	687.5
Inland Rivers	166.4	86.2	130.4	38.6

Source: The Ministry of Water Resources of PRC, *Water Resources in China*.

uneven distribution of water resources, with serious water shortage in some areas, particularly in the northern and northwestern parts of China.

China is among the countries with the longest history of building water resources projects. Among the splendid historical achievements are the legendary flood harnessing led by the Great Yu, the construction of flood prevention embankments along the Yellow River during the Spring and Autumn Period (BC 770–BC 476), the Grand Canal, and the Dujiang Weir irrigation system, , all showing the importance of water projects in the development of the Chinese nation.

Since the 1949 revolution, China continued her tradition of large scale water projects. By 2000, China built 85,000 dams, with a total water storage capacity of 518 billion cubic meters. Of these, 397 are large-sized with a total storage capacity of 326.7 billion cubic meters and another 2,634 are medium-sized with a total storage capacity of 72.9 billion cubic meters.[5] China's water engineering achievements also include 270,000 kilometers of river embankments and 7,900 kilometers of sea embankments, 31,742 sluices, 98 flood storage or detention zones for the Yangtze, the Yellow and the Huai rivers, with a total area of 34,500 square kilometers and a total storage capacity of 100 billion cubic meters.

The Three Gorges Project (TGP) is one of the key projects for improvement and development of the Yangtze River. The construction of the main body of the Three Gorges Water Conservancy Complex includes 102.83 million cubic meters of rock-and-earth excavation and installation of 26 turbine-generator units, each with a capacity of 700 mega watts. The project can effectively adjust the upstream flood of the Yangtze River. Although there are concerns regarding its ecological and environmental impact, the TGP will provide China with an annual average power supply of up to 84.7 TWH (Terawatt Hour), helping thereby to reduce the current power shortage. By not requiring China to obtain this additional power supply from coal fired power stations, and thus allowing to avoid aggravation of acid rain and Green House Gas (GHG) emission, TGP may have a benign influence on China's environment, particularly that of East and Central China. Balancing the rapidly increasing demand for hydro-electric power with the need to preserve the local ecology and environment is a difficult challenge facing Chinese decision makers, hydraulic engineers, environmentalists and local populations.

The total water use in China in 2002 was 549.7 billion cubic meters including 440.4 billion cubic meters of surface water, 107.2 billion groundwater, and 2.1 billion cubic meters of water from other sources. There are in place large water transfer projects affecting the water use in some river basins. For example, 4.6 billion cubic meters of water was transferred from the Yellow River to the Hai River, and 6.09 billion cubic meters and 2.03 billion cubic meters, respectively, from the Yangtze and the Yellow to the Huai River. Water used in a year also depends on the available water storage at the end of last year, precipitation and river flow in the current year.

The ratio of the water use to the volume of water available is used to examine the current degree of exploitation of water resources in a river basin. The overall exploitation of water resources in China is at present not very high, standing at about 19.5 percent in 2000. (Table 12.2) However, the exploitation ratio for the

Table 12.2 Water uses in 2000 and degree of exploitation of water resources by river basin

| River basin | Water use (10^9 m³) | | | Total water use | Water resources (10^9 m³) | Degree of exploit-ation (%) |
	Surface water	Ground water	Others			
China	440.436	107.242	2.049	549.728	2812.4	19.5
Songhua-Liao River	30.751	25.853	0.00	56.604	192.8	29.4
Haihe River	12.795	27.017	0.171	39.983	42.1	95.0
Huaihe River	42.084	18.947	0.187	61.218	96.1	63.7
Yellow River	25.130	13.544	0.187	38.861	74.4	52.2
Yangtze River	159.368	8.174	0.689	168.231	961.3	17.5
Pearl River	80.502	4.169	0.408	85.078	470.8	18.1
Southeast Rivers	30.886	0.895	0.150	31.931	259.2	12.3
Southwest Rivers	9.933	0.278	0.119	10.330	583.3	1.8
Inland Rivers	48.988	8.365	0.138	57.491	130.4	44.1

Source: The Ministry of Water Resources of PRC, *Water Resources in China*

Hai, Huai, and Yellow River basins were much higher than the national average, indicating a very high degree of exploitation of river water in those basins.

Of the 549.7 billion cubic meters of water used in China in 2000, 373.6 billion cubic meters were used for agriculture, accounting for 68 percent of the total, and 90.3 percent of agricultural water use was for irrigation. Of the rest, 114.2 billion cubic meters were used for industries, accounting for 20.8 percent, and 61.9 billion cubic meters for domestic uses, accounting for 11.2 percent. Agriculture (irrigation) remains the biggest water user, but its share has been declining since the 1980s, while industrial and domestic water uses have increased rapidly (Table 12.3).

12.4   Challenges regarding water resources

In the last more than 50 years, the capacity of controlled water supply in China has increased by about five times. However China still faces a serious challenge in the development and utilization of water resources.

First of all, there is an increasing gap between water supply and demand. This is primarily caused by the growth of population, progress in industrialization and urbanization, and also global climate change. At present, the annual water shortage for the agricultural sector in the country as a whole is about 30 billion cubic meters, and the annual average area of farmland affected by drought is

Table 12.3 Water uses and water consumption by river basin in 2000 (10^9 m^3)

River basin	Agriculture	Industry	Domestic	Total water use	Water consumption	Consumption rate (%)
China	373.618	114.236	61.874	549.728	298.5	54
Songhua-Liao River	40.825	10.517	5.262	56.604	31.0	55
Haihe River	28.649	6.179	5.154	39.983	27.9	70
Huaihe River	44.739	9.321	7.158	61.218	39.3	64
Yellow River	29.896	5.472	3.493	38.861	22.0	57
Yangtze River	93.389	53.290	21.552	168.231	76.2	32
Pearl River	54.916	18.256	11.907	85.078	39.3	46
Southeast Rivers	18.439	9.011	4.481	31.931	16.5	52
Southwest Rivers	8.757	0.642	0.932	10.330	7.1	69
Inland Rivers	54.007	1.548	1.935	57.491	39.0	68

Source: The Ministry of Water Resources of PRC, *Water Resources in China*, also see: www.chinagate.com.cn

20 million hm^2, resulting in an average grain yield reduction of between 10 to 25 billion kilograms. The annual water shortage in the urban area and industrial sector is about 6 billion cubic meters, resulting in an estimated reduction in industrial output by 230 billion RMB Yuan. Among the 660 cities in China, there are more than 400 suffering from water shortage, affecting 160 million people.

Over the last ten years, the total rainfall in China declined by 1.1 per cent compared to the normal years.[6] Water resources in northern China have been decreasing over the last 20 years as the average annual runoffs in the Yellow, Huai and Hai Rivers have dropped by 10 to 40 percent. Consequently, drought and water scarcity have become a bottle-neck for economic development, particularly in the Northern provinces of China. It is predicted that by 2030, per capita water supply in China may drop from the current 2,250 m^3 to 1,700 m^3, a level that as per World Bank's definition would designate China as a water scarce country.[7]

As already mentioned, the uneven distribution of water resources, arable land, population, and economic activities makes the situation worse. There are sufficient water resources and insufficient land in the South but abundant land and insufficient water in the North[8]. As much as 80.4 percent of water resources in China are distributed in the Yangtze River basin and to the south of it, which is an area that contains 53.5 percent of the population and 35.2 percent of the farmland and contributes 54.8 percent of the national GDP. Water availability in this area is 3,480 m^3 per capita and 4,300 m^3 per mu (1/15 of a hectare). By comparison, areas to the north of the Yangtze basin contains 44.4 percent of the population and 59.2 percent of the farmland, and contributes 43.4 percent of the national GDP. However, this area has only 14.7 percent of the country's water resources, which amount to a water availability of 747 m^3 per capita and 471 m^3 per mu. In the plain areas of the lower reaches of the Yellow, Huai and Hai rivers, the average per capita water use is only 332 cubic meters and the annual water shortage is up to 18 billion cubic meters ranking these areas among those with the most serious water shortage in China. In addition, there are more than 24 million rural people without access to adequate drinking water supply.

To solve her water problems, China will need to restructure her entire economy to make it more water efficient. As observed by the Worldwatch Institute, it is necessary to shift to more water-efficient crops and livestock products, move to less water-intensive energy sources, and make big jumps in saving water used in the industrial sector.[9]

Ensuring grain security for 1.3 billion Chinese is always a key task for the government. China's policy is to raise water use efficiency and guarantee water supply for agricultural production through water saving, so as to realize zero-increase of total water consumption in the agricultural sector.[10] It is reported that in the last decade, 30 billion cubic meters of water was saved annually, while agricultural production capacity has increased by 40 billion kilograms. China plans to increase its water-saving irrigation areas by 10 million hectares by 2010. Despite these gains, China lags behind many developed countries in terms of water efficiency. In 2000, China's national integrated irrigation water efficiency was 0.43, as compared to 0.7 for developed countries. Similarly, the rate of industrial water reuse in China was 0.55, as compared to 0.75 to 0.85 in developed countries. The average amount of water consumed nationwide in China in order to produce industrial added value of 10,000 RMB Yuan (about US$1,280) in 2005 was 169 cubic meters, which was about five to ten times higher than in developed countries.[11] As expected, there are regional variations in this regard. For example, in hinterland provinces, such as Guizhou, Anhui and Hunan, water consumption for 10,000 Yuan of industrial added value exceeded 360 cubic meters, while in coastal Shandong Province,and the cities of Tianjin and Beijing, the analogous requirement was only 23, 24, and 38 cubic meters, respectively.[12]

The currently implemented South-to-North Water Transfer Project is another huge water engineering project aimed at solving the water shortage in northern China while professedly observing the following principles: (a) water saving, (b) pollution control, and (c) protection of ecology and environment. The project includes the Western Route Project (WRP), the Middle Route Project (MRP), and the Eastern Route Project (ERP) to divert water from the upper, middle, and lower reaches of the Yangtze River, respectively, to meet the developing requirements of the Northwest and North China. By the end of 2006, a total of 21 billion RMB Yuan has already been invested in the project.[13] However, the project remains disputed on both ecological and efficiency grounds, and it has been pointed out that the achievements of engineering methods in China's water management must now be accompanied by institutional reforms in water policy.[14]

Apart from the water shortage, there are other problems in China's water sector, including water pollution, flood control, and erosion. China is among the countries of the world with the most serious soil erosion. As in other countries, in China human activities have combined with natural factors to aggravate the problem. Since the founding of the People's Republic of China, the Chinese government has invested a lot of resources in soil erosion control, but the problem continues to worsen. According to the second national survey of soil erosion, conducted using remote sensing, the area currently affected by soil erosion in China as a whole was 3.56 million square kilometers[15] accounting for 37 percent of the country's land area. In some areas, particularly the western areas, there has been an acceleration of the ecological deterioration process. In other parts, ecologically damaging activities coexist with remedial efforts.

Serious flooding remains a threat to millions of the Chinese people. The capacity for flood control in China is still limited. Most of the current embankments along the major rivers of the country are designed to withstand flooding that may occur in every ten to twenty years. The development of flood storage and retention zones has lagged behind the plan. Since the early 1990s, incidence of extraordinary floods has increased, resulting in a total economic loss of about 1,000 billion RMB Yuan. Floods occurring in 1998 in the Yangtze and Songhua river basins alone caused a direct economic loss of more than 250 billion Yuan.

China is a country with a large number of wetlands. However, under pressure from population growth and economic development, the wetlands have been shrinking and deteriorating. In the last few decades, the total area of lakes in the country has decreased by 1.30 million hm^2, and on average 20 lakes have disappeared each year. The over-exploitation of river flow in the major rivers results in silting up of river channels or mouths, drying up of their middle or lower reaches and lakes in these areas, reduction or disappearance of natural vegetation, desertification, and serious damage to aquatic wildlife. Meanwhile, groundwater overdraft has created 72 depression cones in China, with a total area of 61,000 square kilometers causing ground subsidence, cracking, and other geological hazards and environmental problems.

The natural quality of river flows in China is generally good, but the rivers have been polluted to a great extent as a consequence of human activities, including increased discharge of domestic, industrial, and agricultural waste. According to a research conducted by the US Department of Commerce, the total discharge of sewage and wastewater in China was 62 billion tons in 2000 of which only 24 percent was treated up to the national standard, and the rest was not treated or treated inadequately before being discharged or used for farmland irrigation.[16] The same report also shows that about half of the major rivers and more than 75 percent of the lakes have been polluted. An investigation on drinking water of 118 cities indicates that of 97 percent of them the groundwater is polluted and for 64 percent of them the pollution is serious. Growing pollution of water bodies therefore remains to be a serious challenge facing China in the future.

12.5   Availability of energy resources (fossil fuels)

The general situation of China with regard to oil and gas resources may be characterized as follows: insufficient quantity, per capita shortage, uneven distribution, and poor quality. By 2001, China had conducted oil and gas exploration in 25 out of her 30 provinces, as well as offshore areas, discovering 576 oil fields and 193 gas fields in 23 oil and gas basins and setting up 25 oil and gas production bases (Table 12.4).

In 2002, the average explored ratio in China for oil was only 42.5 percent as compared with the world's 73 percent, and the average explored ratio for gas was 24.5 percent, as compared with 60 percent on average for the world. Recent exploration has been focusing on areas that are geologically complicated, and hence involve greater difficulty and higher technical requirements. Explored reserves and output in offshore areas have been increasing steadily. The offshore oil production in China began in 1967 and by 2001 produced 18.72 million tons, accounting for 11.5 percent of national output.

As of 2002, China's remaining proven oil reserve was 2.5 billion tons, ranking 11th in the world. The remaining proven gas reserve of China was 1,510 billion cubic meters, ranking 21st in the world. China's R/P ratio[17] for oil was 15 versus the world's 40.6, while the ratio for gas was 46.3 and 60.7 for China and the world, respectively. Since the 1990s, China's explored oil reserves have increased by 0.75 to 0.8 billion ton annually. Nevertheless, the per capita remaining proven reserves of oil and gas in China are rather low, only 8 and 6 percent of the world's average, respectively.

China's oil and gas exploration and exploitation are mainly conducted in large-scale basins such as Songliao and Bohai Gulf, and some medium and small-scale basins such as Jiuquan and Erlian. Oil and gas in offshore is concentrated in seven basins, namely Bohai Sea, Southern Yellow Sea, East Sea, Pearl River Estuary, Southern Qiong Sea, Yingge Sea, and Beibu Gulf. On the whole, China's oil and gas reserves are located geographically in undeveloped areas of China. In terms of

Table 12.4   Overview of China's oil and gas resources/reserves

		Total geological resources	Explored geological reserves	Proved reserves	Remained proved reserves
Oil (10^8 tons)	Inland	874	202.69	59	22
	Offshore	225	14.9	3.53	2.21
	Total	1,099	217.59	62.53	24.21
Gas (10^8 m³)	Inland	391,300	25,563	17,000	12,560
	Offshore	157,900	4,460	2,830	2,540
	Total	549,200	30,023	19,830	15,100

Source: China Energy Development Report 2001.

quality, conventional oil accounts for 56.45 percent of total explored oil, and the remaining 43.55 percent are unconventional oil, with hypo-osmotic and viscous oil accounting for 22.41 and 21.14 percent, respectively.

Coal resources account for 95 percent of Chinese total fossil energy and 90 percent of the reserves. According to the latest statistics of China National Administration of Coal and Geology (CNACG), the total volume of coal resources of China is about 5.57 trillion tons, of which more than 1 trillion tons have been identified. China probably has the largest coal resources in the world, comprising about 1/4 of the global total. However, China's coal resource per capita (774 tons) is far below the world average because of her large population. In terms of proven reserves of coal, China in 2002 ranked third in the world,[18] and accounted for about 11.6 percent of world total. The R/P ratio of coal in China in that year was 82, in contrast to 204 on average for the world.

Every provincial unit of China, except Shanghai, has some kind of coal reserve. Among 2,100 towns across China, more than 1,200 have discovered coal resources, and in over 1,100 towns, exploitation efforts have been carried out. In general, northern China is rich in coal resource, while southern China and eastern China lack coal reserves. Thus, coal-rich regions and major coal-consumption regions are different. For example, coal resources are mainly concentrated in Shanxi, Shaanxi, west Inner Mongolia, north Xinjiang provinces, and areas lying along the boarders along Yunnan-Guizhou-Sichuan. These four provinces are under-developed, but hold 85.3 percent of national coal resources. On the other hand, 13 developed coastal provinces and cities only possess 3.4 percent of China's total coal resources. Also of note is that most of China's coal reserves are located in regions with inhospitable terrain, making it difficult to transport coal from points of origin to points of consumption.

12.6 Production and consumption of energy resources

China has gone through three stages in oil production: (a) a soaring increase from 1950s to 1970s, (b) a steady increase from 1980s to the early 1990s and (c) minor fluctuations in the middle and late 1990s. China's oil output was 160 million ton in 2000, and has since increased to 180 million tons in more recent years (Figure 12.4).

Natural gas industry in China made important strides in terms of both reserves and output over the past years. Explored reserves increased from 559.6 to 3,000 billion cubic meters between 1989 and 2001, and gas output exceeded 25 billion cubic meters in 2000. With completion of such gas transportation projects as "West-to-East" and "Out of Sichuan" in the past years, gas production experienced further rapid growth, mainly in central and western China. Xinjiang autonomous region alone produced more than 20 billion Cubic meters of natural gas in 2006, and the total gas output in China in that year reached 60 billion cubic meters (Figure 12.5).

Production of raw coal increased steadily from year by year until 1996. However, the production shrank between 1997 and 2000 due to the sharp decline in the

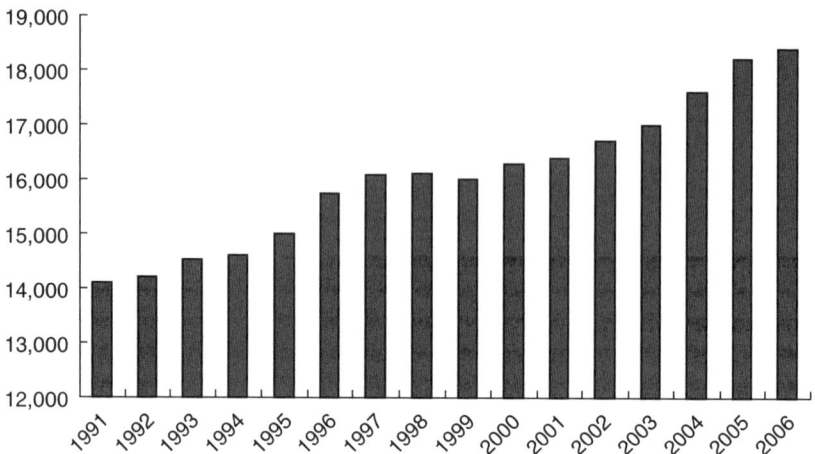

Figure 12. 4   Chinese oil output in recent years (in ten thousand tons)
Source: China Energy Statistical Yearbook, China Statistics Press. Annual 6

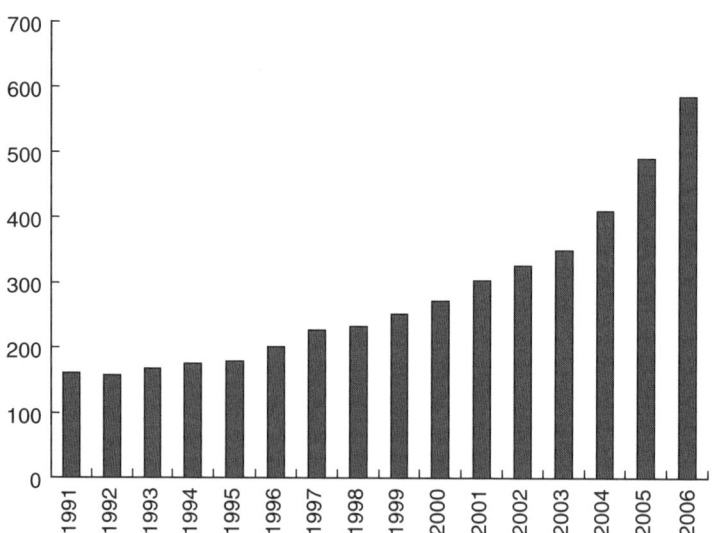

Figure 12.5   Chinese gas output in recent years (10^8 m^3)
Source: China Energy Statistical Yearbook, China Statistics Press. Annual 6

consumption of coals. After 2000, coal production, as well as its share in China's primary energy production, bounced up again (Figure 12.6). China's raw coal output comes mainly from state-owned key mines, but private local mines should not be ignored. In state-owned key mines, excavation is highly mechanized, recovery ratio is high, and safety measures are more strictly implemented. By contrast, private local mines are small and scattered, with low mechanization level

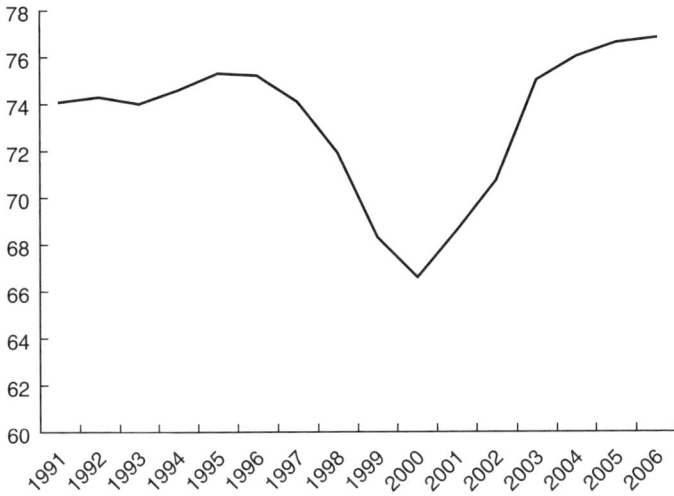

Figure 12.6 Percentage of coal in primary energy production in recent years
Sources: China Energy Statistical Yearbook, China Statistics Press. Annual 6

of excavation. The quality of management of such mines is generally poor, and safety is a big problem. The recovery rate in small mines is only about 10 percent, compared to 30 percent in medium scale mines and above 50 percent in large-scale mines. A lot of coal resources are wasted during the production.

In 2002, China's total primary energy output was 1.387 billion tons of standard coal, the third highest in the world. China's oil output in that year stood at 0.167 billion tons (fifth highest in the world), and natural gas output at 32.66 billion cubic meters (ranking sixteenth), and of raw coal at 1.67 billion tons (highest in the world). China's total energy consumption increased by 4.3 times from 570 million to 2.46 billion tons between 1978 and 2006. In 2006, coal accounted for 69.4 percent of the total energy consumption, oil 20.4 percent, gas 3.0 percent, hydro electricity 6.4 percent, nuclear power 0.8 percent. By comparison with the rest of the world, which derives 25 percent of energy from coal, China's dependence on coal is very high (Figure 12.7).

China's total energy consumption has been rising steadily over the years, with exception for the period of 1997–2000, when it dropped mainly due to the reduction in coal consumption. The second half of 2001 witnessed a shortage of coal supply, prompting recovery of coal production. From 2003 onwards China faced serious regional and seasonal shortages of electricity generation capacity. The shortage contributed to the rapid rise in oil and coal consumption as industrial users turned to diesel generators and small-scale coal-fired plants. While China is importing more to meet her oil demand, the growth in Chinese gas output has been slow. The government has set a target of increasing the share of natural gas in the energy mix to 10 percent by 2020, but this will require a major acceleration of its Liquefied Natural Gas (LNG) imports and other adjustments necessary to

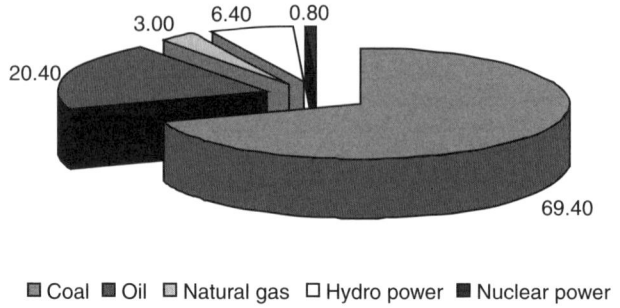

□ Coal ■ Oil □ Natural gas □ Hydro power ■ Nuclear power

Figure 12.7   Consumption of primary energy by type in China in 2006
Source: China Energy Statistical Yearbook, China Statistics Press. Annual 6

orient toward gas and away from coal. So far as coal is concerned, China is able to meet additional need by increasing domestic production (Table 12.5).

It is disconcerting that China's rapid increase in energy consumption is accompanied by low efficiency of energy utilization. The energy requirement of GDP per unit in China is 3.9, 6.3, and 9.2 times higher than that in the United States, Germany and Japan, respectively. The consumption tax on oil in China is extremely low, amounting to only 10 percent of oil price, as compared with 75, 60, and 32 percent in the European Union, Japan, and the United States, respectively. Moreover, China has not paid much attention to the development of oil substituting fuels, such as liquefied coal, biological fuel, and liquefied natural gas. At the same time, poor public transportation systems and surging use of private automobiles have been causing demand for oil to rise rapidly. Unfortunately, China so far has also not been keen in promoting energy-saving and environment-friendly automobiles.

Inefficiency plagues China's coal consumption too. The share of coal used for terminal consumption is too high and is almost ten times of that in developed countries. According to statistics in 2000, the share of coal used in China for power generation was only 41 percent, as compared with 90, 84, and 90 percent in the United States, Australia, and South Africa, respectively.

12.7   China's energy challenge

China has low proved reserves of mineral energy sources to backup her rising demand. Oil consumption in China has more than doubled over the past ten years, and, at some 7m barrels/day is now close to 10 percent of total world consumption. At present, China's per capita energy consumption is 1.7 tons of standard coal, as compared to 11.7 in United States of America, 5.5 in Japan, 6.8 for Organization for Economic Cooperation and Development (OECD) countries, and 2.1 as the world average. However, Chinese energy consumption will continue to

Table 12.5 Oil consumption, import, and export in China from 1993 to 2002 (10⁴ tons)

	1993	1995	1996	1997	1998	1999	2000	2001	2002
Consumption	1,4721.3	1,6064.9	1,7436.2	1,9691.7	1,9817.8	2,1072.9	2,2439	22,838.3	24,242
Import	3,615.7	3,673.2	4,536.9	6,787	5,738.7	6,483.3	9,748.5	8,170	8,976
Export	2,506.5	2,454.5	2,696	2,815.2	2,326.5	1,643.5	2,172	1,679	1,792
Net import:	1,109.2	1,218.7	1,840.9	3,971.8	3,412.2	4,839.8	7,576.5	6,491	7,184
Reliance on import %	7.53	7.59	10.56	20.17	17.22	22.97	33.76	28.29	29.64

Note: Reliance on import is net import divided by consumption of that year.

Data sources: China Energy Statistical Yearbook, International Petroleum Economics Monthly 2003, 3.

rise in the coming years, as the economy grows, putting more pressure on the supplies. Based on current trends, China's per capita energy consumption may exceed 3 tons of standard coal by 2050.

Based on authors' projection, China's oil production will peak during 2010–2020, reaching a total output of about 170–210 million tons, after which oil output will decline to about 100 million tons by 2050. On the consumption side, total oil consumption is projected to reach 320 million tons in 2010, and may reach 630 million tons in 2050. It is therefore clear that the gap between China's consumption and domestic oil production will increase over time (Table 12.6), implying that China will have to rely heavily on oil imports. The dependence on imported oil will make China vulnerable to fluctuations in the world energy market, affecting thereby the stability of her future economic growth.

Responding to the situation, China is making efforts to diversify the source of her oil and gas imports. She is encouraging both state and private oil companies to harness oil and gas supplies both locally and from abroad to meet her rising domestic demand.[19] It is reported that in the first nine months of 2006 China's oil imports rose, compared with a similar period of the previous year, by 24 percent to 3.3m barrels per day. Almost half of this came from traditional suppliers such as Saudi Arabia, Iran and Russia, but increasing amounts of crude oil are now imported from Africa. For example, Angola has now moved up to the third place among China's oil suppliers, and Sudan and Congo (Brazzaville) are ranked sixth and seventh respectively.[20]

China has also become active in investing in foreign oil assets, as it will be more cost-effective to import oil produced by Chinese companies' overseas assets than purchasing from the international market. It is estimated that in 2005, China's oil companies imported about 50 million metric tons of crude oil from their overseas assets, and China's oil companies are expected to double imports of crude oil they produce overseas by the year 2010.[21]

At present, industry consumes two thirds of the total energy in China. The situation will however change, and households will gradually consume more energy than before. An emerging urban middle class and increasing modernization of the national infrastructure have already brought about radical changes in lifestyle, including widespread use of cars. The automobile industry will therefore

Table 12.6 Projection of oil consumption in China, in hundred million tons

	2010	2020	2030	2040	2050
Total demand	3.20	4.20	5.00	5.80	6.30
Domestic production	1.93	1.85	1.63	1.36	1.08
Shortage	1.27	2.35	3.37	4.44	5.22
Self-reliance (%)	60	44	33	23	17

Source: Author's estimation.

has to be a major target for innovating energy-saving technology. In addition, environment-friendly urban planning and introduction of new technology and methods of housing construction should be promoted.

12.8 Energy related environmental problems

China suffers from some serious energy-related environmental problems, such as emissions from inefficient fossil energy uses in urban areas and deforestation caused by wood collecting in rural areas. There is a clear divide in energy consumption pattern between urban and rural China. China's roughly 700 million rural inhabitants still use traditional biomass or briquettes to meet nearly 80–90 percent of their energy need, and about 70 million Chinese have no access to electricity. This energy divide is the result of relatively low cash income of rural households, high price of commercial energy, and an imperfect energy supply system. However, this energy divide is not compatible with the goal of harmonious development, improvement in the quality of life of rural households, and overcoming rural-urban inequality.

Moreover, the traditional method of utilization of biomass energy is not efficient, and is a major cause of pollution in rural China. Indoor pollution caused by inefficient burning of bio-mass is a serious threat to health in rural areas. The high rates of respiratory disease among Chinese women, who smoke far less than men (10 percent vs. 75 percent), can be attributed, to a great extent, to indoor pollution of the above source. The age-specific mortality rates from air-pollution-related lung and heart disease in China are seven to ten times higher than in the United States. Several studies by Chinese researchers ascribe most of the 1.4 million deaths from chronic obstructive pulmonary disease to indoor air pollution.[22]

At a broader level, China's carbon dioxide emissions in recent years have experienced the most rapid absolute growth, making her now the biggest emitting country.[23] Earlier, the United Nations Framework Convention on Climate Change (UN-FCCC) had put China in its non-Annex I list, implying that she was not required to undertake binding targets for reduction of carbon dioxide emissions under the Kyoto Protocol. However, China is now taking initiatives of her own to reduce CO_2 and other Green House Gas (GHG) emissions, so as to contribute to the global effort to reduce such emissions and thus arrest and avert debilitating climate change.[24]

While the Chinese government is concerned with global environmental issues, such as climate change, it tends to be more focused on local issues, such as particulate matter and sulphur dioxide emissions. It is estimated that damages to environment and human health caused by these pollutants translate into economic losses of 110 billion Yuan (US$13.3 billion) per annum. According to a report by the World Health Organization (WHO), seven of the world's ten most polluted cities are in China. China is therefore undertaking various measures to lower emissions of particulate matter, sulfur dioxide, and nitrogen oxide. To this end, she is both imposing pollution controls on power plants and pursuing policies designed to increase the share of natural gas in the country's fuel mix, particularly around major metropolitan areas.

12.9 Conclusions

China's economic growth is faced with serious challenges arising from various material resource constraints. Water and energy shortage is already affecting economic growth in many parts of China, and the situation may deteriorate further in the future. China's growing demand for energy and raw materials has profound international implications. China's growing demand for various resources is often driving up the international prices of these items and is also affecting China's diplomacy in the international arena. Although this process has the potential for generating conflicts, the Chinese leadership seems to be keen on avoiding them. The recent declaration by the Chinese leadership regarding "peaceful rise" of China is indicative of such a desire.

The Chinese government is responding to China's growing vulnerability of oil price volatility and supply risk through a mix of measures, including the development of a strategic oil reserve, acquisition of upstream oil assets, and increase of fuel efficiency standards for vehicles. Steps are also taken to promote the development and use of renewable energy. In February 2005, China passed a groundbreaking law to promote renewable energy, and the implementation of the law started from January 1, 2006. The law provides for a long-term development plan, R&D, geographic resource surveys, technology standards, and financing mechanisms in support of renewable energy. The China Renewable Energy Scale-up Program (CRESP) has been developed by the Government of China in cooperation with the World Bank and the Global Environment Facility to facilitate implementation of the renewable energy policy and undertake the necessary investment program.[25]

It is clear that to confront the resource and environmental challenges faced, a resource-saving and environment-friendly mode of production and life style need to be promoted. It is encouraging to see some reflections of the awareness of this need. For example, the Chinese Government is now strongly promoting recycling, and the State Council of China has put forward concrete recycling targets to be achieved during the 11th Five-Year period, from 2006 to 2010. According to the Plan, by 2010, China's per unit GDP energy consumption will be reduced by 20 percent, water consumption per unit of industrial output will be cut by 30 percent, the utilization ratio of mineral resources will be increased by five percentage points, use of industrial solid waste will be up by 60 percent, and emissions of major pollutants will be curtailed by 10 percent. Some concrete measures towards these goals have been taken. For example, solid clay bricks are now facing a ban in urban areas beyond 2010, and all coal-fired generators are slated to be equipped with sulfur-removal systems before 2015. However, China will have to take even bolder steps in the coming years in order to overcome the twin problems of resource constraint and environmental degradation.

Acknowledgements

The authors would like to thank all participants of the ICSEAD China growth project and other colleagues who provided comments and suggestions, support

and technical help. Special thanks are due to Nazrul Islam for his advice, encour
agement, and patience.

Notes

1 One of the main factors for the shrinkage of cultivated land was the return of cultivated land for ecological purpose, such as reforest projects. More information can be
found in "Communique On Land And Resources Of China 2003". Published by The
Ministry of Land and Resources, P.R. China.
2 Technical details of the footprint account can be found in various footprint websites
and publications, for example: The Living Planet Report 2004, published by WWF and
can be found in http://www.panda.org (accessed on October 11, 2007).
3 Materials in this section come mainly from a research done by Liu Yuhui under the
supervision of one of the co-authors, Xizhe Peng, of this volume. See also in: Liu Yuhui
and Peng Xizhe. 2004. Acta Ecologica Sinica, 10, pp. 2257–62.
4 See Mathis, Wackernagel and William, Rees. 1996. Our Ecological footprint: Reducing
Human Impact on the Earth, Gabriola Island: New Society Publishers, BC.
5 The Ministry of Water Resources of PRC, Water Resources in China, http://www.mwr.
gov.cn/english1/20040802/38161.asp (accessed on October 11, 2007).
6 See The Ministry of Water Resources of PRC, China Water Resource Bulletin 2006.
7 Turner, Jennifer and Otsuka, Kenji. 2006. *Reaching Across the Water*, Washington, D.C.:
Woodrow Wilson Center.
8 Frederick W. Crook and Xinshen Dia, Water Pressure in China: Growth Strains Resources,
Agricultural Outlook, January–February, 2000, Economic Research Service, USDA.
9 Lester R. Brown, Water Shortage Could Shake World Grain Markets, Worldwatch
Institute – April 21, 1998.
10 China's Water Policy and Practice, A speech given by Dr. Jiao Yong, Vice Minister of
Water Resources of China in New Delhi on November 22, 2005.
11 Report released by China's National Development and Reform Commission (NDRC) on
December 12, 2006.
12 Ministry of Water Resources Planning Department. (ed.) (2004). *Water Resources
Sustainable Development Strategy Research*, Beijing: China Waterpower Press.
13 http://www.nsbd.gov.cn/zw/zqxx/tzjh/20061207/200612070026.htm (accessed on
October 11, 2007).
14 Seungho Lee, China's Water Policy Challenges, Discussion Paper 13, November 2006,
China Policy Institute, University of Nottingham.
15 http://www.hw-sd.com/Article.asp?NewsID=437 (accessed on October 11, 2007).
16 See "Water Supply and Wastewater Treatment Market in China", published by U.S.
Department of Commerce, International Trade Administration Washington, D.C. in
January 2005.
17 Reserves/Production (R/P) ratio: the reserves remaining at the end of any year are
divided by the production in that year, and the result is the length of time that those
remaining reserves would last if production were to continue at that level.
18 Proved reserves of coal are generally taken to be those quantities that geological and
engineering information indicates with reasonable certainty can be recovered in the
future from known deposits under existing economic and operating conditions.
19 China's Oil and Gas Import Strategy to 2020, http://www.emerging-markets.com/PDF/
ChinaOilGasStrategy.PDF (accessed on October 11, 2007).
20 See China's energy challenge, http://microsites.rss-uk.net/economist/shell/past-de-
bates/chinas-energy-challenge/forum/single_thread/1/5/31.html (accessed on October
11, 2007).
21 China to Double Oil Import from Foreign Assets, China Institute, April 23, 2006, Dow
Jones Energy Service.

22   Florig. K. 1997. "China's Air Pollution Risks," in Environmental Science and Technology News, November 6, 1997, Carnegie Mellon University.
23   The Netherlands Environment Assessment Agency reported that China's 2006 CO2 emissions surpassed those of the USA, but Chinese government denied the claim. See http://www.mnp.nl/en/dossiers/Climatechange/moreinfo/Chinanowno1inCO2 emissionsUSAinsecondposition.html (accessed on October 11, 2007).
24   Barbara Finamore, Qian Jingjing and Robert Watson, China Is Aggressively Reducing Its Carbon Dioxide Emissions, http://www.global-warming.net/china.htm (accessed on October 11, 2007).
25   Details of the program can be seen in its website: http://www.cresp.org.cn/english/index.asp (accessed on October 11, 2007).

Bibliography

China's Energy Development Report edition committee. 2001. *China Energy Development Report 2001,* Beijing: China Measurement Press (in Chinese).

China National Administration of Coal Geology (Additional Edition. 2001). *Coal Geology of China: Trend Analysis of Effective Supply Capacity of China Coal Resources,* Beijing (in Chinese), China Coal Industry Publishing House, 2001.

Department of Industry and Transport Statistics, National Bureau of Statistics, China and Energy Bureau, National Development and Reform Commission, China. 2005. *China Energy statistical Yearbook 2004,* Beijing: China Statistics Press (in Chinese).

Hu, Tianyu and Li Ruilin. 1995. *Prospect Prediction of Coal Resources in China,* Beijing: Geology Pres (in Chinese).

Liu, Yuhui and Xizhe Peng. 2004. "The Estimation and Evaluation of China's Ecological FootPrints", *Acta Ecologica Sinica*, 10, pp. 2257–2262 (in Chinese).

Mathis, Wackernagel and William Rees. 1996. *Our Ecological Footprint: Reducing Human Impact on the Earth,* Gabriola Island: New Society Publishers, BC.

Mao, Jiehua and Huilong Xu. 1999. *Prediction and Evaluation of China Coal Resources,* Beijing: Science Press (in Chinese).

The Ministry of Land and Resources, P.R. China, "Communique on Land and Resources of China 2004," Beijing. http://www.lrn.cn/basicdata/communique/200611/t20061123_5924_4.htm

The Ministry of Water Resources of PRC, Water Resources in China. http://www.mwr.gov.cn/english1/20040802/38161.asp (accessed on October 11, 2007).

The Ministry of Water Resources of PRC. 2007. China Water Resource Bulletin 2006, Beijing: China Waterpower Press.

Ministry of Water Resources Planning Department (ed.) 2004. Water Resources Sustainable Development Strategy Research, Beijing: China Waterpower Press.

National Bureau of Statistics. Selected years. China statistical Yearbook, Beijing: China Statistics Press.

Qian, Dadu, Binxian Wei, and Yu Li. 1996. *Introduction to Coal Resources of China,* Beijing: Geology Press (in Chinese).

Seungho, Lee. 2006. China's Water Policy Challenges, Discussion Paper 13, November 2006, China Policy Institute, University of Nottingham.

Turner, Jennifer and Otsuka Kenji. 2006. Reaching Across the Water, Woodrow Wilson Center: Washington, D.C.

U.S. Department of Commerce. 2005. " Water Supply and Wastewater Treatment Market in China", Washington, D.C.

World Widelife Fund, The Living Planet Report 2004, http://www.panda.org/downloads/general/lpr2004.pdf (accessed on October 11, 2007).

13
Urban Air Quality in China: Historical and Comparative Perspectives

Thomas G. Rawski

13.1 Introduction

Economic growth creates wealth, employment, and also effluents. In China, as in other rapidly industrializing economies, pollution poses serious challenges to both citizens and governments. High growth rates, high population density, and China's long history of intense human pressure on the land magnify environmental hazards. It is therefore no surprise that Chinese episodes now join the Donora Pennsylvania air inversion of 1948, the smoke emergencies of the 1950s in London, New York City, and Belgium's Meuse Valley, multiple conflagrations on Cleveland's Cuyahoga River, and Japan's Minamata disease in the annals of environmental disasters associated with industrial growth.

Environmental discussions typically castigate China for allowing pollution levels that exceed present-day limits in the service-dominated economies of North America, Western Europe, and Japan. Since effluents are the mirror image of rapid industrialization, accusing China of generating serious pollution amounts to little more than acknowledging China as "the workshop of the world." The two, as John Gray observes, are "different parts of the same process" (2006, p. 21). As India moves toward Chinese-style dynamism, it is no surprise to learn that "Indian air is highly polluted" (*NY Times*, June 4, 2006, p. 4).

Focusing on urban air quality, this essay aims to deliver a balanced perspective on one dimension of the environmental consequences arising from rapid Chinese growth. We consider three basic questions. How bad is air quality in major Chinese cities? Is urban air quality improving or deteriorating? How does the path of urban air quality in China compare with the experience of Japan and Korea, which, like China, combined rapid industrialization with high population density?

The answers proposed in what follows are unambiguous and, in the context of current public discourse, somewhat unexpected. Although Chinese cities suffer from serious air pollution, air quality has improved dramatically and shows a clear upward trend. Information about urban air pollution situates China on a path resembling the experience of previous industrializers. Indeed, China's achievements in controlling ambient air pollution often run ahead of Japanese and Korean attainments at comparable stages of their national development.

13.2   How bad is China's urban air quality?

No one can doubt the seriousness of China's problems with urban air quality. The World Bank's summary, prepared ten years ago, continues to provide an accurate overview:

> [Despite past improvements] ambient concentrations of suspended particulates are ... extremely high in most cities, and ambient sulfur dioxide concentrations and acid rain are also high in areas where high-sulfur coal is consumed. ... northern cities have more serious particulate pollution ... while southern cities have serious sulfur dioxide pollution. ... concentrations of particulates and sulfur dioxide in many Chinese cities are among the highest in the world. (Johnson et al., 1997, pp. 7–9)

These high levels of airborne effluents resemble historical circumstances in other industrializing nations. Writing in 1993, Vaclav Smil notes that particulate levels in Chinese cities "resemble the Western means of fifty to ninety years ago" (1993, p. 117). Kazuo Hishida notes that urban particulates in China during the mid-1980s resembled Japanese conditions of the late 1960s, when dustfall in Japan exceeded Chinese readings from the mid-1980s (1986, pp. 57–58). When this author lived in Tokyo during the late 1960s, Tokyo policemen inhaled oxygen while directing traffic, "vendors sold oxygen on Tokyo's streets, and children wore masks on their way to school" because Japan "may have been the world's most polluted country" (Schreurs, 2002, p. 36).

At that time, Tokyo recorded ambient concentrations of 0.440 milligrams of particulates (1968) and 0.220 milligrams of sulfur dioxide (1965 and 1966) per cubic meter of air. The average particulate level for a group of 36 major Chinese cities exceeded the Tokyo peak in 1986 and 1987. Although this average has subsequently declined (see Figure 13.4), individual cities continue to record high levels of ambient pollution. In 2004, particulates exceeded the 1968 Tokyo level in 11 Chinese cities, all in China's northwest region, where sand rather than industrial effluents predominates (Environment Yearbook, 2005, 773). During the late 1990s, Taiyuan exceeded Tokyo's peak levels for sulfur dioxide; Shijiazhuang's 2003 readings matched Tokyo's mid-1960s figures for sulfur dioxide. In 2004, Linfen and Yangquan, both in coal-rich Shanxi province, exceeded Tokyo's peak levels of 0.220 mg per cubic meter for sulfur dioxide (Ibid., 769).

Figure 13.1 presents international data on the particulate content of urban air samples. We compare the arithmetic average of annual measurements of "Total Suspended Particulates" (TSP) for 36 Chinese cities[1] with figures for Pittsburgh,[2] Tokyo, Kitakyushu,[3] and Seoul. The comparison shows that, on average, ambient TSP concentrations in Chinese cities exceed current figures for the other cities by a large margin. Comparison of recent Chinese results with earlier international figures, however, changes the picture. The Chinese averages never reach the peak Pittsburgh level recorded in the 1920s, rest consistently below the 1968 Tokyo peak beginning in the early 1990s, and are now approaching the levels recorded in Seoul during the late 1980s.

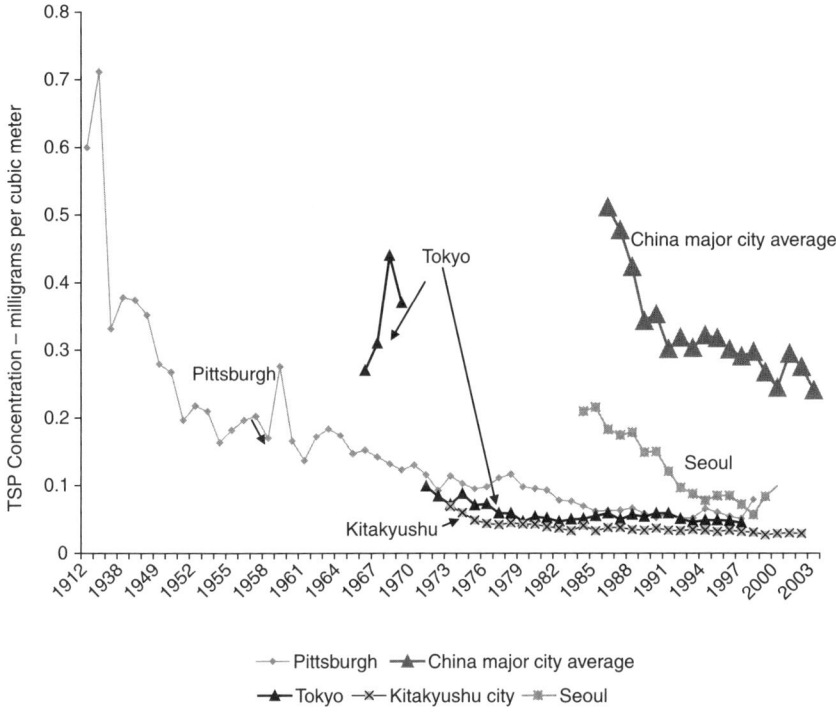

Figure 13.1 International air quality comparison – TSP

Source: Author's calculations.

Figures 13.2 and 13.3 provide more detail on the location of high TSP readings in China. Figure 13.2 directs attention to administrative cities by comparing Beijing, Shanghai, and Guangzhou with Tokyo and Seoul. Trends for Guangzhou and Shanghai from 1990 resemble the trend for Seoul beginning in the mid-1980s. The two Chinese cities begin with higher TSP levels than Seoul's, but drop quickly from peak levels of 0.30–0.35 mg per cubic meter. Recent figures for Shanghai and Guangzhou appear to track Seoul's situation ten years previously. Beijing reports TSP levels that are higher than those for Shanghai and Guangzhou and remain quite stable prior to a big drop in 2002/03. The Beijing figures, however, remain well below the peak levels recorded by Tokyo in the late 1960s.

Dustfall, measured in tons per square kilometer per month, is closely correlated with airborne particulates. Chinese dustfall statistics present a pattern similar to TSP. Chinese readings are high by contemporary international norms, but hardly unusual by historical standards. In 2000, 57 Chinese cities reported dustfall above 10 tons per square kilometre per month, of which 18 scored above 20 tons. The 2004 data indicate very slight improvement, with the numbers falling to 54 and 16. The highest figures approach 40 tons: 38.4 tons for Baoding in 2000, 37.6 tons for Handan in 2004 (Environment Yearbook, 2001, pp. 601–602; 2005, pp. 774–775).[4] Historic peaks for dustfall elsewhere include 70 tons for Pittsburgh (1923/24; the post Second World War peak was 34 tons in 1948),

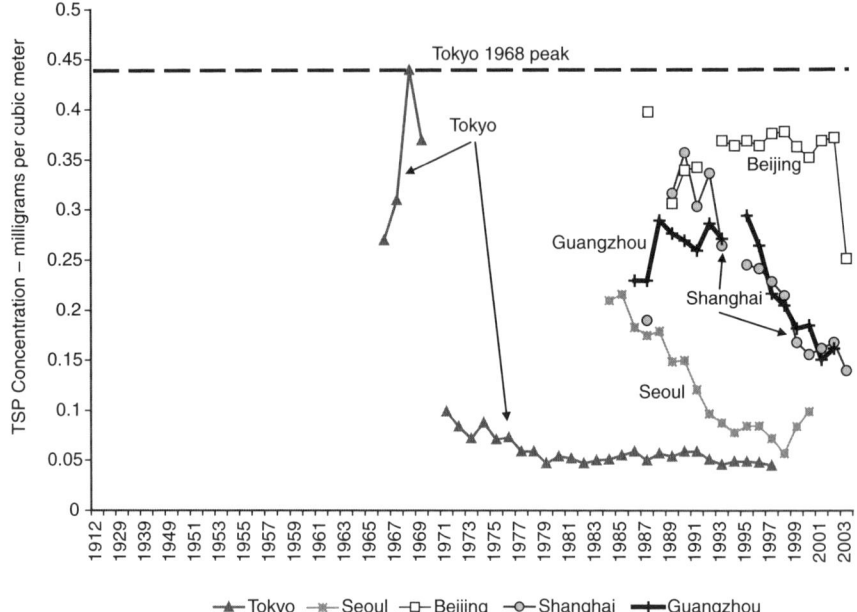

Figure 13.2   Comparative TSP levels – administrative centers

Source: Author's calculations.

33.9 tons for Tokyo (1967), 23.7 tons for Kitakyushu (1959), and Japanese readings that "exceeded 100 tons" elsewhere in Japan during the 1960s (Hishida, 1986, p. 58).[5] Beijing reported dustfall of 15.1 tons per square kilometer in 2000 and 11.5 tons in 2004 (Environment Yearbook 2001, p. 602; 2005, p. 775). By comparison, the most recent observation of dustfall in excess of 10 tons occurred in 1975 for Tokyo, for 1972 in Kitakyushu, and for 1981 in Pittsburgh.

Figure 13.3 shifts the comparison to Chinese industrial cities, of which Chongqing, Lanzhou, Shenyang, and Taiyuan can serve as examples. In the late 1980s, each of these cities reported levels of TSP far above the peak Tokyo levels of the 1960s. For Taiyuan and Lanzhou, the figures for some years even surpass the peak Pittsburgh figures from the early 1920s, which surely qualify as extreme levels of contamination. Three of the four Chinese cities show a sharp downward trend for TSP concentration, with recent figures well below the Tokyo peaks of the 1960s and, for Chongqing and Shenyang, approaching the readings for Seoul during the mid-1980s. In Lanzhou, by contrast, the TSP readings fluctuate at levels close to the peak Pittsburgh figure, with no visible downward trend.

Figure 13.4 provides an international comparison for concentrations of sulfur dioxide. As with TSP, recent annual averages of SO_2 measurements for major Chinese cities are substantially higher than current readings in Tokyo, Kitakyushu, or Seoul. From a historical perspective, however, Chinese measures for urban SO_2 concentrations seem quite moderate. During the early 1980s, average readings for major Chinese cities were similar to observations in Pittsburgh. Recent Chinese

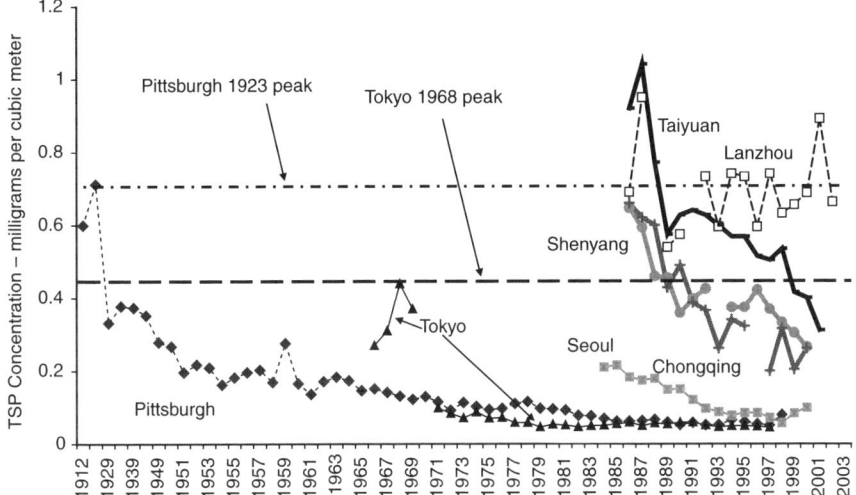

Figure 13.3 Comparative TSP levels – industrial centers
Source: Author's calculations.

averages are far below the historic peaks for Tokyo and Seoul, and slightly below the (much lower) peak for Kitakyushu.

Figure 13.5 focuses on NO_X, the combined quantity of two compounds, NO and NO_2, per cubic meter of air. Here the Chinese readings fall near or below contemporaneous measures for Tokyo, Kitakyushu and Seoul, apparently because Chinese cities still lag behind their Japanese and Korean neighbors in the density of motor vehicle traffic, which is the main contributor to NO_X. Data from individual Chinese cities bear out this correlation between automotive transport and NO_X: the highest Chinese figures come from Beijing, Shanghai, and Guangzhou, cities that lead China in household incomes and auto ownership. Beginning in 2001, China followed international practice by measuring NO_2 separately, rather than reporting the combined concentration of NO and NO_2. The new series resemble the earlier data for NO_X: they show no strong trend, with the highest concentrations of NO_2 observed in China's richest cities.

These observations confirm that many Chinese cities experience levels of air pollution that far exceed today's norms for the advanced economies of East Asia. When compared with historic pollution levels during earlier periods of peak industrialization in Japan, Korea, and the United States, however, these Chinese figures appear routine rather than exceptional. We will return to this subject below.

13.3   Is urban air quality improving?

Figures 13.1–13.5 offer clear evidence of general, but not universal improvement in urban concentrations of particulates and of sulfur dioxide, the main effluents from industrial operations, power plants, and other forms of stationary

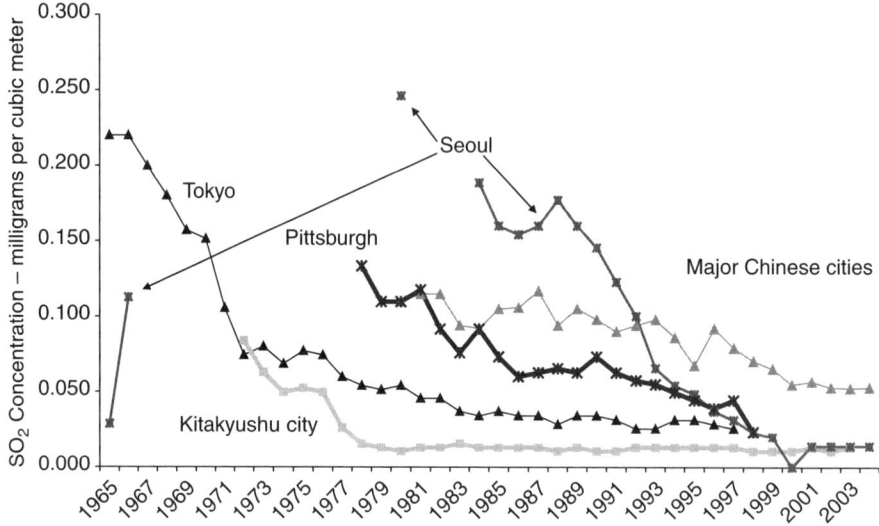

Figure 13.4   International air quality comparison – SO_2
Source: Author's calculations.

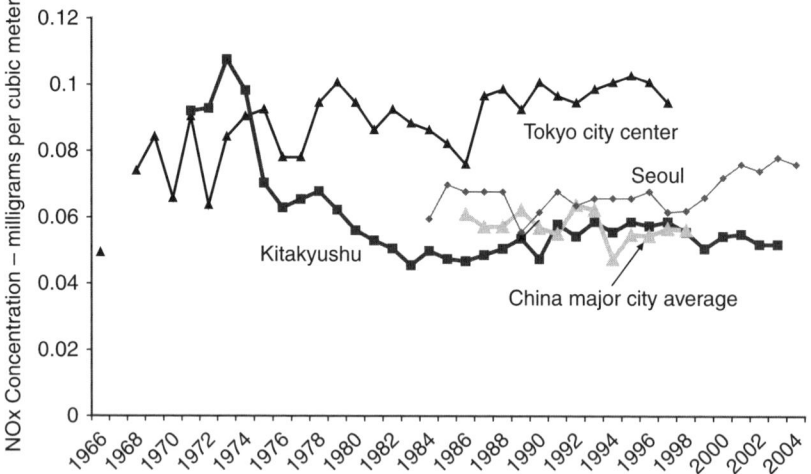

Figure 13.5   International air quality comparison – NO_x
Source: Author's calculations.

combustion. Ambient concentrations of nitrous oxides, which are associated with motor vehicle traffic, have not declined.

Figure 13.6 explores the magnitude of the decline in ambient concentration of particulates. Both average readings for (approximately) 36 major cities and the maximum annual figure within this group dropped sharply between 1986 and 2004. The average figure, which initially exceeded the Tokyo peak level for 1968, dropped below that level in 1988 and has remained well below that figure ever since. In 1999, and again in 2003, the major city average approached the TSP level recorded for Pittsburgh in 1957 following that city's ten-year cleanup campaign. The average Chinese figure for 2003 is less than half the reading for 1986. The maximum annual figure reported for major Chinese cities has dropped even faster. Peak figures for the late 1980s include readings well above 1,000 mg per cubic meter, levels associated with air contamination crises in Europe and North America during the 1950s and 1960s (Goklany, 1995, 346). Since the late 1980s, TSP concentrations in the most polluted major cities have declined by approximately two-thirds, to levels that approximate Tokyo's 1968 peak.

Results for sulfur dioxide, displayed in Figure 13.7, are equally dramatic. After fluctuating around 0.1 mg per cubic meter during the 1980s, the average of figures reported for major Chinese cities dropped below that figure in 1990. Further decline ensued. During the late 1990s and into the current decade, the average of SO_2 readings for major Chinese cities moved below the New York City reading for 1972. The Chinese urban average now regularly dips below Pittsburgh's SO_2 figure for 1984, which presumably informed the selection of this U.S. steel center as "America's most livable city" in the following year. The annual peak figure for major Chinese cities has also dropped sharply, though irregularly.

Table 13.1 summarizes long-term trends in ambient concentrations of common air pollutants in Chinese cities. The data record the arithmetic average of annual readings for large numbers of cities. The results show a strong downward trend for particulates, sulfur dioxide, and dust. Starting from initial levels above Tokyo's peak figures from the late 1960s, average Chinese readings for particulates in major cities decline sharply. The current Chinese average approximates figures for earlier industrializers 5–10 years after the start of serious efforts to reduce environmental hazards: late 1950s Pittsburgh (dustfall 12.8 tons in 1959), mid-1970s Tokyo (dustfall 13.3 tons in 1972), mid-1980s Taipei (dustfall approximately 14 tons in 1985 and 1991).[6] For sulfur dioxide, the decline begins from levels far below the Tokyo peak of the 1960s. Recent figures approximate Tokyo figures of the mid-1970s and, as noted above, are consistently below New York's SO_2 levels of the early 1970s and Pittsburgh's of the mid-1980s.

NO_X offers the lone exception to the general improvement in urban air quality for major Chinese cities, evidently because the rapid growth of motor vehicle traffic has offset what appears to be a general decline in untreated emissions.

13.4 China's development path: normal or aberrant?

Studies of multiple economies suggest that an "environmental Kuznets curve," in which pollution first rises, and then declines during the course of economic growth, provides a plausible expectation of the historic path of environmental hazards during the course of development.

If this formulation description accurately describes the long-term relationship between growth and effluents, we should expect the spread of new technology and of new ideas to accelerate the shift from growth-with-more effluents to growth with reduced environmental damage. The concept of environmental stewardship

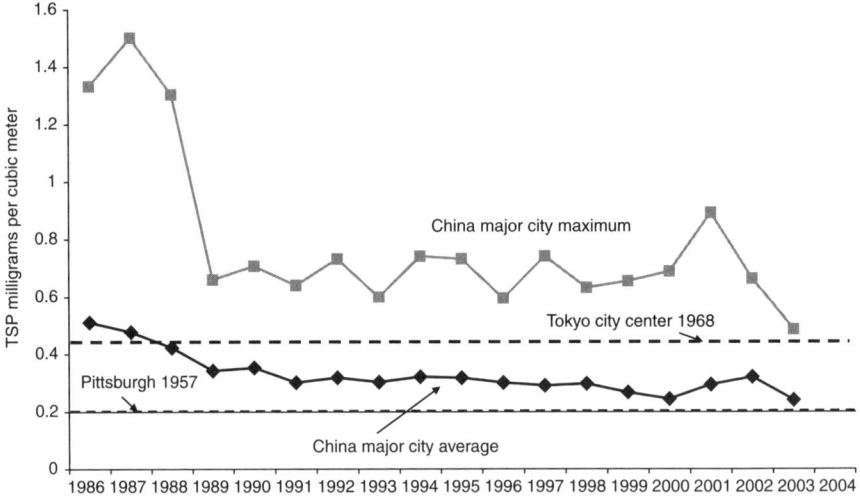

Figure 13.6   China: TSP levels in major urban areas, 1986–2003
Source: Author's calculations.

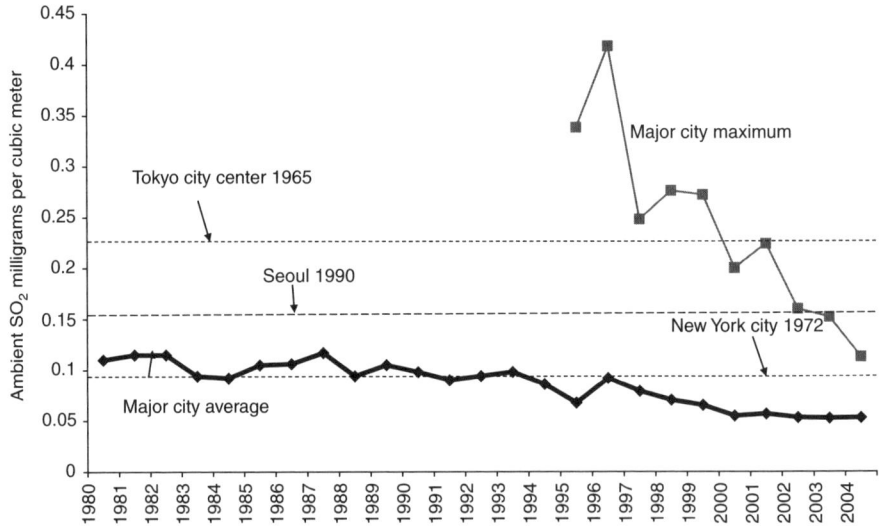

Figure 13.7   China: SO_2 levels in major urban areas, 1980–2003
Source: Author's calculations.

as an important objective of national policy is very recent. National environmental protection agencies did not appear until the early 1970s in the United States and Japan (Schreurs, 2002, pp. 35, 45–46). The subsequent trend toward globalization means that nations like China experience both domestic and international pressures to mitigate environmental damage from economic growth much earlier in the development process than occurred in Japan or Korea.

Figures 13.8 and 13.9 use East Asian evidence to illustrate this systematic shift toward earlier control of environmental damage during the industrialization process. To avoid the complexities associated with cross-national comparisons of national product, we employ the share of labor in the primary sector (farming, forestry, and fishing), which declines regularly with the growth of aggregate and per capita incomes, to index the process of national development.[7]

Figure 13.8 plots primary sector labor force shares for China, Japan, and Korea against urban TSP concentration for Tokyo, Kitakyushu, Seoul, and the arithmetic average of readings for 36 major Chinese cities.[8] All three nations show a declining trend in atmospheric concentration of particulates. In Japan, the decline begins when the primary sector labor force share stands in the range of 20–30 percent. In Korea, the decline starts with primary labor share in the 25 percent range. In China, by contrast, ambient concentrations of TSP begin their downward march much earlier in the development process, when the share of primary sector workers in the national labor force is approximately 50 percent. This result confirms our expectation that new technologies and new thinking will encourage latecomers to tackle the environmental difficulties associated with rapid growth at progressively earlier stages of the development process.

Figure 13.9, which provides a parallel analysis for sulfur dioxide, points in the same direction. Pollution from sulfur dioxide in Chinese cities never reaches the high levels experienced in Japan and Korea. Reduction of ambient concentrations of SO_2 begins far sooner in the development process for China than for either Japan or Korea. Recent readings for urban SO_2 pollution in China, where the primary sector's labor force share is 35–40 percent, match those attained at much later stages in Japan and Korea when primary sector labor occupied less than 15 percent of the work force.

These findings regarding urban air quality indicate that the relationship between economic growth and environment in China strongly resembles the development processes observed elsewhere in East Asia. In China, as in Japan and Korea, an initial phase of high growth with rising pollution intensity yields to a more attractive combination of ongoing growth with declining ambient concentration of major industrial effluents. Figures 13.8 and 13.9 show that the second stage of China's development process, in which the trend of pollution intensity turns downward, begins at an earlier phase of industrialization than occurred in Japan or Korea. We attribute this improvement in the trade-off between growth and environment to the spread of new technology and to increased awareness of the negative environmental consequences of unbridled industrial growth.

13.5   What about air quality outside China's major cities?

Rising awareness of the environmental costs associated with rapid growth has encouraged Chinese policy-makers to increase efforts to limit harmful effluents. Not surprisingly, major cities have become the initial target of new controls. This raises the possibility that improved urban air quality has come at the expense of

Table 13.1   Long-term trends in ambient air quality in Chinese cities

Year	TSP	SO$_2$	Dust	NO$_x$	Number of cities
1980	0.610	0.110	35	0.043	
1981	0.703	0.115	35	0.050	
1982	0.729	0.115	32	0.045	
1983	0.600	0.094	32	0.046	
1984	0.660	0.092	27	0.042	
1985	0.590	0.105	28	0.050	
1986	0.570	0.106	25	0.048	
1987	0.590	0.117	24	0.056	
1988	0.580	0.094	25	0.045	
1989	0.432	0.105	22	0.047	
1990	0.379	0.098	19	0.043	
1991	0.325	0.090	18	0.046	70
1992	0.323	0.094	19	0.048	76
1993	0.329	0.098	19	0.050	77
1994	0.329	0.086	18	0.047	88
1995	0.317	0.081	17	0.047	88
1996	0.308	0.080	16	0.046	90
1997	0.287	0.066	15	0.045	94
1998	0.282	0.057	15	0.045	96
1999	0.259	0.056	14	0.045	97
2000	0.261	0.052	14		94
2001	0.277	0.052	15		97
2002	0.269	0.051	14		98
2003	0.256	0.066	12		113
2004	0.245	0.065	13		113

Notes:
TSP, SO$_2$ and NO$_x$ measured in milligrams per cubic meter.
Dustfall measured in metric tons per square kilometer per month.
Number of cities: figures are for SO$_2$; numbers for other measures vary considerably.
Systematic collection of data for NO$_x$ apparently ended in 1999.

Source: for 1980–1999, *China Energy Databook* , chapter 8.
When the source reports two figures, we use the average of the the two.
For 2000–2004, *Environment Yearbook*, issues for 2001–2005.

environmental deterioration outside major cities, where government and party leaders are strongly motivated to maximize local economic growth.

Extending the present study beyond China's major cities is not possible because systematic quantitative information about air quality appears limited to urban sites.

In a separate project, Zixia Sheng (Carnegie-Mellon University), Wei Wang (University of Pittsburgh) and I use information about emissions, which includes

Figure 13.8 Trend of primary labor force share vs. urban TSP concentration
Source: Author's calculations.

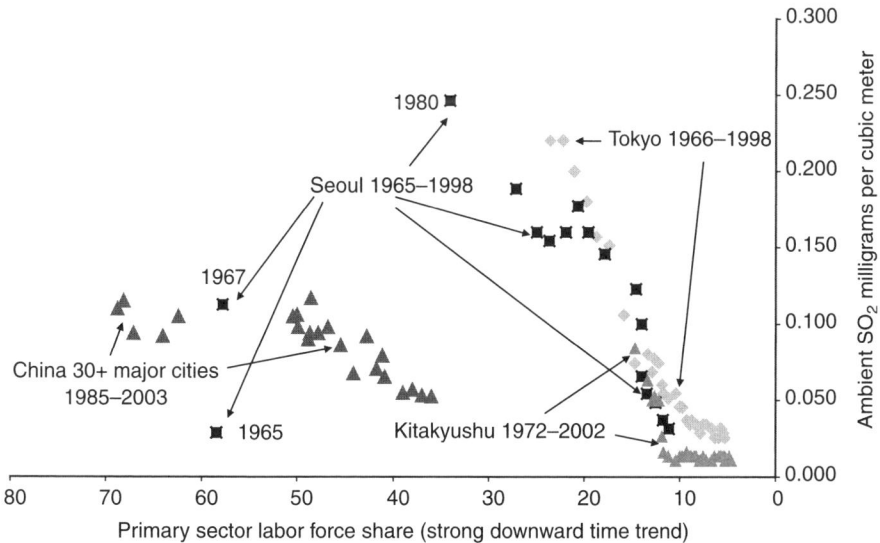

Figure 13.9 Trend of primary labor force share vs. urban SO_2 concentration
Source: Author's calculations.

localities down to the county level, and about the output of township and village enterprises, to construct measures of air quality outside China's major cities. Preliminary results show that ambient concentrations of particulates, soot, and sulfur dioxide increased during the decade ending in 2003, but that concentrations of particulates and soot began to decline around 2000.

These findings suggest that the environmental Kuznets curve dynamics visible in urban China may apply beyond Chinese cities, but with a considerable time lag.

13.6   Conclusions and implications

Our analysis of urban air quality examines only one dimension of the multiplex interaction between economic growth and environmental consequences during China's long economic boom. Extension of our review to encompass water quality, solid wastes, and airborne contaminants outside China's major cities could alter the picture presented here. With this qualification, what conclusions follow from our study of urban air quality?

Air quality in China's major cities falls far short of contemporary standards prevailing in advanced nations. Although studies linking air pollution with negative health outcomes routinely tilt toward alarmism,[9] Xiping Xu's observation that air pollution in China's major cities "is significantly associated with both acute and chronic adverse health effects" appears to provide a realistic and objective summary (1998, p. 281).

From a historical perspective, however, China's environmental circumstances appear routine rather than exceptional. In China, as in every other nation that has experienced sustained economic growth, development produces soot, smoke, and smog as well as new employment opportunities and rising incomes. The levels of airborne pollutants observed in major Chinese cities are not extraordinary when compared with historical circumstances in Pittsburgh, New York, Tokyo, Kitakyushu, Seoul, or Taipei.

What does appear different about the relationship between Chinese economic growth and air pollution is that the downward trend in ambient concentrations of particulates and sulfur dioxide (but not nitrous oxides) begins at an earlier stage of the development process, as measured by the primary sector's labor force share, than occurred in the United States, Japan, or Korea. This reflects the impact of new technology and the spread of concern over the negative environmental consequences of economic growth.

To emphasize the magnitude of China's achievements in limiting the negative environmental consequences of rapid growth, Figure 13.10 compares trends in GDP growth and aggregate energy consumption with changes in average SO_2 concentrations in major cities.[10] The data show that, despite the presence of dirty industries and widely publicized gaps in enforcement of environmental regulations, China's economy has attained huge reductions in effluents per unit of GDP and of energy consumption. Ambient concentrations of sulfur dioxide have dropped by one-half between 1980 and 2003 (left scale). At the same time, GDP has risen by a factor of ten and energy consumption has nearly quadrupled (right scale). Taking

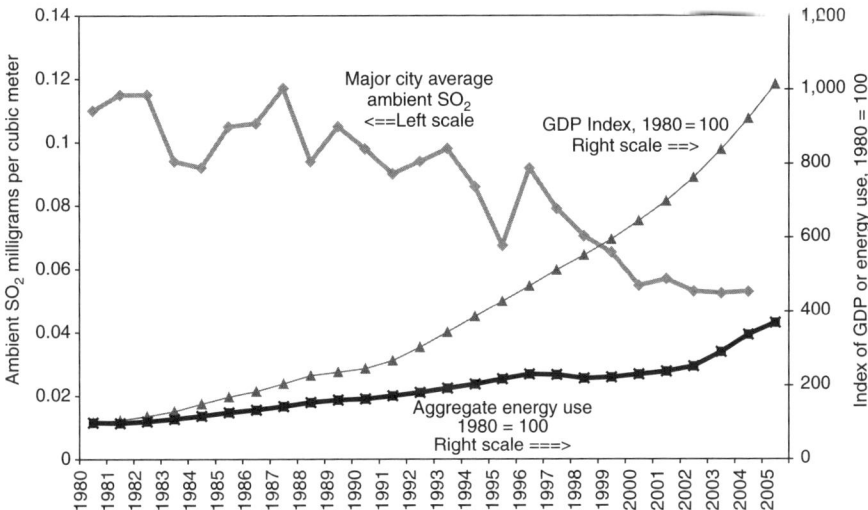

Figure 13.10 China: GDP, energy use, and ambient SO₂ levels in major cities, 1980–2003
Source: Author's calculations.

1980 as 1, these observations imply that ambient urban concentrations of sulfur dioxide in the early years of the current century amount to approximately 0.5/10 or .05 per unit of GDP and approximately 0.5/4 = 0.125 per unit of energy use – indicating respective declines of 95 percent and 87.5 percent in ambient urban sulfur dioxide per unit of GDP and per unit of energy consumption over a period of 20–25 years. Even though the preliminary findings noted above indicate that air quality outside China's cities maintained a downward trend until about 2000, it seems likely that the trend of declining air pollution per unit of GDP or energy use applies, though on a more modest scale, to the entire Chinese economy.

These observations invite speculation on the larger issue of whether environmental degradation is likely to pose a serious obstacle to China's future economic growth. Our findings indicate that health hazards arising from air pollution are unlikely to act as an important constraint on China's future growth. Several considerations reinforce this conclusion.

China has already achieved substantial declines in urban concentrations of major pollutants associated with industrial production. This achievement has occurred without imposing major constraints on China's ongoing high-speed growth. Together with similar experiences in other nations, this result makes it unlikely that either the health hazards associated with current levels of pollution or the expenses tied to future efforts to reduce effluents will place overwhelming burdens on China's economy.

It is difficult to doubt that China's dynamic economy can provide the resources needed to deliver further reduction of effluents. Vermeer writes that "with adequate investment ... larger facilities can be upgraded and [effluents] controlled at a net profit" (1998, pp. 971–972). Even if such investments are not profitable, international experience indicates that costs of environmental cleanup and protection are modest. Japan's governments and corporations spent 1.3 percent of GDP on environmental protection and pollution control in 1990. The Federal Republic of Germany spent 1.6 percent of GDP for the same purposes in 1987. The United States devoted 1.8 percent of its GDP to pollution abatement and control in 1989 (O'Connor 1994, pp. 177–178). China, which currently devotes over 40 percent of annual GDP to investment spending, can easily assign comparable (or much larger) GDP shares to environmental objectives without slowing the economy's progress.

Both Vermeer, writing about China, and O'Connor, focusing more broadly on Asia, indicate that environmental management is more difficult and remediation often less economical for small factories than for large plants (Vermeer 1998, p. 971; O'Connor 1994, pp. 167–174). In China, both market forces and official policy seem likely to push industrial operations in the direction of large-scale facilities. Between 1980 and 2005, the offsetting consequences of entry and consolidation produced a standoff, with no overall trend toward industrial concentration or dispersion (Brandt, Rawski, and Sutton 2008). Continued improvements in domestic transport and communication, ongoing commercialization of the financial system, increased privatization of state enterprises and the gradual removal of legal and administrative restrictions surrounding mergers and bankruptcy all seem likely to encourage a trend toward industrial concentration. In addition, Chinese official policy strongly favors the pursuit of scale economies as well as the closure of small-scale polluters (e.g., "Heavily Polluting Factories to be Demolished," *China Daily* June 13, 2006, p. 3).

Changes in economic structure seem likely to ease the burden of reducing effluents. Table 13.2 shows the sectoral breakdown of China's GDP growth for five-year periods beginning in 1980. The share of the secondary sector (mostly industry and construction) in aggregate growth reached what will probably stand as a historic peak of 54.8 percent of incremental growth during 1990/95. The share of the services sector, which jumped from 35–40 percent of incremental growth during 1980/1995 to over half in 1995/2000, will in all probability increase further. This will lessen the pressure of growth on the environment because of the low energy consumption and effluent generation associated with sectors like education, finance, health care, commerce, and public administration.

Rising costs will surely encourage Chinese manufacturers to reduce unit consumption of energy and materials, which often lags far behind international norms. In addition, structural change within the industrial sector will continue to reduce the ratio of effluents to outputs. As O'Connor observes, at some point in the industrialization process, "the leading growth sectors tend to be ones of low to intermediate pollution intensity – for example. electronic/electrical equipment, general machinery, and transport equipment" (1994, p. 28). This description is highly relevant to China's current development phase.

The Beijing Olympics promise to make a major contribution to raising Chinese environmental standards. China's government, following the lead of South Korea's preparation for the 1988 Seoul Olympics, has embarked upon a massive environmental cleanup for its capital.[11] The decision to remove Capital Steel, a nationally prominent firm employing over 100,000 workers, from Beijing's western suburbs underlines

Table 13.2   Sectoral shares in annual GDP and in GDP growth, 1980–2005

Year	GDP Index	Sectoral shares in annual GDP (%)		
		Primary	Secondary	Tertiary
1980	100.0	30.1	48.5	21.4
1985	169.7	28.4	43.1	28.5
1990	245.8	27.0	41.6	31.3
1995	427.7	19.8	47.2	33.0
2000	645.2	14.8	45.9	39.3
2005	1014.8	12.5	47.3	40.3
Period	**Total**	**Sectoral share of 5-Year GDP growth (%)**		
		Primary	Secondary	Tertiary
1980/1985	100.0	25.9	35.4	38.7
1985/1990	100.0	24.1	38.2	37.6
1990/1995	100.0	10.0	54.8	35.2
1995/2000	100.0	5.0	43.3	51.7
2000/2005	100.0	8.4	49.7	41.9

Sources:
Annual GDP shares (based on nominal values) for 1980 and 1990 from Fifty Years (1999, p. 3), for 1995 and 2000 from National Bureau of Statistics (2006), and for 2005 from Abstract (2006, p. 22).
   GDP index based on officially estimated real growth for the primary, secondary, and tertiary sectors using prices and nominal sector weights for the year 2000, taken from author's file GDP 1980–2005.062506.xls

the scope of the cleanup and the government's determination to achieve a flawless performance on the world stage. With cities and provinces locked in fierce competition for talent and investment resources, Beijing's new, higher environmental standards have already begun to influence other regions. Thus Shenyang now styles itself as "an ecologically and environmentally friendly city" that is "no longer ... polluted by industrial waste," while Benxi seeks "to become a model city of environmental protection" (*China Daily* 20 September 2006, p. S6 and 23 June 2006, p. 3).

   We conclude that China's urban air quality, although low by current international standards, seems quite typical of circumstances in fast-growing economies during peak periods of industrialization. China's urban air quality has improved substantially during the past quarter-century. This improving trend began at an earlier stage of the development process than in Japan or Korea. The cost of further improvements in air quality seems well within the reach of China's economy. Changes in economic structure, policy, and thinking seem likely to push in the direction of further reductions in airborne pollutants. The constancy of urban concentrations of ambient nitrous oxide stands as the lone exception to this generally favorable outcome. China's recent ban on leaded gasoline and promulgation of auto emission standards beyond those currently in force in the United States indicate that the Beijing authorities are both aware of the problems posed by the spread of car ownership and are prepared to take remedial action. In China, as elsewhere, we cannot yet predict the environmental consequences of humanity's love affair with the automobile.

Acknowledgements

The author has benefited from Nazrul Islam's comments on two drafts and from conversations with Gene Gruver, Gary Jefferson, Cynthia Kinnan, Yihong Qian, Wei Wang, Xiao Zhang, Yisheng Zheng and Yuxin Zheng. Ying Fang, Tingting Huang, Karla Wetzig, and Yifan Zhang provided imaginative research assistance. Special thanks to Loren Brandt, Cliff Davidson, Shobhakar Dhakal, Michael Greenstone, Hiroyuki Good, Xuelian Wang, Shoichi Yamashita, Xiao Zhang and the Kitakyushu Municipal Government for generous assistance with data. Responsibility for what follows rests solely with the author.

Notes

1 The number of cities included in the sample varies from year to year because of data gaps. The number of included cities declines sharply after 2000 as the focus of measurement, following international practice, shifts to small particles, which pose the greatest health hazard. The standard metric has changed from TSP (including particles up to 40 microns) to PM-10 (limited to particles of 10 microns or smaller).

2 The Pittsburgh air quality data used here were provided by Professor Cliff Davidson. Professor Michael Greenstone kindly supplied additional data used in Chay and Greenstone (2005).

3 Environmental data for Kitakyushu, the original home of Japan's steel industry, were provided by the Kitakyushu municipal government through the kind assistance of Professor Shoichi Yamashita. Data shown Figure 13.1 and elsewhere describe conditions in Kitakyushu City. The highest effluent readings, and therefore the steepest improvements in air quality, occurred in the Shiroyama industrial district.

4 The highest reading in 2004, 41.9 tons for Yinchuan, probably is associated with sand rather than industrial pollution (Environment Yearbook, 2005, p. 774).

5 The highest reading I have found for Seoul, 7.35 tons per square kilometer-month for 1988, comes after Korea's preparatory cleanup in advance of the 1988 Olympics and is probably not a peak figure.

6 Taipei data from Hsiao et al, 1993, p. 67. Data for Pittsburgh and Tokyo from author's file AirPollution.TRmod.062506.

7 Labor force data for Japan and Korea come from standard official sources. Standard Chinese data appear to overstate the share of primary workers in the national total (Rawski and Mead, 1998). I therefore use Loren Brandt's unpublished estimates of sectoral labor force attachment. Use of official Chinese labor data would accentuate the results described below.

8 The Chinese data are from China Energy Databook (to 1994) and, beginning from 1995, from data provided by Professor Zhang Xiao and Ms. Wang Xuelian of the Chinese Academy of Social Sciences' Institute of Quanti-Economics. The number of cities included varies from year to year due to gaps in available data.

9 Conclusions about increased mortality associated with environmental hazards, for example, typically neglect to analyze the life chances of persons whose deaths are linked to pollutants. In addition, the risks associated with environmental hazards are seldom compared with other dangers (smoking cigarettes, riding in automobiles, etc.) to which citizens routinely expose themselves.

10   GDP data: real growth in 2000 prices computed from official data on real growth in the primary, secondary, and tertiary sectors using 2000 value-added weights. See author's file GDP and Component Indexes 1952–2004. Energy consumption data from Abstract, 2006, p. 145 and Yearbook, 1990, p. 487.

11   I am indebted to George Schoenhofer of Industry Canada for alerting me to the importance of the 1988 Olympics for environmental policies in Korea.

References

Abstract. 2006. *Zhongguo tongji zhaiyao 2006.* [China Statistical Abstract 2006], Beijing: Zhongguo tongji chubanshe.

Brandt, Loren, Thomas G. Rawski, and John Sutton. 2008. "China's Industrial Development," In Loren Brandt and Thomas G. Rawski (eds.) *China's Great Transformation.* Cambridge and New York: Cambridge University Press.

Chay, Kenneth Y., and Michael, Greenstone. 2005. "Does Air Quality Matter? Evidence from the Housing Market," *Journal of Political Economy,* Vol. 113, No. 2, pp. 376–424.

China Energy Databook. 2001. v.5.0, May.

Environment Yearbook. *Zhongguo huanjing nianjian* [China Environment Yearbook]. Beijing: Zhongguo huanjing kexue chubanshe, issues for 2001–2005.

Fifty Years. 1999. *Xin Zhongguo wushinian tongji ziliao huibian.* [Fifty Year Statistics of the New China]. Beijing: Zhongguo tongji chubanshe.

Goklany, Indur M. 1995. "Richer Is Cleaner: Long-Term Trends in Global Air Quality," In Bailey, Ronald (ed.) *The True State Of The Planet*, New York: Free Press.

Gray, John. 2006. "The Global Delusion," *New York Review of Books*, April, 23, pp. 20–23.

Hishida, Kazuo. 1986. "Japanese Report Views China's Pollution, Environmental Protection," *Nitchû keizai kyôkai kaihô*, August, pp. 34–30. Translated in JPRS-CST-86–046 dated November 5, 1986, pp. 54–66.

Hsiao, Hsin-huang (Michael H. H. Xiao). 1993. *Taiwan 2000 nian.* [Taiwan in 2000]. Taipei: Tianxia wenhua chuban gufen youxian gongsi.

Johnson, Todd, Feng Liu, and Richard, S. Newfarmer. 1997. *Clear Water, Blue Skies: China's Environment in the New Century, China 2020 Series.* Washington, D.C.: World Bank.

National Bureau of Statistics. 2006. "Announcement on Revised Result about Historical Data of China's Gross Domestic Products," issued January 10. See http://www.stats.gov.cn/eNgliSH/newsandcomingevents/t20060110_402300302.htm (accessed on 7 February 2006).

O'Connor, David. 1994. *Managing the Environment with Rapid Industrialisation : Lessons from the East Asian Experience, Development Centre Studies.* Paris: OECD Development Centre.

Rawski, Thomas G., and Robert W. Mead. 1998. "On the Trail of China's Phantom Farmers," *World Development,* Vol. 26, No. 5, pp. 767–781.

Schreurs, Miranda A. 2002. *Environmental Politics in Japan, Germany, and the United States.* Cambridge and New York: Cambridge University Press.

Smil, Vaclav. 1993. *China's Environmental Crisis : an Inquiry into the Limits of National Development.* Armonk, NY: M.E. Sharpe.

Vermeer, Eduard B. 1998. "Industrial Pollution in China and Remedial Policies," *China Quarterly*, No. 156, pp. 952–985.

Xu, Xiping. 1998. "Air Pollution and Its Health Effects in Urban China," In Michael B. McElroy, Chris P. Nielsen, and Peter Lydon (eds.), *Energizing China: Reconciling Environmental Protection and Economic Growth,* Cambridge: Harvard University Committee on Environment.

Yearbook. 1990. *Zhongguo tongji nianjian 1990.* [China Statistics Yearbook 1990], Beijing: Zhongguo tongji chubanshe.

Author Index

Note: Page numbers in **bold** denote multiple citations, whereas f, n, and t denote figure, note, and table, respectively.

Subject Index

Notes: Page numbers in **bold** denote extended discussion or heading emphasized in the main text, whereas those with f, n and t denote figure, note and table, respectively.